Greece in the Ancient World

Greece in the Ancient World

Jeremy McInerney

University of Pennsylvania

First published in the United Kingdom in 2018 by Thames & Hudson Ltd, 181A High Holborn, London WC1V 7QX

Reprinted 2021

Greece in the Ancient World © 2018 Thames & Hudson Ltd

Text © 2018 Jeremy McInerney

British Library Cataloguing-in-Publication Data
A catalogue record for this book is available from the British Library

ISBN 978-0-500-25226-0

Printed and bound in China by
C & C Offset Printing Co. Ltd

Be the first to know about our new releases, exclusive content and author events by visiting
thamesandhudson.com
thamesandhudsonusa.com
thamesandhudson.com.au

Contents

Preface

This book was written with some very specific goals in mind. The first was to bring the story of the Greeks to life for a modern-day audience, showing how this ancient civilization played a crucial role in shaping who we are today. Their history is one of remarkable achievement, but it also encompasses issues that are very present in our modern life, such as inequality, social justice, complicated notions of gender and sexuality, and xenophobia and nationalism. The first chapter—"Why Study the Greeks?"—explicitly discusses and evaluates the relevance and legacy of the ancient Greeks today.

I also wanted to write a book that would balance textual and archaeological evidence, including some of the very latest discoveries that have recently come to light. Scholarship keeps advancing our knowledge of the Greek world and in the last decade we have had the discovery of the spectacular Griffin Warrior's grave at Pylos (see Chapter 3), the new Mycenaean palace at Aghios Vasileios in Lakonia (Chapter 3), the mass sixth-century burials at Phaleron (Chapter 6), and the publication of the Derveni papyrus (an allegorical commentary on an Orphic text; see Chapter 10), to name only a few. I have tried to include as many references to this recent work as possible, in order to reinforce the point that our knowledge of ancient Greece is still expanding and that our field of study is vibrant. I have also prefaced the Persian Wars—a key moment in Greek history—with an introduction to Persian culture, highlighting both the similarities and differences between the Persians and Greeks prior to this landmark conflict.

Instructors will recognize that this book corresponds broadly to the chronological parameters of many introductory survey classes in Greek history, and the book certainly reflects my own experience of teaching such a class at the University of Pennsylvania for over twenty-five years. I also, however, wanted to present a personal vision of Greek history, one that would engage readers and students. I do not mean that the views here are completely idiosyncratic, but I do believe that a textbook about a human society should have a distinctive voice. Historians are invested in the world they study, and care about it; for me, it made sense to write a book that shared that enthusiasm and interest, as opposed to producing a book so bland as to offend no one.

Teachers may therefore occasionally find themselves teaching "against" the book because they disagree with an interpretation or point of view, but I see nothing wrong in that. Students should be aware that no textbook is omniscient, and that a robust and healthy skepticism about a textbook's interpretations is an essential part of the historian's toolkit. Sometimes students are puzzled that one professor may emphasize the importance of personality, another the centrality of military affairs, while a third looks for economic factors to explain historical change. But history does not resemble physics, in which a formula is simply right or wrong. History is a combination of evidence and interpretation, and every historian interprets the available evidence in different ways, building his or her argument upon the foundations of primary sources.

Primary Sources: Archaeological Evidence and Written Texts

Primary sources can be either archaeological or written. In the case of Greece, we have access to archaeological evidence (i.e. the physical evidence of a society) that goes back even before the Bronze Age (3100–*c.* 1100 BC). This period is the subject of the first chapters of the book, where our sources consist almost exclusively of archaeological evidence. Tombs, graves, fortified sites with massive walls, buildings adorned with frescoes, grave goods, precious objects in gold, silver, gems, as well as more mundane objects, such as cooking vessels and utensils, all contribute to the story.

Without a contemporary to guide us, however, the archaeological evidence of the early Aegean world can seem opaque. Is the route from the outside to the center of Knossos designed to be a labyrinth? Is this a sign that the ceremonies that took place here were those of a ritualized, hieratic state, ruled by a priest-king? Or is that an interpretation that suits our fantasies of the Minoans? We have no ancient person whom we can interview to answer such questions. In fact, given the ancient Greek appreciation for cunning deception, even if we did have such a person to interview, his testimony would probably not be reliable anyway. After all, it was a Cretan, Epimenides, who said, "All Cretans are liars." As we shall see, from the walls of Mycenae to the layout of Knossos, most of the history we recount of the Greek and Aegean world in the Bronze Age is, in fact, a narrative based on inference, deduction, and interpretation.

The second type of primary source on which we rely is written. In the case of the Greeks, this means that we can use a wealth of inscriptions, from the Linear B tablets at the palace of Knossos to the Lapis Primus tribute stele found on the Akropolis, and a large archive of legal speeches that offer eye-witness evidence of the political upheavals affecting the Greek world. We can also draw upon some of the greatest literature ever written, including the poems of Homer, the *Iliad* and the *Odyssey*, works that have influenced over two thousand years of Western culture. In the work of such Greek dramatists as Aristophanes and Euripides, we are presented with topical events transformed into powerful plays that resonate to this day. We can even utilize the works of the first historians, Herodotos and Thucydides, who attempted to capture both the events of the past and those of the world they lived in.

We do, however, need to treat these written sources with caution. The Homeric poems were orally transmitted for hundreds of years before being written down sometime around 700 BC, and purport to deal with the Trojan War, an event that (if it happened at all) probably took place around 1200 BC. Can poems loosely based on an event of dubious historicity five hundred years earlier be considered sources? In Greece, literary sources are the products, almost exclusively, of the male, propertied elite and by and large display a consistent worldview: land and status are desirable, wealth is problematic, women are subordinate, non-Greeks are inferior, while slaves are barely worth consideration. Legal speeches, another valuable source of information for the Classical period, have to be treated with caution for other reasons. They were delivered before a massed jury and had to appeal to the broadest common denominator in order to be persuasive. As a result, they reflect normative attitudes—those of the thinking man in the street, as it were—but on matters of fact they may be distorted, exaggerated, or in other ways unreliable.

Nor is the work of the ancient historians Herodotos and Thucydides, near or exact contemporaries of the events they describe, free from complicated and sometimes intractable problems of interpretation. Their works contain narrative features, such as dreams and omens, and generic *topoi* (or thematic set-pieces), such as speeches and battle descriptions, that also reflect the expectations of their audience and the social milieu in which they were produced. Even the inscriptions of the Athenians, a rich source of information about the democracy and the Athenian empire, have to be used carefully. Do the decisions made by the Athenian Assembly allow us to infer how Athens' allies viewed these political arrangements? Often one has to read against the grain, to ask what has been left unsaid, and to rely on a degree of speculation and imagination in order to understand exactly what such sources are telling us.

Wrestling with these kinds of problems is what serious scholarship does, and that requires deep and sustained engagement with the archaeology and literature of the Greek world. A volume such as this can touch only lightly on many of these complex areas and developments, since it is intended for undergraduates or the interested general reader looking for a convenient and (I hope) easy-to-read guide to the world of the Greeks. The reader should recognize, then, that behind many of the statements and claims made here there are scholarly debates that often go back to the origins of Ancient History as an academic discipline created in the early nineteenth century AD. This volume is an introduction to the world of the ancient Greeks, the tip of the iceberg of a fascinating and complex culture.

Overview and Features of the Book

This book encompasses the whole of ancient Greek history, from the earliest beginnings in prehistory and the Bronze Age to the Roman conquest of the Greek East. In between, I will cover the Iron Age and Archaic period, followed by the two centuries of the Classical Age from the Persian Wars at the beginning of the fifth century BC, and on into the age of Alexander and the Hellenistic world created by his conquest of the ancient Near East. In the course of the narrative, readers will encounter such significant conflicts as the battles of Thermopylae and Marathon, and the extraordinary cultural flourishing of Classical Athens under Perikles.

In order to emphasize both traditional topics and newer approaches, I have supplemented each chapter with a Spotlight feature designed to focus attention on some particularly salient or interesting aspect. In certain instances, this consists of a short exploration of new research, as in the recent excavations near Pylos highlighted in the Spotlight to Chapter 3 ("New Discoveries around Mycenaean Pylos"). In another case, the Spotlight to Chapter 7, I offer a glimpse into the reception of the Classical tradition, focusing on David's famous depiction of Leonidas at Thermopylae. These Spotlights are intended to pique the reader's interest and to encourage readers to investigate more on their own.

A general Timeline is located at the front of the book to show key events and periods in Greek history. Each chapter also has a Timeline to complement the narrative of the book and reinforce the chronology of Greek history, while numerous maps and plans should make following the narrative easier as well.

I have included a list of Further Reading at the end of the book, again blending standard scholarly works that have become fundamental to serious study of ancient Greece with newer works designed to illustrate the directions of more recent scholarship of the last generation. In addition, glossary terms are styled in bold at their first mention in the text and brief definitions given in a full Glossary at the end of the book. I thank Ben Abbott, Tim Warnock, Kyle Mahoney, and James McInerney for their diligence in helping me with these.

A Note on Spelling and Dates

Most Greek names and expressions have entered English through Latin. Hence, readers may be familiar with such names as Socrates or Aeschines, but a more accurate rendering of the original Greek would be Sokrates and Aischines. In common with many historians I have tried to return to the Greek spellings, or at least a transliteration that stays as close as possible to the Greek.

But consistency here can lead us into troubled waters. Few readers would be comfortable with Platon (for the more familiar Plato), or Thoukydides for the already difficult Thucydides. Accordingly, I have chosen to be consistently inconsistent: Greek spellings where possible, but Latin or English spellings if the Greek version produces something unrecognizable.

All dates in the book are BC ("before Christ") unless specifically marked otherwise; accordingly the dates count down toward the end of the first century BC.

Instructor and Student Resources

There are dedicated resources available to instructors and students, including:

- Bulletpoint chapter summaries, outlining key events and concepts.
- Flashcards: Students can test themselves on vocabulary and concepts with our interactive flashcards.
- The Test Bank, written by the author, covers all concepts and artwork in the textbook. It features 20 questions per chapter: 16 multiple choice, 4 short essay.
- All images in the book available as PowerPoint slides and JPEGs.
- Video created by Thames & Hudson: "The Acropolis and Parthenon of Athens."

This book is also available as an ebook.

Acknowledgments

The thousands of students who have taken AncH 26 over the years were the guinea-pigs for this book. In 2016, in fact, a draft of the entire manuscript served as the textbook for the class and the responses of the students helped improve the final version considerably. The graduate students in Penn's Ancient History graduate group have also been my most lively critics, and to them I owe my thanks. Although a small army of graduate students has taught with me over the years, the crew from 2016 deserve special thanks for conveying to me specific feedback regarding the earlier draft. It is a pleasure to thank Gavin Blasdel, Jordan Rogers, Bryn Ford, Cindy Susalla, Greg Callaghan, and Ryan Pilipow for their contributions.

I also wish to thank the many reviewers whose comments helped me further improve the manuscript while it was at the development stage:

- George L. Armantrout, Portland State University
- Eric Cline, George Washington University
- Paula Debnar, Mount Holyoke College
- Denise Demetriou, University of California, San Diego

- Sviatoslav Dmitriev, Ball State University
- William Duffy, University of Texas, San Antonio
- Kendra Eshleman, Boston College
- Lucien Frary, Rider University
- Greg Golden, Rhode Island College
- Vanessa B. Gorman, University of Nebraska Lincoln
- Greg Halfond, Framingham State University
- Benjamin Haller, Virginia Wesleyan College
- Sarah Harvey, Kent State University
- Susan Hussain, Montclair State University
- Elias Kapetanopoulos, Central Connecticut University
- Nikolaos Lazaridis, California State University, Sacramento
- Jonathan Perry, University of South Florida, Sarasota Manatee
- Emily Rush, Miami University
- Matt Waters, University of Wisconsin, Eau Clare
- David Yount, Mesa Community College

I also wish to thank the team at Thames & Hudson for their hard work when it comes to the book's presentation and layout. Compared with many other volumes this is a book rich in images, and for that I am grateful. Mark Sapwell and Alex Goodwin encouraged me to be lavish, and their production department produced a work that is a pleasure to look at. I thank Sally Nicholls for her work finding many of the images used and Martin Lubikowski for the creation of the many standardized maps. I also thank Managing Editor Lucy Smith for overseeing the editorial process from start to finish. It has been a pleasure working with the Thames & Hudson staff.

Timeline

Paleolithic and Neolithic Ages	c. 38,000–c. 3200	Franchthi Cave
Middle and Late Neolithic Ages	c. 5000–c. 3200	**Sesklo** and **Dimini**, **Dikili Tash**
Early Bronze Age (3100–2100 BC)	c. 3100	Beginning of the Bronze Age
Middle Bronze Age (2100–1600 BC)	c. 1900	First Cretan Palaces
	c. 1700	Destruction of First Cretan Palaces
	c. 1650	Second Cretan Palaces
	1628	Eruption of Thera
Late Bronze Age (1600–c. 1100 BC)	c. 1550	Shaft Graves at **Mycenae**
	c. 1470	Destruction Horizon at Second Cretan Palaces
	c. 1450	Linear B first recorded at **Knossos**
	c. 1450	Griffin Warrior Tomb at **Pylos**
	c. 1425	Warrior Graves at **Knossos** and **Chania**
	c. 1400–c. 1300	Iklaina absorbed by **Pylos**
	c. 1250	Fortification of **Mycenae** and **Tiryns**
	c. 1200	Destruction of Mycenaean Palaces
	c. 1200–c. 1100	Movements to interior of Crete
	1184	Traditional date for the fall of **Troy**
	c. 1150	Upheavals in Eastern Mediterranean
Iron Age (c. 1000–700 BC)	c. 950	Heroon of **Lefkandi**
	c. 800–c. 700	Emergence of the *polis*
	776	First Olympic Games
	c. 725–c. 700	*Iliad* and *Odyssey* written down
	c. 750–c. 500	Greek Diaspora
	c. 720	Invention of the Greek Alphabet
	c. 706	Foundation of Taras (**Tarentum**)

Archaic Age (c. 700–480 BC)	c. 700	**Hesiod**, author of *Theogony* and *Works and Days*
	c. 700–c. 675	Second Messenian War
	700–600	Orientalizing Period of Art
	683/2	First annual Archon at **Athens**
	669	Battle of Hysiai (Sparta versus Argos)
	c. 657–c. 627	**Kypselos**, Tyrant of Corinth
	c. 650	**Tyrtaios**, Spartan poet, associated with Spartan warrior ethos
	c. 650–c. 600	**Alkman**, Spartan poet, associated with choral performances by young women
	632	**Kylon**'s Conspiracy, early attempt to seize power in Athens
	c. 624–c. 546	**Thales** of **Miletos**, first Presocratic philosopher
	621/0	Drako's Law on homicide
	c. 610–c. 546	**Anaximander**, philosopher
	594	**Solon's** first Archonship
	592/1	**Solon's** Legislation
	c. 585–c. 525	**Anaximenes**, philosopher
	c. 570–c. 467	**Xenophanes**, philosopher
	561–528	Career of the tyrant **Peisistratos**
	r. 558–c. 530	**Cyrus the Great**
	c. 550–c. 500	Formation of the Peloponnesian League
	r. c. 530–522	**Cambyses**, son of Cyrus the Great
	546	Battle of Pallene, establishing **Peisistratos's** tyranny in Athens
	c. 535–c. 475	**Herakleitos**, philosopher, author of *On Nature*
	525–456	**Aischylos**, tragedian, author of *Oresteia* and *Persians*
	r. 522–486	**Darius I**
	c. 520	Vix Krater
	514	Assassination of **Hipparchos**
	513	**Darius I** crosses to Europe
	510	Expulsion of **Hippias**
	508/7	Reforms of **Kleisthenes**
	499–493	Ionian Revolt

Chapter 1

Introduction: Why Study the Greeks?

Cultures in Dialogue

Faced with the challenges of understanding a complicated and sometimes frightening modern world, students might pick up this textbook with some skepticism. Why bother to study the Greeks, an ancient civilization scattered around the Mediterranean that existed more than two thousand years ago? Why should we study a dead culture? Surely it is more important to study practical subjects, such as engineering or medicine? After all, those are the foundation of solid careers, and allow you to improve the world. Building bridges or curing sickness—these are worthwhile endeavors. Can studying the Greeks make you a better nurse, or help you to design more energy-efficient housing?

Truthfully, probably not, but aside from the sheer pleasure of getting to know a culture that was rich and vibrant, the connections between us and the Greeks constitute a form of cultural DNA that serves to make the Greeks a society with whom we are, whether we know it or not, in dialogue. Democracy, medicine, architecture, astronomy, ethics, poetry, dance, mathematics—to name only a selection—are all areas of thought and practice in which, as we shall see, we have a debt to the Greeks. Could the

atom have been split without the atomic theory of Demokritos (c. 460–370 BC) and Leukippos, who postulated that the cosmos was comprised of tiny particles, invisible to the eye, known in Greek as atoms? Could engineers and mathematicians have designed and built our world without the mathematical theorems of Euclid? The word "democracy" is derived from two Greek words (*demos*, people and *kratos*, rule), and even our concepts of truth and beauty owe much to the ancient Greeks. By examining these different areas we will discover that, far from being dead, ancient Greek culture is very much alive and present in our society today.

Truth and Beauty

The Greeks valued truth and beauty. Sometimes this can be difficult for us to grasp; the beauty of their poetry, for example, often eludes our ears, since it depends on complex metrical schemes that are closer to opera than our beat-driven meters. Even in translation, however, there are moments that help us to understand why every well-educated Greek man grew up immersed in the *Iliad*, Homer's epic poem that evoked the world of the heroes who fought at

1.1 Kritios Boy *c.* 480–460 BC. Marble, H: 1.17 m (3 ft 10 in.)

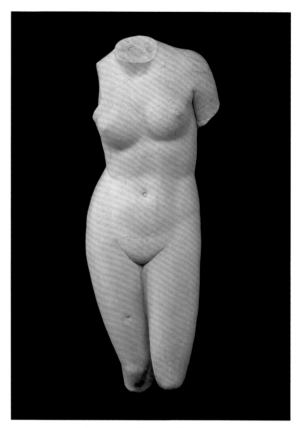

1.2 Female nude of the Aphrodite of Knidos type, Roman copy after Praxiteles, *c.* second century BC. Marble, H: 1.22 m (4 ft)

Troy. Take, for example, the speech of Andromache to her husband Hektor, Troy's mightiest defender. One evening, when he has returned home from the battlefield, she gives voice to the fears of every wife or husband who has seen their loved one leave for war:

My dear husband, your warlike spirit
will be your death. You've no compassion
for your infant child, for me, your sad wife,
who before long will be your widow.
For soon the Achaeans will attack you,
all together, and cut you down. As for me,
it would be better, if I'm to lose you,
to be buried in the ground. For then I'll have
no other comfort, once you meet your death,
except my sorrow.

(Homer, *Iliad* 6.405–17, trans. Johnston)

Another kind of beauty is to be found in the sculpture produced by the Greeks, especially in the fifth and fourth centuries BC. Having learned from the Egyptians how to cut and sculpt limestone and marble, the Greeks quickly mastered the art of rendering the human form in stone, producing masterpieces that are at once lifelike, yet almost perfect in proportion and execution (**1.1** and **1.2**). The Greeks acquired a canon of proportions from the Egyptians, but within a century had radically modified this approach. Instead of entirely stylized representations of the human body, they opted for a revolutionary form of naturalism.

The Greeks were acutely aware of the importance of truth and beauty. In fact, in Plato's *Symposium*, the philosopher Sokrates (469–399 BC) relates a speech of his teacher Diotima, in which he describes how the seeker of truth will hunt for the beauty to be found in all things, beginning with physical beauty but moving on toward something more profound. The seeker will find beauty, not just in bodies, but even in laws and civil institutions. The search continues:

And after laws and institutions he will go on to the sciences, that he may see their beauty, being not like a servant in love with the beauty of one youth or man or institution, himself a slave mean and narrow-minded, but drawing towards and contemplating the vast sea of beauty, he will create many fair and noble thoughts and notions in boundless love of wisdom; until on that shore he grows and waxes strong, and at last the vision is revealed to him of a single form of knowledge, which is the knowledge of beauty everywhere.

(Plato, *Symposium* 210c, trans. Jowett)

When we look at these images and read these sentiments, especially the transcendental and mystical contemplation of truth and beauty advocated by Plato (*c.* 429–347 BC), we would do well to contrast

1.3 Torso of Apollo, *c.* 480–470 BC. Marble, H: 1.32 m (4 ft 4 in.)

them with the popular culture—frequently vapid, often pointless—that surrounds us every day, often resembling the cultural equivalent of sugar: addictive, unfulfilling, and focused on short-term gratification. The solution? A diet of high-fiber Mediterranean culture (**1.3**).

This is not to say that we should put all Greek culture on a pedestal; that would be a mistake. After all, Aristophanes' comedies make it clear that farts and masturbation were part of Greek humor—the Greeks could be every bit as vulgar as us—but at the opposite end of the spectrum, there is something life-changing, almost transcendental, about coming into contact with the profound beauty of Greek culture. The German poet Rainer Maria Rilke (1875–1926) expressed it best in this sonnet, which was inspired by seeing an ancient Greek sculpture:

We cannot know his legendary head
with eyes like ripening fruit. And yet his torso
is still suffused with brilliance from inside,
like a lamp, in which his gaze, now turned to low,
gleams in all its power. Otherwise
the curved breast could not dazzle you so, nor could
a smile run through the placid hips and thighs
to that dark center where procreation flared.
Otherwise this stone would seem defaced
beneath the translucent cascade of the shoulders
and would not glisten like a wild beast's fur:
would not, from all the borders of itself,
burst like a star: for here there is no place
that does not see you. You must change your life.

(Rilke, "Archaic Torso of Apollo,"
trans. Mitchell)

What Greek history shows us, as Rilke understood, is that we have a choice. In our daily lives there is a continual battle between significance and triviality; between things that matter and things that do not; between thoughtful, ethical engagement with the world, and bland superficiality. Studying the Greeks represents an antidote to settling for superficiality, a way of enhancing our appreciation both of this ancient culture and the world around us in general. Knowing the Greeks better means necessarily knowing ourselves better.

Yet despite the influence of the Greeks upon the modern world, their culture is separated from ours by more than two millennia. Consider this *kore* (statue

1.4 Kore (Akr. 674), *c.* 520–500 BC. Marble, H: 92 cm (3 ft)

and indispensable; only in them do we find the ideal of that which we ourselves should like to be and to produce.

(W. von Humboldt, *Geschichte des Verfalls und Unterganges der griechischen Freistaaten* pp. 1807–8, trans. McInerney)

This philhellenism, with antecedents going back to the Renaissance, was not just a philosophical tendency of the eighteenth and nineteenth centuries; it also produced a university system in Germany that laid the foundation for the systematic study of Classical languages, Classical civilization, and Greek and Roman ancient history. This tradition has resulted in a tendency to view the Greeks as a model of perfection, an approach nicely summed up in Edgar Allan Poe's famous reference to the Classical achievement in his poem "To Helen," in which he writes of "the glory that was Greece,/And the grandeur that was Rome."

As a result, every book about the Greeks, including this book, has roots in a particular moment in European intellectual history, both shaping and being shaped by the nationalist agenda of the eighteenth and nineteenth centuries. As a result of this heavy identification of European nations with the Classical world, in most significant areas of modern life we have a real and tangible connection to the Greeks, but it is a complicated relationship that needs to be evaluated and scrutinized.

of a young woman), dating to the late sixth century BC (**1.4**). Beautiful and enigmatic, she compels us to ask questions of her society, a society both strange and recognizable. Who was the girl? Who erected this statue? What function did it and other similar statues serve? How are we to understand her world?

This Western fascination with Greece has an extensive history, and there has been a long tradition of claiming that the Greeks stand at the head of Western culture. The fullest expression of this idea is to be found in the words of Wilhelm von Humboldt, the Prussian minister of education, who in AD 1807 wrote:

In the Greeks we have before us a nation in whose fortunate hands everything, which, according to our deepest feelings, sustains the noblest and richest aspects of human existence, matured to the utmost perfection.... To know them is for us not just pleasant, advantageous

Democracy, Ancient and Modern

A good example of this complicated relationship is to be found in the notion and practice of democracy, one of the most significant Greek innovations. In the English-speaking world, we generally recognize two models of democratic government: the parliamentary and the presidential system. Whichever system you are familiar with, there are certain characteristics that we equate with democracy. Generally, we believe that the franchise should extend to both men and women over the age of eighteen, that citizens elect governments to represent them, and that these governments are answerable to the people, "deriving their just powers from the consent of the governed," as stated by the Declaration of Independence.

Were one to ask an ancient Greek to describe his or her democracy, however, the results might come as a surprise. Compared to our understanding of the concept, no Greek would ever have entertained the notion that women could be active participants in the democracy; they were merely the vessels by which citizen men bred legitimate children. Foreigners were rarely given the chance to win citizenship, and the entire democratic system relied on the existence of large numbers of slaves who made it possible for free citizens to participate in democratic life. In some respects the Athenian democracy resembled an exclusive men's club, the very existence of which depended on the exclusion of many of the inhabitants of Athenian territory. Furthermore, no Greek would recognize the concept of representation in relation to the democratic assembly. In Greek democratic states, all male citizens were eligible to vote, and in the *Ekklesia*, the Athenian assembly that met forty times a year, all present voted on matters as varied as public contracts, taxes, and declarations of war. This was a direct democracy, closer to the model practiced in the cantons of Switzerland than in Washington or Whitehall. It is true that members of the *Boulê*, or Council, were elected representatives from their tribe, but since they were elected by a process of random selection, served for only one year, and could not serve again for another ten years, in practice a very high proportion of Athenians probably served as members of the Boulê at least once during their lifetime.

It is almost impossible, therefore, to find a Greek translation of our word "government" in the sense of the institutions that legislate our lives, since the Athenians, to use the best-known case, *were* the government. You could blame public speakers or generals for bad decisions, but not the government as a separate entity, because ultimately all political decisions were made directly by the people. (Contrast this with the notion that the government is something separate from the people, a distinctly modern point of view.) Democracy was not, however, a model that found favor with all Greeks, as demonstrated by the opening of the essay "On the Constitution of the Athenians," by pseudo-Xenophon (*c.* 400 BC): "Now, regarding the constitution of the Athenians, and the type or manner of constitutional arrangement that they have chosen, I shall not praise it, because the very choice of constitution favors the welfare of the poor as opposed to that of the better class" (1.1).

This is a denunciation of democracy on the grounds that it favors the poor. We cannot even dismiss this judgment as the sentiment of one person alone, as pseudo-Xenophon (who was often called the Old Oligarch) goes on to add that his opinion was common among the aristocracy: "All the world over, the cream of society is in opposition to the democracy." In contrast to modern democracy—which is often divided by concerns over bloated bureaucracy and the invasiveness of "big government"—the fault lines in Greek political thinking, then, concerned whether too many people were included in the running of the state and whether the democracy showed too much support for the poor.

In the main, however, the Greeks were proud of their way of life, which they regarded as based on principles, such as the rule of law, accountability, and the enfranchisement of male citizens, and which they increasingly preferred to monarchy or tyranny. Take, for example, the famous account of democracy contained in the speech of the Athenian general and statesman, Perikles (*c.* 495–427 BC), as recorded by the fifth-century historian Thucydides (*c.* 460–*c.* 400 BC) in Book 2 of his *History of the Peloponnesian War*. The speech is delivered on the occasion of the funeral of those who died in the first year of the war between Athens and Sparta, in 431/430 BC. In this masterpiece of political rhetoric, Perikles explains what it means to be an Athenian. Leaving aside the conventions of these public speeches—normally an orator would evoke such mythological actions as the defeat of the Amazons, or earlier historical episodes, such as the defeat of the Persians—Perikles instead depicts contemporary Athenians as far superior to their Spartan enemies, not because they are braver soldiers, but because they live lives of harmony and balance. He claims:

We rely not upon management or trickery, but upon our own hearts and hands. And in the matter of education, whereas they from early youth are always undergoing laborious exercises which are to make them brave, we live at ease, and yet are equally ready to face the perils which they face....For we are lovers of the beautiful, yet simple in our tastes, and we cultivate the mind without loss of manliness. Wealth we employ, not for talk and ostentation, but when there is a real use for it. To avow poverty with us is no disgrace; the true disgrace is in doing nothing to avoid it.

(Thucydides, *The Peloponnesian War* 2.39–40, trans. Jowett)

1.5 Leo von Klense, *The Akropolis at Athens*, AD 1846. Oil on canvas, 1.03 × 1.48 m (3 ft 5 in. × 4 ft 10 in.)

At one point in his speech, Perikles challenges the living to be a match for the men who died:

Any one can discourse to you forever about the advantages of a brave defence, which you know already. But instead of listening to him I would have you day by day fix your eyes upon the greatness of Athens, until you become filled with the love of her; and when you are impressed by the spectacle of her glory, reflect that this empire has been acquired by men who knew their duty and had the courage to do it, who in the hour of conflict had the fear of dishonour always present to them, and who, if ever they failed in an enterprise, would not allow their virtues to be lost to their country, but freely gave their lives to her as the fairest offering which they could present at her feast.

(*The Peloponnesian War* 2.43, trans. Jowett)

Imagine yourself gazing up at the **Akropolis** as you see Perikles gesture toward its gleaming new temples, such as the Parthenon. Only in a supremely confident society could a leader dare the populace to gaze upon the city's beauty as if beholding its

lover (**1.5**). In similar fashion, though perhaps a little less boldly, presidents of the United States, from Kennedy to Obama, have referred to the United States as a "Shining City on a Hill," evoking John Winthrop's 1630 sermon that called upon the Puritans to create a society living to a higher standard of morality. They use rhetoric to present democratic society in the best light, as did Perikles.

Perikles' speech is a hymn of praise to the Athenians, and the clearest statement we have of the democratic ideology of Classical Athens, but Thucydides then surprises the reader by plunging his audience into a bloody and graphic description of the plague that tore through Athens only months later, killing thousands of Athenians—including Perikles—and reducing the city to chaos. His account starts with a clinical description of symptoms:

Many who were in perfect health, all in a moment, and without any apparent reason, were seized with violent heats in the head and with redness and inflammation of the eyes. Internally the throat and the tongue were quickly

1.6 Evelyn Turner, right, with friends and family, waiting with the body of her common-law husband, Xavier Bowie, after he died in New Orleans, August 30, 2005

At the same time, however, just as Thucydides saw the plague as a brutal reminder that the Athenians were capable of savagery, impiety, and lawlessness, so too we have been reminded that democracies frequently fail to live up to their own standards of decency. The terrible Hurricane Katrina of 2005 is a recent example of a natural disaster, the deeper significance of which lies in the way it revealed underlying social tensions. Not only did it cause massive destruction in New Orleans, but it also provided hundreds of graphic images of social breakdown. Scenes at the Superdome resembled Athens in the grip of the plague. The disaster also prompted a vigorous public debate over inequalities in American society, dramatically demonstrated by the disproportionate impact of the hurricane on the African-American community (**1.6**). It is true that every country at some time or other will undergo a natural disaster, and the lessons to be drawn from it may reveal a great deal about that society's values, whether it be Chinese thinkers equating famines with a withdrawal of the mandate of heaven or Western fundamentalists viewing the AIDS epidemic as God's punishment for immorality. Thucydides would have interpreted Hurricane Katrina as a sign that America falls short of its aspirations.

suffused with blood, and the breath became unnatural and fetid. There followed sneezing and hoarseness; in a short time the disorder, accompanied by a violent cough, reached the chest; then fastening lower down, it would move the stomach and bring on all the vomits of bile to which physicians have ever given names; and they were very distressing.

(*The Peloponnesian War* 2.49, trans. Jowett)

After describing (in excruciating detail) the sufferings of those who contracted the plague, Thucydides then shifts the focus of his description to the social breakdown that accompanied the epidemic. At first this breakdown took the form of impious actions, such as hauling corpses off the funeral pyres that had been prepared for them, but it quickly gave way to a deeper crisis, as despair led more people to lose their fundamental humanity.

The reason that this account of the plague is so important is because Thucydides is doing more than describing the physical signs of an epidemic. By contrasting the idealized vision of Athens in Perikles' speech with the outrages committed during the plague, he is giving expression to a paradox that faces every democratic country proud of its values and accomplishments. That paradox is simply this: free societies are capable of the highest aspirations but must confront their own shortcomings; they are compelled to experience the tension between altruistic aspirations and conspicuous failures.

Greek Architecture and Philosophy

The similarities, then, between Athens and the modern world are neither casual nor coincidental, but reflect a significant interconnectedness between us and the Greeks. We have already noted the ways in which democracy reveals the complex relationship between ourselves and the Greeks. Other areas also bear out the assertion that we are their descendants. In architecture, for example, it is hard to imagine the modern Western world finding an expression for power and national identity without the model of the Greeks. Part of an architect's training involves learning the different orders of Greek architecture: Ionic, Doric, and Corinthian. Similarly, the vocabulary of architectural decoration—egg and dart, bead and reel, cyma reversa—derives from the styles and forms used by the Greeks and, later, the Romans throughout hundreds of years of building temples, **stoas**, and **basilicas**.

Here again, however, superficial similarity can mask significant differences. Take, for example, the Parthenon—the iconic building of Classical Greece—and consider one of its more recent offspring, the Second Bank of the United States, built in Philadelphia between AD 1818–24 (**1.7** and **1.8**).

A quick comparison shows that the designer of the American building was steeped in the conventions of architectural design that, since the Renaissance, have used Greek models as their template. Both buildings have eight Doric columns along the front, and both exhibit the same Doric **entablature** consisting of **metopes** and **triglyphs**. Quite simply, the nineteenth-century building evokes and recalls its Classical predecessor. Yet despite the deliberate visual echoes, the function of the two buildings is different. The Parthenon was built to house a massive gold-and-ivory statue of Athena, and was located within a sanctuary, the Akropolis, that was the religious and symbolic center of the Athenian state and territory. The Second Bank of the United States was, as its name suggests, built as a financial institution designed to guarantee the stability of the new nation's money supply. (It was not a success and its charter lapsed in 1836.) One could argue that the Parthenon served as a repository for the Athenians' gold and silver reserves, so that in function the buildings were not quite as different as they might seem, but no god or goddess was ever worshiped in William Strickland's Greek Revival Building other than the spirit of Commerce.

Similarity and difference are, in fact, the recurring motifs in our relationship with the Greeks. It is an unusual dynamic that also exists in the area of philosophy and ethics, one of the main legacies of the Greeks to Western intellectual thought. Indeed, the philosopher Alfred North Whitehead once observed that "the European philosophical tradition…consists of a series of footnotes to Plato," suggesting that Western philosophical inquiry has merely continued along lines laid down by the Greeks, and in truth the questions the Greeks asked still inform our thought today. From observations of the natural world to the exploration of metaphysical questions—what is the

nature of reality?—and ethical questions—how can one lead a just life?—the Greeks of the sixth and fifth centuries BC established a type of philosophical investigation that became the basis of a whole range of disciplines from physics, biology, and the hard sciences, to humanities subjects, such as history, literary criticism, and philosophy.

Here as elsewhere, the foundational status of the Greeks is not in question. But that is not the same as saying that we should venerate the Greeks. In the case of political thought and philosophy, for example, it is surprising to find that there is no systematic discussion of slavery in Plato's work, and that when slaves are mentioned, it is clear that Plato regarded them as intellectually inferior to freemen.

For Plato, the mental operations of slaves consist of ***doxa*** (opinion or belief), but not ***logos*** (rational thought). Plato developed this into an entire theory of leadership, according to which "some men are by nature fitted to embrace philosophy and lead in the state, while others are unfit to embrace it and must follow the leader" (*Republic* 474c).

Developing the notion of being fitted by nature for either freedom or servitude, in the *Politics* Aristotle (384–322 BC) posed the simple question: "But is there any one thus intended by nature to be a slave, and for whom such a condition is expedient and right, or rather is not all slavery a violation of nature?" Having asked the question in these stark terms, Aristotle answers in a brutal manner: "There is no

1.7 (top) Parthenon, *c.* 447–438 BC
1.8 (above) William Strickland, Second Bank of United States, Philadelphia, 1818–24

difficulty in answering this question, on grounds both of reason and of fact. For that some should rule and others be ruled is a thing not only necessary, but expedient; from the hour of their birth, some are marked out for subjection, others for rule" (*Politics* 1254a). Aristotle proceeds to outline a binary theory, according to which free adult men are seen as superior to women, slaves, and minors, all of whom are understood by Aristotle to be fitted by nature to be ruled. In the *Economics*, his casual discussion of how to treat slaves also reveals how conventional his views were: "We may apportion to our slaves work, punishment, and food. If men are given food, but no punishment nor any work, they become insolent" (1344a).

If it is true that European philosophy does consist of footnotes to Plato, it is also true that Plato and his followers are not always well suited to teaching us to navigate the complexities of modern life. Democratic societies that reject slavery and recognize the rights of women and minorities would have to search long and hard to find philosophical guidance from the ancient Greeks, whose political and moral thought remained stubbornly elitist and restrictive. That too is part of our inheritance from the Greeks.

East versus West?

The Greeks deserve to be studied not because their accomplishments were always and everywhere the stuff of genius, but because for better or for worse they are the touchstone to which we return. It is important to recognize this, not only to prevent ourselves from championing the Greeks at the expense of other cultures and traditions, but also because knowing the Greeks inculcates the historical consciousness that is a necessary part of living a thoughtful, engaged existence in the modern world. The importance of this lies not only in counteracting the corrosive effects of popular culture, but also because it involves an understanding of the contemporary world and the ability to view events from a historical perspective.

Does historical consciousness really matter? Consider the following: in the aftermath of the 9/11 bombings, when shock and anger were still fresh in the United States and around the world, Osama bin Laden (1957–2011) released a video denouncing the United States in the following terms: "What

America is tasting now is only a copy of what we have tasted. Our Islamic nation has been tasting the same for more than eighty years, of humiliation and disgrace, its sons killed and their blood spilled, its sanctities desecrated."

Notice that rather than simply relying on traditional anti-American rhetoric and calling the United States "the Great Satan," Bin Laden drew a parallel between current events and events that had occurred at the end of the First World War. Referring to the British and French settlement of the Middle East, Bin Laden found a direct equivalence between the Sykes–Picot Agreement (1916), the Treaty of Sèvres (1920), and the abolition of the last Muslim caliphate in Istanbul (1924) on the one side, and the destruction of the Twin Towers of the World Trade Center on the other. In each case, these events signaled (in Bin Laden's view) momentous shifts in power, but his words had to be glossed by experts in Middle Eastern politics in order to explain these references, so radically different was his historical consciousness from ours. Events that were historical footnotes in the West, remembered only by university professors, were still a source of aggravation to a man who hated everything about Western culture. In fact, his historical frame of reference was utterly at odds with ours. His attack on the West continued with this claim: "Let the whole world know that we shall never accept that the tragedy of Andalusia would be repeated in Palestine. We cannot accept that Palestine will become Jewish."

It is not only the ferocity of the rhetoric that is notable, but also the way in which events that occurred more than five hundred years ago are spoken of as if they had only just taken place, and as if there were a direct and immediate link between the *Reconquista* in 1492 (when Christian armies defeated the Islamic rulers of Spain), and the declaration of the state of Israel in 1948. For Bin Laden, there had been a continuous war between Islam and Christianity lasting at least five hundred years, without even taking the Crusades into account. If Britain and Spain were two of the Christian powers that assaulted Muslim power, then America was, in Bin Laden's eyes, just the latest Christian oppressor.

Now Bin Laden is dead, but headlines each day make it clear that particularly vicious forms of fundamentalism continue to thrive. A caliphate has been declared in Syria and Iraq, Hezbollah and Israel

1.9 Funerary marker commemorating the Spartans at Thermopylae, with the text of Simonides' epigram: "Go tell the Spartans, Stranger, that here we lie / Obedient to their orders"

trade rockets, and from Afghanistan to Nigeria girls are forced to leave school, adopt the veil, and in some cases are kidnapped. In every case the cost in terms of innocent human lives is terrible.

How does this concern the question with which we began: why study the Greeks? Many people are rightfully wary about any rhetoric that posits a continuous battle between East and West, with the two sides endlessly replaying age-old historical conflicts. Yet modern conflicts have deep roots; deeper, perhaps, than even Bin Laden claimed. The war between Greece and Persia may be said to be the first instance of a confrontation that has manifested itself at various times over the last 2,500 years. It is not always the same conflict, to be sure, but modern conflicts have deep roots. Quite simply, if we are going to ask young men and women to risk injury or death in defense of our liberties and our way of life, especially facing enemies who are fundamentally opposed to what they see as the corruption of Western society, we have an obligation to understand our own societies better: we cannot know where we are going without knowing where we come from.

One final comparison will serve to make the case that studying the Greeks is important and timely, and once again it is a story with more than one side. In 480 BC, as the combined forces of the Persian empire were descending upon Greece, the Spartan king Leonidas (*c.* 530–480 BC) marched up into central Greece and fortified the position at Thermopylae, where the mountains come down to the sea, and where a bottleneck would make the Persian advance difficult. Over the space of three days the Spartans and their allies successfully repulsed the Persians, until a Greek traitor showed the Persians a track through the mountains, allowing them to trap the Spartans. Vastly outnumbered and knowing that to remain meant to die, the Spartans chose to do so. The fifth-century historian Herodotos (*c.* 485–*c.* 424 BC) described what came next:

Xerxes and the barbarians attacked, but Leonidas and the Greeks, knowing they were going to their deaths, advanced now much farther than before into the wider part of the pass. Throughout the day before they had sallied out into the narrow way and fought there, guarding the defensive wall. Now, however, they joined battle outside the narrows and many of the barbarians fell, for the leaders of the companies beat everyone with whips from behind, urging them forward. Many of them were pushed into the sea and drowned. Far more were trampled alive by each other, with no regard for who perished. Since the Greeks knew they must die at the hands of those who had come around the mountain, they displayed the greatest strength they had against the barbarians, fighting recklessly and desperately.

(Herodotos, *Histories* 7.223, trans. Godley)

That heroism quickly became legend. Even today, you can visit the marker at Thermopylae commemorating the sacrifice of the Spartans and find it adorned with wildflowers, left by men and women still moved by the story of Leonidas (**1.9**; see p. 25).

The Persians would be defeated by the Greeks a short time later at Salamis, and again a year later at Plataia, but the Spartan sacrifice had already helped to shape the way the entire war would be remembered. The effect of their actions was immediate and galvanic. Victor Davis Hanson, a noted modern historian, describes the aftermath of the Spartan defeat at Thermopylae:

So almost immediately, contemporary Greeks saw Thermopylae as a critical moral and culture lesson. In universal terms, a small, free people had willingly outfought huge numbers of imperial subjects who advanced under the lash. More specifically, the Western idea that soldiers themselves decide where, how, and against whom they will fight was contrasted against the Eastern notion of despotism and monarchy—freedom proving the stronger idea as the more courageous fighting of the Greeks at Thermopylae, and their later victories at Salamis and Plataea attested.

("History and the Movie '300'," *Private Papers*)

This is one side of the story. The other is less heroic, yet it deserves to be told as well. The victory of the Greeks led to the flowering of Athenian culture in the fifth century BC, to be sure. The dramas of Aischylos (525–456 BC), Sophokles (497–406 BC), and Euripides (*c.* 485–406 BC), for example, would be hard to imagine without the vibrant cultural life of Athens that resulted from victory over the Persians, but the same Athens that took pride in defeating the Persians at Salamis was, by the end of the fifth century, a city that mocked the enemy.

The Eurymedon Vase (**1.10**), a jug commemorating the defeat of the Persians in 467–465 BC at the Battle of Eurymedon, shows a Greek man holding his penis as he advances on a frightened archer in oriental dress. The Persian holds up his arms in alarm, as he is about to be sodomized by the Greek.

There is no hint of Olympian calm or moderation in this imagery. Victory over the Persians prompted an ugly, jingoistic delight in their defeat, and the demeaning and dismissive attitude of the Greeks toward the Persians reflected a response to victory over them that was just as profound as the glorious accomplishments of the fifth century. If we are the

1.10a Eurymedon Vase, *c.* 460 BC. Ceramic, H: 23.8 cm (9⅜ in.)

1.10b Eurymedon Vase, reverse view

1.11 Darius (seated) and his son, Xerxes, holding audience. Persepolis, *c.* 490 BC. Limestone, H: 2.54 m (8 ft 4 in.)

heirs of the Greeks and can claim the sculpture of the Parthenon as part of our patrimony, then our capacity to lump Islam, Iran, and the varied cultures of the Near East into a catch-all category of "Other," or "the Bad Guys," is unfortunately another part of our Greek legacy. Either way, it is the same patrimony. The development of the Western stereotype of the Eastern Other is illustrated by these contrasting images depicting fifth-century Persians.

The relief sculpture shown in **1.11**, created about ten years before the start of the Persian War, depicts the Persian king, Darius I (*c.* 550–486 BC), and his successor Xerxes (the victor at Thermopylae) on the treasury wall at Persepolis. Drawing on conventions of Near Eastern royal iconography, the image emphasizes the Great King's authority by showing him seated, while his subjects stand before him, some bowing. He and his son are also shown as greater than life-size, emphasizing their special status. Darius holds a staff, a symbol of his royal authority. Both he and his son hold lotus blossoms, a popular motif in Achaemenid (i.e. royal Persian) art. The impression created by this iconography is, as we would expect of royal art, one of gravity, order, and sophistication. The king and the royal prince preside over a stable court, in which each group, from all corners of the empire, knows its place.

Contrast this depiction with the portrayal of Xerxes (520–465 BC) in Zach Snyder's film adaptation of Frank Miller's graphic novel *300* (**1.12**). In this recent example, the "Persian" king is depicted as bald, clean-

1.12 Rodrigo Santoro as Xerxes in Zack Snyder's *300* (2006)

shaven, studded, and pierced. It need hardly be said that this has nothing to do with Persian iconographic traditions. Instead, this modern version of Xerxes serves as a caricatured projection of the Eastern threat. Vaguely "black," slim-hipped, and suggestively bisexual, with a serious addiction to bling, this updated Xerxes is very different from his Achaemenid predecessor, and his exchanges with the Spartan king are laden with sexual menace. It is hard not to notice that the exaggerated images, with their confusing mixture of homoeroticism and homophobia, are the product of Athens and Hollywood, while the Eastern iconography is, by comparison, sober and serious. In the early twenty-first century, it seems, we are capable of producing images of the East that perpetuate the category of "barbarian." We might well ask, to what end?

Paideia

The answer to the question, why study the Greeks, can be summarized by the following propositions. All learning is an antidote to the "fluff" of pop culture, and all study of history feeds historical consciousness, helping us to reach a better understanding of our societies and how they came to be as they are. In that respect, studying the early history of China, or the Maya, or any other cultural group, also qualifies as valuable. But given that any active engagement with the past makes us more thoughtful, alert, and engaged, the study of the Greeks is akin to research into our own families, and the relationship we have with the Greeks is similar to the complicated relationship that exists between family members of different generations. Love them or hate them (or both), they remain undeniably a part of our cultural DNA.

In the fourth century BC, Isokrates (436–338 BC), an Athenian thinker and rhetorician, addressed the new realities of being Greek at a time when old powers were fading and new ones emerging. He offered a new, more inclusive definition of being Greek, writing, "We call Greek those who share our *paideia* [education]." The paideia to which he referred was not only education in the narrow sense of learning poetry, music, and mathematics, but also something more broad: culture. To explore ethics honestly, to debate policy vigorously, to value beauty deeply, and to do all these things openly and in a spirit of generosity and civility, with respect for one's opponents: these are the hallmarks of the civilized, engaged citizen. This is the paideia we share with the Greeks. We keep returning to the Greeks, I think, because we will never be as good, as heroic, as decent, as honorable as we would like to be. How could we? We are human, and therefore flawed. But the Greeks offer us a glimpse of something better, and having ideals even when

your models are flawed may not be such a bad thing after all. In David's painting of the men about to die at Thermopylae (see Chapter 7), the victors' wreaths are being offered to the man who carves the words of Simonides' epigram into the rock face:

Go tell the Spartans, Stranger, that here we lie
Obedient to their orders.

So, the Greeks are like the Greatest Generation: better than we are, a model for what we would like to be, and a reminder that whatever flaws a society may have, it can distinguish itself by its accomplishments and create a legacy worth cherishing. In the last year of his presidency, Barack Obama addressed the challenges facing modern societies and spoke of the threats to our "pluralism and...openness, our rule of law, our civil liberties: the very things that make [the United States] great, the very things that make us exceptional." Whether intentionally or not, the President was signaling that we share the paideia of the Greeks. We are the Greeks.

Spotlight
The Afterlife of Monsters

At a spot in southwestern Turkey called Yanartaş, or Fire Mountain, travelers can see rock vents from which flames continuously burn, fed by natural gas (**1.13**).

The ancient name for the region is Lycia, and it is here that the hero Bellerophon, mounted on the winged horse Pegasus, slew the monstrous fire-breathing Chimera. The creature—who, according to myth, was kept by the king of Lycia, Amisodaros, in order to destroy his enemies—is probably based on the peculiar natural phenomenon of these perennial fires. The transformation of natural gas fires into the mythical Chimera illustrates the many ways in which the Greeks used myths. Just as many indigenous people use songs, dances, and rituals to explain the natural world, so too the Greeks used myths inventively to make sense of the world around them.

According to the poet Hesiod (*c.* 700 BC), writing in the eighth or seventh century BC, Chimera was a three-headed monster. Homer offers a fuller description in the *Iliad*:

First Iobates sent Bellerophon away with orders to kill the Chimera, a creature none might approach; a thing of immortal make, not human, lion-fronted and snake behind, a goat in the middle, and snorting out the breath of the terrible flame of bright fire. He killed the Chimera, obeying the portents of the immortals.

(Homer, *Iliad* 6.179, trans. Lattimore)

This passage is a good example of storytelling in the Greek world during the Archaic period, from 700 to 480 BC. The Greeks of that period viewed earlier times as an age of gods and heroes, when threatening monsters everywhere had to be tamed or destroyed. Herakles and the Nemean Lion, Zeus and Typhoeus, and Theseus and the Bull of Marathon are just three examples of gods and heroes defeating the forces of chaos. The Chimera of Arezzo, an Etruscan bronze statue cast around 400 BC, corresponds to this

1.14 The Chimera of Arezzo, *c.* 400 BC. Bronze, L: 1.29 m (4 ft 3 in.)

1.15 The Boread Painter, Lakonian black-figure kylix, *c.* 570–565 BC. Ceramic, D: 14 cm (5½ in.)

1.16 Corinthian stater with Pegasus and Swastika (solar symbol), *c.* 550–500 BC. Silver, 8.6 grams

Homeric version of the creature (**1.14**). It probably comes from a larger statue group that also showed Bellerophon attacking the monster.

As early as the sixth century BC, black-figure vessels depicted Bellerophon and Pegasus battling with the Chimera (**1.15**). But as the story's popularity grew, the Chimera's special association with Lycia faded into the background and other elements became more prominent. Besides being a Lycian monster, the Chimera also became part of a cycle of stories told in Corinth on the Greek mainland. The Corinthians claimed a special connection with Pegasus in particular: it was in their land that Pegasus used to drink at the Peirene fountain, and Corinthian coins used Pegasus as a symbol to stand for the city, just as owls stood for Athens and turtles for Aigina (**1.16**). In response, the Sikyonians—the Corinthians' neighbors (and frequent enemies)—adopted the Chimera as their emblem; if Corinth had the winged horse, the Sikyonians would have an equally distinctive symbol: the fire-breathing lion-goat-serpent hybrid (**1.17**). After 400 BC they began minting coins with the Chimera as their emblem. The Lycian story had been adapted to express local rivalries in mainland Greece.

The Chimera's travels did not end in Corinth and Sikyon. It proved to be a very durable monster, and as Greek culture spread across the Mediterranean, the representation of Bellerophon defeating the Chimera would turn up in many places all over the Roman empire, becoming one of the most popular images from the repertoire of stories and images taken from Greek myth. Mosaics showing this scene have been found as far afield as Nîmes, in southern France, and Palmyra in the Syrian desert, where this mosaic was found by Polish excavators in AD 2003 (**1.18**). The excavators noted the similarity between the composition of the scene and later depictions of St. George and the Dragon.

The many transformations of the Chimera, from a natural gas fire in Turkey to the natural enemy of England's patron saint, nicely illustrate the fact that Greek myth continues to connect us (often in unexpected ways) to the ancient world. Chimeras have appeared in modern culture both in the world of J. K. Rowling's series of Harry Potter novels and also as the title of a live action role-playing game based on the *Chronicles of Narnia*. Chimeras, along with the other creatures of Greek myth, are a part of our cultural DNA. As with the genes that make up our actual DNA, the chimeras we have inherited can be a mixed blessing. The analogy with genetics is even more apt when one considers how scientists in the 1980s began to create creatures with various combinations of human and animal genes in order to study human biological processes at a cellular level and to provide incubators for human organs. Such creations are known in the scientific community as "chimeras." The ethical complexities of such scientific research are profound, and the disquiet that many people feel at the violation of the boundaries between species is surely the same for us as it was for the Greeks when they gave thought to monsters with bodies of different species. Perhaps our scientific chimeras are not far distant from their Classical ancestors.

1.17 Sikyonia drachma with Chimera and Dove, *c.* 330 BC. Silver, 11.9 grams

1.18 Bellerophon and Pegasus slaying the Chimera, Palmyra, *c.* AD 260. Mosaic

Chapter 2

Early Greece and the Minoans: The Labyrinth and the Minotaur

This chapter concerns the world of Minoan Crete. We first move through Early Greece, in order to understand the development of agriculture, trade, and hierarchical society that contributed to the development of a Minoan civilization. The site plan of Knossos anchors a discussion of the Minoan redistributive economy and we explore the notion of Minoan palatial culture as essentially priestly and theatrical. The phases of Minoan culture are also introduced, with special attention paid to Thera and the volcanic eruption that destroyed it. We also use comparative evidence from the ancient Near East to locate the Minoans within the broader range of eastern Mediterranean cultures. An important theme is the intimate connection between the Greek world and the ancient Near East. The chapter closes by discussing a key methodological issue regarding the ability to draw inferences from non-textual material.

Greece in the Neolithic: The Origins of Complex Societies

How far back does Greek prehistory go? Recent research by a Greek–American team studying stone tool production in southwest Crete has shown that early hominins reached Crete by sea no later than 130,000 years before the present, many thousands of years earlier than was thought even ten years ago. At the Franchthi Cave in the Argolid, in southern Greece, seasonal occupation goes back to 18,000 BC, in the Paleolithic. Here, even before the introduction of domesticated plants and animals, hunters and gatherers were subsisting on a diet rich in meat from the red deer that they also hunted for skins, sinews, antlers, and bone. After 11,000 BC, there is evidence for the consumption of lentils, vetch, pistachios, and almonds; after 7000 BC, wild oats and wild barley are also present in the botanical record. Gradually, the people who dwelt in the cave began to exploit the coastal waters nearby: fish bones include those of deep-water species, such as tuna. Human occupation of the cave continues down to the end of the Neolithic, c. 3200 BC, constituting an extraordinary period of occupation lasting almost fifteen thousand years.

Other early communities reveal a similar story of long development. At Dikili Tash in northern Greece, French excavators have unearthed a **tell**, or hill, occupied continuously from 6400 BC to 4000 BC, and again in the Bronze Age, while cave-dwelling communities (similar to those at Franchthi) lived around the southern Peloponnese, the landmass situated below the Isthmus of Corinth, at such sites as the Alepotrypa Cave by the bay of Deros. Here, current excavations have brought to light evidence for occupation of the cave in the Middle and Late Neolithic period, from 5000 BC to 3200 BC. The cave is also notable for its burials: 161 individuals have come to light, some cremated but others buried in shafts 5 meters (16 ft) deep close to the mouth of the cave. As at Franchthi, the community chose a secluded and defensible spot close to the water's edge.

Connectedness and the Beginnings of Pottery

These Paleolithic and Neolithic communities did not live in isolation, but were able to trade over long distances. At the Franchthi Cave, obsidian (a dark, glass-like volcanic rock) from the island of Melos was used for making arrowheads, blades, and scrapers. Since Melos is 150 kilometers (93 mi.) away, the presence of obsidian confirms that even in prehistoric times people were in contact with other communities, including those that could be reached only by boat.

In the fifth and fourth millennia BC, two sites attest to the continuing evolution of complex societies in central Greece. At Sesklo, in southern Thessaly, the population lived in a village comprised of mud-brick huts, built on a small rise overlooking a river valley where the population grew the domesticated crops of wheat and barley. Sesklo marks the introduction of pottery into the Greek world, and is particularly notable for the terra-cotta female figurines that probably attest to fertility cult. At Dimini, a site 5 kilometers (3 mi.) to the east where occupation may have overlapped with Sesklo, the Neolithic site is

2.1 Spherical vase with polychrome decoration, Dimini, Late Neolithic or Final Neolithic (5300–3300 BC). Ceramic

2.2 VRML (Virtual Reality Modeling Language) model of Dimini

situated above a fertile plain running down to the sea, which in the fifth millennium was only about 1 kilometer (0.6 mi.) away, giving the inhabitants access to a trade network that reached across the Aegean. The high quality of the polychrome pottery from Dimini attests to the vitality of the culture (**2.1**).

Both these communities were agro-pastoral villages. The floral and faunal evidence shows that people lived by farming and herding, usually sheep, goats, and pigs. Some hunting and gathering of wild grains supplemented the diet, but in comparison with the earlier communities at Franchthi or Deros, these communities reveal the growing complexity of Neolithic culture in Greece. They occupied sites overlooking the areas they farmed and the inhabitants lived in these villages year round. The earliest houses were usually simple wattle and daub affairs, but were later replaced by mud-brick walls built on a stone socle and topped by pitched roofs. Interpreting the structure of these Neolithic communities is not easy, but the presence of thick circuit walls is suggestive. As the reconstruction in **2.2** shows, the walls at Dimini were built in concentric circles, between 1 and 1.7 meters (3–5 ft) high, arranged radially and intersected by four passageways. What was the purpose of the construction? They were built either for defensive purposes or possibly as retaining walls. In either case, they reveal central planning and a clear demarcation of space. The existence of a single larger building at the center of the settlement, referred to as a *megaron*, has been plausibly interpreted as a sign of an emerging central authority, a "big man," or chieftain. As social stratification took place, we can infer the

emergence of status and class distinctions of the type that would later characterize Minoan society.

The Third Millennium: The Bronze Age

Sesklo and Dimini illustrate the growing complexity of the cultures of the Greek mainland. This picture becomes even richer with the widespread adoption of bronze metallurgy in the third millennium BC and the growing connectivity of the Aegean world at this time as the circulation of goods and people increased. For example, a spectacular graveyard has been excavated at Tsepi in the plain of Marathon, dating to the Early Helladic periods I and II (**2.3**). ("Early Helladic" is a term used to describe a sequence of periods that delineate the changing cultural history of Bronze Age mainland Greece.) The cemetery consists of sixty-four graves, arranged in neat rows and according to a template: the rectangular graves are lined with either river stones or schist, and covered by slabs, indicating that the entire cemetery was carefully planned. The pottery assemblages point to connections with the Cyclades, and the presence of litharge (a form of lead oxide) is some of the earliest evidence for the refining process of cupellation and the smelting of lead and silver. The Tsepi cemetery brings us tantalizingly close to a third millennium community that traded with the Aegean islands.

Another important site from this period is Lerna, at the head of the Argolic Gulf. Here excavators have identified six separate phases of occupation and

2.3 Chamber tombs from the Tsepi cemetery, near Marathon, Attica, dating to between 3200 and 2000 BC

construction. Around 2500 BC, the people of Lerna erected a monumental building of the "Corridor House" type. Buildings of a similar style are found on Aigina (an island in the Saronic Gulf; see **2.4**), as far north as mainland Thebes, and at a handful of other sites in the Argolid (such as Zygouries). These impressive structures, which often feature a second floor and staircases, suggest both the control of labor and centralized authority. At Lerna, the main building was notable for its roof of baked terra-cotta tiles and was surrounded by a double ring of defensive walls. When the building was destroyed by fire, the local people constructed a circle of stones around the central part of the ruin and erected a **tumulus,** or earthen mound, over the center. Was this meant to commemorate a powerful chief? Quite possibly, yet some interpret these not as chieftains' palaces but as communal buildings. As with many aspects of Bronze Age culture, interpretation is often difficult due to the sparseness of evidence.

Elsewhere in the Aegean there are also signs of change in the third millennium BC, but again these also raise questions of interpretation. Excavations at Phylokopi on Melos; Poliochni, Myrina, and Koukonisi on Lemnos; and Skarkos on Ios (**2.5**) have brought to light both buildings and fortification walls that could only be the work of complex, hierarchically organized societies, although there are no signs of the monumental central buildings of the mainland. Recent excavations at Skarkos, however, have revealed the existence of many buildings that were two stories high, with stone-paved floors, and a drainage system; clearly the work of a centrally organized community.

The coastal site of Myrina on Lemnos illustrates the complexity and sophistication of these early

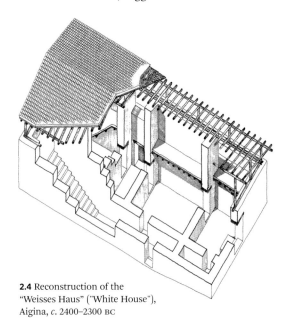

2.4 Reconstruction of the "Weisses Haus" ("White House"), Aigina, *c.* 2400–2300 BC

2.5 Circuit and terrace walls at Skarkos, Ios, *c.* 2500 BC

communities. Here, well protected from the prevailing winds, a settlement developed shortly before 3000 BC. By 2500, after the transition from the Final Neolithic to the Early Bronze Age, the settlement would grow to cover an area of 80,000 square meters (900,000 sq. ft), and at its height had a population of between three and four thousand people. They built dwellings out of stone and engineered a sewerage and drainage system using stone-built channels that ran down the cobbled lanes between the houses.

Pottery is also important for reconstructing the history of the Aegean world in the Early Bronze Age. The term Keros-Syros culture, for example, is used to describe a number of sites in the Cyclades that share the same type of pottery and building design. The intensification of exchange that produced this homogeneous culture was not necessarily a peaceful process. The same period and region also produced many depictions of longboats, rowed by crews of at least twenty-five men, and these appear to represent the assertion of power by the larger communities, such as Chalandriani on Syros, over smaller, outlying communities.

Another body of evidence from the Bronze Age in the Aegean that is hard to understand clearly is that of the marble sculptures usually known as Cycladic figurines (**2.6**). Those that come from secure archaeological contexts, usually burials, can be put into a typological sequence (a method of classifying artifacts according to shared characteristics), showing whether they date from early or late in the third millennium, but the function of these figurines remains difficult to identify. Most are schematic representations of the female body, less than 1 meter (3 ft) tall, with arms folded across the chest, rudimentary breasts, and pubic triangle.

Are they idols and objects of veneration, suggesting a cult of female fertility, or are they no more than dolls? The fact that they are carved of marble and found all over the Aegean and even further afield attests to the importance of these figurines, but questions remain. Were they handled? Were they displayed? Do they represent deities? Ancestral or household spirits? Might they have been used in the same way as Hopi *kachina* dolls, to represent the spirits of families and the local communities? Architecture, walls, pottery, and iconography all require interpretation, and without literary sources to help us, how confidently can we reconstruct the

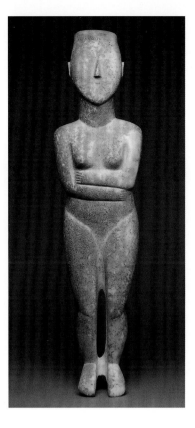

2.6 Cycladic figurine, Spedos type, *c.* 2600–2400 BC. Marble, H: 49 cm (19¼ in.)

communities that left us these physical remains? As with much of Greek prehistory, a first step toward answering these questions depends on assembling as much information as possible, but the interpretation of these data still relies on inferences and comparisons. The gaps in our knowledge are considerable. For example, we simply do not know if these figurines were used as part of a ceremony, or if there was a prayer or an invocation or a ritual that was focused on any of these figurines.

So far we have witnessed a gradual increase in the complexity of Greece's prehistoric communities. As they grew in size, they appear to have become more stratified, and the degree of connectivity between them (measured by the appearance of trade goods and pottery styles turning up across locations far apart) points to a unique feature of the Greek world: hundreds of communities were kept in close proximity by the water. The water did not separate the communities of Greece, but rather encouraged communication: of goods, of people, and of ideas. The intensification we see in the Neolithic would lead straight to the hierarchical social order of Bronze Age societies, first on Crete.

Minoan Crete

The one region of Bronze Age Greece that has captured the modern imagination most completely is Crete. This is due in part to the dramatic way in which the central site of Crete, Knossos, was uncovered. Heinrich Schliemann's excavations at Troy and at Mycenae in the 1870s (discussed at greater length in Chapter 3) had demonstrated that there was a material culture that could be associated with the world of the Homeric poems, and which archaeology could recover. At the end of the nineteenth century AD, it seemed as though archaeology could turn the myths and stories told by the Greeks into tangible history.

Along with Troy and Mycenae, Crete had long held a special place in the myths of the Greeks as the home of the legendary king Minos and his monstrous son, the Minotaur (conceived when his mother seduced a bull), and the labyrinth in which the Minotaur feasted on the flesh of young Athenians sacrificed to the beast. Beginning in AD 1900 at Knossos, the British archaeologist Sir Arthur Evans (1851–1941), with the help of a large team of Cretan workers, began uncovering a vast palace of the Bronze Age, and here, as at Troy, it seemed as though archaeology had discovered the actual remains of a civilization that until then had existed only in myth. They uncovered a vast building complex with dozens of rooms and winding corridors that would baffle anyone not familiar with the layout: it seemed as though Minos's Labyrinth had been discovered at last.

Over the past one hundred years, study of the material culture of the Cretan Bronze Age has allowed us to refine the basic chronology first proposed by Evans. There is still some dispute over terminology, and exact dates are subject to change as more refined techniques of dating are developed, such as dendrochronology (dating using tree rings), carbon-14 (dating using a radioactive isotope of carbon), and thermoluminescence (heating an ancient material and measuring the light emitted). The broadest categories of Minoan chronology concern the development, acme, destruction, and rebuilding of its palaces. As we shall see, however, the palaces are not the only sites of interest in Crete's Bronze Age.

The society that inhabited Evans's Knossos was sophisticated and complex. This is reflected in the ground plan of the site, with its attention to regularity and strict adherence to axial design (2.7). Notice that access to the center of the complex is restricted and controlled: to reach the throne room, one must penetrate to the very heart of the palace, having entered through a monumental structure at the northern or southern end. A similarly carefully designed palace is also known from Ugarit, in Syria, and it too dates from the middle of the second millennium BC. This similarity between Syrian and Cretan palace design is important as it is the first evidence of Cretan culture participating in a wider world of complex, hierarchically organized states. (Evidence for this involvement in a wider world builds through the second millennium.) The corridors that led toward the central plaza were decorated with large frescoes, depicting human figures in processional poses (such as the so-called Prince of the Lilies fresco), or charging, life-size bulls. The impression created by the controlled access, sumptuous frescoes, and heraldic gryphons flanking a throne, is that of a powerful central authority, although we do not know whether it was

2.7 Ground plan of Knossos

a king, a queen, a priest, or a priestess who sat on the throne. The entire complex, however, displays a highly theocratic character, so much so, in fact, that some scholars have suggested that no one lived here continuously, and that these "court-complexes," as they prefer to call the palaces, were ceremonial and ritual centers, not palaces in the modern sense of the word. The ground plan of Knossos is repeated at other major Minoan sites, namely Malia, Phaistos, and Zakro, and the consistency of this planning is significant, since it suggests a homogeneous Cretan culture. In each case, the entire complex is designed with a large, open court at the center. To the east were rooms that are often interpreted as royal apartments. Deep airwells and broad staircases gave access to large, well-lit rooms that were decorated with beautiful frescoes depicting delightful scenes, such as dolphins cavorting. Some of these rooms were also equipped with baths, and they give the impression of a sophisticated and refined elite who lived in comfort. To the west were a throne room, a lustral basin (used for ceremonial purification), and rooms where the decoration and small finds suggest ceremonial and ritual functions. Beyond these lay the magazines (long, narrow storage chambers).

Bull-leaping

The central court around which all these sections of the palace were laid out was probably the venue for the most significant ritual in Minoan religion.

A comparable phenomenon can be observed in the plazas of Mayan cities, but unlike the ball game of the New World sites, the Minoan ritual focused on a cult of the bull, and particularly the performance of bull-leaping, often incorrectly called a sport. Although it required superb athletic skill, it is unlikely that bull-leaping was done purely for entertainment. Instead, it is much more probable that the performance was a reenactment of an astronomical story explaining the movement of the stars. Just as the constellation of Perseus "leaps over" the Bull to rescue Andromeda in the night sky, so too young Cretan athletes leapt over a bull, in a reenactment of the cosmological episode. As with much else in Minoan culture, our interpretation is based on inference and is not confirmed by literary texts, but the immense importance of bull cult is not in doubt. Wealthy Cretans wore signet rings with scenes of bull-leaping carved into precious stones, and the cult performance is known from frescoes and terra-cotta figurines. The horns of consecration (a symbol representing the horns of the sacred bull) found everywhere in Minoan art also attest to the popularity of bull cult on Crete. Nor was this confined to Minoan Crete. Recent excavations at the Hyksos capital of Avaris in Egypt have revealed that bull-leaping was practiced there too (**2.8**).

The presence of bull-leaping at Avaris alerts us to an important feature of Minoan Crete's role in the wider Mediterranean, namely that the Cretans

2.8 Reconstruction of bull-leaping wall paintings, Tell el-Dab'a (ancient Avaris), sixteenth century BC

2.9 Cretans bearing gifts. Wall painting in the tomb of Rekhmire, 1475–1425 BC

2.10 Detail of Agia Triada sarcophagus, depicting a scene of cattle sacrifice

2.11 Rhyton, Knossos, 1550–1500 BC. Steatite, H: 30.5 cm (11¾ in.)

on their backs, requesting the breath [of life], wanting to be loyal to His Majesty, so that His Majesty's might would protect them.

> (*Urk* IV, 1098: 14–1099: 3, trans. Galán)

The expression "breath of life" was used by the Egyptians to signify a group's willingness to become vassals of the Egyptian king, so that the gifts they brought should be thought of as part of an exchange with the pharaoh. What did the Cretans receive in return? A reference to "Keftiu" (the Egyptian name for Crete) ships being constructed at the royal dockyard of Peru-nefer has been interpreted to mean that the Minoans received aid from the pharaoh: Egyptian-built fleets may have helped to project Minoan power well beyond Crete.

Although depictions of bull-leaping on Crete and elsewhere do not show the bulls being slaughtered, it is likely that they were both sacrificed and venerated. A sarcophagus from Agia Triada, for example, shows a bull trussed and hoisted on to a table, blood pouring from a wound in its neck where it has just been stabbed by a priestess (**2.10**). Rhyta were carved out of steatite to represent the bulls' heads (**2.11**), and it has been shown that these rhyta were then ritually destroyed and buried, constituting a kind of second sacrifice. It has also been suggested that the rhyta, which would have been too heavy to drink from, were used to hold the blood of the sacrificial bulls. Taken together, the presence of the open courts in the middle of these palaces, the clear evidence of coherent planning and design, and the location of a throne room nearby allow us to imagine a Minoan society that had developed an elaborate hieratic, or priestly, character. Still, whether the king (or queen) was also a high priest (or priestess), or was even regarded as the embodiment of a god (or goddess), we do not know.

participated in a much broader range of cultural relations than simply with the Greek mainland or the islands nearby. Wall paintings in tombs of the Egyptian New Kingdom depict Cretans bearing gifts to the pharaoh. The tomb of Rekhmire, for example, dating either from the reign of Thutmosis III or Amenhotep II in the middle of the fifteenth century BC, shows men wearing the distinctive Cretan kilt and holding *rhyta* (large stone vessels that weighed up to three kilograms [6 lbs 10 oz.] when full) and sheets of copper in the shape of oxhides (**2.9**), comparable to those found on the Uluburun wreck (see below). The painting is accompanied by a text that reads:

The coming in peace of Keftiu chiefs and the chiefs of the islands of the sea, humbly, bowing their heads down because of His Majesty's might, the king Menkheperre [Thutmosis III]—given life forever! When they heard his achievements in every foreign land, their *jnw* [gifts] were

Minoan Religion

What we can say about Minoan religion is that, despite connections with the Near East as exemplified by the layout of the palaces themselves and the ubiquity of bull cult, in other respects Crete was different from the rest of the eastern Mediterranean. There do not appear to have been temples to the gods, or "gods' houses" (as they are styled in other Bronze Age cultures). Furthermore, gold rings frequently depict figures hovering in the air, and it has been suggested that these represent a moment of epiphany, and the arrival of a divine spirit. Some scholars have speculated—and this really is speculation—that frescoes appearing to show goddesses seated on a throne actually represent priestesses impersonating the goddess, and this has led to the notion that Minoan religion involved rites and practices that resulted in altered consciousness and spiritual possession. Minoan iconography is suggestive: this goddess figurine, shown wearing a crown of poppies, has led to speculation that opiates derived from poppies may have been part of religious practice (**2.12**).

But the reality is that we know very little about the practices and much less about the beliefs of the men and women who used these objects in their religious lives. Snake goddesses—faience figurines showing women wearing Minoan skirts with snakes wrapped around their arms—were relatively common (**2.13**), but whether these were equivalent to the snake handlers in the south of the United States, or were some kind of ancestor worship—the snake being a symbol of regeneration—we cannot say with certainty.

We are on surer ground when it comes to another ritual that can be inferred from the ceramic evidence and iconography: feasting. The significance of the feast as a crucial social institution has become better understood in recent years as archaeologists have drawn on anthropological studies and comparative evidence. It is at the feast that the community is most vividly on display, and it is an opportunity for elites to advertise their power most dramatically, particularly in the act of distributing food and wine. These "patron-role" feasts, as they are known, encouraged social bonding and can often be identified by distinctive ceramic assemblages, including large **kraters**, or bowls, in which wine was presented before being poured in to individual **kylikes** (a type

2.12 Poppy goddess, Gazi, Crete, c. 1350 BC. Terra-cotta, H: 79 cm (31 in.)

2.13 Snake goddess, Knossos, *c.* 1600 BC. Faience, H: 34.2 cm (13½ in.)

2.14 Linear B tablet found at Knossos, recording precious metal vessels in the shape of bull's heads and cups, *c.* 1375–1350 BC. Clay

a syllabic and ideographic system that was employed by scribes to record the produce that came in to the palaces and the goods that were dispatched. Unfortunately, too little of Linear A survives to be translated with certainty, and what there is amounts to little more than requisition lists and receipts. A fuller corpus of material, however, exists from the later part of the Bronze Age in Linear B, the second writing system used on Crete, and one that has been successfully translated. Using many of the same symbols as the earlier script, Linear B was scratched into the wet clay of tablets that were used to keep track of the palace's goods. When the palaces were destroyed by fire, any tablets present were baked, rendering permanent records that were originally just daily accounts (**2.14**). Although the Linear B records are disappointing from the point of view of poetry and literature—there is no Cretan equivalent, for example, of the Mesopotamian *Epic of Gilgamesh*—the translated documents have nevertheless been a treasure trove for scholars trying to understand the palatial economy. Taken in conjunction with the great storerooms found on the western side of the Knossos complex, the Linear B tablets reveal that the palace was the center of a redistributive economy.

of shallow cup). Other distinctive types of pottery, conical cups and bowls in particular, which occur in volume at the sites of the feasts, also indicate communal feasting. At Phaistos, where the evidence of feasting has been studied closely by Italian excavators, it appears that feasting was carried out as part of funerary rites as well as on the occasion of religious festivals. The palaces, then, should be viewed as venues for religious performances and social institutions, all of which gave expression to a rich and complicated social structure.

Given the rich material culture uncovered by Evans at Knossos, the lack of any surviving Minoan literature comes as a surprise, and highlights a real challenge to our understanding of Bronze Age culture. Despite sharing much in common with the other great Bronze Age cultures of the eastern Mediterranean (notably Egypt, Assyria, and the Hittites), the Minoans did not record liturgical texts, legal documents, or historical chronicles in any semi-permanent forms, such as on clay tablets or papyrus. This is puzzling, since it is hard to imagine that they did not produce such a literature. It is especially odd considering that the highly developed, hierarchically organized society of Minoan Crete did develop a writing system known as Linear A,

Minoan Economy

The term "redistributive economy" requires definition. When historians employ this term, they are referring to a complex economic system based on the regular accumulation of surpluses of staple goods. Whether farmers contributed a percentage of their land's production, or worked the palace's land (either as serfs or as corvée laborers) is uncertain, but the surplus could be used two ways: to support such specialized craftsmen as goldsmiths, armorers, and perfume manufacturers in the palaces; and to support farmers in times of crop failure and food shortage. Such a system, therefore, depended on a delicate balance of relations between the palace elites and the farmers and laborers whose work produced both staple items and luxury goods. The former included oil, grain, and wine, items that were stored in *pithoi*, clay vessels that were arranged inside the magazines of the palace (**2.15**). Luxury items might include such precious metals as gold, silver, copper, and tin (copper and tin were used for making bronze). The presence of manufactured items, such as perfume, spears, and chariots, also shows that the palaces were centers of production and manufacturing, a fact also made clear by the extraordinary jewelry found in Minoan excavations. So, just as the palaces were the center of religious life, they were also at the heart of a complex economic system.

This can hardly have operated according to the rules of a market economy based on supply and demand. Rather, the system appears to have relied upon the control of the population by the palace, yet it was not necessarily a coercive or exploitative system. There were good reasons for cooperation between the shepherds and farmers in the countryside and the soldiers, goldsmiths, and officials of the palace. In such an economy based on reciprocity, peasants might give up a certain number of days of corvée labor (digging irrigation channels, constructing walls, even bringing in the harvest [**2.16**]), and in return have received food and supplies from the palace's surplus, both as payment in kind and as emergency rations

2.15 Pithoi inside a magazine (storage room), Knossos

2.16 Harvesters Vase, Agia Triada, *c*. 1500 BC. Steatite, H: 46.5 cm (18¼ in.)

in times of need. Given the regular failure of crops in the Aegean, such an arrangement would have been mutually beneficial. If the palace was viewed as the home of a god-king or the god's representative, then giving labor and produce to the palace would have served as a form of devotion to the gods.

Beyond the Palaces

Despite the significance of the palaces, there were many people on Crete in the Bronze Age who did not live in or next to a palace the size of Knossos or Phaistos and for whom life was structured very differently. In terms of religion, for example, Crete is dotted with mountain peaks and caves where sacrifices and dedications going back to the Early Minoan period (2500–2000 BC) have been found. This sacred landscape predates the palaces, and although it has been proposed that the courts were often built on alignment with peak sanctuaries, there is no suggestion that the palaces controlled all local religious practices. Perhaps the most dramatic example of local religion comes from Anemospilia, south of Knossos, where in the late 1970s, Greek excavators unearthed a shrine in which were found four bodies, one of whom seemed to have been crushed by falling rocks during an earthquake and another of whom appeared to have been in the process of being sacrificed at the time of the earthquake.

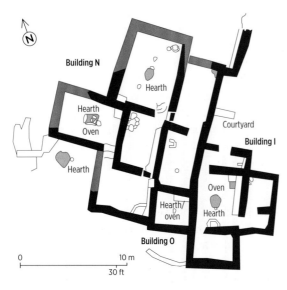

2.17 Plan of Building I-O-N at Vronda

It is not solely in the area of religion that we should look beyond the palaces of Bronze Age Crete. In the eastern parts of the island, an extensive survey around the Gulf of Mirabello has revealed a landscape in which farms and hamlets grew up around reliable water sources and arable land, but without any clearly identifiable regional center, at least during much of the Middle Minoan period (2000–1550 BC). One of these hamlets, at the site of Vronda (**2.17**), by the modern-day village of Kavousi, allows us a glimpse into the lives of non-elite people at the time the town flourished, in 1200–1100 BC. Here we find clusters of modest household units that display a consistent architectural pattern: north-facing courtyards, a core of three to five rooms, with a large central room with a hearth or oven as well as a bench. In addition, a high concentration of cookingware is usually found in these rooms, as well as evidence of the slaughter of sheep, goats, pigs, rabbits, and (more rarely) cattle. These households show signs of stable growth over time, expressed architecturally by the gradual addition of more and more rooms (first I, then O, then N), which would be consistent with occupation over a number of generations by a growing family.

Separate from these household units, there was a two-room structure, Building G, notable for the larger boulders used on its western facade and for the very different assemblage of materials found inside. Instead of the typical signs of food preparation, eating, and drinking associated with the domestic buildings, Building G has a distinctive ceramic assemblage: snake tubes, plaques, and terra-cotta figurines of the Goddess with Upraised Arms. This was a shrine, and it appears to have served the entire community. Yet here, too, excavation raises as many questions as answers. Discussing the cult performances associated with this building and the terra-cotta figurines, Kevin Glowacki observes,

What is unknown, however, is the occasion and frequency for such an offering. Were the goddesses and other articles of cult equipment dedicated and/or displayed during periodic rituals? Were these rituals public or private? Were the sets of ritual equipment offered by individuals, by the community as a whole or by a clearly recognisable subset of the community, such as an individual household or family?

(Glowacki, "House, Household and Community at LM IIIC Vronda, Kavousi")

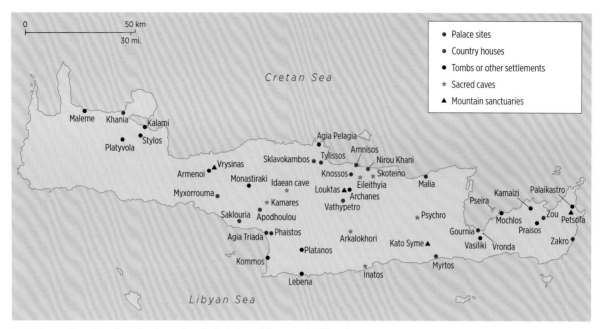

2.18 Minoan Crete: Location of major archaeological sites of the second millennium BC

These are important questions, since they remind us that there is still a great deal to be learned about the lives of ordinary people in the Bronze Age.

Over time, many of these inland hamlets diminished in size. At Kavousi, the inhabitants appear to have moved up to another site in the hills, at Kastro. In other cases, the depopulation of the hinterland may be connected to the growth of the local port town of Pseira, which is unlike the modest settlement of Vronda. Pseira shows signs of expansion in the Late Minoan period. Some of the buildings are decorated with rich frescoes, and the ceramic record points to trade with the Cyclades, Cyprus, and the Levant; a cache of more than two hundred vases, including transport amphorae, all dating from 1800 BC to 1675 BC, supplies evidence of seaborne trade in oil and wine. In addition, luxury materials, such as gold, silver, quartz crystals, copper, tin, and pigments, are consistent with Pseira's role as a trading station in the expanding network of eastern Mediterranean trade. Yet here, as in the case of Kavousi, questions remain. Was the elite that dominated Pseira subject to authority from Malia or Zakro? Or is its location between these last two a sign that it was an autonomous community, outside the direct control of any palace?

In some cases, elites from the palaces may have reproduced the palace system on a smaller scale in the countryside (**2.18**). At Vathypetro, for example, a country estate has been identified, comprising a villa, a kiln, and presses for making wine and manufacturing olive oil. Here the authority of Knossos was probably not exerted directly, although the master of the estate may have sent a tithe of his wine, oil, and wool to the palace. A good example of a palatial center on a smaller scale is to be seen in the town of Gournia. First excavated in the early 1900s by Harriet Boyd Hawes (1871–1945), the site has been studied for more than one hundred years and offers us another glimpse of daily life for ordinary people in eastern Crete. In the Bronze Age, well-constructed streets made of cobblestones separated the town into various quarters, with the palatial center located in the southwest of the town. Harriet Boyd Hawes excavated a shipshed by the water's edge and a street that connected the town to its harbor. From here, ships sailed around the Aegean, taking goods manufactured at Gournia— which included bronze vessels and weapons—all over the eastern Mediterranean. There is also evidence for textile-weaving, wine-making, and the manufacturing of ceramics and stone vessels.

Similar evidence for intense maritime trade has been found at Kommos, on Crete's southern coast. Here, excavators have found Cypriot and Egyptian pottery, pointing to trade routes east and south, as well as Italian, Sardinian, and Peloponnesian pottery

2.19 Late Bronze Age settlement at Koukonisi, Lemnos. The excavator, Christos Boulotis, refers to this as the 'Minoanizing" sector because of the high concentration of Minoan pottery and artifacts in the area.

2.20 Excavating oxhide ingots on the Uluburun shipwreck

from the north and west. The last generation of excavations has demonstrated that even modest settlements on Crete were part of a much greater network of maritime connections that enmeshed the entire eastern Mediterranean during the age of great empires, especially from *c.* 1700 to 1200 BC. In the northern Aegean, for example, Minoan artefacts and pottery have turned up in excavations conducted in 1990s on the small island of Koukonisi (located in Moudros Bay, Lemnos), as well as on the island of Samothrace. The excavator of Koukonisi believes that the Minoans had sailed this far north in search of metal (**2.19**). The site may well have served as a trading post.

Some of the most spectacular evidence of this network comes from shipwrecks, and although Bronze Age shipwrecks are rare, they can reveal a great deal about trade and conditions in the second millennium BC. An especially spectacular find is the Uluburun shipwreck (**2.20**), found in 1982 off the coast of southwestern Turkey by a sponge diver. The wreck has been dated to the late 1400s BC. The cargo of this wreck reflects a zone of connectivity that encompassed the entire eastern Mediterranean. We cannot say with certainty where the Uluburun boat was headed when it sank, but its cargo reveals that it had put in at ports all over the eastern Mediterranean.

Part of the Uluburun cargo, such as Baltic amber, African blackwood, and ostrich shells, had entered the Mediterranean via overland routes, but once these objects reached a port, whether on the African coast or in the Adriatic, they became part of the great movement of goods that flowed around the Mediterranean (**2.21**). This system of port-to-port trading, referred to as **cabotage**, relied on a simple principle: goods increased in value as they became more scarce and exotic. Accordingly, the natural conditions of the eastern Mediterranean favored a system designed to move goods considerable distances. A turquoise ingot or an Egyptian scarab is not difficult to transport by sea, but will be highly prized when it reaches a place where there is no local source of production. When studying any site in the Minoan world in the second millennium, it is therefore important to recognize the interconnectedness of all Minoan sites: major and minor sites alike were part of an eastern Mediterranean trade network.

Thera: A Minoan Settlement

Shipwrecks and exotic trade goods attest to Crete's position in a Bronze Age network. Just as goods flowed in to Crete, so too Cretan culture was exported beyond the island, as the frescoes from Avaris in Egypt make clear. The site that most powerfully evokes Bronze Age life, however, is the remarkable site of Akrotiri, on today's island of Santorini, known in antiquity as Thera, where astonishing archaeological discoveries have been made. Here, before its destruction around 1628 BC (although the exact date is still hotly debated), the town of Akrotiri was a flourishing settlement that may have been founded as a Minoan colony. In common with the other Bronze Age settlements on the island, Akrotiri overlooked the **caldera** (or crater) of a volcano that had erupted in the past. Whether the people of the town were aware that they were living on top of an active volcano we cannot say. We do know, however, that when the volcano erupted in the Bronze Age, the town was destroyed by an explosion that carried the intensity of one hundred and fifty hydrogen bombs. The site lay hidden and forgotten until the 1860s,

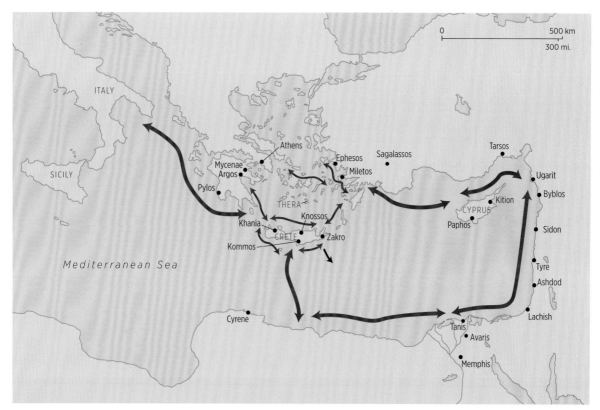

2.21 Crete and the major trade routes of the eastern Mediterranean

2.22 (above) A reconstruction of the West House, Akrotiri, as seen from the north

2.23 (right) Akrotiri frescoes in the National Archaeological Museum of Athens

2.24 (opposite) Saffron gatherer, Akrotiri. Fresco

when engineers began stripping the soft volcanic ash deposited by the eruption for use in making the hydraulic cement needed for the construction of the Suez Canal, and while doing so, exposed the tops of the walls of a Bronze Age town. Systematic excavations did not begin until AD 1967, but in the following years the Greek excavator, Spyridon Marinatos, gradually uncovered a series of finely decorated private and public buildings (**2.22**). The wealth of this decorative program, and the wide provenance of the associated finds, have led the current excavator of the site, Christos Doumas, to describe Thera as a cosmopolitan merchant harbor.

Of special importance is the high quality of the frescoes, although the question, once again, is how to interpret them. In some of the frescoes at Akrotiri, for example, there appears to be a deliberate exploration of the theme of opposition: in Building Beta, for example, boxers trade punches on one wall, while adjacent to them stand two antelope in positions suggesting that they are about to lock antlers (**2.23**). Even the famous swallows depicted in a fresco located in Building Delta are two sparring males. Other frescoes appear to celebrate the splendor of nature: crocuses and lilies are common motifs.

Can these be read together as a pictorial program, in which the frescoes are more than simply

decorative? Some scholars, for example, have noted an age progression in the figures on the Theran frescoes, especially among the female figures, suggesting perhaps an association with rituals that mark the life cycle. In another building at Akrotiri called Xeste 3, most of the frescoes depict women, some young (with shaved heads), others older with their hair tied up in a bun. Some are collecting crocuses or the saffron growing on their stamens (**2.24**), which is then presented to a goddess who is attended by a gryphon. Other depictions of women also suggest religious scenes: they are shown making supplication and burning incense. These scenes have

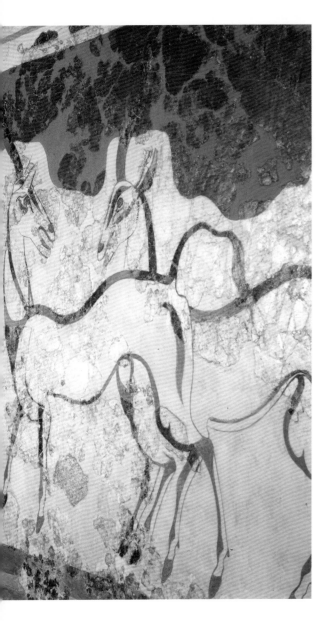

suggested to some scholars that the frescoes can be read together as a celebration of the fecundity of nature and its regenerative power.

The Destruction of Thera

Standing on the caldera of Santorini today, one can look down into the heart of the volcano that blew up at some point in the second millennium BC and destroyed the Bronze Age community on Akrotiri. When the ruins of the Bronze Age city were uncovered by archaeologists, the scale and violence of the destruction suggested that the effects of the eruption could have been felt hundreds of miles away.

As recently as 2006, a National Geographic study of the eruption emphasized its ferocity: "During the eruption, the material that formed the deposits would have plunged into the sea as pyroclastic flows—hot, fast-moving mixtures of gas, ash, and molten rock. As these hit the water, they would have kicked up massive tsunamis."

Thera is 150 kilometers (90 mi.) from Crete, and it was a reasonable suggestion that Crete might have felt the impact of the volcanic explosion and the tsunami that followed, perhaps leading to the collapse of Minoan culture. Modern comparisons have also been adduced: the eruption of Krakatoa in 1883 created an ash cloud that deposited volcanic material thousands of miles from the epicenter of the eruption, and contemporary accounts emphasized the powerful effects of the natural disaster: disruptions in weather patterns, blocked sunlight, earthquakes, and tsunamis were all caused by the volcanic eruption.

One more body of evidence also fits the theory that a volcanic eruption had destroyed Minoan culture: Greek myth. Just as the story of Theseus and the Minotaur might contain a kernel of historical memory, of a time when the Greeks had sailed to Knossos, so too the story of Atlantis recalled a time when a powerful civilization had been destroyed by

2.25 Marine Style octopus vase, *c.* 1450 BC. Ceramic, H: 28 cm (11 in.)

a volcano and earthquakes, and was then swallowed up by the sea. The story is told in Plato's *Timaeus*, and, allowing for obvious poetic exaggeration—Plato locates Atlantis beyond the Pillars of Herakles, in the Atlantic Ocean, but Crete and Thera are in the eastern Mediterranean—one could again argue that the myth contained the kernel of an historical memory.

The nub of the issue has always been the date of the eruption. Pottery sequences establish the relative chronology of the Cretan palaces, and, when taken in conjunction with the evidence from the palaces for destruction and rebuilding, have allowed archaeologists to reconstruct with reasonable certainty the following scenario. The Minoan palaces were first built around 1900 BC and continued to function, with some fluctuations, until the end of the Old Palace period, between 1700 and 1650. In the generation that followed the end of the Old Palace period there was a hiatus, after which the palaces were rebuilt and continued to be in use during the

New Palace period until *c.* 1450 BC. After this, most of the palaces went out of use, except for Knossos and Khania (which show signs of Mycenaean occupation down to the middle of the thirteenth century BC).

According to the theory of volcanic destruction, an eruption *c.* 1450 BC would therefore fit the evidence from Crete neatly. As the island was hit by a series of natural disasters—from a tidal wave demolishing coastal sites and fleets, to an ash cloud disrupting agriculture and precipitating widespread famine, disease, and social breakdown—Minoan culture collapsed, leaving the island vulnerable to attack from the Mycenaeans of the mainland. Exploiting the disaster and the weakened state of the ruler at Knossos, the Mycenaeans invaded and seized control.

The attraction of the volcanic explanation has always been that it is grand and all-encompassing, wedding evidence from hard science with myth. Unfortunately, it is wrong. There are three major problems with attributing the end of Minoan civilization to a volcanic eruption: in the first place, a distinctive form of Minoan pottery, the so-called Marine Style, is not found on Thera, although earlier Minoan pottery styles are found there. Marine Style pottery is distinctive, with elaborate and fluid marine motifs covering the entire vessel (**2.25**). The fact that none of these vessels is to be found at Akrotiri suggests that Marine Style pottery postdates the Theran eruption. This form of pottery, however, is found at Knossos, Malia, Phaistos, and other Minoan sites, suggesting that they continued to flourish *after* Thera had been destroyed. In fact, more careful study of the maritime networks before and after the Theran eruption shows that there was a pronounced shift in the pattern of trade, but that it was not terminated by the eruption.

A second chronological difficulty for the volcanic explanation arises with the deposition of the ash layer associated with the eruption. On the north coast of Crete, at Pseira, excavations by the Institute for Aegean Prehistory have identified this ash layer. It covers layers containing pottery from the earliest periods of Minoan settlement, but *above* the ash there are more recent buildings, evidence of continuing civilization after the natural disaster occurred. Most recently, tree ring data from North America, and European oaks in Sweden and Ireland, have been used to fix the date of the eruption with greater precision. The tree rings suggest a date *c*. 1628 BC, too early to explain the collapse of palaces *c*. 1450 BC. Other studies have resulted in similar dates. Researchers examining Arctic ice cores have suggested a date around 1645 BC, radiocarbon dating of samples from Thera is consistent with a date between 1660 and 1613, while in AD 2006 a Danish team studying an olive tree buried in the eruption found a date between 1627 BC and 1600 BC. The evidence, however, remains stubbornly inconclusive. There are also difficulties reconciling this with the chronology of Egyptian pottery: Minoan pieces appear in contexts that, according to the Egyptian chronology, would be much later. This remains a problem for experts to resolve. For our purposes, a date approximately one generation before 1600 seems most likely, and this rules out the eruption as the cause of the end of the Minoan palaces in *c*. 1450.

It is noticeable, however, that the high date for the eruption does correspond to the end of the Old Palace period around 1650 BC, and here we may be on firmer ground. The Theran eruption was enormous and the effects certainly catastrophic. Both sectors of the palatial system—the production and storage of staples, and participation within a broader Mediterranean trade network—would have suffered major disruptions as a result. It is not hard to imagine crop failure, the loss of ships, and a breakdown in supplies of such precious goods as copper and tin. Taken together, these may have precipitated a total systems failure, as each segment of the economy broke down. Crop failure drained surpluses and diminished the capacity of the palaces to guarantee security and sustenance. Similarly, a disruption to supplies of gold, copper, and tin also meant a diminution of the palace's capacity to participate in Mediterranean trade. But it was not the end of Minoan culture. The Cretans, and particularly the elites who controlled the palaces, reasserted order, and a new palatial period saw the recovery of the society, even surpassing their earlier accomplishments. In part, this was due to the fact that other participants in the eastern Mediterranean had not been as dramatically affected, and the help of such major powers as the Egyptian pharaoh may have contributed to Crete's recovery.

The End of Minoan Culture

If the eruption of Thera was not responsible for the end of Minoan palatial culture, how do we account for the collapse of this extraordinary civilization? The story of the end of Minoan palatial culture cannot be separated from the rivalry that existed between the Minoans and Mycenaean Greeks from the mainland. Before exploring that relationship, however, we should note some basic details. First, there is general agreement that most Minoan sites, both palatial and lower down the hierarchy of size and complexity, suffered catastrophic destruction that put an end to the complex social and economic system of which they were the center. This "destruction horizon" has been traditionally dated to around 1470 BC. More recently, however, a closer study of the destruction horizon has produced a more nuanced picture in which the destruction appears to have been spread over a period of perhaps as long as fifty years. Rather than a single invasion or uprising, it now seems as though Crete was subjected to a generation or more of civil strife, during which we can imagine waves of marauders attacking the palaces and causing ordinary people to retreat to the hills. Pastoralism has always been part of the Greek economy, and in periods of strife, a retreat to the hills with a flock of sheep and goats represents a reasonable response to breakdown in the urban center. In time, as we saw at Vronda and Kastro, entire communities would move into the hills, and from 1200 BC to 1100 BC, this phenomenon occurred in a number of places. At Karphi, for example, an earlier Middle Minoan site was extensively developed into a refuge site at this time. Located high above the Lasithi plateau in eastern Crete, Karphi is protected behind a rise from which it is possible to watch the entire coastal plain 1,000 meters (3,300 ft) below.

Most of the Cretan palaces, other than Knossos and Khania, ceased functioning completely sometime shortly after 1470 BC. While this so-called destruction horizon is now thought to have been spread over a generation or more, there can be no doubt that a principal cause of this was the arrival of the Mycenaeans. The current scholarly debate concerns whether it is appropriate to label this an invasion, and whether there was an active process of "Mycenaeanization" by the new overlords of Knossos. The fact that the disruption to Minoan culture took place over a drawn-out period of time may point to a process of infiltration, but the effects were still profound. To understand how the Bronze Age culture of Crete was dramatically altered, we turn our attention in the next chapter to the second complex culture of the Greek Bronze Age, the Mycenaeans, but first it is time to address some of the particular challenges of interpreting the Bronze Age.

Interpreting the Past

Much of the evidence for life in Bronze Age Crete presented in this chapter derives from sources that raise difficult questions of interpretation. How does the ground plan of an architectural complex, such as a palace, allow us to draw inferences about the society that used these buildings? How do we populate that palace? With kings, queens, and an elite? With workers and slaves? With worshipers? And outside the palace, how do we reconcile the modest settlement of Vronda, which housed a population of farmers and herders, with a broad, eastern Mediterranean world-system in which staples and luxury goods circulated over hundreds of miles as part of an elaborate maritime network? Each piece of evidence, from a wall painting depicting blue monkeys on Thera to an Egyptian scarab turning up on a shipwreck off the coast of Turkey, raises as many questions as answers. These challenges aside, there is a particular pitfall, however, that faces anyone trying to reconstruct the world of the Bronze Age Aegean: the enormous influence of the first generation of archaeologists, whose imagination and interpretations established the broad narrative we still employ today. We shall see this in subsequent chapters, in which our understanding of the Mycenaean world and the Trojan War will be almost indistinguishable from the ego of Heinrich Schliemann, but in the case of Minoan Crete, it is the life, work, and vision of Arthur Evans that continues to shape our appreciation of Bronze Age Crete. The very fact that we call that world "Minoan" and that we still refer to the court-complexes as "palaces" demonstrates Evans's hold: it was he who coined both terms.

Evans was the son of a middle-class mill-owner and antiquarian. After Oxford, where he studied

2.26 North Portico, Knossos, extensively restored by Evans in the twentieth century

archaeology, he went on to a successful career that included excavating in England and abroad, as well as serving as Keeper of the Ashmolean Museum in Oxford. After the death of his wife, however, he turned his attention to the Mediterranean, combining a passion for archaeology with a keen interest in the politics of his own day. He spent time as a journalist in the Balkans where he reported on the gradual dissolution of Ottoman power. On Crete, he denounced the persecution of Christians and Muslims by each other and immersed himself in the affairs of the island. Both inspired by Schliemann's discoveries at Mycenae and Troy, yet also in reaction to the warrior spirit of the culture Schliemann uncovered, Evans turned his attention to the site of Kephala, south of the modern-day capital of Iraklion, where earlier excavations by Minos Kalokairinos had brought to light pottery, walls, and inscribed clay tablets. The possibility of finding a literate Bronze Age culture caught Evans's imagination, and having purchased the site, Evans set to work with a crew of Cretan farmers.

The excavation was immediately successful. Within months, not only had he uncovered a cache of inscribed tablets, which he classified as Linear B to distinguish them from an earlier style, Linear A (categories we still recognize today), but also had unearthed much of the complex of Knossos. Designating the various chambers as the Queen's Quarters, the Throne Room, and so forth, Evans established the plan of Knossos as we know it. It is almost impossible to describe Knossos now without resorting not just to his plan, but to his designations as well.

This is understandable: the archaeologist inevitably shapes interpretation. Evans, however, went a good deal further. His reconstructions far overshadow the original work, and since the practice in 1900 was to merge reconstruction with the original, it is often difficult to tell where the Bronze Age stops and the twentieth century AD begins. Worse still, with the century that has passed since Evans rebuilt Knossos, the "restorations" have themselves weathered and are now virtually indistinguishable from the original traces. Looking at **2.26**, one would be hard-pressed to identify how much of the North Portico is original.

In some cases, the restorations were demonstrably wrong. For most of the twentieth century, visitors

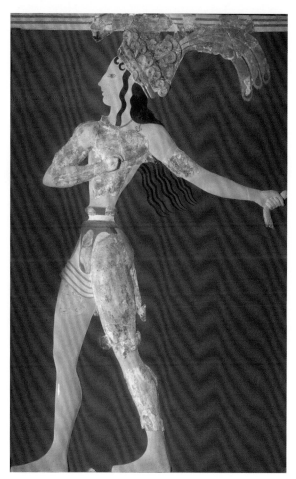

2.27 Prince of the Lilies, Knossos, *c.* 1550 BC, restored AD 1905. Fresco, H: 2.1 m (6ft 11 in.)

to the Iraklion Museum could see a fresco of a blue figure delicately collecting saffron, restored by Evans as a slim-waisted youth, a suitable image of the peace-loving Minoans conjured up by Evans's work. It was only when a similar fresco was uncovered on Thera that Evans's mistake became apparent: the blue figure had a tail and was a monkey! Even today, visitors to Knossos swoon over the figure of the Prince of the Lilies, a life-size fresco depicting Evans's "priest-king" with a glorious feathered headdress that experts now say is probably from a completely separate figure, possibly a gryphon or sphinx (**2.27**).

If one looks at the fresco and Evans's restoration, one cannot help noticing that the headdress does not connect with any part of the human figure, that no part of the original face is preserved, and that most of the bodily proportions (slim waist, toned thighs, flat stomach) are the result, with the exception

2.28 Dolphin fresco, Knossos. Restored by Emile Gilliéron and Piet de Jong

of one leg, of imaginative reconstruction. As early as the 1920s, some visitors were expressing serious doubts about Evans's methods and the way that his restorations were shaping modern perceptions of the Minoans. Evelyn Waugh noted astutely that when one considered the amount of restoration compared to the original material, it seemed as if the restorers had spent a good deal of time looking at the cover of *Vogue* magazine. The influence of Art Nouveau, popular in Europe at the turn of the century, is evident everywhere.

To be fair, the artists employed by Evans, a father and son both named Emile Gilliéron, were painstaking and talented, but a curator of a recent exhibition of their work at the Metropolitan Museum of Art dubbed their restorations "clever," not perhaps the most encouraging description of a restorer's talents. Similar criticisms have been made of another influential artist from the generation after Gilliéron père et fils. Piet de Jong did extensive work at both Mycenae, and, from the late 1940s until the 1960s, at Knossos, where some of his work included restoring earlier restorations of Gilliéron. Once again, the talent of the artist overshadows the reliability of the restoration.

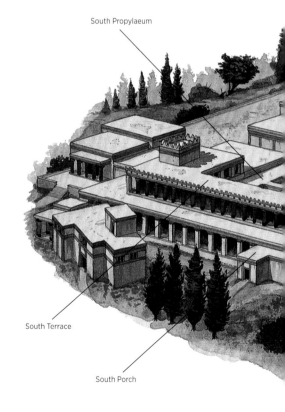

South Propylaeum

South Terrace

South Porch

When one looks at the dolphins in the Queen's megaron at Knossos, one is really seeing a palimpsest, a document in which successive generations have recorded their own vision of the past (**2.28**). It is fair to give Evans credit for having rescued Bronze Age Crete from obscurity, and it is certainly important to recognize the intellectual acumen and brilliance of Evans. At the same time, the vigor and vision of these early archaeologists is a mixed heritage. Evans, for example, was unbending in his belief that Minoan civilization had colonized the mainland, a view that has been disproved but to which he held throughout his career.

Evans not only uncovered much of the Bronze Age civilization of Crete, but also shaped our understanding of it. The palaces ruled by priest-kings, the cult of the bull, even the lack of fortification walls, which Evans took as a sign of the peaceful and harmonious way of life of the Minoans: these "facts" are shot through with the desires of the archaeologist to bring to life a culture that corresponded to his imaginings (**2.29**). It is a sign of Evans's extraordinary influence that his vision is in many respects still ours. It is also a measure of the skill of Evans as an archaeologist, and that of his collaborators (notably Duncan Mackenzie), that so much of that vision remains intact.

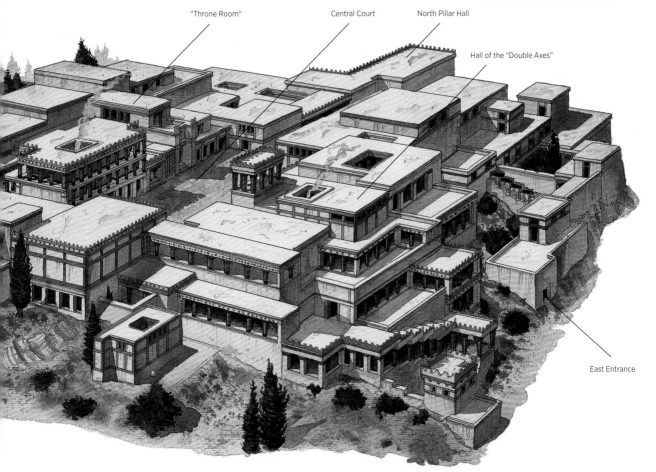

2.29 Reconstruction of Knossos

"Throne Room"

Central Court

North Pillar Hall

Hall of the "Double Axes"

East Entrance

2.30 "Crocus Gatherers" fresco, Akrotiri. H: 1.83 m (6 ft)

The Theran Frescoes: Art and Life in a Minoan Settlement

The dramatic discoveries made by the Greek Archaeological Service on the island of Santorini since the 1960s have provoked a great deal of scholarly debate regarding art and life in the Bronze Age Aegean. Many scholars, for example, now argue that the scenes in the frescoes show the actual landscape of Bronze Age Thera, rather than generic, exotic, or imaginary scenes. According to this view, the landscapes with clumps of papyrus, blooming lilies, blue monkeys leaping across rocks, and women in Minoan-style dress in procession all reflect the lives and experiences of the Therans. Clairy Palyvou, the former architect of the excavations at Akrotiri, juxtaposes pictures of modern-day women collecting crocuses near the site of Akrotiri in the late twentieth century AD with depictions of Theran women collecting saffron from crocuses to suggest a powerful continuity in how local people have experienced the Theran landscape (**2.30**).

There can be little doubt that the Theran artists observed nature closely. In the case of the Fisherman fresco, for example, we see a youth holding two handfuls of recently caught fish (**2.31**). As a result of excavations at Akrotiri, we know that the Therans

2.31 Fisherman fresco, Akrotiri. H: 1.1 m (3 ft 7 in.)

2.32 Flotilla fresco, West House, Akrotiri. H: 43 cm (16⅜ in.)

ate fish caught close to the shore, but the fish he holds are dolphinfish, *coryphaena hippurus,* a deep-water species that could be caught only by fishermen with a special knowledge of the habits of these fish as well as the skill to catch them in the open water. The youth's catch therefore represents evidence of his skill, but how exactly should this be interpreted? Some scholars see the fresco as comparable to a photo taken by a fisherman today in order to commemorate a truly memorable catch. Others think that he is a worshiper taking his offering to a god in thanks. A third proposal is that the youth has undergone a rite of passage and that the painting records his initiation. The range of possible interpretations demonstrates that we are still a long way from understanding these beautiful images.

With these ambiguities in mind, it is worth examining some of the famous frescoes of Thera's West House. This was a two-story structure in which the rooms on the ground floor appear to have been reserved for daily use, consisting of a kitchen, a workshop, and a storeroom. The second floor, however, was decorated with a remarkable set of frescoes. Principal among these is the so-called Flotilla fresco, which depicts ships sailing along a shore and passing by two cities overlooking the water (**2.32**).

A clear interpretation of the fresco is difficult, since unlike contemporary wall paintings from Egypt, there are no hieroglyphs or labels accompanying the visual scenes. Are they a narrative, read as the visitor walks around the room? Would the viewer have recognized that the fresco depicted a ceremony, and that the scene corresponded to an actual maritime procession that took place regularly? Alternatively, the scene may commemorate the return of a specific naval expedition. Another possibility is that the scene might be a pictorial representation of a story told in verse, the story perhaps of a great naval expedition, such as, say, Homer's story of the Achaians' expedition to Troy.

With these questions in mind, one panel of the frieze on the north wall of Room 5 is particularly noteworthy (**2.33**). Here, armed men equipped with plumed helmets and tower shields are arrayed before a town; in the water beneath them dead bodies float in front of a ship as it comes ashore. Above the town, cattle can be seen in the top right-hand corner, either being driven into the hills for safekeeping or having already been seized; are we looking at a cattle raid, as onlookers within the city gaze out from behind their walls? Homer refers frequently to such cattle raids, which were commonplace in the heroic world, and some would see the Theran frescoes as confirmation that the world of Homer—the world of epic—is more than a fantasy, and that he describes a world that is firmly rooted in the actual practices of the Bronze Age.

2.33 North wall frieze depicting a naval engagement, Room 5, West House, Akrotiri. Fresco

c. **1550** BC
Shaft Graves
at Mycenae

c. **1450** BC
Linear B first recorded
at Knossos

c. **1450** BC
Griffin Warrior
Tomb at Pylos

c. **1425** BC
Warrior Graves at
Knossos and Chania

c. **1400**–*c.* **1300** BC
Iklaina absorbed
by Pylos

Chapter 3
Mycenae: Rich in Gold

In the previous chapter on the Minoan world, we encountered serious questions regarding the interpretation of material culture. Similar issues arise when we turn to the second complex civilization to emerge in the Bronze Age Aegean world: Mycenae. How much is to be inferred from the presence of massive Cyclopean walls and graves with weapons? What can we learn from the Grave Circles at Mycenae, and the massive *tholos* tombs outside the walls? And whence came the gold for which Mycenae was famed in Homer? This chapter introduces the notion of a warrior culture located in the Argolid, dominated by warlord mercenaries whose field of operation extended from the Black Sea to Egypt. Following Schliemann, this chapter also poses the question of whether archaeology can be used to "prove" Homer. The concept of cultural memory is introduced and its role in relation to epic is considered.

Schliemann and the Creation of the Bronze Age

If Arthur Evans was responsible for the discovery (and in some respects the invention) of the Minoan world, or at least our way of interpreting the Bronze Age on Crete, then it is certainly true that we owe our view of the Bronze Age Aegean to the German businessman and archaeologist, Heinrich Schliemann (1822–1890). So completely did his work at Troy and Mycenae change the modern Western world's approach to archaeology and the study of the past that it is hard to imagine a time when the epic world of heroes, as described in Homer's poems, was regarded as a glorious fiction and no more. Schliemann, however, was a believer, and had the fervor of a fanatic when it came to the *Iliad* and the *Odyssey*; for Schliemann, Agamemnon, Achilles, and Odysseus had been living, breathing men whose deeds had been commemorated in Homer's poems. It was that unshakable faith that led him to recover the material evidence for Homer's Troy when professional scholars were content to treat Homer's evocation of a heroic warrior age as poetry alone. It is equally true that Schliemann was frequently unscrupulous, faked records, and embellished the accounts of his work, all with a view to promoting himself and his accomplishments.

As a young man, Schliemann made his fortune in Russia by supplying munitions to the Russian government during the Crimean War, and also in California, where he made a second fortune in

63

banking. By the late 1860s he was in his mid-forties, prosperous, and ready to indulge his passion for the heroic world of Homer's poems. Using the *Iliad* as if it were a guidebook to the topography of the heroic world, in 1868 he visited the mound of Hisarlik, in northwestern Turkey, a site that he and others speculated corresponded to Homer's description of Troy. The English amateur archaeologist Frank Calvert had already made some preliminary soundings at the site, but he lacked Schliemann's resources. Paying for a small army of laborers, Schliemann excavated the mound of Hisarlik in 1872 and 1873, almost immediately finding traces of ancient occupation, and eventually uncovered a series of layers that included Roman, Classical, and Bronze Age levels, which he named the successive levels of Troy. Excavations continue there to this day, although in a slightly more scientific manner than in Schliemann's time. His own breathless account, for example, of the discovery of "Priam's Treasure" captures the thrill of archaeology before it had become the scientific discipline it is today:

3.1 Sophia Schliemann wearing the "Jewels of Helen"

In excavating this wall further and directly by the side of the palace of King Priam, I came upon a large copper article of the most remarkable form, which attracted my attention all the more as I thought I saw gold behind it.... In order to withdraw the treasure from the greed of my workmen, and to save it for archaeology...I immediately had "paidos" (lunch break) called....While the men were eating and resting, I cut out the Treasure with a large knife....It would, however, have been impossible for me to have removed the Treasure without the help of my dear wife, who stood by me ready to pack the things which I cut out in her shawl and to carry them away.

A partial catalogue later published by Schliemann of the material that made up Priam's Treasure reveals how extensive was the find that Schliemann claimed to be protecting: a copper shield, a copper cauldron with handles, an unknown copper artifact, perhaps the hasp of a chest, a silver vase containing 2 gold diadems (the "Jewels of Helen"), 8,750 gold rings, buttons and other small objects, 6 gold bracelets, 2 gold goblets, a copper vase, a wrought gold bottle, 2 gold cups (one wrought, one cast), the key to a chest, silver cups, copper axes, and copper spearheads.

Never one to miss an opportunity for promotion, Schliemann famously posed his wife Sophia in the "Jewels of Helen" and published the photo in his account of the excavations (**3.1**). Most of the treasure was acquired by the Berlin Museum and removed to Germany, where it remained until the Second World War. With the collapse of the Third Reich, the treasure disappeared until 1993, when it resurfaced in the vaults of the Pushkin Museum in Moscow.

The same revisionist charges leveled at Evans have also been directed at Schliemann, but in the case of the latter the charges are more serious. Falsification of records, the possibility of theft of objects from sites, and the manufacturing of archaeological material are all claims that have been made against Schliemann. Perhaps tellingly, a pattern of deception and outright lies also emerges from a close study of his life. Some are comparatively trivial, such as his supposed eyewitness account of a fire in San Francisco in June 1851, when he was actually in Sacramento, but some are more serious. He obtained American citizenship and divorced his Russian wife in 1869 having not only lied about his residency, but also having bought the perjured statements of a witness. The difficult question for archaeologists is to what degree Schliemann's reliability regarding archaeological matters is compromised by his persistent dishonesty in other areas of his life.

For example, Schliemann was forced to admit that his wife Sophia was not present when Priam's Treasure was found, and that the story of her hiding the jewels in her shawl was a complete fabrication.

After his successes at Troy, Schliemann turned his attention to Greece in 1876. His excavations at Mycenae brought to light evidence for an advanced, complex Bronze Age culture on the Greek mainland dating back to the middle of the second millennium BC. The relationship between this and the other contemporary cultures of the Aegean and Near East would remain hotly contested for decades to come, but Schliemann's discoveries at Mycenae were dramatic and revolutionized the scholarly world's understanding of Homer. Homer had described Agamemnon as coming from Mycenae, rich in gold, and here was the undeniable proof that there had been a wealthy ruler's fortress at Mycenae, protected by huge walls and accompanied by heroic burials in deep shafts or massive **corbeled** tombs. So impressive are the ruins there that historians still use the term "Mycenaean" to refer to the entire civilization of the Late Bronze Age in Greece, although the fortress at Mycenae did not rule the entire country. Not since Pompeii—the Roman city buried by the volcanic eruption of Vesuvius—had an archaeological discovery so captured the popular imagination. For the fledgling modern state of Greece, only fifty years independent from Ottoman rule, the excavations were a source of deep national pride, and Greek archaeologists, including Christos Tsountas and later Spyros Iakovides, extended Schliemann's work at Mycenae and at other Late Bronze Age sites.

If Evans shaped our view of the Cretans, Schliemann may be said to have given the poems of Homer a tangible materiality. Nowhere is this more true than at Mycenae, the place from which Agamemnon was supposed to have departed for Troy at the head of a massive coalition designed to win back his brother Menelaus's wife, Helen. Schliemann was aided by the fact that Mycenae had never faded completely from memory: the massive walls of the Late Bronze Age citadel, so monumental that later Greeks claimed they could only have been built by the Cyclopes (hence "Cyclopean") were still visible in the early nineteenth century AD, as Edward Dodwell's watercolor shows (**3.2**).

3.2 Edward Dodwell, *View of Mycenae*, AD 1821. Watercolor

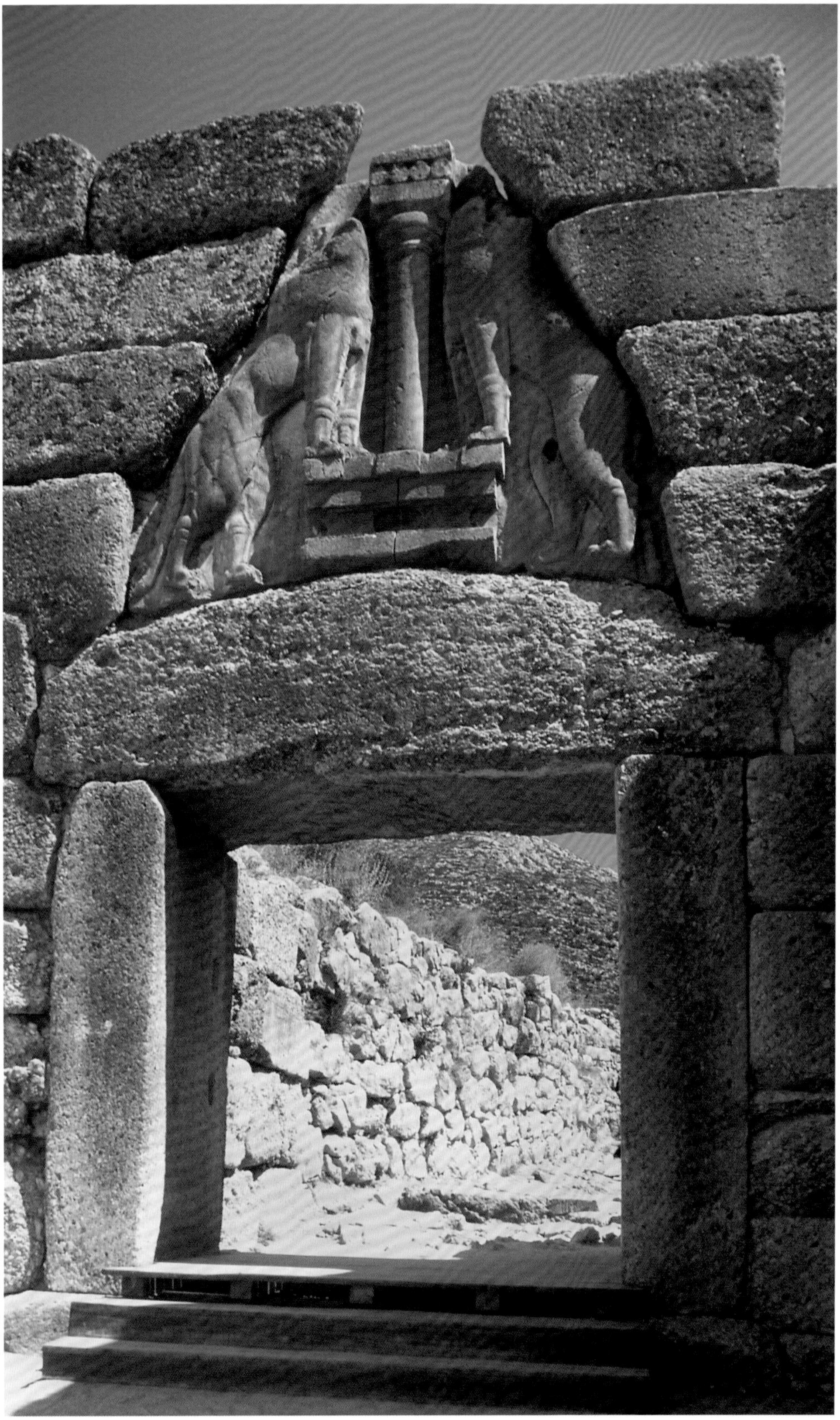

3.3 The Lion Gate, Mycenae, thirteenth century BC

In front of the visitor to Mycenae stood a monumental gateway, over which loomed two heraldic lions (**3.3**). Their feet rest on altars and they flank a column that perhaps represents the royal palace within; the entire sculptural group sits on a massive lintel block weighing 20 tons. This is the earliest piece of monumental stone sculpture in Greece, clearly meant to intimidate the visitor as he or she approached the entrance to the fortress. Recent studies have shown that the drills and saws used to carve the lions were of the same variety as were used in the Hittite kingdom of central Anatolia, where heraldic lions similarly stood beside the entrance to the Hittite capital at Hattusa. Schliemann could not have known this in 1876, but as much as his excavations brought Homer's world to life, they would also supply evidence for the place of the Mycenaeans in the larger world of the eastern Mediterranean at the end of the second millennium BC. We shall look in more detail at Homer's world later, but before doing so we will examine the world of Mycenae uncovered by Schliemann.

The Origins of the People of the Shaft Graves

Do the Mycenaeans revealed by archaeology correspond to Homer's Greeks? To judge by their material culture, they were a society ruled by a warrior aristocracy. We can infer this from such structures as the monumental tholos tombs they built, the massive walls that protected Mycenaean sites, and the central megarons (or ruler's halls where the king sat). Particularly notable is the royal burial ground known as Grave Circle A that is found just inside the Lion Gate (**3.4**). Here, two circles of stones delineated a formal burial space in which were six shaft graves containing nineteen burials. The earliest graves date as early as *c.* 1550 BC, and the entire graveyard predates the erection of the Lion Gate, which was built around 1250. When the massive circuit walls (still visible) were raised around Mycenae in the thirteenth century, the builders chose to incorporate the area of the shaft graves within the fortress, and carefully articulated the space of the grave circle with the addition of the two rings of upright stones with cover slabs still visible today. Were the spirits of ancestors being honored and treated as guardians of the fortress? Most probably.

At Mycenae, within Grave Circle A, the shaft graves were also marked by ***stelai*** (stone markers) of engraved limestone, on which were depicted warriors in chariots wielding spears (**3.5**; see p. 68). The scenes depicted on these stelai resemble those carved on the walls of Egyptian temples that show

3.4 Grave Circle A, with back of Lion Gate visible to the right

pharaoh slaying his enemies, and remind us that, in a similar way to the Minoans, the Mycenaeans were connected to a world of cultural contact that went far beyond the Aegean. With respect to the layout and construction of the shaft graves, however, closer parallels are found in Albania, and there is still considerable debate over whether the shaft graves represent the arrival of a foreign culture in Greece or are a purely local development. In fact,

this question is part of the larger conundrum of the Mycenaeans. Their culture appears suddenly in the middle of the second millennium BC, and it is hard to reconstruct the conditions under which their society so quickly coalesced. Were they foreign invaders? If so, one would expect that their material culture would give an indication of their place of origin. Were they indigenous? If so, then what led to the sudden explosion of building, engineering, wealth, and display that characterizes Mycenaean society?

The shafts contained multiple burials, having been repeatedly reused, and the burial goods also indicated that the people interred were warriors. Many of the men were buried with weapons, including daggers made of bronze beautifully inlaid with a combination of silver and gold (**3.6**). The black highlight used on the daggers is known as **niello** (a substance employing copper, silver, and lead sulphite), and both this and the decorative technique were probably learned from Egypt. Images on the blades show men engaged in such heroic feats as lion hunts. They often carry "figure of eight" shields, a popular motif in Mycenaean wall paintings, or tower shields that protect them from head to toe (and which recall Homer's description of the Greek hero Ajax's shield, which Homer likens to a tower).

Over 15 kilograms (33 lbs) of gold were found in the shaft graves, and this abundant wealth is another puzzle for archaeologists. Where did it come from? The Argolid, where Mycenae and other major Mycenaean sites (such as Tiryns and Midea) are located, was the heartland of the Mycenaean world. It was here that the Mycenaeans built impressive fortresses, stone bridges, and even massive canals to control torrential flooding in the Argive plain. This is not, however, a region rich in mineral wealth,

3.5 Burial stele, Grave Circle A, *c.* 1550 BC. Stone, H: 1.34 m (4 ft 4¾ in.)

3.6 "Lion Hunt" dagger, Mycenae, shaft grave IV, *c.* 1550–1500 BC. Bronze with inlay of gold, silver, and niello, L: 23 cm (9 in.)

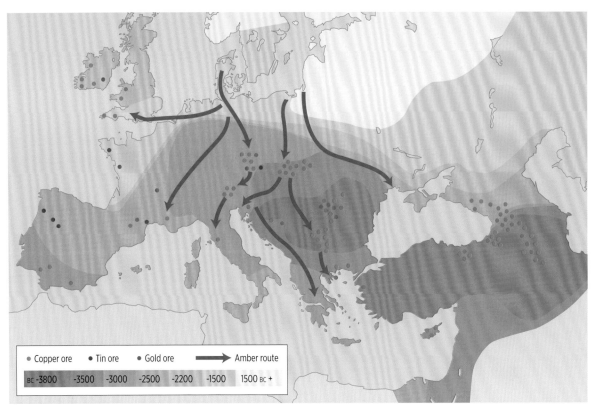

3.7 The diffusion of metallurgy and amber in the Bronze Age between 3800 BC and 1500 BC

so how did the Mycenaeans acquire so much gold that they could cover entire bodies with gold foil in their royal burials? For many years scholars supposed that the answer lay in connections with Crete and Egypt. Evans believed that the Minoans had colonized the mainland, and that the gold was that of the conquerors. But at this time gold vessels are rarer on Crete than at Mycenae, and there is nothing stylistically in common between the culture of the shaft graves and that of the Minoan palaces. The Egyptian thesis depends on the notion that Mycenaean warriors were being rewarded for mercenary services by pharaohs of the Eighteenth Dynasty, who employed them to drive out the Hyksos and help establish the New Kingdom. This thesis, however, also has its problems. The Mycenaeans do not show signs of having been a well-organized naval force at this time, and the Hyksos controlled the Delta region *between* the Theban pharaohs and the Mycenaeans, making coordinated military action difficult, though not impossible to imagine.

Recently, another explanation has been offered that fits the evidence better than the other theories.

In the sixteenth century BC, local people in Romania began mining gold in large quantities and trading it for bronze goods, especially Aegean-style swords: a Mycenaean sword has been found at Dumbrăvioara in northern Romania. The presence of large quantities of gold goods at Mycenae and Pylos, along with amber from northern Europe, when taken in conjunction with Aegean bronze in Transylvania, points to the sudden formation of a highly profitable exchange network between southern Greece and the Danube basin in the sixteenth century BC (**3.7**). Eventually Aegean goods (especially swords) would be found as far north as Scandinavia, and although we do not need to imagine large, organized Mycenaean expeditions into central Europe, the exchange of these goods attests to a rich web of connections between the Aegean and central and northern Europe that the Mycenaeans were better placed to exploit than the Cretans. When these developments are placed alongside the Minoan record we can fairly conclude that, prior to 1600, the two great Bronze Age cultures were fundamentally oriented in different directions: Minoan Crete to the south and east, in the

3.8 The Mycenaean world

Mediterranean and Levant; Mycenaean Greece toward the north. In the Late Bronze Age, however, this would change, and the two cultures would eventually confront each other violently.

The Mycenaean World

Whatever the source of their wealth, from the middle of the second millennium BC the Mycenaeans quickly developed a complex society that controlled much of southern and central Greece (**3.8**). Citadels were built in central Greece at Thebes and Gla, and the Argolid had major centers of Mycenaean power at Mycenae, Tiryns, and Midea. At Messenia in western Greece, the excavations at Pylos have revealed the remains of another palace complex. Since 2010, excavations at Aghios Vasileios in Laconia have added another administrative center to the list.

The focal point of these citadels was the tripartite structure known as the megaron, the design of which was consistent. In each case, a forecourt led to an antechamber and on into the main room, where a central hearth was surrounded by four columns that carried the roof. (The throne was also situated in this main room.) As this reconstruction of the citadel of Mycenae shows (**3.9**), beneath the megaron were

located houses, religious buildings, and areas given over to the manufacturing of luxury goods made of alabaster, gold, and silver. In the case of Mycenae, the entire hilltop was surrounded by a fortification wall built *c.* 1250 BC.

Many of the rooms, especially in the palace complex on the crown of the hill, were decorated with brilliant frescoes. The scenes on these wall paintings, at Mycenae and at other sites (such as Tiryns), reflect the preoccupations and the self-image of the Mycenaean elite: at Tiryns we have hunting scenes—such as the boar hunt shown in **3.10**—and processions of women in chariots; processions of women on foot at Mycenae; and at Pylos, colorful frescoes depicting singers performing to the accompaniment of a lyre, processional scenes with a bull being led to sacrifice, and gruesome battle scenes in which Mycenaean warriors are slaying their enemies.

In the Late Bronze Age, especially in the thirteenth century BC when these citadels were at their peak, the ruling elites advertised their powers not only by building massive fortification walls but also by burying their dead in carefully constructed tholos tombs outside the walls of the citadel. The so-called Treasury of Atreus (or Tomb of Agamemnon, as it

3.9 Reconstruction of the citadel of Mycenae as it would have appeared *c.* 1250 BC

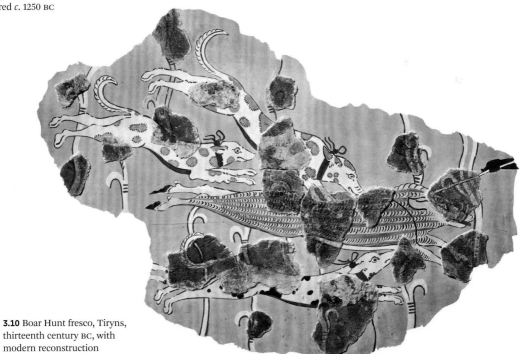

3.10 Boar Hunt fresco, Tiryns, thirteenth century BC, with modern reconstruction

3.11 Treasury of Atreus, *c.* 1250 BC

is sometimes referred to) at Mycenae is a good example (**3.11**). Named by Schliemann for the founder of the dynasty that included Agamemnon and Menelaus, the tomb was built by a member of the Mycenaean elite around 1250 BC. The tomb consists of a great corbeled chamber 14 meters (46 ft) in diameter, constructed with concentric circles of cut stone blocks rising to a height of 13 meters (43 ft) above the ground level. The tomb is approached by a passageway, or ***dromos***, 36 meters (118 ft) long, leading to the entrance, or ***stomion***, where two ornate columns of exotic green stone stood on either side of the doorway. A massive lintel block lay above the door, the weight over it being dispersed by a relieving triangle. The tomb was buried under a man-made mound, or tumulus. The tomb, in common with others at Mycenae, serves as a dramatic advertisement for the power of its occupant: the size and the resources needed to construct it allow us to identify it as the site of an elite, and probably royal, burial.

3.12 Piet de Jong, reconstruction of the interior of the megaron of the Palace of Nestor. Watercolor

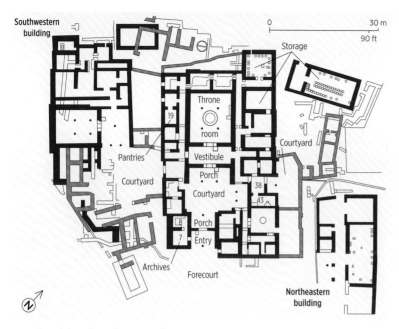

Southwestern building

Storage

Throne room

19

Courtyard

Pantries

Vestibule

Courtyard

Porch

Courtyard

38

43

8

Porch

7

Entry

Archives

Forecourt

Northeastern building

0   30 m
90 ft

3.13 Plan of the Palace of Nestor, Pylos

What was life like in the Mycenaean centers? Recent surveys and excavations at Mycenaean sites have gradually modified the picture painted by Schliemann and his collaborator, the great German excavator Wilhelm Dörpfeld. At Mycenae, for example, it has now emerged that—in addition to the citadel, its megaron, and associated buildings reserved for cult purposes and specialized artisanal work—there was an entire lower town outside the walls of the palace. Survey and excavations between AD 2007 and 2011, beginning with geophysical prospection, have identified a town extending over approximately 30 hectares (75 acres). A fortification wall with at least three gates protected the area, and inside were domestic and commercial buildings, as well as administrative structures. The entire region outside the walls of the citadel has now revealed evidence of a network of roads, dams, and bridges, as well as various building complexes, such as the Oil-Merchant complex and the House of the Wine Merchant. Taken as a whole, the evidence demonstrates that Mycenae was not the lone, isolated mountain citadel that greets today's visitor, but the center of a thriving urban environment, where specialized manufacturing and trade carried on under the protection of the palace within the walls of the citadel.

A recently excavated Mycenaean site that has added to our understanding of this Late Bronze Age society is Korphos-Kalamianos, on the Saronic Gulf. Korphos demonstrates that Mycenaean settlements were not always organized around palaces and citadels. Here, a Mycenaean harbor and town have been revealed by intensive survey. Between AD 2007 and 2010, more than 60 buildings and 120 rooms were identified and plotted by the survey team from the University of Pennsylvania. The town was defended by a wall and in the immediate vicinity was a smaller settlement, terrace walls, and a series of small fortified enclosures, possibly associated with the exploitation of pastoral resources in the hinterland.

A third site that allows us to see the way Mycenaean society was organized is Pylos. Here, as at Korphos-Kalamianos, we encounter a form of social organization that is somewhat different from Mycenae. For example, the Palace of Nestor, as the Mycenaean site at Pylos is sometimes called—once again, the Homeric poems provide the identification, whether their descriptions are accurate or not—was not protected by a fortification wall (**3.12**). In this respect it was not unlike a Minoan palace, and in common with the Cretan palaces Pylos clearly functioned as a center of redistribution (**3.13**). There are indications that goods were stored and dealt out to the population. Some of the rooms in the palace clearly had specialized functions associated with them, which can be inferred from the material finds, including Linear B tablets. For example, a great cache of tablets indicates that Rooms 7 and 8 were archive rooms, while nearly three thousand drinking cups were found in Room 19, clearly pointing to feasting on a grand scale at Pylos. In Room 43, a terra-cotta bathtub was discovered, and in Room 38, records of perfumed oil appear to have fallen into the room from the floor above when the palace was destroyed around 1200 BC.

Mycenaean Industry and Labor
Perfume and textile manufacturing were major Mycenaean industries. The tablets that record oil

manufacturing are particularly useful for showing the industrial scale of these operations. Take, for example, a tablet recording a transaction between a prominent individual named Alxoitas (*A-ko-so-ta* in Linear B) and a perfume maker called Thyestes:

1. As follows Alxoitas gave
2. to Thyestes the unguent-boiler
3. spices for the boiling
4. of oil
5. coriander AROMATIC 576 liters
6. cyperus AROMATIC 576 liters
7. FRUITS 240 liters WINE 576 liters HONEY 58 liters
8. WOOL 6 kilograms MUST 58 liters

(Pylos Un 267, trans. Christidis)

Olive oil would be boiled with these aromatic ingredients before being steeped with rose, sage, or other fragrances. Not only does the list shed light on the process of perfume making, but also it reveals the scale of production: the transaction recorded in Un 267 resulted in hundreds of liters of perfumed oil being produced. Stored in thousands of stirrup jars, this perfumed oil was traded far from Pylos. If we recall the Uluburun wreck discussed in Chapter 2, we can recognize that Pylos and the other Mycenaean centers were participating in the trade network that, as we have seen, tied the Aegean into an even larger world of commodity exchange.

The palaces also had specialized metalworkers who made silver, gold, and copper vessels and jewelry; potters, weavers, dyers, artists, and scribes were also part of the personnel of the palace. In Room 99 of the Palace of Nestor, tablets record the work done on chariots, suggesting that this was the palace's workshop. In the same room a thin strip of bronze has been found and subsequently identified as a wheel rim, corresponding to other Mycenaean texts that describe wheels "bound with bronze." As with the perfume industry, the scale of activity is impressive. One tablet records the transference from the woodcutters to the chariot workshop of fifty saplings (possibly for draught poles) and fifty axles.

Aside from the workers who manufactured staple and luxury items, and who made up the lower ranks of the social hierarchy, there are others among the elite of the Mycenaean world who are attested in hundreds of Linear B tablets at Pylos and elsewhere. For example, the tablets speak of a figure known

as the **wanax**, a term used later in Greek to mean "king." Some workers are described as **wanakteros**, presumably meaning "royal." Another person of very high rank was the **lawagetas**, whose title translates as "leader of the people," possibly a war-leader whose role was separate from that of the king. Below these leaders there were persons of lesser importance: the **koreter**, who had authority over a district in the manner of a governor; the **telestai**, probably landholders, but who may have been religious officials; and the **heqetai** ("Companions"), who may have been a military caste associated with chariot warfare. At the very bottom of the social pyramid were slaves, known as **doeroi** (male) and **doerai** (female), who worked the fields and did a great deal of the manufacturing. The textiles and perfumes produced at the palaces, for example, were the result of this slave labor. It should also be noted that two other words occur in the tablets that point toward a form of social organization separate from the palaces: **geronsia** and **damos**. In Mycenaean times, these terms refer to a council and a corporation of landholders, but both reappear in Classical Greek hundreds of years later: "damos" will come to mean both village and even "the people," eventually forming part of the term that denotes a new kind of government in Classical Greece: democracy.

One controversial category of people in the Linear B tablets is that of the "Collectors" or "Owners," who are sometimes listed in connection with tracts of land, flocks of sheep, the production of olive oil, or teams of slave workers. The scale of their ownership was extraordinary: the tablets record numbers of sheep in the tens of thousands and oil production sometimes reaching over 5,000 liters (1,320 US gallons). Although the exact position of the Collectors in Mycenaean society is not certain, it has been plausibly suggested that they were part of the palace elite, perhaps from families close to the center of power, and that they controlled much of the Mycenaean economy, both as producers and traders. The Mycenaean economy was complex, and such a role for the Collectors suggests that the central authority of the palace relied on the cooperation of middlemen. One such Collector was *A-ko-so-ta*, for example, mentioned above in Un 276, where he appears supplying aromatics to a perfume maker. In other tablets he is an inspector of fields; a receiver of at least sixty-two items that appear to be beds;

3.14 HV Rb 1 recto. Linear B tablet from Aghios Vasileios. Clay

a Collector of livestock; and a distributor of flax. The Linear B evidence reveals a surprisingly complex and sophisticated society, with many social strata and with economic activity occurring on a scale that far exceeds the relatively modest palaces and halls described by Homer. The heroic world of epic is in many ways simpler than the commercial realities of the Late Bronze Age.

The complexity of the Mycenaean economy has been graphically demonstrated by recent archaeological work in the region of Lakonia, south of the Mycenaean heartland of the Argolid. Excavations began in AD 2009 near the village of Aghios Vasileios, less than 20 kilometers (12 mi.) from Sparta, after a Linear B tablet was found in a pit that proved to be part of a collapsed tomb. Earlier surveys had detected Mycenaean pottery in the area, and it was believed that a major Mycenaean center was probably located in the vicinity, but it was the evidence of the tablets that first showed that this was an administrative center of considerable size and power. Subsequent excavations revealed the ground plan of a Mycenaean palace, comparable in size to those known at Thebes and Gla, and located on a hilltop reminiscent of the site of Pylos, which sits on the hill of Epano Englianos in Messenia. The excavator, Adamantia Vasilogamvrou, describes the importance of the Lakonian palace this way: "a palace of such type and size would have administered some thousands of population, in and around it, hundreds of functionaries and tens of scribes making tablets, labels and nodules."

The tablets from Aghios Vasileios mention textiles and weapons, items familiar from other palaces (such as Pylos). HV Rb 1—the very first Linear B tablet found in Lakonia— proved especially interesting (**3.14**). It contains clearly incised signs that read *e-pi-zo-ta*, followed by the symbol for 500. At this point the tablet breaks and an even higher number may have been recorded. The term *e-pi-zo-ta* has been found on tablets from other sites and corresponds to a later Greek word that signifies a scabbard. The tablet appears to indicate the manufacturing and storage of weapons on a large scale, a fact confirmed by the discovery of a room in Building A containing sixteen bronze swords, a dagger, a knife, spearheads, a bronze helmet, and the remains of a boar's tusk helmet (**3.15**).

Here, as in the case of the other Mycenaean sites excavated over the last one hundred years, the shadow of Homer looms large. In the epic poems, Menelaus, brother of Agamemnon, is referred to as the king of Sparta. His wife is Helen, whose abduction by Paris precipitated the Trojan War. If, therefore, we want to marry the evidence of archaeology to the narrative of the epic poems, then it is hard to resist seeing the remains at Aghios Vasileios as anything other than the palace of Menelaus and Helen, and to imagine that it was here that Telemachos was entertained by the royal couple when he went in search of his father, Odysseus. Even if we do not accept such a direct link between poetry and

3.15 Bronze sword blades, Building A, Aghios Vasileios

3.16 Piet de Jong, reconstruction of the Warrior fresco, Pylos, *c.* 1250 BC

archaeology, the Homeric poems do seem to recall in some fashion the political geography of the Mycenaean world. Pylos, for example, is described as the homeland of Nestor, the wise counselor of the Achaians (the Homeric term for the Greeks), and it is the site of a major Mycenaean palace. In each case, the difficulty for us as interpreters of the past is to decide whether archaeology can or should be brought into alignment with epic poetry. Can one field help enrich our understanding of the other, or should pots and poems be kept entirely separate?

Linear B: Solving the Riddle

From the very beginning of the era of modern archaeological research, the fundamental challenge to archaeologists was to clarify the exact relationship between Crete and Mycenae, and to determine whether either or both cultures were Greek. The discoveries of Schliemann, Evans, Blegen, and Tsountas kept forcing scholars back to one unavoidable fact: there were strong affinities between Mycenaean culture and that of Crete. This is most readily demonstrated by the presence of Minoan artifacts, especially pottery and stone vessels, in Mycenaean burials and domestic settings, suggesting that the Mycenaeans favored Minoan styles. Mycenaean wall paintings often depict figures who would not look out of place in the art of Minoan palaces. In fact, so pronounced is the Minoan influence on Mycenaean art that Evans was convinced that the Minoans had conquered the mainland and that Mycenae was originally a Minoan colony. The equation of style with ethnic identity, however, is potentially deceptive: driving a Mercedes does not make the driver German any more than wearing jeans makes one American. Furthermore, there are also stylistic differences that suggest the people of the mainland thought of themselves quite differently. The frescoes from Pylos, for example, depict a scene in which kilted Mycenaean warriors wearing boar's tusk helmets are shown slaughtering their enemies dressed in animal skins, a far more graphic and violent scene than one would find in Cretan art (**3.16**).

As long as the principal source of information about Minoan and Mycenaean society remained the material culture recovered by archaeology, the question of the exact relationship between Minoan Crete and the Mycenaean mainland could only be answered by inference. For example, the Mycenaean practice of building tholos tombs seemed to point toward a significant connection with Crete, where tholos tombs in the southern region of the Mesara go back to the Middle Minoan period. But even these tangible, material connections were open to differing interpretations. Either the Mycenaeans were descended from the Cretans, or were a separate people who had adopted Cretan style in their decorative schemes, their burial practices, their dress, and their social organization. The on-going underwater excavations at Pavlopetri, in southern Lakonia, will shed further light on this. The site is now submerged, but preliminary investigations carried out between AD 2009 and 2013 by the University of Nottingham suggest that this was a major Mycenaean port, with a built area of more than 9,000 square meters (100,000 sq. ft), raising the likelihood that this was the port from which Minoan goods reached the Mycenaean mainland.

The answer, however, to the fundamental question of how Crete and Mycenaean Greece were related lies not in palaces, sunken cities, fortresses, or precious objects, but in the hundreds of nondescript clay tablets, incised with the script identified as Linear B, that turned up in the excavations of Knossos on Crete, and at Mycenae, Tiryns, and Pylos on the mainland. The translation of these tablets finally gave the inhabitants of the Bronze Age Aegean a voice. A number of scholars spent years attempting to decipher the code, but the most important was Alice Kober (1906–1950), an American scholar who, between AD 1930 and her death, meticulously assembled more than 180,000 transcriptions of the signs on the tablets. In doing so, she managed to establish the basic syllabic structure of the language and to show that it exhibited a consistent pattern: words were made up of syllabic roots to which were added various endings. This meant that the language of Linear B was inflected, a feature of Greek, although until then most scholars had dismissed the possibility that the language of Linear B was Greek. Two years after Kober's death, and building on her work, a British amateur, Michael Ventris (1922–1956), definitively deciphered the language and showed that it was Greek. Ventris demonstrated that many familiar toponyms (place names) and the names of deities known from later periods were found in Linear B. For example, *po-se-da-wo-ne* and *ar-te-mi-to* were clearly Poseidon and Artemis. More tablets have

recently come to light in western Crete (at Khania), on the mainland in Thebes, and within the last five years at Aghios Vasileios. These tablets, found after Ventris first deciphered Linear B, have all consistently confirmed that the language of the Mycenaeans was Greek, and that many place names in the Linear B record accorded with later, known toponyms. A tablet from Thebes that was transcribed and published in 2001, for example, refers to a place called *e-u-te-re-u*, which corresponds to the later toponym Eutresis, a Boiotian town mentioned by Homer.

In some respects the translation of Linear B was a disappointment. No poems or literary texts survive in the script, but as a source of information about the economic conditions and political organization of the Mycenaean world, they have proved to be invaluable. Take, for example Un 2, a tablet that sheds light on ceremonial practices:

9. At Sphagianes, on the occasion of the king's "initiation,"
10. the man in charge of the establishment[?] released:
11. 1,575 liters of barley; 14.5 liters of cyperus; 8 liters of "O" [another type of cyperus?]
12. 115 liters of flour; 211 liters of olives; 19 liters of [?] 132; 10 liters of honey
13. 96 liters of figs; 1 ox; 26 rams; 6 ewes; 2 he-goats; 2 she goats
14. 1 fattened pig; 6 sows; 586 liters of wine; 2 pieces of [?] 146 cloth

(PY Un 2, trans. Castleden)

Despite the fact that some of the signs remain untranslated (as indicated by [?]), there is enough that can be read to show that the document records details of the coronation of the new king, an event that was celebrated by a great public feast organized and supplied by the palace. A single ox, served up with nearly 600 liters (160 US gallons) of wine, would have been enough to supply hundreds of people without even taking into consideration the sheep and goats also culled from the palace flocks. When we associate this text with the hundreds of drinking vessels within the palace storerooms, we begin to see the redistributive economy in action: the entire community assembled at Sphagianes (*pa-ki-ja-ne* in Linear B), a place of sacrifice, to celebrate the king's initiation by killing the ox and then enjoying a banquet provided by the central authority. Ritual slaughter and feast, which would continue to be the backbone of Greek sacrifice and religious practice for centuries to come, clearly have their roots in Mycenaean practices.

Linear B also shed light on other important aspects of Mycenaean political organization. Pylos, as it was known in later Greek—*pu-ro* in Linear B—was actually divided into two regions, the Hither and Further Provinces, separated by Mount Aigialeon. The tablets also demonstrate that within these regions there were many other administrative units, each with a governor or mayor. Jn 829, a Linear B tablet found at Pylos, for example, contains the names of sixteen locations in the Hither Province and reveals how these communities related to the central authority at Pylos. According to this document, each community was allocated an amount of bronze to supply to the palace to be made into spearheads and arrowheads. In another case, the outlying communities were given piglets to fatten for a public feast, and in yet a third case they received distributions of wine from the palace. In addition to these accounts, the tablets also record tax payments as well as records of the detachments of soldiers sent to keep watch up and down the coast. In other words, although the Linear B tablets are essentially bureaucratic and do not offer us a view of the beliefs or attitudes of the inhabitants of the kingdom of Pylos, they do allow us to see a highly organized state apparatus at work, in which the palace operated as both the symbolic, ritual center, and as the central node in an economic network. Here, as in the Cretan palaces, the entire system was based on a balance between the production, storage, and redistribution of staple goods on the one hand, and the manufacturing, trade, and consumption of luxury items on the other. The first of these spheres was primarily local, the second international. It was a system of some complexity, and the Linear B tablets reflect the complex organization of Mycenaean society. It is hard to image anyone in the kingdom of Pylos whose life was not bound up with the fortunes of the palace.

Mycenaean Knossos

If the decipherment of Linear B revealed the workings of the Mycenaean palaces, it also helped to settle the issue of the Mycenaean world's relations with Crete. Throughout the second millennium BC, the Minoan world underwent a series of fluctuations that corresponded to the building and destruction of the major palatial centers. Around 1470 BC, the palaces were destroyed a second time; in the generations that followed, most of the palaces were not used as either ceremonial or administrative centers. Knossos, however, was rebuilt and returned to its role as a center of the redistributive economy, but the records kept by the scribes at Knossos in the fourteenth century BC were written in Linear B, which, as we now know, was Greek. It follows then that the rulers of Knossos in its final phase of occupation were Greek, since it would have made no sense for indigenous Cretan rulers to have imported Greek-speaking scribes when there already existed a Cretan script, Linear A, which had been developed locally by their own scribal class. The implications of Linear B tablets being used to keep inventories and lists at Knossos are enormous. If Greeks were ruling at Knossos, then it made sense that it was mainland Greeks who had been responsible for the destruction of the Cretan cities, almost certainly as a result of an invasion. So Evans had not only been wrong to guess that the Minoans had colonized the mainland, but he had also inverted the actual situation: the Mycenaean Greeks had taken over Minoan Crete, destroying much of the palatial system, and ruled at Knossos in the final years of the Bronze Age.

This explanation not only fits with the distribution of Linear B tablets but also accords with other evidence. It has long been recognized, for example, that at sites outside of the Greek mainland and Crete, such as Miletos and Rhodes (where Minoan pottery is found in high quantities in the sixteenth century BC), the proportion of Minoan pottery drops considerably in relation to Mycenaean pottery over the course of the next two hundred years. It is not difficult to imagine competition between the two peoples for dominance in the Aegean. As Mycenaean power waxed, Minoan power waned. An invasion of Crete itself, where previously the cities had been unwalled, since their defense lay in their ships, could thus be seen as the final act in a protracted period of hostility, once the balance of power had changed.

Further confirmation of this notion comes from a variety of sources, some unexpected. One is Greek mythology. Later Greek tradition associated Crete and specifically the legendary king Minos with a naval empire, and this is a tradition based on fact.

3.17 Vapheio cup (1), *c.* 1400– 1350 BC. Gold, H: 7.8 cm (3⅛ in.)

We have already noted in the last chapter that the Egyptian evidence, both textual and iconographic, confirms that the Minoans sailed widely around the eastern Mediterranean. The evidence from Thera, as well, demonstrates that the Cretans projected their power and presence into the Aegean world by means of a navy. These same traditions concerning the Minoan naval empire also maintained that Minos had required a tribute from the mainland each year: seven Athenian youths and seven maidens had been sent to Knossos and were sacrificed to the Minotaur, Minos's monstrous son. Only Theseus, coming from the mainland, had entered the Labyrinth and slain the beast, liberating the Athenians. The myth looks very much like a justification of an invasion from the mainland, a story in which the Cretans were demonized, their glorious palace made into a charnel house, their bull cult reviled and recast as a perversion. The Minotaur was said to have been born of the unholy union of Pasiphae, Minos's wife, with a bull after she had been punished by Poseidon with an unnatural urge to mate with the animal. It is unlikely that this was how the Cretans regarded the cult of the bull. Near Eastern parallels suggest that the bull would have been treated reverentially, and that perhaps the king or high priest was seen as an incarnation of that same power. But in this final, Mycenaean phase, the

bull cult was altered, with some scholars noting a change in the iconography associated with the bull cult. One wonders if shamans dressed in bull's-head masks were the basis for the story of the Minotaur. If so, the transformation of a long-standing cult into the story of the Minotaur could well be due to the stories brought back to the mainland by Greeks who had witnessed the cult in its last days.

Some recent archaeological work on Crete offers support for the view that Knossos in its last days was the center of a Mycenaean kingdom on Crete. In AD 1990, excavations by the Danish Institute at Chania in western Crete uncovered Linear B tablets, pointing to the presence of Mycenaeans there as well. Subsequent excavations in 2010 revealed the building associated with the Mycenaean ruler of Kydonia, the Mycenaean name for Khania. In this building were found five seal stones of the type used by the Mycenaeans to seal documents and vessels, as well as an ivory knife and a bronze knife. Some rooms have implements associated with textile manufacturing, and this may have been one source of wealth in the area. Even more dramatic was the realization that some of the Khania Linear B tablets came from secure contexts much later than the period of 1425–1375 BC, the dates usually assigned to the Knossos tablets, and that at least one of them was written by the same

3.18 Vapheio cup (2), *c.* 1400–1350 BC. Gold, H: 7.8 cm (3⅛ in.)

scribe as produced some of the Knossos material. As a result, it now seems that the Mycenaean period on Crete may have continued until 1250, overlapping with the same period on the mainland when the Mycenaeans were using Linear B to record their economic documents. Whether the Mycenaeans and Minoans were able to fashion a single identity (or saw each other as implacable enemies) is difficult to say; archive rooms at Knossos appear to have been used first for Linear A and later Linear B tablets, and this continuity of function has been interpreted as a sign of cooperation between the new Mycenaean elite and their subjects.

Other excavations in Crete have largely confirmed the view that the final phase of palace culture after 1450 BC was Mycenaean. By 1425, new types of burials appear, the so-called "warrior graves" at Khania and Knossos, which involved the inhumation of single bodies accompanied by luxury goods and weapons. The pottery associated with the burials is labelled Ephyraean after the type-site of Ephyra (in the Peloponnese) from which it originated, and DNA studies have demonstrated that in the Late Bronze Age the Cretan population witnessed an influx from the Peloponnese and central Greece.

The effect of this Mycenaean phase in the last years of Knossos was considerable, and not just on Crete where Mycenaean Greeks took control. In many ways, Cretan palatial culture was so well suited to the organization of territory and the exploitation of resources on a massive scale—more than one hundred thousand sheep were owned by the central authority at Knossos—that what the Mycenaeans encountered was an apparatus far more complex and developed than their own. Not only did the Greeks enjoy drinking from vessels decorated with Minoan motifs and employing Cretan craftsmen to decorate their palaces, but also—and more importantly—they developed a form of state organization and control that clearly mimicked the Cretan model. Warrior chieftains with a taste for war and booty, in the thirteenth century the Mycenaeans also became the kings of principalities that developed the same model of storage, manufacturing, luxury trade, redistribution, and scribal record-keeping that had been the hallmark of Minoan Crete.

The complexity of this relationship can be illustrated by two cups found in a tholos tomb south of Sparta by Christos Tsountas in AD 1889. The Vapheio cups (**3.17** and **3.18**) depict bulls being captured and tamed. The style, composition, and execution of the scenes point to the work of master-craftsmen, and there has been a debate for more than one hundred years regarding the cups' provenance.

Are they of Minoan manufacture, buried with the tomb's occupant as two of his most treasured luxury items? Or, as many scholars now believe, are they of separate origin, one Cretan and one Mycenaean? There are subtle difference of technique and composition that suggest they were not manufactured together. In fact, it has been plausibly suggested that the cup depicting the rampaging bull may be an answer to the cup with the peaceful scene of the bull being gently tethered and tamed. If the latter is the Cretan scene, with its idyllic view of nature, then the rampaging bull may represent the Mycenaean assertion of a harder, more brutal attitude to life.

Reading identity and cultural value of this sort into the iconography of a single item, however, is fraught with danger. There are more satisfactory approaches. One is to examine entire assemblages, in order to evaluate the overall context in which burial goods are found, and another is to consider the distribution of goods over a wide area.

An example of what can be learned by the first approach is the Mycenaean cemetery excavated at Dendra, in the vicinity of the Mycenaean citadel at Midea, where a tholos tomb was uncovered by the Swedish excavator, Axel Persson, in AD 1926. Sixteen chamber tombs have also come to light, many used for multiple burials. Two aspects of the Dendra cemetery are striking: the first is that in one of the tombs a full panoply, or suit, of bronze armor and boar's tusk helmet were found (**3.19**), along with rich grave goods: a bronze jug, basin and spouted conical bowl. The second is that some of the Dendra graves were characterized by horse burials, in which the bodies of the slaughtered animals were arranged carefully facing each other on their sides as if heraldically. A similar phenomenon occurs in a Mycenaean tomb from Marathon in Attica. It is hard to escape the impression that the local chief who was buried here was from an elite who regarded military prowess as the supreme expression of their power. In common with the Homeric heroes, the horse-lords of Dendra and Marathon were proud to proclaim their status as warriors.

A good example of the significance of distribution patterns can be seen when we plot the find-spots of Mycenaean "Type D" swords (**3.20**). These swords, sometimes up to 70 centimeters (2 ft 4½ in.) in length, are of a distinctive type, with a central rib,

3.19 Panoply and boar tusk helmet, Dendra, *c.* 1200 BC. Bronze and boar tusk

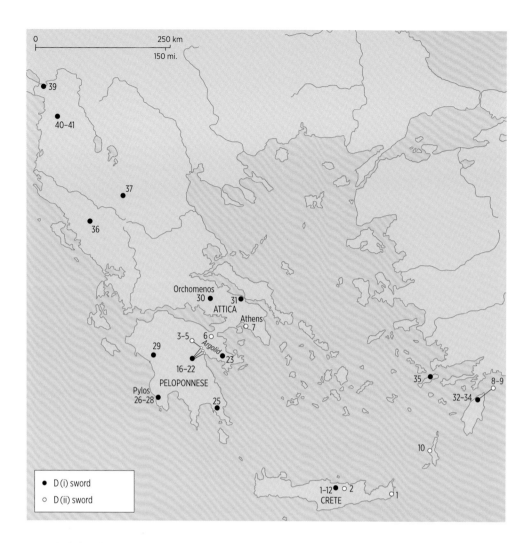

0   250 km
      150 mi.

- 39
- 40–41
- 37
- 36
- Orchomenos 30
- 31
- ATTICA
- Athens 7
- 3–5
- 6
- Argolid
- 29
- 23
- 16–22
- PELOPONNESE
- Pylos 26–28
- 25
- 35
- 8–9
- 32–34
- 10
- 1–12 2
- CRETE
- 1

● D (i) sword
○ D (ii) sword

rounded shoulders, and a flanged extension of the tang, to which wood or ivory could be attached for a handle. The distribution of the swords closely approximates the borders of the Mycenaean world. The heavy concentration of sites in the Peloponnese, especially the Argolid, corresponds to the rest of our evidence, while other known Mycenaean sites, such as Pylos, Orchomenos, and Athens, are also represented. The presence of Type D swords does not guarantee the existence of a palace nearby, nor does the absence of such swords mean the absence of any Mycenaean presence in an area, but by collecting data of different categories—weapons, architecture, tholos tombs, Linear B tablets, and so forth—we are able to build up a more complete picture of the Mycenaean world.

Troy and Homer

We reconstruct Mycenaean Greece using archaeology, but as we have seen, the Bronze Age also exists in the myths and memories of the Greeks. The site that most completely bridges archaeology and myth is Troy, and any interpretation of Greece in the Bronze Age must deal with the many questions that surround Troy. Homer locates Troy close to the coast and near the Scamander River in the region that is situated in modern-day Turkey, close to the Hellespont, the long seaway that links the Aegean to the Bosporos and eventually the Black Sea. As we have already seen, Heinrich Schliemann excavated at Hisarlik in the early 1870s and demonstrated, dramatically, that Troy was more than a poetic fiction. Nearly one hundred and fifty years have passed since the first systematic excavations at Troy and we are now in a position to understand the history of the site much more fully than when Schliemann first dug here.

It is now clear that there were many phases of occupation on the same site (**3.21**). The earliest, Troy I, goes back to the Early Bronze Age and has been dated as early as the beginning of the third millennium BC. The levels that best correspond to the traditional date of the Trojan War, which according to Eratosthenes of Alexandria occurred around 1184 BC, are either Troy VI or Troy VII. There are indications that Troy VI was destroyed by an earthquake, and there are no signs of destruction as a result of warfare; Troy VII, on the other hand, may have been destroyed as the result of a siege and attack. It is this archaeological layer that most scholars traditionally identified with Homer's Troy.

This was the consensus until about AD 1988. In the last generation, however, the debate over Homer's Troy has become increasingly rancorous. On the one side stands the German excavator, Manfred Korfmann (1942–2005). Claiming to have found evidence for a ditch and a fortification wall around the lower city, Korfmann claimed that Troy VI and VII were ten times bigger than had previously been thought. More than just a regional center, Korfmann's Troy would have been one of the largest trade emporia of the Late Bronze Age. To explain Troy's importance, Korfmann drew attention to the city's location. Situated in antiquity closer to the water, the city would have profited from the trade that passed up and down the Hellespont between the Black Sea and the Aegean. Grain, wine, oil, hides, slaves, and luxury items of precious metal were exchanged between the two zones: the Black Sea was the entry to a Danubian zone leading into central and northern Europe as well as Ukraine and east into the Urals, ancient Georgia, and central Asia. Small precious items, such as lapis lazuli from Afghanistan, passed by

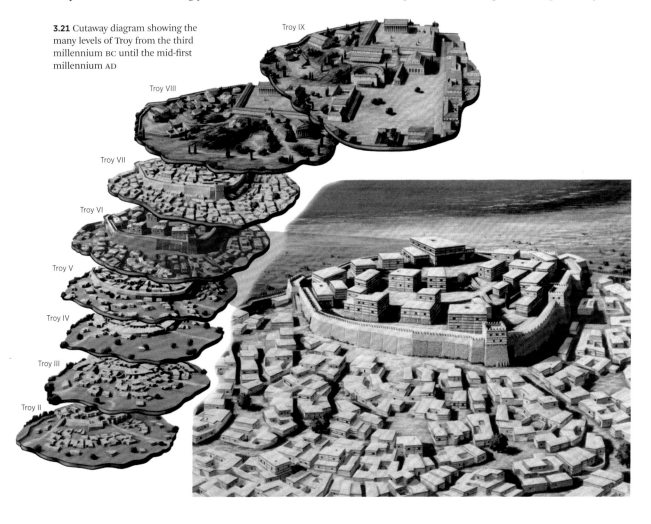

3.21 Cutaway diagram showing the many levels of Troy from the third millennium BC until the mid-first millennium AD

Troy IX

Troy VIII

Troy VII

Troy VI

Troy V

Troy IV

Troy III

Troy II

land routes until reaching the Black Sea, from where they could be easily traded down into the Aegean and Mediterranean. The central node where these two networks intersected was the Hellespont, where natural conditions favored the site of Troy.

Opposing this reconstruction has been Korfmann's Tübingen colleague, Frank Kolb (1945–), who has dismissed the evidence of the lower city as a fanciful reconstruction. Furthermore, Kolb notes that there are few luxury items from the Black Sea found at Troy, and that unlike the other great palatial centers of the Late Bronze Age, no archive has ever been found associated with the citadel of Troy VI or VII. Most scholars, however, believe that Korfmann's version is not an exaggeration, and that the features he identifies below the citadel of Troy are consistent with major defensive works, such as ditches designed to impede chariots. Korfmann's work has been endorsed by such leading scholars as Joachim Latacz, who has used an Egyptian geographic list on the temple of Amenophis III to show that Mycenae and Thebes were regarded by the Egyptians as major kingdoms in the Late Bronze Age; kingdoms that, in his view, vied with the Hittites for control of western Anatolia. Troy would thus have been located in an area contested by the Mycenaeans and Hittites.

There are other reasons to believe that Troy VI and VII were more than two different levels of a small, unimportant city in northwestern Anatolia. Diplomatic correspondence from the Hittite capital of Hattusa repeatedly makes mention of the site of Wilusa, the Hittite version of the Greek toponym of Ilion, an alternative name for Troy. Furthermore, these letters, which date from the late fourteenth century BC to the late thirteenth, contain a great many names similar to names that occur in the *Iliad*. There is mention, for example, of a local renegade by the name of Piyamaradu who has thrown off loyalty to the Hittites. Some scholars would see in his name the historical antecedent of Homer's Priam, king of Troy. Another person named in the Hittite documents is Alaksandu, king of Wilusa; in the *Iliad*, Paris is often referred to as Alexandros. Finally, the neighboring region from which Piyamaradu launched his raids on Hittite territory is called Ahhiyawa, whose king in one letter is said to have given an order to hand over Piyamaradu to the Hittites. Many scholars would identify Ahhiyawa with Homer's Achaians (and the Ekwesh of the Egyptian records). In a letter from

the Hittite king Hattusili III from around 1250 BC, the king alludes to the fact that the king of Ahhiyawa has been supporting Piyamaradu, and even notes that the Hittites and Ahhiyawa have resolved their differences regarding Wilusa, over which they once went to war.

It should be stressed that the Hittite diplomatic corpus does not prove the factuality of Homer's account of the Trojan War. The historical figure of Piyamaradu may lie behind the epic character Priam, but they are hardly identical. What it does suggest, however, is that many elements of the epic poems derive from conditions at the end of the Bronze Age without necessarily describing historical events. It was in the regional confrontations of western Anatolia in the thirteenth century BC that a real Troy found itself sandwiched between ambitious local dynasts and even more powerful kingdoms and empires. Those conflicts would provide the nucleus for a version of the events described in Homer's poems. The question for historians, then, becomes this: what aspects of the poems reflect a historical reality and what elements are fiction? Is Paris closer to Alaksandu or to Alexandros?

To answer this question we must return to the subject of epic poetry. Composed orally, employing a strict metrical scheme of dactylic hexameters (see below), the Homeric poems were first written down sometime after 750 BC. Prior to this date, however, the poems were transmitted purely by oral performance. Studies of Slavic bards by Milman Parry and Alfred Lord in the AD 1920s and later have demonstrated that poets singing an oral composition are capable of extraordinary feats of memory and performance. Even more important was the discovery that oral composition is a fluid and ever-changing process: no two performances will be identical. The poet cuts and shapes and expands his material based on his audience and the reception of his work. Aided by strict metrical schemes—in the case of Greek epic a system called dactylic hexameter, employing six measures, or "feet," composed of combinations of long and short syllables such as dactyls (-ˇˇ) and spondees (--)—the poet constructed lines and sometimes entire passages using formulaic set pieces to help him. Some of these might be half lines ("Swift-footed Achilles"), others might be ten or more lines long, such as the descriptions of warriors arming for battle, in which each instance will include a description of the cuirass, the greaves, the shield, the spears, and the helmet worn by the warrior. When the poems were finally written down sometime after 750 BC, this organic style of composition gradually, though not immediately, ossified, and eventually by the Hellenistic period had reached the form in which we know the poems today.

The oral transmission of the poems means that there is a gap of more than three hundred and fifty years between the writing of the poems and the events they purport to describe. During the intervening centuries, the stories and the poems evolved continuously. Scholars studying oral composition have noted that it is almost impossible for a poet to describe accurately social institutions and abstractions from a century earlier. Accordingly, when Homer describes Telemachos calling an assembly on Ithaca before leaving to find his father, or when Andromache speaks of the dowry paid for her when Hektor courted her, the marriage arrangements and the governmental practices described are likely to be those of the poet's own day. On the other hand, descriptions of specific items, such as chariots, shields, and helmets, are well suited to being described in passages as set pieces that delighted the audience and were repeated many times over the generations. Here, for example, is the poet's description of Nestor's cup:

Beside these she set a cup,
a magnificent work Nestor had brought from home,
studded with gold. There were four handles on it,
around each one a pair of golden doves was feeding.
Below were two supports. When that cup was full,
another man could hardly lift it from the table,
but, old as he was, Nestor picked it up with ease.

(Homer, Iliad 9.629–37, trans. Johnston)

Schliemann found a magnificent gold cup in Grave Circle A at Mycenae that corresponds in some ways to this description, and it is easy to imagine a poet elaborately describing such a vessel to delight his audience, especially if in their own day they had not seen such a precious object (**3.22**). Such passages are examples of **ekphrasis**, the detailed descriptions of rare and special objects, and they can result in fossils turning up in the poems' texts. Homer describes Ajax fighting behind a tower shield, such as the one depicted in Theran wall paintings, but which had not been used in Homer's day for three hundred years.

This method of analysing the poems, according to which there is a poetic stratigraphy that matches the archaeological layers of a site (such as Troy), is complicated, however, by other factors: the poet singing his poems had to appeal to audiences and patrons who often had their own traditions of local heroes. As a result, episodes might be woven into the poems that had originated separately. Diomedes, for example, plays a prominent role in Book 5 of the *Iliad*, and this entire portion of the poem may derive from a separate cycle of epic poems in which his **aristeia**, or heroic accomplishments, were the central focus. Furthermore, in the tenth, ninth, and eighth centuries BC, when the poems were being retold on countless occasions, the audiences were often living in settings much more humble than the palaces of the Bronze Age, and the poet appealed to this audience by imbuing the world of the heroes with a heroic grandeur that was very much the product of fantasy and imagination. It would be difficult to find a precise and accurate historical antecedent, for example, for the Cyclops. And just as the heroes encounter magical monsters, they themselves have superhuman qualities precisely because those qualities made them entertaining: even in antiquity critics observed that Homer's heroes only ever ate meat, remarkable in a world where bread, olives, and cheese were the staples. Spare ribs are more heroic than salad.

The searches, therefore, for a historical Trojan War and for a "Homeric society" are extremely complicated. It is likely that the town of Troy was fought over and sacked early in the twelfth century BC, and, given the upheavals of the time, it is equally likely that Mycenaean Greeks participated. For every point of convergence between the archaeology of Troy and the world described in epic, however, there is a comparable divergence. Consider, for example, the role of Helen. The incentive for Mycenaeans participating in an attack on Troy is more likely to have been the wealth of the strategically located city, rather than the winning back of Menelaus's errant wife. And far from being the *femme fatale* of the *Odyssey* and Athenian drama, Helen was worshiped in Lakonia as a heroic ancestor of the Spartans; her shrine at Therapne, just outside Sparta, was in continuous use throughout the Classical and Archaic periods. Perhaps the most glaring discrepancy concerns the very people whose records gave us

a glimpse of Bronze Age Wilusa: the Hittites. Even though the Hittite empire dominated the territory of Anatolia throughout the thirteenth century, in the *Iliad* Homer shows no signs of being aware of them. In the catalogue of Trojan allies in Book 2 of the *Iliad* we are given a list of the ethnic groups who fought the Achaians, including Lycians, Lydians, and Mysians from Anatolia, but the greatest empire of the region, and one that was contemporary with the Mycenaeans, is not mentioned. Yet the Hittites did leave their mark in the literary traditions of other Levantine societies— the Hebrew Bible, for example, refers to an alliance between Israel and the King of the Hittites at 2 Kings 7.6—but the Hittites lie outside Homer's geographical

awareness. If the largest empire of Anatolia in the Bronze Age cannot find a place in Homer's account of the Trojan War, then we should not expect to find much history in the *Iliad*.

The Collapse of Mycenaean Culture

If Homer's poems are any kind of guide to the Aegean in the Bronze Age, then the fall of Troy signaled the beginning of the end of the Bronze Age. And whether or not Homer can be read as a mythopoetic treatment of that collapse, it remains true that Mycenaean culture—in so far as it was also based on great, fortified palaces, such as Mycenae and Tiryns, and the smaller palaces, such as Pylos—did collapse dramatically shortly after 1200 BC. As in the earlier case of Minoan Crete, this is evident in a horizon of destruction visible in the stratigraphy of the major Mycenaean sites, and the consistency of this demands an explanation. What happened to Mycenaean culture?

There are many competing theories. They range from the suggestion that climate change, and drought in particular, produced a catastrophic breakdown of the Mycenaean economy, to the notion that the Mycenaean system was so coercive that it prompted a backlash from the slaves and farmers upon whose labor it rested. Alternatively, some scholars have looked for evidence for foreign invasion, while others have tried to identify major changes in the technology of warfare, such as the emergence of mobile infantry replacing heavy chariots as the preferred formation for armies in the eastern Mediterranean. According to this theory, as chariot-based warfare was replaced by infantry combat, the elites identified with chariot fighting found their hold on power challenged. An interesting echo of this change may be found in the Homeric poems, where the warriors ride to battle in chariots but dismount to fight. Perhaps the heroic associations of the chariot persisted long after it became obsolete as a battle vehicle.

Although these explanations appear mutually exclusive, a closer examination suggests that each has some merit and that they may all have played a role. For example, although there is no compelling evidence for a prolonged drought in the Mycenaean world, tree-ring data from Anatolia does suggest that a dry spell may be associated with the collapse of Hittite civilization around 1200 BC, and it is reasonable to extrapolate this to Greece as well. Furthermore, excavators at Mycenae, Tiryns, and Midea are convinced that all three sites were hit by massive earthquakes around 1200, and there is also evidence that a flood destroyed the lower city outside the walls of Tiryns. In combination, these events would have caused disruptions to the food production in the Argive plain and could easily have had a flow-on effect, fueling discontent and raising internal tensions within the palace communities. In the period between 1300 and 1200, there is evidence of fire at some of the houses outside the walls at Mycenae, and for the burning of the citadel of Gla in Boiotia, although whether these were deliberate or accidental has not been established.

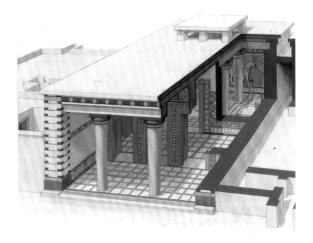

3.23
Reconstruction of Tiryns c. 1200 BC, showing (from top) the extension of the circuit wall, interior views of the palace and megaron, cross-section of wall

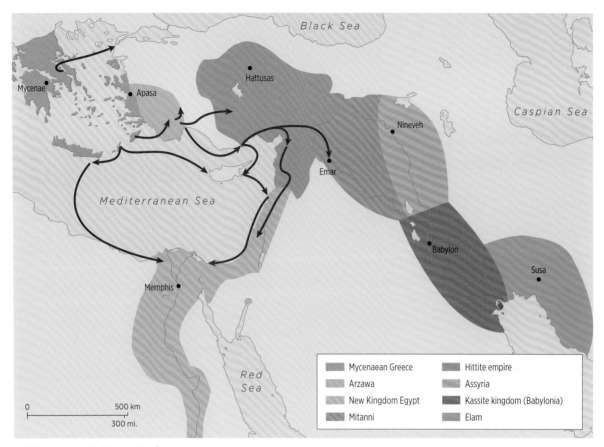

3.24 Regions attacked by Sea People

Even as these disasters were hitting the Mycenaean power centers, there are signs that the ruling elites were in the grip of anxiety. At both Mycenae and Tiryns, the fortifications were extended. At Mycenae this allowed access to a cistern now within the walls, while at Tiryns the citadel was doubled in size, allowing for a large increase in the storage capacity of the citadel (**3.23**). These and other construction programs hint at the ruling class preparing to withstand sieges, while Linear B tablets from the period sometimes mention "the watchers by the sea," suggesting that there was a fear of attack from the sea.

The fear of being attacked by sea was not unwarranted, because there is evidence that attacks by marauding groups were a widespread phenomenon in the eastern Mediterranean around 1200. The evidence for this comes from Egypt and concerns groups known collectively as the Sea People. The map **3.24** shows the regions impacted by the operations of the Sea People. Most historians believe that they were a loose coalition of tribes and ethnic groups who exploited tensions

between the great eastern Mediterranean states of Egypt, Mitanni, and the Hittites to plunder coastal territories around the Levant. They are mentioned in a variety of Egyptian sources, from the Amarna Letters (a royal Egyptian archive dating from the Late Bronze Age) onward, but it is an inscription on the walls of Ramses III's temple at Medinet Habu that has supplied tantalizing evidence regarding their identity. The inscription reads:

The foreign countries made a plot in their islands. Dislodged and scattered by battle were the lands all at one time, and no land could stand before their arms, beginning with Khatti, Kode, Carchemish, Arzawa and Alasiya...They came, the flame prepared before them, onwards to Egypt. Their confederacy consisted of Peleset, Tjekker, Sheklesh, Danu, and Weshesh, united lands, and they laid their hands upon the lands to the entire circuit of the earth...

(Gardiner, *Egypt of the Pharaohs* 284–85)

Even allowing for the exaggeration likely in a text celebrating Ramses' victory, this account is still evidence of the widespread destruction caused by these marauders in the years prior to their defeat in 1184 BC. Their victims, according to the Egyptian text, include the Hittites ("Khatti"), the inhabitants of northern Syria ("Kode"), "Carchemish" (by the headwaters of the Euphrates), "Arzawa" in western Anatolia, and "Alasiya" (an ancient name for Cyprus).

The names of the tribes within the confederacy have caused the greatest interest. Most scholars have interpreted the "Peleset" (or more accurately "PLST," since the Egyptian writing system did not use vowels), as the Philistines named in the Hebrew Bible. This group ended up occupying five major sites in the land of Canaan, and the pottery they brought with them appears to be originally indistinguishable from Mycenaean pottery in the period 1200–1100 BC. The Tjekker may have come from the region of Troy (associated in later sources with a tribe called the Teucri), or from east Crete, their name being related to the site of Zakro. The Shekelesh may be identified with the later Siculi from Sicily. If these names do point to the place of origin for these groups, then one plausible hypothesis would be that these groups originated west of the Levant. In that case, the presence of the Danu and Weshesh in the list allows us to include Mycenaean Greeks among the Sea People, since these names correspond to the ethnic labels used in Homer's poems, where he refers to the Greeks as the Danaans and the Achaians. On this hypothesis the Sea People included Mycenaeans in their ranks, a theory that gains support from the crested helmets and Mycenaean kilts worn by some of the Sea People in the Medinet Habu reliefs (**3.25**). Even so, speculation about the ethnic origins of the Sea People is hardly conclusive, and other theories would connect them with Anatolia and Syria. All that

3.25 Peleset prisoners, relief in the temple of Medinet Habu, *c.* 1180 BC. Stone

can be said with certainty is that their presence attests to the massive upheavals that took place across the Levant shortly after 1200.

Although the Mycenaean hypothesis is not universally accepted, the notion that the Sea People included Mycenaean bands is worth considering seriously. But if it is correct, it raises a question: if there were Mycenaean Greeks among the Sea People, then can we attribute the collapse of the Mycenaean centers to the Sea People? This would seem to make them both victims and aggressors.

One way to resolve this problem would be to postulate the following scenario: around 1200 BC, the central regions of the Mycenaean world in the Peloponnese and central Greece entered a period of protracted crisis: the eastern Mediterranean saw an increase in population movements by various groups eager for land and attracted by the prospect of plundering the wealth of the great empires and their palaces. Coming from the central Mediterranean—in addition to Sicily, the ancient inhabitants of Sardinia also appear in the records—these piratical bands passed by the Peloponnese, causing the kings of Pylos and Mycenae to post lookouts by the sea and where possible to add to their fortifications. At the same time, the Mycenaean economic and social system was threatened by natural disasters, environmental change, and a fraying of the social fabric. Each calamity had a flow-on effect. When Gla burned, for example, there were not enough men to save the citadel, nor to repair the canals and drainage works that had reclaimed the fertile agricultural plain below. Unsupervised, the engineering needed to maintain the system failed, and in short order what had once been a fertile agricultural plain became a lake, as it had been before the land was reclaimed by Mycenaean engineers. As a result of this period of crisis, bands of Mycenaean Greeks joined the groups who had taken to the sea. Quitting Greece they sailed east, to Cyprus and further east and south, to the coastal regions of Syria and Canaan and even the Nile Delta. This process was not a single invasion, but episodic and variable. Some of the people involved were mercenaries, in the pay of pharaohs and kings; others were pirates, roving the coastal regions and sacking such places as Ugarit. Others seized land and settled at such places as Tel Dor in Israel.

Whichever way we explain the end of the Mycenaean world—be it from natural disaster, external invasion, or internal systems collapse— by 1100 BC, the world of the complex Bronze Age civilizations was over. Nevertheless, myth gave the Bronze Age an afterlife. In the subsequent period, the Iron Age, the stories of the heroes who went to Troy would serve to mark the loss of that Golden Age. Palaces would fall, squatters would occupy the megaron of the wanax, and the massive stone galleries where staples were stored would become sheep pens used by poor shepherds, but story telling, and especially epic poetry, kept the memory of this glorious past alive. As we shall see, the Bronze Age remained a presence in the centuries that followed, thanks to Homer.

New Discoveries around Mycenaean Pylos

Over the last decade, new and continuing excavations in the vicinity of Nestor's Palace at Pylos have added to our understanding of this powerful and important region of Mycenaean Greece. The new excavations have been conducted at Iklaina, only 5 kilometers (3 mi.) south of Nestor's Palace (but separated from it by a series of ridges and valleys), where a joint team of Greek and American excavators working since 2006 has brought to light evidence of an unexpectedly complex site. Buildings and features uncovered include a monumental Cyclopean Terrace Complex and a second monumental building, as well as indications of a very advanced urban infrastructure (featuring paved roads, paved piazzas, extensive drainage system with stone-built drains, and water distribution system with terra-cotta pipes; see **3.26**). These features, combined with the existence of administrative records (written in Linear B) and the clear separation of activity areas into separate zones (administrative, industrial, and residential) suggest that Iklaina was a primary center before its annexation by the rulers of nearby Pylos. (The date of the annexation is still being investigated, but was

3.26 Aerial overview of the recent excavations by the joint Greek and American team at Iklaina

probably between 1400 and 1300 BC; detailed study of the pottery should resolve the question.)

Although the date of Iklaina's annexation to the domain of the Palace of Nestor is uncertain, it does mark an important stage in the expansion of Pylos, which (as Linear B tablets have shown) culminated in the control of the entire southwestern Peloponnese. So great was the extent of the kingdom of Pylos—reaching as far north as the Neda River—that administrative records refer to Hither and Further Provinces. Further excavation and analysis of the site may help to clarify the relationship between Iklaina and Nestor's Palace, but this computer reconstruction of the Cyclopean Terrace Complex certainly serves as a powerful reminder of the

3.27 Reconstruction of the Cyclopean Terrace Complex at Iklaina

3.28 Comb from the Tomb of the Griffin Warrior, Pylos, c. 1500 BC. Ivory, L: 15 cm (5⅞ in.)

authority of the Mycenaean kings of this region (**3.27**).

Another testament to the power of the ruler of Pylos came to light even more recently. Although the Palace of Nestor was first systematically excavated by Carl Blegen in AD 1939, much of the surrounding area remained untouched olive groves. Excavators from the University of Cincinnati, however, made an extraordinary discovery in AD 2015: excavating 150 meters (492 ft) from the Palace of Nestor, they uncovered a Mycenaean stone-built grave on the very first day of excavations, close to a Mycenaean tholos tomb that had already been unearthed by Blegen. Further research revealed that this was in fact the unplundered burial of a chieftain dating from around 1450 BC, the earliest days of Mycenaean civilization. The tomb contained the burial of a single male aged between 30 and 35, whose remains were located at the bottom of the shaft and surrounded by fifteen hundred objects, including jewelry, sealstones, and vessels made of gold, silver, and bronze, as well as other precious items, such as ivory combs (**3.28**), bronze mirrors, a bronze sword, and gold rings clearly manufactured on Crete. The discovery quickly became known as the Tomb of the Griffin Warrior, and its significance is still being evaluated.

The presence of so many items manufactured on Crete in such an early Mycenaean tomb came as a surprise to the excavators. The Minoan items may have been booty from raids but the excavators believe that they were purposefully acquired; certainly they demonstrate a taste for Minoan goods among the Mycenaean elite. Particularly striking are the gold rings worn by the Mycenaean chieftain. One shows five female figures (who may be priestesses) clearly wearing

3.29 Ring depicting women before a shrine, Tomb of the Griffin Warrior, *c.* 1450 BC. Gold, L: *c.* 3 cm (1⅛ in.)

3.30 Ring depicting bull-leaping, Tomb of the Griffin Warrior, *c.* 1450 BC. Gold, L: *c.* 3 cm (1⅛ in.)

Minoan-style dresses and standing before a shrine (**3.29**), while another depicts a charging bull and a bull-leaper behind him, a favorite scene on Minoan gemstones (**3.30**). The finds at Pylos show that the Mycenaeans freely employed Minoan objects and Minoan style to enhance their prestige and reinforce their status.

Chapter 4
The Iron Age

Beginning with an evaluation of the current debate over collapse or continuity from the Bronze to the Iron Age in such areas as demography, religion, economic activity, and writing, this chapter deals with the major developments of the so-called eighth-century-BC renaissance: the increase in population, the growth of the early *polis*, renascent trade networks, and the beginning of the great colonial movement of the Greeks around the Mediterranean. This chapter also argues that Homer's poetry reflects both the hold of the heroic ideal in the worldview of the early Greeks and their deep disquiet regarding its suitability for civil society. We also investigate the ethnographic imagination of epic, arguing that early colonial encounters are reflected in the demonizing of non-Greeks in epic as monsters and giants, and conclude with a description of one of the most recognizable Greek institutions: the Olympics.

Center and Periphery in the Early Iron Age

Homer's poems, as we have seen, recast the Bronze Age into a world of heroes. Some details in Homer's descriptions of battle (such as shields, helmets, and chariots) may recall Mycenaean warfare, but the world depicted in epic poetry does not resemble the actual palaces of Minoan Crete, or even the fortresses of the Mycenaean mainland. Instead, the material world of the Homeric poems is much closer to the humble reality of the Early Iron Age. Take, for example, the houses in which Homer's kings reside. Far from being magnificent palaces (such as had existed at Knossos), or even the massive citadels of Mycenae and Tiryns, Homer's royal households are more akin to long halls. Nestor's Palace, the royal residence of Menelaus, and the house of King Alcinous on Scheria are often described by the poet as glorious, but on closer examination of the text, the buildings appear relatively simple in design. In the poetic rendering of Sparta, for example, it seems that only Menelaus and Helen sleep inside the royal building, and that their guests have beds made up for them in the forecourt.

The Early Iron Age building discovered at Lefkandi, on the island of Euboia, offers an archaeological example of the type of hall described by Homer. Lefkandi is the largest tenth-century-BC building yet excavated in Greece, modest compared to the palaces of the Late Bronze Age, but illustrative of how a society ruled by chieftains, or "big men,"

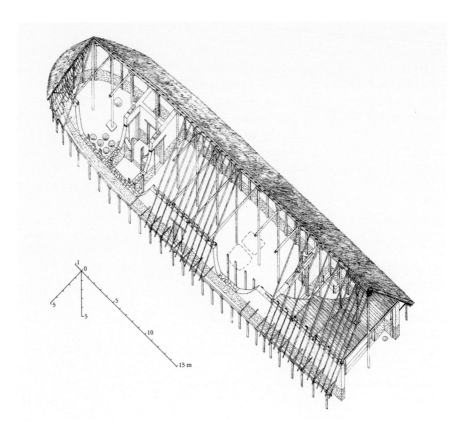

4.1 Reconstruction of the apsidal building at Lefkandi, tenth century BC

was emerging in the Proto-Geometric period. (The Iron Age [1000–700 BC] is often referred to as the Geometric period because of the preference for geometric designs in the pottery; the Proto-Geometric period is the earliest subdivision of this sequence.)

The building at Lefkandi measures 50 by 13.8 meters (164 × 45 ft), and is known as an **apsidal** building due to one end being semi-circular (**4.1**). Around the mud-brick walls, which sit on stone foundations, runs a set of postholes that suggests a porch surrounded the building. The internal layout of the building consists of a forecourt, an antechamber, and a large main room, with smaller storage rooms at the western end of the building.

Despite the diminished scale of the building at Lefkandi when compared to Mycenaean palaces, there is also evidence of continuity with the earlier period. A startling feature of the Lefkandi structure is that, shortly after it was constructed, the entire building was reused for a heroic burial. In the center of the main chamber two pits were cut. The cremated remains of a warrior chieftain (along with his armor) were laid into one, and, next to him, the corpse of a woman with her jewels. Four horses were buried in

the second pit, presumably slaughtered to honor their dead master, a practice that is reminiscent of horse burials from the Mycenaean world, such as at Dendra (see Chapter 3, p. 82), and also closer to Euboia in a Mycenaean tholos tomb at Marathon. At the same time, the tenth-century-BC horse burial from Lefkandi recalls the sacrifice made by Achilles for Patroklos in Book 23 of the *Iliad*, when Achilles throws four horses, two dogs, and twelve Trojans on the funeral pyre. (One wonders if the Lefkandi female burial was also an act of human sacrifice.)

Once the chieftain, his companion, and his horses were placed in the burial pits, the entire building was buried beneath a mound. The area immediately outside the mound was used as a large cemetery, consisting of eighty-three tombs and thirty-four pyres. The excavators have plausibly suggested, based on the wealthy goods found in the shafts and the later cist graves, that the cemetery was used by a kin-group claiming descent from the hero buried inside the apsidal building.

The Lefkandi building has forced scholars to re-examine the entire question of the Greek world after the collapse of Mycenaean civilization. Until a generation ago, the end of the Mycenaean citadels seemed so abrupt and so catastrophic that it was conventional to speak of the subsequent period as the Greek Dark Ages. At such sites as Nichoria in the Peloponnese, surveys seemed to suggest that people had returned to a simpler way of life based on herding. Instead of complex, hierarchically organized states, the Greek world appeared to have been inhabited by poor farmers and herders. We now know, thanks to such sites as Lefkandi, that the story is much more complicated. The palaces *did* cease to function, but the worst effects of the collapse of the Mycenaean world were felt in a central corridor running south from Thebes and Gla down to the Argive plain. Even in this central corridor, there is now evidence of continued occupation in the lower citadel (**Unterberg**) at Tiryns.

On the periphery of the Mycenaean world, by contrast, decline was much less dramatic, and recovery swifter. At Kalapodi, in central Greece, recent excavations by the German Archaeological Institute have shown that cult activity continued in the same location from the Middle Helladic (*c.* 2000–1650 BC) down to Roman times without interruption, good evidence for continuity, at least of cult (**4.2**). Similarly,

the American excavations at the sanctuary of Zeus on Mount Lykaion in the Peloponnese reveal continuity of cult from the Bronze Age to the Roman period. It is on the Euboian Gulf, however, that archaeological work in the last ten years has shown a surprising continuity of settlement from the Late Bronze Age into the Early Iron Age. At Mitrou, Kynos Livanaton, Atalante, and at the Alonaki cemetery near Elateia, the evidence from settlements and burials shows that there were very few disruptions from the end of the Mycenaean period down to the Iron Age. Goods were being traded from here to Thessaly and out to the Cycladic Islands, even as far away as Crete. As the Belgian and Greek excavators of Mitrou put it: "Thus it appears that the inhabitants of this region of east-central Greece, unlike those living in areas further south from Boeotia to the Peloponnese, did not experience a major cultural break at the transition from the final Bronze Age to the Early Iron Age, and suffered much less of a decline in material culture than did their southern neighbors."

We are now in a better position to understand the relationship between the world of Homeric epic and the world of the Iron Age. The people of Iron

4.2 West facade of Archaic temple, Kalapodi. A succession of structures have been identified on the same spot, including an apsidal structure visible under the Archaic temple.

4.3 Tholos tomb, Menidhi, Attica, *c.* 1400 BC

Age Greece actively created memories of their past, taking stories of a dimly remembered Trojan War but recasting those stories with local heroes whose values were very much those of the princes and kings—or ***basileis,*** to use the Greek term—of the Early Iron Age. Nor were the poems the only vehicles for making this connection to the past. Burial markers from the Bronze Age, such as tholos tombs and chamber tombs, were found all around Greece, powerful evocations of an early age of glory. In the ninth and eighth centuries BC, it became increasingly common for local people to reuse earlier tombs or to venerate the original occupants with dedications from much later periods. At the Menidhi tomb in Attica, for example, the first burial dates to around 1400 BC and is remarkably rich; grave goods included jewelry, weapons, and even an ivory lyre (**4.3**). But equally significant is the fact that the burial chamber was left intact in antiquity; in the dromos leading down to the tholos, excavators found pottery in a continuous sequence from the Iron Age to the Classical period.

Tombs were the physical evidence of a heroic past. By making dedications at these sites, the men and women of later periods transformed them into locations of memory and thereby asserted their own connections to that heroic past. These Iron Age peoples often claimed that the original occupants of the tombs were their own ancestors, many of whom were figures known from epic. As late as the sixth century BC, a certain Euthykrines was making dedications to Menelaus, the legendary king of Sparta, at the Menelaion outside Sparta. Even lesser-known figures allowed communities to establish Homeric credentials: the obscure town of Panopeus in central Greece claimed that a figure named Schedios, named in the Catalogue of Ships (Homer's list in the *Iliad* of the Greek contingents that fought at Troy), had been an early king of their town, though two other small communities also claimed his tomb lay in their territory. The Homeric poems may not offer a very accurate picture of the Bronze Age, but they certainly helped shape the Iron Age by rendering into narrative form a connection between the present and the heroic past.

Society and Identity in the Iron Age

Other features of Lefkandi shed light on the Early Iron Age. Even though the ***heroon*** (as the main building was called because of the heroic burial it contained) was no Mycenaean palace, the descendants of the hero of Lefkandi, far from being backward squatters living in the shadows of a ruined Mycenaean palace, participated in a trade network that reached to Phoenicia and Egypt. Scarabs, seals, gold jewelry, faience vessels, and iron weapons found in the tombs reveal that, within one hundred years of the end of the palaces, the eastern periphery of the Mycenaean world had recovered. The wealth of the tombs brings to mind Menelaus's description in the *Odyssey* of how he restored the wealth of his own household after the Trojan War:

I carried riches back
inside my ships, after we'd endured so much
while we were wandering. We made it home—
it took us more than seven years. We roamed
to Cyprus, Egypt, and Phoenicia.
We even reached the Ethiopians,
Sidonians, and Erembi—Lydia, too,
where lambs are born with horns and ewes give birth
three times in one full year.

(Homer, *Odyssey* 4.81–89, trans. Johnston)

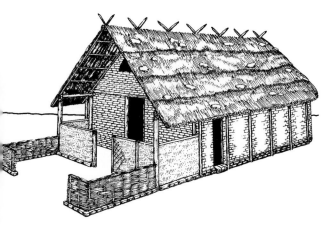

4.4 Early Iron Age apsidal house, Nichoria

But only in Homer's imagination would the palaces be restored. In some places, such as Mycenae and Troy itself, later communities would build over the Bronze Age remains, but a new form of social organization would develop to replace the highly centralized authority of the Bronze Age power centers. The predominant social institution of the Iron Age would be the *oikos* or household, a patrilinear family unit centered on the big man, the head of the clan. These men would style themselves princes, or basileis, and it was the highly competitive society they dominated that provided the actual social milieu in which the Homeric poems were shaped before they were written down. It is for this reason that despite the Bronze Age grace notes that occur in the epic poems, the world they most accurately evoke is the Early Iron Age. The hieratic states and redistributive economies of the thirteenth century left little impact on Homer's descriptions of a world of heroes. Menelaus may be a figure from epic and seem to come from Mycenaean Sparta, but his "palace," his wealth, and his adventures belong to the Proto-Geometric world of Lefkandi.

We rely to some degree on the Homeric poems to reconstruct the social world of this big man society, centered on families, clans, and chieftains, each ruling his own oikos and vying for power. Material culture is the other source of our information and can be used to fill out our view of Iron Age Greece. At Eretria, across the Euboian Gulf from Attica, Swiss and Greek excavations have brought to light evidence of the Early Iron Age community. Although there are no city walls before 700 BC, clear indications of communal organization are to be found in the elaborate system of canals constructed to drain the central coastal plain where the city developed. Similar types of pre-urban agglomerations have been found at Nichoria in Messenia (**4.4**) and Emborio on Chios.

In these Early Iron Age communities, simple apsidal houses, often consisting of a single room, are typical; the same type found at Nichoria and Eretria is also to be seen at old Smyrna on the other side of the Aegean. At other Early Iron Age settlements, such as Athens, Argos, and Corinth, multiple hamlets appear to have existed in close proximity to each other and point to competing clans, each dominated by a chieftain. Most scholars would see this society as comprised of a warrior elite controlling larger numbers of dependent farmers. Not by coincidence, weapons and figurines depicting warriors are commonplace throughout the period. The small standing figure brandishing a spear and armed with a shield was dedicated by such a warrior from Karditsa in Thessaly, and is typical of the offerings made at sanctuaries by members of the elite (**4.5**).

4.5 Warrior figurine, Karditsa, Thessaly, *c.* 700 BC. Bronze, H: 28 cm (11 in.)

4.6 Centaur figurine, Lefkandi, *c.* 920 BC. Clay, H: 36 cm (1 ft 2 in.)

Just as the warrior from Karditsa reflects his society's preoccupations, other notable objects can shed light on the Early Iron Age world. One such evocative object is a terra-cotta figurine depicting a centaur that comes from the Toumba cemetery at Lefkandi (**4.6**). Some scholars have suggested that it represents Cheiron, the centaur who raised Achilles, but there is insufficient evidence to identify it so confidently.

It does remind us, however, that this was a richly imaginative age, and that the monsters and hybrid creatures of Greek myth were vividly present in the Iron Age. Later myths would locate the centaurs in Thessaly, and it is worth noting that this region was on the edge of the Mycenaean world. Even when Mycenaean Greece was long gone, the association with advanced civilization and the south remained, while the north never lost its reputation for wildness.

A second notable object that reflects the spirit of the age is the Mykonos **pithos** depicting the Trojan Horse (**4.7**). Though this pithos dates from somewhat later, in the early seventh century BC, it reminds us that the stories told in the epic cycle—the abduction of Helen, the war at Troy, the sack of the city, and the unhappy returns of most of the survivors—remained alive in the imagination of the Greeks for hundreds of years, long after any historical events connected to the stories were finished.

The subject of the Mykonos pithos, the Trojan Horse, points to the importance of Homer's stories, a key feature of the Greek Iron Age. Homer's significance is also reflected by a cup found at the Greek colony of Pithekoussai, in the Bay of Naples, which is explicitly labelled as Nestor's cup (**4.8**). The inscription on it reads:

Nestor's cup I am, good to drink from.
Whoever drinks this cup empty, straightaway
the desire of beautiful-crowned Aphrodite will seize.

It is important to note that the cup on which this inscription was found is a humble terra-cotta vessel, not a glorious golden chalice, and that the cup that was once the marker of a great hero is now reimagined as a drinking cup with a message about mixing wine and sex. No longer strictly heroic, Nestor's cup makes a joke that plays on the contrast between the high world of epic and the more mundane world of the eighth century. Yet without a memory of the heroic past, the joke would make no sense.

4.7 Detail of pithos depicting the Trojan Horse, Mykonos, *c.* 670 BC. Ceramic, H (of detail): 35 cm (1 ft 1¾ in.)

4.8 Nestor's cup, Rhodian kotyle, Pithekoussai, *c.* 725 BC. Ceramic

It would be a mistake, however, to see the entire Iron Age through the lens of Homeric poetry. It was an age that saw its own significant cultural developments. In Athens, for example, the middle of the eighth century BC saw the production of dozens of monumental terra-cotta funerary markers by the Dipylon Master and his workshop. These vessels, sometimes over 1.5 meters (5 ft) tall, stood over the graves of the elite and regularly show two funerary scenes: the *ekphora* and the *prothesis*. The ekphora was the procession that escorted the body from the home to the burial. In this example, chariots and armed warriors attend the dead man, whose funerary cortège thus becomes a celebration of his status as a leader and a warrior (**4.9**). The prothesis traditionally depicted the dead person laid out on a funeral bier as attendants from the household stand, kneel, and engage in lamentations around the corpse. The funeral was an opportunity for the great families to assert their status by advertising the prowess of their clan leaders.

On balance, the shift from the Bronze Age to the Iron Age can be summed up as follows. There were widespread upheavals in the eastern Mediterranean around 1150 BC, one consequence of which may have been to jeopardize the regular international trade, and to disrupt the supply of such specialty items as copper and tin that were used for bronze-making. The most vulnerable places were the palatial centres, where centralized control broke down. Although elite control and international trade reappeared in the tenth century BC, some changes were irrevocable. Linear B, the script (but not the language of Greek), was lost forever, and Greece would remain without any writing system for three hundred years. Oral

poetry, however, provided a link to the palatial past and blended it with the new society taking shape in the Iron Age, from around 1000 to 700 BC. This Iron Age society was a society ruled by elites who participated in international trade, even to the point, some have suggested, of monopolizing the new, preferred metal for weapons: iron. As Greece recovered from the collapse of Bronze Age civilization, a new social order would develop, based on the domination of a warrior elite who modeled themselves on Homer's heroes. In the eighth century, as we shall see shortly, Greek culture would face fresh challenges but the Homeric code would remain the basis for how they behaved. Homer gave the Greeks of the Iron Age their identity.

4.9 Dipylon vase depicting ekphora, Athens, *c.* 765–730 BC. Ceramic, H: 1.08 m (3 ft 6 in.)

Heroes and Villains

The Early Iron Age, as we have seen, witnessed the evolution of a new Greek world in which memories of a heroic past helped shape the present. Basileis asserted their status as leaders and warriors, while their families and households frequently fashioned an elite identity by practicing tomb and ancestor cult at sites going back to the Bronze Age. In this aristocratic setting, the Homeric poems expressed a complex attitude to the past, a past both vividly present in the stories of these heroes, yet at the same time gone, in some respects, forever.

The stories called the **Nostoi** told of the returns of the heroes from Troy, but more often than not are tales of shipwreck, betrayal, and death. Throughout the *Odyssey*, for example, Odysseus's homecoming is contrasted with that of Agamemnon, who returned to Mycenae only to be slaughtered by Klytaimnestra and her lover, Aigisthos. So, even if the epic poems express an elite ideology suitable for princes claiming descent from Homeric heroes, they also reflect a society in which there are signs of dissatisfaction with the rule of kings. The institutions of justice and governance often appear rudimentary, as though there was a genuine concern in the eighth-century-BC world in which the poems were written down with how authority operates. In the *Iliad*, for example, Agamemnon's power often appears arbitrary and willful.

This concern over power and authority is reflected in the work of the great eighth-century poet, Hesiod. In his poems, the *Theogony* and *Works and Days*, he explores the question of justice. In one famous episode he shakes his fist at the judges deliberating over his legal case—a land and inheritance dispute with his brother Perses—calling them "bribe-eating basileis," and he shouts at them to deliver straight justice (*Works and Days* 38–41). Whether or not the episode is autobiographical hardly matters; the vignette expresses the rage of those who saw through the Homeric pretensions of the elite and perceived the rulers for what they were: greedy and ready to be bribed. In a parable elsewhere in his poem, Hesiod tells the tale of a hawk and a dove. The inevitability of the hawk's victory over the weaker bird does nothing to make his power more legitimate, and the theme of the story seems to be a familiar lesson that many Greeks recognized, one later articulated by the historian Thucydides: the strong do what they will; the weak suffer what they must.

Even when kings do act boldly, the poems often leave the audience painfully aware of how inadequate the Homeric code is as the basis of a social contract. After his death Achilles will end up in Hades, telling Odysseus that he would rather be the poorest dirt-breaking laborer than king of the entire Underworld; so much for heroism. Odysseus will reclaim his oikos not by recourse to law or the decisions of judges but by slaughtering the Suitors (who have been courting his wife Penelope in his absence) and then hanging the disloyal serving girls. He leaves their bodies dangling, their necks broken, like so many pigeons waiting to be cooked. The end of the *Odyssey* is particularly noteworthy in this respect. When Odysseus realizes that he has been impoverished by the Suitors, he blithely remarks that he will go raiding and replenish his stocks by plundering others, and so the cycle of violence will continue.

Homeric heroism, so magnificent on the battlefield, threatened to condemn Iron Age society to a state of perpetual war. In terms of the psychology of battle, the poems are astonishingly perceptive, recognizing the power of the warrior to lose himself in battle-rage, but the poems also pose a difficult question: can the code that nurtures warriors be reconciled with peace? Odysseus's revenge is completely heroic, as he throws off his rags, strings his mighty bow, and cuts down a dozen men with arrows through the throat and belly, but what happens when, the next day, the families of the dead men want to exact *their* vengeance in turn?

Polis and Ethnos in the Eighth Century

It was in the eighth century BC that many of these tensions were played out and shaped the future direction of Greek society, particularly as the polis, or **city-state**, emerged as the distinctive form of Greek social and political life. The developments of that century contributed to the formation of Archaic Greece and gave the culture a distinctive shape and feel, because the changes experienced by the Greeks would be profound. It was the age of the first Olympics; it was the age of the first overseas trade emporia, or trading posts, and along with them the beginning of a diaspora of Greeks throughout the Mediterranean and beyond; and it was the age in which the Greeks acquired their alphabet.

The first of these phenomena was the rise of the polis, or city-state. It was in the eighth century that city-states began to take shape. There is evidence for this at old Smyrna on the coast of modern-day Turkey (**4.10**), and at Corinth, where clusters of houses and specialized production areas (notably for pottery) suggest the growth of complex social organization. Corinth, where American excavations have shed light on the development of the community in the Iron Age, is particularly well documented. A cluster of villages near the site of the later *agora*, or marketplace, witnessed a rapid increase in population, as demonstrated by the rising number of wells and burials. At the same time, Corinthian pottery began to be traded far afield, again suggesting the vigorous commercial life of the community. This proto-city, as we may think of it, still relied on the exploitation of agricultural resources in the plain running down to the Corinthian Gulf, but the city profited from its strategic position at the intersection of the Corinthian and Saronic Gulfs, with harbors at Kenchreai and Lechaion, to export material both east and west. At the same time, colonies were dispatched from Corinth led by Archias (to Syracuse, in Sicily) and Chersicrates (to Corcyra, modern-day Corfu); the fact that both colonial leaders were from the same aristocratic family, the Bacchiads, reflects the oligarchic control of the emerging city by this great clan.

While the polis became the best-known form of community in ancient Greece, synonymous with such leading states as Athens, Sparta, and Corinth, the polis was not the sole form of social organization to emerge in the Iron Age. In many parts of Greece, aggregates of communities asserted a common ethnic identity. These were known as ***ethne*** (sing. ***ethnos***). Many of these formed political federations, known as ***koina*** (sing. ***koinon***). The Aitolians of western Greece, for example, included such towns as Kalydon and Pleuron, whose inhabitants all claimed to be descended from a common ancestor, Aitolos. Some of these leagues were primarily religious networks, such as the Kalaurian League in the Saronic Gulf, and some became important regional organizations. The Delphic Amphiktyony, for example, was a federal body with members drawn from all over Greece. Appropriately, the Amphiktyony administered the panhellenic sanctuary of Delphi and guaranteed the sanctuary's neutrality. Often the koinon served as a regional union. The Greeks of Ionia, for example, met at the Panionion in the sanctuary of Poseidon at Cape Mycale, near Miletos, to deliberate on issues of interest to all the member states. In some instances there was a very clear tension between one or two leading towns and the rest of the region: at times Boiotia was subordinate to the Thebans, while at other times the Boiotian koinon was a genuinely regional organization with representatives and magistrates drawn from all of Boiotia, not just Thebes.

Monumental Temples and the Rule of Law

Closely connected with the increase in urban agglomerations was the development of monumental temples. One site that illustrates the growth of communities and sanctuaries is Prinias in Crete. Here, occupation goes back to the Late Minoan period and is still attested in the ninth century BC. The eighth-century site is characterized by regularly laid-out city blocks divided by streets. It is also notable for two buildings from the seventh century (usually identified as temples) that exhibit strong Egyptian and Near Eastern influence, and which mark the return of monumental stone buildings to the repertoire of Greek architecture (**4.11**; see p. 106). The seated figures on the lintel of Temple A, for example, wear the headdress known as the ***polos***, typical of Near Eastern goddesses, while the relief depicting a procession of panthers reflects the influence of North Syrian temple reliefs. A necropolis near the settlement fell out of use around 550 BC, the same time as the settlement and temples were abandoned. The site thus serves as a kind of time-capsule, showing the

4.10 Reconstruction of Old Smyrna in the eighth century BC

4.11 Prinias, lintel sculpture, Temple A, seventh century BC

typical features of an Early Archaic community and hinting at the external influences affecting Greek culture at a time still often referred to by scholars as the Orientalizing period.

While early temples clearly attest the importance of religious and cult activity in the eighth and seventh centuries, we should also note a distinctive feature of many Early Archaic sanctuaries: the transformation of rulers' huts into temples of the gods. At Eretria, for example, perhaps as early as 800 BC, the site of what would later be identified as the sanctuary of Apollo originally included a number of apsidal huts, possibly houses of the elite or of the ruler. During the Iron Age a much larger building, referred to as a *hekatompedon* ("Hundred Footer") was built in the same location. This was subsequently rebuilt around 670–650 BC in the Early Archaic period, and again in the Late Archaic period *c.* 530–520 BC.

A similar process appears to have occurred at Thermon, in Aitolia (**4.12**). There, Megaron A was in use in the Mycenaean period; in the Early Iron Age another building, Megaron B, was erected close by. Both were probably the rulers' residences. In the Early Archaic period, a temple was constructed directly over Megaron B. Both Megaron B and the Archaic temple were made of wood and mud brick on a stone foundation. The Archaic temple, however,

was not only the last building in the sequence, but also was much larger and more elaborate, impressive both because of its greater dimensions and the colorful painted terra-cotta metopes that adorned the entablature (**4.13**).

In the sixth century BC, the Greeks would go a step further and begin building their temples from limestone and even marble. As a result, there has been a tendency for scholars to look for an evolutionary development in temple architecture—smaller buildings give way to larger, and simple construction materials (such as wood, mud brick, and terra-cotta) give way to limestone and marble—but there is another way of seeing this progression, and that is in terms of function. The change from rulers' palaces to gods' houses suggests not only a change in architecture, but also a fundamental shift in the nature of social hierarchy.

Another profound change concerned the rule of law. As gods emerged as the central focus of the Archaic communities, and as kings declined in importance, communities took the first steps toward establishing regular, codified laws. Governance began to shift from the decisions of basileis, who had modeled themselves on Homer's heroes, and now found expression in the sovereign decisions of the community. At Dreros, for example, where

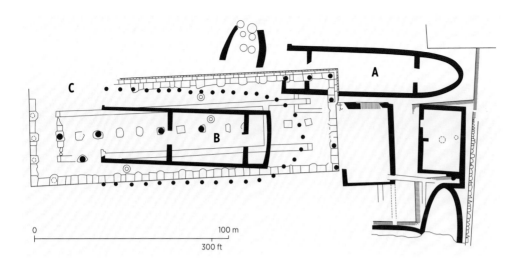

4.12 Ground plan of Thermon. Note Megaron B, a Bronze Age ruler's residence, over which is built the Archaic temple of Apollo (C).

another very early temple to Apollo was built in the mid-eighth century BC, the community passed and wrote down perhaps the earliest inscribed law in Greek:

May God be kind (?). This has been decided by the city: When a man has been Kosmos, for ten years that same man shall not be Kosmos. If he should become Kosmos, whatever judgments he gives, he himself shall owe double, and he shall be useless as long as he lives, and what he does as Kosmos shall be as nothing. The swearers (to this shall be) the Kosmos, the Demioi, and the Twenty of the city.

(BCH.61 [1937] 333/8, trans. Fornara)

Here in the mountains of Crete, an autonomous community established the rules by which legal authority within the community would be exercised. Executive power would rotate and boards of magistrates would guarantee that no single person wielded power exclusively. This represents a fundamental shift away from either the Bronze Age or the Early Iron Age worlds of kings or the ideal Homeric world of heroes.

We know of a handful of early Greek lawgivers—the names of Lykourgos, Zaleukos, Charondas, and Solon are the best known—but their stories tend to follow very formulaic patterns involving an initial crisis, the appointment of the lawgiver, testing of the new laws, and the departure of the lawgiver. The repetition of this pattern suggests that establishing laws with the help of the gods or a semi-divine lawgiver was a stage of social development through

which emerging communities had to pass if they were to survive, although it is important to keep in mind that this process was not uniform and did not occur in every Archaic community. But even allowing for the semi-mythical quality of stories concerning lawgivers, two features of the emergence of law deserve to be emphasized. The first is that early Greek law was primarily procedural, not substantive. This means that most early Greek laws dictated how an

4.13 Detail of metope, Temple of Apollo, Thermon. Terra-cotta

arbitration was to be conducted or what penalty was to be exacted if the law was not enforced, but rarely did early Greek laws lay out any underlying principles. Law was practical, not theoretical. The second notable feature was that the writing down of laws radically altered the operation of law. Those who knew laws through memory and could expound on them (men variously called *exegetai* or *hieromnemones*) gradually lost importance between 800 and 500 BC. The act of writing the laws placed the emphasis on the law, not the legal expert. It is for this reason that some scholars regard the inscription of laws as a step toward democracy.

A Greek Diaspora

What drove these changes was a complex nexus of factors that may have included population growth and greater social complexity, but one agent of change must be the vigorous commercial activity throughout the Greek world that occurred between 750 and 500 BC. During this time the Greeks were trading north into the Black Sea region as far as Ukraine, and also as far south as Egypt. In the east they sought trade contacts on Rhodes and Cyprus, as well as the coast of Syria, and in the west they traveled to Sicily, southern Italy, and along the northern coast of the Mediterranean in the areas of modern-day France and Spain. In most of these places they eventually established permanent colonies, colonies that needed land for growing the crops that fed the colony's population (**4.14**). This complex process has sometimes been viewed by scholars in simple binary terms: did the Greeks send out colonies to relieve population pressure at home and to acquire new land, or did they go in search of trade opportunities, a process which then resulted in the foundation of colonies? The reality is that different conditions contributed, and that to search for a single solution is to oversimplify the phenomenon. It may be more helpful to think of a Greek diaspora, and to ask what general conditions led so many Greeks to leave their ancestral homes.

Names sometimes give a clue. On the coast of modern-day northern Spain, Greek settlers established a colony called Emporio (Ampurias), the very name of which means "trading place." Precious metals, such as silver and tin, were brought from the inland region to this coastal community where

they were traded for Greek products. Other colonies positioned in strategic locations in relation to trade were located at Pithekoussai, on the island of Ischia in the Bay of Naples (which gave the Greeks access to the trade goods reaching central Italy from further north); at Al Mina on the Syrian coast; and at Naucratis in the Nile Delta (a trading place ceded to a group of Greek traders by the pharaoh, thus allowing the Egyptians to maintain a level of control over the flow of goods in and out of Egypt).

Each of these places represents the mercantile drive that took Greeks to the farthest reaches of the Mediterranean world in search of precious metals, luxury items, and eventually even such goods as hides, grain, and slaves. At the same time, however, recent excavations at Pithekoussai have revealed the presence of land divisions from a very early stage, highlighting that land was also a resource sought by the Greeks. Colonists might be officially dispatched from Corinth or Miletos, meaning that the officer in charge was appointed by the mother-city, but the reality was always that these colonies were founded by waves of settlers from different parts of Greece, and that trade and land went hand in hand. The name of the biggest Greek colony in Ukraine is Olbia, meaning "wealth," but that wealth came in various forms: timber, metal, hides, and grain. The last of these had to be farmed: agricultural colonies cannot be classified separately from trading colonies.

At most of the Greek colonies there is clear evidence that land was surveyed and plots of equal size were apportioned to the first settlers. This is particularly evident in Sicily, which, along with southern Italy, was known as Magna Graecia, or "Big Greece," precisely because most of the cities in the region—such as Syracuse, Agrigentum (Akragas), Selinuntum (Selinous), Sybaris and Croton—were actually founded as Greek colonies. Surveys conducted over the last generation have consistently shown that most of these colonies were planned communities from the outset. The two principles governing this planning were the desire to honor the gods (enacted by setting aside areas for their worship), and the need to provide land for the new settlers. But the allocation of land for new settlers raised issues of status and fairness; how could one settler be content with one or two acres while others received dozens or hundreds of acres? The act of founding a colony made it a matter of urgency

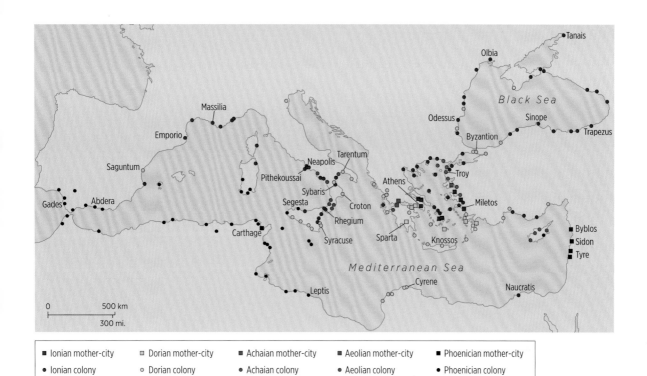

4.14 The Greek diaspora: Colonies around the Mediterranean and Black Seas

Legend:
- ■ Ionian mother-city
- □ Dorian mother-city
- ■ Achaian mother-city
- ■ Aeolian mother-city
- ■ Phoenician mother-city
- ● Ionian colony
- ○ Dorian colony
- ● Achaian colony
- ● Aeolian colony
- ● Phoenician colony

Greek

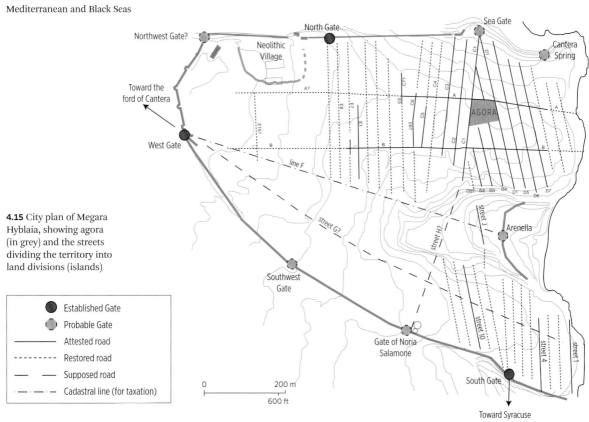

4.15 City plan of Megara Hyblaia, showing agora (in grey) and the streets dividing the territory into land divisions (islands)

Legend:
- ● Established Gate
- ● Probable Gate
- —— Attested road
- ----- Restored road
- – – Supposed road
- –·–·– Cadastral line (for taxation)

that each settler received an equal portion. In the charter of the colony of Corcyra Melaina, for example, the land was divided into one thousand lots (*kleroi*) of three *plethra* each, and this was the standard plot each settler was assigned. The size of these lots deserves comment: as a square measurement, three plethra corresponds to approximately only three-quarters of an acre. This is much smaller than even the most modest subsistence farms in the modern Mediterranean, and even allowing for differences based on both farming equipment and irrigation, the small allocations in the Greek colonial setting can only have been enough for each household to have a market garden and a few domesticated animals. Clearly, these settlers planned on supplementing their livelihoods by maintaining herds and land holdings out of town as well as by trading.

The early colony of Megara Hyblaia, on the east coast of Sicily, demonstrates how these planning principles were put into practice. Here, a survey conducted by French archaeologists has revealed that a central area was set aside at the time of the colony's foundation to house the temples of the gods and an agora, or public space. Running from this central space were roads that divided the community's land into a regular grid of approximately equal plots. The orientation of buildings in these "islands" divided by streets reveals that colonial communities, unlike the "organic" communities of the mainland, were planned from the outset. The same pattern of equal land allocations can still be seen today on the Ortygia peninsula of Syracuse, where the modern-day streets sit atop a checkerboard of ancient roads (**4.15**; see p. 109).

It is interesting to correlate the phenomenon of equal land allocations in Magna Graecia with the poetry of Hesiod, who presents Zeus allocating lots to the gods. In Hesiod's interpretation, Zeus is a generous father-figure, dispensing gifts to those beneath him, just as in the colonies the *oikist*, or founder, distributed lots of land to those who had followed him. These oikists were frequently revered afterwards and given divine honors in the colonies they founded. In the middle of the marketplace of Cyrene, in Libya, the Greek colonists erected an altar where they offered sacrifices to the memory of Battos, the Theran who led the first colonial expedition to North Africa and whose story is discussed below.

Communities, Foundations, and Identities

The diaspora, therefore, had profound effects on the development of Greek culture. Colonies confirmed the authority of a founder and lawgiver who resembled Zeus, but at the same time, colonies helped articulate a notion of equality. This entered Greek thought not as an abstraction but as a reality, experienced by those who made the dramatic decision to quit Greece, face the unknown, and start again in a new place. In recent years a further dimension has been added to the scholarly debate over colonization. Some scholars have suggested that the idea of formal colonial expeditions—organized by the mother-city (or *metropolis*, as the Greeks would call it), authorized by a foundational charter from Delphi, and led by a colonial founder—is a retrojection from later times as these communities sought to gain legitimacy by telling stories of their foundations. Without doubt, such stories became more elaborate and fantastic as generations passed, to the point where myth and history became inextricably entwined.

In one famous case, Cyrene, we have a detailed account of the colony's foundations as told hundreds of years later. Herodotos gives two versions, in fact, of the founding, one told by the people of Thera and the other the account of the Cyreneans themselves. In the Theran account, Herodotos offers an elaborate story going back generations to Sparta and culminating with a visit to Delphi by Grinos, the king of Thera, who is told to found a colony in Libya. The Cyrenean account begins very differently, and involves tales of shipwrecked sailors, but also ends up at Delphi. The eventual founder of the colony, Battos, whose name means "Stammerer," goes to the oracle to inquire about his speech impediment, and receives the following reply:

Battos, thou camest to ask of thy voice; but Phoibos Apollo
Bids thee establish a city in Libya, abounding in fleeces...
(Herodotos, *Histories* 4.155, trans. Rawlinson)

Ignoring the god's order, Battos returns to Thera, but the Therans are punished by Apollo until they once again consult the oracle. The priestess of Apollo, the Pythia, orders them a second time to establish a colony in Libya. The Therans, still unwilling to obey the god completely, now try to satisfy the oracle by founding a colony on an island off the coast of Libya, but still the god is implacable:

In this place they continued two years, but at the end of that time, as their ill luck still followed them, they left the island to the care of one of their number, and went in a body to Delphi, where they made complaint at the shrine to the effect that, notwithstanding they had colonised Libya, they prospered as poorly as before. Hereon the Pythoness made them the following answer:

Knowest thou better than I, fair Libya
abounding in fleeces?
Better the stranger than he who has trod it?
Oh! clever Therans!

(*Histories* 4.157, trans. Rawlinson)

Eventually Battos and the Therans realize they have no option but to colonize the mainland. After further hardships, they are led across the desert by the indigenous people to the site where they will finally establish the colony of Cyrene.

In Herodotos's full account, we hear of Spartan, Theran, and Cyrenean versions, while Samos and Itanos on Crete both play a role too, making it clear that many Greek communities either had their own versions of the founding of Cyrene or sought inclusion in the Cyrenean story. The foundation stories that we simply call "mythology" often rely on elaborate geographies and journeys undertaken by heroes; inclusion in these tales, as with inclusion in the family trees of heroes, allowed Archaic communities to develop affinities based on goodwill, fictional ties of blood, and shared episodes in the tales of heroes' journeys and accomplishments. This is the language of Archaic diplomacy: it might result in shared cults, trade connections, or even military alliances. These stories, in fact, served as a narrative web linking communities all over the Aegean world.

Aside from Herodotos's version, which clearly draws on oral accounts he collected during his travels, we also possess an official version of the Cyrene foundation story. In the fourth or third century BC, the Cyreneans erected an inscription on which they claimed to have reinscribed the text of the oath of the original settlers of three hundred years before. The inscription reads:

Oath of the Settlers: The assembly decided: since Apollo spontaneously ordered Battos and the Therans to colonize Cyrene, the Therans resolve to send out Battos to Libya as a leader and a king, with Therans to sail as his companions. They are to sail on fair and equal terms, according to households, one son to be chosen [from each family?] of those who are in the prime of life; and of the rest of Therans those free men [who wish?] may sail. If the colonists establish the settlement, any of their fellow citizens who sails later to Libya is to share in citizenship and honor, and to be allotted unoccupied land. But if they do not establish the settlement, and the Therans cannot help them, and they are driven by necessity for five years, let them return from the land without fear to Thera, to their own property and to be citizens. But whoever is unwilling to sail, when he has been sent by the city, shall be liable to the death penalty, and his property shall be made public; and whoever receives or protects another, whether father or son, or brother his brother, shall suffer the same penalty as he who is unwilling to sail.

On these conditions they swore a solemn agreement, those who stayed at home and those who sailed to found the colony; and they placed a curse on those who broke the agreement and did not abide by it, either those living in Libya or those staying at home. They molded wax images, and burned them with curses, all of them coming together, men and women, boys and girls: "May he who does not abide by these oaths, but breaks them, melt away and dissolve like the images, himself and his offspring and his property. But for those who abide by these oaths, for those who sail to Libya and those who remain in Thera, may there be abundance and prosperity for themselves and for their offspring."

(*ML*.5, trans. Murray)

Scholars still debate whether or not the Oath of the Founders is an accurate record of an actual eighth- or seventh-century original, although if it is authentic, it would be longer and more detailed than any other written public document of that period. What is more likely is that it represents how the colony of Cyrene in later years wished to see its origins: a colony established by the will of heaven and made real by free men acting on fair and equal terms, swearing in the most solemn fashion to abide by the original agreement. It is in the colonies that the Greeks were therefore forced to ask and answer the basic questions of social life: what constitutes a community? How shall it be governed? What authority will give its laws force? How shall we live?

Delphi and Greek Identity

A further point to emerge in the story of Cyrene's founding is the central role of Delphi. It has been said that colonization did more for Delphi than Delphi ever did for colonization, but the truth is that both the oracle and the diaspora communities profited from Apollo's participation. Droughts, famines, and other natural disasters figure prominently in the accounts of colonial foundations, often undertaken on the advice of the oracle to expiate some wrongdoing in the home community. Whether to discover what they had done wrong or how to placate the gods, the communities of Archaic Greece were compelled to seek the active guidance of the gods through oracles, and so not coincidentally Apollo is both the god of oracular communication and the god who, as the *archagetes*, led many colonial expeditions

to their new home. Accordingly, Cyrene's foundation story draws on Apollo's authority to give the colony legitimacy. Apollo also guarantees that these new communities will abide by laws agreed upon by all, as we see in a decree from a Lokrian colony of the sixth century BC. The decree specifies how land is to be divided between old and new settlers, possibly at Naupaktos, and states unequivocally, "This law shall be sacred to Pythian Apollo, and the gods who dwell with him. May the person who transgresses this law be destroyed utterly" (*ML*.13). At Cyrene, Apollo continued to play a central role as the divine authority whose power lent force to law. In the fourth century BC the people of Cyrene inscribed a series of

4.16 (left) Proto-Attic amphora, Eleusis, *c.* 670–650 BC. Ceramic, H: 42 cm (16½ in.)

4.17 (opposite) Metope of Perseus killing Medusa, Temple C, Selinunte, *c.* 530–510 BC. Limestone, H: 1.47 m (4 ft 10 in.)

between 800 and 500 BC when most Greek colonies were founded, the presence of indigenous people is recorded in a scant sixteen instances. As Greeks spread across the Mediterranean and established more than a hundred diaspora communities, they successfully demonized the indigenous people they encountered, casting them as monsters and inferiors, a colonial mentality that is another part of our Greek legacy. It is for this reason that the Archaic period saw the Greek imagination teem with visions of centaurs, Cyclopes, and sphinxes, vivid projections of the alien, non-Greek world in which these new communities found themselves. A mid-seventh-century terra-cotta amphora from Eleusis (**4.16**) reflects the worldview emerging in the Greek consciousness: on the neck of the amphora the Greek hero Odysseus is blinding the Cyclops, while on the body of the vessel gorgons chase another hero, Perseus. The message of the vessel is clear: beyond Greece there are monsters.

Similarly, on the temples built in these new settings, visitors could see scenes of Greek gods and heroes doing battle with the monsters that represented the strange new world in which the Greeks found themselves. On Temple C at Selinunte, for example, Perseus is shown gruesomely decapitating Medusa (**4.17**). Giants, amazons, and hybrid monsters served as a dramatic reminder of the dangers and threats constantly lurking on the borders of the known world. The message here was complex, since it reinforced the sense of difference between Greeks and others, permitting a state of permanent hostility to exist, even at a time when the Greeks were engaged in such widespread commerce and travel around the Mediterranean that contacts were inevitable.

laws that dealt with marriage, pollution, inheritance, and other legal matters that a community must adjudicate. The code begins,

Apollo declared by oracle: dwell in the land
of Libya forever, performing purifications,
abstinences, and paying tithes.

(*SEG*.IX.72, trans McInerney)

It is important to recognize that the involvement of Apollo in every aspect of the diaspora community's foundation and continued existence shaped the community's Greek identity: the Greeks overseas remained enclaves of Greekness. A mentality of "us" and "them" took root as the Greeks encountered other people around the Mediterranean. In this respect it is worth noting that Herodotos's account of the foundation of Cyrene is one of the few instances in which the indigenous people dispossessed by the Greeks are acknowledged. In the three hundred years

"Orientalizing" and Eastern Influence

The effect of this diaspora on Greek culture was profound and can be seen in the art of the eighth and seventh centuries BC. The prevalence on Corinthian vases of designs derived from the Near East, for example, illustrates the so-called Orientalizing phase of Greek culture, when ideas and motifs from the eastern Mediterranean entered Greek culture. The exotic animals (such as lions and panthers) and strange hybrids (such as sphinxes) on a Corinthian *dinos*, or wine-mixing vessel (**4.18**), gives a glimpse of the Greek response to this new, wider world of cultural interaction.

While these imported ideas and motifs were used to help define a sense of Greekness, they were, however, also materially changing the nature of Greek culture itself. As the Greeks were exposed to other people and cultures around the Mediterranean, especially to the East, they absorbed the stories, poems, and technologies to which they were exposed. The poetry of Hesiod is especially important in this respect. We have already seen that, unlike Homer, Hesiod's poems do not reflect a particularly heroic outlook. Zeus may dispense justice from on high but his human counterparts, the basileis of Hesiod's own day, were more likely to put wealth or power ahead of justice. But Hesiod's poetry, for all its apparent autobiographical and contemporary appearance, is shot through with motifs drawn from the older cultures of the ancient Near East with whom the Greeks were in contact. For example, when Hesiod describes the successive generations of the gods, he is borrowing a well-established Eastern motif. In the Greek version, Kronos castrates his father, Ouranos, and seizes power. In the next generation Zeus is saved from his father, Kronos, who devours his own children, and then returns fully grown to do battle

with his father and the Titans before consigning Kronos to the Underworld. Similarly in the Hurrian and Hittite cosmological poems entitled *Kingship in Heaven* and the *Song of Ullikumi*, the god Kumarbi bites off his father Anu's genitals, swallows them, and takes his place on the throne. In another borrowing from Eastern religions, Hesiod describes Zeus doing battle with the monster known as Typhoeus, an example of the cosmological battles Zeus must win in order to establish his rule and the order of the universe (**4.19**). In similar fashion, the Babylonian god, Marduk, whose heroic deeds were recited each year in a hymn that combined theogony and epic, established his victory by shooting an arrow into the womb of Tiamat, the mother of monsters (**4.20**).

In their Near Eastern settings, from Babylon to Hattusa, these stories function at many levels. They certainly put into narrative form the rivalries of various kingdoms and city-states of the ancient Near East, and they also draw on deeply rooted psychological fears such as castration, birth, and rivalry between the generations. In addition,

4.18 Corinthian dinos (mixing bowl), 630–615 BC. Ceramic, H: 18.4 cm (7¼ in.)

4.19 Black-figure hydria depicting Zeus defeating Typhoeus (Typhon), *c.* 540–530 BC. Ceramic

4.20 Marduk defeating Tiamat. Drawn from a bas-relief from the Palace of Ashur-nasir-pal (King of Assyria, r. 885-860 BC) at Nimrûd.

many of these accounts may have had astrological significance and may have been stories that rendered the movements of constellations into narrative form. Hesiod never speaks directly of the Eastern antecedents to his stories and so it is hard to know exactly in what way this borrowing took place or how deliberate it was, but it is surely closely connected to the other great instance of cultural borrowing from the East that occurred in the eighth century: the adoption of an Eastern alphabet and the reinvention of writing in the Greek world.

The Reinvention of Writing

After the end of the Bronze Age and the collapse of palatial culture, Linear B fell out of use and writing remained absent from the Greek world for more than three hundred years (with the exception of Cyprus, where a modified syllabic writing system based on Linear A continued in use). The widespread loss of the writing habit is understandable when we consider that Linear B had been used to record transactions in the palatial economies of the Late Bronze Age. With the end of that economic system, record-keeping also stopped, and so the practice of writing simply withered (although of course the language of Greek was still spoken). Sometime around 720 BC, however, the Greeks adapted a script borrowed from northwest Semitic. This was a writing system used in the region of Al Mina on the Syrian coast where Greeks traded, and it would also have been familiar wherever Phoenicians from the same region traded. It makes sense, therefore, that some of the earliest written Greek turns up where Greeks and Phoenicians traded, notably at Syria and Sicily. Perhaps some clever Greeks realized that labels helped keep track of trade goods, and adapted a Phoenician system encountered when merchants exchanged goods. Another idea, ultimately unprovable but worth considering nonetheless, is that the bilingual children of marriages between Greeks and Phoenicians adapted the writing system of one language to represent the sounds of the other.

Whatever the exact point of origin (and there may be more than one), and the circumstances under which Greek speakers adopted an alphabet to write down their language, the practice caught on very quickly. This has been underscored by recent excavations at Methone in northern Greece, where dozens of vessels inscribed with Greek names and even lines of verse have been found between AD 2003 and 2007 in an rectangular structure labeled by Greek archaeologists the "Ypogeio" ("Underground"). The structure is unusual, and it is unclear why a construction 11.5 meters (38 ft) deep was first built.

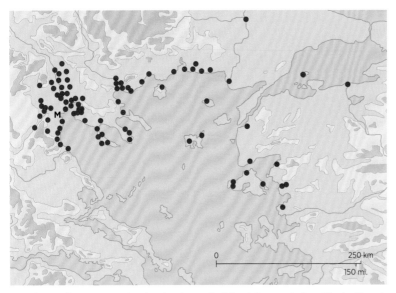

4.21 The Northern Aegean, showing the places of origin of clay vessels found in the Ypogeio, Methone (marked "M" on the map)

northern Aegean, even into the central Balkans. This can be seen in **4.21**, which shows the points of origin for the vessels found at the bottom of the Ypogeio.

The inscribed vessels include Chian transport amphorae; locally made and Euboean *skyphoi* (drinking cups); a Dipylon *oinochoe* (wine jug) from Athens; and other drinking cups with the names of their owners. The cup of Philion (**4.22**) may be of Lesbian manufacture, and in common with the other inscribed vessels, dates to the late eighth century. Another vessel, a Euboean skyphos, contains an inscription that recalls the cup of Nestor from Pithekoussai discussed above. The inscription on the cup of Hagesandros reads, "I am the cup of Hagesandros...[whoever steals] me will lose his eyes!"

Neither a well nor a building, it may have been intended originally as a storage facility or silo. Shortly after 700 BC, however, it seems to have been turned into a rubbish dump: timber, mud brick, stone, copper and iron slag, crucibles for gold-working, and thousands of pieces of broken pottery were thrown to the bottom. The pottery included both transport vessels and drinking cups associated with *symposia*, or drinking parties.

The provenance of this material, from various parts of the Greek and Phoenician world, attests to the importance of Methone. Lying on the Thermaic Gulf, Methone was settled around 730 BC by settlers from Euboia, and profited from its strategic location. From here, the settlers had access to an interior rich in timber, the metal reserves of Macedonia, and a point of entry to trade networks that crossed the entire

These are among the earliest pieces of written Greek, dating from shortly after the middle of the eighth century. In some cases Greek letters appear to have been used to label transport vessels; in other instances they are used to identify the owner of drinking paraphernalia. If these uses reflect the adoption of the alphabet, we should conclude that the Greeks adapted a Semitic alphabet in two settings: for use in trade and in the symposium. The alphabet would soon be used for writing down the Homeric poems, but since discussions of poetry were a regular feature of symposia, this is not an unexpected development. Methone, in common with other colonies of the eighth and seventh centuries, reveals a Greek culture tightly bound into Aegean and Mediterranean worlds characterized by intense degrees of interaction. Cultural exchange between Greeks and non-Greeks made this a period of ferment with profound consequences for Greek culture.

The Olympics

If the diaspora experience stimulated change in Greek culture because of the intense contact with non-Greeks, the same period witnessed an equal and opposite impulse toward asserting Greek

4.22 Cup of Philion, late eighth century BC. Ceramic

identity. This found expression in one of the most distinctive cultural institutions of the Greek world: the Olympics. Founded in 776 BC (by Herakles, according to Olympic tradition), for more than a thousand years the Olympics would remain one of the key institutions for determining inclusion within the community of Greeks, and by extension, the exclusion of those who were not Greek. The officials who ran the games were known as the **Hellanodikai**, or "Judges of the Greeks," and when in the late sixth century BC King Alexander I of Macedon (an ancestor of Alexander the Great) sought to participate, he was barred from the games until he produced a family tree showing that the Macedonian royal house, the Argeadai, was in fact Argive by descent.

The games were held every four years in an open area at the foot of Kronos Hill adjacent to the sanctuary of Zeus at Olympia (**4.23**). The sanctuary lay in a region of western Greece far from the direct control of any major power, which may have contributed to the success of the Olympics. Although in the early years of the games the Spartans dominated the athletic events, they appear not to have sought to take control of the sanctuary. Instead, along with Delphi, Nemea, and Isthmia, Olympia emerged as a panhellenic sanctuary, one of the few places where Greeks from anywhere could mingle

and mix freely. The panhellenic sanctuaries were therefore critical in the emergence and the shaping of Greek identity. It was, ironically, by competing as Athenian versus Corinthian, or Megarian versus Arkadian, or Spartan versus Argive, that each competitor reinforced a common Greek identity, since only Greeks competed with Greeks. This was especially important since the emergence of a shared culture, confirmed by shared language and shared myths, served in place of political unification. There were no united states of Greece, but all Greeks could be proud of their Olympic champions. Throughout most of their history, the sanctuary and the games were under the administrative control of the people of Elis, the state that lies to the north of the site, although for a brief period in the fourth century the nearer state of Pisa seized control of the sanctuary. Olympia and the other panhellenic sanctuaries were the principal places for the expression of a shared Greek identity, and if Delphi profited most from its role in authorizing colonial enterprises, Olympia's status depended on the competitive culture that characterized Archaic Greece.

When we think of the Olympics it is hard not to use the modern games as a point of reference, and there are some very real similarities, but the most distinctive feature of the ancient Olympics was that

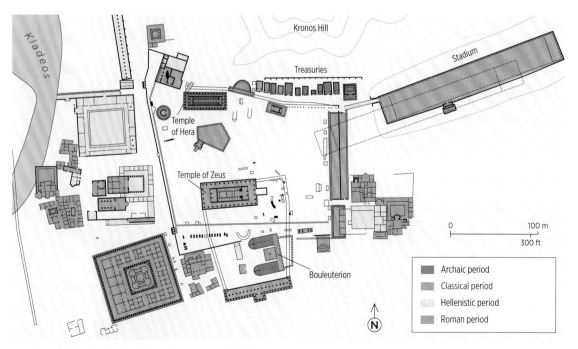

4.23 Plan of Olympia, showing the various stages of development

they were a sacred event: the games were conducted for the glory of Zeus, as much as for the athletes. The month leading up the games was a time of truce throughout Greece, the *ekecheiria*, during which wars were suspended so that athletes and spectators could travel freely to Olympia. Once at Olympia, spectators found a stadium (extended in at least three phases) located right next to the sanctuary. To reach the warm-up area, or Palaistra, in the stadium, athletes had to cross the center of the sanctuary, walking past the temple of Zeus with its monumental statue of the god, the work of Phidias, and long considered a wonder of the ancient world. They also passed the temple of Hera, a beautiful Doric temple dating to the late sixth century BC, and the Altis, the monumental ash altar in the center of the sanctuary. The Altis was the spot where athletes and visitors, both as private individuals and representing the states of Greece, made sacrifices to Zeus. The thousands of statues that filled every inch of space around the Altis and the temples commemorated these sacrifices. Passing these temples, altars, and dedications, the athletes then proceeded to the tunnel leading into the stadium. Here the athletes walked below a terrace dominated by treasure houses in which many more dedications were stored. In front of the treasuries stood a line of sixteen statues of Zeus, known as the *Zanes*, paid for by the fines imposed on athletes for cheating. The games may have been sacred, but the athletes were all too human.

The format of the games changed over the more than one thousand years of the games' existence, but a core of activities remained fundamental and sheds important light on the values of the Greeks. Among the oldest events were the simple running races. These included the *stadion*, which, as the name suggests, was a straight sprint the length of the stadium (192 meters [630 ft]). Next came the *diaulos*, a sprint to the end and back, almost equivalent to the modern-day 400-meter race. Another running event was the *dolichos* (**4.24**), a long-distance race of 20 stadia, the equivalent of just under 4,000 meters (13,100 ft). The marathon, however, was not an event in the ancient Olympics; it was introduced in the modern Olympics to commemorate the legendary run from Marathon to Athens by Pheidippides when bringing the news of the defeat of the Persians.

In addition to the running races, the ancient Olympics also included a series of combat

4.24 Dolichos runners, Panathenaic vase, *c.* 330 BC. Ceramic, H: 84 cm (2 ft 9 in.)

4.25 Red-figure kylix, 500–490 BC, depicting athletes training with halteres (stone weights), used to extend the distance of their jumps. Ceramic, D: 22.5 cm (8⅞ in.)

competitions. Boxing resembled the modern version, with the boxers using leather thongs wrapped around their hands to serve as gloves. Holding, however, was not allowed since this was considered part of the second combat sport: wrestling. This event consisted of two forms: upright and ground wrestling. In the former, a wrestler won if he threw his opponent three times. In ground wrestling, victory came by forcing the opponent to submit, which he signaled by raising his finger, the equivalent of tapping out. The third combat sport was the popular event known as *pankration*. This was a combination of boxing and wrestling, and closely resembled modern-day mixed martial arts. All wrestling holds and boxing styles were permitted; the only moves disallowed were gouging, biting, and grabbing the genitals. The Olympics also included the pentathlon, comprised of discus, javelin, standing jump (with the aid of weights, called *halteres*; see **4.25**), running, and wrestling.

It is not uncommon for the ancient Olympics to be held up as a paradigm of amateurism in contrast to the crass commercialism of the modern games, but this is to misrepresent the purpose of the ancient Olympics and to ignore their long history. In the first centuries of the games there was a very strong association between aristocratic status and Olympic victory. This is reflected in the epinician poems, or victory odes, composed by the Theban poet Pindar in the fifth century BC, which frequently honor not only the Olympic victor but also other victorious members of his family. Many of these victors were dynastic rulers on the mainland, on Aigina, and in the Sicilian cities, and their Olympic victories were bound up with the claims to legitimacy of these families. For this reason Pindar's poems cast the victors as Homeric heroes. In his seventh Olympian ode, for example, Pindar tells of Diagoras of Rhodes, victor in the boxing competition at Olympia in 464 BC, and lists his many other victories at Nemea, Isthmia, and various lesser competitions. He begs the gods to grant Diagoras favor "from citizens and from strangers," pairing the victor's triumph with his family's and his community's prosperity. "When the Eratidai rejoice," says Pindar, in a reference to Diagoras's clan, "the city also is feasting." Similarly, in his second Olympian ode, Pindar praises Theron of Akragas for winning the chariot race (another sign of the aristocratic origins of the games—a chariot and four horses were not the possessions of a farmer), as follows:

Pisa belongs to Zeus, the Olympian feast
Herakles founded, the loot of war,
But of Theron let your voices ring,
For his victorious four-in-hand.
He is courteous and kind to guests,
The bulwark of Akragas;
In him his famous fathers
Flower, and the city stands.
> (Pindar, *Olympian Odes* 2.3–10, trans. Bowra)

The connections are significant. As Olympia is to Zeus and Herakles, Akragas is to Theron. His chariot race victory is a confirmation of his *arête* (a term meaning virtue or excellence), and he displays *xenia*, or the spirit of hospitality, in the manner of a good host in Homer. Finally, his excellence affirms and extends his family's nobility, and thanks to these qualities the city flourishes. Even in the fourth century BC, long after Homer's day, Aischines could write,

Victory is rare...and because of the competition and the honor, and the undying fame that victory brings, men are willing to risk their bodies, and at the cost of the most severe discipline to carry the struggle to the end.

(Aischines, *Against Ktesiphon* 180, trans. Adams)

One cannot help noticing that the reward for victory, according to Aischines, is "undying fame," the very same *kleos aphthiton* sought by Homer's heroes. The funeral games for Patroklos in Book 23 of the *Iliad* include most of the Olympic events, another sign that the Olympics served as a kind of Homeric performance. It would not be wrong to say that the Olympics began as an attempt by aristocratic families to find a way of demonstrating their prowess and to assert the claim that they embodied the very virtues they found in Homer's poems.

Over the course of time, however, the strictly aristocratic character of the games waned, and professional athletes emerged. No longer awarded simply an oak-leaf crown, Olympic victors in the Classical period might be rewarded by their home cities in cash (in some cases the equivalent of more than a year's pay for a laborer) or by such rewards as free meals for life. Once again, however, it is not enough to note the similarity with modern-day professional athletes. Successful Olympians in the Classical world exerted enormous influence in their communities, serving as political and military leaders, and even being worshiped as demi-gods after their death. In the case of Milo of Croton (located in Magna Graecia), his great strength and enormous appetite threatened to make him no more than a caricature—he was supposed to have carried a bull the length of the stadium before stunning it with a blow and consuming the entire beast—but he was also remembered for having led the Crotonians in battle and to victory over their neighbors from Sybaris. Another famous champion, Theagenes of Thasos, won both the boxing and pankration at Olympia in 480 BC, and was said by his fellow citizens to have been the son of Herakles. Pausanias,

in a lengthy description of the statues of victorious athletes, tells of what became of Theagenes after his death. The story, set on Thasos, is worth closer examination:

After Theagenes died, one of those who were his enemies while he lived came every night to the statue of Theagenes and flogged the bronze as though he were ill-treating Theagenes himself. The statue put an end to the outrage by falling on him, but the sons of the dead man prosecuted the statue for murder. So the Thasians dropped the statue to the bottom of the sea, adopting the principle of Drako, who, when he framed for the Athenians laws to deal with homicide, inflicted banishment even on lifeless things, should one of them fall and kill a man. But in course of time, when the earth yielded no crop to the Thasians, they sent envoys to Delphi, and the god instructed them to receive back the exiles. At this command they received them back, but their restoration brought no remedy of the famine. So for the second time they went to the Pythian priestess, saying that although they had obeyed her instructions the wrath of the gods still abode with them. Whereupon the Pythian priestess replied to them:

But you have forgotten your great Theagenes. And when they could not think of a contrivance to recover the statue of Theagenes, fishermen, they say, after putting out to sea for a catch of fish caught the statue in their net and brought it back to land. The Thasians set it up in its original position, and are wont to sacrifice to him as to a god.

(Pausanias, *Description of Greece* 6.1.16, trans. Jones)

Athletes, even long after Homer's day, continued to enjoy the status of superheroes, honored for their accomplishments and revered for their powers. Such figures as Herakles, men of semi-divine parentage, were not unique to the Greek world. Gilgamesh, Samson, and Melqart all shared qualities in common with Herakles, but in the Olympics the Greeks devised an institution that, despite its Heraklean associations, has no parallels in the ancient Near East. The origins of the games and the growth of such panhellenic sanctuaries as Olympia and Delphi reflect the exciting climate of vigorous change that characterized Greek culture in the Archaic period.

Spotlight
Epic, Vases, and the Symposium

In the sixth and fifth centuries BC, vase painters (notably in Athens) were drawn to scenes from the epic poems of Homer. They painted these scenes on a wide variety of vessels that were used as part of the aristocratic practice of the symposium, the drinking party at which members of the elite would sing, recite episodes from the epic poems they had learned by heart, and engage in philosophical discussion. Many of these symposia were also boisterous affairs that involved entertainment by slaves, flute players, and female companions,

but some were also more restrained. The prevalence of epic episodes in the decoration of these drinking and symposiastic vessels confirms the place of Homer in the culture of the Greeks. These poems were recited, discussed, and argued over because they were the foundational texts of Archaic and Classical Greek culture.

In **4.26** we see the Companions of Odysseus in the process of being transformed into animals by Circe, who can be seen in the center of the composition pouring her magic potion into a drinking cup. (The vessel on

which the scene has been painted is also a drinking cup, known as a kylix, so that the scene can be read as an amusing warning about the effects of drinking; not all references to epic need be serious.)

The famous amphora depicting Achilles and Ajax playing dice is one of the best-known painted vessels from the sixth century BC, and shows a scene that was widely copied (**4.27**; see p. 122). The popularity of the scene stems from the fact that it reveals the human side of the heroes. Even though both were known for their strength

4.26 Black-figure kylix depicting Circe and the Companions of Odysseus, 560–550 BC. Ceramic, H: 13.2 cm (5¼ in.)

4.27 Exekias, detail of black-figure amphora depicting Achilles and Ajax playing dice, 530–520 BC. Ceramic, H: 61 cm (2 ft)

and valor, here they are taking a well-earned break from battle. Although both are still wearing their armor, they can be seen throwing the dice. The words "three" and "four" are painted close to their mouths: when we read the words we hear the heroes as they call out their throws. Once again, the counterpoint between the heroes' epic status and the human, even mundane, quality of the scene adds to its power. The scene also has more than a hint of pathos and irony: any Greek viewer would also have known that Ajax would claim Achilles' armor as a

mark of his own status after Achilles' death. He failed to convince the rest of the Greeks, and after going on a murderous rampage, would commit suicide. This was another epic scene used by the vase-painter Exekias and widely copied: in the famous example shown here, Ajax can be seen planting his sword in the ground before falling on it in despair (**4.28**).

One final scene illustrates the popularity of epic scenes in later periods. This red-figure kylix from Chiusi shows Odysseus, dressed in the manner of a traveler, placing

4.28 Exekias, black-figure amphora depicting the suicide of Ajax, c. 530 BC. Ceramic, H: 24 cm (9½ in.)

his foot in a basin while Eurykleia, his old wet-nurse, lifts her face in recognition (**4.29**); she has seen the scar on his leg that reveals his identity. A commonplace ritual of hospitality—washing the dust from the traveler's feet—has become one of the most powerful recognition scenes in Greek art.

Some scholars read such scenes as the suicide of Ajax as politically charged, as if the hero's death can be interpreted as a symbol of the passing of the old aristocratic order. Whether or not this is correct, it is clear that the symposium for which these vessels were intended as cups, mixing bowls, and storage vessels was a place for members of the elite to perform their roles as aristocrats: drinking, conversing, and referring back to the world of Homer as the model for their own. Little wonder, then, that Homeric scenes were the preferred artistic episodes for the decoration of vessels: potters understood their patrons' tastes.

4.29 Penelope Painter, detail of red-figure kylix depicting Odysseus and Eurykleia, from Chiusi, *c.* 440 BC. Ceramic, H: 20.5 cm (8 in.)

Chapter 5

The Archaic Age: Sparta

The Archaic period, from *c.* 700 to 480 BC, was one of increasing prosperity yet also rising tension, both between classes and between aristocratically dominated clans. In this and the next chapter we will explore the dramatic changes Greek communities underwent during the two centuries before the Persian Wars, and examine the response to these challenges in two very different states: Sparta and Athens. The response to the social upheaval in Sparta, in particular, was remarkable and distinctive. We shall see that, contrary to our expectations and running counter to the usual image of Sparta as a military state, there is evidence, in the form of an early constitutional document entitled the Great Rhetra, for a distinctly proto-democratic impulse in early Sparta. This was suppressed, we shall see, and power was increasingly concentrated in the hands of the leading magistrates known as *ephors* and the top echelons of Spartan society. Another key factor that shaped the unusual trajectory of Sparta's development was the role of the Messenian Wars, which left Sparta virtually the only Greek territory in which one ethnic group became the permanent overlords of another, neighboring people. Through a process of what some have called internal colonization, the Spartans enslaved the Messenian population, reducing them to the status of **helots**, or serfs. The effect of this was to transform Sparta into a state with a dominant ideology of permanent readiness for warfare, in which all Spartan institutions were devoted to training warriors. Before looking at Sparta's distinctive response to the challenges of the Archaic Age, however, it is necessary to describe the wider Greek world at this time.

Archaic Crisis: Wealth, Strife, and Tyranny

The Archaic period was a time of profound change throughout the Greek world. As in the eighth century BC, the Greeks experienced long and sustained contact with other cultures, both as a result of goods and ideas coming into Greece and also as a result of Greek communities establishing themselves around the Mediterranean.

In the Archaic period, this penetration of Greek culture would become profound, influencing every aspect of life from Greeks' conception of the gods to their style of dress. The Greeks experienced an increase in trade in the search for resources, land, and luxury items, as is revealed in the archaeological record by such items as Euboian pottery, which has been found in various parts of the Mediterranean. The age was remarkable for the formation of a Greek diaspora extending from the Black Sea to the far end of the Mediterranean. Greeks were found at Naucratis in the Nile Delta, at Cyrene on the coast of Libya, at Al Mina on the coast of Syria, in the Bay of Naples and around the coast of Sicily, up the coast of the Adriatic, and around the edges of the Black Sea. The alphabet adopted from northern Phoenicia exemplified the new developments occurring in Greece because of the contact between cultures. The Greeks expanded the scope of their world, telling stories, for example, of Herakles traveling to the very end of the Mediterranean, as far as Gibraltar. For the Greeks, the wider Mediterranean world was a place of communities connected by trade, commerce, and the establishment of colonies, but it was also a world of wonders, threats, and anxieties brought about through contact with other peoples and places. The widespread appearance of monsters in Greek art and mythology during the Archaic period surely represents some of the uncertainty that accompanied this cultural change. The *Odyssey*, telling of the return of Odysseus from Troy, expresses the challenge of navigating a strange, wondrous, and sometimes frightening new world (**5.1**).

Inevitably, this contact with the wider world prompted important changes in mainland Greece, where city-states were growing larger and where regional powers (such as Athens, Thebes, and Sparta) began to emerge. Internally, wealth, status competition, and rivalry (both aristocratic and between communities) became more prevalent. Different communities, however, responded to these developments in different ways. Corinth, for example, would profit from its location by the narrow isthmus that separates the Saronic Gulf from the Corinthian Gulf. The city, in addition to possessing a well-fortified akropolis high above the city (the *Acrocorinth*), had two separate harbors, as we saw in Chapter 4: Kenchreai, an emporium for trade coming from the East; and Lechaion, well located to control the western trade. (The *diolkos*, a limestone road across the Isthmus, may have been used for transshipping between the two bodies of water; a canal would not be successfully dug until the late nineteenth century AD.) So much wealth flowed from east to west through the city that it became proverbial for the delights to be enjoyed there. Famous for its courtesans (sex workers who were actually temple slaves to Aphrodite), the city grew rich as an emporium between Italy and Sicily on the one hand and the eastern Mediterranean on the other. It was an attractive destination, but as the geographer Strabo would write later, "Not for every man is the voyage to Corinth" (*Geography* 8.6.20).

In the early part of the Archaic period, Corinth was firmly under the control of a single aristocratic family, the Bacchiads, who supplied first kings and later annual magistrates, as well as the colonial leaders who founded new colonies. Toward the middle of the seventh century BC, however, a single, unelected ruler, Kypselos, seized power and ruled as tyrant. This pattern was repeated in many parts of Greece, where tyrants used the social and political tensions of the age as opportunities to take control of their communities. Because of the highly negative associations with the word "tyrant" in modern times, earlier scholarship often treated tyranny solely as a symptom of disorder and the weakness of early Greek city-states, but more recent studies have suggested a more nuanced view of the phenomenon. Many tyrants acted as lawgivers and their rule was often relatively benign. In fact, as we shall see in the discussion of the tyrants of Athens in the next chapter, a case can be made that tyranny in some places put an end to regional factionalism. By providing a generation or more of stability, tyrants may have left an important legacy, measured not by political rights but by freedom from social upheaval and increasing economic prosperity. Nevertheless, it remains true that the widespread phenomenon of tyrants claiming neither the birthright of kings nor the mandate of election by the community attests to the political upheavals affecting many Greek city-states in the Archaic period.

The unsettled conditions of social and economic life at this time are reflected in an emphasis in poetry on **stasis**, or internal civil conflict. In many communities we hear of men killed or exiled because of factional disputes within the emerging city-states. Some historians therefore characterize the Archaic period as one in which more and more people were subject to the compulsion of a few, leading to a class struggle between the richest and poorest citizens. They point, for example, to the fact that in many states an elite can now be identified in the poetry of the time: men who call themselves the *aristoi*, the root of the word "aristocracy," meaning "the rule of the best." At the same time, we now begin to hear of whole subject groups, such as the *penestai* of Thessaly (who appear to have been serfs, tied to the land); the *klarotai* in Crete; and the helots in Sparta. On the other hand, when we have more precise details about actual instances of stasis or civil disorder—as we do on the island of Lesbos and at Halikarnassos or in Megara—it transpires more often than not that it is competing groups of aristocrats or gangs who are the warring parties; in other words, not entire classes of society but clans. To put it simply, some historians see the divisions of Archaic society as horizontal (class), while others see them as vertical

(status). We will return to the question of aristocratic rivalry in the next chapter, where we will see that Athens was nearly torn apart by stasis.

The tensions of the age were expressed in other ways as well. On Euboia, where commerce flourished and the early cities of Chalkis and Eretria profited from trade around the Aegean and beyond, increasing prosperity also fueled competition between these neighboring communities. The Battle of the Lelantine Plain, named for the fertile plain that lay between Chalkis and Eretria, was fought between the two cities in the eighth or seventh century BC, and was long remembered as one of the epochal events of the Archaic Age. For much of the next four hundred years, the history of Greek interstate relations would

5.1 Detail of red-figure *stamnos* depicting Odysseus and the Sirens, Vulci, *c.* 480–470 BC. Ceramic, H: 35.6 cm (1 ft 2 in.)

be indistinguishable from a continuous series of wars, fought between neighboring cities, regions, and alliances. How and why the Greeks remained addicted to conflict is still one of the most salient questions historians must address in relation to the Archaic period. It may be that the very same agonistic culture that was expressed in athletic competition and encoded in the heroic values of epic emphasized individual worth to such a degree that it worked against the emergence of loyalty to any group beyond family, clan, and immediate community. Certainly Greece was never a united country, in political terms, except in cases of emergency, such as the Persian Wars, or when under the domination of such powers as Macedon or, later, Rome.

If competition, strife, and conflict were the defining features of the age, it was also marked by increasing trade and commercial activity, which also contributed to the spread and transformation of Greek culture. As we saw in Chapter 4, in Egypt,

5.2 The Taygetos mountain range, with Sparta below

the pharaoh Psammetichos permitted a consortium of Greek trading states to establish an emporium in the Delta region at Naucratis, and it is surely no coincidence that techniques of stone-cutting and the sculpting of life-size statues of humans (well-established practices in Egyptian religious and funerary settings) now became a feature of Greek culture too.

One last development should be noted if we are to understand the shifts affecting Greek culture in the two centuries prior to the Persian Wars: the introduction of coinage and the emergence of a monetized economy. Coins were first minted in Anatolia (modern-day Turkey) in the sixth century BC. Made of electrum, an alloy of silver and gold, these coins made it possible for trade to bypass the cumbersome process of barter, in which goods were exchanged directly. The practical advantages of money were obvious: bartering could be difficult to conduct efficiently, especially when the underlying value of the goods to be traded was estimated very differently by the parties to the exchange. The process was long, uncertain, and hazardous: Herodotos has an account of Greek traders in Africa laying out their merchandise on the strand in exchange for local goods; day after day, the Greek traders stack up their goods in increasing quantities until the locals agree to take the imported goods in exchange for their own. In contrast, coins allowed traders to negotiate over the value of merchandise without having to render it into an equivalent in wine, precious metal, or luxury goods. Typically, Greek accounts of this important change in economic practice claimed that it was a Greek, Pheidon of Argos, who introduced coinage by taking a handful of iron spits from the Argive Heraion (an ancient temple at Argos) and then cutting them into pieces, thereby producing the first coins. Although Pheidon's dates are uncertain, and the whole tradition has an apocryphal air to it, the story is not without significance. The small denomination of Greek coins was called the *obol*, from the word for a spit, and a bunch of these was referred to as a *drachma*, literally a "handful." Spits dedicated to Hera were also found at the American excavations of the Argive Heraion in AD 1900, so that even if Pheidon did not invent coinage, he may have contributed to the adoption of the practice.

In whatever way coinage became a feature of Archaic commerce, the results were profound. In the poems of Theognis of Megara, for example, we find a continuous complaint raised against those who put profit ahead of nobility. Traditional notions of wealth equated this with land and the tangible goods that one could pass on to one's descendants, but the shift toward monetary exchange threatened to replace aristocratic birth with monetary wealth as the highest good to which one could aspire. It is worth recalling that in the *Odyssey*, when the Phaeacians, denizens of a heroic world about to disappear, insult Odysseus for his unwillingness to compete in their aristocratic games, they dismiss him as a merchant, calling him,

...a captain
in charge of merchant sailors, whose concern
is for his freight—he keeps a greedy eye
on the cargo and his profit. You don't seem
to be an athlete.

(Homer, *Odyssey* 8.161–65, trans. Johnston)

The poet of the *Odyssey* saw that, in his world, money and heroism were very much at odds.

Early Sparta

Different parts of Greece, as we have seen, responded to the tensions of the Archaic Age in different ways, but the Spartan response was unique. Throughout the history of Sparta, its citizens boasted of being "hostile to tyrants" (**misotyrannos**). Instead, the Spartans claimed that their political and communal life was based on **eunomia**, or good order, which they attributed to the work of a semi-legendary lawgiver, Lykourgos. The notion of an early lawgiver was not unique to Sparta—the Athenians saw Solon in the same light, even as Moses served the same purpose for early Israel—but the Spartans went on to fashion a social and political contract that diverged sharply from the trajectory followed by other Greek communities. Here the emphasis was on a strict social hierarchy, at the top of which was a warrior class known as Spartiates.

The historical reasons for Sparta's unique social organization are complex, but geography played a part. Located on the banks of the Eurotas River, the city is overshadowed by Mount Taygetos (**5.2**), a steep ridge that cuts the region of Lakonia off from its western neighbors in Messenia. To the northeast, Mount Parnon separates Lakonia from the plain of

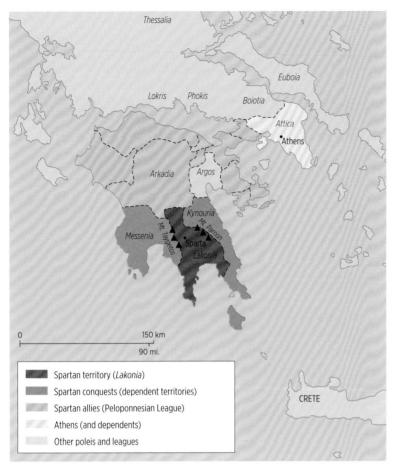

from the name for their region, Lakonia); would stand in battle until the last man was cut down; prized honor and a glorious death more than life; and were trained under the harshest possible conditions, wearing the simplest of clothes in the cold and eating such food as Spartan black broth, which other Greeks found disgusting. "I bore him so that he might die for Sparta, and now my wishes are fulfilled," said one Spartan mother upon hearing that her son had died in battle. This was an image of Sparta that was cultivated and grew over time. In the late first century AD, for example, Plutarch (AD 46–126) collected many such one-liners, pithy remarks designed to illustrate the unwavering courage of Spartan men and women. The result of this self-mythologizing is that the line between reality and myth is blurry at best.

One way of dealing with this difficulty is to use the material culture of the region to shed light on Sparta's early history. As discussed in Chapter 3, the palace

5.3 Map of the Peloponnese, showing Lakonia and neighboring regions. Note, in particular, Kynouria, the borderland between Lakonia and Argos, and the region of Messenia to the west

Argos (**5.3**). This sense of physical isolation helped foster the belief that Sparta was unique, a society which, thanks to Lykourgos and his constitution, had managed to avoid the stasis that afflicted so many other Archaic communities. While other cities fell prey to tyrants, who arose to power amid the brawls of civil unrest, the Spartans applied themselves to a strict and unyielding code of conduct designed to raise generation after generation of unbeatable warriors.

Or so they believed. The problem for the historian is that it is almost impossible to disentangle the early history of Sparta from the later mythologizing that grew up around every aspect of Spartan life, creating what has sometimes been called "the Spartan mirage." In time, this legendary image of Sparta was happily embraced by the Spartans themselves: the Spartans were terse in speech ("laconic" is derived

at Aghios Vasileios proves that Lakonia, the region in which Sparta was situated, was completely integrated into the Mycenaean world. Similarly, the tholos tomb at Vapheio and the gold cups found inside the tomb would not be out of place in a Mycenaean burial from any other part of the Peloponnese. At Therapne, only 5 kilometers (3 mi.) to the southeast of Sparta, a complex of Late Helladic (1650–1050 BC) houses was excavated by the British School in AD 1909, offering further evidence that the culture of Bronze Age Lakonia resembled the Bronze Age culture of other regions of the Mycenaean world. After the end of the Bronze Age, however, Lakonia was affected by the same abrupt changes that impacted the Mycenaean centers in the Argolid. Later traditions associated these upheavals with the return of the Herakleidai, the descendants of Herakles who were believed to have inhabited the Peloponnese once upon a time and who then had quit the region. Such stories of population movements belong to the semi-mythical time of heroes and, despite the details recorded in the work of much later historians, the legends are not a reliable guide to early Spartan history. Many scholars prefer to see such legends as evidence of societies in transition, especially when emerging elites sought to claim distinctive genealogical origins to distinguish themselves from those they ruled. The society that subsequently took shape in Sparta during the Archaic period looked very different from other Greek city-states. The city center, for example, seems to have been physically unimpressive and probably consisted of a loose amalgamation of five villages: Limnai, Pitana, Kynosoura, Mesoa, and Amyklai. Such amalgamations are themselves not unusual; Athens, for example, probably had similar origins, but while the *synoecism*, or unification, of Athens culminated in a fully developed city center, it is hard to identify civic buildings or a city center in Sparta before the Roman period. In the fifth century BC, Thucydides famously observed that in the future people might be deceived by the physical remains of Athens and Sparta: Athens with its magnificent temples was not as powerful as it seemed, while Sparta's humble architectural remains belied the city's true strength. In this respect, as in so many other areas, Sparta seemed anomalous to other Greeks of the Classical Age.

Spartan Religion

Religious practices also point to the emergence of a distinctive Spartan culture. At Amyklai, for example, the Spartans engaged in the worship of a hero, Hyakinthos, and the god Apollo. While the pairing of hero and god was not unique (Apollo and Asklepios would enjoy a similar relationship at Epidauros), the monument built at Amyklai was extraordinary. Designed by Bathykles of Samos, it was constructed around the middle of the sixth century BC and took the form of a massive throne (**5.4**). The current Greek excavator of the site, Angelos Delivorrias, emphasizes that the structure (which was in effect a two-story building) was meant to echo visually a piece of furniture, and describes it as "a totally unorthodox architectural creation." Pausanias saw the throne in the second century AD and his description suggests that the entire structure was decorated with painted wooden panels depicting mythological scenes. He also describes a standing cult statue of Apollo 14 meters (46 ft) tall. The reconstruction by Roland Martin is consistent with Pausanias's account and illustrates how strange the structure was.

Spartan religion was distinct and different in many respects from that practiced throughout the rest of Archaic Greece. Take, for example, the notorious figure of Helen of Troy. In the *Iliad* we encounter her at Troy where she has fled with Paris, abandoning her husband and children. She also appears in the *Odyssey*, reunited with Menelaus but depicted as a woman capable of drugging men and unbound by the conventions of xenia, or hospitality. The negative presentation of Helen in epic was echoed in Athenian drama, but in Sparta she enjoyed the high status not only of a heroine but also of a goddess. Along with her husband Menelaus, she received sacrifices and dedications at a massive shrine known as the Menelaion, only 5 kilometers (3 mi.) southeast of the Classical town, on a hill overlooking the

5.4 Reconstruction of the Throne of Amyklai, after Roland Martin (1976)

Eurotas River (**5.5**). Cultic worship of both Menelaus and Helen continued for hundreds of years at the site, which is located only 100 meters (328 ft) away from Late Bronze Age houses at Therapne.

Similarly unusual, when compared to religious practice in the rest of Greece, is the religious activity associated with the Sanctuary of Artemis Orthia at Sparta, where more than one hundred thousand small lead figurines have been found. Many depict ***hoplites*** (warriors), female worshipers, and animals; the figurines were probably dedications to the goddess by soldiers, hunters, and women, given in recognition of her help. Also found in this sanctuary were terracotta masks that portray grotesque faces suggesting demons, possibly associated with the initiation of young men into secret societies (**5.6**). The nearest parallels for the masks are not from mainland Greece but from Cyprus and Punic (or Carthaginian) sites in the western Mediterranean or Phoenicia.

The goddess herself, depicted on ivory plaques wearing a polos, or crown, looks not unlike Phoenician goddesses, such as Tanit, perhaps pointing to early connections between Sparta and the East. Some scholars have gone so far as to suggest that the cult of Artemis Orthia was brought to Sparta by Phoenicians, although the evidence for this—namely the small plaques and other ivory objects—actually points to a connection with workshops on Crete.

The best-attested ritual associated with the cult of Artemis Orthia was particularly strange and brutal: boys were charged with stealing large wheels of cheese from the altar but were savagely whipped while trying to do so, in the belief that the blood they shed would appease the goddess, whose statue became unbearably heavy to those holding it if the whippers were too lenient. The practice continued throughout the Hellenistic and Roman periods, and was so popular with Roman tourists in late antiquity that a theater was built facing the temple and altar so that visitors could watch the ritual flagellation. Similarly, it has been suggested that a Lakonian kylix depicts an early version of the flagellation ritual (**5.7**). The figure being sodomized at the top of the scene bears the marks of a whipping on his back, while the figure on the left defecates in fear as he runs away.

Even the architecture of temples in Lakonia is unusual when compared to the rest of Greece: while most Greek temples were peripteral, meaning that the central chamber was surrounded by an external colonnade of columns, in Lakonia the practice of erecting non-peripteral temples persisted. In appearance these were simpler and less ornamental, a suitable expression of the Spartans' image of themselves as hard and uncompromising. In each of these instances one could make the case that Spartan practice represents a variation on norms

found throughout the Greek world: elsewhere boys and girls underwent initiation in sometimes unusual ways (in Arkadia one ritual may have involved swimming across a lake and living in the wilderness with the wolves); in other states Homeric characters were treated as local heroes; and throughout the Greek world Artemis had various avatars that were just as bloodthirsty as her Spartan incarnation. Nevertheless, even the Greeks themselves believed that Sparta was distinctive and different. Perhaps it is better to conclude that the panhellenic view of Greece that has come down to us from the Homeric poems has obscured the extraordinary degree of local variation in Greek culture and religion. In addition to the panhellenic cults familiar to us from Delphi, Olympia, and elsewhere, there were local and regional versions of the Greek gods who are much less readily recognizable. Consider Athena and Demeter, two well-known goddesses. Athena, dressed for war with helmet and breastplate, is easy to recognize; Demeter, on the other hand, with the head of a horse (as she was depicted in a cult statue at Phigaleia) hardly fits our conventional view of the Greek gods.

Spartan Exceptionalism

What led the Spartans to chart a course so at odds with the rest of mainland Greece? One answer may lie in a series of wars that the Spartans fought with their western neighbors, the Messenians, beginning as early as the mid- to late eighth century BC. Exact dates are difficult to establish with certainty, but the foundation of the Spartan colony of Taras at Tarentum in southern Italy is the key to establishing

5.6 (above) Clay mask dedicated at the Sanctuary of Artemis Orthia between *c.* 600 and 450 BC. The masks may be terra-cotta representations of linen or wooden masks used in either theatrical performances or initiatory rites.

5.7 (right) Drawing of Lakonian kylix that may depict an initiation scene.

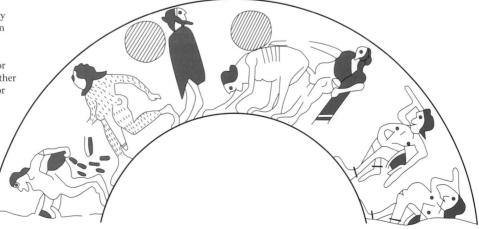

the time period. The foundation of the colony appears to be reliably dated archaeologically to the years immediately before 700 BC, and Spartan tradition maintained that the founders were Spartans known as the Parthenioi, men who were born to Spartan women while their husbands were away during the Messenian Wars. Their questionable legitimacy and status were a source of considerable tension at Sparta, and the solution to the problem they posed was to deport them to Italy. How reliable is the story? Probably not very. Some scholars, in fact, would prefer to see the Parthenioi as an aristocratic secret society, one of the many that characterized Archaic Sparta, who had fled Sparta after an abortive coup. But the evidence for such secret societies in Archaic Sparta is slim and the theory is little better than a rationalization of the story of the Parthenioi. Regardless, however, of who exactly the Parthenioi were, the stories connecting them with the foundation of Taras give us a chronological peg, which allows us to date the beginning of the Messenian Wars to the late eighth century, some time before 700 BC (although even this date has been recently challenged by P. J. Shaw, who believes that this and other early Spartan events should be down-dated by more than 170 years).

The second Messenian War, fought sometime in the first quarter of the seventh century BC, proved to be a turning point for Sparta's internal development. This is because, having conquered the Messenians, the Spartans took the unusual decision to permanently subjugate them and thereafter treat them as a servile class in their own territory. In previous wars (and most subsequent wars as well), the habitual practice of the Greeks was to raid their neighbors' territory during the campaigning season, which corresponded to the summer months. Cattle and other livestock could be carried off, and any people too slow to avoid such raids would end up enslaved. Pitched battles were, for the most part, avoided or settled quickly. After the initial contact, the shoving of shields, and thrusting of spears, one side would break and run away, leaving the victors to strip the dead and erect a trophy at the point where their enemies had turned. Vicious campaigns might entail burning crops or cutting down trees, but at the end of the campaigning season the war essentially came to an end. The Spartan treatment of Messenia was different. Instead of quitting Messenia,

the Spartans annexed the territory to Lakonia. For more than three hundred years the Spartans acted as absentee landlords, with the broad rich plains of Messenia—"good to plow" in the words of the Spartan poet Tyrtaios—supplying the *syssitia*, literally groups of those "eating together," or messes, in which Sparta's warrior citizens lived. The land was worked by the slaves of Sparta, the helots, a population that included the original owners of Messenia.

The significance of this process, by which one part of the Peloponnese was forcibly and permanently subjugated to another in a process that could be described as internal colonization, cannot be overestimated. It transformed Messenia into occupied territory and made it both possible and necessary for Sparta to become a society dedicated to the raising of elite warriors. The threat of a helot uprising was ever-present, and every institution of Spartan society was directed toward the creation of this warrior elite, the Spartiates, whose rank, privilege, and status depended on the continuing subjugation of another Greek ethnic group. Nor were the Spartiates especially popular among the other citizens of Sparta. When, in the fourth century BC, a disaffected Spartiate named Kinadon was arrested by the state's magistrates (known as ephors) and was asked who was part of his conspiracy, he remarked that when any of the lower classes of Spartans met, they agreed that they would gladly have eaten the Spartiates raw.

It was the institutions of Spartiate training that evolved in the aftermath of the Messenian Wars that made Sparta so unusual even in the eyes of other Greeks. Spartan boys, for example, were taken from their families at the age of seven and raised with other boys of their own age. This age-class system, the *agoge*, was practiced in more recent times by the Maasai, another culture that has placed a high emphasis on military training, hardiness, and, some might say, a kind of hypermasculinity. According to some sources, in the Spartan system, boys were encouraged to steal, live by their wits, and resist any weakness. Later accounts, however, designed to illustrate this uncompromising code, strain credulity. Here, for example, is Plutarch's account of the conduct of a Spartan boy, written toward the end of the first century AD:

In the case of another boy, when the time had arrived during which it was the custom for the free boys to steal whatever they could, and it was a disgrace not to escape being found out, when the boys with him had stolen a young fox alive, and given it to him to keep, and those who had lost the fox came in search for it, the boy happened to have slipped the fox under his garment. The beast, however, became savage and ate through his side to the vitals; but the boy did not move or cry out, so as to avoid being exposed...when they [those who had lost the fox] had departed, the boys saw what had happened, and blamed him, saying that it would have been better to let the fox be seen than to hide it even unto death; the boy, however, said, "Not so, but better to die without yielding to the pain than through being detected because of weakness of spirit to gain a life to be lived in disgrace."

(Plutarch, *Sayings of the Spartans* 35, trans. Babbitt)

It is possible that the notion that boys were meant to steal is actually part of some kind of initiation, comparable to the hazing experienced by boys at boarding school or in fraternities, but the entire episode is so bound up with the performance of being Spartan in the Roman period, when Plutarch collected these stories, that it is almost impossible to distinguish the original behavior from the *Boys' Own* stuff of the anecdote.

Boys graduated from their adolescence into the ranks of the Spartan army along with the others of their age class. As they continued to train and to serve, they lived in the syssitia. Recent studies suggest that the syssition had between fifteen and twenty members from all age groups, and that new members were boys, around the age of twelve, who were introduced by their older lovers, young men around the age of twenty-two. Since the group included, in turn, one or two older generations of former lovers, the result was an unusually cohesive group, bound by the closest possible ties. (A similar type of bonding existed in the Theban Sacred Band.) Membership of these messes, as they are normally called in English, required contributions from each member, not only in the form of game caught by hunting, but also such staples as barley and wheat, the produce of the lands farmed by the Spartiates' helot slaves. Failure to make the necessary contributions to the syssition could lead not just to expulsion, but demotion from the ranks of the Spartiates to the lower rank of the **Hypomeiones** ("Inferiors").

The syssition may offer a clue to the origins of Sparta's distinctive institutions. Although other mainland states generally did not resemble Sparta's social organization, some communities on Crete did. According to one source, the people of Lyktos on Crete pooled their produce into a system of collective messes, also called syssitia, by having the state keep a share but dividing the rest among the households of the citizens. This system may represent an early attempt to use state regulation and intervention as a way of helping the community survive the threat of crop failure. Whatever its intention, the institution appears to have provided a model to the Spartans. In other areas, too, the Spartans were said to have enjoyed a close relationship with the Cretans. Both were speakers of the Doric dialect of Greek, and traditions regarding the semi-mythical Spartan lawgiver, Lykourgos, maintained that he had traveled to Crete to learn how to draft a set of laws for Sparta. Plato went so far as to refer to Sparta and Crete enjoying "kindred law codes" (**adelphoi nomoi**). When we recall the Cretan origin of some of the ivory plaques from the Orthia sanctuary, a Cretan origin to some of Sparta's characteristic institutions becomes more plausible.

In conjunction with the distinctive training system, which effectively turned the top tier of Spartan society into professional warriors, the Spartans also established other institutions that advertised their separation from the rest of Greek society. In most Greek states, for example, young men underwent military training during late adolescence that was designed to prepare them for taking their place in the hoplite **phalanx** of citizen warriors. Such youths were known as **ephebes**, and their term of service might involve both specialized training and particular service, such as at Athens, where they served as border guards for two years. In Sparta, however, they also served in an institution known as the **krypteia**, which functioned as a kind of secret police, not unlike the paramilitary squads in recent South American civil conflicts. Their function was to terrorize the helot population. Armed with knives, they were dispatched to patrol Sparta, killing any helot found outside after dark.

While the rigid order of Spartan society was dictated by fear of helot rebellion, the Spartans were also morbidly afraid of innovation from abroad. The free flow of ideas, encouraged by debate, disputation, and discourse, would become a hallmark of Athenian democratic culture. In the repressive oligarchy of

Sparta, however, open discussion was discouraged. *Aidos*, or reserve, was prized as a virtue, the mark of a real man, but was also used rhetorically to distinguish Spartans from others. In Thucydides' account of the outbreak of the Peloponnesian War, an Athenian embassy delivers a speech six chapters long, justifying the history of Athenian policy since the Persian Wars fifty years earlier. In response, the Spartan ephor Sthenelaidas delivers a short and ferocious speech one chapter long, in which he responds to the prolix language and convoluted arguments of the Athenians by saying, "If they behaved well in the Persian War and are now behaving badly to us they ought to be punished twice over, because they were once good men and have become bad" (*Peloponnesian War* 1.86).

This taciturnity is closely linked to a suspicion of discussion, so pronounced in Sparta that periodically the Spartans would simply expel all foreigners, a practice known as *xenelasia*. In one famous episode in the late 460s BC, the Athenians sent an expeditionary force to Sparta to aid the Spartans after an earthquake had hit the Peloponnese, prompting the helots to revolt. Yet after some months in Lakonia, the Athenians and their pro-Spartan commander, Kimon (*c.* 510–450 BC), were asked to leave. According to Thucydides, the Spartans were afraid of the "new thinking" of the Athenians, and the effect it might have in Sparta. Though vulnerable to a slave revolt, the Spartans still preferred to expel the Athenians rather than run the risk of having the word "democracy" uttered in Sparta. Nothing more dramatically reveals how closed a society Sparta had become by the middle of the fifth century.

The Great Rhetra

The irony of Sparta's devolution into a police state is that during the Archaic period there were still signs that political and constitutional developments might have gone in a different and more democratic direction. To understand the curious development of Spartan constitutional history, we need to recognize the distinctive shape of Spartan government. In Sparta, kingship was retained long after most Greek city-states abolished kings or reduced their role to a ceremonial function. Furthermore, Sparta was ruled through the historical period by two royal families, the Eurypontids and the Agiads. Kings wielded real power, especially since the Spartan army was nearly always led by one of the kings. They appear to have been known as the *archagetai*, or leaders, an interesting title since it is also an epithet used of Apollo, who was believed to lead colonial expeditions to their new lands. The expression occurs in an enigmatic text, known as the Great Rhetra, preserved much later by Plutarch in the first century AD and purporting to be an oracle given by Delphi to the lawgiver Lykourgos, when he sought the god's help in establishing a constitutional code for Sparta. According to Plutarch, the text read as follows:

Having established a cult of Syllanian Zeus and Athena, having done the "tribing and obing" [the division of the state into tribes and villages] and having established a Gerousia of thirty including the kings, then season in and season out they are to hold Apellai between Babyka and Knakion; the Gerousia is both to introduce proposals and to stand aloof; the Damos is to have power to give a decisive verdict.

(Plutarch, *Life of Lykourgos* 6, trans. Cartledge)

Virtually every clause of this so-called Great Rhetra has excited heated scholarly debate. Some dismiss it as a complete fiction, others regard it as an authentic document of the seventh century BC. The division of the state into *phylai* (tribes) fits with what is known of Sparta's later history, when all male citizens were members of one of three tribes—Hylleis, Dymanes, and Pamphyloi—so it is entirely possible that such tribal divisions were also a part of early Sparta's social organization. Similarly the division into *obai*, or villages, seems to correspond to early Sparta. The **Gerousia** was a senate, made up of Spartan elders, and such councils were a common feature in Archaic communities. It is not unreasonable, therefore, to take the Great Rhetra as a guide to the constitutional arrangements adopted in Sparta in the Archaic period. It is difficult to determine what kind of social tensions may have fueled pressure to shape a constitution: was Spartan eunomia a way of moderating aristocratic competition, channeling it into fixed and predictable institutions? Aristotle certainly believed that at the time of the Messenian Wars, Sparta was an aristocratic state riven by factions, but he also claims that this resulted in demands for the redistribution of land, so, once again, it is difficult to separate the "horizontal" divisions of rich and poor from the "vertical" division of aristocratic feuding.

Whichever way we reconstruct early Sparta, two features of the Great Rhetra are very important. The first is that there is no mention of the magistrates known as the ephors, five of whom, in later periods, were elected each year to administer the city's affairs; and the second is that the Great Rhetra states clearly that sovereign power resides with the Damos, or People: "the Damos is to have power to give a decisive verdict." If the document were a later fabrication, it is likely that the forger would have included reference to the ephors, since in any later period this would have seemed a natural feature of the Spartan system. Instead, the absence of any such mention suggests the authenticity of the Great Rhetra: we seem to have a document going back to the early stages of Sparta's constitutional development, to a time when it was agreed and publicly proclaimed that the Damos would have ultimate authority. In other words, early Sparta was on the path to democracy, and under different circumstances would surely have evolved a system closer to the open, discourse-driven, egalitarian government of Athens, had it not been diverted.

Plutarch goes on to report that a rider was subsequently added to the Great Rhetra: "But if the Damos speaks crookedly, the Gerontes and Kings are to be removers." The Damos is a clear reference to the community of adult male Spartan citizens, while the reference to the members of the Gerousia and the kings as **apostateres** ("removers") suggests they had been given the power of a veto. It is possible to combine these clauses and reconstruct Sparta's constitutional history broadly as follows: in the seventh century BC, the nascent Spartan community fixed upon a proto-democratic form of government that retained kings as war-leaders and heads of state while stating firmly that final legislative power lay in the hands of the community of adult male citizens. At a later time, however, probably in the sixth century and the aftermath of the Messenian Wars, aristocratic power and privilege successfully reasserted control of Sparta, using the threat of helot revolt to fashion a closed political and military elite. The ephors ("overseers") oversaw political decision-making, while the time spent on political debate in assemblies of the people in other Greek states was instead directed toward the military training of the elite (**5.8**).

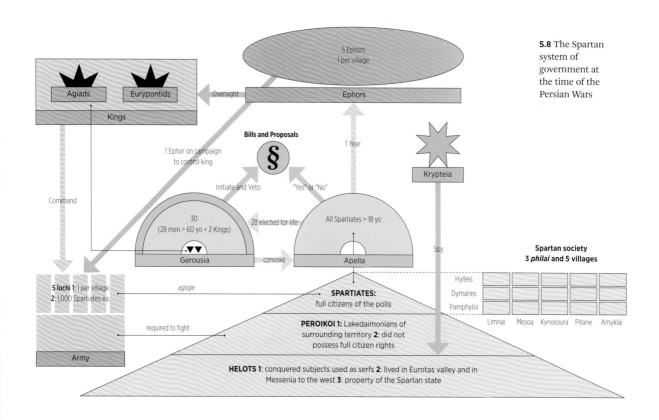

5.8 The Spartan system of government at the time of the Persian Wars

Spartan Culture

This relentless focus on military excellence skewed the development of Spartan society. In one area—athletic contests, unsurprisingly—Sparta excelled. For example, in the thirty-five Olympic contests held every four years between 720 and 580 BC, Spartan male athletes won forty-four victories, more than athletes from any other state, and Spartan women also dominated the games held at Olympia in honor of the goddess Hera. But the state of permanent internal warfare against the helot population combined to bring about the closing of Spartan society. This is most marked when we look at the vigorous cultural traditions of the Archaic period and compare them with the wasteland of Spartan culture in the subsequent Classical period. Prior to the Persian Wars, for example, Spartan craftsmen distinguished themselves in metalwork. Small bronzes, such as the famous figures of a running girl (**5.9**) and an aristocrat (**5.10**) reclining in a symposium, are the equal of any metalwork produced in the Greek world at this time.

Another artistic area in which early Sparta excelled was in ivory. The Sanctuary of Artemis Orthia, already mentioned for its unusual terra-cotta masks and many miniature lead figurines, was also notable for dedications carved from ivory. One famous plaque depicts a ship on which soldiers can be seen with their shields (**5.11**). In the center, two men appear to be unfurling the sails, while on the left a man appears to be holding a woman by the wrist. This posture is repeated on a number of painted vases, and the scene quite probably represents one of the several abductions common in Greek epic: Jason and Medea, or even Paris and Helen.

5.9 Figure of a running girl, *c.* 520–500 BC. Bronze, H: 11.4 cm (4½ in.)

5.10 Figure of a reclining banqueter, *c.* 520 BC. Bronze, L: 10 cm (4 in.)

5.11 Ivory plaque from the Sanctuary of Artemis Orthia, seventh century BC

In poetry too, the early Spartans were originally innovators and masters. For example, the poet Alkman, writing in the seventh century BC, produced hymns for choruses of young girls that were rich, complex, and beautifully suited to performance at religious festivals. In one choral song that compares the beauty of a young woman to various luxury items as well as to different breeds of horses, the chorus leader (a woman) appears to speak frankly of her companion's power to exhaust her sexually:

For abundance of purple is not sufficient for protection, nor intricate snake of solid gold, no, nor Lydian headband, pride of dark-eyed girls, nor the hair of Nanno, nor again godlike Areta nor Thylakis and Kleësithera; nor will you go to Ainesimbrota's and say, "If only Astaphis were mine, if only Philylla were to look my way and Damareta and lovely Ianthemis"; no, Hagesichora wears me out!

> (Alkman, fr. 1 trans. Campbell,
> emended by Hutchinson and Stehle)

The poem becomes even more powerful and enigmatic if a recent study of the text has interpreted it correctly: Gloria Ferrari has convincingly argued that the young women named in the song should be interpreted as heavenly bodies—planets, stars, and such constellations as the Hyades and Pleiades—that the chorus is praising in an elaborate metaphor of cosmic movement. The poem commemorates the gods, heroes, and heroines of Sparta, and identifies them with the orderly annual movement of the heavens. The imagination of the Archaic Spartans, it seems, in common with their material culture, was rich and beautiful.

If Alkman's poems reflect an unusual blend of the astrological and the erotic, by contrast it is Tyrtaios who seems to encapsulate the martial ideology that would eclipse every other aspect of Spartan life. In his poems, the old Homeric code is reconfigured for a new age, in which entire battalions of citizen soldiers, rather than individual heroes, are urged on into battle:

Let us advance, then, behind our hollow shields like a hoard of locusts, or flock of cranes, Pamphyloi, Hylleis, Dymanes, savagely wielding our ash-wood spears that bring death to men. And thus placing everything in the hands of the Immortal Gods, let us obey our holy leader for ever without end. But in a moment one and all together

shall we be wielding the flail, standing up to spearmen; and dire will be the din when both sides clash rounded shield against rounded shield, and awful the shrieks as they fall one upon another, piercing men's breasts with the spear; and no whit will they draw back for the pounding of the missiles, nay, despite the battery of great hurlstones, the helms shall abide the rattle of war unbowed.

> (Tyrtaios 1.2.2, trans. Edmonds, modified)

In Homer's poems death in battle occurs everywhere and constantly, but the poems never urge the listener to go to war. In Tyrtaios, on the other hand, the poems deliberately evoke battle as the arena in which men must test themselves, since it is only in this way that they can win glory for themselves and avoid the shame of defeat and disgrace. There is no other choice. His most famous formulation of this pitiless understanding of war has reverberated through Western culture for centuries: "It is a fine thing for a good man to fall and die fighting in the van for his native land." Horace's rendering of this in Latin, "dulce et decorum est, pro patria mori," adorns countless funerary monuments from the wars of many ages in many lands, but it is worth noting that the original lines in Tyrtaios do more than extol the virtues of noble death in battle. They also hold up the prospect of a single alternative to taking up a position in the front rank, and it is not a happy picture:

...whereas to leave his city and his rich fields and go a-begging is of all things the most miserable, wandering with mother dear and aged father, with little children and wedded wife. For hateful shall such a man be among all those to whom he shall come in bondage to Want and loathsome Poverty, and he shames his lineage and belies his noble beauty, followed by all evil and dishonour.

> (Tyrtaios, cited by Lykourgos, in Leocr. 107,
> trans. Edmonds, modified)

In recent years some scholars have argued that, as with Spartan religion, Spartan culture was not really exceptional, and that many of the features of Spartan life were paralleled in other states, especially Dorian cities (located in those regions of Greece, especially in the west and south, that spoke a distinctive dialect of Greek). After all, other states owned slaves or serfs; other cities had similar political institutions, such as councils, magistrates, and lawgivers; and if free Athenians were proud of their democracy in the fifth and fourth centuries BC, the Spartiates were equally proud of their equal status and called themselves *homoioi*, or "equals." The pro-Spartan Athenian orator Isokrates even claimed that the Spartans were "particularly democratic," by which he meant that equality prevailed among those in the top tier of Spartan society. But even allowing for the Spartans' own image of themselves as unrelenting warriors and taking into consideration the problem of retrojecting later images and ideas onto earlier periods, we would be wrong to interpret Sparta as no different from other Greek city-states. Contemporary Greeks of the fifth and fourth centuries, from Thucydides to Xenophon and Aristotle, all described aspects of Spartan culture that struck them as peculiar, because the Spartans diverged from the pattern of cultural and political development that we find in most other Greek city-states. Time and again the cause of this divergence is to be found in the relentless militarization of Spartan society.

Women in Sparta

It is worth exploring further this militarization of Sparta and the impact of the annexation of Messenia on the role of women in Spartan society. Take, for example, the view repeated in many ancient sources (including Xenophon, who had first-hand experience of Sparta) that women in Sparta were more powerful than women in other Greek states. According to Aristotle they could inherit, own, and administer property. This was certainly at odds with common practice in most Greek states, and was seen as a weakness of the Spartan system. Aristotle must have summed up the opinion of many when he wrote, "In the days of Sparta's supremacy, a great deal was managed by women. What difference is there between women rulers and rulers ruled by women?" (*Politics* 1269b). Related to this was the claim that the Spartans practiced a particular form of polygamy, according to which women might have more than one husband: **polyandry**. According to sources from the fourth century BC onward, under some circumstances men could father legitimate children by Spartan women who were not their wives. In effect,

then, these women had more than one husband. In a variation of this, Polybios describes Spartan families in which brothers were married to the same woman, a practice known as fraternal polyandry (and still widely practiced in Tibet). How should we interpret these reports? In antiquity they contributed to the view that Spartan women were outspoken, promiscuous, independent, and wielded far too much power. Aristotle's conclusion, echoed at various times by later writers, is that because of the status and rights of women, Sparta suffered from *oliganthropia*, a shortage of men, and that women were indirectly the cause of Sparta's downfall. Conversely, and drawing on the same evidence, some recent scholars have likened Spartan women to what one historian has condescendingly called "the liberated women of modern times." Both approaches suffer from a similar flaw: they interpret the Spartans in the light of contemporary values and biases. A better interpretation, and closer to the evidence, is that the Spartans were interested in selective breeding and practiced eugenics. In a hierarchical society, those in the most exclusive class, the Spartiates, were jealous of preserving both their privileges and their land. Women who had proven themselves fertile were therefore prized, since they could provide heirs and guarantee the household's continuation. Women shared within a large family were even better: where inherited land might otherwise be split between many offspring descending from brothers with different wives, a shared wife meant fewer lines of descent and therefore less pressure to divide the family's property. Added to these concerns was the biological belief that strong, hardy women would produce equally powerful sons.

So unusual were all these arrangements by the standards of the rest of the Greek world that Spartan women gained notoriety. While most citizen women in the Greek world were kept respectably covered, Spartan woman exercised and were known as "thigh-flashers." But the tendency of the ancient sources to moralize should cause us to be wary. What struck Aristotle and Xenophon as odd and exceptional makes sense when viewed in relation to the peculiar circumstances of Spartan life. Recent studies of Spartan economic practice have emphasized that the militarization of Spartan society and the demands of overseeing distant estates meant that Spartan men were compelled to delegate household control to their women and to leave them with much greater autonomy than in other parts of Greece. In other words, the traditions that speak of powerful Spartan women should not be rejected as untrue simply because they come down to us packaged in moralizing and sexist vignettes, recounted by men horrified by the notion of strong women. Instead, we should ask how the unique position of Spartan women reflects the unusual conditions of Spartan society. Far from ruining their homeland, the women of Sparta enjoyed comparatively greater freedom because this made it possible for their menfolk to maintain their distant estates and to engage in constant military training. As with Rosie the Riveter, Spartan women enjoyed a degree of autonomy because without their contribution their society could not have functioned.

Sparta and the Peloponnese

The other area in which the militarization of Sparta had an important effect was in Sparta's foreign relations and dealings with other states, particularly in the Peloponnese. A glance at a map of the Peloponnese (see p. 130) shows that the mountain ranges of Taygetos and Parnonas effectively separated Lakonia from Messenia to the west and Argos to the northeast. Nevertheless, regional conflict involving both these regions occupied the Spartans throughout the Archaic period.

We have seen that a series of wars with Messenia resulted in the annexation of that territory. Though less successful against their Argive neighbors, the Spartans were nevertheless just as preoccupied with them. Their enmity focused on the strip of territory southwest of Argos on the coastal plain below Mount Parnon, a region known as either Kynouria or the plain of Thyrea. According to Herodotos, in the middle of the sixth century BC the two sides were feuding over the territory, and hit upon a novel way of settling the dispute: a battle of their respective three hundred best warriors. The two contingents engaged and fought until only three men were left, a situation that led to an ambiguous outcome:

Neither could gain advantage in the battle; at last, only three out of the six hundred were left, Alkenor and Chromios of the Argives, Othryades of the Lacedaemonians: these three were left alive at nightfall.

Then the two Argives, believing themselves victors, ran to Argos; but Othryades the Lacedaemonian, after stripping the Argive dead and taking the arms to his camp, waited at his position. On the second day both armies came to learn the issue. For a while both claimed the victory, the Argives arguing that more of their men had survived, the Lacedaemonians showing that the Argives had fled, while their man had stood his ground and stripped the enemy dead. At last from arguing they fell to fighting; many of both sides fell, but the Lacedaemonians gained the victory.

(Herodotos, *Histories* 1.82, trans. Godley)

According to Herodotos, the Argives shaved their heads and swore never to grow their hair long until they had recovered Thyrea, while the Spartans ever after wore their hair long.

Even allowing for the embellishments of storytelling, Herodotos's account captures the absolutely implacable hatred that kept the Spartans and Argives at odds for hundreds of years. When Sparta stood against the Persians—almost alone at Thermopylae in 480 BC, and one year later at Plataia as leader of the combined Greek forces—the Argives refused to participate, and during the Peloponnesian War against Athens, the Argives sided with Sparta's enemies. The Battle of the Champions, as the battle described in Herodotos is often called, was not the only confrontation between Sparta and Argos. Earlier in the Archaic period, perhaps as early as 669 BC (although some would date it much later) and again later in the Peloponnesian War in 418–417, the Spartans fought the Argives in battle at Hysiai. On the latter occasion the Spartans took the male citizens of Hysiai captive and then slaughtered them all.

Sparta's treatment of its Peloponnesian neighbors was therefore frequently (and brutally) confrontational. At the same time, for close to two hundred years, the Spartans also managed a loose alliance of Peloponnesian states usually referred to as the Peloponnesian League, which Sparta treated much more leniently than the Athenians dealt with their allies. No tribute was imposed on these Peloponnesian allies, except wartime levies, and they met with equal voting power in a congress. But these apparently benign aspects of Sparta's **hegemony** should be viewed cautiously. It is noteworthy that the Peloponnesian states most distant from Sparta, such as Elis in the northwest, and Corinth and Epidauros in the northeast, were treated with respect and

5.12 Figure of an athlete with the Thyreatic crown, mid-sixth century BC, stolen from the Museum of the Olympic Games in AD 2012. Bronze, H: 17.7 cm (7 in.)

but the Tegeans never lost their antipathy toward the Spartans.

What are we to make of Sparta's Peloponnesian hegemony? The consistent theme running through the sixth century BC is the desire of the Spartans to amass as much land as possible, to subjugate other Greek states wherever possible, and to solidify the borders of Lakonia by any means possible. Ridding Corinth of tyrants earned Sparta an ally in that wealthy state, while supporting the Elian claim to control Olympia also brought a beneficial alliance, but nearer to home the Spartans used direct, ruthless military intervention to pacify or at least neutralize the neighboring states of Messenia, Argos, and Arkadia. Religion, too, was a weapon for negotiating borders. In the pass leading across Mount Parnon to the contested area of Kynouria at the southwestern end of the Argive plain, the Spartans established a sanctuary of Apollo Maleatas (near the modern-day town of Kosmas). Here, in addition to worshiping a version of Apollo who probably originated in the Lakonian territory of Cape Maleas, they held games in the god's honor.

A famous Spartan athlete of the fifth century BC, Damonon, recorded his many victories in various games around the Peloponnese, and boasted of winning the stadion and diaulos races there as a boy. Similarly to the other victors he was awarded a "Thyreatic crown," commemorating the defeat of the Argives (**5.12**).

In addition to athletes marking their victories, Spartan warriors also advertised their presence with dedications at the sanctuary, such as the bronze figurine of a Spartan hoplite shown in **5.13** (see p. 144), reinforcing the message that Sparta owned this territory. Here, cult activity and athletic games staked territorial claims. Dedications from this sanctuary reflect the ways in which borders were marked by both a military and religious presence.

Relations between the Spartans and the Messenians also shaped religious practice. The goddess most widely worshiped throughout the southern Peloponnese was Artemis, and her sanctuary on Mount Taygetos, the border between Lakonia and Messenia, was a site where both Messenians and Spartans came to worship. But as a religious location where two hostile peoples shared the same space, it was also hotly contested. The Spartans claimed on one occasion that

generally stayed loyal to their alliance with Sparta, while the cities of Arkadia, immediately north of Lakonia (namely Tegea and Mantineia) were in a much more precarious position. In the middle of the sixth century the Spartans marched on Tegea, bringing with them fetters with which to enslave their northern neighbors. Instead, the Tegeans were victorious and dedicated the fetters at the temple of Athena Alea, thereby avoiding becoming yet another helot population (such as the Messenians). Eventually, some twenty years later, the Spartan king Anaxandridas succeeded in bringing Tegea into the Peloponnesian League, and thereafter the city served as a sort of garrison on Lakonia's northern border;

Messenian youths had attacked Spartan girls who had gone to the sanctuary to worship the goddess, even going so far as to kill the Spartan king Teleklos. The Spartans retaliated and the Messenian Wars ensued. The Messenians, however, claimed that it was not Spartan girls but young, beardless men who had entered the sanctuary of Artemis, and that it was Spartan provocation that began the war. Eventually the Spartans established a cult of Artemis on the outskirts of Sparta, at Limnai, once again using a sanctuary to demonstrate their territorial ambitions.

Repeatedly, then, in the Archaic period, we find evidence of the Spartans oppressing and attacking nearby communities, asserting a hegemony that extended over much of the Peloponnese and which was especially coercive in the territories bordering Lakonia. Unsurprisingly, as soon as they had the chance to throw off Spartan suzerainty, the Peloponnesian states needed little prompting. At the end of the first phase of the Peloponnesian War in 421 BC, Athens formed an alliance with Argos. In 418, the Arkadian city of Mantineia (which had, along with Tegea, been forced to submit to Spartan control) joined the anti-Sparta alliance, and it was here that Sparta's enemies came closest to defeating the Peloponnesian superpower in one of the bloodiest battles of the war. The Spartans, however, were victorious and never forgot Mantineia's betrayal. In the 380s, during a period of renewed Spartan aggression, they compelled the Mantineians to abandon their city and disperse to the five smaller villages that had formed the city. But the Spartan hegemony was one of only two regional power clusters to emerge from the Archaic period, and it is to the other, Athens, that we should now turn. As we shall see in Chapter 6, Athens would unify the territory of Attica, but would eventually look to the islands for a sphere in which to exercise hegemony. Perhaps more important was the protracted period of stasis that afflicted the city, and the unusual steps whereby the Athenians moved from disorder to tyranny and, finally, democracy.

5.13 Lakonian hoplite warrior statuette, discovered at Aghios Kosmas in Kynouria, sixth century BC. Bronze

5.14 Vix Krater, c. 520 BC.
Bronze, H: 1.63 m (5 ft 4 in.)

The Vix Krater

Alhough Sparta became a society dedicated to the training of warriors and the constant suppression of the helot population, the Spartans also had a long tradition of excellence in a variety of arts and crafts. Notable among these was the Spartan skill in bronze-casting. An extraordinary example of this is the Vix Krater (**5.14**), a monumental bronze urn 1.63 meters tall (5 ft 4 in.) and weighing over 200 kilograms (440 lbs). Discovered in northern France in AD 1953, the krater was part of a remarkably rich burial tumulus that contained the body of a Celtic woman of high status (**5.15**). Her body was laid out on the bed of a wagon, the wheels of which were placed against it. Other objects in the burial included Attic black-figure vases, electrum torques (neck ornaments of twisted metal), Etruscan earrings, and pieces of Baltic amber, but the enormous urn is by far the most impressive of the grave goods. It is a testament to the skill of the Spartan craftsmen who made it, and the fact that it is the biggest, most luxurious,

5.15 Reconstruction of the interior of the tomb of the Vix princess

5.16 Detail of gorgon's head set into volute handle of the krater

5.17 Detail of the neck of the Vix Krater depicting hoplites, a chariot, and horses

and most conspicuous item among the burial goods confirms that Spartan craftsmanship was valued for its exceptional quality.

Details of the vessel reveal the superb skill of the craftsmen. The gorgon's head, set into the volute handle of the krater, is decorated with tight curls, long locks, and a scaly skin that evokes snakes and suggests that the figure had an apotropaic function, designed to ward off evil influences (**5.16**). Similarly, the figures in relief on the neck of the krater show charioteers, hoplites, and horses (**5.17**) in a manner that beautifully blends naturalism and the slightly exaggerated style of late Archaic art.

To understand the full significance of the Vix Krater, it is important to place it in context. The burial site has been the subject of intensive study since the early 1990s, and we now know that the Celtic tribe who lived here occupied a well-fortified stronghold on Mount Lassois, from which they controlled a strategic corridor connecting the Seine and Loire river systems, permitting the transportation of goods from the Mediterranean all the way to the Atlantic. The goods from the burial can thus be seen as the luxury items belonging to one of the wealthiest and most powerful rulers in central France in the late sixth century BC.

In AD 2006, a palatial complex associated with the burial was also uncovered. The main building, which measures 35 by 21 meters (115 x 69 ft), has an apsidal end and a porch at the entrance, and resembles the megaron buildings from Iron Age Greece. The palace and the burial were both located within a space that was heavily fortified with ditches and walls 8 meters (26 ft) thick. The settlement was carefully laid out, and included houses and storage areas. It is one of the most impressive *oppida*—as these fortified settlements are known—in Celtic Europe.

683/2 BC
First annual Archon
at Athens

632 BC
Kylon's Conspiracy

621/0 BC
Drako's Law
on Homicide

594 BC
Solon's first Archonship

592/1 BC
Solon's Legislation

Chapter 6

The Archaic Age: Athens

In contrast to Sparta, Athens responded to the Archaic crisis not by emphasizing exclusion and hierarchy, but by creating an open and inclusive society. The road to this, however, was rocky. The state experienced a prolonged period of crisis until Solon (*c.* 640–*c.* 560 BC) began the process of constitutional and legislative reform in the early sixth century BC. Even so, and ironically, civic instability returned after Solon's departure from Athens, and Athens was subsequently dominated for more than forty years by one family of tyrants, Peisistratos and his sons. Peisistratos, however, ruled mildly, maintained the rule of law in general, oversaw a period of prosperous growth, and substantially quelled the aristocratic rivalry that threatened Athenian society. With the end of the tyranny, the Athenians avoided a return to civil upheaval by electing Kleisthenes who, extraordinarily, instituted a systematic constitutional reform that remained the basis of the Athenian democracy for hundreds of years.

Competition and Rivalry in the Archaic World

The Archaic Age (700–480 BC) was, as we saw in the last chapter, a time of foment and change throughout Greece. In most places kingship was abolished, but in many communities tyrants emerged to counteract the effects of aristocratic rivalry that, though partially channeled into athletic competition, was potentially destructive.

One story illuminates the age: Herodotos has an amusing account of suitors from all over Greece vying for the hand of a young woman of high birth, Agariste of Sikyon. At a feast before the winner was announced, an Athenian aristocrat named Hippokleides got drunk and danced on his hands—an alarming image given the nature of Greek clothing—and was told that he had danced away his marriage. "Hippokleides doesn't give a damn!" was his cavalier response (*Histories* 6.129–30). The story reflects a world in which a small cadre of great families from various cities vied with each other for status and standing—no laughing matter. Many of the famous statues of young men and young women found on the Akropolis, for example, were dedications made by these aristocratic families competing with each other to glorify the young and beautiful sons and daughters of the elite (**6.1**; see p. 150).

In this world, Sparta and Athens represented two starkly different responses to the threat presented by aristocratic rivalry and stasis. While Sparta evolved toward a highly rigid, hierarchical system centered on the training of warriors, the suppression of dissent, and the maintaining of eunomia, or good order, developments in Athens followed a very different path. First came unification. In the seventh and sixth centuries BC, the city changed from a series of hamlets and villages scattered around the south side of the Akropolis to become a more unified urban agglomeration. (Confusingly, the term demos, or **deme**, refers both to these local communities and to the people of Athens as a whole.) The Athenians attributed this unification, or synoecism, to Theseus, but in common with many of the traditions involving semi-mythical founder-figures, there is little to support the truth of the claim.

6.1 Kore (Akr. 675), *c.* 520–510 BC. Marble, H: 55 cm (21⅝ in.)

Despite the emergence of this larger society, the basic unit of social life remained the oikos, or household. When listening to descriptions of the palace of Helen and Menelaus in performances of Homer's poetry, many families in the Archaic Age would still have recognized households not dissimilar to their own. The household included retainers and slaves as well as the family, and related households were aggregated into clans known as **gene** (singular: **genos**). Athenian men were usually part of other social groups: **phratries**, or "brotherhoods," were supposed to consist of men related by blood, although over time these ties may have been more fictive than real, just as today "frat brothers" are usually not actual brothers.

Other groups, known as ***thiasoi*** and ***orgeones***, were religious groups consisting of men bound by a shared cult, often sacrificing to local heroes about whom we know next to nothing.

All these corporate groups could own land and property, the result of which was a society in which individual men were implicated in complex networks of social engagement. As in other Archaic communities, most Athenian men were also members of a tribe, or ***phyle***, although the view that these were holdovers from an earlier stage of social development loses sight of the fact that these grew and changed along with the emerging city-states. Most of these aggregations were flexible and were capable of adapting to change.

Reconstructing life in the Archaic period in Athens is not easy, but there are signs of significant change and increasing social tension. One gruesome piece of evidence concerns the discovery of more than fifteen hundred graves in the Phaleron district of Athens. First uncovered one hundred years ago, the Phaleron cemetery was systematically excavated by the Greek Archaeological Service between AD 2012 and 2016. The excavations brought to light approximately eighty skeletons from the third quarter of the seventh century BC; of these, thirty-six were buried with their arms shackled (**6.2**). Thucydides recounts details of an attempt by the Athenian Kylon who attempted to establish himself as tyrant in 632 BC, but whose

6.3 (top) Athenian tetradrachm, an example of Wappenmünzen, or heraldic coinage, c. 515 BC. Silver. 16.98 grams

6.4 (bottom) Aiginetan "Turtle," (silver stater), c. 530–525 BC. Silver, 12.3 grams

supporters were subsequently butchered by the Athenians. The Greek excavators of the site have tentatively proposed that the Phaleron skeletons are the supporters of Kylon; whether or not the excavators are correct, the skeletons still testify to a violent episode in the history of Athens.

One cause of tumult affecting Archaic Athens may have been the introduction of coinage and the consequent changes in the economy. While Sparta rejected the use of coins, many other Greek states adopted the practice from Anatolia, where electrum coins were produced as early as 600 BC. The Athenians began minting coins sometime around the middle of the sixth century. The earliest Athenian coins appear to be decorated with heraldic blazons and are known as ***Wappenmünzen*** ("Heraldic Coins"), although the precise associations of many of the devices are unclear (**6.3**). (One compelling theory is that these blazons represented the leading families of Athens.) Communities would soon start to assert their separate identities through their coins: the people of Aigina used "turtles," appropriate given the island's maritime trade (**6.4**), while Corinth fixed on the mythical figure of Pegasus to serve as their emblem. By the end of the sixth century the Athenians had settled on the owl, Athena's symbol, to stand for Athens.

The beginning of a monetized economy, in which wealth could be measured not just in sheaves of wheat or amphorae of wine but also in gold and silver, caused alarm in many circles. The sixth-century-BC poet, Theognis of Megara, summed up these anxieties:

Many bad men are wealthy, and many
    good men are poor;
But we shall not exchange with them
Our goodness for their wealth, because
    the one is sure forever,
While money belongs to different men
    at different times.

(Theognis, *Elegies* 1.315–18
[=Solon fr. 15], trans. Miller)

The antagonism between virtue (often equated with aristocratic birth) and wealth is a common theme in Archaic poetry, and suggests that, for many, society appeared to be undergoing a very unwelcome transition. Typically, elegiac poets treated this as a matter of moral decline, but occasionally they hinted at political breakdown as well. Theognis, for example, saw his city on the brink of collapse. In a poem addressed to his lover, Kyrnos, he complains:

Kyrnos, this city is pregnant, and I fear
    that it may give birth to a man
Who will chastise and correct our wicked
    arrogance.
For though the citizens are still of sound
    mind, their leaders
Are on a fixed course to fall into great
    wickedness.

                  (*Elegies* 1.39–42, trans. Miller)

The "Corrector" he feared was a man who would emerge from civil chaos and take control of the city on his own: a tyrant in the shape of Kypselos of Corinth or Pittakos of Mytilene. In another poem, Theognis makes an impassioned plea against the prospect of tyranny:

Once base men set their hearts on things
    like these,
Gains that come with hurt to the people,
From these things come factions (*stasis*),
    the internecine slaughter of men,
And tyrants. May they never be pleasing
    to *this* city!

                  (*Elegies* 1.49–52, trans. Miller)

The Rule of Law

One response to the threat of stasis was to emphasize the rule of law. It is not a coincidence that many communities in the Archaic period set about replacing the customary law administered by elders and priests, which had been the hallmark of earlier communities, and devised the first written legal codes in the Greek world. In some cases—such as Zaleukos of Epizephyrian Lokri, Charondas of Katania, and Lykourgos in Sparta—the lawgivers responsible for these codes are semi-legendary and little is known about them that is not apocryphal. In most stories, for example, the lawgiver is called in to settle civil strife but his commitment to his own code is tested, as in the case of Charondas, who realizes he has absentmindedly entered the marketplace with a dagger, thereby violating his own laws. (To maintain the law, Charondas stabs himself.) In one intriguing

instance, however, we have not only the lawgiver, but also one of his laws. In the late seventh century BC, the Athenian lawgiver Drako promulgated a law on homicide that was reinscribed on stone in 409 BC. By this date the Athenians had instituted quite sophisticated procedures for dealing with a variety of legal situations, from disputes over property to the impeachment of public officials, but in the case of homicide they chose to stick to an arcane and antiquated procedure, expressed in language difficult to understand; the inscription therefore is evidence of the Athenians' respect for this important document of (for them) high antiquity. The preserved section of the law reads as follows:

First axon.

Even if someone kills someone else not from forethought, he shall be exiled. The kings shall pronounce responsible for homicide [the one who himself killed or the one?] who planned it; the ***ephetai*** shall decide it. There shall be reconciliation, if there are a father or brother or sons, to be granted by all, or the objector shall prevail. If these do not exist, then as far as cousinhood and cousin, if they are all willing to grant reconciliation, or the objector shall prevail. If none of these exists but he killed unintentionally and the fifty-one ephetai decide that he killed unintentionally, let ten members of the phratry allow him to enter if they are willing: let these be chosen by the fifty-one on the basis of their excellence. And those who killed previously shall be liable to this ordinance. There shall be a proclamation against the killer in the agora by those as far as cousinhood and cousin; there shall join in the prosecution cousins and cousins' sons and brothers-in-law and fathers-in-law and phratry members...is responsible for homicide...the fifty-one...convict of homicide.... If anybody kills a killer, or is responsible for his being killed, when he is keeping away from a frontier market and Amphiktyonic contests and rites, he shall be liable to the same things as for killing an Athenian; the appeal judges shall decide...he is a free man. And if he kills a man by defending immediately when the man is forcibly and unjustly taking and removing, that man shall have been killed without penalty...

        (*IG* I³ 104, trans. Lambert and Rhodes, adapted)

This inscription gives us a glimpse of how the early Athenian community practiced law. It is striking, for example, that the procedure seems to envisage the kings acting as prosecutors and the judges confirming the denunciation, presumably after an investigation or appeal by the killer. The victim's family plays a critical role in deciding the case. If they agree, then a compromise can be worked out; if not, the decision stands. So powerful is the pressure to reach a settlement that the law also envisages the involvement of a larger social group, the phratry, which is supposed to act on behalf of the victim if there are no family members to speak for him. It would be fair to conclude that the law on homicide is profoundly concerned with restoring equilibrium and making sure that as many of the people affected as possible should play a role in resolving the disruption caused by homicide. This is not the same as vengeance, and if the mechanisms seem to us weak (no professional prosecutors or defenders; no select juries of peers; few laws spelled out in detail; no details of how investigations were to be conducted), it is worth remembering that, for societies undergoing the transition from face-to-face communities to larger and more complex stages of development, judicial institutions may be as fragile and vulnerable as the people they serve.

This was certainly the case in Athens in the early years of the sixth century BC. Aristotle, in his work *The Athenian Constitution* (the *Athenaion Politeia*, a short history of early Athens probably compiled by one of his students), lists 595–594 BC as a year of stasis, or upheaval, and 590–589 BC as a year of **anarchia** (that is, a time of "no archon," or ruler), again because of civil turmoil. In the midst of these unsettled conditions, in 594 the Athenians elected Solon as archon, with a mandate to address the strife afflicting Athens. Solon saw the issue as primarily a question of economic malaise. Too many Athenians had fallen into debt-bondage as a result of a system of tenant farming in which they paid a percentage of their produce, probably one-sixth, to the owners of the land they worked. These **hektemoroi** ("one-sixth men"), as the tenants were known, were vulnerable. Crop failures, marginal land, famine, drought, or sickness—all of which were not uncommon in the ancient Mediterranean—could drive them so far into debt that many ended up losing their livelihood, their land, and, in the worst instances, being sold into slavery. Solon's solution was to cancel debts, an event known as the **Seisachtheia**, or "Shaking off of Burdens." Details are murky; one source, for

example, thought that debts were merely lowered, not cancelled, and our best sources, Aristotle and Plutarch, wrote hundreds of years after these events, but Solon's own poems reveal the broad outlines of the crisis:

Of all the purposes for which I gathered the
　　demos together,
which of them had I not achieved when I quit?
On this point the greatest mother of the
Olympian spirits, black Earth, might best bear
witness in the court of Time, she from whom I once
lifted the boundary stones that had been fixed
　　everywhere:
before she was in slavery, now she is free.
And many Athenians sold into slavery—some
　　justly, some not—
did I bring home to their god-founded land,
　　while others,
having fled their debts under Necessity's
　　compulsion, no longer
spoke the Attic tongue (since they wandered
　　to all parts of the earth),
and others here, bound in shameful servitude
　　and trembling before the harsh
character of their masters, I set free. I achieved
　　these things,
forcefully yoking force and justice together,
and I proceeded on the course that I had promised.

(Solon, fr. 36, trans. Porter)

It is important to keep in mind that Solon's poems are not a journalistic account of economic reforms, and also that the poems rely heavily on metaphorical language. The poems are not a blueprint for political action, but instead reflect the mindset of the lawgiver whose primary intention was to find a cure for the stasis afflicting Athens. Along with Theognis of Megara, he comes from a tradition of wisdom poetry—a genre well established in the ancient Near East—that places a heavy emphasis on justice and moderation, so that most of his poetry is concerned with the moral quandaries posed by wealth and poverty. Even allowing, however, for the requirements of the genre in which he writes, the broad issues seem clear: land was encumbered by debt and those who could not repay their mortgages (i.e. the loans they had secured on their land) were in dire straits. Some had fled Attica and others had been

6.5 Athenian (Attic) Geometric chest with five model "granaries" on the lid, mid-ninth century BC. If the five cone-shaped objects represent granaries, they may refer to the buried woman's status as a member of the pentekosiomedimnoi. H: 25 cm (10 in.)

sold into slavery. With little hard evidence to support this bleak picture, it is tempting to dismiss Solon's claims as poetic exaggeration, but were his poems a complete fabrication they would have struck his contemporaries as very odd indeed.

Solon's Social Reforms

Nevertheless, despite Solon's efforts, economic reform was not immediately successful. The wealthy felt he had gone too far; the poor felt he had not gone far enough. As Solon himself wrote in one poem, "In undertakings of great import, it is difficult to please all" (Solon fr. 7). Unrest continued after Solon's term as archon had ended, and (under circumstances still largely opaque) around 592–591 BC he was called upon to serve as archon a second time. In his second term he introduced a series of reforms, both economic and constitutional, that would have profound effects on the future development of Athens. To begin with, the Athenians were subjected to a census, and were divided into four classes based on the amount of produce yielded by their land:

Pentekosiomedimnoi	> 500 measures
Hippeis	> 300
Zeugitai	> 200
Thetes	< 200

The measure referred to here is the Attic *medimnos*, equivalent to approximately 52½ liters (14 US gallons). At the upper end of the scale were *Hippeis*, or Knights, cavalrymen whose wealth was sufficient for them to be able to afford horses. Next came the *Zeugitai*, or yokemen, farmers who could afford a pair of oxen. At the bottom were *Thetes*, the poorest class, who were subsistence farmers. Notably, members of the very top class were not referred to by a label suggesting their social status but were dubbed the *Pentekosiomedimnoi*, or "500-measure men," a term that refers specifically to their measure of wealth. They were the super-rich, and the uniqueness of their name suggests that this was probably a new designation coined by Solon, although the existence of chests with five model granaries on the lid in burials going back to the mid-ninth century BC has been taken by some as an indication that the Athenians were already employing this category at that time (**6.5**).

The significance of the census system is that eligibility for the archonship was specifically tied to the top two census classes, and that all classes were permitted to attend the popular assembly. Although aristocratic privilege had not been swept away, birth was no longer the sole or even major criterion for access to office. It is worth asking what principles guided this reform: were they designed to curb the powers of the aristoi? Or was the Solonian arrangement designed to secure aristocratic privilege by excluding the lower classes from top office? In fact, neither is at the heart of the matter. Solon established a set of arrangements that made political life predictable and orderly. In the short term that

would prove an elusive goal, but in the long term it would make the rule of law secure and help Athens institute a stable democracy.

Solon's reforms went further. Recognizing that a guaranteed food supply was critical to the stability of the community, he banned the export of grain from Attica. In time Athens would grow dependent on foreign grain, but already in the early sixth century Solon had determined that self-sufficiency was desirable. Unable to export their wheat and barley, the Athenians would increasingly look to olive cultivation for export, and would become famous for this. Attempting to encourage a diversity of skills in the community, Solon also offered citizenship to foreign craftsmen who came to Athens. Recognizing that trade could increase prosperity, he compelled the Athenians to adopt Euboian weights and measures, a system widely used around the Aegean. Athenian coinage would come to be widely accepted, and the fact that it could easily be exchanged for other currencies minted on the same standard increased its value. In legal matters Solon instituted a formal distinction between public and private law, making it simpler for both magistrates and those who had recourse to the courts to know how cases should be managed. Finally, although this is not certain, some sources maintain that he was responsible for establishing a Council of Four Hundred to advise the Ekklesia, or Assembly, and prepare its agenda.

Taken together, the reforms are comprehensive. What is very clear is that they do not favor any of the traditional antagonists, and no interest group, as we might say, was given special treatment. Instead, the underlying principle that emerges time and again is a tendency toward moderation and consistency, making both government and economic activity rational, orderly, and, as far as possible, predictable.

Other areas of social life attracted Solon's attention. Later sources preserve scattered details of a series of laws dealing with the care of the weak and the disadvantaged: Solon believed that orphans and heiresses needed to be supported, and in the latter case, provided with dowries. Solon enacted laws guaranteeing that the archon would supervise these cases and ensure that kinsmen met their familial obligations. (These may be classified as laws promoting social cohesion.) Similarly, Solon implemented regulations that carefully circumscribed how the Athenians buried their dead (**6.6**). These regulations have recently been summarized by the Dutch scholar Josine Blok as follows:

1. The body must be laid out for burial (prothesis) within the house.
2. The funeral procession (ekphora) shall take place the next day before sunrise.
3. The corpse is to be adorned and buried with no more than three garments.
4. In the procession (ekphora) the men walk in front, and the women behind.
5. Only women over the age of sixty may enter the house of the dead person and participate in the ekphora, unless a relative closer than the degree of second cousin.
6. Mourners may not self-inflict wounds or grieve excessively.

7. No dirges or lamentations are permitted at the grave.
8. No ox sacrifice is permitted at the grave.
9. No grave is to be disturbed or used for a stranger's burial.
10. Deceased are to be mourned at the **Genesia** Festival.
11. No one is to speak ill of the dead.

Scholars have often suggested that this funerary legislation was designed to curb expenditure on conspicuous funeral ceremonies by aristocratic families, but this is not the central focus of the legislation. Instead, Solon appears to have put limitations on every kind of excess, from the number of shrouds and garments permitted to the corpse to limiting where, when, and how mourners could perform their dirges. Aristocratic funerals were opportunities for clans to celebrate their chiefs' rank and to assert publicly their status; funerary songs celebrating the dead might have been politically charged, so legislating against public performances may have served to curb yet another potential cause of strife in the early Athenian community. In the climate of factionalism that perpetually threatened stability, Solon's funerary legislation made sense.

Underpinning all of Solon's actions, from the Seisachtheia to the funerary laws, we find a consistent theme: capricious decisions, unpredictable policies, unstated laws, and vested interests represent a threat to the community. They undermine confidence and are a recipe for unrest, as events in many modern political crises have shown again and again. Solon has been revered at various times in history as the very model of the wise reformer, and the reputation is thoroughly deserved: he was probably the first Greek statesman to attempt a comprehensive constitutional and economic reform.

It is interesting to compare the career of the great Athenian lawgiver with his Spartan counterpart, Lykourgos. The latter is a shadowy figure whose story is shrouded in a veil of semi-divinity. His Rhetra, for example, is supposed to have been delivered to him by the Delphic oracle; in Sparta, as in quite a number of other Archaic states, the laws were seen as ultimately deriving from the will of heaven. In relatively weak states, religious authority gave laws their force. As a result, the Spartans forever attributed to Lykourgos the eunomia (good order) they associated with their society's legal apparatus. In Athens, by contrast, Solon was never viewed as semi-divine, and his laws were always regarded as very much his own invention. It is true that the Athenians did have a semi-mythical figure in the manner of Lykourgos, namely Drako (whose name, meaning "The Snake," suggests a connection with ancestor worship), but in later times it was reported that Solon had repealed all of Drako's laws except (as we have seen) the law on homicide. In other words, Solon was very much a flesh-and-blood character, whose laws were devised by human intelligence and intended as a compromise solution to human problems.

In this respect, Solon's law against tyranny is especially notable. According to this law, Solon prescribed as the punishment for anyone who tried to establish a tyranny the penalty of being declared ***atimos***. This denied the aspiring tyrant all rights of protection, so that they could be put to death by anyone without penalty. Yet the punishment could only be inflicted if the person had been prosecuted. In other words, even the protection of the state and the execution of persons guilty of treason were matters that were to be handled by due process of law. So great was Solon's belief in the power of the law that he enacted one last, extraordinary piece of legislation, the terms of which are recorded in the Aristotelian *The Athenian Constitution*: "When the city is in conflict, whoever takes up arms with neither side shall be disenfranchised and have no share in the city" (8.5).

A great deal of ink has been spilled trying to explain how the great mediator could enact a legislative ban on neutrality. Was he not condemning the Athenians to yet more stasis? The problem of interpretation is very real. Some scholars have tried to read the language figuratively, suggesting that he wanted citizens to be involved in the political processes of the state rather than watching from the sidelines, but another possibility is that the language of the law, unlike his poems, was meant to be taken literally. If everyone, rather than a few rowdy faction fighters, were compelled to take a side, the city would face only two possible outcomes: either complete civil war and the annihilation of the entire community, or a collective decision to refer their differences to the legal and political institutions of the state: the Assembly, the Council, and most especially the venerable court of the **Areopagus**. Only by guaranteeing that no one was above the law could he ensure that the law was above everyone.

Stasis and Tyranny after Solon

The fruit of Solon's labors, however, would be a long time coming. If he laid the foundation for Athenian prosperity of later years, the immediate aftermath of his rule was far less auspicious. Twice in the decade following his archonship the Athenians experienced such chaos that no archon was elected: the state of anarchy. Emerging from this period of stasis, Athens lurched toward tyranny. In 582–581 BC, an individual named Damasias was elected archon but refused to give up power until driven out in 580–579 BC. Some scholars, citing Solon's reforms, have seen the threat facing Athens in the early sixth century BC as a form of class warfare, in which the poorest class, comprised of subsistence farmers, chafed against the oppressive rule of the wealthiest landowners. Yet throughout the sixth century, the actual episodes of political violence known to us always involved competing clans and families, often associated with particular regions of Attica. Their goal, just as we saw in the case of Kypselos and the Bacchiads at Corinth (see Chapter 5, p. 126), was simple: power, in the hands of

6.7 *Pelike* depicting the apotheosis of Herakles, *c*. 410 BC. Ceramic, H: 43 cm (17 in.)

the family or its leader. Around 561, one such regional clan leader, Peisistratos, whose family hailed from the central coastal region of eastern Attica, made the first in a series of attempts to establish himself as tyrant of Athens. Herodotos maintains that Athens at this time was riven by strife between factional groups, namely the men of the coast (led by Megakles) and the men of the plain led by Lykourgos (who was, rather confusingly, not the Spartan lawgiver of the same name). Peisistratos, having formed a third faction, entered the Agora after tearing his clothes, and announced that his rivals had attacked him. He asked the Athenians to authorize the formation of a bodyguard consisting of club-bearers, whereupon he seized the Akropolis and set himself up as tyrant. As far-fetched as the story sounds, subsequent episodes in the saga of Peisistratos are even more bizarre. Expelled sometime later by the combined forces of his opponents, Peisistratos made a second attempt in 558 BC. Exploiting a disagreement between Megakles and Lykourgos, Peisistratos accepted an invitation from Megakles to marry his daughter. To bolster his standing among the Athenians, he hired a tall young woman, Phye, from outside Athens to dress in armor and to escort him in a chariot into Athens: the goddess Athena herself was bringing Peisistratos back. The story sounds ludicrous, but Peisistratos may have been relying on the heroic overtones of the episode: 44 percent of scenes on vases from Athens in the sixth century depict Herakles, and one of the most popular of these scenes was the apotheosis of the hero, when Athena herself escorted him into heaven in a chariot (**6.7**). But even this bit of political theater proved farcical: according to Herodotos, Peisistratos refused to have sex with his new wife "in the usual way." When Megakles found out he repudiated his new son-in-law and reconciled with his political enemies. Peisistratos escaped from Athens and spent the next ten years in the northern Aegean acquiring the means to raise a private army. He returned in 546 BC and defeated his enemies at the Battle of Pallene. He was now once and for all tyrant of Athens, and the city would be ruled by Peisistratos or his sons for nearly forty years.

The Legacy of Peisistratos

In later times the Athenians would venerate the men who liberated Athens from the tyrants, suggesting that democracy in the fifth century BC emphasized the differences between tyranny and the democratic rule of law in such a way as to validate democracy and discredit the tyrants, but the evidence from the period of Peisistratid rule tells a very different story. Peisistratos maintained laws and held elections every year. In this respect, the regularity and predictability necessary for prosperous development was enhanced, not undermined, by the tyranny. In modern times the successful democratization of many societies has followed the expansion of middle class prosperity. Viewed in this way, the Peisistratid tyranny may have done more to enhance the subsequent years of democratic government than any of the reforms of Solon. Peisistratos, for example, appointed rural magistrates, making it possible for citizens to engage in litigation without having to travel to and from the city center, a burden that favored the rich. He made loans to the poor at low interest and introduced a 5 percent tax on produce. For a state emerging from the chaos of clan warfare, such taxation set public finances on a firm footing, as did his expansion of silver mining both in Attic territory at Laureion and in the northern Aegean at Mount Pangaion.

In common with other tyrants, Peisistratos also used capital works both to enhance the city's infrastructure and to give work to craftsmen and laborers. To this end he embarked on a building program in Athens. The Agora, located north of the Akropolis, was now for the first time clearly articulated as public space (previously the area had been used for burials and private habitation). The boundaries of the Agora were indicated by stelai (known as **horos** inscriptions) that were engraved with the words, "I am the boundary (horos) of the Agora," indicating that the area had now been set apart as the new public space at the heart of Athenian life (**6.8.**)

Another important Peisistratid construction was an outdoor shrine to the twelve gods in the northwest corner of the Agora. The origins of this sanctuary are recounted by Thucydides, who notes, "Amongst those of the Peisistratids who held the annual magistracy at Athens was Peisistratos, son of Hippias the tyrant [named after his grandfather], who during his archonship set up the Altar of the Twelve Gods in the Agora and the Altar of Apollo in the shrine of Apollo Pythios" (*The Peloponnesian War* 6.54.6–7). But along with other Peisistratid benefactions to Athens, the tyrannical associations of the monument were

6.8 Boundary stone of the Athenian Agora

later effaced: the inscription that explained that Peisistratos had erected the altar was covered up by the new democracy. Thereafter, inscriptions giving the distances from the altar mentioned only the city, not the Peisistratids. One such road sign reads: "The city set me up, a truthful monument to show all mortals the measure of their journeying: the distance to the altar of the Twelve Gods from the harbor is forty-five stades" (*IG* 1³ 1092 bis).

The older Peisistratos was also responsible for beginning work on the Temple of Olympian Zeus southeast of the Akropolis, although the work was never completed under the tyrants and was still half-finished when the Roman emperor Hadrian revitalized the project in the second century AD. Peisistratos or his sons were also responsible for the building of a fountain house in the southeast corner of the Agora called the ***Enneakrounos***, supplying the area with a reliable source of water. On the Akropolis, although the precise chronology of the sixth-century-BC buildings remains controversial, a number of buildings and precincts can be attributed to the Peisistratids. Notable among these is a sanctuary dedicated to Brauronian Artemis, a

6.9 Pedimental sculpture group, c. 550–540 BC, from either the Old Temple of Athena or the Hekatompedon, built on the site of the later Parthenon. The monster usually known as Bluebeard has three human torsos that meet in a triple-twisted snake tail. The figures appear to hold representations of the elements: water, fire and a bird (air). Limestone, W: 3.25 m (10 ft 8 in.), H: 0.78 m (2 ft 7 in.)

sacred precinct on the Akropolis that essentially duplicates the sanctuary to the same goddess in the traditional Peisistratid territory of Brauron. In addition, an early temple to Athena, in which was displayed the cult statue of the goddess, was built in the middle of the Akropolis. (The foundations of this temple are still to be seen between the Erechtheion and the Parthenon, and even after the Persian sack of Athens in 480 BC, a part of this temple, referred to in inscriptions of the time as the **Archaios Naos**, or Old Temple, still stood.) Pedimental sculpture (**6.9**) also survives from the middle of the sixth century BC, probably associated with a monumental temple called the Hekatompedon ("The Hundred Footer") that stood either where the Old Athena Temple was later erected, or a short distance to the south where the Parthenon was later built. Along with the hundreds of statues and dedications made on the Akropolis, these sacred buildings are dramatic proof of the transformation of the Acropolis under Peisistratos and his sons.

Aside from the Peisistratid buildings in the Agora and on the Akropolis, Peisistratos's expansion of such festivals as the **Dionysia** and **Panathenaia** were also important accomplishments. The Panathenaia in particular helped to foster a growing sense of Athenian identity: it was, as the name suggests, an "All-Athens" celebration commemorating Athena's victory over the Giants in the cosmic conflicts that came before the Olympian order was established. Celebrated every four years with special grandeur as the Greater Panathenaia and in other years as the Lesser Panathenaia, it was open to all citizens of Attica. Regardless of the region of their origin, whether the plain, the coast, or the city, they were all **Athenaioi**: Athenians. The Panathenaia included a procession through the heart of the city and on up to the Akropolis. Hundreds of Athenians took part in the grand procession as marshals, water carriers, weavers, cavalrymen, and wranglers while the rest looked on. The culmination of the procession was the presentation of a new robe, or **peplos**, to the goddess. Once the cattle had been led up to the Akropolis they were sacrificed on a massive scale and their meat distributed to the thousands of families who had participated. It was an occasion to celebrate the cohesion of the Athenian community.

Drawing on smaller festivals from the Peisistratid territory of Brauron, Peisistratos expanded the

Panathenaia to include both musical and athletic contests. Details of the musical contests in the sixth century BC are scarce, but by the fourth century, the musical contests included five separate categories. The first was rhapsodic performance, which consisted of recitations of the Homeric poems by poets, who were known as **rhapsodes**. A number of passing references to Athens, all favorable, are scattered through the *Iliad* and the *Odyssey*, and even in antiquity there was serious debate over whether or not Homer's epics had been largely shaped by this so-called Peisistratid recension. If it is true that the performances at the Panathenaia served as a filter, establishing which episodes were retained and which others were dropped, then Peisistratos's importance, not only for the history of Athens but also for the reception of epic, cannot be overestimated. The second and third categories were singing performances accompanied by the **kithara** and **aulos** respectively, instruments similar to guitars and flutes. The fourth and fifth categories were instrumental performances of the kithara and aulos. We still possess inscriptional records for these contests and know that prizes were awarded in the kithara contest for the first five places. (First prize was a gold crown worth 1,000 drachmas, approximately the equivalent of three years' wages for a skilled workman.) In time, the Panathenaia would come to rival the panhellenic games at Olympia, Delphi, Nemea, and Isthmia, and would advertise the status of Athens as the premier cultural center of the Greek world. In athletics, too, the Athenians fashioned the Panathenaia as a rival to the games held at the panhellenic festivals. Events included the stadion, pentathlon, wrestling, boxing, and pankration. For men, there were also the middle-distance races, the diaulos and the dolichos. The **hoplites**, a race in full armor, added a martial tone to the athletic contests and was in keeping with the festival's theme: the defeat of the Giants. The Panathenaia was also distinctive for offering valuable prizes in addition to crowns. Oil from the olive trees sacred to Athena was packed in distinctive Panathenaic amphorae and given to winners, who could either keep the oil or sell it (**6.10**). By the fourth century BC, 1,450 of these amphorae of Athena's oil were being given as prizes at each festival, with the oil worth about 6 drachmas per amphora. At today's rates, the total value of prizes for athletics was well over $500,000.

It is important to recognize that the Panathenaia grew over time and that the evidence for the festival in Plato and Aristotle's day cannot be applied directly to the early days of the festival, but it is clear that by promoting the event that was the single most significant celebration of Athenian identity, Peisistratos paved the way for the egalitarian ethos and cohesive community that made democracy possible. Athens in the sixth century BC was a vibrant community and, thanks to Peisistratos, a stable one. With this growing confidence and prosperity also came a new assertiveness overseas. While Peisistratos conducted peaceful relations with other tyrants, such as Lygdamis of Naxos and Polykrates of Samos, he also annexed the island of Delos, thereby bringing the most important sanctuary in the Aegean firmly under Athenian control.

The Fall of Tyranny in Athens

After his death in 528 BC, Peisistratos was succeeded by his sons, Hippias and Hipparchos, who ruled until 514. In that year Hipparchos was assassinated as the Athenians were preparing to celebrate the Panathenaia. Accounts in the fifth century speculated that the assassination arose from a lovers' quarrel. According to the version recounted by Thucydides, for example, Hipparchos made sexual overtures toward an Athenian aristocrat named Harmodios and was rejected. To spite him, Hipparchos then banned Harmodios's sister from serving in a position of honor at a festival. To avenge this slight, Harmodios and his older lover Aristogeiton waited till the next Panathenaia, when they could assemble under arms without causing suspicion. Seeing one of their fellow conspirators talking to Hippias, they panicked and slaughtered the first of the Peisistratids they encountered: Hipparchos. Harmodios was killed on the spot and Aristogeiton was executed. Hippias ruled in increasingly autocratic fashion for four more years until he was driven from the city by the Spartans and an Athenian clan that claimed to have been in exile under the tyrants, the Alkmaionidai. Eventually Hippias reached the court of the Persian king, where he would serve as an advisor to Darius leading up to the Persian invasion of Greece in 490. In the years after the expulsion of the tyrants, the Athenians would celebrate the deeds of the tyrannicides, Harmodios and Aristogeiton, and sang drinking songs in their honor:

I shall bear my sword in a branch of myrtle
Like Harmodios and Aristogeiton
When they killed the tyrant
And made Athens a place of equality before
   the law (*isonomia*)
                 (Athenaios, *Deipnosophistae* 15.50, trans. Fornara)

But the notion that the tyrannicides liberated an Athens ruled oppressively by the Peisistratids is an oversimplification. The Alkmaeonids and other noble families may have tried to distance themselves from the tyrants in the waning years of Hippias's reign, but before this final phase there is evidence of collaboration and cooperation between the great aristocratic families and the tyrants. The American excavator, Benjamin Meritt, published a fragmentary inscription from the Athenian Agora in AD 1939 that cast the last years of the Peisistratid era in a new light. Fragment C of the inscription reads as follows:

[On]eto[rides]	(527/6)
[H]ippia[s]	(526/5)
[K]leisthen[es]	(525/4)
[M]iltiades	(524/3)
[K]alliades	(523/2)
[...]strat[os]	(522/1)
	(ML 6, trans. McInerney)

The inscription is a copy of the Athenian archon list, and Fragment C covers the years immediately after the death of Peisistratos in 528–527 BC. As the inscription clearly shows, the heads of leading families, such as Kleisthenes of the Alkmaionidai and Miltiades of the Philaidai, were in Athens and holding the office of archon, no doubt with the approval of Hippias, who had inherited his father's position as tyrant.

Kleisthenes and the Foundation of Democracy

In the aftermath of Hippias's expulsion, civil strife once again threatened to engulf Athens. Just as in recent times the removal of an autocrat has sometimes fueled sectarian violence, so in Athens, the old regional, aristocratic factions reemerged and the city faced a return to the clan-based political violence that had afflicted it in the time of Solon. How the Athenians avoided this was largely thanks to the genius of a single man, Kleisthenes, head of the Alkmaionid clan. Herodotos describes how Kleisthenes made a pact with the people in exchange for power:

Athens had been a powerful state before, but after the expulsion of the tyrants it became even more so. Two men were preeminent at this time: Kleisthenes and Isagoras. A struggle for power broke out between the two of them. As he was being beaten Kleisthenes turned to the common people and made an alliance with them. Previously the Athenians had had four tribes, but now he changed these for ten new tribes.
                 (Herodotos, *Histories* 5.66.1–2,
                 adapted, trans. McInerney)

Behind this simple description lies a complex story of the institutional origins of Athenian democracy. As near as we can tell, Kleisthenes found himself on the losing side of a traditional aristocratic faction fight, but instead of resorting to violence or duplicity he made a direct appeal to the Athenian demos. Herodotos's actual words are that "he took the people into his political club," which can only mean that, for the first time, a politician appealed directly to the community of Athenian citizens rather than to an alliance of other aristocratic chiefs. Recognizing that the general population was eager to participate in political life and to avoid a return to the old ways, he proposed a comprehensive and systematic reform of the Athenian tribal and electoral system. Where there had been four tribes, dominated by powerful families whose influence was strongest in particular regions, Kleisthenes proposed a complex system that broke up many of the old regional power-clusters. The electoral map of Attica, so to speak, was redrawn. (See the Spotlight section, p. 168.) The new system fixed every Athenian male citizen to the deme (the community, town, or village) where he was born. He could move and own land elsewhere, but the deme remained his place of registration. At the time of Kleisthenes' reforms there were 139 of these demes, some large, such as Acharnai, and some small, such as Probalinthos. The small ones were aggregated into clusters and treated as a single unit. Each cluster—whether of one, two, or more demes—comprised what was called a **trittys** (pl. **trittyes**), meaning "a third," so called because all ten tribes were made up of three "thirds": one from the city, one from the plain, and one from the coast.

The ten tribes so constituted were fundamental to the political and military life of Athens. The army mustered by tribes, and many of the trittyes were located so that demesmen from the countryside could quickly get to Athens and join their fellow tribesmen from the city. Similarly, the new Council of Five Hundred, which drew up the agenda of the Assembly and oversaw the day-to-day running of the state, was composed of ten units of fifty councillors; each unit, once again, representing and being selected from one tribe. Throughout the following centuries of Athenian greatness and long into the periods of Macedonian and Roman domination that followed, the basic political map created by Kleisthenes endured, as did the institutions (notably the Council) that were an outgrowth of the system of tribes and trittyes.

It is important to emphasize the oddity and the complexity of the Kleisthenic system because understanding his intentions has been the source of endless argument among historians. Some scholars have argued, for example, that the Kleisthenic system was a kind of gerrymandering by which demes dominated by Alkmaionid families were seeded throughout a number of trittyes, and therefore across the tribes. In this way, runs the argument, Alkmaionid influence would exert itself not in one tribe but in three or four. The evidence for this, however, is slight, and it is possible that spreading Alkmaionid membership across several tribes would have had the opposite effect, dissipating Alkmaionid power instead of boosting it. Another interpretation emphasizes the military aspect of the reforms, and draws attention to the existence of a road network that would have facilitated the movement of tribal units from the demes to the center of Athens. This may have been part of Kleisthenes' plan, although the argument depends heavily on inferring Kleisthenes' intentions from the consequences of his reforms. It is not clear, for example, why Kleisthenes should have promulgated such complex internal reforms during a time of upheaval if he was actually concerned with long-term military readiness, an issue that presumably was more pressing when a foreign foe loomed.

What can be said with the greatest confidence is that local and regional rivalries had been the bane of Athens for a century, and that Kleisthenes' reforms addressed that problem directly. By separating demes from their neighbors, Kleisthenes made it harder for the established aristocratic families to organize block votes of their dependents. Consider the deme of Philaidai, for example. This deme takes its name from the powerful family of the same name, the family of Miltiades and Kimon, yet we know that the ancestral territory of that family was on the western side of the city of Athens, at Lakiadai, while the deme named Philaidai by Kleisthenes had formerly been the Peisistratid stronghold of Brauron, far to the east of the city. As a result of the reforms the deme was cut adrift. It was not strongly connected to the family of Miltiades and Kimon, and at the same time, Peisistratid influence in the wider area around Brauron was also weakened. Their sphere of influence would have extended to the neighboring demes of Kytheros and Steiria, which were less than 5 kilometers (3 mi.) away, but thanks to the Kleisthenic reforms Philaidai was now allocated to the tribe Aigeis, while all of its nearest neighbors were placed in Pandionis. Controlling the votes of these neighboring demes as a bloc in tribal assemblies and elections was now impossible, because the local people of these demes assembled and voted in different tribal assemblies. Even in the general assembly of the entire demos, the ties between a regionally powerful clan and its neighbors would be weakened. In one notable case of artificially manipulated boundaries, an ancient religious agglomeration from the northeast of Attica, known as the Tetrapolis (comprised of the demes of Marathon, Trikorythos, Probalinthos, and Oinoe), was allowed to continue functioning as an independent religious union, sending its own embassies to Delphi, but Probalinthos was separated from the other demes in the new tribal structure. Oinoe, Trikorythos, and Marathon were placed in tribe 9 (Aiantis), while Probalinthos was paired with the city deme of tribe 3 (Pandionis). Whatever political strength the Tetrapolis had as a regional cluster was thus broken.

One way of understanding the novelty and importance of Kleisthenes' reforms is to study them from the bottom up. Stanford's Josiah Ober has examined the deme of Prasiai, a coastal deme in the tribe of Pandionis. Ober characterizes the deme, a face-to-face community in which most of the citizens would have known each other well, as an example of "the cliquish strong-tie local networks that characterized ordinary Athenian social life." But with the advent of the Kleisthenic reforms, in addition to those local ties, the men of Prasiai mustered alongside fellow members of the tribe of Pandionis from the inland demes and the city, men with whom they had previously had few, if any, connections. In addition to serving with them in the army, they participated together in tribal activities including religious festivals, sacrifices, and feasts, and voted with them in tribal assemblies. Ober emphasizes the effect of this intermingling: "The system very literally 'inter-mixed' Athenians from different geographic/economic zones in a variety of psychologically powerful activities. Over time, the experience of marching, fighting, sacrificing, eating, and dancing together in this newly 'inter-mixed' grouping would, according to Kleisthenes' plan, lead to a strengthened collective identity at the level of the polis."

Kleisthenes disappears from history soon after instituting this system, but not before it was severely challenged. Isagoras, in perhaps the last gasp of the old aristocratic rivalries of the Archaic Age, called upon the Spartans to remove Kleisthenes, dismantle the Kleisthenic system, and disband the Council of Five Hundred. Kleisthenes slipped out of Athens, and (if Herodotos is correct) a total of seven hundred families were banished as well, but then a momentous event occurred: the Athenians rose up and besieged the Spartan king, Kleomenes, for three days on the Akropolis. The Spartans sued for terms and were permitted to leave Athens along with Isagoras. Kleomenes made one more attempt to invade Attica and avenge his ignominious defeat, but his army was riven by dissent and eventually dispersed. The Athenians, meanwhile, fought and won a series of battles against the neighboring Boiotians and Chalcidians. They dedicated the spoils of war on the Akropolis, and from the ransom paid by their prisoners they erected a bronze four-horse chariot beside the entrance to the Propylaia.

Ostracism

One last reform of the Athenian political system that is commonly attributed to Kleisthenes deserves mention. This was the practice of **ostracism**, a process by which the Athenians could expel a leading figure for ten years. The man ostracized did not lose his citizenship or his property; he was simply expected to quit the city and to stay away for ten years. The institution was designed to identify prominent men who might become tyrants, and the details of the

6.11 Ostraka, early fifth century BC. Terra-cotta, maximum dimesions 7–10 cm (3–4 in.)

ostracism process reveal how quickly democratic procedure had become ingrained in Athenian society. In the middle of the winter, during the sixth month of the civic year, the Assembly held a simple vote on whether or not the people wished to hold an ostracism. If the answer was yes, then two months later the ostracism proper was held. There is some confusion in the ancient sources about what came next. We know that citizens voted by scratching the name of the person they wanted to ostracize on a piece of broken pottery (an **ostrakon** in Greek; **6.11**), but it is not clear whether there needed to be a quorum of 6,000 votes to make the vote valid—in which case the name with the most votes lost—or if 6,000 was the minimum number of votes that the losing name had to have. In either scenario the procedure was not cavalier: impetuous decisions were avoided by inserting a gap between the first and second vote, and the fact that the Athenians did not resort to ostracism every year also reveals that they only used this safety valve when there was a good deal of apprehension about an individual. Between 487 and 415 BC, for example, only about thirteen men were ostracized.

The early recorded instances of ostracism—of Hipparchos son of Charmos, a Peisistratid, in 487 BC, and of Megakles, nephew of Kleisthenes, in 486 BC—both suggest that the demos was wary of the sort of big men whose conflicting ambitions had caused such unrest in the previous century. Moreover, these ostracisms came at a time when Athens had just survived the Persian landing at Marathon, where the exiled tyrant Hippias had served as a guide for the Persians, doubtless in the expectation that he would be reinstalled as tyrant if the Persians were successful. Nor had the Persian threat been decisively defeated at Marathon: by the end of the same decade Darius's successor, Xerxes, would assemble a vast army and descend on Greece by land and sea. The Athenians' desire to protect their young democracy from subversion and treachery was therefore entirely understandable. The threats they faced were real.

Some scholars have been troubled by the fact that the first recorded ostracism did not occur until twenty years after Kleisthenes' other reforms were enacted, and have therefore speculated that the institution was set in place after Kleisthenes. We may never know for certain whether ostracism was a Kleisthenic invention, but it should be remembered that the years around 500 BC are not well recorded: we do not know, for example, when or under what circumstances Kleisthenes died. It is possible that there was an ostracism before that of Hipparchos son of Charmos, or that the procedure was introduced by Kleisthenes in around 508 but underwent further refinements in the following years. Whatever the case, such leading politicians as Xanthippos (the father of Perikles) and Kimon (the son of Miltiades) were both ostracized during their lifetimes. Given the aristocratic temper of Athenian politics in the Archaic period, ostracism was a valuable tool for inhibiting the otherwise unbridled ambitions of men who might be aiming at tyranny. After all, Kimon's father, Miltiades, had ruled as tyrant in the Thracian Chersonese and had helped the Persians in their first forays into European territory, so the fear that the next generation might also harbor similar aspirations was not unreasonable. Ostracism is also interesting in that it shows the democracy using a similar strategy to that employed by tyrants against those who threatened their supremacy. In a well-known story the tyrant Thrasyboulos, when asked how he secured his rule, walked through a field of wheat chopping off the heads of the tallest stalks, grimly illustrating the principle that tyrants must not tolerate rivals. Adopting a similar attitude, but a gentler practice, toward the tall poppies in their midst, the Athenians of the fifth century would avert the danger of tyranny.

Whether or not the institution of ostracism can be attributed to Kleisthenes, his importance in the history of Athens and the development of democracy is second to none. His career, however, also raises a question. As we look back to the tumultuous history of Athens between 600 and 500 BC, should we see democracy as the culmination of a century of gradual legal and institutional reform, beginning with Solon and culminating in the complicated electoral map of Attica created by Kleisthenes? Or should we see democracy as the institutional face of a prosperous, stable, egalitarian society that was the legacy of a generation of Peisistratid rule? In modern times, Western states have championed the holding of elections in such states as Iraq and Afghanistan as proof that nation-building and democratic institutions can work anywhere, but if the Athenians tell us anything, it is surely that steady, sustained economic growth and prosperity, and a commitment to the rule of law, are the foundations on which democracy is built. In Athens, however, in the generation after Kleisthenes, such questions would become entirely academic, as the Athenians faced an altogether more pressing threat: the Persian invasions.

The Political Reforms of Kleisthenes

To appreciate how complex the system of Kleisthenes was, consider this map of Attica, showing the demes and trittyes of the ten tribes (**6.12**).

The basic unit of the political map is the deme, a community that might be as small as a hamlet consisting of a few houses, or could be as large a township, such as Acharnai, which rivaled downtown Athens itself. The demes whose locations are reasonably well known are indicated on the map as circles. They were organized by Kleisthenes into clusters, shown on the map by the lines that join various demes into a larger unit. As mentioned above, these aggregate clusters were known as trittyes, or "thirds," because each of the ten new tribes comprised three such clusters: a trittys from the coastal zone, a trittys from the inland zone, and a trittys from the **asty**, downtown Athens. Taken together, then, the map illustrates how every town, big and small, across all of Attica, was incorporated into a complex system of thirty trittyes that constituted ten tribes.

The map depicting these units also helps us to see how the trittyes fitted together. Trittyes from the same tribe are shown in the same color, so that one can quickly see, for example, the location of the coastal trittys of Tribe 1, Erechtheis, shown in red. One can also see the demes clustered on the southeastern side of the city that constituted the asty trittys of the same tribe, once again shown in red. Finally, one can see another cluster of demes north of the city, which together formed the inland third of the same tribe.

The numbers inside the circles refer to the bouleutic representation of the deme, that is, the number of councillors that the community needed to supply every year to serve on the Council (or Boulê). The Kleisthenic Council numbered five hundred, but can be thought of as consisting of ten tribal contingents of fifty men each, serving for one-tenth of the year. Deme quotas must have broadly equated with population: large demes, high quotas; small demes, low quotas. We can imagine the system in action if we look at one tribe as an example. Take the second tribe, known as Aigeis, shown on the map in yellow. The tribe's three trittyes had to supply fifty councillors every year. The tribe had a city trittys that comprised a number of small demes, one within the city walls at Kollytos (with a bouleutic quota of three), then a cluster of demes just outside the city walls in an arc that ran around the northeast edge of the city, from Diomeia and Upper and Lower Ankyle to Kolomos. Together their quotas add up to twelve, but add councillors supplied by the inland demes of Ikarion and Plotheia, which were artificially artificially connected to the city trittys, and the quota of councilors for the trittys reaches an acceptable seventeen. If each trittys supplied sixteen or seventeen, then the tribe could meet its total quota of fifty.

This tribe's trittys of the plain was located around the northern spur of Mount Hymettos. Then, just beyond that region, the coastal trittys comprises a cluster of demes on the coast from Araphen up to Myrrhinoutta. In this way, Kleisthenes' system built on natural networks growing out of neighboring demes within regions, but also created networks of weaker affiliation between trittyes that often had no prior relationship and were not geographically contiguous. Aristotle was therefore correct when he observed that Kleisthenes' aim was "to intermix the residents of Athenian territory" (*Ath. Pol.* 21.2–3).

The massive complexity of the Kleisthenic plan has prompted, as we have seen, various explanations; for some it is a military reform, for others an assault on the regional factionalism that had bedeviled the Athenians for one hundred years. Recently, two experts in the field of management studies have used the language of business school to explain Kleisthenes' program:

Kleisthenes' tribal innovations represent, probably, the world's first formal matrix organization structure. Traditional geographic divisions were crossed with the new tribal project teams who came together for specific functions. The Athenian reformer sought benefits similar to those that managers today seek by employing such a structure: enhanced co-ordination, better communication and improved motivation and commitment, precisely the things that would be required of the new system if *demokratia* through unity was to be achieved.

(Cummings and Brocklesby, "Towards *demokratia* - myth and the management of organizational change in ancient Athens")

Although it is unlikely that Kleisthenes ever thought of demes as "tribal project teams" the comparison is a valuable one, since it draws attention both to the complexity

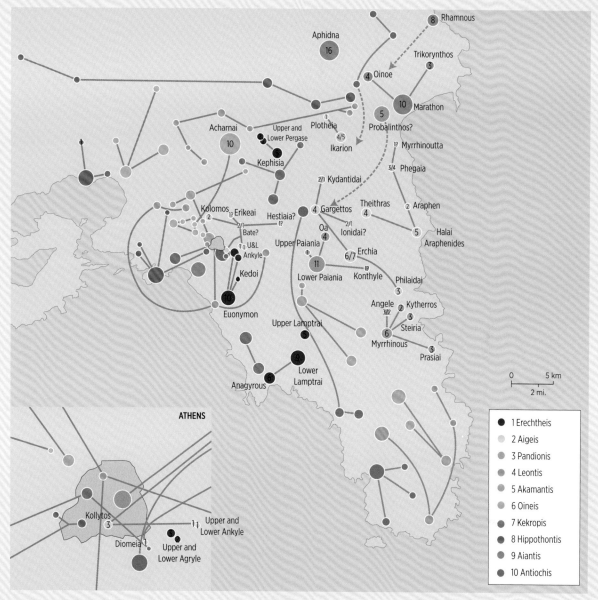

6.12 The political organization of Attica under Kleisthenes. Deme names and bouleutic quotas have been supplied for only a few tribes. In fact, every deme was integrated into the new Kleisthenic plan.

Legend:
- 1 Erechtheis
- 2 Aigeis
- 3 Pandionis
- 4 Leontis
- 5 Akamantis
- 6 Oineis
- 7 Kekropis
- 8 Hippothontis
- 9 Aiantis
- 10 Antiochis

and the undeniable intentionality of Kleisthenes' program, which was carefully and deliberately engineered. The question for historians is how much emphasis to place on the Kleisthenic system in explaining the origins and success of Athenian democracy. Can democracy be engineered by an elaborate set of institutions, or does it depend on a deeper, more fundamental commitment to such principals as equality and the rule of law? As Western societies continue to try to build nations and grow democracies in various parts of the world, these questions have taken on a new urgency: would we be better served aiming for economic justice and greater prosperity, instead of holding elections? Is the success of democracy the result of careful planning, or are the circumstance of its survival no more than a fluke?

r. 558–c. 530 BC
Cyrus the Great

r. c. 530–522 BC
Cambyses

r. 522–486 BC
Darius I

513 BC
Darius I crosses to Europe

499–493 BC
Ionian Revolt

Chapter 7

Persia

The story of the Persian Wars is a stirring tale of heroism and military courage, which, as we shall see, is illustrated by the various battles of Marathon, Thermopylae, Salamis, and Plataia. Furthermore, the Persian Wars were also hugely important for the Greeks' sense of their own cultural identity. But before we can assess the impact of the Persian Wars on the Greeks, it will be necessary to look at the Persians themselves. Only once we have a clearer sense of Persian culture and the Achaemenid dynasty that ruled Persia will we be able to evaluate the legacy of the Persian Wars. As we shall see, this would be a double-edged sword: on the one hand the defeat of the Persians ushered in a new era of cultural flowering in Athens—the Classical Age—but victory would come at a cost: the demonizing of the East, a cultural division that has recently assumed significance in the contemporary world.

Greece on the Eve of the Persian Wars

Athens, in common with other parts of Greece, underwent profound changes in the Archaic period. The rivalry of ambitious men, the introduction of coinage, and the disparities of wealth distribution brought hardship for some and enormous wealth for a few. In Athens the problem was especially acute for those who had lost their land and were reduced to debt-bondage. Along with many other states, the Athenians responded to the crises of the age by experimenting with various ways of establishing eunomia, or good order, in an attempt to break the cycle of stasis (civil disorder). First they appointed a special lawgiver, Solon, who set down a series of laws designed to ease tensions and avert further conflict, as did other lawgivers in Sparta, Lokris, and in Sicily. But despite Solon's reforms, the threat of tyranny was ever-present in Athens throughout the sixth century BC, and the city was, in fact, ruled by the family of the Peisistratids from 546 BC until the last tyrants were banished in 510 BC. It was in the shadow of the tyrants' banishment and the threat of a reversion to stasis that Kleisthenes managed to establish a fully participatory democracy. The system designed by Kleisthenes dispersed power as widely as possible through the demes and tribes of Athens. Power was not to be concentrated in the hands of one man or family, but spread evenly across the state. This democratic experiment came into being in 508 BC, but it very nearly died before the passing of the generation that instigated the reforms. In less than twenty years Athens was subject to a foreign invasion, and in less than thirty years Athens had been sacked by these same foreigners. And yet Athens retained its independence, as did the rest of Greece, and instead of becoming the western outpost of the Persian empire, the Greeks came to see themselves as the very antithesis of the Persians.

We have already seen that in the Bronze Age and even later into the Archaic period the people of Greece were very much a part of an eastern Mediterranean world that experienced significant cultural contact between Greeks, Phoenicians, Egyptians, Canaanites, and Hittites. In the centuries before the Classical Age, the Greeks traded and shared material culture with the other peoples of the eastern Mediterraenean in the form of precious objects in metal and ivory, as well as less tangible items: ideas, religious beliefs, poems, and songs. In that world, prior to the Persian Wars, the Greeks were aware of ethnic differences, but, leaving aside the indigenous people whose territories they colonized, they also recognized that the settled people from Ugarit or Lydia, or any of the other people whom they encountered in the Mediterranean world, lived in city-states not unlike those of Greece. In this polyglot world the Greeks primarily identified themselves as the people who spoke Greek, and thought of others who spoke roughly or thickly as "barbarians" (i.e. their speech sounded like babbling: "ba, ba, ba"). After the Persian Wars of the 480s BC, however, "barbarian" comes to mean something not just different, but inferior. The first-century-BC writer Strabo put it this way:

Accordingly, when all who pronounced words thickly were being called barbarians onomatopoetically, it appeared that the pronunciations of all alien races were likewise thick, I mean of those that were not Greek. Those, therefore, they called barbarians in the special sense of the term, at first derisively, meaning that they pronounced words thickly or harshly; and then we misused the word as a general ethnic term, thus making a logical distinction between the Greeks and all other races.

(Strabo, *Geography* 14.2.28, trans. Jones)

The victory of the Greeks would have both a positive and a negative side. The upside of the Greek victory over Persia was the enormous self-confidence of the Greeks, capable of building such majestic yet simple buildings as the Parthenon, and composing plays of spine-chilling brilliance, such as the *Medea* by Euripides. The downside was that this society of small city-states, factious and quarrelsome, transformed their triumph over the Persians into an instance of triumphalism, a gaudy and at times racist celebration of all things Greek and the demonization of all things foreign. The culture created by the Greeks in the aftermath of their surprising victory over Persia became the benchmark by which civilization was measured, and Europe (which culturally speaking includes the entire Anglophone world) has never looked at Africa, the Middle East, or Asia the same way since. If European, British, and American cultures all share an adulation of the Greeks, treating them as the foundational civilization from which Western culture derives (however problematic the term "Western" may be), the reverse of this is a predisposition to see "Eastern" cultures and states as antithetical to the values of the West. This process of "Othering," as it is sometimes called, is neither fair nor unbiased, but it is a feature of our cultural make-up. It is what allows some people, for example, to frame contemporary tensions involving Islam, immigration, and integration in terms of the clash of cultures. Similarly, Herodotos offers us the first portrait of an Eastern despot in his presentation of Xerxes madly whipping the sea when his bridge of boats has been destroyed. He is a type that we readily recognize in our own times when evaluating such foreign dictators as Saddam Hussein or Kim Jong-un. Whether we have read Herodotos or not, the mixture of petulance and megalomania we find in such autocrats could come straight from the pages of the Greek historian. Accordingly, in order to understand how deeply the Persian Wars matter to us still today, we need to interrupt the story of the Greeks and for a moment turn our attention to the Persians.

Who Were the Persians?

East of the Greek world lay territories that witnessed the rise of numerous complex states from the fourth millennium BC onward (**7.1**). Prominent among these were the civilization of Egypt, which grew up along the fertile strips of land on either side of the Nile River, and the various city-states and empires centered in the valley between the Tigris and Euphrates Rivers. Ancient Mesopotamia, named

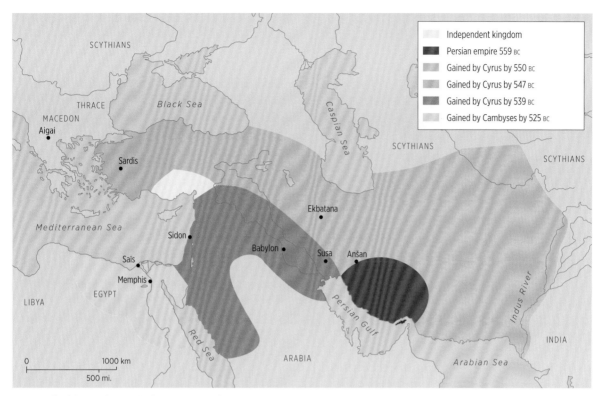

7.1 Growth of the Persian empire between 559 and 525 BC

from the Greek term for "the land between the rivers," corresponds to the territory of modern-day Iraq, and was home to a succession of civilizations beginning with Sumer and Akkad, including many complex city-states such as Babylon, Uruk, and Ur, some of which are familiar as sites in the Hebrew Bible. Advances in mathematics, astronomy, writing, law, poetry, and monumental architecture were among the many cultural accomplishments of this part of the ancient world. Successive waves of cultural growth, invasion, and destruction set the pattern of history in the Bronze Age and Early Iron Age, as each new power—such as the Assyrians (who, in Byron's words, "came down like the wolf on the fold"), Hittites, Babylonians, Neo-Babylonians, and Neo-Assyrians— swallowed up the civilization that came before.

The Persians originated even further east, in the steppes of Central Asia north of modern-day Iran. They were speakers of an Indo-European language; that is to say, from the same language family that includes Sanskrit and Greek. Their language and culture were distinctly different from the older civilizations of Mesopotamia (in much the same way as modern-day Iranians are unrelated to Arabs).

7.2 Luristan horse bit and cheek pieces, ninth to seventh century BC. Bronze, L: 12 cm (4¾ in.)

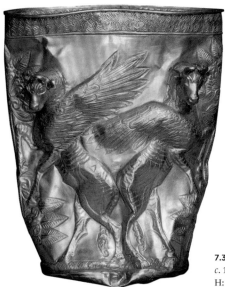

7.3 Marlik bowl, *c.* 1000 BC. Gold, H: 18 cm (7 in.)

years established the basis of the Persian empire by conquering the Medes, a neighboring people. From here he continued the expansion of Persian supremacy to the east and west, and by the time of his death in *c.* 530, the Persian domain reached almost from Afghanistan in the east to the Ionian coast in the west. All of Asia Minor, with the exception of the Greek cities on the coast, was now subject to Persian control, and the various independent kingdoms were swallowed up into the new provinces, or ***satrapies***, of the Persian empire.

The precise relationship between Cyrus, king of Anshan, and the foundation of the Achaemenid dynasty in Persia remains a difficult problem. In the Cyrus Cylinder, a clay document on which the king recorded his ancestry, he claims to have been descended from the Anshanite king, Teispes, while the Persepolis Fortification Tablets also appear to

Originally, they were a semi-nomadic people who probably came out of the great open steppes of southern Russia into the high Iranian plateau some time before 700 BC. As they entered Iran, they came into contact with, and absorbed by marriage and conquest, other nomadic groups, such as the inhabitants of Luristan, whose elaborate bronzework also reflects their nomadic origins (**7.2**; see p. 173). There were other cultures in the same area, many of which had reached a high level of sophistication in their material culture, such as the people of northern Iran known as the Marlik culture. Tombs from the region they inhabited have yielded such masterpieces as this gold bowl (**7.3**), depicting winged bulls flanking a palm tree, delicately manufactured in repoussé (a method of hammering metal to produce a relief image) sometime around 1000 BC. Unfortunately the cemeteries that yielded this material have been only poorly excavated and subject to considerable plundering. As a consequence, the history of the Persians' arrival in Iran is still only imperfectly understood.

The Origins of the Achaemenids

At the beginning of the sixth century BC, the entire Iranian region was still composed of various tribes and small kingdoms, among which was the kingdom of Anshan in western Fars. It was here around 600 BC that the true founder of Persian power was born: Cyrus the Great (600–*c.* 530 BC). He succeeded to the throne in 558 BC and in the course of the next few

7.4 Relief depicting Darius I, Apadana, Persepolis, *c.* 490 BC. Stone

refer to his grandfather (Cyrus the Elder) as "Cyrus the Anshanite, son of Teispes." Based on this, it has been suggested that Cyrus and his family were Anshanite or Elamite, not Persian. This does not lessen the accomplishments of Cyrus, but it does mean that the genealogical descent of the Achaemenids may conceal struggles and disputes over Persian kingship that are hidden from us.

Upon his death *c.* 530 BC, Cyrus was succeeded by his son, Cambyses, who ruled only until 522, but was remembered for undertaking the conquest of Egypt. On his death, Darius I came to the throne, and it is clear that he ruled this vast kingdom as an absolute monarch, modeling his authority on that of the great Sky God Ahura Mazda. Images from the reign of Darius depict him as either larger than any other human, or else place him above the other figures, thereby visually suggesting that everyone else was subordinate to the Achaemenid king (**7.4**). On the stairway of the Apadana (the Audience Hall) at Persepolis, Darius receives tribute from vassals who are both smaller than the king and stand on a lower level. Only Xerxes, the king's son and heir, is permitted to share the dais with the king.

Achaemenid Religion

The empire created by Cyrus covered a vast amount of territory, from the Caucasus mountains between the Black Sea and the Caspian in the west to Afghanistan and the edge of the Indus Valley in the east. Ruling such a large empire presented serious challenges to the Achaemenid kings, who responded with intelligent and flexible policies. Subject peoples were for the most part treated humanely and their religious practices tolerated. Furthermore, the administration of the empire was placed in the hands of provincial governors, or satraps, usually drawn from the Achaemenid clan, who could be expected to be loyal to the king and were required to follow the dynasty's policies of tolerance. One source for our understanding of Achaemenid tolerance is the Hebrew Bible, in which Cyrus is remembered as a liberator of the Jews in exile in Babylon:

In the first year of King Cyrus, Cyrus the king issued a decree: "Concerning the house of God at Jerusalem, let the temple, the place where sacrifices are offered, be rebuilt and let its foundations be retained....And let the cost be paid from the royal treasury. Also let the gold and silver utensils of the house of God, which Nebuchadnezzar took from the temple in Jerusalem and brought to Babylon, be returned and brought to their places in the temple in Jerusalem; and you shall put them in the house of God."

(Ezra 6: 3–5 [New American Standard Bible])

A similar policy is reflected a generation after Cyrus in a letter from Darius to a satrap of one of the western provinces, in which the Great King balances encouragement and anger in the manner of a stern parent:

The King of Kings, Darius son of Hystaspes, says this to his slave Gadatas: "I find that you are not obeying my commands in all respects; insofar as you are cultivating my land and planting the furthest parts of Asia with the fruit trees from across the Euphrates, I praise your design and as a result great favour will lie in store for you in the house of the King, but insofar as you are flouting my disposition with respect to the gods, I shall make you experience the wrath of my spirit unless you change your course; for you are exacting tribute from the sacred gardeners of Apollo and ordering them to cultivate profane land, ignorant of my ancestors' attitude to their god, who enjoined strict uprightness on the Persians..."

(Meiggs and Lewis 12, trans. Crawford and Whitehead)

That the Great King praised his subordinates for increasing the productivity of the land comes as no great surprise, but to find a Persian monarch explicitly calling for his officials to show respect to a sanctuary within his territory dedicated to a Greek god is a powerful reminder of the Achaemenids' high regard for piety and correct conduct toward the gods.

The Greeks had difficulty understanding the religious system of the Persians. Herodotos told his fifth-century-BC audience that the only gods the Persians worshiped were the sky, sun, moon, earth, fire, and water—that is, the elements—and that the Persians later added other gods as they came in contact with other people. There was, however, also an ethical component to Persian religion. Zoroastrianism, named after the prophet Zarathustra, focused on free will, and relied on three ethical imperatives: good thoughts, good words, and good deeds. Underpinning this was a theology that postulated the existence of a just supreme being— the Sky God Ahura Mazda—who was believed to

7.5 Faravahar, a visual representation of Ahura Mazda, from Persepolis, 486–465 BC. Stone

be in contention with the forces of evil (sometimes simply referred to as "the Lie"). Darius and Artaxerxes II both referred to Ahura Mazda in their public proclamations and employed images of Ahura Mazda, usually in the form of a winged disk, in conjunction with inscriptions and palace architecture (**7.5**). In the colossal inscription on the cliff at Behistun, for example, Darius states, "By the grace of Ahura Mazda am I king; Ahura Mazda has granted me the kingdom."

Just as the Egyptian pharaohs aligned themselves with Maat, the spirit of truth, order, and justice, so too the Persian kings presented their rule as an expression of (and authorized by) divine order. It is worth noting that Hesiod's poems make it clear that in early Greece, the chieftains, or basileis, of the Greek world employed a similar ideology, identifying their rule with the order created by their supreme god, Zeus, after his defeat of the Giants. Despite these similarities, however, there is remarkably little evidence of Greek writers in the Classical period exploring the cosmogonies of the Persians. There is a passing references in a Platonic text to the teachings of "Zarathustra, son of Ahura Mazda"

(Ps. Plato, *Alcibiades* 122A), and such Greeks as Xenophon and Ktesias of Knidos—who was a doctor at the court of Artaxerxes II *c.* 400 BC—knew that there was a priestly caste of religious experts whom the Greeks called ***magi***, but in general the Greeks were not overly curious about the empire to their east, except when Persian customs differed from Greek practice. This emerges in Herodotos's account of the sacrifices conducted by the magi:

As for ceremonial, when the Persians offer sacrifice to the deities...they erect no altar and kindle no fire. The libation, the flute music, the garlands, the sprinkled meal—all these things, familiar to us, they have no use for. But before a ceremony, a man sticks a spray of leaves, usually myrtle leaves, into his headdress, takes his victim to some open place and invokes the deity to whom he wishes to sacrifice. The actual worshiper is not permitted to pray for any personal or private blessing, but only for the king and for the general good of the community.

(Herodotos, *Histories*, 1.132, trans. de Selincourt)

Each of the elements in this account—altars, fire, libations, music, and so on—is presented by

Herodotos as an indication of how different the Persians were. Perhaps the scale of Persian power in the late sixth and fifth centuries BC so far eclipsed anything the Greeks had ever experienced that Herodotos and his contemporaries were compelled to dwell on what made the Persians different from the Greeks. The Persian king was the very model of an all-powerful ruler, a figure that did not exist in the world of competitive Greek city-states. Even Agamemnon, who had led the Greeks at Troy, had ruled as the first among equals and had never succeeded in uniting all of Greece. Certainly no tyrant—Kypselos of Corinth, Peisistratos of Athens, or Polykrates of Samos—had ever extended his rule beyond his own small piece of Greek territory, so that to the Greeks, whoever sat on the Achaemenid throne represented something unique, a king of kings, whom they referred to as "the Great King," and sometimes simply as "the King."

Administering an Empire

If Greece was small and divided, Achaemenid Persia was vast. Unity demanded an effective administration and the frequent use of force. Revolts on the periphery were not uncommon, and even within the ruling dynasty internecine feuds broke out between competing factions. In the Behistun Inscription, Darius offers details of a rebellion by the so-called "False Smerdis," a magus named Gaumâta who impersonated a member of the royal family, the real Smerdis, after the assassination of Smerdis by his brother the king, Cambyses (**7.6**). Darius records how he slew Gaumâta and restored the kingdom to Darius's family. The language Darius uses to explain these events is revealing:

The kingdom that had been wrested from our line I brought back and I reestablished it on its foundation. The temples which Gaumâta, the Magian, had destroyed, I restored to the people, and the pasture lands, and the herds and the dwelling places, and the houses which Gaumâta, the Magus had taken away. I settled the people in their place, the people of Persia, and Media, and the other provinces. I restored that which had been taken away, as it was in the days of old. This did I by the grace of Ahura Mazda, I labored until I had established our dynasty in its place, as in the days of old; I labored, by the grace of Ahura Mazda, so that Gaumâta, the Magus, did not dispossess our house.

(*Behistun Inscription* col. 1. 14, trans. King and Thompson)

7.6 The Behistun Inscription, depicting conquered rebels in front of King Darius

Darius casts the events leading to his ascent to the throne as a reassertion of the ancestral ways, linking his legitimacy to his dynastic connections and to the favor of Ahura Mazda. Similarly, he records suppressing revolts in the regions of Persia, Elam, Media, Assyria, Egypt, Parthia, Margiana, Sattagydia, and Scythia. In each case the revolt ended in the defeat of the rebel, who was usually mutilated, tortured, and crucified. The lesson was clear: cooperation with the Achaemenids was rewarded, but revolt was suppressed without hesitation. It was a lesson the Greeks would come to learn for themselves.

Less dramatic than Darius's campaigns but just as important for the Achaemenids' successful rule was the network of well-maintained roads that crossed the territory of the Persian empire. This network was unlike anything known to the Greeks, and facilitated communication between the Great King (residing in his royal capitals at Persepolis, Susa, and Ekbatana) and the satraps located on the peripheries of the empire. Herodotos was familiar with a major segment of this network, the Royal Road running from Sardis (in modern-day Turkey) to Susa (in Iran), and gives details of a route divided into stages at regular intervals. After describing the various satrapies through which the road passed, he calculates the length of the road:

This is the number of stages with resting-places, as one goes up from Sardis to Susa. If the royal road has been rightly measured...the number of kilometers from Sardis to the palace of Memnon is 2500. So if one travels 30 kilometers each day, some ninety days are spent on the journey.

(*Histories* 5.52–53, trans. de Selincourt)

It has been suggested that the Achaemenids were exploiting a road that had already been used by the Assyrians to conduct trade in the area of modern-day Syria, northern Iraq, and eastern Turkey. This does not, however, diminish the Persians' accomplishment. Not only was the road broad and well maintained—6 meters (20 ft) wide near Phrygia in central Anatolia—but also it was equipped with a network of horse-changing posts, a system termed

7.7 Plan of Persepolis, *c.* 465 BC

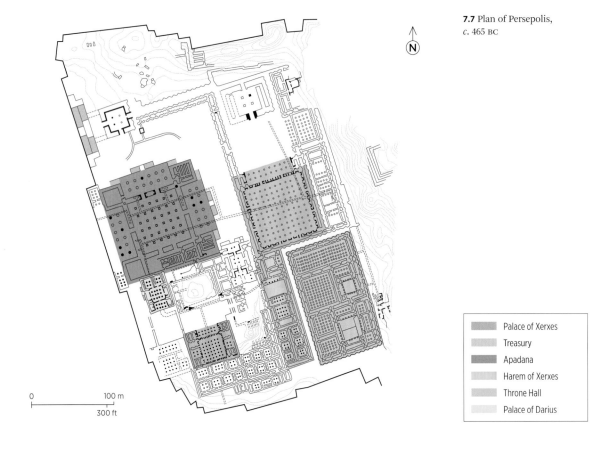

	Palace of Xerxes
	Treasury
	Apadana
	Harem of Xerxes
	Throne Hall
	Palace of Darius

0   100 m

300 ft

7.8 Relief sculpture from the Apadana, Persepolis, depicting an Armenian delegation being led to the King by a Persian officer, seventh century BC. Stone

pirradaziš, that made overland communication across ancient Persia probably as fast as any system before the Industrial Revolution. Once again, Herodotos offers the details:

> There is nothing mortal which accomplishes a journey with more speed than these messengers, so skillfully has this been invented by the Persians. For they say that according to the number of days of which the entire journey consists, so many horses and men are set at intervals, each man and horse appointed for a day's journey. Neither snow nor rain nor heat nor darkness of night prevents them from accomplishing the task proposed to them with the very utmost speed. The first one rides and delivers the message with which he is charged to the second, and the second to the third; and after that it goes through them handed from one to the other, as in the torch race among the Greeks, which they perform for Hephaistos.
>
> (*Histories* 8.98, trans. de Selincourt)

The official position of the Achaemenid kings regarding this vast territory was that it was a domain made up of distinct nationalities and ethnic groups who all paid tribute in an orderly fashion to the royal authority that bound the empire together; the worship of Ahura Mazda, as we have seen, reinforced this hierarchy by legitimizing the King. The Achaemenids therefore represent a fascinating phenomenon: a society with mixed agrarian and nomadic roots successfully adopting the habits of the large, complex, sedentary, bureaucratically organized, hierarchical states of the ancient Near East. As long as tribute was paid, the Achaemenid system operated well.

The coherence of Achaemenid ruling power, so dissimilar to any rulership or state bureaucracy in the Greek world, found an even more dramatic expression in the architecture and decoration of the royal capitals built by Darius and Xerxes. At Persepolis, for example, the Achaemenid worldview was monumentalized in a fashion designed to leave the visitor awestruck by the power and reach of the Achaemenid rulers (**7.7**). The earliest building within the royal complex was the Apadana, a vast audience hall built by Darius shortly after 518 BC on a levelled-off terrace, on which stood seventy-two columns, each more than 20 meters (66 ft) tall. Just as imposing as its dimensions were the extraordinary relief sculptures carved on the staircases leading up to the hall itself, which still survive. In addition to these sculptures—which comprise combat scenes depicting lions attacking bulls (employing the same motifs as the pedimental sculptures from the Hekatompedon on the Athenian Akropolis)—there are also relief sculptures facing the steps that show the various tributary people of the empire bringing gifts to the king. Each is distinguished by a particular form of attire (**7.8**), creating a visual catalogue of the ethnic groups subject to Persia, including Ionian Greeks.

7.9 (right) Staircase from the Apadana, Persepolis, depicting a lion attacking a bull, late sixth century BC. Stone

7.10 (below) East pediment of the Hekatompedon in Athens depicting a lioness attacking a bull-calf, *c.* 570 BC. Stone

The Apadana sculptures reveal a great deal about the Persian empire. The undeniable similarities between the Apadana lion and bull scenes (**7.9**) and those on the Athenian Akropolis (**7.10**) remind us that Greeks and Persians were in cultural dialogue with each other, as craftsmen and artists moved from the center of the Persian realm to the Mediterranean (and vice versa). The stark lines of separation between Greece and Persia *after* the Persian Wars can blind us to the fact that *prior* to the Persian Wars the two cultures were by no means entirely at odds. Indeed,

members of the aristocratic elite in Archaic Athens had a taste for clothing and such objects as drinking cups that were associated with Eastern luxury. Achaemenid bowls were especially popular, first made of beaten metal and later copied in terra-cotta. Cultural relations between Persia and Greece were not close, but the Greeks had to be aware of the existence of a powerful empire in the east. As we shall see, the bloody encounter with that empire would crystallize more sharply the Greeks' own identity, recasting the Persians as "barbarian" in every sense of that word.

Expansion and Empire

Each of the Achaemenid rulers sought to add to the lands conquered by Cyrus. As we have seen, Cambyses spent much of his reign from *c.* 530 to 522 BC campaigning to subjugate Egypt, and Darius followed a similar policy, annexing territory to the east in the region of modern-day Pakistan and to the west in Libya. In 513 BC he also took an army across the Bosporos into Europe and continued to the Danube River, which he crossed by means of a bridge of boats. The rear of his army was protected by various subordinates, including the Athenian Miltiades, whose family had established themselves as tyrants in the Thracian Chersonese. Although Darius's expedition across the Danube did not result in any lasting territorial acquisitions, by 500 BC Persian territorial control had reached the coast of the Aegean (**7.11**). In Greek cities on the mainland, from newly democratic Athens to Thebes, Corinth, and Sparta, there must have been those who felt it was but a matter of time before Persian emissaries came demanding the obeisance of the Greeks.

Given the continual expansion of the Persian realm, conflict with the Greeks of the mainland was almost inevitable. The instigators of this conflict, however, were not the Persians. In 499 BC, the various cities of the coast of Asia Minor revolted against the Persians and the tyrants who in some places ruled as pro-Persian puppets. The revolt culminated in the burning of Sardis in 498, with a contingent of Athenians joining the other Ionians. It is tempting to cast the Ionian Revolt as the first assertion by freedom-loving Greeks of their willingness to resist the Persians, but the Ionian Revolt was more complex than such a simple reading would suggest. The revolt was fomented by Aristagoras, a Greek who ruled as tyrant of Miletos. He had convinced the Persian satrap Artaphernes to undertake the invasion of Naxos. When the invasion failed, Aristagoras, fearing that his own position was threatened, gave up his tyranny, declared Miletos a democracy, and began stirring up rebellion among the other Greek cities of Ionia. Since the rest of Ionia was convinced to revolt there must have been a high degree of discontent in

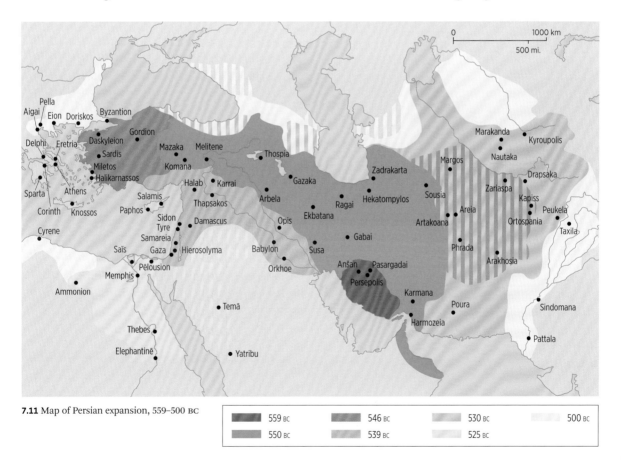

7.11 Map of Persian expansion, 559–500 BC

| 559 BC | 546 BC | 530 BC | 500 BC |
| 550 BC | 539 BC | 525 BC | |

the air, but most historians believe that the Greeks objected more to the imposition of tyrants in their communities than to the Persian presence. In the aftermath of this struggle, after the defeat of the Ionians at the Battle of Lade in 494, the Persians replaced many of the tyrannies with democracies. As long as tribute flowed and Ionia was stable, the Persians were not concerned with democracy or the finer points of constitutions; there were no deep ideological differences between Greeks and Persians. Similarly when Athens later liberated many of these cities, the Athenians exacted taxes at exactly the same rate as the Persians. Accordingly, Persian control of Ionia was probably no more irksome than Athenian domination.

Marathon

No Persian king, however, would tolerate outside interference, revolt, and insurrection, and in 490 BC, Darius sent ambassadors to Athens demanding earth and water (tokens of the Athenian submission). The Athenians responded by tossing the emissaries into a well. Darius then organized an expedition to cross the Aegean and punish the Athenians. In September 490, the Persians landed at a town called Marathon 44 kilometers (26 mi.) from Athens, and it is no exaggeration to say that events here changed history. We do not have a Persian version of the battle or the events leading up to it, and Herodotos's account was

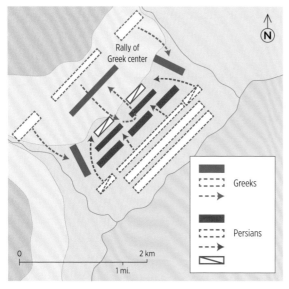

7.12 Battle of Marathon, 490 BC

composed half a century later, so many details of the battle are obscure or controversial, but in broad outline the story of Marathon is clear. The Persian forces came ashore at the wide bay of Marathon, northeast of the city of Athens; the Athenian army, consisting of around ten thousand hoplites (heavily armed infantrymen clad in bronze armor from head to foot), took up a position a little more than 1.6 kilometers (1 mi.) inland. The Persians, whose army numbered at least twenty-five thousand lightly armed bowmen and spearmen, remained close to their ships that were drawn up on the beach. (Ancient sources give impossibly high numbers ranging from two hundred thousand to half a million men for the Persians.) The Athenians waited for five days before forcing the battle. This delay is puzzling, but a Byzantine source explains that the Persian cavalry was absent. The reason is not clear, but if the Persians had embarked their horses with a view to ferrying them to Athens by sea, the Athenian commander, Miltiades, may have decided that the Persians had lost the tactical advantage.

The plan **7.12** shows the initial Greek position in dotted lines. Forming a line of battle across the plain from the Persians, the Athenians charged across the open terrain. Over the last 200 meters (650 ft) arrows rained down on them, but instead of either halting or retreating, the Athenians broke into a run and crashed headlong into the Persian ranks. To the consternation of the Persians, when the center of the Athenian line appeared to give way, drawing the Persians forward, the wings of the Athenian battle order encircled the center of the Persian line. As the Greek center rallied and resumed battle order (shown by the solid blue line), the Persians found themselves facing a wall of bronze and iron in front while being attacked on either side of their line. The Greek maneuvre caused the Persian line to falter, break, and run. In the ensuing rout, according to Herodotos, nearly six and a half thousand Persians were killed. The survivors took to their ships and fled.

In total, 192 Athenians perished on the field of battle, where they were buried in a huge tumulus called the Soros in the manner of Homeric heroes (**7.13**). For generations to come, the Athenians would look back on these *Marathonomachoi* ("The Men who fought at Marathon") as heroes in the full sense of the word: men whose deeds had earned them an honored place in the Afterlife, and who received cult offerings in commemoration of their superhuman accomplishments. Aischylos's brother Kynegiros, for example, was remembered for storming the Persian ships and seizing hold of the prow of a boat. When his hands were cut off by an axe, he fought on, according to some accounts, using his teeth "like a wild animal" until he died.

Almost as soon as the battle was over, the business of commemoration began. According to some later accounts the news was brought to Athens by a runner, Pheidippides, who, having covered the 44 kilometers (26 mi.) from Marathon to the city, cried out, "Rejoice, we are victorious," then fell down dead. (The story probably conflates the news reaching Athens with a much longer run, before the battle, when an Athenian ran for two days to Sparta to ask for help.) Not long after the battle, the Athenians cut an inscription along the front of the stoa they erected just below the temple of Apollo at Delphi that read in large letters: "The Athenians [dedicate] these spoils to Apollo [taken] from the Medes [the Persians] at the battle of Marathon." The celebration of this unexpected victory continued for centuries: an epigram recently excavated at the second-century-AD villa of Herodes Atticus in Lakonia shows that the Marathonomachoi were still being honored more than six hundred years later. It reads:

Good report indeed, as it reaches the
    furthest ends of
Well-lit earth, will learn of the aretê
    of these men, how
They died fighting against the Medes
    and crowned
Athens, a few having awaited the attack
    of the many.

(*Marathon Epigram* [*SEG* LVI, 430],
trans. Hartnett 2010)

These and other commemorative epigrams reveal that the older Homeric and aristocratic habits of personal commemoration were giving way to celebrations of the entire community's glory. If the political developments of the sixth century BC fashioned Athens into a fully functioning democracy, the victory at Marathon cemented the identity of Athens as a single, cohesive community. This unity would be tested in the next phase of Greece's confrontation with the Persians.

7.13 The Soros, or funeral mound, of the Athenians who died at Marathon

Xerxes and the Invasion of Greece

In the aftermath of the battle there was little time to celebrate. Although Darius was occupied with the suppression of a revolt in Egypt, and subsequently died in late 486 BC before he could exact vengeance on the Athenians, his son Xerxes immediately set about planning a massive invasion that would dwarf the punitive expedition his father had dispatched to Marathon. In 483, Xerxes began amassing a vast army in western Anatolia, modern-day Turkey, drawn from all over his empire. In the late 480s, reports began filtering in to Greece of an army assembling in the satrapies of western Asia Minor. It was so huge that it was to be supported as it marched northwest by a fleet of Phoenician ships, the sheer scale of the invasion designed to strike fear into the hearts of the Greeks. In 480 the army crossed the Bosporos from Asia into Europe on a bridge made by lashing together hundreds of boats. As the Persians advanced across northern Greece they drank whole rivers dry. Before reaching the Chalkidike (the triple-pronged peninsula located in the northern Aegean), Xerxes ordered his engineers to dig a tunnel through the Athos peninsula rather than have the fleet face open water and the threat of storms. Every action demonstrated the Great King's semi-divine power. When Herodotos calculated the total size of the army, he concluded that it numbered 5,283,220 men.

We know of these details thanks to Herodotos's account, although, as with his descriptions of Marathon, we have to recall that he was writing more than a generation later and in the knowledge that the Greeks had defeated the Persians. Many of the stories told of Xerxes may have originated in the awe

7.14 The Gorge of Tempe, between Thessaly and Macedonia

felt by the Greeks in the face of the sheer might of Persia, but in hindsight these anecdotes also came to convey a lesson: the Persians were undone by their *hubris*, or pride. Power easily leads to overconfidence, and in trying to understand how they had managed to defeat the Persians, many Greeks intepreted their miraculous deliverance as evidence that the defeat of the Persians had been divinely ordained. According to this view, power meant nothing if it was not restrained by humility and piety. Herodotos is quite explicit in attributing the Greek victory to the gods: when the Persian fleet was hit by a deadly storm off the Hollows of Euboia, for example, Herodotos says that this was Heaven seeking to balance the scales that otherwise had favored the Persians. According to Herodotos's interpretation of the Persian Wars, the Athenians are the agents of heaven, although the Persians are ultimately responsible for their own destruction. Even before the invasion takes place, for example, Herodotos offers a lengthy account in Book 7 of Xerxes' decision to attack, in which (having been persuaded by his uncle, Artabanos), Xerxes decides to call off the invasion, after reaching the conclusion that it is a costly and hazardous undertaking. When a phantom appears to him in a dream and demands that he attack, however, he realizes that heaven has ordained the invasion. Dreams are not usually cited

by modern-day historians as part of their explanations for historical events, but Herodotos is reflecting the popular thinking of his day. Many of his readers will have nodded their heads and understood the point of the dream sequence: the Persians had aimed too high, had acquired too much territory, had grown over-confident, and the gods had decided to punish them. If a single ruler tried to avoid that punishment, even if his reasoning was sound, then the gods would force him back to the path fate had chosen for them. The Persians *had* to be defeated, so they *had* to attack.

Once the decision to invade was made, the Persian king had a clear role to play in Herodotos's account: the despot. When the first bridge at the Hellespont was destroyed by a storm, Xerxes not only built another, but also ordered his men to scourge the waters with three hundred lashes for having defied his authority. Any Greek reader would have understood: this was hubris, arrogance on a scale to match the Persians' power. Punishment would not be delayed long. Shortly after this episode, three hundred Spartans would defy Xerxes at Thermopylae, their valor and sacrifice in stark counterpoint to Xerxes' megalomania.

Greek preparations for the coming war were slow, half-hearted, and badly coordinated. When, for example, the congress of Greek states decided to send a force north to face the Persians at Tempe, a narrow defile between the mountains and the sea leading from the southern part of Macedonia into Northern Thessaly and central Greece (**7.14**), the army had no sooner arrived than it surveyed the enormous Persian host and promptly withdrew. They had been warned by Alexander of Macedon (an early ancestor of Alexander the Great) that there was a western route from Macedon into Thessaly and that they would be surrounded, but Herodotos is probably right in concluding that it was simply fear that caused them to leave. The one bright spot in the Greek preparations was thanks to a decision made only a few years earlier by the Athenians. An especially rich vein of silver had been discovered at Laurion, in southern Attica, and the Athenians had held an open discussion about how the silver should be used. Most people initially favored distributing the money among the citizen population, 10 drachmas per man, but a newly prominent politician named Themistokles successfully argued that the money should be spent on building a new fleet of ***triremes***, ships powered by both sail and oar. At the time Athens was in a state of open hostility with its neighbor, Aigina, and

Themistokles may have intended the ships for that war, but, once again, with hindsight it was possible to say that he had really had the Persian threat in mind all along. Whatever the truth of the matter, the Athenians were in the lucky position of facing the Persian invasion not only with their hoplite army, but also with a newly constructed fleet of two hundred triremes.

Thermopylae

The Greek forces retreated to the Isthmus of Corinth after the withdrawal from Tempe. Here, the leaders of the Greek states met and decided to assemble their forces at Thermopylae, the "Hot Gates," named for the thermal springs nearby. It was here in central Greece that the mountains dropped sharply toward the Gulf of Malis. At its narrowest, the pass through the Hot Gates was only wide enough for a single cart. To the south were steep mountains, to the north shallows and mudflats. (Today, alluviation in the Gulf of Malis has changed the shoreline dramatically, but Edward Lear's 1848 watercolor gives a sense of the environment; see **7.15**.) At Thermopylae, however, disagreements between the Greeks still threatened

7.15 Edward Lear, *Thermopylae*, 30 June 1848. Watercolor, 17.5 × 28 cm (6⅞ × 11 in.).

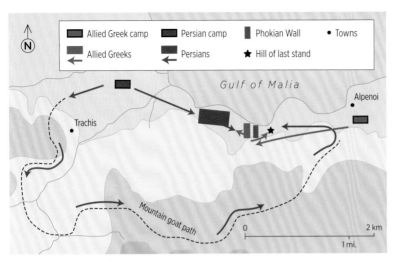

7.16 Battle of Thermopylae, 480 BC

to make resistance impossible. Some regions, such as Macedon, Thessaly, and the Ionian Greeks, had already ***medized***, the term used by the Greeks to mean changing one's allegiance to the Persians. Others wanted to withdraw south of the Isthmus of Corinth and make their stand at the choke-point between the mainland and the Peloponnese. Facing the prospect of the Greek resistance crumbling, the Spartan king Leonidas decided to stay at Thermopylae. Here, with a small contingent of three hundred Spartiates and nearly seven thousand troops from other Greek states, Leonidas prepared to use the narrow terrain and a wall built by the Phokians to nullify the Persians' numerical superiority and to block the advance.

For three days, they succeeded, even against the vaunted elite of the Persian army, Xerxes' Immortals (a corps ten thousand strong of the bravest and best-equipped of the Persians, according to Herodotos). Fighting from behind a fortified position in the middle of the pass, the Greeks held out until a local shepherd named Ephialtes betrayed them, revealing to the Persians a mountain track that wound through the hills and debouched into the plain east of the Greek position (**7.16**). Learning that their position was about to be turned, Leonidas dismissed the rest of the Greeks and prepared to make a final stand, along with his three hundred men and seven hundred men of Thespiae, who also chose to stay. Outnumbered, surrounded, and certain of death, the Spartans and Thespians fought until their arrows were spent and their spears broken. They moved into the center of the pass and fought exactly as Homeric heroes:

prizing glory more highly than life itself. Leonidas would fall, his men fighting over his body (the eventual desecration of his corpse, as recounted by Herodotos, would also have resonated with his Greek audience as another sure sign that Xerxes' impiety would call down divine punishment on the Persians). Herodotos claimed to have taken great care to learn the names of all three hundred Spartans who died at Thermopylae "on account of their great worthiness"; along with Hektor and Achilles, they had won undying glory. The award for bravest man in the battle went to Dienekes, who was also famous for his quips. Told that the arrows of the Persians would block out the sun, he replied, "So much the better, my friend, we'll fight in the shade."

When we try to separate the tactics and strategy of the battle from the collective memory and mythologizing that quickly accreted around this extraordinary act of heroism, the story becomes much harder to explain. Some scholars have dismissed the entire episode as impossible, arguing that the pass at Thermopylae was not even open in 480 BC. They have argued that the military road through central Greece lay further inland and that fortifying Thermopylae made no strategic sense, but cores taken from the region showing that the modern-day plain was largely underwater around 500 BC prove that Herodotos was right: this was a choke-point. After their victory the Persians did turn inland, but Herodotos also explains that this was because the Thessalians led the Persians this way so that they could destroy all the towns of the Phokians, their ancestral enemies, along the way. A more difficult question to answer is this: what did Leonidas hope to accomplish by blocking the pass? Surely not the comprehensive defeat of the Persians? Herodotos maintains that the Spartans were prevented from sending their full army because of a religious festival, the Karneia, but that they hoped that a show of Spartan force would inspire the Greeks to fight. A strategic consideration also deserves attention. The entire Thermopylae campaign may have been intended as a delaying action, designed to give the Greeks time to mount a coordinated defense further south on a battlefield that suited their style of heavy infantry warfare, such as the plain of Chaironeia or Plataia. A second possibilty is that Leonidas took seriously a prophesy recorded in Herodotos, that Sparta would only avoid destruction if one of its kings perished. Is it beyond plausibility that a Spartan king truly believed his life was the price of Sparta's survival?

Salamis

The theater of operations now shifted from the land to the water. On the same day that the Persians finally took Thermopylae, their navy engaged the Athenians at the Battle of Artemision. The engagement ended indecisively, and the Greeks withdrew to the Saronic Gulf, closer to Athens. Among the Greeks, many repeated the wish to withdraw to the Isthmus and abandon all territory north of Corinth. The Athenians, aware that the advance of the Persian army into Attica could not be stopped, voted to abandon their city. Women, the elderly, and children were evacuated to Troizen; all available men reported to the ships. In doing so, the Athenians were again following the advice of Themistokles: when the Delphic oracle offered the Athenians the slimmest of chances to avoid calamity by declaring, enigmatically, that the Wooden Wall alone would remain intact, it was Themistokles who convinced the Athenians that the oracle was referring to the ships of the Athenian navy. The oracle had spoken of "Divine Salamis"; Themistokles argued that if the oracle were foretelling disaster it would have used an expression along the lines of "Cruel Salamis." There were, however, still some who preferred to interpret the "Wooden Wall" as the palisade that had once surrounded the Akropolis. They remained, and were later slaughtered by the Persians.

The Athenians therefore assembled their ships along a narrow neck of land called Kynosoura ("The Dog's Tail") on the island of Salamis, opposite Athens, where they were joined by the rest of the Greek forces (**7.17**). Herodotos preserves details of the confusion prevailing in the Greek ranks: some were close to panic while others tried to persuade the waiverers to stay. The hero of his account is the Athenian leader, Themistokles. Later, just as stories circulated of the heroism of Leonidas, there would also be many tales of Themistokles' cunning. One such story had Themistokles writing to the Persian king on the eve of the battle, warning him that the Greeks were planning to disperse during the night. As a result the Persians spent the night rowing back and forth in an attempt to keep the Greeks bottled up in the straits of Salamis, rendering them exhausted the next day. The truth of such stories can neither be proved nor disproved, but it is worth noting that if Leonidas was destined to play the role of the doomed hero, such as Achilles or Hektor, Themistokles was just as easily cast as Odysseus, the hero who survived by his wits.

When the two fleets engaged after daybreak, Xerxes watched from his throne, set up on a hill outside the city of Athens. Behind him, Athens was a burned ruin. The Athenians had been in the process of building a massive temple to Athena on the south side of the Akropolis (where they would later erect the Parthenon); parts of its columns and architectural decoration would later be put on display in the walls of the Akropolis as a permanent reminder of the Persians' impiety. Whatever the tolerance shown by the Persians to their subjects, they showed no forgiveness to those who resisted the King, so that on the eve of Salamis Athens was in ruins, the temple of the goddess destroyed, together with

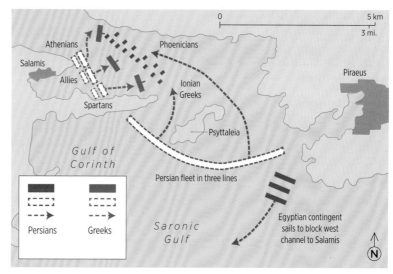

7.17 Battle of Salamis, 480 BC

hundreds of smaller shrines, statues, and dedications that had also been torn down by the Persians. The Athenians could still see smoke hanging over the city as they rowed into position to engage the Persians, reminding them that without defeating the Persians they had no city to which they could return.

The ships in the Greek navy were bigger but, even numbering more than three hundred, they were still far fewer than the Phoenician boats of the Persian fleet, which probably numbered somewhere around six hundred boats. Themistokles argued that an engagement in a narrow space would suit the Greeks better than an encounter in open water, and in this he was proved correct. After holding their position by gently backing water for some time, the Greeks opened the attack as a single trireme surged forward and engaged a Persian ship. As more and more boats entered the fray the discipline of the Greek ships, especially that of the Athenians and Aeginetan contingents, proved superior to that of the Phoenicians. The greater numbers of Persian ships actually hindered their maneuverability and in the mounting confusion, according to Herodotos, the Persians abandoned their battle plan. Herodotos credits the Persian ships with determination and bravery, but the tactics and experience of the Greeks put them at an advantage. It is possible that Herodotos's reference to the heaviness of the Greek ships may mean that they were more sturdily constructed and could withstand being rammed. It is also possible that the bigger Greek ships were well manned with marines. Many of the Persians' boats were captured by the Greeks, and this may reflect the fact that when two boats grappled with each other, the presence of the Greek marines effectively transformed the naval engagement into a land battle. Details are hard to confirm, but the outcome is not: the Persians were decisively defeated. Xerxes and his land forces immediately withdrew from Attica altogether. The Persians set up winter quarters in central Greece, but the King returned to Susa, leaving his general Mardonios to renew the campaign the following summer.

Plataia

After leaving their winter quarters in Thessaly, the Persians returned south to continue the campaign against the Greeks in 479 BC. Once again we rely on Herodotos for an account of the events of that year, and his narrative makes clear that the Greeks were still not truly unified. Some states had fallen into the hands of the Persians and had medized—Thebes, for example, now supplied heavily armed hoplites to the Persian army—and there were several competing voices concerning the best course of action to take against the renewed Persian threat. Many still wanted to remain behind the wall at the Isthmus, but adopting such a policy meant abandoning Attica, while the size of the Athenian forces (which included an army of ten thousand men and the largest naval contingent in the Greek fleet), guaranteed that Athenian interests were not ignored. For their part, the Athenians were determined not to see the Greek alliance retreat to the Peloponnese. When the Persian general Mardonios dispatched Alexander of Macedon to offer the Athenians a treaty, the Athenians prolonged the proceedings so that Spartan ambassadors would be on hand to hear. The terms they were offered included an amnesty for harming the King, as well as autonomy. In addition, Xerxes offered to allow the Athenians their choice of any territory in Greece to add to their own. The Athenians rejected the offer, and the explanation they offered to the Spartans for their decision sheds light on the profound changes that the Persian Wars had wrought on the Greeks. First, said the Athenians, the destruction of the temples of the gods by the Persians meant that they were duty-bound not to enter into an alliance with the Persians but to seek revenge. Furthermore, they said:

> there is the fact of our Greekness: we are one in blood and one in language, and we have temples to the gods and religious rites in common, and a common way of life.
>
> (Herodotos, *Histories* 8.144, trans. Waterfield)

Even if the Greeks still struggled to offer a united front in councils of war or on the battlefield itself, a common Greek identity was being fashioned by the shared danger they faced. In years to come, the Athenians would often refer to the Mede, as if all the many peoples of the Persian empire were a single enemy, but the single identity really being forged by the Persian Wars was a Greek identity. The Persian threat had forced them to recognize that what bound them together was more powerful than what separated them.

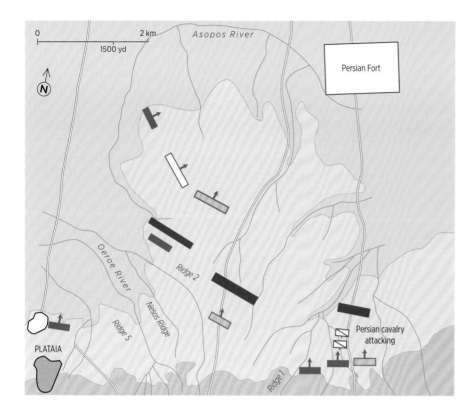

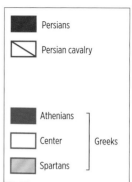

0

2 km

1500 yd

Asopos River

Persian Fort

(N)

Oeroe River

Ridge 2

Nesos Ridge

Ridge 5

PLATAIA

Ridge 1

Persian cavalry attacking

Persians

Persian cavalry

Athenians ⎤

Center ⎥ Greeks

Spartans ⎦

The campaign of 479 BC saw the Persians advance south from Thessaly into Boiotia, the region dominated by Thebes and now under Persian control. It is worth remembering this, because as the Greek forces moved north of the Isthmus, they assembled at Plataia, on the slopes of Mount Kithairon, in territory that lay close on the Boiotian side of the border with Attica. The Greeks could not expect supplies to reach them from the rich wheat fields of Boiotia and were forced to replenish their supplies from further south. At Plataia, therefore, the advantage lay with the Persians. Mardonios may well have understood the Greeks' predicament, because for ten days he refused to offer battle, even though both armies were drawn up facing each other. Once again, numbers favored the Persians, whose army modern-day estimates put around one hundred thousand, compared to a Greek force of probably fewer than forty thousand hoplites.

Mardonios had also seen what happened when the linen armor and wicker shields of the Persian spearmen encountered the bronze shields and iron swords of Greek hoplites. Wisely, he relied on his cavalry to harass the Greeks and threaten their supply lines. He also managed to capture the Gargaphian Spring, the source of the Greeks' water supply. He was also helped by indecision among the Greeks. The Spartan commander, Pausanias, consistently received poor omens and refused to advance his forces. There was dissent, too, between the Athenians and Tegeans as to who would have the honor of leading the left wing of the army. As a result, the Greeks decided to withdraw, and the battle almost did not take place. Seeing the Greeks leaving, Mardonios ordered his troops to cross the Asopos River. Many of the allied contingents had in fact already begun their retreat when Pausanias, alerted to the Persian advance, led the Spartans into battle. In the general engagement that followed Mardonios was killed and the Persians routed (**7.18**). In what was almost a completely separate battle, the Athenians prevailed in a particularly savage encounter with the Thebans who had medized. After the death of Mardonios, the Persian survivors withdrew to their fortified camp, until the Athenians and Tegeans fought their way over the walls and slaughtered most of the Persians who had not escaped. The victory soon turned into a rout. Only a few thousand Persians, led by Artabazos, managed to get away.

Aftermath of the Persian Wars

It is not easy to separate fact from fiction in surviving accounts of the Persian Wars. Herodotos's numbers exaggerate the discrepancy between the armies, and historians have rightly been suspicious of the coincidences in his account: the sea battle at Artemision was fought on the same day as the last day of the battle at Thermopylae; similarly, the land battle at Plataia is supposed to have taken place on exactly the same day as the sea battle at Mykale, near Samos, where a Greek fleet destroyed the Persian navy. More than just a record of the events of the war, Herodotos's account reflects the traditions and stories that grew up in the generation after the Persian Wars, when many states were vying for credit. This emerges in both literature and art. A monument, for example, erected at Delphi by the victorious Greek states reflects this desire to share in the glorious victory. In Apollo's sanctuary, close to the temple entrance, the Spartan king Pausanias dedicated a golden tripod sitting atop a massive bronze column made of the entwined bodies of three serpents, on which he engraved a two-line poem claiming personal credit for defeating the Persians (**7.19**). The rest of the Greeks objected, however, and the engraving honoring Pausanias was replaced with a list of the Greek states that had participated in the war. The serpent column stood outside the temple of Apollo at Delphi for more than eight hundred years until it was moved by the Roman emperor Constantine to his new capital; parts of the column can still be seen in Istanbul.

The impact of the victory can also be seen in Aischylos's play *Persians*, produced in 472 BC, only eight years after the Battle of Salamis. In the course of the play, Xerxes' mother Atossa recounts a dream in which she sees two beautiful women standing in front of her son's chariot:

I dreamed of two women in beautiful clothes, one in Persian garb, the other in Dorian attire....He yoked them both to his car and placed the collar-straps upon their necks. The one bore herself proudly in these trappings and kept her mouth obedient to the rein. The other struggled and with her hands tore apart the harness of the car; then, free of the curb, she dragged it violently along with her and snapped the yoke in two.

(Aischylos, *Persians* 180–95, trans. Smyth)

Atossa's dream points to a dramatic shift in Greek thinking. Before the Persian Wars, the Great King's power and dominion had dwarfed anything the Greeks could imagine, but in the immediate aftermath of the Persian Wars, the Greeks (and the Athenians in particular), quickly came to see themselves as on a par with the Persians. Other references to the Athenians in the play reflect a desire to assert that it was the Athenians who were most responsible for defeating the Great King. When

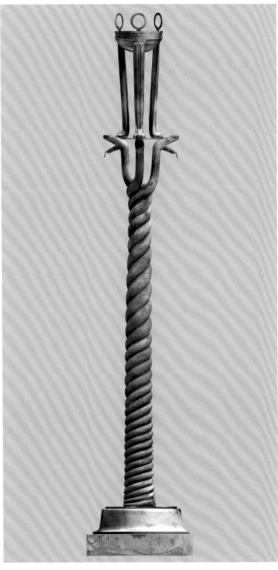

7.19 Reconstruction of the serpent column and golden tripod, Delphi. The golden cauldron was later melted down but the bronze column was transferred to Constantinople, where a large portion of it can still be seen in the Hippodrome. H: *c.* 9 m (29 ft 6 in.)

the Persian Queen Atossa asks, "What man do they [the Athenians] call master?" she is told "Of no man are they called slaves or vassals." The play is a celebration of freedom, performed by Athenians in front of an Athenian audience, many of whom would have been the men who fought at Salamis. In fact, it is around this time that "freedom" begins to enter Greek discourse with increasing frequency. Prior to the Persian Wars, freedom had been thought of as the status that a person enjoyed who was not a slave; in the aftermath of the Persian Wars it came to mark the way that the Greeks thought of their separate political communities as states "free" from outside interference.

There were other significant changes triggered by the Greek victory during the Persian Wars. "Barbarian" was, we have seen, a term formerly used to characterize those whose speech was unintelligible or whose accent was thick. Now it came to take on a more ominous meaning: the "barbarian" was inferior. This increasing sense of Greek racial superiority over the Persians is also reflected in a treatise by Hippokrates (c. 460–c. 377 BC) entitled *Airs, Waters, and Places*, in which he considers the role of environment in shaping culture:

And with regard to the cowardice of the inhabitants of Asia, the principal reason they are more unwarlike and of gentler disposition than the Europeans is the nature of the seasons, which do not undergo any great changes either to heat or cold, or the like; for there is neither excitement of the understanding nor any strong change of the body whereby the temper might be ruffled and they be roused to inconsiderate emotion and passion, rather than living as they do always in the state. It is changes of all kinds which arouse understanding of mankind, and do not allow them to get into a torpid condition. For these reasons, it appears to me, the Asiatic race is feeble, and further, owing to their laws; for monarchy prevails in the greater part of Asia, and where men are not their own masters nor independent, but are the slaves of others, it is not a matter of consideration with them how they may acquire military discipline.

(Hippokrates, *Airs, Waters, and Places* 16, trans. Adams [modified])

In art, too, we find evidence of an increasingly xenophobic attitude toward the East. In the introduction to this book we saw the Eurymedon

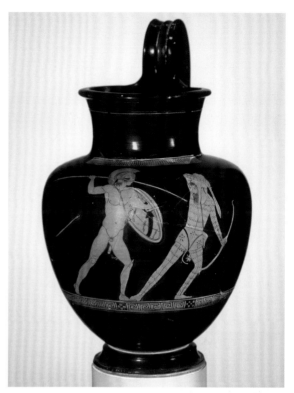

7.20 Red-figure oinochoe depicting a Greek fighting a Persian, c. 450 BC. Ceramic, H: 24 cm (9½ in.)

Vase, in which a Greek is shown about to sodomize a Persian, who holds his hands up in alarm. Other images of the soft Easterner also began to appear on Greek vases, such as the oinochoe, or wine jug, shown in **7.20,** which depicts a Greek, heroically naked, lunging toward a Persian attired in trousers and soft hat and armed with a sword and bow. Both figures are, in fact, generic types of image manufactured in the fifth century BC, giving a face to the Eastern enemy recently routed by the Greeks.

The period ushered in by the Greek victory over the Persians corresponds to the epoch of greatest cultural accomplishment achieved by the Greeks. In architecture and literature, from the Parthenon to the plays of Sophokles and Euripides, from the philosophy of Plato to the history of Thucydides, the Classical Age would be a time of extraordinary richness, but it will be important to recall as we survey the accomplishments of the Classical Athenians that victory in the Persian Wars was achieved at a price.

7.21 Jacques-Louis David, *Leonidas at Thermopylae*, 1814. Oil on canvas, 3.95 x 5.31 m (12 ft 11½ in. x 17 ft 5 in.)

Spotlight
David's *Leonidas at Thermopylae*

Jacques-Louis David (1748–1825) was one of the most important painters of the late eighteenth and early nineteenth centuries. His career spanned the aristocratic political system of the *ancien régime*, the French Revolution, and the rise and fall of the Emperor Napoleon (1769–1821). During much of this turbulent period David was in Rome, where his exposure to Classical culture had a profound effect upon his work. In particular, he was influenced by the German art

historian and archaeologist, Johann Joachim Winkelmann, who believed that art should strive to reach the "noble simplicity and calm grandeur" that was found in Classical art. In earlier times, artists had often added ancient ruins to their landscapes in order to enhance the atmosphere of their paintings, but David was drawn to the human drama of episodes in antiquity and to stories of self-sacrifice in particular, as is evidenced by such paintings as *The Oath of the*

Horatii (1784; **7.22**) and *The Death of Socrates* (1787; see **12.3**, p. 302). His austere vision of antiquity was deeply influential and helped make the worlds of Classical Greece and Republican Rome models for the new regime in revolutionary France. The Neoclassicism of David and other artists would confer on Greek and Roman art the elevated status it still enjoys today.

Preliminary drawings show that David was at work on *Leonidas at*

Thermopylae (**7.21**) for fifteen years before he finished it in 1814, but David's painting, for all that it helped fix Leonidas's position as the very embodiment of heroism, is not an illustration of Herodotos's story so much as a reimagining of it. Leonidas is positioned at the center of the painting, seated on his red Spartan war-cloak, looking contemplatively but firmly at the viewer, as if having at that very moment made the fatal decision to stay. Along with the other warriors he is depicted heroically nude; swords and scabbards are strategically placed to suggest the men's virility. Unlike many of the figures—who are dramatically leaping, gesturing with wreaths, or urgently blowing their trumpets—he remains still and resolved, aware of his fate

and calmly ready to accept it. Behind him the baggage train departs, and to the side a single man has climbed the rock face in order to inscribe the Spartans' famous last words onto the rock mentioned in the Introduction of this book: the perennial testament, together with the painting itself, to the Spartans' heroism and sacrifice:

Go tell the Spartans, Stranger,
    that here we lie
Obedient to their orders.

In October of 1814 the painting was not exhibited at the Salon, the usual venue for major new works by established artists, but in David's own studio, and the short note he added perhaps helps us to understand how he intended the painting to be received:

"This commitment of Leonidas and his companions made a greater impact than the most brilliant victory: it revealed to the Greeks the secret of their power, and of their weakness to the Persians." Earlier that same year, in March, Paris had fallen to the Allied armies, and in April Napoleon had abdicated. The painting, therefore, was completed and exhibited during the brief period before Napoleon's unsuccessful return from exile in Elba when it looked as though, in the manner of Leonidas, he had been nobly defeated. The circumstances of the painting's creation and exhibition are worth noting, since they remind us that past and present are in constant dialogue: the past is always a part of the present, a past that we reinvent, rediscover, and reuse.

7.22 Jacques-Louis David, *The Oath of the Horatii*, 1784. Oil on canvas, 3.30 x 4.25 m (10 ft 10 in. x 13 ft 11⅜ in.)

461 BC
Reforms of Ephialtes

460–445 BC
First Peloponnesian War

451 BC
Perikles' Citizenship Law

449 BC
Peace of Kallias?

437 BC
Foundation of
Amphipolis

Chapter 8

Democracy and Empire

In the previous chapter we examined the confrontation of Greece and Persia between 490 and 479 BC. Given the enormous size and power of the Persian empire, the Greek victory in the Persian Wars had been unexpected. A tiny, disunited region had managed to defeat the Persians by land and by sea. In this chapter, we explore the effects of this victory in Athens, the state that emerged as the most powerful polis in Greece in the Classical Age (480–338 BC). The narrative covers the period from the Persian Wars down to the outbreak of the Peloponnesian War (431–404 BC), a period usually referred to as the *Pentekontaetia*, or fifty-year period, and deals with the recovery of Athens from the utter destruction of the Persian War till the point at the end of the fifth century when Athens was at the zenith of its power. As we shall see, the story of Athens in the Classical Age is also the story of influential statesmen, such as Kimon and Perikles, whose rivalry would precipitate fundamental changes in the orientation of Athenian policy, as Sparta replaced Persia as the focus of Athenian hostility.

Aside, however, from personal rivalries, more profound changes were at work in the fifth century. To understand how Athens was transformed by the Persian Wars, we need to explore two contradictory features of Athenian life in the Classical Age. On the one hand, democracy became more firmly established as a result of a series of reforms designed to maximize the number of citizens playing an active role in the democracy. We will examine in detail the organs of democratic government at Athens: assembly, council, magistracies, and law courts. As we explore the peculiar features of this system, we should note the lengths to which the Athenians went in order to ensure that power was diffused broadly across many sectors of society. Random selection, the rotation of office, and annuality guaranteed that a broadly egalitarian ethos prevailed.

On the other hand, Athens quickly assumed the role of hegemon, or leader, of an alliance of Greek states eager to continue the war with Persia, and in doing so emerged as an imperial power. In contrast to the emphasis on democracy at home, the Athenians created an increasingly coercive system of imperial hegemony abroad that relied on garrisons, military governors, the exaction of tribute, and the brutal suppression of dissent and revolt. The ambiguity and tension between democracy and empire is a central theme of the chapter.

Introduction: From Ruin to Recovery

In the immediate aftermath of the defeat of the Persians at Plataia (479 BC), the Greeks immediately undertook a campaign against the Great King, according to Thucydides, to compensate themselves for the ravages perpetrated by the Persians. Xerxes had been defeated, but, contrary to Greek claims that his empire had collapsed, would reign until 465 BC. (His dynasty would continue to rule Persia, in fact, until overthrown by Alexander the Great more than a century later.) The Greeks agreed to plunder Xerxes' territory and liberate those islands and coastal cities of the eastern Aegean that had been under Persian control for the previous twenty years. The Athenians began by campaigning in the Hellespontine region, where they captured Sestos in 477 BC after a winter-long siege. After the arrival of the Spartan king Pausanias, the combined forces of the Greeks continued the assault on Persian positions, reaching as far north as Byzantion, close to the entrance to the Black Sea, and as far east as Cyprus.

The Greek decision to wage war on the King was entirely understandable—the Persians, after all, had sacked temples, burned cities, and conducted a brutal war in Greece—but it was also a decision that had unforeseeable consequences. No one could have predicted, for example, that the Spartan victor at Plataia, Pausanias, would soon be discredited. It was rumored that, after taking charge of the Greek forces, he began behaving in the manner of a tyrant, exhibiting a tendency toward violence and coercion; he even dressed in the same way as a Persian and had a retinue of Egyptian and Persian bodyguards. In short, he was beginning to resemble the very Persian king whose army he had defeated.

As a result of this worrying development, the Ionian cities implored the Athenians to take command of the allied forces. Certainly by dialect and ancestry the Ionians felt a stronger affinity with the Athenians than with the Dorian Spartans, and having Athenian generals in command may have seemed more natural than answering to a Spartan who was suspected of aiming at tyranny or, even worse, medizing.

Whether the stories told regarding Pausanias were accurate or not is unclear. He was recalled to Sparta and, although initially acquitted of the most serious charges, was found guilty of conspiring with the Persians in a second investigation. As punishment, he was walled up inside a temple and left to starve to death. The Spartans were rarely inclined to conduct protracted foreign campaigns, and the debacle involving Pausanias only strengthened the Spartans' aversion to campaigns far afield. When the Ionians refused to accept the authority of Pausanias's successor, Dorkis, the Spartans chose not to contest the issue further, seemingly content to allow the Athenians to assume command. Athens duly became hegemon of the new alliance, usually referred to as the Delian League because the Athenians set up the alliance's treasury on Delos. The Athenians also elected treasurers, **_Hellenotamiai_** (Treasurers of the Greeks), who assessed the allies' tribute. This tribute, says Thucydides, was ostensibly to pay for the campaign in which the Athenians and the allies would take revenge for the sufferings the Persians had inflicted on them by plundering the King's land. In reality, however, it meant that the Athenians had been handed subjects, ships, revenues, and a justification for a continuing, open-ended military operation at a single stroke.

It did not take the Athenians long to act upon the opportunity they had been given. Upon assuming command, they did indeed begin a vigorous campaign to cleanse the Aegean of the Persian presence, but it quickly became noticeable that Athenian leadership of the League, shaped by Kimon, son of Miltiades, was focused on asserting Athenian interests. Their first target in 476 BC was the site of the Persian garrison at Eion, on the Strymon River in northern Greece. The expulsion of the Persian garrison was unquestionably necessary, but whether the enslavement of the entire population was also necessary is less obvious. What is clear is that the seizure of Eion gave Athens access to the gold and silver of Mount Pangaion, as well as the timbers of the Macedonian hills which were good for ship-building. A decade after capturing Eion, the Athenians made their first attempt to colonize the area, dispatching ten thousand colonists to the site of Ennea Hodoi (Nine Ways) around 465 BC. Within a short period of time, however, these colonists were massacred by the local tribe, the Edonians, "to whom," in Thucydides' understated description, "their [the Athenian] occupation of the place was a hostile act."

The Athenian presence in the vicinity of the Strymon River was also viewed with apprehension by the people of Thasos, a Greek island and a member of the Delian League that controlled much of the Thracian mainland opposite the island. According to Thucydides, a quarrel arose between Athens and Thasos over the markets and mineral resources of the region, and the Athenians defeated the Thasians in a sea-battle. After the Thasians surrendered, they were forced to tear down their walls, hand over their ships, and give up their possessions on the mainland. A generation later the Athenians would renew their attempt to colonize the region, founding the town of Amphipolis around 437 BC, a town that would become a key battleground in the Peloponnesian War. The Delian League had already begun to show signs of internal division.

At the time of the Eion campaign in 476 BC, the Athenians also seized the small island of Skyros and enslaved its population, a tribe known as the Dolopians. The island had no strategic significance in relation to the Persian campaign but lay directly in a line from Athens to Lemnos and up the Hellespont to the Black Sea (**8.1**). This was the route by which grain was shipped to Athens, and the seizure of Skyros in 476 is clear evidence that the Athenians had been quick to realize the potential of their naval supremacy. But outward appearances were still important, and a religious pretext for the campaign was provided by stories that Theseus had died on the island. Kimon arranged for the bones to be returned to Athens for proper burial, thereby masking the seizure of the island with an outward show of piety and pomp. It was not unusual for Greek states to cite such religious concerns as curses and the expiation of guilt as the reason for a campaign, but the truth was simpler: Athenian policy placed Athenian interests ahead of all other considerations.

This was made even clearer by subsequent events. The Athenians overwhelmed the people of Karystos (a city at the southern end of Euboia, also

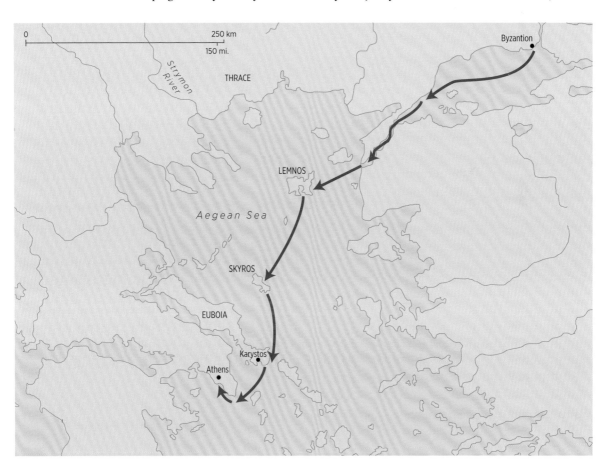

8.1 Map of the Northern Aegean showing the grain route from the Black Sea to Athens, and the principal areas of Athenian activity, 479–465 BC. Note the importance of securing the stations along the grain route, as well as establishing control of the mineral- and resource-rich region of Thrace by the mouth of the Strymon River.

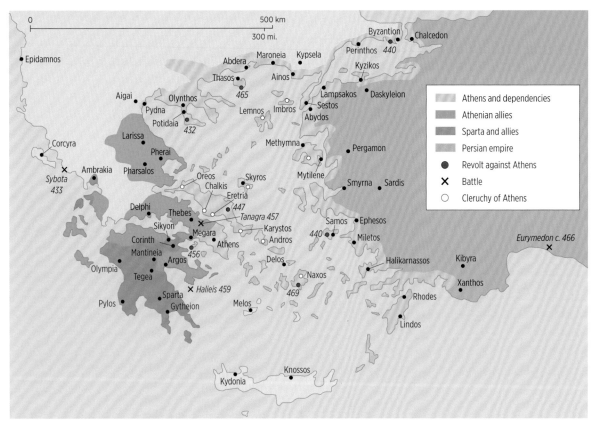

8.2 Map of the Aegean showing the extent of the Delian League as well as the sites of battles and revolts. Eurymedon is located at the eastern edge of the map.

on the grain route from the Black Sea to Athens) in 473 BC and forced the city to join the Delian League. Later in the fifth century BC, the Athenians placed a cleruchy—essentially a colony of Athenians who remained Athenian citizens—at Karystos. Then, sometime around 470 or 469 BC, the Athenians put down a revolt by the island of Naxos, an allied state which had sought to quit the Delian League.

Historians have often debated whether or when the Athenians became harsher in their treatment of the Allies over the course of the fifth century, but the pattern of Athenian rule was apparent from the outset. Seizure and massacre were the vocabulary of empire, and the Athenians spoke this language from the very beginning. Even in its first decade of existence the Delian League was little more than an instrument of Athenian policy. By the time of the Battle of Eurymedon, fought sometime between 467 and 465 BC when Kimon destroyed a Persian fleet of two hundred triremes, the Delian League had been transformed into an Athenian naval empire (**8.2**).

Democratic Institutions

If the Athenians had acquired an empire as a result of the decision to continue the war against Persia, they had also survived the Persian Wars with the institutions of democracy intact. The relationship between the empire abroad and the democracy at home was a critical feature of the story of Classical Athens, and in order to understand how Athens reconciled this seeming paradox, it is necessary to examine how exactly the Athenian democracy functioned and how this intersected with the running of an empire.

The Ekklesia and Archonship

Sovereign power lay with the people, the demos. As we have seen in Chapter 6, shortly before the Persian Wars, in 508 BC, Kleisthenes devised a complicated system of demes, trittyes, and tribes that was designed to organize the citizen body and to distribute power throughout the demos, confronting the factionalism that had so often pushed Athens, along with many other Greek states, to the brink of anarchy during the sixth century. An important mainstay of Athenian democracy was the Ekklesia or Assembly. In the fifth century, whenever the citizen body met collectively, it did so as the Ekklesia. Meetings were held forty times per year: four times during each of the ten months of the civic calendar. Each month, one of these meetings was designated the *Kyria Ekklesia*, at which matters of particular importance, such as declarations of war or proposals from foreign embassies, were discussed. (It was at the Kyria Ekklesia, for example, that the allies' tribute was formally presented to the Athenian people, dramatically demonstrating that the democracy was the beneficiary of Athens' imperial power.)

Since this was a direct, participatory democracy, ordinary citizens heard reports from magistrates and city officials on every sort of civic matter at meetings of the Ekklesia, from proposed renovations to temples to the price of grain in the market. An agenda was prepared by the Council, or Boulê, but procedural rules were simple. An executive board of nine men, the *proedroi*, whose membership rotated with each meeting, watched over proceedings, but anyone present was entitled to speak. Meetings were usually held southwest of the Agora, at an open-air location called the Pnyx. Participation was open to any Athenian citizen, provided that the participating citizen had performed his military training.

This system functioned throughout the Classical period, but it did not remain unchanged: democracy continued to evolve in the fifth century. In the first generations after Kleisthenes, it had been permissible for an Athenian citizen to have a non-Athenian wife and for his sons still to inherit citizenship. The leading statesman of the first generation after the Persian Wars, Kimon, was the product of just such a marriage. His father was Miltiades, from the aristocratic clan of the Philaidai, but his mother was Hegesipyle, daughter of the Thracian king, Oloros. The Athenians, however, changed the requirement for citizenship in 451 BC; now to inherit this privilege, an Athenian had to be the child of both a citizen father and an Athenian mother too. Was the change designed to ensure the exclusivity of Athenian citizenship more generally, or was it an attack by Perikles (who proposed the new law) aimed squarely at his political opponent, Kimon, and other aristocrats who married non-Athenians? The answer is probably a mixture of both.

In addition to the Ekklesia, the democratic system also depended on various boards of magistrates to supervise the affairs of the city. The most important were the three archons, literally the "Rulers" of Athens. One was in charge of the army and was known as the Polemarch or War-Archon. Another was the Archon Basileus, or King Archon, who was the chief priest of Athens and conducted sacrifices on behalf of the entire community. The third and most important archon was the head of state for his one year of office. The year was named for him, and we often refer to him as the eponymous archon. Athenian official records would begin with the dating formula, "In the year when Hagnon [for example] was archon." Once again, although this arrangement lasted for hundreds of years—eponymous archons were still being elected well into the Roman period, six hundred years later—it would be a mistake to think of the archonship as an unchanging institution.

The Athenians had modified the way in which archons were chosen as early as 487 BC. Before, only men from the top two classes in Solon's census ratings were eligible, and they were elected to office. After 487, rather than standing for popular election, candidates now submitted their names to a list of eligible candidates from which the winners were chosen by random selection (*klerosis ek prokritôn*). The archonship was then opened up to men from the third rank of Solon's four classes (the Zeugitai) in 458/7, making the archonship more democratic and egalitarian. No longer the pinnacle of an aristocrat's public career, it was a position now available to a great many ordinary Athenians.

Not long after the opening up of the archonship, probably between 454 and 451 BC, the Athenians also introduced *misthos*, or payment for service on the juries. Jury payment was only one of a series of such expenditures undertaken by the state. Along with the citizenship law, the phenomenon of payment for service not only reflects a broader application of democratic practice in the mid-fifth century, but also seems to have arisen as a result of the rivalry between Kimon and Perikles. Writing five centuries later, Plutarch explained misthos this way:

In the beginning, as has been said, pitted as he [Perikles] was against the reputation of Kimon, he tried to ingratiate himself with the people. And since he was the inferior in wealth and property, by means of which Kimon would win over the poor—furnishing a dinner every day to any Athenian who wanted it, bestowing garments on the elderly men, and removing the fences from his estates that whosoever wished might pluck the fruit— Perikles, outdone in popular devices of this sort, had recourse to the distribution of the people's own wealth. And soon, what with festival-grants and jurors' wages and other fees and acts of largesse, he bribed the multitude completely.

(Plutarch, *Life of Perikles* 9.2, trans. Perrin, modified)

The "festival-grants" cited by Plutarch were payments made from a state fund known as the **theorikon**; citizens too poor to afford the price of a theater ticket at the major religious festivals were subsidized by the state. Plutarch condemns this as a form of bribery, but we should remember that most of the historians and philosophers who describe the democracy of Classical Athens were fundamentally hostile to it; it is no surprise that Plutarch regarded the theorikon and other forms of payment to citizens as nothing more than bribes designed to pander to the masses. Another way of looking at these state funds—the theorikon and the **dikastikon** (the fund that paid for jury service)—is to see in them proof that the institutions of democracy were evolving to give more and more ordinary men a greater investment in Athenian civic life, at the same time as older, more elitist offices (such as the archonship) were being opened up.

The Boulê and the Areopagus

In the day-to-day running of the state, the most important institution of the Athenian democracy was the Boulê, the Council of Five Hundred established by Kleisthenes. As with citizenship and the archonship, the Council did not remain unchanged during its long history. Originally comprised of ten tribal contingents of fifty men per tribe, on various occasions in the Hellenistic and Roman periods the Council grew or shrank as the Athenians added to or subtracted tribes from the original ten, and adjusted the size of the Council accordingly. From its inception in 508 BC, however, the Boulê remained a Council of Five Hundred for two hundred years, thereby providing Athens with a high degree of administrative stability.

The Council met in the period of the early fifth century BC on the west side of the Agora in the Old Bouleuterion (**8.3**), and later in the hall built behind this, the New Bouleuterion. The composition of the Council reflected the principles of the Kleisthenic democracy in action. Membership of the Boulê was not by election but appointment by lot. Each deme within a trittys and tribe was allocated a fixed number of candidates that it supplied each year. From this pool of candidates, the tribe would then select (by lot) fifty councillors to serve as its tribal contingent for the year. Because there were ten tribes, and therefore ten contingents of fifty, the total number of councillors was five hundred. The fifty councillors from a single tribe were known as the **prytaneis** (sometimes called "presidents" in English), and the ten tribal contingents took turns serving for one month of the civic year (which was divided into ten months). Once a citizen had been selected as a councillor he was not eligible for selection for another ten years, so that in practice the vast majority of Athenian men must have served as councillor at least one time in their lives.

The Council's position at the heart of the democracy was the result, once again, of a curious conjunction of general conditions and specific political events that could not have been predicted. Southern Greece was rocked by an earthquake in 464 BC, and soon after Sparta's helot population went into revolt and withdrew to Mount Ithome, where the Spartans prepared to lay siege to them. At the behest of Kimon, whose aristocratic family had long seen Sparta as a natural ally, the Athenians (who were well experienced at siege warfare) offered the Spartans assistance. Whatever tensions may have existed between Sparta and Athens in the post-Persian War

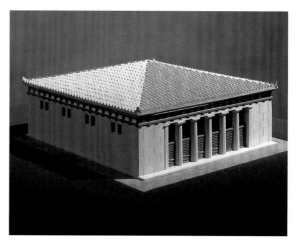

8.3 Model of the Old Bouleuterion, *c.* 500 BC

period, the prospect of a slave uprising was enough to unite them initially, but the Spartans soon grew apprehensive at the presence of so many brash Athenians in their midst. Fearful that the presence of the Athenians might sow the seeds of a democratic revolution in the Spartan homeland, the Spartans dismissed them.

Responding to the Spartan insult, the Athenians ostracized Kimon. The decision forcefully interrupted Kimon's tenure as the foremost citizen of Athens and paved the way for the supremacy of his rival Perikles, but there would also be more sweeping changes. Kimon's ostracism and the sharp Athenian response to the dismissal from the Peloponnese meshed with the growing power of democratic institutions at Athens. In the vacuum created by Kimon's absence, newer, more radical politicians with an even more democratic agenda quickly came to the fore in Athens. Among these was Ephialtes, whose name is associated with a series of reforms but who is otherwise a shadowy figure. The focus of his attention was the Areopagus, an ancient Council that (unlike the Kleisthenic Boulê) was made up of life-long members. It was comprised of ex-archons, and served in both an advisory role and as a homicide court. It had also, according to Aristotle, acquired unspecified extra powers that it employed in safeguarding the constitution. It was these extra powers that Ephialtes stripped away. The nature of these powers (and the larger question of what exactly the reforms of Ephialtes amounted to) have been much debated. A good argument can be made that the focus of his attack was the authority of the Areopagus to examine candidates' suitability (**dokimasia**) and to review the performance of outgoing magistrates, powers now transferred to the Council of Five Hundred. To understand why there might have been democratic resistance to the Areopagus holding these powers, we should keep in mind that the Areopagus, as a council of ex-archons, was not only populated with the most prominent men in the city but also was accountable to neither the Ekklesia nor any other democratic body. According to one view, its existence illustrated the so-called "iron law of oligarchy," which holds that all democratic organizations inevitably develop oligarchic tendencies. In the case of the Areopagus, however, it may be more accurate to say that as a democracy grows in confidence, hold-overs from a

8.4 Model of the Tholos, the building that served as the official residence and dining room of the Prytaneis of the Boulê

more oligarchic stage of development must either adapt or be swept away.

The reforms of Ephialtes in 461 BC mark the full emergence of the Kleisthenic Council of Five Hundred as the center of power in the Athenian state. It drew up the agenda for the Assembly, reviewed the suitability of elected officials, and scrutinized the accounts of the outgoing magistrates, an examination known as the **euthyna**. In addition, it oversaw the construction and maintenance of all public buildings, as well every aspect of fleet readiness, from tackle, timber, and sail to the upkeep of the triremes and the commissioning of new ships. All leases, taxes, and revenues that came into the state's coffers were handled by specific boards of officials, but all of these answered to the Boulê. They even conducted a review of the horses owned by the Athenian state. The Council's supervision extended to every corner of civic life, and it was on call twenty-four hours per day, seven days a week. On any given day there were fifty serving councillors, or prytaneis, on hand, every hour of the day for the entire month of their service. They lived, slept, and dined in the Tholos, a round building on the western side of the Agora, ready to respond to any crisis (**8.4**).

The success and resilience of this arrangement is demonstrated by the fact that the democracy of Demosthenes' time, in the 330s BC, very closely resembled the system first envisaged by Kleisthenes nearly two hundred years earlier. It was a system that worked by balancing the collective power of the Assembly with the administrative expertise of the

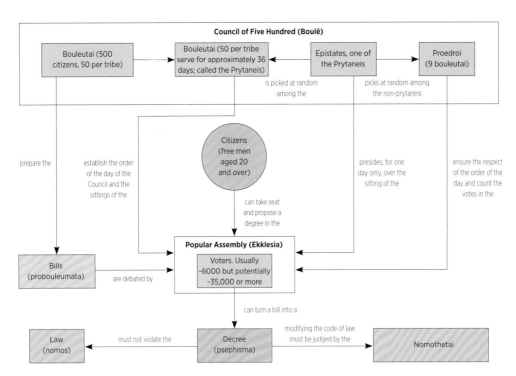

Council of Five Hundred (Boulê)

Bouleutai (500 citizens, 50 per tribe)

Bouleutai (50 per tribe serve for approximately 36 days; called the Prytaneis)

Epistates, one of the Prytaneis

Proedroi (9 bouleutai)

is picked at random among the

picks at random among the non-prytaneis

Citizens (free men aged 20 and over)

prepare the

establish the order of the day of the Council and the sittings of the

presides, for one day only, over the sitting of the

ensure the respect of the order of the day and count the votes in the

can take seat and propose a degree in the

Popular Assembly (Ekklesia)

Voters. Usually ~6000 but potentially ~35,000 or more

Bills (probouleumata)

are debated by

can turn a bill into a

Law (nomos)

must not violate the

Decree (psephisma)

modifying the code of law must be judged by the

Nomothetai

Council (**8.5**). It also relied on the existence of a small army of minor officials. As well as the three archons, who, as we have seen, were the commander-in-chief, the high priest, and the chief operating officer of the Athenian state, there were six other important magistrates who supervised the running of the law courts and were known as the **Thesmothetai**, the "Law-Setters," although they were responsible for seeing that the law was enforced, not for drafting laws. In addition to these major magistrates, there was a wide variety of other, more junior office holders, who oversaw everything from the public auctions of confiscated goods (the **Poletai**), the use of legitimate weights and measures in the marketplace (the **Agoranomoi**), to the monitoring of the grain supply to prevent price-fixing (the **Sitophylakes**). Each year, magistrates who handled public funds had to give an account of their expenditures, which was then reviewed by the state's accountants, the **Logistai**, who published the results of their audit. One such inscription survives from *c.* 434 BC and reveals how scrupulously the Athenians kept track of revenues and expenses, especially when the money concerned belonged to the gods:

And for the future let the treasurers in office inscribe on a stele and give an account of the treasures in hand and the income of the gods and anything expended during the year, to the Logistai, and let them render their accounts. And let them give their account from Panathenaia to Panathenaia, in the same way as those responsible for the treasures of Athena.

(*IG* 1³ 52, trans. Lambert and Rhodes)

Democracy in Principle and in Action

The Ekklesia, Boulê, and magistrates together made it possible for Athens to function as a large, organized state, in which accountability and oversight—the fundamental principles of orderly, civic life—operated. Without this combination of institutions and offices, Athens would have remained a small and insignificant community of scattered farms and villages. At the same time, after their experience with the tyranny of the Peisistratids and more recently the threat of Persian domination, the Athenians were rightly wary of the accretion of power in the hands of a single man. For this reason, all official positions, whether magistracies or Council membership, were held for one year only, and those serving were always part of a board of officials, power being distributed and therefore dissipated. Collegiality and annuality were the bedrock principles of Athenian office-holding, and, like ostracism, reflect the deep ambivalence felt by the Athenians toward powerful individuals. The complexity of this system is suggested by a flowchart showing the institutional arrangement of the Athenian democracy (**8.6**).

There are other aspects of the democratic system that deserve comment. One is that the practice of deliberating in an assembly was not restricted to the Ekklesia. The ten tribes of Athens also held their own assemblies, and were responsible for electing not only their own magistrates, the Phylarchs, but also the ten generals of the Athenian army (which also assembled by tribes). The demes of Athens, too, held communal meetings, conducted sacrifices according to a deme calendar, and elected their own officials, the Demarchs. The existence of these organizations and the replication of the democratic system from the local level of the deme all the way up to the full Ekklesia of the democratic polis were critical to the continued existence of the democracy. Quite simply, the civic identity of an Athenian resembled a set of matryoshka dolls: from deme (little) to tribe (middle) to polis (big), it was built on the replication of the same forms, practices, and habits.

The Lawcourts and Oratory

One feature of the system that was central to the operation of Athenian democracy was the lawcourts, and it was these that the Athenians saw as the crowning glory of their democracy. With juries of 500, 1,000, or 1,500 men, the courts of Athens did not at all resemble modern courts. Trials were conducted with minimal attention to rules of evidence or procedure, and surviving examples of court speeches include arguments and assertions that suggest trials could be brutal affairs. Demosthenes (384–322 BC), for example, did not hesitate to slander the parents of his opponent, Aischines, offering details that were designed simply to destroy his opponent's reputation. Addressing his adversary directly he asks:

Should I begin with your father, Tromes, who was a slave in the house of Elpias...and how he was shackled and wore a wooden yoke? What about your mother, how she ran a love chapel by the hour in a lean-to near the shrine of the Hero Kalamites, making enough money to raise you, her pretty doll, the finest hack actor ever?

(Demosthenes, *On the Crown* 18.133, trans. McInerney)

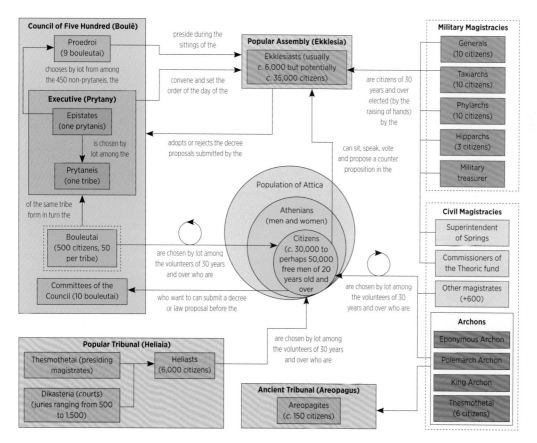

8.6 The arrangement of the Athenian democracy

Aischines, it should be noted, frequently resorted to innuendo about Demosthenes' relationships with good-looking young men. Watching the two of them in court would have been entertaining at least, if not edifying. In the fifth century, Aristophanes recognized that the courts were the bedrock of the democratic system, as well as a source of entertainment. In Aristophanes' play, *Wasps*, which takes its name from the chorus of Athenian jurors who enjoy "stinging" their victims, Philokleon has this to say about how the jurors are treated by plaintiffs:

Oh! What tricks to secure acquittal! Ah! There is no form of flattery that is not addressed to the jury! Some groan over their poverty and exaggerate it. Others tell us anecdotes or some comic story from Aesop. Others, again, crack jokes; they fancy I shall be appeased. But if we are not even then won over, why, then they drag forward their young children by the hand, both boys and girls, who prostrate themselves and whine with one accord, and then the father, trembling as if before a god, beseeches me not to condemn him out of pity for them, "If you love

the voice of the lamb, have pity on my sons"; and because I am fond of little sows, I must yield to his daughter's prayers. Then we relax the heat of our wrath a little for him. Is not this great power indeed, which allows even wealth to be disdained?

(Aristophanes, *Wasps* 563–75, trans. O'Neill)

There is always a healthy amount of comic exaggeration in Aristophanes, to be sure, but one feature of Philokleon's speech should be kept in mind: the actor playing Philokleon was performing before his audience in the theater in exactly the same way as, in real life, a speaker addressed a jury or a politician spoke before the Assembly. Accordingly, when Philokleon claims that the Athenians are supremely powerful as a collective body he is again affirming democratic practice. Speaking to (and for) the Everyman in the audience, he continues:

As to power, am I not equal to the king of the gods? If our assembly is noisy, all say as they pass, "Great gods! the jury is rolling out its thunder!" If I let loose the lightning, the richest, aye, the noblest are half dead with terror and crap for fright. You yourself are afraid of me, yes, by god! you are afraid. But may I die if you frighten me.

(*Wasps* 629–30, trans. O'Neill)

Athenian democracy was less an ideology or collection of ideas and more a set of habits and practices that reinforced democratic behavior again and again in different settings, in every court, every theater, every assembly, and every sacrificial feast where Athenians met as a body. One of the most striking instances of these democratic practices was the funeral oration, the event held at the end of the campaigning season when the Athenian community met to listen to a eulogy to the dead delivered by a leading orator. The most famous example was delivered by Perikles in 431 BC to commemorate those who

8.7 Excavation of Demosion Sema, Athens

had died in the first year of the Peloponnesian War. As we saw in Chapter 1, Perikles' speech is remarkable for challenging the living to see the glorious buildings of Athens as evidence of the sacrifice of the dead. When we contrast the collective excellence of the war dead eulogized by Perikles with the praise of personal courage, arête, and the urge to win individual glory, **kleos**, which we find in the Homeric poems, the communal ethos of the fifth-century speech is striking. No individual was named by Perikles. Instead, once again, a single speaker stood before an audience of Athenians, his words binding them as one. His message was that all living Athenian men were honor-bound to replicate the sacrifice of the glorious dead, to fight and if necessary to die for Athens, as if the city were a woman whose beauty has inspired these men to their acts of heroism. The erotic overtones are remarkable, as is the personification of Athens, yet the underlying theme is even more so: Homeric warriors fought for their personal glory; Athenians fight for Athens. Tyrtaios had expressed the same idea for the Spartans, but in Athens the theme took on a distinctly democratic flavor, one that was part of the very fabric of the city itself. Recent rescue excavations have brought to light the **Demosion Sema** (public cemetery), just beyond the Dipylon Gate, where the bones of the Athenian dead were collectively interred (**8.7**). The egalitarian spirit of the Athenians was present even in death.

Powerful rhetoric, both scurrilous and noble, characterized ancient democracy, but it also raised the spectre of a prominent and persuasive individual harboring ambitions of tyranny. The fear of this explains some of the most distinctive features of Athenian democracy, particularly in relation to juries and the courts. In the first place, the enormous size of juries made tampering with the jury and rigging trials virtually impossible. Furthermore, candidates for jury service were chosen by lot. They presented their tokens, which were placed in the slots of a voting machine (**8.8**). Colored markers were then dropped

8.8 Voting machine (*kleroterion*), third century BC. Stone, H: 59 cm (22⅞ in.)

down a tube beside the tokens, with the colors representing selection or rejection. The result was the random selection of some tokens and rejection of others. Those selected could present their tokens for payment.

Although the system was designed to give a vote and a voice to as many men as possible, there is sometimes a tendency among modern-day writers to romanticize the Athenian democracy. One obvious qualification was that participation was not open to women, slaves, or, except under exceptional circumstances, foreigners resident in Athens. Even among the forty thousand or so freeborn Athenian men who constituted the citizen body (out of a total population of perhaps three hundred thousand), there were also some who were more active participants than others. Success in the Assembly depended on the power to speak convincingly, loudly, and colorfully; stuttering and timid speakers were liable to be ridiculed. The Athenians enjoyed stimulating oratory, and rhetorical training was the mark of an educated man. The hurly-burly of Athenian democratic life is captured in one anecdote regarding the arrival in Athens of an embassy from Philip of Macedon that Demosthenes recounts. The episode comes from the fourth century, but vividly captures the rambunctious quality of debate in the Ekklesia:

The other day some Thessalians and envoys from Philip came to ask you to vote for Philip's admission to the Amphiktyonic Council. When you [the Assembly] raised a clamour, and refused to hear him, Aischines came down from the speaker's platform, and, in order to make a fine display in front of Philip's ambassadors he yelled, "Plenty of shouters, but not many soldiers when it comes to the crunch."

(Demosthenes 19.111–13, trans. Vince, modified)

Aischines was trained as an actor, with the skill and confidence to shout down the thousands of listeners grumbling during his speech, but in such a climate of abuse, taunting, and vilification, the average farmer was not likely to answer the herald's cry, "Who wishes to speak?"

Oratory aside, a second feature that worked against the egalitarian ethos of democracy was the military component. Generals could be elected year after year, the only office in the democracy that was not subject to annual rotation. Accordingly, a man who was a powerful speaker, worth listening to and capable of riveting his audience's attention, and who was also a successful general, could expect a long and distinguished career. Such men tended to come from wealthy and high-born families; they often referred to themselves as the *Eupatridai*, "men of good birth." Perikles perfectly illustrates how the combination of a good background, eminence as an orator, and a record of successful military campaigns could translate into political power; it is no coincidence that he dominated Athens for more than twenty years. Wealth and aristocratic birth might seem antithetical to the values of democracy, but the Athenians were not the last people to reconcile dynastic politics with democracy. The world's largest democracy, India, has been led for forty of the last sixty years by a member of the Gandhi–Nehru family, while in the United States, dynastic names such as Adams, Roosevelt, Kennedy, Bush, and Clinton have similarly enjoyed prominence even within a democratic political system.

The Imperial Democracy

The eclipse of Kimon's career and policies, the emergence of more popular democratic leaders (such as Ephialtes and Perikles), and the various reforms relating to eligibility, pay, and the strengthening of the power of the Kleisthenic Boulê, all suggest that by the mid-fifth century BC, the *politeia*, or constitution, of Athens was growing more thoroughly egalitarian with each passing year. In part, this was to be expected: a state that prides itself on democracy should, at some level, encourage as many citizens as possible to participate. At the same time, the impetus toward active participation by more people in the democracy was also spurred by the involvement of more and more citizens in the running of the Athenian empire. According to Aristotle, at its height the Athenian empire required 700 magistrates to be dispatched from Athens every year to supervise affairs in the allied states, particularly the collection of tribute. These magistrates were selected by the Athenian state and it was to Athens that they were beholden, not the allies. Each year a fleet of no fewer than ninety triremes patrolled the Aegean, ferrying Athenian troops and garrison commanders to different locations, collecting tribute and reminding both allies and non-Greeks alike of the Athenians' ability to project power by sea throughout the Aegean. With each trireme needing a complement of at least 150 men, the fleet employed a minimum of 13,500 rowers throughout the sailing season. Many were citizens from the lowest class of Thetes, but slaves too were deployed. (For slave owners this was another source of revenue and, as in other areas involving manual labor, such as the construction industry, slaves and low-born freemen often worked side by side.) Add the boatswains, petty officers, shipwrights, carpenters, sail-makers, and suppliers based in the Piraeus (the port of Athens) to the magistrates, surveyors, officers, and garrison troops constantly moving between Athens and all corners of the Aegean, and a complicated picture of the Athenian empire emerges: the machinery of empire—bureaucracy, fleet, army, and tax collection—involved Athenians from every level of society. As a result, the Athenians developed the most fully democratic system at home, yet were uniquely equipped to assert imperial control over the greatest number of other Greeks abroad. The Athenian democracy and the Athenian empire depended on each other.

The sphere of Athenian influence was primarily the Aegean, but the ascent of Perikles and a cadre of leaders of the generation after Kimon coincided with a new and aggressive policy towards other states located in many different regions. The first was

8.9 Athenian relief crowning a list of casualties, 394/3 BC. Marble, W: 1.03 m (3 ft 4½ in.)

central Greece. The disgrace of Kimon had turned public opinion against Sparta, and Athenian attempts to extend their influence into central Greece also brought them into conflict with Thebes. The result was a period of fluctuating hostilities and various pitched battles fought between the Athenians on one side and the Spartans and Thebans on the other. These campaigns, although fought primarily in Boiotia, are collectively known as the First Peloponnesian War (460–445 BC), but the war was inconclusive. (Unfortunately, while historians refer to this as the First Peloponnesian War, the subsequent conflict from 431 to 404 BC is simply called the Peloponnesian War.) A Spartan victory at Tanagra in 457 BC, for example, was followed by an Athenian victory only two months later at Oinophyta.

The Athenians continued to undertake military expeditions on many other fronts, a fact that is revealed by the inscriptions put up at Athens recording the names of the fallen. For example, the tribe Erechtheis erected a memorial to the 180 men who fell in 460–59 BC that lists the theaters of operations as follows:

Of Erechtheis
These died in the war, in Cyprus, in Egypt,
In Phoenicia, in Halieis, in Aigina, at Megara
In the same year.

(IG I³ 1147, trans. Lambert and Osborne)

These casualty lists were erected in public places, such as the public burial ground of Athens, and were adorned with reliefs depicting the fallen as heroes (**8.9**).

Many of these are campaigns not mentioned in our literary sources, reminding us that there are significant gaps in our knowledge of where the Athenians were fighting in these years. We do know, however, that in 460 BC, the Athenians dispatched a naval expedition to Cyprus that was then instructed to sail to Egypt in support of an insurrection against the Persians led by the native Egyptian leader Inaros.

Although initially successful, the Athenians were eventually besieged by the Persian general Megabazos and their entire force of two hundred ships was destroyed. Worse still, an auxiliary fleet of fifty ships was dispatched in 454 BC and arrived unaware of the fate of the earlier expedition; it also was destroyed.

Delian League in Crisis

In a very short period of time Athens had plummeted from the height of its power. In the first twenty years after the Persian Wars the Athenians had projected their power across the Aegean and had vigorously prosecuted the war against Persia. They had eradicated Persian influence from the Aegean entirely and had established the mechanisms of empire, thanks to their naval power and the allies' tribute. But by the mid-450s BC the Athenians faced a very different political landscape abroad. If Persia was no longer an immediate threat, Sparta was also no longer a firm ally. Thebes and Megara were hardly friendly neighbors. More significantly, resistance to Athens from disaffected allies lurked beneath the surface. The Egyptian disaster had cost the Athenians dearly in both ships and manpower, and so there followed a period of adjustment, as the Athenians took stock of hard realities. In the aftermath of the failures in Egypt the treasury of the Delian League was physically removed from Delos and transferred to Athens. This was a necessary precaution because, in the aftermath of the Egyptian disaster, revolts broke out in important allied states, such as Miletos and Erythrai, which the Athenians suppressed. An inscription found on the Akropolis of Athens (now lost) reveals that when the Athenians put down the revolt on Erythrai, they intervened in the internal constitutional order of the state. The terms of the settlement are revealing:

There shall be a Council appointed by lot of a hundred and twenty men; a [man who is appointed shall be examined?] in the Council, and...shall be possible to be a councillor if he is not less than thirty years old; [anyone rejected in the examination?] shall be prosecuted. No one shall be a councillor twice within four years. The overseers and the garrison commander shall allot and install the Council for now, and in future the Council and the garrison commander shall do it, not less than thirty days before the Council's term of office ends.

(*IG* I³ 14, trans. Lambert and Rhodes)

Here are unambiguous signs of Athenian interventionism, both constitutional and military. The council set up on Erythrai was modeled on the Kleisthenic Council of Five Hundred, and the same principles and practices of official scrutiny, annuality, and rotation of office were imported from Athens; but at the same time, the Athenian overseers and garrison commanders were clearly the men in charge. The constitution may have been democratic, but it was inextricably linked to imperial power.

Kimon's ten-year ostracism was over by 451 BC and he returned in time to negotiate a five-year peace treaty with Sparta. His return also signaled a resumption of hostilities with Persia, and shortly after the peace with Sparta was signed, Kimon led an expeditionary force of two hundred ships to Cyprus. The details of this campaign are murky but it is likely that this was an opportunistic campaign designed to take advantage of revolts and disaffection across the western reaches of the Persian empire, from Syria to Egypt. Cyprus lies at the very intersection of the Greek world and the eastern Mediterranean regions inhabited by the sea-going Phoenicians. Kimon used the opportunity to assert Athenian influence even further afield, exploiting a moment of relative weakness in the hold of the Persians and Phoenicians. He died, however, during the siege of Kition, on Cyprus, after which the allied forces returned home and abandoned further attempts to liberate Cyprus.

A Peace of Kallias?

The middle of the century saw Athens at a crossroads. At home, democracy was secure, but with Kimon dead, Perikles now enjoyed a position of supremacy that was distinctly undemocratic. (Ephialtes, according to the ancient sources, had been assassinated shortly after the reforms of 461 BC.) Perikles was not unchallenged, but most of the major policy decisions of the next two decades were his and it is for this reason that historians speak of the third quarter of the fifth century BC as the age of Periklean Athens. (We will return to the cultural life of the fifth century in the next chapter.)

In this Periklean Athens, the pro-Spartan, anti-Persian policies associated with Kimon were beginning to look old. Was Sparta still the ally of the Athenians from the days of the Persian Wars? Recent history had seen the Athenians and Spartans fighting on opposite sides in central Greece. Was Persia still the common enemy of all Greeks? Quite possibly, but if the Athenians stayed out of Persian business, there was a decent chance Persia would stay out of theirs. The time was ripe, then, to begin exploring the possibility of peace with Persia. Whether a formal peace was negotiated, however, has become one of the key problems of fifth-century history.

A powerful argument for a formal peace is to be found in the reconstruction of the records of the Delian League known as the Athenian Tribute Lists. A monumental stele, known as the *Lapis Primus* ("The First Stone"), records payments made to Athena from the tribute paid by the allied states from 454 BC down to 440 BC and these records allow us to calculate how much tribute they sent to Athens each year. (Athena was given one-sixtieth of all tribute.) Attempts conducted in the 1930s to restore the inscription from the many fragments in which it was found strongly support the view that there are only fourteen lists in that fifteen-year period; in other words, there seems to be a missing year of tribute. The editors of the Athenian Tribute Lists suggested that the missing year was 449 BC, and offered an elegant reconstruction of events to explain the omission. The death of Kimon in 450 BC, they argued, opened up the opportunity for negotiations with Persia, which were conducted in 450/449 BC and resulted in a treaty. Later sources refer to the ambassador who negotiated the treaty as Kallias, and so it is usual to refer to this treaty as the Peace of Kallias. The Athenians could scarcely justify collecting tribute for their war chest when they had just negotiated a peace treaty with the common enemy, and so for one year no tribute was collected. Since the Athenians had no intention of giving up their empire, however, tribute collection resumed the following year, although fluctuations in the annual Tribute Lists point to increasing resentment among the allied states at paying for Athens' imperial ambitions.

Despite the attractiveness of this reconstruction, it has not convinced everyone. Perhaps the biggest stumbling block is that Thucydides—the major historian of fifth-century events—never mentions the Peace of Kallias. Since Thucydides was interested in charting the growth of Athenian power from the end of the Persian Wars in 479 BC to the outbreak of Peloponnesian War in 431, it is hard to fathom how he

could leave out a peace treaty in 449 that marked the formal end of the first of these momentous conflicts. Furthermore, it is a cause for some suspicion that once references to the Peace of Kallias do begin to appear in our sources, it is often in the context of speeches by such fourth-century-BC rhetoricians and orators as Isagoras and Lykourgos, who explicitly contrast the (glorious) Peace of Kallias with the craven peace treaties negotiated by their contemporaries. In other words, our sources are often tendentious, and in their descriptions of the geographical limits established by the treaty (specifying, for example, how far west Persian troops and ships could come into Greek space) they are also inconsistent and, frankly, unbelievable. Writing in the 380s, Isokrates suggested that the Great King was bound by a treaty that would not allow him west of the Halys River, a detail that, if true, would have meant ceding the entire western half of Asia Minor. This is simply inconceivable, and contradicts what we know of Persian territorial control in the fifth and fourth centuries. Short of a dramatic archaeological discovery, there may never be a conclusive way to prove whether or not a formal Peace of Kallias was ever signed by the Athenians and the Great King of Persia. Certainly the fourth-century-BC historian Theopompos believed that it was a forgery and that no authentic treaty ever existed. There is, however, one tantalizing alternative still to consider. Herodotos tells us that a certain Athenian named Kallias was in Susa on business when an Argive delegation came to ask whether King Artaxerxes regarded the treaty the Argives had signed with his father as still binding. Artaxerxes reigned from 465 to 424 BC, so the Argive visit could have occurred in 449. Could discussions of a broad peace treaty between Greeks and Persia have prompted the Argives to send an embassy to Susa, to clarify the status of their own specific treaty with Persia? And if Herodotos's testimony places Kallias in Susa at this critical moment, some have wondered what Kallias's business was if not to discuss the cessation of hostilities between Athens and Persia. Furthermore, one way of reading the episode, recently advocated by Loren Samons, is that the discussions resulted not in a formal treaty but in an informal understanding between the two sides. To be sure, this is not stated in any source, but then neither Kallias nor Perikles were likely to boast about such an agreement if by its nature it was never subject to formal ratification. Such an explanation would be consistent with a missing year of tribute—why pay for a war while its cessation was being negotiated?—and with an understanding that only in later years was informal agreement elevated to the status of a formal peace.

Colonies and Cleruchies

Many scholars believe that the decade of the 440s BC marks a hardening of the Athenians' attitude toward their allies, or perhaps more accurately, their subjects, as they sought to reestablish firm control of the League. It may be that our view of the Athenian empire is skewed by an accident of preservation, namely that we have much more evidence in the form of inscriptions from the second half of the century than the first, but what is not in doubt is that the Athenians developed a clear set of practices that served to confirm their imperial control of the Aegean. These included intervening with their superior military and naval forces, founding colonies, establishing cleruchies (see below) in allied territory, imposing Athenian weights and measures, and making the allies subject to Athenian courts in any legal disputes. Each of these features of the Athenian empire is demonstrated by the rich epigraphic record and by Thucydides' account of the Pentekontaetia, the period between the Persian and Peloponnesian Wars.

Colonies

Colonies became a means for Athens to assert its control over members of the League. Different sources of evidence, however, provide different perspectives on the Athenian attitude. For example, in Thucydides' *History of the Peloponnesian War*, we learn that while the Athenians were campaigning in Boiotia in 446 BC, they captured the city of Chaironeia and enslaved the entire population (1.113–15). The Athenians were subsequently defeated by a Boiotian army shortly after at the Battle of Koroneia, and, as with Athenian reversals in the 450s BC, the defeat sparked unrest among the Athenian allies. The cities of Euboia went into revolt, and Perikles led a major Athenian expedition to the island to suppress the rebellion. The city of Histiaia was sacked, its population enslaved, and the land given over to Athenian colonists. The other cities sued for peace, and we possess a lengthy inscription that shows exactly how the Athenians used judicial

arrangements to enforce their rule. Having quelled the uprising on Euboia, the Athenians decided on the terms of their future relationship with the people of Chalkis, the largest city on Euboia. They made an oath to the Chalkidians that they inscribed on a stone stele:

I shall not expel the Chalkidians from Chalkis, nor shall I lay waste the city, nor shall I deprive any individual of civic rights nor punish any with exile nor take any prisoner, nor execute any, nor confiscate the money of anyone not condemned in court without the authority of the Athenian People; and whenever I am a prytany member I shall not put anything prejudicial to the interests of an individual or the community to the vote without due notice, and any embassy that is sent I shall bring before the Council and People within ten days, as far as I am able; and I shall maintain this while the Chalkidians obey the Athenian People.

> (*IG* I³ 40 4–10, trans. Lambert and Osborne)

This is an extraordinary piece of evidence, and reflects the complex attitudes of the Athenians to the members of the Delian League. In the first place, the oath suggests the importance to the Athenians of at least the appearance of legality in their dealings with subject states. Furthermore, the oath is framed as a series of guarantees of fair practice by the Athenians (which must make us wonder whether actual Athenian behavior was more coercive). The oath, however, leaves no doubt about where power was located in any transaction between Chalkis and Athens. The Athenian people were the final arbiters, and the contract implicit in the oath was contingent on Chalkidian obedience. Far from being a treaty between two equal states, this is a set of regulations spelling out what Chalkis can expect from the imperial power.

As a corollary to the Athenian oath, every Chalkidian of military age also took an oath, the terms of which were spelled out by the Athenians:

I shall not revolt from the People of Athens by any means or device whatsoever, neither in word nor in deed, nor shall I obey anyone who does revolt; and if anyone revolts I shall denounce him to the Athenians, and I shall pay to the Athenians whatever tribute I persuade them to agree [is fair], and I shall be the best and fairest ally I am able to be and shall help and defend the Athenian People, in the event of anyone wronging the Athenian People, and I shall obey the Athenian People.

(*IG* I³ 40 22–31, trans. Lambert and Osborne, modified)

The subordination of the Chalkidians is laid out starkly here. Not only did they have to forswear future revolts, but also they promised to denounce any talk of insurrection. They agreed to continue paying tribute and could do little more than hope for fair treatment. Furthermore, two addenda to the original decree contain other details and provisions that underscore the weakness of the Chalkidian position. An oblique reference suggests that the Athenians had taken hostages upon suppressing the Euboian revolt. When the Chalkidians petitioned for their release, the Athenian response was a polite and measured refusal:

And on the matter of hostages, [the Athenian ambassadors] shall reply to the Chalkidians that for the moment the Athenians have decided to leave matters as they have been voted, but when they decide to do so they will deliberate and make an exchange on terms which seem suitable for the Athenians and the Chalkidians.

(*IG* I³ 40 47–52, trans. Lambert and Osborne)

Behind this diplomatic language there lurks a fundamental imbalance of power: the Athenians could dismiss or postpone petitions that, from the point of view of the plaintiffs, were matters of life or death. Similarly, other imbalances of power are baldly stated but deserve consideration. In another clause, the Athenians stipulate:

...and the foreigners in Chalkis—except those living there who pay no taxes to Athens, and anyone who has been given tax exemption by the Athenian People—the rest shall pay taxes to Chalkis, just like other Chalkidians.

(*IG* I³ 40 52–57, trans. Lambert and Osborne)

Various individuals and perhaps entire groups enjoyed different tax statuses on Chalkis. The power to determine which tax regime one was bound by in Chalkis was in the hands of the Athenians, and it was probably the case that there were Athenians in Chalkis who not only owned land there and resided there, but also paid no taxes there. Colonies and cleruchies enjoyed privileges not available to subject states.

We catch a glimpse of how colonies functioned as an instrument of Athenian policy in the regulations for the founding of a colony at Brea, in the northern Aegean (possibly on the Chalkidike peninsula), dating from not long after the suppression of the Euboian revolt. The north was always of strategic interest to the Athenians, as we have seen, because of its natural wealth in mineral resources and timber. The establishment of an Athenian colony here, as with the colony at Amphipolis, was designed to secure an Athenian presence in the region. Nor was the colony simply dispatched to fend for itself. Provided the colonists met their obligations to the mother city, by sending a cow (probably a bull calf or steer) and a set of armor every four years to the Greater Panathenaia, the Athenians would be ready to render assistance:

If any one attacks the land of the colonists, the cities shall come in support as quickly as possible, in accordance with the instructions drawn up.

(*IG* I³ 46 17–19, trans. Lambert and Rhodes)

Accordingly, the colony served as a beachhead for the Athenians. Yet it was a reciprocal arrangement. If a conflict were to arise involving either non-Greek tribes or other Greek cities in the region, such as the Corinthian colony of Potidaia, the contractual arrangement spelled out in the colony's charter bound Athens to intervene on the colony's behalf.

Other features of the Brea regulations deserve note. The first is that it is fairly clear that the incentive for leaving Athens was land. The establishment of the colony went hand in hand with the dispatch of ten land surveyors to divide the territory into parcels for the colonists. This makes particular sense when we consider the final clause of the regulations: the colonists are drawn from the bottom two tiers of the Solonian property classes: Zeugitai and Thetes. These were the very men who were either landless or owned the smallest plots and most marginal land. For them, ten good acres in a potentially hostile region was better than two acres of guaranteed hardship. It appears from the terms of the inscription that soldiers serving in the Athenian army were all given the opportunity to sign up for the colonial expedition; a clause in the inscription stipulates that after they return to Athens (presumably from their current campaign), they have thirty days in which to go to Brea as additional colonists. In short, colonies were an opportunity for many to start again, but in the knowledge that they retained significant ties with Athens.

Cleruchies

Continued connections to Athens were also central to the other demographic instrument of Athenian imperialism: the cleruchy. Cleruchies resembled colonies, in that they involved the allocation of land in allied or foreign territory to Athenians, but the cleruchs retained their Athenian citizenship and their obligation to military service. Accordingly, cleruchies have sometimes been described as a cross between a colony and a garrison. By putting Athenians in non-Athenian territory, cleruchies constituted an effective tool for imperial control of the Aegean by Athens. Cleruchies flourished in the late 450s and 440s BC, and are attested on Euboia, in the Chersonese, as well as on Andros and Naxos. This was during a period, as we have seen, when Athens was in real danger of losing control of the Delian League. As the Persian Wars passed into memory, the justifications of the Athenians for their empire would have sounded more hollow with each year. As the Persian threat receded, the hegemonial power of the Athenians became both more onerous to the allies, and at times more vulnerable to resistance. By seizing land, Athens both pacified states that had proved restive or rebellious, and at the same time imposed a unique form of punishment. When we examine the tribute quotas of the states that received cleruchies, we often observe sharp drops in their payments, which have been plausibly interpreted as evidence that after the arrival of the Athenian cleruchs the original communities were incapable of paying at their earlier, higher rates. With their best land now in the hands of Athenians, rebellious allies were paying the price of revolt. A good example is the island of Andros: the Andrians paid 12 talents in tribute in 450 BC, but in 449 that rate dropped to 6 talents, and stayed at that rate for years afterwards. Similarly, in 453 Karystos on Euboia paid 12 talents, but over the next four years their tribute was reduced twice until they paid only 5 talents.

Aside from these scattered epigraphic attestations, there is also powerful evidence of the use of cleruchies as an instrument of imperial control in Thucydides' account (3.50) of the aftermath of the revolt of Mytilene on Lesbos in 427. After the

surrender of the city, the Athenians put to death one thousand of the leaders of the revolt, tore down the city walls, and seized the Mytilenians' ships. They then divided the land of Lesbos into three thousand lots, consecrated the three hundred choicest lots to the gods, and gave the rest to Athenians (that is, themselves) with the remaining population of Lesbians working the land that they rented from the Athenians at the rate of 2 minas of silver per lot per year. The Athenians thus took in 100 talents per year in private revenue from a single island, much more than they took in as tribute from any allied state. Some scholars have argued that in general the Athenians were absentee landlords and therefore not an intrusive presence in the day-to-day life of the cleruchies, but what is not in doubt is that cleruchies profited the richest Athenians, who gained productive land overseas where they could grow grain for sale back in Athens. It is not a coincidence that by the late fourth century BC the island of Lemnos was largely in the hands of Athenian cleruchs, and that the island produced four times as much wheat as all of Attica, especially the preferred variety of bread wheat. Cleruchies were a key feature of the Athenian control of one of the primary economic resources of the Aegean world: productive land.

Coercion

Although there were many aspects of Athenian imperial control that rankled with their subjects, Thucydides is adamant that one factor was by far the most irksome: tribute, or **phoros**. He states:

Of all the causes of defection, that connected with arrears of tribute and vessels, and with failure of service, was the chief; for the Athenians were very severe and exacting, and made themselves offensive by applying the screw of necessity to men who were not used to and in fact not disposed for any continuous labour. In some other respects the Athenians were not the old popular rulers they had been at first; and if they had more than their fair share of service, it was correspondingly easy for them to reduce any that tried to leave the confederacy. For this the allies had themselves to blame; the wish to get off service making most of them arrange to pay their share of the expense in money instead of in ships, and so to avoid having to leave their homes. Thus while Athens was increasing her navy with the funds which they contributed, a revolt always found them [the allies] without resources or experience for war.

(Thucydides, *The Peloponnesian War* 1.99, trans. Crawley)

In his contemplation of the realities of power, Thucydides was always fascinated by the behavior of unequal parties, and his analysis of the allied resentment of tribute fits a pattern, according to which he saw weaker parties as responsible in part for their own enslavement. Even so, it is hard to find a reason not to accept his analysis. Tribute was the most obvious sign of the allies' subordination, both real and symbolic. One wonders how people from the allied states felt when they looked at the Lapis Primus, the stele recording payments to Athena from the tribute exacted from the allies, and saw the name of their state. Pride, occasioned by piety? Or chagrin at the Athenians reveling in the subjugation of other Greek states?

The allies were not the only ones dissatisfied with the nexus of democracy and empire. Athenians hostile to the democracy also recognized that the democracy and the empire went hand in hand. The link between the two was the navy: it was both a tool of imperial control and an expression of the egalitarian spirit of Athens. There were also those who were hostile to the idea of empire itself, and who claimed that the greatness of imperial Athens was inextricably linked to its moral decline. In the *Gorgias*, Plato depicts Sokrates lamenting the moral corruption that resulted from Athens' rise to imperial greatness in terms that focus on naval power:

You, Kallikles, praise those men who have given the citizens everything they ever wanted. They say that they made the city great, but they do not understand that thanks to those men of old there is a tumor swelling in the city's belly. Because without a thought for temperance or justice, they stuffed the city with harbors and dockyards and walls and tribute and crap of that sort; as a result, whenever the city in its weakness stumbles, they blame their current crop of political leaders, all the while praising Themistokles and Kimon and Perikles, who are the real cause of all their woes.

(Plato, *Gorgias* 519a, trans. McInerney)

Not for the last time conservative thinkers would view power and prosperity as indications of moral decline. Just as in recent times the moral decline of the United States, Great Britain, or the West in general, have been tropes of conservative discourse, so too in the Athenian case, the defeat of Athens in the Peloponnesian War would also color the view of later thinkers, leading them to look back nostalgically upon an earlier time when Athens was poorer and more humble, less powerful but more upright. Such nostalgia usually yearns for a less egalitarian time as well: every age needs its Downton Abbey.

By the time the Peloponnesian War broke out in 431 BC, the Athenians had grown to rely on their empire to keep them supplied with grain and to provide the city with a steady source of revenue. They had accomplished this by increasing their control of trade throughout the Aegean. Over the course of the fifth century BC, for example, the number of states in the Delian League minting their own coinage had dropped from seventy-nine in 478 to thirty-four by 420. Since minting one's own coinage was, and still is, a mark of a community's autonomy, the steady diminution of local mints is a handy diagnostic for growing Athenian economic power. Once war broke out in 431, however, both revenues and grain were threatened. In addition, there were concerns regarding unpaid tribute in arrears and it was believed that insufficient tribute was coming in. Little wonder that the Athenians took measures to strengthen their grip on the allies. Leading politicians such as Kleonymos, Thoudippos, and Kleinias all proposed ways of improving revenue collection. Then, around 414 BC, the Athenians made two important decisions. The first was to cancel tribute altogether and to replace this with a 5 percent tax on import and exports. The second was to require every state within the Delian League to adopt Athenian weights and measures. This last requirement also involved melting down all local coins and reminting the metal on Athenian standards. It is perhaps one of the ironies of Greek history that political and economic decisions that were moving the Aegean toward increasingly free trade coincided with the war that would break Athenian imperial control of the same region. We shall trace the course of that war in Chapter 11, but first the culture that became synonymous with Classical Athens at its height commands our attention.

The Lapis Primus and Recovering the Athenian Empire

Responding to the destruction of their naval expedition to Egypt and ensuing revolts throughout the empire, the Athenians moved the treasury of the Delian League from Delos to Athens around 454 BC. For the next forty years, the Athenians would take one-sixtieth of the tribute they collected from the allies and offer it as a gift to Athena. The Athenians called these payments *aparchai*, or first fruits, and scholars often refer to the annual records of these payments as tribute lists or quota lists. With their habitual concern for record-keeping and accountability, the Athenians inscribed the amounts of aparchai on large marble blocks. The first and most important of these is known as the Lapis Primus, a massive block that contained lists of money paid from 454–453 down to 440–439 BC. The Lapis Primus provides vivid details about how the Athenians organized their empire.

The Lapis Primus is reconstructed from more than 180 separate pieces of marble found on the Akropolis over the course of the nineteenth and early twentieth centuries. Three scholars— H. T. Wade-Gery, Benjamin Merritt, and Malcolm McGregor—reassembled the fragments in 1927 in what is essentially a gigantic three-dimensional puzzle, at which point the pieces were set in a plaster matrix reinforced by iron bars on the interior (**8.10**). Their work was painstaking and many of their insights into the arrangement of the fragments were brilliant, allowing us, for example, to see how the Athenians organized their tribute

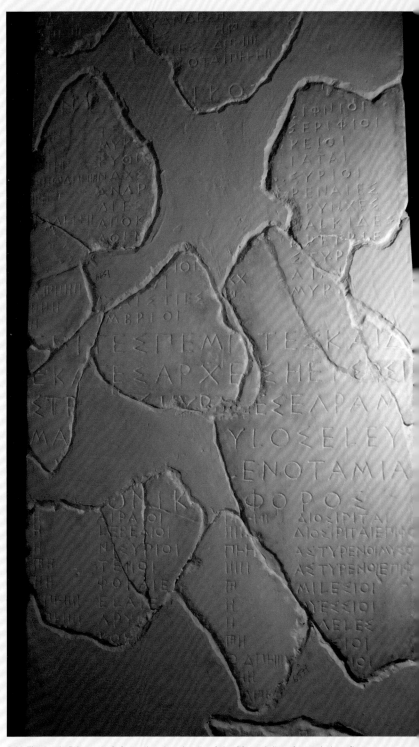

8.10 The Lapis Primus. Left face, showing details of the fifteenth list of aparchai, or first-fruit offerings to Athena, taken from the tribute paid to Athens by the allies, 440–439 BC. Marble, H: 3.5 m (11 ft 6 in.)

8.11 Reconstruction of the Akropolis on the eve of the Persian invasion of 480 BC. The Temple of Athena Polias, center right, had just been built under the new Athenian democracy, c. 510 BC. The Older Parthenon, started after Marathon, was under construction. The site, on the south side of the Akropolis, was later occupied by the current Parthenon, built under Perikles. Note that at the time of the destruction, the building site would have been surrounded by wooden scaffolding, thus accounting for the fire damage done to many of the marble architectural blocks.

collection by regions. But the physical reconstruction of the Lapis Primus also presents problems. New fragments, for example, have continued to come to light, and reintegrating them into the reconstructed block is not simple. Second, setting the fragments into plaster has meant that the backs of fragments are not available for study, making measurements of the thickness of the reconstruction approximate and preventing the possibility of finding internal joins between fragments not visible on the surface. Finally, the iron rods holding the reconstructed stele together are deteriorating. The Director of the Epigraphical Museum has announced plans to disassemble the entire reconstruction, meaning that it will soon be possible to study this vital inscription afresh, using new techniques unavailable in the 1920s

to measure and read the Athenian tribute lists.

Even in its present state, the Lapis Primus is extraordinarily impressive. Standing more than 3.5 meters (11 ft 6 in.) tall, the inscribed block is twice the height of most of the people who would have seen it prominently displayed on the Akropolis in antiquity. The block is at least 1.14 meters (3ft 9 in.) wide and nearly 0.4 meters (1 ft 4 in.) thick. (A second monumental block, the Lapis Secundus, also stood on the Akropolis and displayed the aparchai for the years from 439–438 to 432–431; after 432–431 the Athenians began entering the annual records each on separate, smaller stelai.)

The sheer size of the Lapis Primus, inscribed with fifteen years of quotas, has been investigated recently by an American archaeologist,

Margaret M. Miles, who has argued persuasively that the block on which these first quota lists were inscribed was, in fact, originally brought to the Akropolis to serve as an architrave block in the Older Parthenon. The Athenians were building this earlier Parthenon (a new temple for Athena begun after their victory at the Battle of Marathon) and it was still under scaffolding when the Persians invaded a second time and burnt it down, along with the new Temple of Athena Polias (**8.11**).

The suggestion that the Lapis Primus is a reused architectural block fits well with what we know of Athenian practice after the Persian Wars. What was offered to the goddess became her property, whether sculpture, architecture, or smaller objects. Even though the material was damaged by the Persians, it had to remain on the Akropolis, so the Athenians either buried it there or reused it. If Miles' theory is correct, then in the 450s the Athenians had at hand a number of marble architectural pieces from the destroyed temple of Athena. How better to put them to use than in structures that visually emphasized the recovery and the piety of the Athenians? The argument is also strengthened by the fact that this is exactly what the Athenians did with other pieces of the Older Parthenon, as any visitor to Athens can still see today when she or he looks up from the Agora below. The north wall of the Akropolis (**8.12**) conspicuously uses column drums from the Older Parthenon. Other sections of the same wall show triglyphs and metopes from the Temple of Athena Polias, so that the wall of the Akropolis both recalls the impiety of the Persians and attests to the piety of the Athenians.

Had the Lapis Primus been a piece of sculpture rather than an architrave block, it might have suffered a slightly different fate. In the 1860s French excavators on the Akropolis made an extraordinary discovery: a trove of Archaic sculptures that had been pulled down by the Persians and then reverently buried by the Athenians. More burnt and broken sculpture and painted pottery was subsequently excavated by Greek and German excavators in the 1880s, and the entire deposit is usually referred to as the *Perserschutt*, or Persian Debris (**8.13**). This is not a garbage dump. Rather, it is evidence that the Athenians looked upon the Akropolis as the goddess's own place in Athens. Everything that had ever been deposited there was the property of the goddess, and remained sacred whatever became of it. Along with the Lapis Primus, the Perserschutt tells a story with many aspects, combining power and piety in a way typical of Athens in the fifth century.

8.12 Column drums of the Older Parthenon incorporated in the northern wall of the Akropolis

8.13 Sculpture from the Perserschutt, including the Moscophoros (Calf-Bearer; *c.* 560 BC), photographed at the time of discovery in 1866

| 525–456 BC | 497–406 BC | c. 485–406 BC | c. 450–c. 386 BC | >454 BC |
| Aischylos | Sophokles | Euripides | Aristophanes | Transfer of treasury from Delos to Athens |

Chapter 9

Inclusion and Exclusion: Life in Periklean Athens

What was life like in the Athens of Perikles? In this chapter we will focus on two areas in which Athens witnessed significant cultural change during the fifth century BC. The first area is that of drama, one of the most significant Greek cultural innovations. Although tragedy and comedy are important genres of literature, we will also emphasize the social context of drama, presenting it as a "parademocratic" institution, that is, as a socially constructed performance which by its form and nature reinforced the egalitarian ethos of the Athenian democracy. The second significant area of change was in the transformation of the Akropolis, begun under Perikles, whose leadership of Athens defined the period. As we shall see, the Akropolis was the primary location in Athens where the Athenian community defined its identity, memorialized its past, and exalted itself as a democratic empire. Finally, in order to present a balanced picture of Athens in its heyday, we will also examine the three groups whose exclusion from democratic participation nevertheless made democracy possible: women, slaves, and resident aliens.

Drama

A key institution in Athenian life was theater. Through tragedy, comedy, and a third genre known as satyr plays, the Athenians gave expression to a complex worldview that was at times pessimistic, at times hilarious, but always unflinchingly direct in its portrayal of the whole range of human experience. Modern productions allow us to recapture something of the fierce honesty of tragedy and the riotous anarchy of comedy, but viewed from the perspective of its social function, ancient drama was quite different from its modern counterpart. Plays in Athens were performed as parts of festivals in honor of Dionysos, and were witnessed by most of the citizen population. They were civic and religious events, but above all else they were communal events.

Origins of Drama

The origins of Athenian drama go back to the sixth century BC, and probably lie in the agricultural festivals that celebrated the harvest. On round threshing floors, lines of young men and women would perform songs and dances called **dithyrambs** in honor of Dionysos, the god of nature and wine. According to legend, a certain Thespis of Ikaria

(a deme in northern Attica), was the first to add a speaking part (later known as the protagonist); with the addition of a second character (the antagonist), the transition from purely choral performance to drama had begun. In its developed form, Greek drama consisted primarily of odes sung by the chorus that were punctuated by sections (known as episodes) in which two characters would exchange alternating lines of dialogue. Such exchanges, called ***stichomythia***, lent themselves to the sharp expression of opposing viewpoints, so that by its very structure, Greek drama encouraged and expressed agonistic or combative exchanges between characters. Many of the central dramatic pairings of Greek drama—such as Antigone and Kreon, Medea and Jason, and Helen and Hekuba—all conform to this very simple principle of dramatic conflict.

Eventually a third actor was added, and with the use of heavy robes, costumes, and masks it was possible for these three actors to assume different roles (**9.1**). Standard character types and roles recurred, such as the powerful ruler, the messenger, the nurse, and the heroine. The chorus, too, was a kind of character, often identified as town elders or as more subordinate characters, such as the Corinthian women in the *Medea*. It seems that in the earliest

periods the chorus served as a kind of Everyman, offering normative reactions couched in conventional terms that responded to the chaotic and subversive actions of the principal actors. Over time, the chorus would offer less commentary, but the choral components of song and dance were always present.

Most plots for tragedy were taken from either the story of the Trojan War (and its aftermath) or the Seven Against Thebes cycle (see p. 222). With such conventional and familiar plots, as well as the simplicity of the plays' structure and the almost total lack of special effects, it is worth asking the question, what made these plays so powerful? Any answer must certainly take into account the serious topics that tragedy dealt with—murder, incest, parricide, and execution regularly figure in the plays—but there are other important features of drama that contributed to its impact.

Drama was first and foremost an aural experience. The Greeks were keenly aware of how combinations of long and short syllables in words and phrases could be artfully employed to create metrical schemes that were associated with dirges, marches, dances, and stately hymns. Playwrights used these different meters, and it was the poetic quality of their language more than anything else that engaged an audience. Sometimes the beat of the meter matched the natural emphasis of a word; sometimes it clashed with it. Either way, it did not resemble our own modern experience of drama. We watch it; the Greeks, raised on hearing Homer's poetry, listened to it. (Opera is on some ways the modern-day equivalent, and the closest we can come to experiencing the pleasure of listening to the poetic crafting of language.) Accordingly, when we judge a dramatic performance based on the actor's ability to imbue a character with emotion through posture, facial expression, and diction, we are reacting to elements that are virtually meaningless in the context of Greek tragedy. The use of masks sums up the difference between our aesthetic and theirs. With no facial expressions to respond to, the audience relied much more on the aural experience (**9.2**).

Katharsis

Despite the absence of what we might call naturalism, these plays worked powerfully on the audience's feelings. For Aristotle, the key to effective drama was **katharsis** (also spelled "catharsis"). Katharsis is the process by which the audience, by being forced to contemplate the unthinkable, are cleansed of their worst impulses and fears. In Sophokles' *Oidipous Tyrannos* (usually called Oedipus Rex in English), we watch and hear as Oidipous learns of his horrific actions, namely having killed his father and fathered two children by his own mother. By forcing his audience to confront the taboos of incest and parricide, Sophokles allows the audience to experience katharsis. It is this utter honesty that makes Greek tragedy so compelling. The plays do not propose that all humans are killers or incestuous, but they do suggest that anyone could do horrific things. The katharsis we experience is partly the relief we feel at having avoided the terrible fate of Oidipous.

Greek tragedy challenges its audiences not only through the confrontation between characters, but also by dramatizing conflicts between fundamentally irreconcilable value systems. Consider, for example, Antigone's dilemma in the eponymous play by Sophokles. Her two brothers, Eteokles and Polyneikes, have fallen out with each other, and both perish in battle before the walls of Thebes. Only Eteokles has been given a decent burial by his successor, Kreon; Polyneikes, the rebel who had led a coalition of heroes (known as the Seven Against Thebes), lies in disgrace outside the city walls, his burial forbidden by Kreon.

What should Antigone do? Obey the king and allow her brother's corpse to be picked clean by scavenging animals (thereby flouting the dictates of natural law, which demands honoring her brother with burial), or obey the obligations of blood and family, bury her brother, and thereby break the state's law? There is no possibility of compromise, no way of satisfying both natural and human justice: she is in an untenable position. She ends up burying her brother, and for this deed of natural goodness is buried alive in a tomb. Nor do the deaths finish there. When Kreon's son, Haimon, tries to release her, he finds she has hanged herself, whereupon he stabs himself. We have a mania for closure and reconciliation, but the Greeks saw each tragedy as only a way station on a much longer trail of tears.

The Dionysia

Greek drama was also distinctive from modern-day drama in other respects. While for us, television and movies can be streamed onto laptops, telephones, or big-screen televisions, anywhere and at any time, tragedy in Athens was performed only under very particular conditions at two festivals, the Dionysia and the Lenaia. Tragedians would present their works in advance for selection, and magistrates would select only three tragedians for a single festival. Each tragedian produced a trilogy for performance at the festival, and the three plays would be performed over the course of a single day. (In addition to the tragic trilogy, a satyr play, which mixed comic and burlesque elements, was staged at the end of the day in order to lighten the atmosphere.) Tragedy was also distinctive in this respect: the festival was a competition as well as a religious event, and at the end of the three days a crown was offered to the tragedian whose trilogy was judged the best. Aischylos, Sophokles, and Euripides were all, at different times in their careers, winners at the Dionysia.

It is important to keep the festival setting of tragedy in mind for two reasons. The first is that tragedy had a meaningful connection to the worship of Dionysos, who was a god who did more than bless humans with the gift of wine. For the Greeks, Dionysos was a god associated with transgression. Often depicted with luxurious hair and feminine clothes, he and his worshipers represented threats to social order: transvestism and drunkenness challenged normal behavior. But his major celebration, the Great Dionysia, was also a festival that celebrated the normative roles of men and women in society. By purging the most antisocial and dangerous drives in us, the plays of the Dionysia offer the audience the prospect of a truly communitarian experience. In binary and paradoxical fashion, Dionysos stands for what makes us crudest and most savage, and also what makes us orderly and capable of civilized behavior. Theater is his space, both the place where we meet as a community and where we explore transgression against that community, the actions that arise from our human passions that threaten order and society (**9.3**). Through tragedy, theater created a setting in which Greeks could explore the worst, most anti-social psychoses. By enacting the very worst possible human crimes and purging us of the drives that make these possible, theater served to bind the democratic community together.

Drama, as a social institution, therefore has everything to do with Dionysos. For this reason many plays explore dilemmas of piety and obligation, but not just at the level of the individual, as in the case of Antigone. There is also an important relationship between traditional notions of piety and the entire community. Exploring this is at the core of theater's function in Classical Athens. Consider, for example, the dilemma of Pelasgos, king of Argos, in Aischylos's *Suppliants*. The play relates the story of the daughters of Danaos who have returned to Argos, their ancestral home, fleeing from undesirable marriages to their Egyptian cousins, marriages which the women refer to as a man-made prison. Pursued by their would-be husbands, they beg for protection from the men of Argos:

Shall one who sits before her own kind
   pleading heaven's law
Find no relief mandated
In the laws of men? Zeus Suppliant's anger
Burns unquenchable though its victim
Lament to the end.

          (Aischylos, *Suppliants* 476–82, trans. Lembke)

Pelasgos must weigh up the request for asylum from the daughters of Danaos with the likelihood that granting their supplication will bring war down on his people from the Egyptians. Even though the women of Argos chide the suppliants, saying in effect that marriage is a woman's destiny, Pelasgos chooses to honor the request of the suppliants. Taking in refugees is a profound ethical obligation, even if it means provoking further anger from the Egyptians. In an extraordinary speech, Danaos reports to his daughters that their salvation has been accomplished, not just by the decision of Pelasgos, but by a vote of the Argive assembly, which has been persuaded by their king. His report begins with the words, "It has been decided by the Argives," closely imitating the beginning of a formal Athenian decree, "It has been decided by the Athenians." So the salvation of the Danaids results from two factors: suppliants are protected by the will of Zeus, and the case of the Danaids has been decided by a democratic vote of the civic body. The play reinforces the idea that the Athenian community is both a political entity (a democracy), and a community bound by shared religious beliefs and ethical imperatives.

The universal power of Greek drama is rightly praised, but we would do well to remember that these

9.3 The Theater of Dionysos, Athens, seen from the Akropolis. The original theater dates to the sixth century BC and was extensively rebuilt in the fourth century and later in the Roman period. The marble orchestra (the semicircular space where the chorus performed), thrones for priests and dignitaries, and parts of the scene building are all visible.

plays were produced in a specific time and place: democratic, fifth-century Athens. The plays therefore often reflect their contemporary setting and deal with contemporary issues.

Take, for example, Euripides' *Medea*. First performed in Athens in 431 BC, the play deals with the dilemma of a foreign woman, Medea, brought to Greece by her lover, Jason, and then abandoned by him so that he can make a more advantageous marriage to the daughter of the king of Corinth. Enraged and powerless, Medea arranges for the death of her rival, then slaughters her own children before disappearing in a fiery chariot. On one level, her denunciations of the powerlessness of women, who, she says, purchase their own servitude through marriage, resonate with anyone who has experienced prejudice against women in society, but quite aside from this universality, the play has a very particular point to make: twenty years earlier, the Athenians (under the direction of Perikles) had passed a law according to which every legitimate Athenian had to be the child of both an Athenian father *and* mother. As we saw in Chapter 8, this law may have been an attempt to safeguard the exclusivity of Athenian citizenship, or it may have been aimed specifically at those aristocrats, such as Perikles' opponent Kimon, who married non-Athenian women. Whatever the conditions behind the passage of the law in 451 BC, however, its consequences were becoming clear by 431. At precisely the moment when the play was performed, a generation of boys were reaching manhood only to find that those with mothers who were not Athenian (such as Medea) were ineligible for citizenship. The numbers may not have been great, although according to Plutarch five thousand individuals were disenfranchised by the law. Whether this figure is reliable or not, Euripides' play addresses an issue that was very much in the minds of his contemporaries. The greatest tragedies can be as timely as they are timeless.

Comedy

As was the case with tragedies, comic plays were also staged at the Dionysia and Lenaia, and were also performed in competition. But if tragedies explored our deepest passions, comedy investigated prevailing habits and attitudes, satirized foolishness, and tested tolerance. This is perhaps more true of the comic plays of the fifth century, collectively called

9.4 Movie poster for Spike Lee's *Chi-Raq* (2015)

Old Comedy, than the milder plays of the fourth century, known to us from the romantic comedies of Menander. Old Comedy is more robust, to judge from the fragments we have from the poets Kratinos and Eupolis, and the eleven surviving plays by Aristophanes. Taken together they give a good idea of Old Comedy's preoccupations, and show that comedy was a thoroughly democratic genre. The plays ridicule politicians, such as Kleon, whose gigantic ego and violent language both amused and alarmed his contemporaries, and use contemporary events such as the Peloponnesian War as the inspiration for wild fantasies: in the *Lysistrata*, for example, the women of Athens go on a sex strike to force the men to make peace. The recent popularity of this plot device, in the Lysistrata Project and Spike Lee's film *Chi-Raq*, suggests that Aristophanes' humor (in a similar way to Euripides' tragedies), speaks equally to Athenians of the fifth century BC and modern-day audiences (**9.4**).

Even in its most far-flung mode, Old Comedy still manages to strike modern-day audiences. Aristophanes' plays, for example, often feature fantastically absurd plots, as in *Birds* when two Athenians fly off to Cloudcuckooland to avoid the war. Many commentators have noted that in the twentieth century the Theater of the Absurd and Monty Python both demonstrated the attraction of silliness. When the world is senseless, so, it seems, is the humor it creates. The language of comedy, too, can be crazy, although this presents a special challenge to the translator. Aristophanes uses a dialect close to ordinary Greek, but also invents ridiculous new words, the longest of which is a 171-letter word for a meat and seafood dish. (Surf'n'turf looks tame by comparison.) The advertisement for Spike Lee's *Chi-Raq* shows how often translating Aristophanes is less about finding an exact English equivalent for his peculiar Greek and more a matter of catching the spirit of the comedy: the tagline of the film, "No Peace/No Piece," is not a line that occurs in Aristophanes, but it is perfectly Aristophanic in spirit. Aside from crazy language, Aristophanes' plays also frequently feature gags that revolve around farting and masturbation (**9.5**). There is a direct line from Aristophanes to *Animal House*.

9.5 Detail of red-figure bell-krater depicting a choral scene from Aristophanes' *Birds*, *c*. 415–400 BC. Note the outlandish costumes and prosthetic penises. Ceramic, H: 18.7 cm (7⅜ in.)

The Democracy of Drama

If the language and subjects of Old Comedy were distinctively democratic—satirizing politicians and lampooning Athenian war policies—the festival setting reinforced the plays' democratic impact. Both comedies and tragedies were experienced by the entire community together in the theater of Dionysos, not privately. As in attending the courts or the assembly, going to the Lenaia repeated a familiar pattern: the community of citizens assembled to witness a performance by a select few speakers. The performers were the professionals, or at least trained, but their status was balanced by the large, anonymous audience, who, like jurors, exercised a controlling power by voting on the performance. The result was that the theater replicated the social dynamic of the democratic assembly. Furthermore, the individuals being ridiculed in the plays were often right there in the very audience, and the tradition that Kleon prosecuted Aristophanes reflects the fact that comedic satire was just as much a feature of Athenian political life as the scurrilous invective that characterized forensic and deliberative oratory. The roots of this abusive language lie in the iambographic tradition, a genre that used insult and abuse to attack one's rivals, not unlike playing the dozens in contemporary African-American communities. The iambographic tradition went back to the sixth century BC or earlier, but in democratic Athens there were plenty of opportunities for abusing one's opponents.

Tragedy and comedy helped to constitute the inclusivity of the Athenian community, and reinforced the shared belief that reverence for the gods was characteristic of the Athenians and flowed on into communal relations. This is a theme often used by Athenian orators to castigate their enemies: if a man didn't know how to behave toward the gods, how could he be trusted to behave honorably toward other citizens? Demosthenes develops this idea in a speech delivered against his opponent, Meidias, when he distinguishes between a private insult delivered against Demosthenes personally and an insult against Demosthenes the public figure, whose activities were directed toward the gods on behalf of the city. Demosthenes explains the distinction as follows:

Now if I had not been chorus-master, men of Athens, when I was thus maltreated by Meidias, it is only the personal insult that one would have condemned; but under the circumstances I think one would be justified in condemning also the impiety of the act. You surely realize that all your choruses and hymns to the god are sanctioned, not only by the regulations of the Dionysia, but also by the oracles, in all of which, whether given at Delphi or at Dodona, you will find a solemn injunction to the State to set up dances after the ancestral custom, to fill the streets with the savour of sacrifice, and to wear garlands.

(Demosthenes, *Against Meidias* 51–54, trans. Murray)

Demosthenes' words were designed to appeal to the Athenians' way of seeing themselves. He does not dismiss the Dionysia as a mere excuse for performing plays, but rather as an instantiation of the Athenian character: we produce drama, he says, in accordance with the command of heaven. In the eyes of the Athenians, therefore, to be a part of the Athenian community one had to be a participant in all the rituals, sacrifices, and processions that marked everyday life in Athens.

The Akropolis

In fifth-century Athens, participation in the world of drama as producer, actor, playwright, or audience meant inclusion within the Athenian community. Next to the theater, the other principal venue for the performance of Athenian identity was the Akropolis.

When Athens was at the height of its power in the age of Perikles, the Athenian Akropolis would be radically reimagined as an expression of both that power and the shared identity of the Athenians. The Parthenon, Propylaia, and Erechtheion should be viewed not solely as majestic architectural accomplishments but also as tangible proof that in Periklean Athens, democracy, community, and imperial power were inextricably bound to each other through religion.

Although the Athenians had sworn, in common with the rest of the Greeks, to leave unrestored the temples burnt by the Persians as a reminder of the Persians' impiety, under Perikles, the Athenians would begin an ambitious building program on the Akropolis, transforming it into the showpiece of an imperial capital. The funding of the program reveals how these two concerns—religious piety and imperial power—helped pay for the rebuilding. With the transference of the Delian League treasury to Athens in 454 BC, massive amounts of silver were sent directly to Athens each year. The original assessment of 460 talents in 478 BC had risen to 1500 talents before tribute was replaced by the 5 percent trade tax during the Peloponnesian War. As we saw in Chapter 8 with the Lapis Primus, from this tribute, aparchai (first fruits) of one-sixtieth were offered to Athena every year and duly deposited in the Treasury of Athena, separate from League or Athenian state funds. From the tribute (excluding the aparchai), the

9.6 Drawing of the Akropolis at the end of the fifth century BC showing the major buildings of the Periklean construction program

Erechtheion

Parthenon

Propylaia

Athena Nike Temple

Athenians, as we have seen, maintained a fleet of at least two hundred triremes each year. But aside from meeting the expenses of the fleet, on a number of occasions over the next twenty years, the Athenians also transferred additional money, beyond the annual aparchai payments, from the Hellenotamiai (treasurers) to the Treasury of Athena, money that helped finance the building program devised by Perikles. In other words, money from the empire was channeled through dedications to the goddess Athena, and then put to Athenian use.

The architectural transformation of the city began immediately after the treasury was moved to Athens around 454 BC. Over the course of a generation the Athenians embarked on an astonishing number of major building projects: the Parthenon, the Propylaia, the Erechtheion, the Nike temple, the sanctuary of Brauronian Artemis, the Chalkotheke (all on the Akropolis; see **9.6**), as well as the Odeion, the temple of Artemis Agrotera (on the Ilissos River), the temple of Athena at Pallene, the temple of Poseidon at Sounion, the temple of Nemesis at Rhamnous, and the Teleusterion at Eleusis. Nor were these buildings cheap. The Parthenon was reported to have cost 469 talents, more than the total annual tribute received by the Athenians at the time the Delian League was founded. Plutarch reports that there was widespread criticism among the allies of Perikles' misuse of money that was intended to pay for their defense, not pretty buildings. He describes the controversy this way:

They said, "The Greeks must be insulted by this appalling act of arrogance and consider it to be clear-cut tyranny, when they see us covering our city with gold and beautifying it with the tribute taken from them by force, for the war against Persia."

(Plutarch, *Life of Perikles* 12, trans. Buckley)

Some scholars have doubted the reliability of Plutarch's account, and have suggested that there is no solid evidence for the use of allied money to finance the Periklean building program, but this takes skepticism too far. The Treasurers of Athena are listed on the Parthenon Building Accounts as the financial officers who paid for the building, and it was they who managed the money given to Athena from the allies' tribute. The allies were right to complain: it was an imperial building program.

9.7 The Parthenon seen from the west as one enters the Akropolis from the Propylaia. The building was begun in 448 BC, shortly after the transfer of the Delian League treasury to Athens *c*. 454 BC.

9.8 Parthenon, Athens: detail of east side showing curvature of stylobate and stereobate levels, 447–438 BC.

The Parthenon and Propylaia

The building that began the beautification of Athens was the Parthenon, a massive temple dedicated to Athena that would house the gold and ivory statue designed by Pheidias. Work started in 448 BC under the supervision of Iktinos and the building was completed in only a decade (**9.7**). The Parthenon has always been an architect's delight, and a great deal has been written about the building's architecture, especially the refinements that give the building a more organic and softer appearance: the curvature of the stylobate (the flat platform on which the columns stood, which actually rises toward the center; see **9.8**), and the ***entasis*** of the columns (the slight bulge toward the center of the column).

Despite these innovations, the Parthenon was also built with an eye to the existing topography of the Akropolis: it was part of a landscape of memory, in which new buildings actively related to their

9.9 Nike Bastion, north face, with view through to Mycenaean phases

is the bloom of perpetual newness, as it were, upon these works of his.

(*Life of Perikles* 13, trans. Perrin)

Plutarch's response, however romanticized, reminds us of an important feature of the building: the Parthenon was both highly conventional and yet radically original. This is best illustrated by the sculptural program. Temples traditionally chose from a fairly limited repertoire of themes for their sculptural decoration, often depicting battles between humans and centaurs, Greeks and Amazons, or Gods versus the Giants (known as centauromachies, amazonomachies, and gigantomachies). These were perennial favorites, each suggesting the cosmic battle between order and chaos, while the deeds of such heroes as Herakles and Theseus were also popular. The Parthenon drew on these stock scenes, along with the Trojan War, for the metopes of the Doric frieze on the outside of the temple, above the columns. (In a Doric frieze, each metope was set off from the others by a triglyph block, and each metope showed a single scene.) What made the Parthenon so bold was that the Athenians chose to complement these exterior metopes with a continuous Ionic frieze 170 meters (557 ft) long, running the length of the *cella* (inner chamber) wall.

High up on the cella wall, the Parthenon's Ionic frieze depicted the procession of the Greater Panathenaia, the great festival held every four years by all Athenians in honor of the city's goddess, Athena. The procession culminated in the presentation of the newly woven robe to Athena, a scene depicted in the middle of the frieze at the eastern end of the temple, immediately over the entrance to the chamber in which stood the magnificent gold and ivory statue of Athena. The cutaway reconstruction shown in **9.10** depicts both statue of Athena and the Ionic frieze.

For the first time, a major Greek temple was adorned by a frieze containing dozens of figures who were not gods, giants, or heroes, but who were idealized versions of the very people visiting the temple: the waterbearers, the musicians, and the herdsmen grappling with the cattle on the frieze were Athenians (**9.11**). That is what makes the Parthenon radical, and a powerful proof of the confidence of the

predecessors, many of which had been destroyed by the Persians but still retained significance. Even the Mycenaean phases of the Akropolis were put on display, including a bastion at the west end that Mnesikles, the architect of the Propylaia, incorporated into his design.

Today, visitors to the Akropolis still walk past a section of fifth-century-BC wall below the Nike Bastion that was constructed with a window in it, allowing visitors to catch a glimpse of the Mycenaean edifice within (**9.9**). The Athenians claimed to be autochthonous (indigenous to a place, as opposed to having arrived as migrants), and the way that both the recent past (the Persian Wars) and the deep past (Mycenaean, "Cyclopean" masonry) were incorporated into the presentation of the Akropolis reflects how seriously the Athenians believed that claim. To be an Athenian meant to claim a ancestral connection both with the past and with a specific locale: the Athenian Akropolis.

And yet, paradoxically, the Akropolis and the Parthenon in particular also represented a new attitude to the present. Plutarch evokes this in an often-quoted assessment of Perikles' architectural legacy:

Each one of [the buildings], in its beauty, was even then and at once antique; but in the freshness of its vigor it is, even to the present day, recent and newly wrought. Such

9.10 Cutaway showing the interior of the Parthenon, with the massive gold and ivory statue of Athena by Pheidias. Note the continuous Ionic frieze high on the exterior of the cella wall depicting the Panathenaic procession.

Athenians at the height of their power. The actual procession and the depiction of it on the Parthenon jointly articulated a distinctive Athenian ideology: the imperial democratic community was embodied as a pious sacrificial community.

The power of the Athenians was also reflected in Pheidias's massive statue of gold and ivory, placed in the cella of the Parthenon. Roman copies and depictions on coins show that the statue of Athena in the Parthenon presented the goddess attired in full armor, a reminder of the warrior qualities that were celebrated also at the Panathenaia. As a personification of the imperial Athenians, she was grand and imposing. She wore a helmet and the snake-fringed *aegis*, a protective goatskin given to her by her father, Zeus, while resting by her leg was a massive shield. In her right hand she held a golden Nike, a winged figure that served as the symbol of her martial victories. Recent research by Manolis Korres, the chief architect of the Akropolis Restoration Project, has revealed that the eastern cella wall of the Parthenon included windows on either side of the door, suggesting that the statue would have been well lit. A gallery running around the interior of the

9.11 South Block XLIV from the Ionic frieze on the south cella wall of the Parthenon, carved between 443–438 BC. The actual Panathenaic procession proceeded along the long northern side of the Parthenon toward the Great Altar, while depicted high on the cella wall was the same procession in stone. Instead of scenes from mythology, the Athenians here chose to portray themselves. Pentelic marble, H: 1.22 m (4 ft)

cella also made it possible for visitors to see the face and upper torso of the goddess from high up. The combination of painted surfaces and torchlight also meant that the statue would have had a dynamic quality. As the soft light played over the shiny ivory surface of the goddess's face, the flickering of the flames would have made the goddess seem alive.

Despite the investment and the innovations that characterize the Parthenon, just as remarkable was the second building of Perikles' program, the Propylaia. A monumental gateway had stood at the western entrance to the Akropolis in earlier times, but the size and scale of Mnesikles' masterpiece eclipsed its predecessor. Begun immediately after the completion of the Parthenon, the Propylaia was erected between 437 and 432 BC (**9.12**). The building uses Salamis as a visual point of reference, and the site of the Athenian naval victory over the Persians becomes the backdrop to the visitor's pilgrimage to the Akropolis, serving as a reminder of how the power of Athens was won.

The Erechtheion

The rebuilding of the Akropolis consistently deployed similar architectural orders and designs, making the visual environment of the Akropolis coherent and harmonious. The best example of the desire to make the Akropolis coherent is also the most peculiar building in Athens or anywhere else in the Greek world: the Erechtheion. Begun in 421 BC during a hiatus in the Peloponnesian War, the Erechtheion was built on the north side of the Akropolis in an area teeming with profound and ancient religious associations, near to the Old Temple of Athena (which had been burned by the Persians but whose back room was still in use during the fifth century as a treasury chamber).

It was here, for example, that an olive tree and a spring of brackish water were treated by the Athenians as the physical evidence of the contest between Athena and Poseidon for suzerainty over Athens. Each had offered the Athenians a gift, and the Athenians had chosen Athena's olive. It was here too that the Athenians pointed to a cleft that had been created by Zeus's thunderbolt in the very bedrock of the Akropolis. Aside from these religious associations, it was also here that the Athenians worshiped some of their earliest founder heroes, including Erechtheus, Kekrops, and his daughters Herse, Pandrosos, and

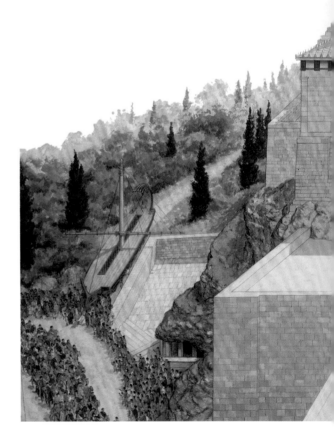

9.12 Peter Connelly's illustration of the Propylaia (center), as it would have appeared in the late fifth century on the occasion of the Panathenaic Festival. Also visible are the Nike Bastion (lower right) and the Parthenon (upper right). The Akropolis is approached from the west. Those exiting would see Salamis in the distance.

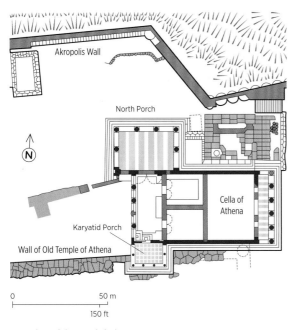

9.13 Plan of the Erechtheion, 421–406 BC

Aglauros. Furthermore, when the Athenians sought Athena's help, the **xoanon**, or olive wood statue, to which they prayed was housed here as well.

This was the most sacred location on the Akropolis. The challenge, therefore, was to design a building to bring architectural cohesion to a spot where there were so many cults and sacred associations, and an examination of the Erechtheion's ground plan reveals Mnesikles' solution (**9.13**). On the east side of the temple was the cella devoted to Athena Polias, where the xoanon was housed. (This statue was believed to have fallen from heaven, and was adorned with a new robe, or peplos, woven by the **Arrephoroi**, every four years.) To the west, but 3 meters (10 ft) lower, were two chambers that did not communicate with the cella to the east; they were instead approached from a porch that runs the width of the building. Their precise purpose is uncertain, but we know of cults of Hephaistos and the early Athenian hero, Boutes (the Plowman) that were housed in the Erechtheion. The north porch was designed to accommodate the cleft in the rock where Zeus struck Erechtheus with a thunderbolt, and so attentive were the Athenians to these physical signs of the gods' presence that the ceiling of the porch was

9.14 Foundations of the Old Temple of Athena, from top of Parthenon, with the Erechtheion to the north.

9.15 The Erechtheion, southwest view. The tree is modern.

constructed with a deliberate hole in the place of one coffer (a sunken panel in a ceiling), to show the path down from heaven taken by Zeus's thunderbolt. To the south is another porch, in which the six columns carrying the roof have been replaced with Karyatids, or, as the ancient inscription calls them, "Maidens" (korai). They probably served as symbolic libation bearers above the tomb of Kekrops. They also recall the Archaic korai of the pre-Persian Wars period, replacing the statues dedicated to the daughters of aristocratic families with anonymous young women of the Athenian democracy. This photograph of the foundations of the Old Athena Temple (**9.14**), (sometimes called the Dörpfeld Foundations after the great German excavator), reveals that the Karyatid porch of the Erechtheion was built so as to touch the older building. The Erechtheion would replicate the peculiar inner layout of the older temple and thus presents itself not so much as new but as a renewal of the ancestral building.

What the ground plan cannot capture is the irregularity of various levels associated with the building. The four different facades of the building hide many of these internal complexities and irregularities: the architect succeeded in tying many diverse and unrelated cults together into a complex that creates an illusion of orderly arrangement. Only outside the western face of the building would the visitor be aware of the different levels, yet it was here that the sacred olive tree of Athena grew, offering a broad, thick coverage of boughs and leaves to conceal the peculiarity of the architecture (**9.15**).

Symbols of Power

It is hard to view these buildings without recognizing in them an ideological statement: Athens' enormous power is deployed in honoring the gods. The greatness of Athens is thereby endorsed. At the same time, the fact that work began on the Propylaia as soon as the Parthenon was finished, and that work on the Erechtheion started as soon as the first phase of the Peloponnesian War ended in 421 BC, should prompt us to consider the impact of Perikles' building program on the Athenian economy. Considering that the daily wage of a skilled workman in fifth-century Athens was 1 drachma, we can calculate that the total cost of the Parthenon—469 talents— was the equivalent of 2,814,000 man-days of skilled labor. Over a ten-year period, this was enough to finance a workforce of nearly eight hundred men. When one considers the flow-on effects of this in the rest of the economy (since these men had to be fed, clothed, housed, and equipped), the Periklean building program begins to look very much like a public works program. Another way of thinking of this is to consider the difference between the tribute paid to Athens, including the first fruits given to the goddess, all of which was paid in coin or bullion and was effectively nothing more than passive wealth, and the money put into circulation by employing a small army of craftsmen, laborers, and slaves to build these temples. Even if part of the total cost went on building materials, such as the pentelic marble used for the temple's columns and entablature (so-called after its source, Mount Pentelikon), ultimately the money spent on these went back into the pockets of those Athenians who supplied them. According to Plutarch, this was a deliberate policy on the part of Perikles. He claims that Perikles responded to his critics by arguing:

It is only right that the city, when once she is sufficiently equipped with all that is necessary for prosecuting the war, should apply her abundance to such works as, by their completion, will bring her everlasting glory, and while in process of completion will bring that abundance into actual service, in that all sorts of activity and diversified demands arise, which rouse every art and stir every hand, and bring, as it were, the whole city under pay, so that she not only adorns, but supports herself as well from her own resources.

(*Life of Perikles* 12, trans. Perrin)

Some scholars have doubted that this represents contemporary thinking and have detected a whiff of Plutarch's experiences of imperial Rome in the account, but again, there is nothing inherently implausible about a democratic leader putting vast amounts of revenue into architectural projects that benefitted both city and workers.

Stimulating the economy was, of course, not the sole purpose of the building program. In place of the smattering of large and small temples, altars, cult spots, and dedications that had dotted the Archaic Akropolis, Perikles' architects fashioned a new sacred topography, making the remodeled Akropolis a unique expression of the unity of religion, democracy,

and imperial power. In place of the many Archaic dedications (and even small temples) that had been torn down by the Persians, the Athenians erected hundreds of stelai containing the decisions, laws, treaties, casualty lists, and honorary decrees of the democracy.

Under Perikles, the democracy had found a visual language for expressing the power, pride, and common identity of all Athenians. When the Panathenaic procession wound its way up to the Akropolis, the religious heart of Athens, the Athenians were borrowing a model of communal performance familiar from the panhellenic sanctuaries—Delphi, Olympia, Nemea, and Isthmia—where the participation of athletes, spectators, and ambassadors added up to the performance of being Greek. The Akropolis served this role for Athens, putting on display both the power and the piety that were the source of Athenian pride. Participating in the procession to the Akropolis and visiting so many spots redolent with mythic associations from the past forcefully marked the participants as Athenians.

Power and Exclusion

If so much of the cultural production of Athens in the fifth century can be read as intimately bound up with democracy, our modern understanding of the term may lead us to assume that this culture was equally available to all the inhabitants of democratic Athens. It was not. While we may celebrate the democratic nature of Athens, it is also surely important to examine the position of those groups in society who were explicitly excluded or marginalized from the democracy. Perikles' Athens, we have seen, was comprised of perhaps forty thousand citizens, counting only adult, freeborn males. Given an overall population of perhaps three hundred thousand, there were many more outside the club than in it. Leaving aside the status of children, we need to look at the place of women, slaves, and foreign residents in Classical Athens.

Women in Classical Athens

Examining the position of women in Classical Athens requires a broader investigation into the construction of sexual and gender identity in ancient Athens. It must be stressed that we have very few female voices from antiquity, so any claims regarding the status of women must be interpreted as representing men's attitudes toward women. Take, for example, Hesiod's explanation of how women were first created by the gods:

"But I will give men as the price for fire an evil thing in which they may all be glad of heart while they embrace their own destruction." So said the father of men and gods, and laughed aloud. And he bade famous Hephaistos make haste and mix earth with water and to put in it the voice and strength of human kind, and fashion a sweet, lovely maiden-shape, like to the immortal goddesses in face; and Athena to teach her needlework and the weaving of the varied web...and golden Aphrodite to shed grace upon her head and cruel longing and cares that weary the limbs. And he charged Hermes the guide, the Slayer of Argos, to put in her a shameless mind and a deceitful nature.

(Hesiod, *Works and Days* 58–68, trans. Evelyn-White)

Zeus orders the creation of women to punish men for the gift of fire, bestowed on mankind by Prometheus after he stole it from heaven. So, in this widespread and popular account, women are man's affliction.

Even more explicitly misogynistic is another poem that was popular in antiquity, Semonides' diatribe *On Women*. The poem consists of a series of descriptions of the various kinds of disgusting and lazy women who are the bane of men's lives. Each is likened to an animal: the ape for an ugly woman, the mare for a vain woman. Here, for example, is the bitch:

One type is from a dog—a no-good bitch,
A mother through and through; she wants to hear
Everything, know everything, go everywhere,
And stick her nose in everything, and bark
Whether she sees anyone or not.
A man can't stop her barking; not with threats,
Not (when he's had enough) by knocking out
Her teeth with a stone, and not with sweet talk either;
Even among guests, she'll sit and yap;
The onslaught of her voice cannot be stopped.

(Semonides, *On Women* 12–21, trans. Svarlien)

The casual violence referred to in the poem reminds us that the values of the Greeks were not always enlightened. The speaker of one speech in the works of Demosthenes makes a remark that might raise eyebrows in another age but clearly made sense to his audience of Athenian jurors, dividing the world into three classes of women whose roles are entirely defined by their relationship to men: "We have courtesans for pleasure, concubines for the daily service of our bodies, and wives for the production of legitimate offspring..." (Demosthenes 59.122).

Wives, who were women from citizen families, served to provide children who could inherit the family's property. This legalistic basis for marriage is made plain by one Greek word for marriage, **engyê**, which meant both a betrothal and a contract. It was a contract that, as the opening of Xenophon's *Economicus* makes clear, was not between man and woman, but between the woman's father and her husband. Preparing to teach his young wife the art of household management, Ischomachos opens the lesson by asking:

Tell me, wife, do you understand why I took you and your parents gave you to me in marriage? Because I am sure that you'll agree there would not have been a problem for either of us to find someone else to share each other's bed. But I gave a good deal of thought on my behalf, just as your parents did on yours, as to who would make the best partner for home and family. So I chose you, and your parents, it would seem, chose me from all the other possible candidates.

(Xenophon, *Economicus* 7.10–11, trans. McInerney)

It would be nice to know the young woman's name, but anonymity was prized by the Athenians when it came to good women. When Perikles addressed the mothers and wives of the men who had died on behalf of Athens, he offered this advice: "Great will be your glory in not falling short of your natural character; and greatest will be hers who is least talked of among the men, whether for good or for bad" (*The Peloponnesian War* 2.45.2).

The image of the anonymous, silent wife, waiting patiently at home for her husband, probably exists somewhere between reality and the Athenian male's vision of an ideal marriage. There is evidence, for example, to suggest that women could participate in the decisions of a family council, but the cloistering of Athenian women is undeniable, although it was not always successful in denying women contact with the world. In one famous case involving a defense speech in a homicide case, the speaker, Euphiletos, had to explain to the jurors why he was sleeping upstairs and his wife downstairs. The jury's expectation was that, under normal circumstances, the woman would be as far from the street as possible, and in a two-story house she would normally have had a chamber upstairs at the back of the house; even domestic space was organized to keep the household's women as secluded as possible (**9.16**). Euphiletos claimed that the reason why his wife was sleeping downstairs was so she would not have to keep going up and down stairs to feed the child. It is worth noting in relation to the domestic arrangements of Euphiletos's house and, in fact, all the details of this case, that we have no way of determining the truth of any of Euphiletos's claims. His descriptions, however, were designed to persuade a massed jury of Athenian male citizens. Even if not true, what he said had to be plausible. Euphiletos's speech sheds a good deal of light on family dynamics, or at least on how an Athenian man speaking to his peers felt he should portray his family life.

The circumstances of the case were that Euphiletos's wife, never named in the speech, had been seduced by a certain Eratosthenes of Oe and brought him home. (The physical arrangement of the household mattered, because Euphiletos had to explain how his wife had managed to entertain her lover within the house.) Euphiletos was informed by an old crone, who found him in the marketplace. Looking back over the last few months, Euphiletos told the jury, he realized that the signs of her infidelity were all there: his wife had first met Eratosthenes while at a funeral, and afterwards began wearing make-up even though she was still supposed to be in mourning. She would lock Euphiletos in his room, pretending that this was to stop him visiting the servant girl during the night, and eventually she changed rooms with him, ostensibly for the sake of feeding the baby but really so she could let her lover into the house. Once Euphiletos had grasped the situation, he threatened the house slave: she could either cooperate and turn informer, or she can be punished by being put to work in the mill. Euphiletos described the climax of the affair:

Eratosthenes, sirs, entered, and the maidservant roused me at once, and told me that he was in the house. Bidding her look after the door, I descended and went out in silence; I called on one friend and another, and found some of them at home. I took with me as many as I could

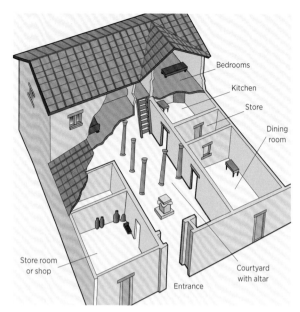

9.16 The layout of an Athenian house

among those who were there, and so came along. Then we got torches from the nearest shop, and went in; the door was open, as the girl had it in readiness. We pushed open the door of the bedroom, and the first of us to enter were in time to see him lying down by my wife; those who followed saw him standing naked on the bed. I gave him a blow, sirs, which knocked him down, and pulling round his two hands behind his back, and tying them, I asked him why he had the insolence to enter my house. He admitted his guilt; then he besought and implored me not to kill him, but to exact a sum of money. To this I replied, "It is not I who am going to kill you, but our city's law, which you have transgressed and regarded as of less account than your pleasures, choosing rather to commit this foul offence against my wife and my children than to obey the laws like a decent person."

(Lysias, *On the Murder of Eratosthenes* 23–26, trans. Lamb)

Thereupon Euphiletos killed Eratosthenes, arguing that he was entitled to do so because he had caught Eratosthenes in the act. In our eyes, Eratosthenes was guilty of adultery, but for Euphiletos, his friends, and the jury, the offence was hubris: Eratosthenes had insulted Euphiletos by seducing his wife. We have already encountered hubris as the fault that characterizes Persian behavior in Herodotos. It is an idea that had remarkable power for the Greeks. Going beyond what was moderate and acceptable, whether marked by lust or violence, was to invite the punishment of the gods, or, in Eratosthenes' case, the retribution of a wronged husband. The integrity of his household, the legitimacy of his children, and the honor of his family were all impugned if another man could have sex with his wife. This provides us with an insight into the Athenians' understanding of marriage and the family, but behind this legal construction of the case, there is a myriad of other elements that remain obscure: the agency of the wife, for example. Her feelings, her motivations and even her actions are largely irrelevant to the legal case, but were certainly a part of the human drama that culminated in the death of Eratosthenes. We only catch a glimpse of the wife's presence indirectly, when Euphiletos raise the legal distinction between seduction and rape: the former is worse, he argued, since it involves the corruption of the woman's soul by the seducer. Her willingness to take a lover, rather than her having been raped, made Eratosthenes' crime worse and was used to justify Euphiletos's decision to kill him.

The dramatic difference in status between men and women was reinforced by the age of marriage: girls were often betrothed before puberty and married shortly after menarchy. Men were more likely to marry at around the age of thirty. Such a construction of marriage produced social relations that bore little resemblance to modern marriages. In the first place, men did not look for companionship in their marriage. Many kept mistresses or resorted to prostitutes, and such arrangements were even semi-formalized. The symposium, for example, was not just a drinking party between men but often involved the participation of flute girls and sex workers, the most accomplished of whom were professional companions, or *hetairai*. Describing one such encounter in *Wasps*, Aristophanes has his character Philokleon drunkenly proposition a flute girl, saying, "Listen, Piglet, if you're good, once my son is dead, I'll get you released and take you as my mistress" (ll. 1,351–53). The term "piglet" is an Athenian colloquialism for a woman's sexual organs, and once again Philokleon's remark reflects the attitude of his fellow citizens. Prostitutes, or *pornai*, everyone could agree, were there to be used, although if she were lucky a porne might work her way up to being a man's mistress. Concubinage was even a recognized category in Athenian law.

Here, as in other cases, the legalistic veneer of the Athenian democracy, in which laws, decrees, and treaties were regularly published and cited, can blind us to a simple truth: there were gross inequalities in the Athenians' treatment of those who were excluded from the benefits of Athenian citizenship. We have seen this in the case of the allies, whose subjugation was barely masked by the bureaucratic apparatus of tribute, record-keeping, and various regulations, but the same danger applies to our understanding of the position of women and slaves. These two classes of subordinates were largely powerless in the face of the Greek man, and their relationships with Athenian men must be viewed as expressions of male Athenian power. This is dramatically illustrated in a legal case involving a woman named Neaira, who was sold into slave prostitution at an early age and began her career in the brothel of a Corinthian woman named Nikarete. She was the favorite of two Corinthian men. Apollodoros recounts the story:

Timanoridas and Eukrates found Nikarete's expenses excessive so they paid thirty mnai for Neaira to be their slave. They kept her and made use of her for as long as they wanted. However, when they were about to get married, they announced that they didn't want to see her plying her trade in Corinth or living in a brothel, but they offered to remit ten mnai and to have her pay them back the remaining twenty mnai when she had the means.

(Apollodoros, *Against Neaira* 29, trans. Freeman)

The amounts of money involved in this commercial transaction are notable. The 30 **mnai** paid for Neaira are equivalent to nearly ten years of salary for a skilled workman. The price of her freedom was two-thirds that amount. This speech was delivered before an audience of hundreds of Athenian jurors. As in the speech of Euphiletos, it contains elements that are salacious and possibly fictitious, but the important feature is that they were seen by the jury of Athenian men as plausible. The idea that two men might buy a slave to keep as their personal sex toy was not incredible, and the notion that they might be embarrassed to have her around once they were married is presented as perfectly reasonable. The audience is not supposed to feel sympathy for the slave-prostitute, but to accept as normal a scenario in which her owners graciously give her a discount so she can buy her freedom, provided she quits Corinth.

When viewed from the point of view of these uneven power relations, many of the images of sex

9.17 Detail of red-figure kylix showing a couple having sex, *c.* 460 BC

on Greek vases emerge as striking less for their graphic depiction of gymnastic flexibility, and more because heterosexual sex is so often depicted as an expression of physical dominance (**9.17**). (For good reason one study of sexuality in the Classical age refers to the "reign of the phallus.")

Pederasty

Interpreting sexuality as another expression of power relations is important for understanding the culture of Classical Athens, particularly so because it helps us grasp the significance of a notable feature of the sexual life of Periklean Athens: pederasty. In our culture, there is no doubt that pederasty is a form of child abuse, which makes it difficult to comprehend this aspect of Greek life. What are we to make of it? Herodotos describes the Persians as adopting more foreign habits than any other people, "including the practice of having sex with boys, which they learned from the Greeks" (*Histories* 1.135). Accordingly, we have to recognize that this was a practice that was distinctively and identifiably Greek, and to some degree normative. By way of comparison, we might take the case of ritualized homosexuality in parts of New Guinea. In one tribe it is believed that masculinity resides in semen, and that for boys to become men they are expected to fellate older youths. As Gilbert Herdt writes, "All males pass through both erotic stages, being first fellators, then fellateds: there

are no exceptions since all...males are initiated and pressured to engage in homosexual fellatio."

Herdt's study reminds us that sexuality is shaped in the crucible of social values and beliefs, and with this in mind, we should ask how pederasty functioned in Greek society. In the first place, the iconography makes it clear that the usual relationship involved clear age differences—even when the younger man is shown with clearly defined musculature, the absence of facial hair serves as a clear marker. The older man, bearded, is the ***erastes***; the younger, unbearded, is the ***eromenos*** (**9.18**). These terms are used whenever ancient sources refer to the partners in a homosexual relationship. The erastes is the active partner, while the passive partner is the eromenos, a word that in Greek is even grammatically a passive participle: the beloved.

There have been various attempts to interpret this particular construction of gender roles. Some scholars have emphasized the seclusion of Greek women and have seen same-sex relationships as a kind of compensation for the lack of affectionate heterosexual relationships. Others point to the intense military

9.18 Detail of black-figure vase depicting a pederastic couple, *c.* 530–520 BC

training of some Dorian societies, such as Sparta, and see this as an expression of the bonding that can occur in hypermasculine settings. In Athens, which was not Dorian, the gymnasium may have been the setting for pederastic encounters (Aristophanes satirizes an old man who falls into a reverie while thinking about the outline of boys' bottoms in the sand of the wrestling ground). Still others note the aristocratic milieu in which pederasty seems to function—Aristophanes' satire, in fact, might be targeting aristocratic Athenians, whose habits would have struck the man in the street as ludicrous—and have emphasized the tutoring element of the relationship: the older man is supposed to train the younger man and prepare him for manhood. Strabo, writing hundreds of years later, reports one version of pederasty practiced on Crete that seems to combine a number of these elements:

[The Cretans] have a peculiar custom in regard to love affairs, for they win the objects with their love, not by persuasion, but by abduction; the lover tells the friends of the boy three or four days beforehand that he is going to make the abduction; but for the friends to conceal the boy, or not to let him go forth along the appointed road, is indeed a most disgraceful thing, a confession, as it were, that the boy is unworthy to obtain such a lover; and when they meet, if the abductor is the boy's equal or superior in rank or other respects, the friends pursue him and lay hold of him, though only in a very gentle way, thus satisfying the custom; and after that they cheerfully turn the boy over to him to lead away; if, however, the abductor is unworthy, they take the boy away from him.

(Strabo, *Geography* 10.4.21, trans. Jones)

Other communities may not have practiced this ritual kidnapping, but there do seem to be two common denominators running through the various versions of pederasty known to us from the Greek world. The first is that in every instance the model of masculinity that underpinned pederastic relations was based on a clear equation of the adult male with penetration; the erastes was a penetrator while the eromenos was penetrated, and therefore played the same role, from the point of view of power relations, as the woman, the slave, or the Persian (see the Eurymedon Vase, p. 26). The second feature of this construction of sexual identity is that, unlike the woman, slave, or Persian, the eromenos will

outgrow his youthful role and will assume his place as an adult, an Athenian, a man, and an erastes. Accordingly, pederasty in Athens served as a kind of sexual initiation, undergone before the youth took his place as a man. Whether every boy or even most boys experienced this is impossible to say, but from the Athenian point of view, the critical feature was that a youth who was praised as *kalos* ("beautiful"; see **9.19**) by his older lover must at some definite point shed that status: one should not be a fully grown man and still be an eromenos. (This would be a deeply shameful position.)

There is an irony here from the point of view of our estimation of Classical culture. To the Athenians, there was nothing shameful in an adult male seeking a boy as his sexual partner, but the notion of two grown men living together in a homosexual relationship was disgusting. In that case, the eromenos became a *kinaidos*, and suggesting that your opponent was involved in such a relationship was a good way of attacking his character, as Aischines well knew when he said of Demosthenes:

There is a certain Aristion, a Plataean, who as a youth was outstandingly good-looking and lived for a long time in Demosthenes' house. Allegations about the part he was playing there vary, and it would be most unseemly for me to talk about it.

(Aischines, *Against Ktesiphon* 3.162, trans. Dover)

9.19 Detail of red-figure kalos vase, *c.* 510–500 BC. Ceramic, H: 7.6 cm (3 in.)

The construction of gender in any society is a complex phenomenon, and hard to tease out, but in the case of the Athenians what makes the matter especially complex is that attitudes toward gender identity served the construction of an Athenian ideal: man as the active master of his household and all his property. Boys could be made into men; women were meant to be subservient and used; and inferior to all, to the point of sometimes being excluded from humanity altogether, were slaves.

Slavery

Slaves were everywhere in Ancient Greece. Agricultural workers and miners, known as ***douloi***, worked the fields and dug silver out of the ground. In the *Ways and Means*, Xenophon explains how investing in such slaves could produce a guaranteed source of revenue:

Those of us who have given thought to the matter have heard long ago, I imagine, that Nikias son of Nikeratos, once owned a thousand men in the mines, and let them out to Sosias the Thracian, on condition that Sosias paid him an obol a day per man net and filled all vacancies as they occurred. Hipponikos, again, had six hundred slaves let out on the same terms and received a rent of a mna a day net. Philemonides had three hundred, and received half a mna.

(Xenophon, *Ways and Means* 4.14, trans. Marchant)

In Attica, as in many other parts of Greece, the agricultural workforce was largely made up of slaves. At Argos these workers were called the ***Gymnetes***, "The Naked Ones," and at Epidauros the ***Koniopodes***, or "The Dusty Feet." Sparta, as we have seen, had a servile population known as the helots, and in Thessaly the slaves were called penestai. In many of these places the slaves were identified as the original inhabitants of the region, suggesting that in these places slave owners tried to identify themselves as ethnically distinct from their slaves. Evidence from Athens points to a much greater range of nationalities, and the prevalence of non-Greek slaves probably made it easier for Athenians to regard their slaves as little more than "income-earning bodies," as they were called. Inscriptions recording the price of slaves refer to people from Kappadokia, Karia, Kolchis, Lydia, Phrygia, Syria, Illyria, Macedonia,

9.20 Vase depicting house slaves (oiketai) weaving, *c.* 550–530 BC. Ceramic, H: 17.1 cm (6¾ in.)

Skythia, and Thrace. It is probable, therefore, that there was a strong ethnic overlay to the slave/free distinction operating in Periklean Athens. Even if skin color did not mark out the entire slave population, pronunciation will have allowed many Athenians to profile the non-Athenians among them.

Within the oikos, household slaves (known as ***oiketai***) wove cloth, cooked, and waited in attendance on the master and mistress of the house (**9.20**). The conditions under which a house slave lived were generally better than those endured by agricultural slaves, but the myth of the Happy Slave is no more true of ancient Athens than it is of the antebellum South.

Another class, known as the ***choris oikountes*** ("those who dwell apart"), appears to have been semi-independent craftsmen, such as shoemakers, whose labor and products supported both themselves and their owners. Aside from these privately owned slaves, there were also public slaves, or *demosioi*, who helped the day-to-day running of Athens as clerks, secretaries, streetsweepers, and even a rudimentary police force. So ubiquitous were slaves in Athenian life that a man petitioning the state for a pension claimed that he was so poor that he couldn't even afford to buy a slave to carry on his business.

As in Sparta, the presence of large numbers of slaves in Athens made punishment and coercion necessary, in order to guarantee compliance. In Xenophon's *Memorabilia*, two Athenian gentlemen discuss the proper treatment of slaves in terms that reveal the conditions under which most slaves lived:

But now let us see how masters treat such servants. Do they not starve them to keep them from immorality, lock up the stores to stop their stealing, clap fetters on them so that they can't run away, and beat the laziness out of them with whips? What do you do yourself to cure such faults among your servants?

(Xenophon, *Memorabilia* 2.1.16, trans. Marchant)

The Athenian treatment of slaves is the clearest expression of the power relations operating through Athenian society. If women's inferiority resides in their treatment as sexual objects, either for bearing children or giving pleasure, and if the allies were relegated to the status of subjects, what underlies the Athenian conception of the slave is that the slave is barely human. One way to mark that inferiority was to create a hierarchy for distinguishing the free man from the slave. Demosthenes declares before his peers:

If, gentlemen of the jury, you will turn over in your minds the question what is the difference between being a slave and being a free man, you will find that the biggest difference is that the body of a slave is made responsible for all his misdeeds, whereas corporal punishment is the last penalty to inflict on a free man.

(Demosthenes, *Against Timokrates* 167, trans. Murray)

The slave was a body, and only a body, so that punishment had to be applied to the body. In the same fashion, you could take testimony from a free person, but a slave was subjected to torture, since they could not be relied upon to use their intellect; either they did not possess it or they had forfeited it upon becoming a slave. The prejudices of slave owners, who were free, toward the enslaved have never, in any society, stood up to close rational scrutiny, but the logical somersaults the Athenians performed to justify slavery were extraordinary. The nub of the matter, Aristotle believed, was power: in every relationship mastery is the *telos*, the proper function of the relationship. Using the examples of bows and horses, Aristotle argued that mastery confers usefulness. An unbent bow is basically a stick, while a bow, bent to the will of the archer, becomes a weapon. A horse running free serves no purpose, but a harnessed horse can be employed as a cavalry charger. As a result, mastery defines all relationships and gives them a purpose:

The master is only the master of the slave; he does not belong to him, whereas the slave is not only the slave of his master, but wholly belongs to him. Hence we see what is the nature and office of a slave; he who is by nature not his own but another's man, is by nature a slave; and he may be said to be another's man who, being a human being, is also a possession. And a possession may be defined as an instrument of action, separable from the possessor.

(Aristotle, *Politics* 1.4 1254a, trans. Jowett)

There were dissenting voices. The fourth-century rhetorician Alkidamas asserted that "God has left all men free; nature has made none a slave" (Schol. ad Aristot. *Rhet.* 1373b). But objections to slavery were muted and the institution went unchallenged through antiquity.

One final observation regarding slavery is in order. It is necessary to recognize that slavery was a feature of Periklean Athens, just as it was in most ancient Mediterranean societies, but it may be possible to go one step further. The culture of Classical Athens, from the philosophy of Plato to the histories of Thucydides, was available to a class of men who had the leisure time to pursue philosophy, poetry, and the other pursuits of high culture. The term for these leisurely pursuits in Greek is *scholê*, the origin of our term "school." The great historian Moses Finley (1912–1986) argued that scholê was only possible because of the presence of a broad class of unfree people, whose labor made time available to the society of slave owners. In answer, then, to the question, was Greek civilization made possible by slave labor, he replied with an absolute yes. Periklean Athens was, without doubt, a brilliant society of astonishing cultural accomplishments, but we will do well to recognize that the glory that was Greece, to use Edgar Allan Poe's phrase again, came at a high price: the dignity and freedom of those enslaved to serve Athenian citizens.

Metics

One last group of disenfranchised people should be included in our assessment of Athenian culture in the fifth century. In a famous section of the Funeral Oration, Perikles remarks, "All good things flow into the city." Here Perikles has in mind the Piraeus, the port of Athens, which in the fifth century became a bustling hub of commerce as goods poured into the city from around the Aegean and beyond: grain, hides, and slaves from the Black Sea; wine from Thasos; fish from the Saronic Gulf and beyond; ivory, perfume, and fabrics from the eastern Mediterranean. There were luxury items too: scarabs and ostrich eggs from Egypt and Africa, as well as amber from the Baltic. Much of the trade and manufacturing that developed in the age of Perikles was conducted by **metics**, resident aliens, who paid a tax to live in Athens but were rarely given the opportunity to become Athenian citizens. Both Solon and Kleisthenes enrolled "new citizens" at key moments in the development of the democracy, but there was no regular path to citizenship. The tax they paid, known as the *metoikion*, was assessed at 12 drachmas per annum for a man, the equivalent of about two weeks' salary for a skilled workman, and 6 drachmas for a woman. They were required to register in an Athenian deme and were also required to have an Athenian patron. There appear to have been approximately 10,000 metics resident in Athens in the late fourth century BC.

In some respects, the term "metic" is a catchall title. Some were freeborn people who had moved to Athens in order to pursue the opportunities provided by the growing economy. One such metic was Kephalos, the father of Lysias, the Athenian orator, who came to Athens and opened a factory manufacturing shields. Others were former slaves, who, upon manumission (the formal process of being released from slavery) acquired freedom. The fourth-century banker, Pasion, for example, had been so brilliant at banking that he earned his freedom and, in time, thanks to his generosity to the Athenian state, was awarded citizenship. Pasion's benefactions and high profile may have worked in his favor, but he was probably the exception rather than the rule. A vivid account of the Athenian attitude to the foreigners in their midst is found in a speech by Lysias concerning a man named Pankleon. The speaker issued an indictment of Pankleon with the Polemarch, the magistrate who dealt with foreigners, on the grounds that Pankleon was a metic. When Pankleon appealed that he was, in fact, a citizen, the speaker started an investigation:

I then went and asked at the barber's in the street of the Hermai, where the Dekeleans resort, and I inquired of such Dekeleans as I could discover if they knew a certain Pankleon belonging to the township of Dekelea. As nobody spoke to knowing him, and I learnt that he was then a defendant in some other suits before the Polemarch, and had been cast in some, I took proceedings on my own part. So now, in the first place, I will produce to you as witnesses some Dekeleans whom I questioned, and after them the other persons who have taken proceedings against him before the Polemarch and have obtained a conviction—as many as chance to be present.

(Lysias, *Against Pankleon* 3, trans. Lamb)

The speaker's strategy—to suggest that his opponent was not an Athenian citizen—is found in many speeches. This is hardly surprising since record-keeping was less stringent than in modern society, but the passage also reminds us of the degree to which Athens was a face-to-face society. The most efficient way of checking on whether Pankleon was, as he said, a member of the deme of Dekelea was to go to the barbershop where the Dekeleans gathered and ask them. Some commentators have also noticed that the question of Pankleon's formal status was difficult to determine: ex-slave, metic, poor freeman? It was difficult to tell the difference at the bottom end of the social scale in Athens, but one thing was clear: life was better if you had won a place within the privileged ranks of Athenian male citizens.

Spotlight
Liturgy and Symposium

An important path to understanding the inner workings of any society lies in identifying its most characteristic institutions. Over the course of the fifth century BC, the Athenians developed two remarkable institutions for which there is no precise modern analogue. The first of these is the **liturgy**, meaning "a public service." Each year wealthy citizens were expected to bear the burden of a major expense, undertaken for the good of the community. These expenses were of three principal types. One was the cost of the upkeep of a trireme in the Athenian war fleet. Although the state paid the crew, the *trierarch*, as the liturgist was called, was responsible for such repairs as the replacement of sail, timber, and cordage. In some cases, the trierarch actually served as the ship's captain, although it was also possible to pay for a more experienced man to

9.21 Detail of the Choregos Vase. Red-figure bell-krater from Apulia, *c.* 380 BC. Two of the figures, leaning on sticks, are each identified as a choregos. The scene depicted is from a burlesque known as a *phylax* play, and the two choregoi are caricatures.

take the trierarch's place. The second type of liturgy was the production of choruses in the dramatic festivals. This liturgy entailed paying for the entire production; the *choregos*, as this liturgist was known, hired the actors and the chorus, and paid for their training, their costumes, and any other expenses (**9.21**). Perikles served as choregos in 472 BC when he was responsible for producing Aischylos's

Persians, one of the first plays to put contemporary events on to the stage. In serving as producer, Perikles was advertising his arrival in the front ranks of Athenian society and politics.

A third, expensive liturgy was that of the *gymnasiarch*. Each year, the ten tribes of Athens selected a man from each tribe to take on the expenses associated with festivals that featured torch races (**9.22**). Once again, the

9.22 Detail of red-figure *pelike* depicting runners at the Lampadephoria (torch race), fifth century BC

9.23 Nikias Painter, detail of red-figure bell-krater depicting a symposium scene, *c.* 420 BC. The symposiasts are shown reclining and playing the wine-tossing game known as *kottabos*, while a flute girl plays music. Ceramic, H: 33 cm (12¾ in.).

liturgist was liable for all expenses associated with training and supplies.

Each of these major liturgies (and the various lesser liturgies as well) involved rich men conspicuously taking on a financial burden, sometimes considerable, for the benefit of Athenian society. There was a pay-off, in that liturgies brought social distinction and honor, but there are signs that some of the wealthiest citizens of Athens were reluctant to be called on, sometimes many times over, to pick up the tab for these expenses. In the fourth century individual trierarchs, for example, were replaced by boards of men, *symmories*, who shared the costs. There appear to have been 1,200 such men, in 20 symmories of 60 men each.

If liturgies represent a public Athenian institution that is distantly related to modern philanthropy, in the private sphere the symposium is also an institution that superficially resembles a familiar modern social event, the dinner party. The symposium, however, was conducted under very different rules and served a different purpose. As a drinking party for men, the symposium originally had strong aristocratic associations and may have grown out of the commensality enjoyed by warrior bands. Even under the democracy the symposium still had aristocratic and elitist associations, and on more sober occasions was an opportunity for discussions of philosophical questions or poetry (see Chapter 4, p. 123). What is the nature of love? Is there a difference between being a good man and becoming a good man? These are the kinds of abstract issues that might be the focus of discussion.

But most symposia, as the name suggests (symposium means literally a "drinking together"), were less philosophical and more devoted to drinking and carousing. Respectable women were not present, and women depicted in symposiastic settings were invariably entertainers, such as flute girls or prostitutes, especially the *hetairai*, sex workers often known for their skill in entertaining men with music, dancing, and conversation (**9.23**). The frequent references to symposia in fifth-century sources suggest that the drinking party was an opportunity for Athenian men to perform their masculinity in settings that were always homosocial and often homoerotic. The symposium proved to be a popular export as well. Etruscan culture, which borrowed heavily from the Greeks, certainly included the practice, as the pictorial program of the Tombe del Tuffatore, discovered in Paestum in 1968, demonstrates (**9.24**).

9.24. Detail of Etruscan wall painting depicting symposiasts, Tomba del Tuffatore, *c.* 470 BC

Chapter 10

Religion and Philosophy: Belief and Knowledge in the Classical Age

Athens in the age of Perikles was a society undergoing rapid and dramatic change. After the establishment of the Kleisthenic democracy, the city found itself embroiled in the Persian Wars. Athens emerged triumphant from the conflict and went on to experience two generations of economic growth at home and imperial power abroad. As a result of these developments, the Athenians of the fifth century BC created the vibrant and vigorous culture that we still refer to as Classical Athens. We have seen, for example, how tragedy and comedy examined contemporary and universal issues, and how the Athenians transformed the Akropolis into a perfect expression of Athenian piety and confidence. We have also found, however, that the egalitarian ethos fostered by the democracy required a corresponding exclusion of foreigners, slaves, and women.

In this chapter, we will examine the institutions and mechanisms that provided the glue that kept Athens together, principally a system of beliefs and practices often referred to as polis-religion. It was religion that bound the city together as a community, and it was the polis that shaped Greek religion. Religious ritual exerted a strongly normative influence over the Greeks, offering them ways to behave that confirmed their piety and pleased the gods, while religious actions also reinforced the cohesion of polis society. We can describe these forces as centripetal: shared sacrifices and religious festivals brought people together, creating common bonds of affiliation. But there were also centrifugal tendencies in the fifth century. Philosophy in particular presented alternative ways of understanding the world that challenged convention. This challenge might have been formulated in abstract terms, but Athens was a society in which the threat of social breakdown was very real: a society characterized by slavery, disenfranchised women, and class tensions between the wealthy and the poor—together with a tradition of factional strife—will always run the risk of civic friction, and perhaps even disintegration. For this reason, as new modes of inquiry emerged —scientific, historical, and ethical—the new learning would call into question many of the accepted conventions of the time.

Polis-Religion

The role of communal religion in shaping the lives of the Athenians began at birth. At the first Apatouria

10.1 Brauron sanctuary. Within the sanctuary there were dining rooms, shown here. Lining these rooms were couches, and it is possible that the girls who had come to "play the bear" (i.e. to be initiated) slept here.

festival falling after the birth of his male child, an Athenian father would introduce the baby to other members of his religious fraternity, the phratry. Those same boys would be reintroduced when they were approximately eighteen years of age, signaling their acceptance by the *phratores* (phratry brothers). After induction into the phratry as a youth, the young Athenian would usually serve as an ephebe, a hoplite in training. These ephebes served as the border guards of Athens for two years. Upon their return from the border they were able to take up their place as soldiers and citizens.

In a real sense, then, one entered the citizen rolls through one's father's religious fraternity. The interplay of individual, familial, and communal relations here is significant. If, for example, a young man's father had died, his father's phratry brothers could attest to the young man's citizenship. This is demonstrated in an important inscription known as the Decree of the Demotionidai, a phratry that, in the aftermath of the Peloponnesian War in 396 BC,

addressed irregularities in its roster. In overhauling the phratry's procedures, the members agreed to a set of elaborate procedures to guard against fraud, which may have become a problem with the death of so many men during the war. Even when a young man was introduced by his father, witnesses were required to confirm the legitimacy of the inductee. They swore as follows:

I witness that the one whom he is introducing is his own legitimate son by a wedded wife. This is true, by Zeus Phratrios. If my oath is good, may there be many benefits for me, but if my oath is false, the opposite.

(*IG* II² 1237, trans. Lambert and Schuddeboom)

In some respects the phratry acted as the individual's extended family, and it was fitting that an Athenian's status as a citizen was conferred through that confraternity, first at birth, and then later upon coming of age.

Coming of age was a particularly important moment of transformation for women. Unlike male rituals, which equated the youth's coming of age with his training as a citizen-soldier, coming of age for women was more closely tied to the onset of menstruation, which signaled the young woman's capacity to bear children. She was now close to assuming her role as a wife and mother. Once again, however, religious ritual provided the medium by which the girl's social identity was transformed. In Aristophanes' *Lysistrata*, there is a reference to young girls (or at least those from the leading families in Athens) taking part in a festival held in honor of Artemis at her rural sanctuary of Brauron (**10.1**). Here the girls ran, danced, ate together, and slept in rooms within the sacred enclosure. They referred to this as "playing the bear" for Artemis, although the exact meaning of the phrase is unclear. The bear was an animal sacred to Artemis and the girls may have engaged in a ritual performance in which they pretended to become the goddess's animal, but we do not possess any detailed descriptions of the cult. Nevertheless, the Brauronia festival has been interpreted as a coming-of-age ritual for these girls, marking a transition from childhood to puberty and advertising that they were now available for marriage, or at least betrothal.

Inscriptions from the sanctuary of Artemis on the Akropolis—a twin of the Brauron sanctuary—reveal that women continued to make dedications to the goddess at later points in their lives, and suggest that major life events, such as marriage and childbirth, continued to be marked by offerings to the goddess, including precious garments which were frequently left in the goddess's sacred precinct. Here, for example, is the text of an inventory kept by the officials of the Artemis sanctuary on the Akropolis listing dedications from the year 347/6 BC:

In the year that Themistokles was archon, Thyaine and Malthake dedicated an embroidered, purple chitoniskos on a frame...Phile [dedicated] a belt. Pheidylla [dedicated] a woman's white himation on a frame...Glykera, wife of Xanthippos [dedicated] a chitoniskos with border, purple but faded, and two small capes. Nikolea [dedicated] a linen chiton, around the base. Aristodamea dedicated an ivory mirror with handle, by the wall.

(*IG* II² 1514 12–24, trans. McInerney)

These were often the women's most expensive garments, and the details of the inscription allow us to imagine the experience of entering the temple and seeing the interior decorated with dozens of pieces of clothing. Some of them are described as half-finished ("on the frame"), and may have still been on the loom when the woman weaving the garment died; the garments may have been subsequently dedicated by the woman's husband or father. Dedicating such a garment to the goddess acted as a concrete way of demonstrating piety and receiving the goddess's favor. Many of the rites practiced here and at other sanctuaries were kept secret, so that reconstructing what went on often involves a degree of speculation, but the presence of sanctuaries everywhere in Greece confirms that religious rites were woven into the fabric of daily life.

Purification and Sacrifice

Major transitions, such as birth, coming of age, marriage, and death, were marked by religious rituals, but a wide variety of religious practices occurred on a daily basis in the Greek world and allow us to glimpse how orthopraxy—correct behavior toward the gods—modified all aspects of life. As well as guiding normative conduct, correct behavior could restore peace and harmony both to society and to an individual. Consider, for example, the troublesome business of haunting. How does one get rid of a ghost or evil spirit, called an **elasteros**, that is haunting one's house? A fifth-century-BC sacred law from the Greek city of Selinous (first published in the mid-1990s) reveals the method. The first column lays out a series of regulations regarding the correct manner and timing of a series of sacrifices offered to some very powerful deities. The gods to whom these sacrifices were made, Zeus Eumenes, the Eumenides, Zeus Meilichios, and the Tritopatores (the Great-Grandfathers), are generally associated with the welfare of the family and other social groups, and with human fertility. The Eumenides, often called the Furies in English, are quite well known, thanks to Aischylos's *Oresteia*, in which they act as avenging spirits hunting Orestes after he has killed his mother. They thirst for blood, and only the intervention of Athena saves Orestes. The Selinous tablet confirms that the Eumenides were not just characters in a play: they were powerful spirits who had to be appeased if the family and community were to thrive.

The sacrifices specified in the ritual consist of two sorts: libations, poured into the earth, suitable for appeasing the spirits of the dead and chthonic deities who resided underground; and burned sacrifices of meat, suitable for pleasing the gods, who were believed to enjoy the smell of burning fat and flesh. The clause forbidding meat from leaving the sanctuary is a common regulation and confirms that these sacrifices would have resulted in a feast, at which the barbecued meat was eaten by the human participants.

Specific instructions laying out how the purification is to be carried out are given in Column B of the inscription:

If anyone wishes to purify himself, with respect to a foreign or ancestral elasteros, either one that has been heard or one that has been seen, or anyone at all, let him purify himself in the same way as the *autorrektas* [a person who has committed homicide] does when he is purified of an elasteros. Having sacrificed a full-grown sheep on the public altar, let him be pure. Having marked a boundary with salt and having performed aspersion with a golden [vessel], let him go away. Whenever one needs to sacrifice to the elasteros, sacrifice as to the immortals. But let him slaughter [the victim so that the blood flows] into the earth.

(*NGSL*[2] 27, trans. Jameson, Jordan, and Kotansky)

In this section an individual who needs to be freed from the attentions of an elasteros is told the procedures for purification. The ritual is compared to that undertaken by an autorrektas (someone guilty of homicide), implying that the person afflicted by the elasteros was in serious trouble and faced complete social rejection. The elasteroi (plural) could come in two forms: from within the family, or from without. A family ghost could be a brother who had died far from home and was seeking a decent burial, or a daughter who had died prematurely before leaving the home as a bride. A foreign ghost might be the soul of a guest who had died under the family's roof, representing a violation of xenia, the protection that any guest might expect. Whatever the circumstances, the individual haunted by the ghost needed to know how to perform an exorcism. First, salt was used to mark out a purified area, then water was sprinkled to signify it was holy ground. Once the sacrificial animal

was killed, the victim's blood was allowed to flow into the earth, thereby feeding and appeasing the angry spirit. Only once this was done could the individual be reintegrated into his family. The Selinous tablet confirms that religious practice served as a way of purifying individuals and bringing them back into the community.

The vivid presence of ghosts and vengeful spirits in the sacred law from Selinous reminds us that, for the Greeks, religion was very much concerned with regulating behavior to ensure a harmonious relationship between the human community and the divine. This harmony could be threatened by pollution, such as bloodshed, or by impious actions. An inscription from the Athenian deme of Eupyridai demonstrates that even the smallest local cults were woven into the great tapestry of polis-religion:

Gods. The priest of Apollo Erithaseos announces and forbids on behalf of himself and the demesmen and the Athenian People, that in the sanctuary of Apollo there be any cutting or carrying out of the sanctuary of wood or branches-with-leaves or firewood or fallen leaves; and if anyone is caught cutting or taking any of the forbidden items from the sanctuary, if the person caught is a slave, he will be flogged with fifty lashes of the whip and the priest will hand him over, with the name of his master, to the king and the Council in accordance with the decree of the Athenian Council and People; and if he is a free man, the priest, together with the demarch, will fine him fifty drachmas and will hand over his name to the king and the Council in accordance with the decree of the Athenian Council and People.

(IG II[2] 1362, trans. Lambert and Schuddeboom)

The priest responsible for the sanctuary is here authorized to safeguard even the most humble aspects of the god's property, and has the weight of both the local deme and the Athenian demos and Boulê behind him. Another potential transgression was oath-breaking. The Athenians, for example, regularly swore oaths including a clause calling down the punishment of heaven on themselves, specifically that their wives might bear monsters rather than children resembling their parents, if they broke their oath.

Sacrifice

This was a religious system in which personal belief was undeniably one aspect of life, but it also involved an understanding of faith that resided in ritual action and repetition: whether concerned with the individual or the community, Greek religion always retained a powerful performative component. This helps to explain the most distinctive feature of polis-religion: the ubiquity of sacrifice. The Athenians regarded **eusebeia**, or piety, as their most distinctive quality, but this required affirmation through action regularly. By one estimate, an Athenian citizen was likely to participate in some kind of communal sacrifice at least once every eight or nine days.

Throughout Attica and Greece, even at the local level, there was a steady stream of sacrifices (**10.2**) and feasts sanctioned by families, clans, tribes, and demes, meaning that the gods were ever-present in the lives of the Greeks. For example, we know of calendars of sacrifice from the Attic demes of Thorikos, Erchia, and Marathon. A fragment of a new sacrificial calendar was found in the excavations of the Athenian Agora and was published for the first time in AD 2007. Face A of the inscription contains a list of sacrifices including the following:

For Apollo Prostaterios, a full-grown victim [probably a sheep]; for Apollo Under the Long Rocks, a full-grown victim; **hierosyna**, [priest's portion]; for Demeter in the city, a sheep; for Pherrephatte, a ram; for [deity] at the

Pythion, a full-grown offering; hierosyna; for Athena Itonia, a sheep; hierosyna; for Demeter at Eleusis, a sheep; for Pherrephatte at Eleusis, a ram...

(*SEG* 52.48A, trans. Lambert, modified)

Apollo, who appears as Protector of the City ("Prostaterios"), is familiar. The expression "Under the Long Rocks" (*Hupo Makrais*) refers to a local cult of Apollo in a cave below the Akropolis. Other major deities mentioned are Athena, Demeter, and Pherrephatte (often referred to as Persephone). On the other hand, in another section the calendar also makes reference to the Hyakinthides, who are not well known, while another reference to "Pankoi--" remains obscure. The combination of both well-known and obscure gods is telling. The same mixture of well-known Olympian deities and quite obscure local heroes, heroines, and minor gods and goddesses occurs wherever long lists of deities are mentioned—in the Selinous regulations or the sacred calendars from Attica—vividly reminding us that the Greeks lived in a world that was populated by dozens, if not hundreds, of spirits, not just the twelve Olympian gods and goddesses with whom we are familiar. Furthermore, each of these religious texts reflects a daily life that was a continuous round of sacrifices to major and minor deities. Making sacrifices to the

10.2 Scene of animal sacrifice on a pinax (votive tablet) from Pitsa, near Corinth, *c.* 540–520 BC. Paint on wood, H: 15 cm (5⅞ in.)

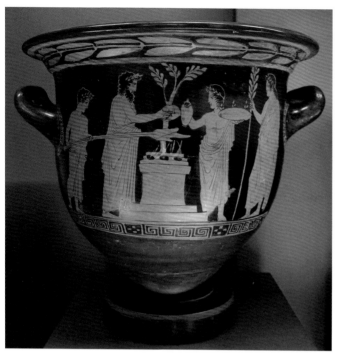

10.3 Pothos Painter, red-figure krater depicting a scene of animal sacrifice, c. 430–420 BC. Young attendants hold the sacrificial meat over the fire on the altar and pour out a libation as the priest observes. Soon the meat will be eaten at a feast or distributed to the participants in the sacrifice. Such scenes were repeated regularly all over the city. Ceramic, H: 33.2 cm (13⅛ in.)

gods regularly and repeatedly constituted the most fundamental civic duty of an Athenian. Sacrifice dominated their lives. The many depictions of sacrifice on Greek vases show scenes familiar to any Athenian: a priest officiates while attendants hold the sacrificial meat over the flames (**10.3**). The actions are formulaic, repeated, and comforting, whether performed by a phratry or by the entire polis.

Religion and Commerce

Sacrifice occurred on a sliding scale, from the Panathenaia involving the entire city, to demes and phratries, and down to even smaller sacrificial groups. One such, the orgeones of Egretes, owned a piece of land that they leased out each year. The terms of the lease shed light not only on farming, but also on the close overlap between religion and commerce:

Gods! The sacrificing associates (orgeones) leased the temple of Egretes to Diognetos son of Archesilas of Melite, for a period of ten years, at an annual rent of 200 drachmas. He may have use of the temple and the houses which are built there as a sanctuary. Diognetos shall whitewash the walls as they require it; he shall build and furnish it whenever he wishes. When the period of ten years elapses, he will depart, taking with him the wooden fixtures and the tiles and the doors, but he will remove nothing else. He shall take care of the trees that have been planted in the sanctuary, and if any should die, he will replace it and return to the lessors the same number of trees. Diognetos shall pay the rent to whoever is the treasurer of the sacrificing associates, each year, one half, or 100 drachmas, on the first of the month of Boedromion, and the remainder, being 100 drachmas, in the first of the month of Elaphebolion. Now when the sacrificing associates sacrifice to the hero in the month of Boedromion, Diognetos shall make available the house, where the shrine is, the open part and the shed and the kitchen, along with couches and tables for two triclinia. If Diognetos does not pay the rent at the times that have been indicated or if he does not carry out the other provisions that are recorded in this lease, the lease shall be void and after the wood and tiles and doors have been removed, the sacrificing associates shall be entitled to re-lease the sanctuary to whomever they wish. If some special tax should be levied, it shall be deducted from the payment due to the sacrificing associates. Diognetos shall inscribe this lease on the stele that belongs to the sanctuary. The lease shall be in effect beginning with the civic leadership [archonship] of Koroibos.

(*IG* II² 2499, trans. Kloppenborg)

It is interesting to ask what this "sanctuary" looked like. From the terms of the lease, it seems as if for most of the year this sanctuary of the hero would have looked very much like a working farm, and that only at the time when the hero received his cult sacrifices, during the month of Boedromion, did it revert to being a locale for sacrifice and feasting. Was it a small, rural sanctuary kept up by the devotees of an obscure hero, or a farm owned by a group of associates who had invested in land that they collectively leased? It was both. This lease and many others resembling it involving demes, phratries, and the city of Athens show that religion cannot be separated from any of the activities of the communities, large and small, that constituted Athens. From farming to festivals, every aspect of Athenian life was modulated by religious practice.

Conventional Belief

How exactly did the Greeks conceive of their gods? What did they look like? How did they behave?

For the Greeks, the universe was ruled by a supreme sky god, Zeus (**10.4**), who reigned with his heavenly consort, Hera. In this cosmology, a family of Olympian deities, including Zeus's brothers Poseidon and Hades, had defeated the primordial Titans and Giants.

They then divided up the cosmos between them, so that each had a particular aspect of the natural and human world under his or her control: Athena, sprung from the head of Zeus, represented wisdom and technical skills, such as weaving; Aphrodite incarnated the power of sexual desire—flowers and grass grew up wherever she walked, so fecund was the force she embodied—while Ares gave a human yet also divine face to the gruesome bloodlust of battle; Poseidon sent earthquakes, while Hades ruled the Underworld. This was the order created by the will of Zeus, an order that represented a triumph over chaos. If heaven and the cosmos reflect the way a society sees itself, then for the Greeks the basic conditions

10.4 The Artemision Bronze, National Archaeological Museum, Athens, *c.* 460–450 BC. The statue depicts Zeus, poised to hurl his thunderbolt. The stance is attested in many smaller statues of the sky god. Bronze, H: 2.1 m (6 ft 10½ in.)

of the universe and the social order by which we live resembled a slightly dysfunctional family requiring the firm hand of a father figure.

When we describe Athena as the goddess of wisdom, Apollo as the god of music, prophecy, or healing, and Artemis as the goddess of the hunt, we are approaching the gods in a way that Herodotos would have understood: they are figures who resemble us and have areas of power that directly intersect with our lives. Knowledge about the Greek gods was transmitted by means of a rich supply of stories told by poets, priests, and even parents teaching their children, stories that have become part of our cultural consciousness. These stories, or myths, shed light on the Greek conception of the mortal and divine realms (and indeed, how the two interact).

When, for example, the Greeks related the story of Aktaion—who saw Artemis bathing in the wild as he was out hunting, and who was then punished by the goddess by being torn to pieces by his own hunting dogs—they were using a myth about the gods to express a deep-seated apprehension about the danger of nature and wilderness, as well as the power of the divine (**10.5**). Yet notice that the myth only makes sense if the audience imagines Artemis as a beautiful woman whose modesty has been compromised by the encounter with the hunter. The situation is both

10.5 Red-figure vase depicting Artemis and the death of Aktaion, *c.* 470 BC. Ceramic, H: 37 cm (1 ft 2⅝ in.)

divine and human, and the players, even when divine, still resemble human actors.

In these stories the gods are remarkably anthropomorphic: they look and behave very much like us. In a famous episode in the *Odyssey*, the bard sings of the time when Ares and Aphrodite were captured in bed by Aphrodite's husband, Hephaistos. Suspicious of his wife's behavior, the god of the forge had fashioned a net to fall from the bedposts to catch the lovers while they were having sex. In this passage, Hephaistos appeals to Zeus as he rages over his wife's undeniable adultery:

Father Zeus, all you other sacred gods
Who live forever, come here, so you can see
Something disgusting and ridiculous—
See how these two have gone to my own bed
And are lying there, having sex together,
While I look on in pain.
     (Homer, *Odyssey* 8.305–7, 312–15, trans. Johnston)

The scene is comic, and suggests that piety and irreverence went hand in hand for the Greeks. In myth, the barriers between human and divine often broke down. Both male and female gods, for example, took human lovers. This was particularly true of Zeus, whose pursuit of young women infuriated his wife. On one level, such stories offered a kind of justification for similar behavior among humans. If the gods behaved badly, then the same was to be expected of mortals, surely? But if the gods were really so similar to us, it also meant that the gods were approachable. Anthropomorphic gods could be consulted, appealed to, and placated in times of uncertainty. When a plague ravaged the city, the Athenians asked Apollo, the god of both plagues and health, to save them. The popularity of healing sanctuaries from the late fifth century onward reflects the same attitude: if the gods are powerful and present, then we can approach them the correct way and have them intercede on our behalf.

The reverse of this urge to win the gods' intercession was a fear of the gods' power. Euripides' *Bacchai*, for example, tells the story of the arrival of Dionysos in Thebes, where Pentheus, the city's ruler, fails to recognize the god's divinity. By the end of the play, Pentheus has been punished for his failure to acknowledge the god's awful power: his mother, Agave, and the other bacchants (female followers of

10.6 Red-figure vase depicting Pentheus being torn apart by bacchants, *c*. 480 BC. Ceramic, H: 12.7 cm (5 in.)

Dionysos) tear the young man to pieces while under the influence of the god (**10.6**). There is no story of redemption or forgiveness here, only the brutal reality of the god's power. The god was to be feared, and the play forcefully juxtaposes the individual skepticism of Pentheus with the bacchants' acceptance of Dionysos. Resisting the god is an act of individual folly; even when the god is murderous, the community must submit to his authority.

Eleusis

For the Greeks, the divine was vividly real, yet even the most personal religious experience, such as an epiphany or direct encounter with a god, fell under the penumbra of polis-religion. This is illustrated by the mysteries of Eleusis. Located approximately 20 kilometres (12.5 mi) west of Athens, Eleusis was incorporated into the political structure of Attica as a deme, but the sanctuary of Demeter, where the origins of agriculture were celebrated, remained under the control of two local clans, the Eumolpidai and the Kerykes. The growth of the sanctuary's significance can be charted in the periodic enlargement of the sanctuary, especially the ***Telesterion***, or Hall of Mysteries, where hundreds of people were initiated each year into a mystery cult connected to the cycle of the seasons and the worship of the Earth Mother. It was not, however, simply a matter of more people undergoing initiation with each passing generation. Each enlargement of the telesterion also contributed to the transformation of what had been a private cult of a genos or clan intoa state cult, collectively paid for by the Athenians. As the plan in **10.7** (see p. 256) illustrates, the earlier phases of the sanctuary, dating to the sixth century BC (shown in blue), were built over as the sanctuary expanded in the fifth century BC (shown in red), an expansion that continued into the Roman period.

Each ***mystes***, or initiate, was supposed to experience the appearance of the goddess Demeter (an epiphany, from the Greek word "to reveal") at the culmination of a ceremony held at night. Purified by fasting, and quite possibly under the influence of mildly hallucinogenic drugs—initiation involved drinking ***kykeon***, a mixture that may have included the fungus ergot—the initiates were primed to

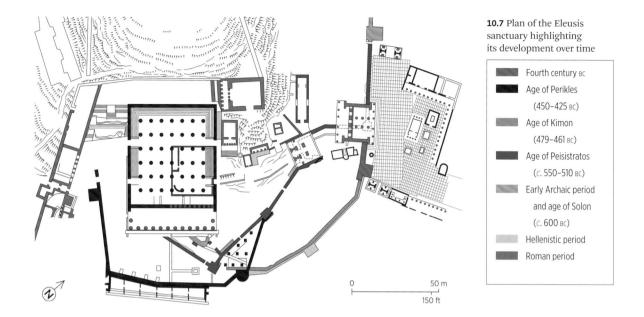

10.7 Plan of the Eleusis sanctuary highlighting its development over time

■	Fourth century BC
■	Age of Perikles (450–425 BC)
■	Age of Kimon (479–461 BC)
■	Age of Peisistratos (c. 550–510 BC)
■	Early Archaic period and age of Solon (c. 600 BC)
■	Hellenistic period
■	Roman period

undergo this epiphany, witnessing the divinity's actual presence. We can reconstruct some sense of how this experience felt by comparing it to the Midnight Mass held in an Orthodox church at Easter. When the priest introduces a candle in the darkness and declares that Christ has risen, the Orthodox ritual powerfully evokes its ancient antecedent. Unlike the later Christian ritual, however, the Eleusinian rites were closely tied to celebrations of the fertility of the land and the origins of agriculture. This was emphasized in the foundation story of the cult, according to which Demeter, wandering distraught at the abduction of her daughter, Persephone, was hospitably received by Metaneira and Triptolemos, wife and son of the king of Eleusis. In return for their generosity, Demeter rewarded Triptolemos by revealing the secrets of agriculture. (Demeter can be seen on her throne in **10.8** as she receives from Metaneira an offering of a sheaf of wheat, just as the sanctuary would receive first-fruit offerings from states and individuals.)

It may seem odd that the Athenian state took such great interest in a mystery cult, since initiation was a private affair. The site of Eleusis, however, had a strategic significance on the western side of Attica, near the border with Megara, a long-standing enemy of Athens. Furthermore, in claiming that Eleusis was the home of agriculture and a territory favored by the gods, the Athenians could claim that it was in their territory that the events took place that made all civilized life possible. As if this were not sufficient, the cult also offered the prospect of a happy afterlife to the initiates, by freeing them from the fear of death. These elements are all found in the *Homeric Hymn to Demeter*, a text dating from as early as the sixth century BC:

Happy is he among men upon earth who has seen these mysteries; but he who is uninitiate and who has no part in them, never has lot of like good things once he is dead, down in the darkness and gloom.

(*Homeric Hymn to Demeter* [2]. 480–83, trans. Evelyn-White)

As a sanctuary the rituals of which dealt with issues of life, death, and the afterlife, Eleusis increased in prestige with each generation. The eagerness of the Athenians to control the sanctuary is therefore not hard to understand. They did so by building a counterpart to the sanctuary within the city of Athens, usually known as the City Eleusinion and sometimes described as a "branch" of the sanctuary at Eleusis. Such a practice was not uncommon: the sanctuary of Artemis at Brauron was also matched by an urban Brauronion on the Akropolis. This twinning of extra-urban and city sanctuaries had the effect of connecting center and periphery, a connection reinforced by the processions that moved from the extra-urban sanctuary to the city and back, transforming the entire region into a religious landscape. Each year the Athenians sent their ephebes, young men doing their first military service, to Eleusis to bring secret, sacred objects back to Athens. Then, after the initiates had paraded to the Piraeus and purified themselves by bathing in the sea, they and those who had been initiated before them marched back to Eleusis. Along the way the initiates were verbally abused at a river crossing—the term for this ritual is the **gephyrismos**, literally "the Bridge"— before reaching Eleusis and undergoing the formal initiation into the mystery cult described above. Comparable to modern-day pilgrimages to such sites as Lourdes or Mecca, these were mass movements of people, requiring planning, preparation, and regulation by the state and religious authorities (which in Greece were often one and the same).

Eleusis was not the only cult that offered its initiates the prospects of a happy afterlife. There were many people around the Greek world who were initiated into a cult that was identified with Orpheus, the figure from myth who could charm the animals with his music and who almost succeeded in bringing his beloved Eurydike back from the Underworld. Those initiated were called *Orpheotelestai* ("Initiates of Orpheus"), and many were buried with small gold plates inscribed with such enigmatic texts as this:

I come from the pure, pure Queen of those below, and Eukles and Eubouleus, and other Gods and Daemons. For I also avow that I am of your blessed race. And I have paid the penalty for deeds unrighteous, whether it be that Fate laid me low or the gods immortal or...with star-flung thunderbolt. I have flown out of the sorrowful, weary circle. I have passed with swift feet to the diadem desired. I have sunk beneath the bosom of the Mistress, the Queen of Hades. And now I come a suppliant to holy Persephoneia, that of her grace she send men to the seats of the Hallowed. Happy and blessed one, thou shalt be god instead of mortal. A kid I have fallen into milk.

(Timpone Piccolo, Thurii, Lamella A1, trans. Guthrie)

Although many of the references remain obscure, the overall meaning of the gold plates is clear. Initiates were being offered an incantation that they were expected to use once they woke up dead. The plate served as a kind of passport, or attestation, that they were worthy of passing into the realms of the pure and blessed, thus avoiding a dreary afterlife, or worse, punishment, such as awaited those who had not been initiated. After death you were received by the judges of the Underworld, and the prospects for what followed varied from grim to horrible. Homer's *Odyssey*, possibly the best-known poem in antiquity, has Odysseus visiting Hades, and it was precisely the sterile, bleak existence of the shades described by Homer that initiates hoped to avoid. They turned instead to initiation, and the promise of a blessed afterlife offered by these cults.

10.8 Demeter and Metaneira, holding ears of wheat. Detail of the belly of an Apulian red-figure hydria, *c.* 340 BC. Ceramic, H: 68 cm (26¾ in.)

Shared Beliefs and Scripture

Eleusis and the Orphic cult demonstrated that religion in the Greek world did speak to the deepest spiritual needs of ordinary people, but as a system of belief and practice, Greek religion was different from most religions in modern societies. First, although the Greeks of the Classical era did believe in divine inspiration for poets, they did not maintain that any of their texts had been handed down directly from any god as straightforward guides to ethical behavior; in other words, they did not regard any poem as the equivalent of scripture. Homer and Hesiod were seen as authoritative, but no Greek or foreigner was ever burned at the stake for denying the words of the poets. Perhaps because Greek religion was not based on a scriptural foundation, it was generally characterized by a tendency to find similarities between the gods of different peoples rather than to assert the superiority of the Greek gods. Herakles, for example, was popular with Greeks around the Mediterranean and was often linked to the Phoenician god, Melqart (**10.9**). In some places the two divinities fused: Herodotos has a lengthy passage discussing the origins of "Tyrian Herakles" (referring to Herakles from Tyre, a Phoenician city), while the modern-day principality of Monaco takes its name from Herakles Monoikos, a blend of Herakles and the epithet of Melqart, Menouakh.

A second feature of Greek religion to keep in mind is that, while there were instances of religious persecution in the Greek world—usually on the charge of *asebeia*, or impiety—these were rare, and were usually aimed at controversial public figures. The trials were motivated as much by social anxieties and political upheavals as by religious scruples. Finally, it is important to remember that the discussions of cosmology we encounter in the writings of Xenophanes, Protagoras, or Plato (about whom we shall have more to say below) are the products of a literary elite; it is not at all clear that ordinary Greeks shared these ideas. Theophrastos was probably describing something closer to the average Greek of the Classical Age when he characterized the behavior of a superstitious man as follows: "Whenever he has a dream he heads off to the dream-interpreters, to the soothsayers, and to those who interpret bird-signs to ask which god or goddess he ought to appease" (*Characters* 16.11). It is not the skeptical philosophers of antiquity who were typical; it was the men and

10.9 Statuette of Herakles/Melqart, early fifth century BC. Limestone

women who worshiped at small local shrines, who were members of religious brotherhoods, who trekked out to Brauron or Eleusis with their friends and family, and who participated in the regular calendars of sacrifice that were observed in every deme and tribe. Sacrifice, festival, and procession were the ingredients of religion, repeated again and again. Together, they constructed community.

Asklepios and Hippokrates: The Splintering of Belief

As a vivid presence in the lives of the Greeks, the gods were feared and respected. They could destroy humans, as Dionysos does Pentheus, or in the manner of Asklepios—the god of healing—they could restore us. Toward the end of the fifth century, the popularity of Asklepios began to grow dramatically. He was formally received into Athens in the 420s BC by a delegation of leading Athenians, headed by Sophokles, and a number of sanctuaries dedicated to him and serving as healing shrines began to spring up during the fourth century. The sick came to the god's sanctuary, where the deity either healed them in their dreams or diagnosed their ailments while they slept. There was very little room for metaphorical interpretations of the god's appearances. It was believed that he was really

present, and the inscriptions put up outside his most famous sanctuary, at Epidauros, were written with the clear intention of convincing people that this god was right there and could be relied upon to cure the sick. Here is a typical inscription:

Ambrosia from Athens, blind of one eye. She came as a suppliant to the god. Going around the shrine she mocked at some of the cures as incredible and impossible, [as] if the lame and blind became whole by having a dream. But when she slept in the shrine the god, standing over her, seemed to say that he would cure her but that he would require her to give to the temple a silver pig as a memorial of her unbelief. Saying this, he cut open her diseased eye and poured in a drug. When day came she went away cured.

(*IG* IV² 1.121, trans. Hamilton, modified)

Other inscriptions tell similar stories of the god's intervention. The attestations to the efficacy of the god were there to convince the skeptical that a cure awaited them inside the sanctuary. The sick would sleep in a dormitory close to the god's temple, and in their dreams the god would appear, as he did to Ambrosia, and as he was shown doing on many relief sculptures, such as in **10.10** from the Piraeus. Asklepios is depicted standing over the figure of the sick woman who is lying asleep on a couch; the god is

10.10 Votive relief for Asklepios, Greek, *c.* 350 BC. Limestone

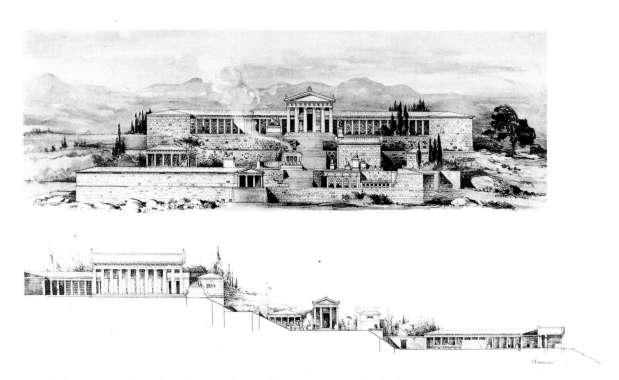

10.11 Modern reconstruction of the Asklepieion of Kos *c.* mid-fourth century BC, showing front and side elevations

performing some type of operation or manipulation of her shoulder. (In other depictions the sacred snake of Asklepios is sometimes seen doing this, licking the sick person.) Behind the god is his daughter, Hygieia ("Health"), while in front, shown smaller than the gods, are the human members of the sick person's family, awaiting the outcome of Asklepios's intervention.

Asklepieia, or sanctuaries to Asklepios, appeared in Athens, Corinth, and Trikka, but nowhere was there a sanctuary to rival the Asklepieion on Kos (**10.11**). The location of this sanctuary is remarkable, because Kos was also the island where Hippokrates and his students laid the foundations for what we would regard as scientific medicine, the opposite, it would seem, of religious intervention. The school of Hippokrates produced dozens of treatises that dealt with the identification and treatment of diseases, ranging from haemorrhoids to epilepsy. The Hippokratics were particularly important for their development of a system of **diagnosis** and **prognosis**, according to which physicians were trained to observe the sick carefully before embarking on treatment. Scholars have sometimes drawn a sharp line between scientific medicine and religious healing in ancient Greece, but this is probably exaggerated.

Both varieties of medicine, the scientific and the religious, seem to have employed diet, exercise, baths and even, on occasion, surgery to cure the sick. Furthermore, when doctors trained by Hippokrates began practicing, the oath they swore (as modern-day doctors still do today) bore witness to the importance they placed on Asklepios and the other gods of healing. The Hippokratic oath begins: "I swear by Apollo, the healer, Asklepios, Hygieia, and Panacia, and I take to witness all the gods, all the goddesses, to keep according to my ability and my judgment, the following oath and agreement...." It is probable that the sick who came to Kos looking for a cure turned both to Asklepios, whose imposing sanctuary sat on a terrace above the city, and also to Hippokrates.

Even if Hippokrates expected his students to honor the god Asklepios, there are signs that the new approach to medicine, based on the observation of symptoms and an accumulation of case-histories, was sometimes at odds with conventional belief and a reliance on the gods to heal disease. This is illustrated by an essay by Hippokrates on hysteria in young women, a problem he attributes to an accumulation of blood first in the womb and then in the heart and lungs. His prescription is for virgins to be wedded as soon as possible and to become pregnant. This, he claims, will cure their insanity by releasing the pent-up supply of blood. Discussing the cure of this affliction, he remarks,

When this person returns to her right mind, women give to Artemis various offerings, especially the most valuable of women's robes, following the orders of oracles, but they are deceived. The fact is that the disorder is cured when nothing impedes the downward flow of blood.
    (Hippokrates, *On Virgins* 8.466, trans. Lefkowitz and Fant)

If we recall the dedications we noted earlier at Brauron, it is clear that Hippokrates was dismissing such instances of piety as misguided. To attribute cures to the intervention of Artemis, even when oracles authorized such cures, was to be deceived and to misunderstand the actual causes of the disease, in his view. Hippokrates' disparaging remarks are a reminder that alternatives to conventional religion were emerging in the fifth century BC. Given the central position of religion both in the lives of individual Athenians and to the Athenian community more generally, these alternatives were potentially subversive. Philosophy challenged convention.

The Challenge of Presocratic Philosophy

Hippokrates was not the first or only thinker to pose a threat to conventional practice. In the sixth, fifth, and fourth centuries BC, a number of philosophers and philosophical schools emerged, especially in the eastern Greek world of Ionia. They are often known as the Presocratics, for the simple reason that they preceded Sokrates. Their inquiries into cosmology were generally speculative and abstract, and the other areas of their inquiries (natural science and ethics) were not explicitly political, but by challenging some of the traditional views of the gods, their rational theology (as it is sometimes called) would offer an implicit challenge to Athenian society and Greek culture more generally. For example, even before Herodotos observed favorably that Homer and Hesiod had provided the Greeks with genealogies of the gods, the sixth-century philosopher Xenophanes had complained that Homer and Hesiod told stories of the gods in which they were liars, thieves, and cheats; deities acting immorally. For Xenophanes, gods in the shape of adulterous humans caught doing "something disgusting and ridiculous," to

use Hephaistos's words in the episode from the *Odyssey* cited earlier, were a farce, a projection of our desire to make the world comprehensible to humans. If cows and horses could paint, said Xenophanes, their gods would look like horses and cows.

Xenophanes was part of a tradition of Ionian philosophers whose cosmological investigations produced remarkable results. A succession of thinkers began with the basic question of the constituent matter of the universe. For Thales (*c*. 624–*c*. 546 BC), writing in the first half of the sixth century, it was water, while for Herakleitos (*c*. 535–*c*. 475 BC), writing a generation later, it was fire. Anaximander (*c*. 610–*c*. 546 BC) speculated that the universe was comprised of four elements: air, earth, fire, and water. The Ionian philosophers then asked what principles determined how the universe took the shape it did. Anaximenes (*c*. 585–*c*. 525 BC), who postulated that air was the basic substance of the cosmos, believed that air differed in essence in accordance with its rarity or density. When air is thinned, Anaximenes argued, it becomes fire, while when it is condensed it becomes wind, then cloud; when still more condensed it becomes water, then earth, then stone. Everything else comes from these. For Anaximander, on the other hand, the four constituent elements did not arise from just one base substance, but were constantly interacting with each other, while beneath them was a primeval principle of chaos. The elements moved in a vortex motion and resolved into oppositions: hot versus cold, wet versus dry, and so forth. The universe created from this motion and these oppositions was, for Anaximander, boundless, **apeiron**. According to Theophrastos,

Anaximander said that the first principle and element of existing things was the boundless; it was he who originally introduced this name for the first principle. He says that it is not water or any of the other so-called elements, but something different from them, something boundless by nature, which is the source of all the heavens and the worlds in them.
    (Anaximander, T15 [=DK 12 A9], trans. Waterfield)

One is immediately struck by the way that speculation based on observation and contemplation, but without the aid of scientific instrumentation, produced results that often appear astonishingly modern. The apeiron is, quite simply, an infinite universe.

The same blend of novel speculation and modern insight characterizes the thought of Thales, who asserted that the Earth floated on a bed of water. Previously, the traditional Greek notion had been that the Earth was surrounded by Okeanos, not that the Earth sat over it. Here Thales is probably reflecting Near Eastern influence, and his idea, while striking in a Greek context, would not have been out of the ordinary in a Mesopotamian context. Thales, however, also believed that living creatures came into being from the action of the sun evaporating moisture, and postulated that humans were related to other living creatures, such as fish. This is an insight that few of his contemporaries would have readily accepted, although it fits with modern evolutionary theory; the concept of the reptilian brain in each of us might not have shocked Thales. Similarly striking were the philosophies of a third pairing of Presocratic philosophers, Demokritos and Leukippos, who together postulated that the universe was made up of tiny particles, much smaller than can be seen by the eye, moving in space. These particles were so small, they speculated, that they could not be cut, and so they dubbed them indivisible, or, in Greek, **atoma**. The Greeks postulated the existence of atoms two millennia before the invention of the electron microscope. Even these few examples of Presocratic philosophy reveal how inventive, how curious, and how fearless early Greek philosophers were in their cosmological inquiries.

Building on these material observations and speculations, the Presocratics wrestled with questions of first principles. Chaos, commotion, and continuous change became some of the key concepts underpinning many of these philosophies. Herakleitos, for example, famously observed that "All is flux," a principle that he was able to convey with the aphorism that you cannot step in to the same river twice. Of course, in one sense you can step in to the same river innumerable times, but in another, more significant sense, the river is constantly changing. Paradox has long been a powerful tool for philosophical thinking.

A number of the Presocratics, however, intuited that there was an order underpinning the cosmos. For Thales, it was logos, a complex term that can mean "word' but also "order" and "meaning." Thales appears to have been proposing that the universe makes sense, an idea that leads directly to the notion of a single intelligence at work. More explicitly theological was the thinking of Empedokles, a Presocratic philosopher from Akragas in Sicily, who postulated the existence of a blissful Sphere from which the cosmos was born thanks to the action of cosmogenic forces of Love and Strife. The former he identified with Aphrodite, but when he speaks of divinities he is really describing transcendent principles rather than the anthropomorphic gods familiar to the Greeks. Such an understanding of the gods is close to rendering the gods as no more than allegories, and would have been little comfort to a traditionalist. Parmenides, for example, composed a lengthy poem in the early fifth century investigating the difference between truth and opinion, employing the allegory of a journey to investigate the soul's ascent to enlightenment. He speaks of the traveler's journey being guided by a goddess, but she is surely unlike any goddess from the usual pantheon. Cautioning the traveler against the false opinions of most people and the absolute truth of enlightenment, she offers advice that is enigmatic at best:

...and it is necessary for you to learn all things,
Both the still-heart of persuasive reality,
And the opinions of mortals, in which there is no
    trustworthy persuasion.
        (Parmenides, *On Nature* C 1 28–30, trans. Coxon)

This is a long way from myths of Athena born from the head of Zeus, or Hera berating Zeus for his lust. Little wonder that even Plato expressed doubt about ever fully grasping Parmenides' meaning.

Aware that there was a growing gap between conventional religion on the one hand, and philosophical speculation on the other, various philosophers approached the question with varying degrees of caution. Herakleitos, for example, chose to claim that philosophical inquiry resulted in a kind of secret knowledge. He argued that the logos of the universe was comprehensible only to a select few:

Although this logos holds always, humans prove unable to understand it, both before hearing it and when they have first heard it. For although all things come to be [or, "happen"] in accordance with this logos, humans are like the inexperienced when they experience such words and deeds as I set out, distinguishing each thing in accordance with its nature (**physis**) and saying how it is.

But other people fail to notice what they do when awake, just as they forget what they do while asleep.

(Herakleitos DK 22 B1, trans. Curd and McKirahan)

This passage is particularly revealing. As well as making the argument that the logos was understandable only by a few, he also posited a single philosophical concept in place of the gods. The scientific observations of the Presocratics harmed no one, and the cosmological speculations that followed were not overtly radical, but as Presocratic thought moved toward monism, the doctrine that all is one, the traditional systems of belief predicated on a polytheistic universe would come into question. This became explicit in the early fifth century, when Xenophanes challenged traditional religion by expounding monotheism, claiming that there was a single, supreme deity. Since traditional beliefs and the religious performances that arose from them were, as we have seen, the glue that kept the city-state together, philosophy would come to present an implicit challenge to the status quo. A late fifth-century play, *Sisyphos*, attributed to Euripides or Kritias (the uncle of Plato), went further and argued that conventional religion was a fiction that had been dreamed up to curb human wrongdoing:

...when the laws prevented men from open deeds of violence, but they continued to commit them in secret, I believe that a man of shrewd and subtle mind invented for men the fear of the gods, so that there might be something to frighten the wicked even if they acted, spoke or thought in secret....So, I think, first of all did someone persuade men to believe that there exists a race of gods.

(DK 88 B25, trans. Guthrie)

Protagoras and the Sophists

By the late fifth century, another philosopher, Protagoras (*c*. 490–*c*. 420 BC), would assert a doctrine that we would recognize as agnosticism: "As to the gods, I do not know whether they exist or not." Furthermore, Protagoras proclaimed that man was the measure of all things. In doing so, he placed humans at the center of the cosmos. This we can see and be sure of, he was saying, but as for the gods? Well, there certainty eludes us.

Such statements can read to a modern audience as little more than moderate agnosticism, but

modern pluralistic societies are built on a tolerance of many points of view. To understand the impact of Protagoras and the other philosophers whose ideas either denied, doubted, or allegorized the gods into insignificance, we must remember that ancient societies tended to equate piety toward the gods with the very idea of being a community. If the gods didn't exist, then what made Athens a community?

Protagoras, therefore, represents a definite break from the certainties of religious convention. If he was right, then traditional practices (such as initiation into various cults) were no guarantee of the gods' favor or a happy afterlife. In fact, philosophers and intellectuals often treated these popular stories about the gods and the Underworld not as literally true but as elaborate metaphors. This is illustrated by a text published as recently as 2006, the Derveni Papyrus, so-called because of its find-spot in Macedonia. The author of the Derveni Papyrus produced a commentary on the poems of Orpheus, in which he tried to explain how stories that could be read literally should actually be seen as allegories of existence. For example, the author claims at one point: "When Orpheus calls Night 'nurse' he is giving a hint that night cools and solidifies those elements which the sun warms and dissolves..." A comparable modern example might be reading the story of Hansel and Gretel and trying to decide if this was the true story of two children abandoned in the forest, or a metaphor for the loneliness of human existence.

Protagoras was one of a new breed of philosophers. Along with such men as Hippias of Elis and Prodikos of Keos, he was known as a sophist. In contrast to the Presocratics, these men taught a wide variety of disciplines, ranging from language and linguistics to grammar, rhetoric, geometry, music theory, and **eristics**. This last subject, similar to debating in the modern curriculum, brought them a good deal of suspicion. Learning to argue that black is white, or as the Athenians put it, making the weaker argument seem stronger, became a conventional charge leveled against the sophists, who had also acquired an unsavory reputation because they accepted pay for their teaching. Sophistic teaching helped to crystalize the misgivings many Athenians felt about philosophy and the threat it posed to convention. Education had up till now been largely a family concern, confined to basic literacy, numeracy, and a knowledge of Homer. Now young Athenians were flocking to hear the

10.12 The Philosophers' Mosaic discovered near Pompeii in 1897, perhaps depicting Plato (third from left) and Aristotle (far right), among others. Mosaic, H: 86 cm (2 ft 9⅞ in.)

latest intellectual lecturing in Athens on topics from astronomy to ethics (**10.12**). The anxiety that arose as a result of new ideas and new teaching is nicely captured in a famous exchange in Aristophanes, when old Strepsiades goes to the "Think-Tank" where Sokrates teaches and gets a lesson in science and religion. Discussing the clouds, Sokrates says:

Sokrates: You see, these are the only true gods, everything else is utter nonsense.
Strepsiades: What about Zeus? How can Olympian Zeus not be a god?
Sokrates: Zeus? Don't be absurd! Zeus doesn't exist.
Strepsiades: What are you saying? Who is it that makes the rain, then?
Sokrates: Why, the Clouds of course! I'll prove it to you. Does it ever rain without Clouds? No, and you would have thought that Zeus could have made it rain on his own if he so desired, without the help of the Clouds.
Strepsiades: And I always thought it was Zeus pissing through a sieve!

(Aristophanes, *Clouds* 364–73, trans. Meineck)

Little wonder that Protagoras was expelled from Athens. Some scholars have doubted the tradition that Protagoras was charged with impiety, and as a specific legal question the issue will probably remain open, but the mood of Athens in the late fifth century was undoubtedly hardening. Conventional believers could be excused for feeling their beliefs were under attack.

Herodotos and Thucydides

The shift away from conventional belief is most clearly demonstrated in the difference in the works of the historians Herodotos and Thucydides. We have already relied on Herodotos for telling the story of the Persian Wars in Chapter 7 and Thucydides will provide the fullest account of the Peloponnesian War in Chapter 11, but it is worth contrasting their histories as literary products of the fifth century. The differences illuminate how rapidly Athenian culture was being transformed.

Herodotos, writing around the middle of the fifth century, was the first historian to offer a sustained inquiry into the causes of a major war from the recent past. (The term "history" actually comes from his use of the term "inquiry" to describe his project.)

His work is detailed and comprehensive, but it is also a work that includes elements that today would scarcely qualify as historiography. The gods, for example, play a major role in the work, as when the fleet of Xerxes is hit by a storm while sailing down the harsh coast of Euboia. Hundreds of ships are sunk, leading Herodotos to explain that the storm was the work of heaven, sent by the gods in order to make the Greek and Persian numbers more even. The entire Persian campaign is presented by Herodotos as an act of hubris, of the overweening pride that leads a man (or a people) to commit an act of folly, but which will also activate heaven's retribution (**nemesis**). There is a deliberate use of literary patterning to give the work a satisfying symmetry. As we saw in Chapter 1, if Xerxes demonstrates his megalomania by whipping the Hellespont with three hundred strokes after the water has dared to destroy his boats, it will come as no surprise to Herodotos's readers that three hundred Spartans will oppose the Persians at Thermopylae and begin the downfall of the Persians. And because Herodotos's work is shot through with religious and moral elements, he uses the literary tools appropriate to these: dreams and portents foreshadow what is to come because there is a divine will at work, shaping the destiny of men and nations. Astyages, king of the Medes, for example, dreams of a vine growing from his daughter's genitals, a vine that will overshadow all of Asia (**10.13**; see p. 266). The actual product of her womb is Cyrus, who will indeed rule all of Asia and establish Achaemenid power, so the dream is a premonition of Persian rule. Similarly, when the banished Athenian tyrant Hippias lands at Marathon with the Persians in 490 BC, he sneezes and loses a tooth. Hippias concludes, fatalistically, that the clod of earth containing his tooth is all he will ever win back. In other words, the gods have sent a sign that he will fail. Perhaps most remarkable of all is a series of dreams in Book 7 when Herodotos describes Xerxes' change of heart. For a short time he decides *not* to invade Greece, until a phantom appears to him in his dream and threatens him if he abandons his plans. After the king's adviser, Artabanos, tests the phantom by sleeping on the throne in the king's regalia—a trick that does not fool the phantom—it is clear to Xerxes, Artabanos, and the audience that the gods have ordained that the Persians must invade. According to Herodotos's way of seeing history, the Persians had to be defeated, so they had to be

10.13 Astyages' Dream, manuscript illustration, *c.* 1475 AD. Tempera colors, gold paint, and gold leaf on parchment

compelled by heaven to invade, thus proving that they deserved to be defeated.

All these elements, from dreams, oracles, and phantoms, to the underlying mechanisms of history, consisting of hubris, folly, and retribution, made sense to an audience of Athenians in the mid-fifth century raised on Homer and tragedy. If Leonidas was a glorious hero who died in battle and Themistokles a cunning hero who survived, any reader or listener could take them as modern, real versions of Achilles and Odysseus, heroes from the world of epic. In these respects, Herodotos was a conventional thinker. His ethnographic interests were wide-ranging, his curiosity endless, and his powers of observation were truly formidable, but the intellectual apparatus he brought to bear on interpreting major historical events were those of a conventional Greek of the mid-fifth century.

Writing only a generation later, Thucydides was an historian of a totally different type. He announced that his work was to be a record of the Peloponnesian War, and in the very second sentence of his history he described the war as the greatest commotion (*kinesis*) ever to occur in the Greek world or anywhere else, employing a word that seems better suited to the language of Presocratic cosmology than historiography. Thucydides explicitly rejected Herodotean storytelling, saying that his work might be less pleasurable to listen to since it lacked the legendary and the fabulous (*to mythodes*), but

that it would prove useful to those who wanted to know how history had unfolded and would unfold again. This predictive quality was due to a basic fact of history: it is made by humans, and human nature being what it is, events will occur in the same or similar fashion in the future. This human element Thucydides called "the human thing" (*to anthropinon*), and it represents a forceful rejection not only of the Herodotean taste for tall tales, but also for the underlying Herodotean notion that history unfolds in accordance with a divine plan. In other words, Thucydides banished the gods from history. Instead there are just flawed, angry, ambitious, calculating humans. The difference between the two historians reflects the fundamental separation between convention and the new learning.

In the next chapter we will see how thoroughly Thucydides has shaped our understanding of the Peloponnesian War (431–404 BC), but one episode in the war itself, and Thucydides' description of it, will serve to illustrate how much Athens was changing with respect to traditional religious practice in the late fifth century. The Peloponnesian War would put the city under extraordinary stress, and the Athenians faced no greater threat than the plague that broke out in the second year of the war. As the city succumbed to the dreadful disease, people sought solace in conventional religion, but Thucydides makes it clear that this was pointless.

No human art was of any avail, and as to supplications in temples, enquiries of oracles, and the like, they were utterly useless, and at last men were overpowered by the calamity and gave them all up.

(Thucydides, *The Peloponnesian War* 2.47, trans. Jowett)

Thucydides proceeds to give a graphically detailed account of the symptoms of the plague, offering a description of the sort we would expect from a Hippokratic doctor, specifically with the aim of equiping the reader to recognize the disease should it recur. As the disease progressed:

...it would move into the stomach and bring on all the vomits of bile to which physicians have ever given names; and they were very distressing. An ineffectual retching producing violent convulsions attacked most of the sufferers....The body externally was not so very hot to the touch, nor yet pale; it was of a livid colour inclining to red, and breaking out in pustules and ulcers. But the internal fever was intense; the sufferers could not bear to have on them even the finest linen garment; they insisted on being naked, and there was nothing which they longed for more eagerly than to throw themselves into cold water. And many of those who had no one to look after them actually plunged into the cisterns, for they were tormented by unceasing thirst, which was not in the least assuaged whether they drank little or much. They could not sleep; a restlessness which was intolerable never left them. While the disease was at its height the body, instead of wasting away, held out amid these sufferings in a marvellous manner, and either they died on the seventh or ninth day, not of weakness, for their strength was not exhausted, but of internal fever, which was the end of most; or, if they survived, then the disease descended into the bowels and there produced violent ulceration; severe diarrhoea at the same time set in, and at a later stage caused exhaustion, which finally with few exceptions carried them off.

(*The Peloponnesian War* 2.49, trans. Jowett)

But the plague was more than an opportunity for Thucydides to demonstrate that he could describe a physical disease as well as any doctor trained by Hippokrates. The plague, in his analysis, also precipitated a breakdown of the body politic, as people rejected both human and divine law.

No fear of Gods or law of man deterred a criminal. Those who saw all perishing alike, thought that the worship or neglect of the Gods made no difference. For offences against human law no punishment was to be feared; no one would live long enough to be called to account.

(*The Peloponnesian War* 2.53, trans. Jowett)

What had been a purely intellectual agnosticism among the philosophers and sophists was now a visceral symptom of the despair of a sick and ailing community. Thucydides would come to apply the same analysis to the breakdown of social order caused by civil wars, and would conclude that the seeds of these disasters lay in human shortcomings, revealed by the exigencies of war and power politics. Earlier, in the sixth and the first half of the fifth century BC, Athens had been a more resilient and open place, but as we shall see in the next chapter, the Peloponnesian War was a hard master, matching the temper of the Athenians to the challenges they faced. The coming war would have many victims, not least of which would be the free and open exchange of ideas characteristic of a great society.

10.14 Albert Tournaire, reconstruction of the sanctuary of Delphi, 1894. Watercolor

Spotlight
The Oracle of Delphi

Visitors today see only the skeleton of Delphi, but this nineteenth-century Beaux-Arts reconstruction (**10.14**), looking north up the folds of Parnassos, evokes the splendor and the awe-inspiring views that pilgrims encountered on the way to consult the oracle. The entrance to the *temenos* (sacred enclosure) was located on the southeast corner (lower right). From here the sacred way climbed gradually west, then turned sharply back near the Treasury of the Athenians, before ascending toward the eastern end of the temple terrace. Passing the Great Altar, the visitor then stood at the eastern edge of the Temple Terrace, with a clear view of the eastern facade of the temple of Apollo (**10.15**).

Close by the temple was the *omphalos*, a stone that represented the Earth's navel. Delphi was considered the center of the world, a belief that may be reflected in the sanctuary's name. Although Delphi was often said to be derived from Apollo Delphinios (i.e. "the dolphin"), Delphi's name may in fact come from the Greek word *delphus*, meaning "womb."

The operation of the oracle remains one of the great mysteries of Greek religion. Many ancient sources refer to a chasm through which fumes are supposed to have risen, causing the Pythia, Apollo's priestess, to become intoxicated with the god's spirit and to utter his prophecies. Until recently, there was no geological evidence to support this, but in the last twenty years an American team of geologists, chemists, and ancient historians has argued that Delphi sits directly over the intersection of two fault-lines, one running north/south and the other east/west. Slippage along these fault-lines, they have argued, released a combination of ethylene, ethane, and methane that would have produced

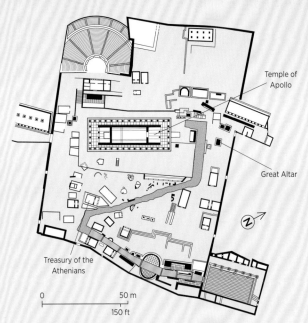

10.15 Plan of the sanctuary of Apollo at Delphi. Visitors entered from the lower right and proceeded up the Sacred Way leading to the temple terrace. Most of the small buildings shown are treasuries and dedications by kings, rulers, and city-states. None of the buildings are governmental, nor do any serve a primarily civic function.

Temple of Apollo

Great Altar

Treasury of the Athenians

0   50 m

150 ft

an intoxicating effect on the Pythia (**10.16**). Other scientists have disputed both the existence of the faults and the presence of hallucinatory gases in sufficient quantities to drug the god's spokeswoman. Investigations will continue, yet there still remains the problem of how drug-induced babble was rendered into complete hexameter poetry, which is how the oracles were transmitted to the inquirers. Apollo's priests, it seems, played an important hand in shaping the god's communications.

The importance of Delphi is reflected in the magnificent

10.16 Detail of a red-figure kylix depicting the Pythia seated on a tripod, fifth century BC. In her right hand is a sprig of laurel, the plant sacred to Apollo. To her right stands a priest, waiting to hear the Pythia's pronouncements. Ceramic, D: 32 cm (1 ft ⅝ in.)

treasuries, statues, tripods, and other dedications that transformed it into the wealthiest and most prestigious location in Greece. Most of these objects have, of course, been looted and plundered over the centuries, but the few pieces that remain, such as the Charioteer, dedicated by the Sicilian tyrant Polyzalos in 478 BC, give us an idea of Delphi's wealth (**10.17**). The Charioteer is life-size, standing 1.8 meters (5 ft 10⅞ in.) tall. It was originally displayed standing in a chariot drawn by a team of horses. The Charioteer was discovered in 1896 in the early days of the excavation of the temple of Apollo by the French School. It is likely that the charioteer and his team were damaged in an earthquake that hit Delphi in 373 BC and that the pieces, in common with other damaged treasures, were buried in the sanctuary. At the height of its power, in the Classical period, Delphi teemed with such treasures.

The earthquake of 373 BC was only one of a number of occasions when the temple suffered natural calamities, but each time the Amphiktyony (the association of Greek cities that controlled Delphi) contributed money toward its rebuilding. Even here, however, political influence and piety were intertwined. It was said that the Athenian clan, the Alkmaionidai, contracted to rebuild the façade of the late Archaic temple in limestone, but did so in marble, in order to curry favor with the oracle and help bring about their return from exile.

Similarly to the other panhellenic sanctuaries at Olympia, Nemea, and Isthmia, Delphi possessed virtually no political power of its own, but was the symbolic center of a network of Greek states. As we saw in Chapter 4, cities planning to dispatch colonies sought the approval of Apollo, whose instructions were normally delivered

10.17 Delphic Charioteer dedicated by Polyzalos of Gela, c. 470 BC. Bronze, H: 1.8 m (5 ft 10⅞ in.)

in the form of an oracle. Over the course of the Archaic and Classical periods, hundreds of embassies came to Delphi from all over the Greek world and beyond. The advice given by the oracle therefore had a powerful effect on the lives of states and individuals. According to Herodotos, for example, Delphi was one of the sanctuaries consulted by Kroisos when he wanted to obtain reliable guidance from the gods when he was contemplating an attack on the growing power of Persia. He tested the god at Delphi by asking him to identify exactly what he was doing on a specific day, although he was in Lydia, hundreds of miles away from Delphi. When Apollo responded through the Pythia, his human acolyte, that he could smell lamb cooking with tortoise meat in a bronze cauldron, which was correct, Kroisos was duly impressed. The oracle went on to predict that Kroisos would destroy a great empire if he attacked Persia, which Kroisos interpreted as a promise of victory. He attacked, but the empire he destroyed proved to be his own.

The story of Kroisos's mistake occurs in a number of sources. In some versions, after his defeat Kroisos was condemned by Cyrus to be burned alive but was saved by Apollo, illustrating both Kroisos's error and the god's forbearance (**10.18**). The entire episode reveals a great deal about how the Delphic oracle operated within the belief-system of the Greeks: the gods listened, and gave signs. They did not lie, but humans still had to interpret the responses of the gods, since they were frequently posed as puzzles, or enigmas. Modern commentators have often ridiculed this, as though the oracle were hedging its bets, but in the context of Greek culture the oracle's behavior made sense: we should not blame the gods if our greed or stupidity leads us to misinterpret the gods' messages.

In addition to offering responses to specific questions, the oracle also offered broad moral guidance expressed in equally pithy utterances: "know thyself" and "nothing in excess" were two simple injunctions that sum up Delphi's role in articulating an ethical code that applied to all Greeks. So, just as the Athenians claimed piety as their most characteristic quality, more generally it was their shared reverence for the gods that the Greeks saw as one of the characteristics that united them, along with shared language and shared blood. It was religious belief and practice, much more than political unity, that defined the Athenians and, more generally, the Greeks as a people. The Peloponnesian War, however, would reveal that not even shared religious beliefs could save the Greeks from a catastrophic conflict.

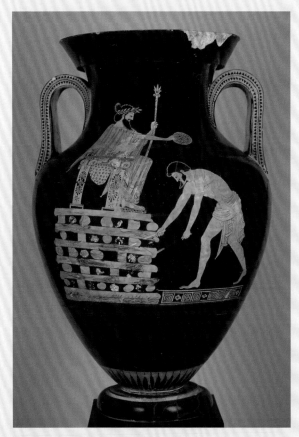

10.18 Kroisos on the Pyre. Red-figure amphora, *c.* 500–490 BC. Ceramic, H: 59.5 cm (1 ft 11⅜ in.)

Chapter 11
The Peloponnesian War

The Peloponnesian War is both the most traumatic episode in the history of the Greeks of the Classical Age and also the subject of the most subtle and complex historical analysis produced by the Greeks, the work of Thucydides. This chapter examines the origins of the conflict, and suggests that Corinth was the state most responsible for setting the Greeks on the path to war. We also explore Thucydides' interest in the dynamic relationship between a people and its leaders in the shape of his psychologically nuanced portrait of bold commanders inspiring conservative followers and restrained leaders checking their impetuous followers. The Sicilian expedition is presented not only as a military defeat, but also as a disaster brought about by misunderstanding and miscalculation. Thucydides' work is a prose tragedy, in which the Athenians are undone by their own shortcomings.

Warfare and the Greeks

The growth of Athenian power was made possible by the unexpected victory of the Greeks during the Persian Wars. That period of political ascendancy came to a close toward the end of the fifth century BC

as a result of a protracted, disastrous war between the Athenians and their allies on one side and the Spartans and their allies on the other. This conflict, which became known as the Peloponnesian War (431–404 BC), reshaped the future direction of Athenian and Greek affairs.

One of the many causes of the Peloponnesian War lay in the changing nature of war itself. Warfare was undeniably a recurring, ubiquitous feature of Greek life, yet prior to the late fifth century, it was usually conducted under certain rules of engagement. As we saw in Chapter 5, throughout antiquity, campaigning was seasonal, generally lasting from April until September, and much of the fighting consisted of skirmishing: pillaging the land of the enemy and raiding were the usual practice. By contrast, mass engagements were less common. When they did occur, the sides fought until one side broke—those who ran away would drop their shields, while the pursuers would often stop to strip the dead. As a result, few battles resulted in slaughter on a massive scale, and casualties were therefore limited.

Archaic warfare was waged by armies levied by the aristocratic leaders of the state, who promised booty or possibly land as incentives for their followers, yet these armies were not necessarily state armies. When Peisistratos defeated his enemies at the Battle of Pallene in 546 BC, for example, it was not the Athenian army that he led but a private force made up of his friends, allies, and retainers. Land was also a primary reason for waging war: prior to the Persian Wars, most wars were escalations of border disputes, and even international wars often had their origins in conflicts over contested territory. The earliest war, for example, to involve networks of alliances on either side was the conflict between Chalkis and Eretria on Euboia (often referred to as the Lelantine War, named for the rich coastal plain that lay between the two cities). Similarly, the principal wars involving the Spartans in the Archaic period were fought with the Messenians, their neighbors to the west, and the Argives to the north. The same phenomenon occurred throughout Archaic Greece: Oropos, for example, on the border between Attica and Boiotia, changed hands so often that in the third century BC, the inhabitants even described themselves as "Boiotian Athenians."

The Hoplite Revolution

During the sixth century BC, however, the face of warfare was changing. The one-on-one combat scenarios familiar from the Homeric poems were gradually giving way to hoplite engagements.

11.1 Detail of a red-figure kylix depicting a hoplite arming, *c.* 500–475 BC

These battles involved men armed head to foot in bronze and iron, soldiers known as hoplites, named for the *hoplon*, or shield, that they carried (**11.1**). Heavily armed, they were able to fight in a massed formation, the phalanx. The hoplite was vulnerable on his right side, as he thrust his spear forward, but the left side of his neighbor's shield offered protection as long as he stayed close. Accordingly, the hoplite's armor favored the phalanx formation. For the phalanx's commanders, the most pressing tactical question was whether to deepen the phalanx so that it hit the enemy in the manner of a massive battering ram, or to lengthen the front line and possibly outflank the enemy's line, allowing one's troops to roll up the enemy from the side and cause them to break. The gradual evolution of the phalanx as the preferred formation for infantry warfare was significant. Hoplite warfare encouraged an egalitarian ethos and a sense of dependence on the other men of similar status: the middle rank of society, above the Thetes yet below the cavalry.

It is easy, however, to exaggerate the tactical innovations of hoplite warfare. On the one hand, these tactical innovations may have been more of an evolution of preexisting strategy. As early as Homer's poems in the late eighth century, there are references to men fighting in serried, or compact, ranks, and mass formations may have been known in Bronze Age battles. On the other hand, Archaic styles of conflict persisted into the Classical era. Even as late as Herodotos's *Histories* (composed in the middle of the fifth century BC) we find men being awarded the prize for valor, having distinguished themselves in battle in the style of Homeric heroes.

Perhaps surprisingly, the greatest impact of hoplite warfare may have been in the arena of democracy. The difference between Greece in 800 BC and Greece in 500 BC was that the scattered, varied, aristocratically ruled communities of the earlier age had become states, political entities where people recognized affiliations that transcended family and clan. The new armies—comprised of hundreds of men, all capable of owning arms, fighting side by side yet unrelated by blood—surely contributed to the solidification of group identities. It should be noted that although hoplites were found in every Greek state, not every Greek state became a democracy, but nevertheless, the idea of a hoplite revolution is worth taking seriously. People were

11.2 Detail of the Chigi Vase showing an early depiction of the phalanx, *c.* 650 BC. Ceramic, H (of decorated band): 5 cm (2 in.)

becoming invested in their states, and the right to participate in orderly decision-making was a peacetime correlate to, and perhaps a condition of, their military service. Hoplites made citizens (**11.2**).

In the fifth century, warfare continued to evolve in new directions. The Athenian democracy used war as an extension of policy and as a means to assert Athenian hegemony. Victor Davis Hanson has correctly observed that during the fifth century, Athens "widened, amplified, and intensified" the waging of war, regularly attacked other democracies, and was "a constant source of death and destruction" among the Greeks. The Athenian demos voted to undertake a new campaign on average every two to three years, each one openly debated and endorsed by the Ekklesia; at the height of its power, Athens frequently engaged in sieges for a full year or longer. More public money was spent on military campaigns than all other activities combined, and during the Peloponnesian War the Athenians were spending between 500 to 2,000 talents every year on their war effort.

Athenian Bellicosity

All of these details raise an important question: was the Athenian democracy inherently bellicose? Thucydides, whose analysis of the Peloponnesian War is fundamental to our understanding of Athenian war policy, characterizes his countrymen as restlessly energetic and recklessly daring. They were born to take no rest and to give no peace to anyone else either, says a Corinthian ambassador, describing the Athenians to the Spartans (*The Peloponnesian War* 1.70).

One way to understand the increasingly militaristic bent of Athenian society is to consider the relationship of warfare to democracy more broadly. Recent sociological studies have compared different political regimes with respect to warfare, and the results are instructive. Edward Mansfield and Jack Snyder have determined, somewhat surprisingly, that states transitioning to democracy start wars more often than established democracies or authoritarian governments. Democracies also win wars (90 percent of the wars they initiate and 80 percent overall), according to Dan Reiter and Allan Stam. And a third finding is pertinent: democracies rarely fight each other. None of these observations amounts to a total explanation of the Athenian democracy's bellicosity, but taken as broad brushstrokes, they paint a picture of an Athenian democracy whose confidence resulted in an increased inclination to wage war. The Kleisthenic reforms had fashioned Athens into a state that, from the military point of view, was well prepared to muster and deploy large numbers of men, but the speed at which this transformation occurred was astonishing. In the two generations after Peisistratos won control of Athens in 546 BC with a private army probably numbering no more than a few hundred men, the Athenians defeated

11.3 The Lenormant Trireme Relief, *c.* 410–400 BC. This is one of the few depictions of rowers on a trireme. Note that while the top tier of rowers (***thranites***) can be seen, two lower tiers sat below them, shown on the relief by their oars. Many of the crew were rowing blind, which required precise training. Marble, L: 54 cm (1 ft 9¼ in.)

Chalkis and Boiotia in 506 BC; sent 20 ships to aid the Ionian Revolt in 499 (requiring the participation of nearly 4,000 men); and deployed more than 9,000 men to Marathon in 490. By then their army was comprised of a body of citizen soldiers equipped in standard armor, trained to fight in formation, and led by competent officers.

Another element of the Athenian practice of war needs to be considered: the Athenians tolerated surprisingly high casualty rates. Consider the casualties of the tribe Erechtheis, cited in Chapter 8. In 459 BC, Erechtheis lost 177 men in campaigns as far afield as Egypt, Cyprus, and Megara. This equals

a potential total of 1,770 across the ten tribes. (Even if we cannot determine with certainty that all tribes that year lost approximately the same number of men, the potential for such losses existed, since no tribe was deployed more often or to more dangerous areas than any other.) Given a total citizen population of approximately 40,000, the Athenians were prepared to tolerate the loss of between 4 and 5 percent of their adult males of fighting age in a single year. In order to grasp how extraordinary this is compared to war in modern terms, consider that in 1968, the worst year of the Vietnam War from the point of view of American casualties, the United States lost 16,899 military

brought about a reorientation of military operations: in quick order the naval contingents of the Aegean states emerged as crucial to the Greek victory (**11.3**).

This transformation suited the Athenians well for the simple reason that naval power built on and reinforced broad-based democracy. A cavalryman needs a horse, a hoplite must be able to afford armor, but a rower needs nothing more than the calluses on his hands and an oar (which was supplied by the state). By shifting the focus of their military from a land-based army of heavily armed infantrymen to the navy, the Athenians were effectively favoring a more democratic form of warfare, or—more accurately—were shifting the class basis of their military forces, with the egalitarianism of the middle-class hoplite phalanx in competition with the lower-class brotherhood of the trireme. As with the hoplite revolution, however, the shift away from heroic, Homeric, land-based combat was met with disapproval by some. Stesimbrotos, a pamphlet writer who lived in the fifth century, put it pithily: "Themistokles robbed the Athenians of spear and shield and gave them oars and cushions instead..." (Plutarch, *Themistokles* 4).

In common with Stesimbrotos, most political thinkers were hostile to democracy, yet the connection between rowing a trireme and serving as a citizen were recognized as two sides of the same coin. A pamphlet that survives in the works of Xenophon, usually ascribed to pseudo-Xenophon, puts the case bluntly:

My first point is that it is right that the poor and the ordinary people there should have more power than the noble and the rich, because it is the ordinary people who man the fleet and bring the city her power; they provide the helmsmen, the boatswains, the junior officers, the look-outs and the shipwrights; it is these people who make the city powerful much more than the hoplites and the noble and respectable citizens. This being so, it seems just that all should share in public office by lot and by election, and that any citizen who wishes should be able to speak in the Assembly.

(pseudo-Xenophon, *The Constitution of the Athenians*, 1.1–2, trans. Moore)

As pseudo-Xenophon correctly points out, naval strength, broad-based democracy, and imperial power all work together.

personnel out of a US adult population at the time of 15,400,000; i.e. *c.* 0.11 percent.

One further feature of the configuration of military affairs in Athenian life looms large in the build-up to the Peloponnesian War. It is unlikely that, before the Persian Wars, the navy had formed the principal military force of any Greek state. Aigina and Athens had fought for dominance in the region of the Saronic Gulf, it is true, and such cities as Chalkis in Euboia as well as the Greek cities in Sicily had fleets, but prior to Xerxes' invasion, most Greeks embroiled in war had fought on land. The Persian invasion, in which the invading army was supported by a massive fleet, had

Athenian Expansion, Spartan Resistance

By the late 430s BC, this restlessly aggressive navy was projecting Athenian power into each corner of the Aegean. This relentless growth, combined with the forced exaction of tribute and the ruthless suppression of rebellion, scared and alienated many of the island states of the Aegean and contributed to the emergence of a land-based coalition of states in the Peloponnese as a counterweight to the power of Athens. The days of common cooperation in the face of the Persian threat were long gone; a veteran of thirty years of age at the time of Marathon would have been nearly ninety years old when the Peloponnesian War broke out in 431 BC.

The two sides were polar opposites: the Spartans were Dorian and spoke a distinctively different Greek from the Ionian Greek of the Athenians; the Spartans exercised their hegemony by land, relying on a professional army of Spartiate warriors, while the Athenians projected their power by sea, relying on rowers often from the poorest ranks of society; at home the Spartans restricted full citizenship to the Spartiate elite, while the Athenian democracy of the fifth century extended participation in the Assembly to every male citizen; abroad, the Spartans showed no interest in enlarging their territorial holdings beyond Lakonia and Messenia, even as the Athenians were seizing territory, sending out colonies and cleruchies; and the Spartans shunned coinage, while the Athenians made the Athenian "owl" the currency of the Aegean (**11.4**).

The Cause of War

The fundamental cause of the conflict was stated by the man who has left us the most detailed account of the war: the Athenian general, Thucydides. He lived through the war, participated in it, and eventually was forced into exile thanks to his failure to secure the Athenian outpost of Amphipolis in northern Greece from an attack by the Spartan general Brasidas. Thucydides was a realist, with little time for the divine interventions or narrative flourishes that Herodotos had employed to describe the Persian Wars. Instead, he offered a penetrating analysis that reflected an often bleak assessment of human nature and political power. Although the ethnic differences of Ionians and Dorians no doubt contributed to the war, Thucydides

11.4 An Athenian tetradrachm, or "owl," *c.* 450–406 BC. Silver, 17.05 grams

is absolutely explicit about the real reason behind the conflict: "The truest cause, although never openly stated, was, in my opinion, this: the Athenians, by becoming powerful and inspiring fear in the Spartans, forced them into war" (*The Peloponnesian War* 1.23).

Thucydides' analysis carries the weight of first-hand experience, so we should take his statement very seriously. Although Herodotos was the first Greek historian to investigate a major historical event from the recent past, the Persian Wars, Thucydides must command our attention as the first historian to analyse a major contemporary event of such importance. So he is surely right when he claims that the growth of Athenian power alarmed Sparta. Even so, in narrating the outbreak of the war, Thucydides recounts a series of events that escalated tensions, and a close reading of this timetable to war offers a more nuanced reading, and suggests that we should refine Thucydides' judgment somewhat.

The Epidamnos Affair

Thucydides traces the beginning of the conflict to a civil war that broke out in 435 BC at Epidamnos (modern-day Durrës, in Albania) between the oligarchs and the democrats. Located near the mouth of the Adriatic, the city was a colony of Corcyra (modern-day Kerkyra) and was well located to give access to trade up and down the Adriatic coast. As a result of the civil stasis in Epidamnos, the two sides sought help from outside powers: the democrats turned to Corinth for help, while the oligarchs were supported by Corcyra (even though the Corcyraeans were themselves a colony from Corinth).

As the conflict escalated, the focus of attention moved from Epidamnos to Corcyra. With a fleet of eighty ships, the Corcyraeans defeated a Corinthian fleet, and at almost the same moment their remaining forty ships forced the Epidamnians to surrender. The Corcyreans' treatment of the prisoners was brutal and presaged events to come: all prisoners (with the exception of the Corinthians) were slaughtered.

Galvanized by their humiliation, the Corinthians set about building a massive new fleet, scouring the Peloponnese for rowers. In response, the Corcyreans sought an alliance with the Athenians, and at the Battle of Sybota in 433, the Athenians assisted the Corcyreans in what proved to be a large but inconclusive battle with the Corinthians. The scale of the engagement was notable, with the Corinthian fleet numbering 150 ships and the Corcyreans 110. The initial Athenian contingent that participated in the battle was only ten ships strong, but a second Athenian force of twenty triremes arrived as the Corinthians were preparing to land and forced the Corinthians to withdraw.

The Epidamnos affair is important for two reasons. The first is that the original conflict between the oligarchic and democratic factions in Epidamnos was irrelevant to the Athenian decision to become involved. The Athenians were not driven by altruism; more compelling to them was the prospect of an alliance with one of the largest navies in Greece. The second reason is that, from a Corinthian point of view, the Athenian involvement was ominous. The theater of operations, the Ionian Sea, lay just beyond the entrance to the Corinthian Gulf, and was an area of interest to the Corinthians.

The Athenian presence represented an unwelcome intrusion into the Corinthian sphere of influence. Furthermore, Corinth was the mother city of Corcyra and the grandmother city, so to speak, of Epidamnos. From a Corinthian point of view, Athens was involving itself in matters that were none of its business. Quite aside from larger issues of Athenian involvement in the western arena of the Mediterranean (since the route to Italy, Sicily, and the Corinthian colonies of Magna Graecia went past Corcyra), the Epidamnos affair was regarded by the Corinthians as a provocation in which Athens' strategic plans collided directly with Corinthian regional interests.

The Siege of Potidaia and the Megarian Decree

Athenian relations with the Corinthians quickly deteriorated. Eager to strengthen their control over every part of the Aegean, and suspecting that the Corinthians were plotting against them, the Athenians singled out Potidaia, a city in the Chalcidike region of the northwest Aegean. The city was in the unfortunate position of being both an Athenian ally and a Corinthian colony with close ties to the mother-city. (Each year, for example, a ruling magistrate was dispatched by the Corinthians to run Potidaia.) In 433/2 BC, two years after the Epidamnos affair, the Athenians ordered the city to tear down its walls and send hostages to Athens, their demands reinforced by the presence of an Athenian fleet and a thousand hoplites. The Potidaians appealed and, encouraged by a promise from the Spartan magistrates to invade Attica should the Athenians attack, went into revolt, whereupon the Athenians began a siege of the city.

Over the next three years, hostilities escalated. The Corinthians dispatched a force of 1,600 hoplites to defend the city. They were joined by mercenaries from the Peloponnese, although during this time the promised Spartan invasion of Attica never materialized. The Athenians responded with successive waves of reinforcements: 2,000 hoplites under Kallias; 1,600 men under Phormio; and finally, in 430 BC, 4,000 men under Hagnon and Kleopompos. The siege ended in 430 when the Potidaians, facing starvation, surrendered, by which point war had already been formally declared between Athens and Sparta.

The Epidamnos and Potidaia episodes show that the two blocs of Greek states arrayed behind Athens and Sparta were moving toward open rupture. The final event that precipitated the formal declaration of war between Athens and Sparta involved, ironically, an old-fashioned border dispute. At some point in the late 430s—it is unclear precisely when—Perikles charged the Megarians with farming the Sacred Land on the border between Megara and Eleusis, at the western edge of Attic territory. When no resolution was reached the Athenians imposed a trade embargo on the Megarians, a decision that became known as the Megarian Decree. In 432 BC, the Corinthians convinced the Spartans to hold a congress in Sparta so that the Peloponnesian allies could air their grievances. The Megarians complained that they had been excluded from the ports and markets of the Athenian empire; among the various complaints against the Athenians, this seems to have carried special weight. After the congress the Spartans sent at least two embassies to Athens in a belated effort to avert war. Describing the second of these, Thucydides says that the ambassadors made it clear that war could be prevented if the Athenians lifted the Megarian Decree. Perikles characterized the demand as at the head of the list of the Spartans' complaints and cautioned the Athenians against giving in. Rescind the Decree, he argued, and you will face a fresh ultimatum. They did not, and the war began in earnest shortly after.

What was at stake in the Megarian Decree? One can suggest that Perikles mishandled negotiations by underestimating Spartan concerns, or more cynically suppose that he understood exactly how significant the embargo was, but neither interpretation adequately explains the nub of the issue. Why should encroachment on some sacred pasture land consisting of no more than a few square miles on the edge of Attica have precipitated an economic war? Surely there was more to the dispute than this?

If we continue examining events from the point of view of spheres of influence then it would seem that the importance of the Megarian Decree was due entirely to Megara's position. Sandwiched between Athens and Corinth, Megara was a Dorian state that often rankled under the influence of its Corinthian neighbors. During the First Peloponnesian War around 457 BC, the Megarians entered the Athenian alliance, according to Thucydides, because they were annoyed about a border imposed on them by the Corinthians. The Athenians had responded enthusiastically, building for the Megarians a set of Long Walls from Megara to the port of Nisaia on the Saronic Gulf, where the Athenians installed a garrison.

During the Epidamnos affair in 435 BC, however, the Megarians supplied a contingent of eight ships to help the Corinthians, and this betrayal is surely what prompted the Megarian Decree. Exclusion from the ports and harbors of the Athenians and their allies carried a message: Athens had built such facilities for the Megarians for their loyalty, and it could take them away just as quickly. By destroying Megara's chance to trade in the Saronic Gulf and the Aegean, the Athenians demonstrated once again that there was a clearly defined sphere of Athenian influence. With the establishment of a similar zone in the Ionian Sea, the growth of Athenian power increasingly alarmed Corinth.

Thucydides' chain of proximate causes shows how a series of localized conflicts quickly engulfed the Aegean, drawing the two main powers of the region into opposition. Thucydides simplifies this by presenting the process as the growth of Athenian power and the fear it inspired in Sparta, but his own narrative suggests a slight modification of this judgment: the truest cause of the war was that the growth of Athens' power scared Corinth. Threatened to the west and to the north, and facing the reduction of Megara on their border as a result of an Athenian embargo, the Corinthians goaded the Spartans into action. "If only you will act," say the Corinthians at the congress in Sparta on the eve of war, "we will stand by you" (*The Peloponnesian War* 1.71.6).

The Archidamian War

With the breakdown of negotiations the war began in earnest. The first phase of the war, which lasted from 431 to 421 BC (**11.5**), is usually named for the Spartan king associated with its outbreak, Archidamos. Cautious and wary of acting precipitously, he represents a model of leadership that stands in contrast to the rashness of the Athenians. For example, in advising the Spartans to avoid an open break, he warns them:

But do not take up arms yet. Let us first send and remonstrate with them: we need not let them know positively whether we intend to go to war or not. In the meantime our own preparations may be going forward; we may seek for allies wherever we can find them, whether in Greece or among the Barbarians, who will supply our deficiencies in ships and money....If [the Athenians] listen to our ambassadors, well and good; but, if not, in two or three years' time we shall be in a stronger position, should we then determine to attack them. Perhaps too when they begin to see that we are getting ready, and that our words are to be interpreted by our actions, they may be more likely to yield; for their fields will be still untouched and their goods undespoiled.

(Thucydides, *The Peloponnesian War* 1.82, trans. Jowett)

Despite his warnings, the Spartans elected to go to war. If much of the Greek world looked on in anticipation of a grand reckoning or a quick result, however, they were to be disappointed. Despite persuading the Athenians to go to war, Perikles adopted a defensive strategy that went against the Athenians' aggressive instincts. Rely on the walls to keep the city safe, argued Perikles. Use the fleet to keep the city supplied with all of its needs, and most importantly of all, do not undertake more campaigns. The Periklean strategy meant that from the outset the Athenians were forced to retreat behind their walls and to become refugees within their own city. Other than wearing the Spartans down by refusing battle,

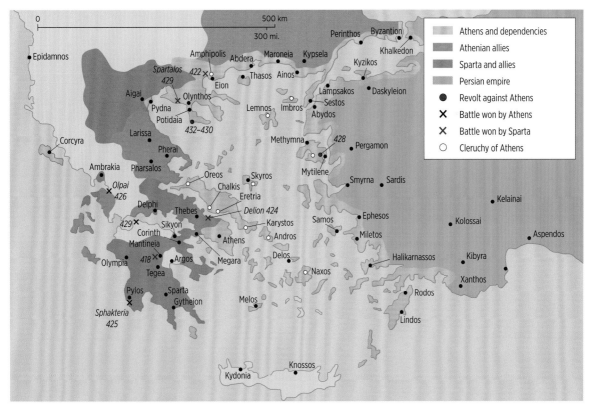

11.5 Map of theater of operations in the Peloponnesian War up to 421 BC

it is not clear how this defensive strategy was likely to win the war. It was not long before the Athenians abandoned their defensive posture, however, primarily because in 430, during the second year of the war, Perikles died of the plague that decimated Athens and changed the course of the war.

Athens in Crisis

Perikles so thoroughly dominated Athenian affairs for at least fifteen years that Thucydides summed up his career by saying that in what was nominally a democracy power was really in the hands of one man, yet Perikles also had a gift for characterizing the mood of Athens before the plague. We have already noted in earlier chapters that Perikles delivered the famous Funeral Oration after the first year of the war, and that his speech represents the clearest statement of what it meant to be a citizen of the Athenian democracy, delivered while Athens was at the acme of its power:

For in the hour of trial Athens alone among her contemporaries is superior to the report of her. No enemy who comes against her is indignant at the reverses which he sustains at the hands of such a city; no subject complains that his masters are unworthy of him. And we shall assuredly not be without witnesses; there are mighty monuments of our power which will make us the wonder of this and of succeeding ages....For we have compelled every land and every sea to open a path for our valour, and have everywhere planted eternal memorials of our friendship and of our enmity.

(*The Peloponnesian War* 2.41, trans. Jowett)

It is also important to note that the Funeral Oration's eloquent testimony to the glory of Athens is immediately followed in Thucydides' work by his celebrated description of the plague, which broke out in the second year of the war, 430 BC. If Perikles' Funeral Oration offers us a shining city on a hill, the plague brings us quickly back down to earth. In the style of a well-trained Hippokratic doctor, Thucydides recounts the symptoms of those afflicted: fever, inflamed eyes, swollen throat, foul breath, hoarseness, chest pains, and a harsh cough. Then followed bile, retching, spasms and ulcers, insatiable thirst, dreadful diarrhea, and, in most cases, death. Recent studies of skeletal remains excavated in AD 1994–95 from a mass grave in Athens have determined that the terrible plague that struck Athens was a form of typhoid. A reconstruction based on one of the skeletons found in the Kerameikos neighborhood of Athens allows us to see once again the face of a young Athenian girl who died of this terrible disease (**11.6**).

For Thucydides, however, the physical damage caused by the disease was not as bad as the social breakdown caused by the plague. Crammed in behind its walls, thanks to the defensive policies of Perikles, the city descended into chaos, and it is this description of Athens that reads as a counterpoint to the vision outlined in Perikles' Funeral Oration:

The bodies of dying men lay one upon another, and half-dead creatures reeled about the streets and gathered round all the fountains in their longing for water....All the burial rites before in use were entirely upset, and they buried the bodies as best they could. Many, for lack of the proper materials, through so many of their friends having died already, had recourse to the most shameless funeral practices: sometimes getting the start of those who had raised a pile, they threw their own dead body upon the stranger's pyre and ignited it; sometimes they tossed the corpse which they were carrying on top of another that was burning, and so went off.

(*The Peloponnesian War* 2.52.1, trans. Crawley)

The Funeral Oration is a eulogy to the Athens that died with Perikles: the Golden Athens could not survive the death of its greatest man. Instead, for Thucydides, a harsher Athens recovered from the plague, and, no longer restrained by the defensive mindset of Perikles, turned to Kleon, who offered a more aggressive strategy that was more naturally in line with the tendencies of the democracy. Certainly the emergence of Kleon, whom Thucydides calls the most violent yet persuasive speaker of his day, marks the emergence of a new level of bellicosity and a possible transformation of the Athenians, although perhaps this transformation was more obvious to Thucydides in hindsight. At the time, the Athenians were focused on surviving the annual invasions of their territory by the Spartans that took place over the course of the next decade. They were also engaged in suppressing rebellions in the Delian League (notably on the large island of Lesbos), raiding parts of Boiotia, participating in dynastic conflicts in Macedon and Thrace, aiding their allies on Corcyra, sending a fleet

11.6 Reconstruction of "Myrtis," an eleven-year-old Athenian girl who died of the plague.

to Sicily, and seizing various opportunities to grab territory in strategic positions. Although the Athenians had to face invasion from the Spartans each year, they managed to campaign in a variety of theaters of war, demonstrating that restless energy for which they were famous. A major focus of Athenian attention was northwestern Greece. From 428 to 426 BC Athenian armies sought to weaken Corinth's influence in the area. The Athenian general Demosthenes also threatened the entrance to the Corinthian Gulf, campaigning on Leukas and at Naupaktos, putting pressure on the trade routes on which Corinth relied. The Athenians also seized Kythera, south of Lakonia, in 424, and in the same year they succeeded in capturing Megara, establishing Athenian military presence on the border of the Corinthians.

In the course of these campaigns, Athenian commanders operated with wide discretion. Phormio in the Corinthian Gulf, Laches in Sicily, Nikias in the Aegean, and Demosthenes in western Greece were all able to form alliances and to choose where and when to campaign with minimal supervision from Athens. The result was that the Athenians found themselves operating on many fronts at any one time. It also meant that in the aftermath of their campaigns, commanders found their decisions being closely scrutinized at home. When the Athenian generals in Sicily, for example, returned to Athens with the news that the Sicilian cities had agreed among themselves to a peace treaty, Pythodoros and Sophokles were banished, and Eurymedon was fined on suspicion of having taken a bribe.

Kleon and the Sphakteria Campaign

One of the key episodes shaped by this odd combination of independent command and popular scrutiny was a campaign that began almost by accident. In 425 BC, the Athenian general Demosthenes was sailing along the western coast of the Peloponnese when bad weather forced him to seek shelter. Pulling in at Pylos, in the Bay of Navarino, he brought his ships and men ashore. Out of boredom his men began building a fortified camp, and Demosthenes realized that this was an opportunity to establish a base from which Athenian forces could harry the western Peloponnese. In response, the Spartans dispatched a force to dislodge the Athenians. Skirmishing followed, and as part of their disposition of forces the Spartans landed a detachment of heavily armed troops on the island of Sphakteria, which faced the bay and allowed entry and exit from only two channels, at the northern and southern ends of the island. In the course of an assault on the Athenian position, the Spartans lost their ships and the men on the island were stranded.

Alarmed at the prospect of a serious defeat, the Spartans sent ambassadors to Athens to sue for peace, but during negotiations the Athenian politician Kleon spoke out vigorously against the proposed armistice, and the talks were abandoned. In the ensuing weeks the Athenians kept up a difficult and exhausting blockade of Sphakteria, while the Spartans took every measure to get supplies to the men on the island, even encouraging helots to run the blockade from the seaward side with the promise of freedom. As the siege dragged on, at Athens the mood grew restive and Kleon faced a rising tide of blame for having killed the peace talks. In a bold move, Kleon tried to deflect the blame on to his political enemy Nikias, and claimed that it would be easy for a real general, such as himself, to finish the siege. A game of brinksmanship followed when Nikias offered to resign his command in favor of Kleon. Kleon demurred, but the more he did so, the more he was called upon to live up to his words. He finally took command of the operation, with yet another flourish. He promised to capture the Spartans within twenty days or kill them on the spot, and—remarkably—he succeeded. In the Spartan force, 420 hoplites had been sent to Spakteria, of which 292 surrendered and were sent to Athens, and of these, 120 were Spartiates. The desperation in Sparta caused by this defeat is significant. The loss of 120 Spartiates was seen as a calamity, and the Athenians' victory demonstrated that, as masters of the sea, they could project their power even to the far side of the Peloponnese.

Despite defeat at Sphakteria, the Spartans prosecuted the war vigorously over the course of the next four years. Perhaps recognizing that they could not expect to make a peace without significant victories, they entrusted their principal effort to a brilliant and energetic commander named Brasidas, who marched north and began a systematic assault on the Athenian holdings in Thrace. Through a combination of deft diplomacy and rapid deployments, he managed to capture Torone and Amphipolis, as well as a string of smaller towns. He was so successful that the Spartans were able to negotiate a one-year truce in 423 BC. The Athenians hoped that the truce would stop the defections of allied states to Brasidas and the Spartans hoped the pause would encourage the Athenians to consider a lengthier peace treaty.

Both sides were wrong. The northern campaign resumed in 422 BC, with Kleon commanding a force of 1,200 hoplites and 30 ships. His goal was to recapture Amphipolis, the key to Athens' control of the north, but in the battle for the city both Kleon and Brasidas were killed. Brasidas was subsequently given a heroic burial and treated as the founder of the city; a recently excavated tomb has been plausibly identified by the Greek archaeologist Chaido Koukouli-Chrysanthaki as belonging to the Spartan

11.7 Silver ossuary (chest holding skeletal remains) and gold wreath from the Tomb of Brasidas, Amphipolis, late fifth century BC

commander (**11.7**). The outcome of the battle was a Spartan victory, but as Thucydides understood, the greater significance was the death of the two men most opposed to peace. Early in the spring of 421, after ten years of war and a winter of prolonged negotiations, the two sides signed a fifty-year treaty, the Peace of Nikias, named after the conservative and aristocratic general who emerged in the years after Perikles' death as a leading advocate for peace.

Neither side, however, was truly committed to a long-lasting peace. The terms of the treaty included the return of contested territories, but the Spartans refused to hand over Amphipolis and the Athenians would not give up Pylos. In addition, the Athenians formed an alliance with three Peloponnesian states hostile to Sparta—Argos, Mantineia, and Elis—but the Spartans under King Agis II defeated the anti-Spartan alliance at the Battle of Mantineia in 418, and for the next two years Sparta was occupied with establishing pro-Spartan oligarchies throughout the Peloponnese in Mantineia, Argos, and Sicyon. During this period there was little the Athenians could do in these campaigns in the Peloponnese, but one naval campaign in 416 against the island of Melos is recounted by Thucydides in such a way as to suggest that he saw it as a perfect illustration of the realities that underlay both the Peloponnesian War and all other wars.

Melos

Melos was a relatively insignificant island in the southwestern segment of the Cycladic Islands, populated in the fifth century BC by colonists from Sparta. They had resisted incorporation into the Athenian empire, and up until 416 BC had remained neutral. Now an Athenian fleet of 38 ships carrying an army of 1,600 hoplites invaded, but before laying siege to the city, the Athenians were invited to state their aims. In the dialogue that Thucydides reports the Athenians offered no moral or ethical justification for their presence. In fact, they stated the heart of the matter with ruthless precision:

> For ourselves, we shall not trouble you with specious pretences—either of how we have a right to our empire because we overthrew the Persians, or are now attacking you because of wrong that you have done us—and make a long speech which would not be believed; and in return we hope that you, instead of thinking to influence us by saying that you did not join the Spartans, although their colonists, or that you have done us no wrong, will aim at what is feasible, holding in view the real sentiments of us both; since you know as well as we do that right, as the world goes, is only in question between equals in power, while the strong do what they can and the weak suffer what they must.
>
> (*The Peloponnesian War* 5.89, trans. Crawley)

In Thucydides' view of the world, equality is not a natural right; power alone determines how states deal with each other. In the rest of the exchange the Athenians dismiss honor, justice, loyalty, and blood as equally empty, and offer point-by-point responses to the Melians' arguments. Submit, say the Athenians, and you'll avoid worse sufferings. Can't we just stay neutral, respond the Melians. No, since if you don't submit we will look weak in the eyes of our subjects. But attacking us when we are neutral will alienate all other neutrals, argue the Melians. No matter, reply the Athenians, people on the mainland don't concern us; we want to secure our rule among the island states like you. And so the rest of the dialogue depressingly unfolds. Just in case the reader is left thinking that this is no more than an essay on the nature of power, Thucydides makes sure that we learn the outcome of the Melians' resistance. The Melians surrendered to the Athenians in the winter of 416/15 BC. The men were all executed, the women and children sold as slaves. The jarring contrast between the cool discussion of political reality in the dialogue and the bloody outcome of the episode is typically Thucydidean. The reader is meant to be affected by the author's reserve.

This understanding of international relations as purely an exercise in the application of power—a conception often referred to as *Realpolitik*—is distinctively Thucydidean, but may also represent the attitudes of many Athenians. For those adverse to such strong-arm tactics, Perikles offered an insight that was both cautionary and pragmatic: "you see, your empire is really like a tyranny—though it may have been thought unjust to seize, it is now unsafe to surrender" (*The Peloponnesian War* 2.63). Remarkably, Thucydides puts the same sentiment in the mouth of Kleon, who, in advising the Athenians to execute every man in Mytilene after the city had gone into revolt, castigated the Athenians, saying, "your softness puts you in danger and does not win you the affection of your allies, and you do not see that your empire is a tyranny" (3.37). Some scholars have argued that having two such different statesmen both liken the empire to a tyranny really means that the words are Thucydides' own, and this is entirely possible, but it is equally possible that his audience was familiar with the sentiment. Any Athenian statesman could remind the Athenians that there was nothing inherently just or justified in Athens ruling the islands. Whatever the pieties of the traditional funeral oration regarding sacrifice, defeating the Amazons, or resisting the Persians, every Athenian knew exactly what Thucydides meant: power is its own justification.

The Melian Dialogue is not the only time that Thucydides used his account of events to illustrate underlying truths regarding warfare. Having witnessed countless campaigns, including civil wars, Thucydides concluded that war is a harsh teacher. He believed that war revealed the brutality lurking behind the veneer of civilization. In his description of the civil war at Corcyra in Book 3, for example, he offered a diagnosis of an ailing body politic:

The sufferings were many and terrible, such as have occurred and always will occur, as long as the nature of mankind remains the same; though in a severer or milder form, and varying in their symptoms, according to the variety of the particular cases. In peace and prosperity states and individuals have better sentiments, because they do not find themselves suddenly confronted with imperious necessities; but war takes away the easy supply of daily wants, and so proves a rough master, that brings most men's characters to a level with their fortunes.

(*The Peloponnesian War* 3.82.2, trans. Crawley)

Thucydides lived to see the end of the war and Athens' defeat, although his work breaks off some years before that. Accordingly, many of the episodes that he records either look forward to the defeat of Athens or are narrated with that defeat looming over them. The events that marked the turning of Athens' fortunes occurred at the half-way mark, when, in 416–15 BC, the Athenians made the momentous decision to undertake a massive invasion of Sicily.

The Sicilian Expedition

Throughout antiquity Sicily was regarded as a wealthy island. The Greek cities of the island were adorned with large and handsome temples, the island was an important producer of grain, and in both the Archaic and Classical periods many of the Sicilian cities were ruled by men who were generous patrons of the arts. Aischylos, for example, was reported to have spent time at the court of Hiero I in Syracuse, and a century later Plato would also live for some time at the court of the Syracusan tyrant Dionysios I. Many of the leading cities were originally Corinthian colonies, and the use of Corinthian-style coins shows that the region retained ties to the mother-city.

Accordingly, when envoys from Segesta arrived in Athens with 60 talents of silver bullion with them to persuade the Athenians to come to their assistance against neighboring Selinous, the Athenians, well aware of the island's wealth, were all too easily persuaded. The deliberations leading up to the Athenians' Sicilian expedition, in fact, are a classic case of Thucydidean analysis, combining venal motives, deception, and ambition with miscalculation. The Athenians were convinced that there was much more money on the island, and were therefore inclined to mount an expedition.

11.8 Archaic herm statue, Siphnos, *c.* 520 BC. Marble, H: 66 cm (26 in.)

Arguing against the war was the cautious, upright, and wholly unimaginative general and statesman Nikias, who had inherited Perikles' defensive outlook, but who lacked Perikles' capacity to persuade the Athenians to restrain themselves. Arguing for intervention was the young, brilliant, and mercurial general Alkibiades (450–404 BC). The two men offered competing visions of Athens' best interests, and when it became clear that most men in the Ekklesia supported the war, Nikias tried to dissuade them by exaggerating the cost and the size of the force needed to subdue Sicily. It was a fatal mistake. The Athenians accepted his inflated estimates and voted for a massive invasion force: 100 triremes and 5,000 hoplites, with an appropriate number of archers and slingers.

The invasion began disastrously, even before leaving Athens. As the fleet was being prepared a disturbing incident occurred in the city. One evening a group of drunk young men mutilated some of the herm statues in the city. (These were stone pillars crowned with the head of Hermes and shown with an erect phallus, used as apotropaic markers and to delineate the commercial space of the agora and bring it under the protection of the god; an example from the island of Siphnos is shown in **11.8**.)

It was claimed in the subsequent inquiry that the men had also performed a mock celebration of the Mysteries, an act of impiety. The rumor mill soon took over, with dark muttering about attempts to overthrow the democracy. Alkibiades was implicated and appealed to have the case heard immediately, but the decision was deferred until after the fleet, full of his supporters, had sailed. Alkibiades continued on to Sicily with the fleet, only to receive a summons shortly after his arrival to return to Athens. He sailed back as far as Thurii in Italy before deserting. Eventually he defected to Sparta and was condemned *in absentia* by the Athenians. It will probably never be possible to determine the truth of what happened. All that can said with certainty is that he had a reputation for wild behavior which sometimes alarmed the Athenians, making it easier to convince them of his impiety.

Along with the failure of many of the Sicilian cities to open their ports and the realization that Segesta had nowhere near the wealth that had lured them to Sicily, the Athenians were now looking at a campaign whose goals were unclear, conducted far from home with uncertain supplies, under the command of a

vacillating general who had opposed the campaign from the start. Their opponents, principally the Syracusans, were well supplied, knew the land, were confident, and possessed an advantage in cavalry that made it possible for them to harry the Athenians at every step. The campaign dragged on from 415 BC into the winter, when the Athenians sent an urgent request to Athens for more money and troops.

Meanwhile, during the winter and into the spring and summer of 414 BC, the Athenians and Syracusans engaged in a construction battle, erecting walls and counterwalls west from Syracuse and up onto the Epipolai plateau behind the city. The Athenians' aim was to encircle the city; the counterwalls of the Syracusans were designed to cross the Athenian circuit wall perpendicularly and therefore make encirclement impossible (**11.9**). During the same season, the Syracusans received support from their allies, the Spartans. On the advice of Alkibiades, who had sought refuge in Sparta, the Spartans had dispatched a capable Spartiate commander named Gylippos to coordinate the Sicilian opposition to the Spartans and bring aid to Syracuse. Facing the

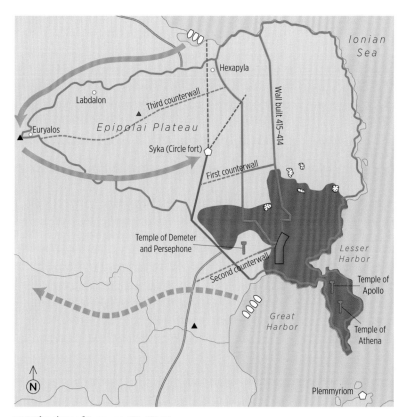
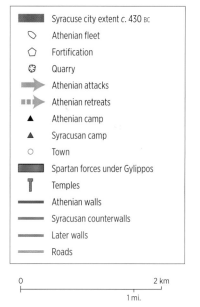

11.9 The siege of Syracuse, 415–413 BC

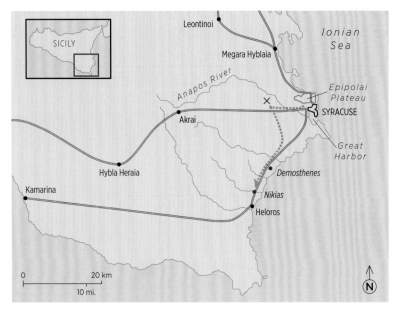

11.10 Final route (dotted blue line) of the escape of Demosthenes and Nikias from Syracuse

night when the Athenians, led by Demosthenes, stormed the heights of Epipolai.

Thucydides' account captures the confusion and the chaos of the Night Battle:

Owing to the rout that had taken place all in front was now in confusion, and the noise made it difficult to distinguish anything. The victorious Syracusans and allies were cheering each other on with loud cries, while the Athenians were seeking for one another, taking all in front of them for enemies, even although they might be some of their now flying friends; and by constantly asking for the watchword, which was their only means of recognition, not only caused great confusion among themselves by asking all at once, but also made it known to the enemy. But what hurt them as much, or indeed more than anything else, was the singing of the Paean, from the perplexity which it caused by being nearly the same on either side: the Argives and Corcyraeans and any other Dorian peoples in the army, struck terror into the Athenians whenever they raised their Paean, no less than did the enemy. Thus, after being once thrown into disorder, they ended by coming into collision with each other in many parts of the field, friends with friends, and citizens with citizens, and not only terrified one another, but even came to blows and could only be parted with difficulty.

(*The Peloponnesian War* 7.44.3–7, trans. Crawley)

The picture that Thucydides paints is meant to be more than an evocation of the confusion of battle. It is the Dorian paean being heard behind the (Ionian) Athenians that confuses them. This should be their enemy's battle cry, but in fact it is the war shout of their own Dorian allies.

Thucydides is making an important point here. The Greeks behaved as if the ethnic distinctions of Dorian and Ionian were clear, and spoke as if all Ionians were naturally always opposed to all Dorians, but the reality was much more complex and confusing. Both alliances included allies from the other ethnic camp, and the two power blocs were not so ethnically distinct at all. The tragedy,

prospect of a joint Spartan and Syracusan alliance, Nikias grew increasingly despondent. Worried that the presence of the Spartans would energize the Sicilians, he wrote to the Athenians, warning them of the imminent unification of the Sicilians against them. He emphasized the difficulty of his position and requested them to accept his resignation. They refused, and voted instead to send a second army and fleet the following spring.

The year 413 BC proved to be the turning point. Following the advice of the defector Alkibiades, the Spartans invaded Attica and established a fort at Dekelea. In time this would prove a decisive move, disrupting the transportation of grain from northeast Attica to the city of Athens, and forcing the Athenians to give up some of their own territory. (Traces of the Spartan fortification wall can still be seen on the grounds of the former royal estates at Tatoi, north of Athens.) In the immediate circumstances, however, the Athenians were primarily occupied by developments in Sicily. A supply fleet on its way to Sicily was captured, and the Athenian forces at Syracuse grew increasingly desperate. Yet their position was not hopeless. Later in the same summer a relief expedition arrived from Athens under the command of Demosthenes, consisting of seventy-three ships and nearly five thousand hoplites. Demosthenes directed the Athenian attack on Epipolai with renewed vigor, until one fateful

for Thucydides, was that all the combatants were Greek: it was a fratricidal conflict.

The Night Battle ended in a rout, but even then the Athenians' woes were not over. The commanders, Demosthenes and Nikias, could not agree on a common plan, and Nikias refused to withdraw immediately because he interpreted an eclipse of the moon as a bad omen for departure. The delay, a crucial twenty-seven days, emboldened the Syracusans, giving their allies time to come to their aid. They engaged the Athenian ships in the Great Harbor of Syracuse, breaking the center of the Athenian line and even killing the Athenian commander, Eurymedon, on the right wing. In a second and final naval engagement the Syracusans were again successful. Their spirits broken, the Athenian sailors refused to man the ships and tried to withdraw by land. Without any clear plan of escape, forty thousand Athenians began the desperate march out from Syracuse (**11.10**). Over the next six days they were harassed by the Syracusan forces until, broken, hungry, and hopeless, they surrendered. Demosthenes and Nikias were executed. The

survivors, numbering no more than seven thousand, were imprisoned in open-air quarries in Syracuse. The bodies of the dead and dying were left where they lay; the survivors were given a pint of grain and half a pint of water each day for two and a half months. Finally, most of the non-Athenian prisoners were sold into slavery. A few of the Athenians escaped death, it was said, by being able to recite lines from Euripides, whose plays were especially popular in Sicily. The story may be apocryphal, but it is a pleasant notion that, at the nadir of its power, a few citizens of Athens were saved by a playwright.

The Dekelean War

With the disastrous end of the Sicilian expedition in 413 BC, it seemed as though Athens was on the brink of catastrophic defeat, yet this proved not to be the case. Over the next seven years the setbacks continued (**11.11**), yet the city struggled on. Following Alkibiades' advice, the Spartans continued to use their fort at Dekelea to disrupt life in Athens. The fort's location was especially well chosen since it

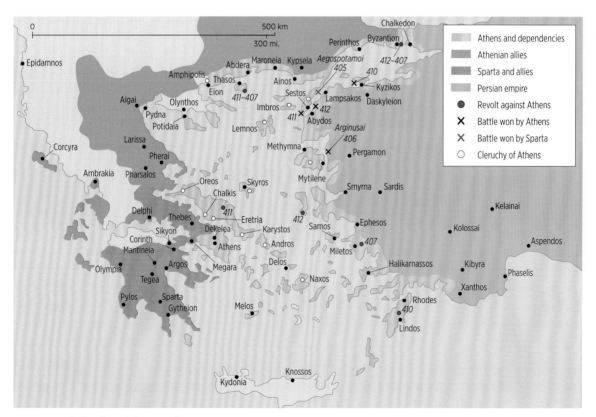

11.11 Greece during the Dekelean War (413–406 BC)

made it impossible for the Athenians to bring their grain supplies overland from Oropos to Athens, meaning that all grain now had to be brought in to Piraeus by sea. To make that more difficult, the Spartans for the first time began to pay serious attention to naval operations in the Aegean. Not long after the Athenians' defeat in Sicily in 413 BC the Spartans commissioned a fleet. Shipbuilding activity continued until 409 and 408 and, relying on the aid of disaffected Athenian allies with fleets of their own, such as Chios, they began frequently dispatching fleets to the Hellespont in an attempt to choke off Athens' grain supply from the Black Sea.

Another development was also ominous. In Persia, Darius II Ochos had ascended the throne in 424 BC after a year of bloody dynastic turmoil that saw the death of two of his older brothers. At the beginning of his reign Ochos stayed out of Aegean affairs, but in 413 the Athenians had given aid to a rebel named Amorges, thereby earning the Great King's anger. In the aftermath of Athens' disastrous Sicilian expedition the Persian king and his satraps began negotiating with the Spartans, which culminated in the Persian satrap Tissaphernes signing a treaty with Sparta according to which the Spartans would regard the king's enemies as their own, including anyone who revolted from the Great King. Sparta now found itself serving as an instrument of Persian policy in western Asia, in return for which their navy was paid for by Persian gold.

Democracy under Threat

There were also plenty of upheavals in Athens itself. An oligarchic coup took place in 411 BC, engineered by a man named Peisander. He and his supporters installed an oligarchic government of the Four Hundred, consciously evoking the council and four tribes that had existed prior to the Kleisthenic democratic reforms one hundred years earlier. The government of the Four Hundred was able to gain power because of the climate of uncertainty in Athens and because it was believed that an oligarchic regime would make it possible to win Persian support and finish the war with Sparta. In order to appease moderates and those who blamed the democracy for Athens' woes, the Four Hundred proposed handing over the state to a broader oligarchic government of 5,000, but for months this remained no more than an empty promise. In fact, thuggery and assassination became the Four Hundred's tools for dealing with dissent.

The Four Hundred's reign of tyranny came to an end with an unexpected and extraordinary event outside Athens. The Athenian fleet and army on Samos, where the Athenians had established a base of operations to suppress the revolt of Chios and Miletos, became embroiled in a civil war between oligarchs and democrats on the island, taking the side of the democrats. When news reached them of events in Athens, the Athenians on Samos declared that they would defend both the Athenian and Samian democracies. Making common cause with the democrats on Samos, they swore to reject communication with the government of the Four Hundred, to support democracy on Samos, and to continue the war with Sparta. Led by Thrasyboulos and Thrasyllos, they held democratic assemblies on Samos. In effect, the Athenians abroad became the democracy at precisely the moment when democracy had been suspended at home. They even recalled Alkibiades. Although he had been convicted of sacrilege and had given helpful advice to the Spartans, his reputation and flair meant that he was still popular in some circles, certainly more with the rowers of the fleet than with the men of property who were suspected of oligarchic sympathies. Nor was Alkibiades above stoking the democrats' hopes by hinting that he would bring the Great King over to the Athenian side. The Persian King could easily afford to pay the men of the fleet, no small consideration when men on service were expected to pay for their own rations.

Meanwhile, the Spartans took the opportunity of the chaos in Athens to sail to Euboia, where they engaged a scratch fleet of Athenian ships manned by inexperienced crews. The Spartans captured twenty-two ships, killing or capturing their crews. Many of the Athenian survivors swam ashore near Eretria, but they were slaughtered by the locals. Once news of the disaster reached the city, the Four Hundred were deposed and a constitution of the 5,000 was drawn up. The franchise was restricted to those who could supply themselves with a suit of armor; in other words, the hoplite class. For a moderate conservative, such as Thucydides, this seemed to be the ideal constitution, and he remarked that Athens was better governed under the 5,000 than at any other time in his life. According to Aristotle, however, the arrangement did not last long, and full democracy was restored soon after. The event that precipitated this final return to democracy was the momentous victory of the Athenian fleet in 410 BC at the Battle of Kyzikos over the Spartans. According to Xenophon, whose account picks up where Thucydides' breaks off, the defeated Spartans wrote home for instructions, saying, "The ships are gone. Mindaros [the Spartan office in command] is dead. The men are starving. We know not what to do." The Athenians once again enjoyed the upper hand in the Hellespont, although such key cities as Byzantion and Chalcedon had not yet been restored to the Athenian empire. In desperation, the Spartans sued for peace.

Had the two sides signed a peace in 410 BC, historians might well wonder what the Peloponnesian War accomplished, since the terms of the proposed treaty were largely an affirmation of the status quo. Having lost Euboia and with the cities of the Hellespont still wavering, the Athenians looked on the treaty as confirmation of their weakness. So they rejected the Spartans' overtures, and in the manner of two tired boxers, both sides paused for the next three seasons. This decision deserves comment. The Athenians had been fighting for more than twenty years, had suffered catastrophic defeats abroad, and had experienced great suffering at home, yet were unwilling to accept a peace treaty that would have at the very least allowed them to retain their sphere of influence. How do we explain this? There are many possibilities, but two deserve special attention. The first is that the Athenians had truly internalized the view that victory in the Persian Wars had entitled them to supremacy within the Greek world. Their empire *was* a tyranny, but it had been won by their ancestors and each generation had inherited not only the empire but also the belief that it was theirs by right. A second possibility that we should entertain—and we will never know the answer for sure—is that after two generations of power and coercion the Athenians were afraid of the alternative. The top dog must never show weakness.

Whichever way we explain the Athenian decision to fight on, once again we have to admire their tenacity. Gradually the Athenians reasserted their control of the Hellespont, but then in 406 BC, while Alkibiades (now once again on the Athenian side) was absent from his command, his lieutenant, Antiochos, forced a rash engagement with the Spartans, which led to the loss of twenty-two ships. Alkibiades was blamed, went into exile, and the war entered its final phase.

Spartan and Athenian fleets engaged twice more in 406 BC. In the first encounter the Athenians under Konon were defeated and the survivors withdrew to Mytilene, where they were blockaded by the Spartans. Once again, responding to catastrophe, the Athenians assembled a massive fleet of 155 triremes, enlisting slaves and metics among the crews, and dispatched the fleet. At the Battle of Arginusai, in the straits between Lesbos and the coast of Asia Minor, the Athenians were victorious, and even succeeded in killing the Spartan admiral Kallikratidas, but in the aftermath of the battle a storm prevented the Athenians from saving many sailors whose ships had been crippled in the battle. At Athens the news of the victory brought elation, but just as quickly joy turned to despair when news of the drownings reached the city. Somehow the deaths of the sailors who had won the battle but had been left to die were worse than if they had lost. Six of the eight commanders returned to Athens, where they were collectively tried and executed. Despite this disastrous outcome, the Spartan position was not much better. An important commander had died, the fleet was in poor shape, and morale at home was close to exhaustion. Once again the Spartans offered peace based on the status quo. Once again the Athenians refused.

The new Spartan commander in the Aegean was Lysander, who was already familiar with the theater of operations, having served there successfully in 407–406 BC. He had also established friendly relations with the Persians and was able to draw on Persian money to refurbish the Spartan fleet. He set out attacking Athenian holdings in the Aegean and even went so far as to campaign close to Attica, attacking Salamis and Aigina. Lysander understood that the key to defeating Athens decisively was to destroy the Athenians' hold on the Hellespont and to starve the city into submission. Accordingly he established a base at Abydos, in the Hellespont.

The Athenians were forced to send a fleet to respond to the threat, and set up their own base at Sestos. Instead of keeping their ships safely within the port at Sestos, however, each day they sailed past the Spartan base in formation, inviting Lysander to engage, and each evening they beached the ships close by, near the mouth of the Aegospotamoi River. There are conflicting accounts of exactly how the final battle unfolded: either a small Athenian detachment of thirty ships was dispatched to tempt the Spartans out, and was destroyed, after which the remaining Athenian ships were caught unawares on the beach; or the Athenians were caught completely off-guard while foraging for food and supplies, and the ships were captured by the Spartans without any fight at sea at all. Either way, the result was the same: 150 Athenians ships were destroyed or captured, and 3,000 men were lost. The scale of the defeat dwarfed anything they had previously experienced, and as soon as the news reached Athens, delivered by the state trireme, the **Paralos**, it quickly became apparent that no emergency measures would allow the Athenians to mount a fresh defense. Xenophon's description of the arrival of the news captures the mood of a great city contemplating its defeat:

It was at night that the *Paralos* arrived at Athens with tidings of the disaster, and a sound of wailing ran from Piraeus through the long walls to the city, one man passing on the news to another; and during that night no one slept, all mourning, not for the lost alone, but far more for their own selves, thinking that they would suffer such treatment as they had visited upon the Melians, colonists of the Spartans, after reducing them by siege, and upon the Histiaians and Skionaians and Toronaians and Aiginetans and many other Greek peoples.

(Xenophon, *Hellenica* 2.2.3, trans. BROWNSON)

The coda that follows Athens' defeat (and which Xenophon alludes to) is an interesting story to which we shall come shortly, but with the Battle of Aegospotamoi, the Peloponnesian War was over (**11.12**). Soon Lysander's fleet would sail into the Piraeus and the Athenians would begin tearing down their walls, the final symbol of the city's defeat and humiliation. The greatest upheaval to afflict the Greek world, as Thucydides called it, had resulted in the complete defeat of its greatest city, Athens. The question facing the Athenians was simple: what was to be their fate?

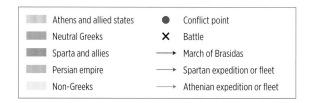

Athens and allied states		●	Conflict point
Neutral Greeks		✕	Battle
Sparta and allies		→	March of Brasidas
Persian empire		→	Spartan expedition or fleet
Non-Greeks		→	Athenian expedition or fleet

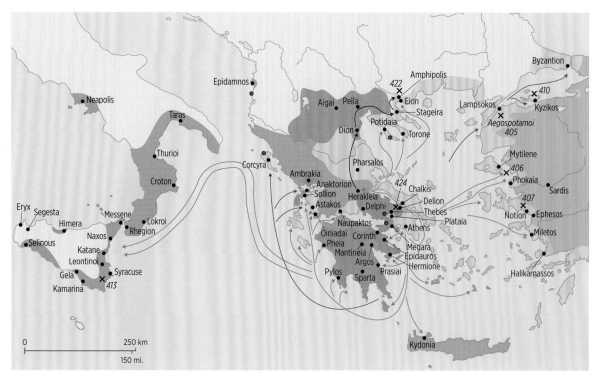

11.12 Map of the conflicts of the Peloponnesian War, including the Sicilian expedition

11.13 Artist's impression of a fifth-century-BC hoplite in full panoply. The shield, or *hoplon*, provides protection from neck to knee. His lower legs are protected by greaves, or **knemides**. His Corinthian-style helmet offers full protection for the head and face. The hoplite wears a short slashing sword, a *xiphos*, but will only use this at close quarters, and carries a spear.

Spotlight
Hoplites and Rowers

We have seen in both Chapter 7 and Chapter 11 that philosophers and political thinkers were often hostile to the connection between naval power, democracy, and empire. Conservative thinkers tended to prefer the sober world of the self-reliant farmer-soldier, and so favored the hoplite class (**11.13**). These were men who regarded land as the basis of real wealth and had little taste for luxury. Coming from the middle ranks of Athenian society, they were not as wealthy as cavalrymen, but were able to provide themselves with a full hoplite panoply in order to take their place in battle. (Aristophanes

makes fun of the conservatism of the citizen-soldier in his play *Acharnians*, named for an inland deme where the men were proverbially as tough as oak.)

Despite the popular attitudes that both favored and made fun of this hoplite class, it was in the trireme that we find the truest expression of Athens' imperial democracy. The discipline needed to row in time, the training needed to perform expert maneuvers, not to mention the good order required for embarking 170 rowers in timely fashion, all served to make the trireme into the naval

equivalent of a miniature phalanx. Early in the fifth century, engagements would often have resembled land warfare, with the trireme as fighting platform, but over time the vessel came into its own as a lethal weapon.

As with the phalanx on land, the trireme needed discipline, training, and good order to perform successfully. Consider, for example, the maneuver known as the **diekplous**, in which an attacking trireme changed the angle of attack and tried to sheer off the oars of the enemy's vessel. To accomplish this required weeks of intensive training. Similarly, the *periplous* required a trireme to circle an enemy boat and ram it from behind. This required not only enormous skill, but also strength, speed and discipline. The aim of these maneuvers, was to deploy the devastating power of the bronze ram attached to the boat's shearwater.

It is worth remembering that all these maneuvers were carried out in the confines of the trireme's extremely cramped interior, where men of the lower ranks rowed with the backsides of the men above in their faces (**11.14**). One can only imagine the degree of solidarity among the rowers. Boris Rankov, an ancient historian, champion rower, and chair of the Trireme Trust that built the *Olympias*, a modern-day reconstruction of a trireme (**11.15**), powerfully evokes the working conditions on board a trireme in this description:

With 170 rowers packed into a hull 37 metres [121½ ft] long and 5 metres [16½ ft] across, accommodation is cramped and sweaty and the oarblades are separated from each other in the water by only about 30 centimetres [1 ft]. Moreover, whilst the top layer of rowers can see out of the ship and watch the oars, the lower two layers are rowing through small portholes and can only see along the interior; in effect, two-thirds of the crew are rowing blind. As a result, the crew need to be given the time by an audible signal on every stroke, especially at the lower rates of striking. But even the rowing master in charge of co-ordinating the rowing and normally standing in the central gangway cannot see the oarblades and the crew at the same time, and in any case his voice will not carry instructions more than halfway through a ship packed with wooden furniture and human flesh.

(Rankov, "The good ship *Democracy*")

During the fifth century the Athenians built and maintained hundreds of triremes, and at the same time transformed the Piraeus into a well-fortified naval base, as well as an emporium for the goods that flowed from around the Aegean into Athens. The Zea Harbour Project, a joint Danish and Greek research project, has been investigating the facilities of the

11.14 Interior of a trireme (modern reconstruction).

11.15 The reconstructed Greek trireme, *Olympias*, under sail and preparing to undergo trials. The bronze ram, visible at the prow, weighs 200 kg (440 lbs). When propelled solely by oars, the *Olympias* can achieve 9 knots.

democracy's arsenal at Piraeus since 2002. Their work has shed light on the three harbors that together made up the Piraeus, and gives us a glimpse of Athens at the height of its power. On any given day, an Athenian walking past the hundreds of shipsheds (**11.16**) built to house the triremes of the Athenian navy would have seen their names proudly on display: *Hegemonia* (Hegemony), *Dynamis* (Power), *Parrhesia* (Free Speech), *Polynike* (Many Victories), *Dikaiosyne* (Justice), *Naukratousa* (Sea Victor), and, of course, *Demokratia*. Each boat in the fleet was a proud advertisement of the hopes and aspirations of its crew, the democratic citizens of Athens.

11.16 Reconstruction of the shipsheds at Zea Harbor.

404–403 BC	399 BC	395–387 BC	387/6 BC	379/8 BC
Rule of the Thirty Tyrants at Athens	Execution of Sokrates	Corinthian War	King's Peace	Formation of the Second Athenian Confederacy

Chapter 12

Panhellenism and the Rise of Philip

Though often dismissed as the Cinderella century of Greek history, a forgettable age overshadowed by the glorious fifth century, the fourth century was, in fact, a period of substantial change and development. Not only was it the age of philosophers, such as Aristotle, and artists, such as Praxiteles, but it was also the age that saw a slew of important constitutional developments: experiments with common peace treaties to break the cycle of intercity warfare, peace with Persia, a growing impulse toward federalism, and the renaissance of Athenian power abroad in a more humane and less coercive fashion. Yet these tendencies would be eclipsed by the growth of regional powers beyond the heartland of Greece, notably in Macedonia, where Philip would combine military genius, newfound wealth, canny diplomacy, and restless energy to bring all of Greece under his control by 338 BC.

Athens in Defeat

In the immediate aftermath of the defeat at Aegospotamoi in 406 BC, the Athenians, fully aware of their shocking treatment of other Greek states, faced the prospect of being enslaved or worse.

The Ekklesia met and undertook preparations for the siege they expected would now take place. In the meantime, they sent Theramenes and other ambassadors to the Spartans to seek the most lenient terms possible for a negotiated surrender. Despite calls from their allies to destroy Athens, the Spartans resisted, insisting that they would not enslave a city that had done such great service on behalf of the Greeks during the Persian Wars. Instead, Xenophon relates that they offered peace on the following terms:

...that the Athenians should destroy the long walls and the walls of Piraeus, surrender all their ships except twelve, allow their exiles to return, count the same people friends and enemies as the Spartans did, and follow the Spartans both by land and by sea wherever they should lead the way.

(Xenophon, *Hellenica* 2.2, trans. Brownson)

The Spartan admiral Lysander sailed into the Piraeus and work commenced on dismantling the Long Walls that ran between Athens and the port. Athens would be defenseless and rendered impotent with the loss of its navy. As punishment this was mild, but then Lysander imposed a new political regime that had the potential to change Athens much more fundamentally. This kind of political intervention, however, was part of the new Spartan foreign policy: around the Aegean, wherever Lysander faced opposition from pro-Athenian democracies, he installed ruling oligarchies of ten men, known as **decarchies**. He also employed a system of military garrisons and governors, called **harmosts**, to guarantee the compliance of Sparta's new allies. At Athens he adapted this model slightly; recognizing that the size of the city made it exceptional, he arranged for thirty men to govern the state. The democracy was disbanded in April 404 BC. The future of Athens was unclear, although the most pressing questions were simple: was democracy an experiment that had failed; was Athens to be ruled by aristocrats allied to Sparta; and what kind of masters had the Athenians acquired as a result of Sparta's victory?

Almost immediately the Thirty, as the new regime came to be called, revealed that it was no better than a junta. They and their henchmen set about seizing property and imprisoning their opponents, terrorizing the city over the course of the next eight months. Inscribed laws were physically torn down, and in a series of show trials jurors were required to show their vote, and were cowed into capitulation. In this climate of suspicion the members of the Thirty even turned on each other. Kritias (c. 460–403 BC), a hardline leader of the Thirty and a former pupil of Sokrates, denounced another of the leaders, Theramenes, and arranged for his execution. One reliable estimate of the people killed by the Thirty puts the number at 1,500 out of a citizen body of perhaps 35,000. Andrew Wolpert argues convincingly that "most Athenians must have experienced a personal loss, if not of a family member or relative, then of a friend, associate or neighbor." In particular, the Thirty targeted wealthy metics—the aliens living in Athens—knowing that they were vulnerable: metics were not citizens and therefore could not take legal action without the help of a patron, and were less likely to have familial and social networks of support. One such man was a speechwriter named Lysias, who was awarded citizenship at a later date and used his new status to prosecute the men who had killed his brother. His eyewitness account includes this graphic description of the Thirty's behavior:

They found me entertaining guests, and after driving them out they handed me over to Peison...I asked if he would save me for a price and he agreed. I said I was prepared to pay him one talent of silver, and he accepted. When he had sworn, invoking annihilation upon himself and his children if he did not save me on receipt of the talent, I went into my bedroom and opened the money-chest. Peison noticed it and came in; on seeing its contents he called two of his underlings and bade them take what was in the chest. Since he now had, instead of the agreed amount, gentlemen, three talents of silver, four hundred cyzicenes, a hundred darics and four silver cups, I begged him to give me money for my journey; but he declared that I should be glad enough to save my skin.

(Lysias, *Against Eratosthenes* 11, trans. Lamb)

The tyranny of the Thirty eventually provoked a response from the Athenians, and a resistance movement was organized by the democrat Thrasyboulos (c. 440–388 BC) in January 403 BC. The democrats assembled at a fort in the hills north of Athens at Phyle, and successfully repulsed an attempt by the Thirty to dislodge them (**12.1**). Throughout the spring of 403, Thrasyboulos continued to attract men to the democratic cause. Eventually, with the support of more than one thousand men, he marched on the Piraeus. In the engagement fought there the democrats defeated the forces of the Thirty and killed Kritias.

Sensing a turn of the tide, the Thirty withdrew in May 403 BC to Eleusis. When news reached the city that the remaining members of the Thirty were hiring mercenaries, the rest of the Athenian populace rose up against them. A final bloody confrontation was avoided by the arrival of a Spartan army under King Pausanias, who negotiated a settlement between the two sides. Democracy was restored in Athens and the few remaining adherents of the Thirty were allowed to resettle at Eleusis. A general amnesty was declared by late 403. Athens had survived a brief, bloody civil war, and the democracy had proven its resilience.

The decision to declare an amnesty was an instance of the generosity and good sense of the Athenian democrats. In a similar way to South Africa at the end of the Apartheid era, the Athenians were dealing with a turbulent and traumatic period in their history, and, just as the Truth and Reconciliation Commission in South Africa helped avoid a civil war, so too the Athenian amnesty provided a necessary step toward the healing of wounds. Amnesty in Greek means "non-remembering," and this was what the

Athenians chose to do: to forget or ignore criminal actions done while the Thirty were in power. As far-sighted as this was, it could not completely assuage the anger and frustrations of the Athenians who had seen their democracy overthrown. Perhaps the most curious outcome of the sequence of events from the Peloponnesian War to restoration of the democracy following the fall of the Thirty is that it culminated in the trial and execution of the most famous philosopher in Western history: Sokrates.

Sokrates

We have many portraits of Sokrates, from the intellectual gadfly in various dialogues composed by his student, Plato, to the comic caricature in Aristophanes' *Clouds*, a play that mercilessly satirizes the intellectual pretentiousness of Athenian intellectuals, as we saw in Chapter 10. For anyone who has seen a production of this play, and has watched Sokrates hanging in a basket so that he can mix his *nous* ("intellect/mind") with the more rarefied air of the **aither** ("atmosphere," also spelled **aether**), the notion that this silly, harmless windbag was in any way connected with the political upheavals of the Peloponnesian War may seem incredible, but that is precisely the context of his execution (**12.2**; see p. 300).

Consider this exchange from the play and ask whether the philosopher here represents a threat to Athens:

Strepsiades: Hey look, who is this fellow hanging from the hook?
Student: Himself!
Strepsiades: Who him?
Student: Sokrates!
Strepsiades: Sokrates! Could you call him for me?
Student: Call him yourself.
Strepsiades: Sokrates, oh Sokratiddly-poo!
Sokrates: Why callest thou upon me, creature of but a day?
Strepsiades: Well, first off, what are you doing up there?
Sokrates: I tread the air and contemplate the sun.
Strepsiades: If you want to show contempt towards the gods, why do it hanging from a basket? Why not here at ground level?
Sokrates: I would never discover the truth of astrological phenomena if I did not suspend my mind and combine my thoughts with the aither.

(Aristophanes, *Clouds* 218–48, trans. McInerney)

How did this absent-minded professor ever come to deserve execution? We saw in Chapter 10 that Athens had witnessed developments in the

12.2 Manuscript illustration depicting Sokrates hanging in a basket, *c.* sixteenth century AD

intellectual life of the city over the course of the fifth century BC that left many unsure about their traditional understanding of the world. As we have already seen, such philosophers as Xenophanes and Protagoras challenged conventional religion, and other thinkers began building on the natural science and ethical inquiries of the Ionian philosophers of the sixth and fifth centuries BC. Anaxagoras, for example, speculated that nous caused all elements to move, and that the sun was a whirling hot stone giving off light reflected by the moon. Ideas that challenged convention were a threat, however, and in 430 BC Anaxagoras was charged with asebeia (impiety). More prosecutions were to come: Ninos was executed for conducting initiations into cults not yet sanctioned by the state, while another prosecution was brought against a man charged with cutting down some of Athena's sacred olive trees. Protagoras was banished for his anthropocentric views in 411 BC. Yet the prosecutions did not prevent a new generation of philosophers from emerging, men who came to Athens and taught for pay. Prodikos, Gorgias,

and Hippias, among others, offered lectures on linguistics, ethics, and (in particular) eristics, or the study of how to construct effective arguments. They were known as sophists, and they were looked upon in some circles with suspicion (democracy and anti-intellectualism are no strangers to one another).

It is not easy to tease out each of these threads in the rich tapestry of Athens' cultural history, but this much seems clear: Athens at peace was more resilient and more tolerant than Athens during and after the Peloponnesian War. The last three decades of the fifth century saw Athens barely survive annihilation and as the fabric of Athenian society began to fray, the old leniency of the Athenians (at home, if not abroad) gave way to a harsher temper and increasing intolerance.

The Philosophy of Sokrates

It was in this turbulent intellectual and social climate that Sokrates' career intersected with the great events of the day, propelling him from the sidelines of Greek history to the center. His own philosophy was hardly a call for revolution. He taught that all virtues—bravery, loyalty, temperance, and justice—were in essence the same thing: goodness. (This doctrine is often referred to as the Unity of all Virtues.) He also believed that no man knowingly does wrong. It follows then, that the purpose of philosophy is to educate people into recognizing what is good, in the sure belief that if genuine knowledge replaces ignorance or unchallenged opinion people will behave well. Neither of these doctrines was particularly seditious; what was more troubling was the manner in which he went about educating his fellow citizens. Sokrates became famous for a technique known as **elenchos**, which was a form of cross-examination. Here is a typical example: can you feel pleasure and pain at the same time? No, because they're opposites. Are hunger and thirst painful? Yes. Are eating and drinking pleasurable? Yes. Do we eat and drink when we are hungry and thirsty? Yes. So we experience pleasure and pain at the same time (contradicting the opening proposition)? The final question in these exchanges is usually answered by the interlocutor admitting that he doesn't know what he is talking about. The technique may have demonstrated Sokrates' greater intelligence, but showing up other people's intellectual inadequacies rarely wins friends, in particular among those solid, traditional families who found their sons coming home and showing off their borrowed intelligence. After one such exchange involving a young Alkibiades, who would go on to notoriety in the Peloponnesian War, his older interlocutor answers in frustration, "Alkbiades, when we were your age we used to be very clever at these sorts of things too..." (Xenophon, *Memorabilia* 1.46).

We catch echoes of this frustration in the official charges brought against Sokrates in 399 BC by two private citizens, Meletos and Anytos. In their indictment they produced a mishmash of charges, championing conventional religion and resorting to innuendo with respect to his teaching: "Sokrates is guilty of not recognizing the gods whom the polis recognizes and of bringing in other, novel deities instead; he is also guilty of corrupting the young" (*Memorabilia* 1.1.1).

Corrupting the young was exactly what people feared was happening as the city was exposed to and infected by philosophy, or worse, sophistry. And as to the claim that he was impious in relation to the gods, this seems to be no more than an overreaction

to Sokrates' habit of referring to his **daimonion** (little spirit), the inner voice of conscience with which he carried on a constant interior dialogue. In the context of the asebeia trials noted earlier, however, these complaints all began to add up: Sokrates was classified among those thinkers whose philosophy was seen as a threat.

Yet we might still wonder whether the climate in Athens in 399 BC was so fraught that a relatively harmless, albeit annoying, minor celebrity was really a danger to Athens. A shrewd remark, preserved in the speeches of Aischines some fifty years later, allows us to glimpse the undercurrents beneath the trial of Sokrates. Aischines asks, "Since you executed Sokrates the sophist because it was clear that he had been the teacher of Kritias, one of the Thirty who put down the demos, is Demosthenes to succeed in snatching his friends from your hands?" (1.173).

The real target in Aischines' speech a half-century after the trial of Sokrates is his political enemy Demosthenes, and the trial in which Aischines delivered his speech had nothing to do with Sokrates, but the analogy with the case of Sokrates clearly presupposes that most Athenians in the audience would nod their heads in familiarity: yes, we must hold Demosthenes accountable, just as we held Sokrates accountable. For what? For the Thirty and Kritias. The connection between Sokrates and the Thirty was probably tenuous, but the Athenians remembered the trauma inflicted on the city by the Thirty a generation earlier. Kritias would have been a young man when he was Sokrates' student, quite probably as early as the 430s, long before he served as the leader of the anti-democratic faction that ruled Athens after the war, but guilt by association seems to have transformed Sokrates from a harmless public figure into the focus of Athenians' pent-up frustrations after the Thirty were overthrown. The amnesty following the restoration of democracy made overtly political trials impossible, but the intellectual midwife of the Thirty's oligarchic revolution could be attacked. Sokrates therefore became the public face of the Thirty, particularly after the death of Kritias and the dissolution of the oligarchy. Was this accurate or justified?

Almost certainly not, but in the feverish aftermath of the suppression of democracy and its subsequent rebirth, Sokrates was there, in their midst, resolutely continuing his practice of interrogating ordinary

Athenians and reminding them of their moral and ethical obligations.

To judge by Plato's presentation of Sokrates as he faced death, Sokrates pugnaciously continued to teach an uncompromising view of philosophy as the preparation of the soul for death. On the day he drank hemlock, he discussed the nature of the soul with his students as follows:

So long as we keep to the body and our soul is contaminated with this imperfection, there is no chance of our ever attaining satisfactorily to our object, which we assert to be Truth....If we are ever to have pure knowledge of anything, we must get rid of the body and contemplate things in isolation with the soul in isolation....True philosophers make dying their profession.

(Plato, *Phaedo* 67e, trans. Tredennick)

Were this the whole story, Sokrates would definitely merit his reputation as an intellectual martyr prepared to die rather than waver in his adherence to the truth, yet there is also something off-putting about his need to continue baiting the Athenians during his trial. He calls Apollo at Delphi as his witness; since Apollo declared him the wisest man alive, who were they to challenge the god? This neatly answered the charge of impiety, but further provoked the Athenians. Describing his technique of cross-examination and its effects he claims with false naiveté, "From that time on I interviewed one person after another. I realized with alarm that I was making myself unpopular, but I felt compelled to put the god's business first" (Plato, *Apology* 21e).

Eventually he likens the entire city to a fat, lazy horse that needs him to sting it into action. These arguments failed to convince the jurors, although they surely demonstrated to anyone who did not already know that he was supremely irritating. In the usual custom of Athenian trials, having been found guilty, Sokrates was permitted a second speech in which to suggest an appropriate sentence:

I set myself to do to you individually in private what I hold to be the greatest possible service: I tried to persuade each one of you not to think of more practical advantages than of his mental and moral well-being....

12.3 Jacques-Louis David, *The Death of Socrates*, 1787. Oil on canvas, 1.29 × 1.96 m (4 ft 3 in. × 6 ft 5 in.)

What do I deserve for behaving like this?...I suggest free maintenance by the State.

(Plato, *Apology* 36b, trans. Tredennick)

Sokrates' suggestion was rejected and he was sentenced to death instead. Provocative to the end, Sokrates refused to escape when the chance was offered to him, and stayed to see the sentence of the court carried out. He drank hemlock, and in the closing minutes of his life told his student Krito to offer a cock to Asklepios, a neat touch for a man charged with impiety: as he lay dying, his gift was to the god of healing.

Because of the supreme importance of Plato in shaping Western philosophy, we have tended to view Sokrates through a Platonic lens, seeing the philosopher as Plato saw him, a martyr for philosophy. The execution of Sokrates has resonated through the years. The painter David, for example, who often depicted feats of martial valor from antiquity (see Chapter 7, p. 192), gives us a vigorous and alert Sokrates lecturing even as he is about to take the cup of hemlock. In contrast to images in antiquity, which tended to show a rotund and comical Sokrates, David's figure is absolutely heroic, a suitable image for a man whose uncompromising commitment to the truth has made him a hero to many (**12.3**).

This is fair, but there is also another way of understanding Sokrates. In the context of events after the Peloponnesian War, his sacrifice takes on an unexpected significance. Sokrates' trial took place in 399 BC, only four years after the overthrow of the Thirty, when the trauma was still fresh. We know that affairs in the city were still unsettled thanks to a speech by Andokides delivered in the same year as Sokrates' trial, in which he offers details of the Athenians' efforts to decide which laws were still in effect and which were not. By providing a scapegoat to an Athenian population desperately trying to return to democracy and the rule of law, Sokrates may have saved the Athenians from themselves. His death brought an end to the threat of civil war by symbolically doing away with the last connection with the Thirty, and did so in a fashion that confirmed the rule of law. In that respect he was a martyr to the one thing he loved as much as philosophy: Athens.

The Spartan Hegemony

As Athens struggled through the civil war and the reign of the Thirty, Sparta was free to exploit their victory in the Peloponnesian War, but squandered the opportunity. The system of decarchies installed by Lysander proved unpopular, although the Spartan commander himself received divine honors on Samos, where he had established an oligarchic regime at the end of the war. Conceptually, there was a long tradition in Greek culture of men achieving divine status for their accomplishments—Herakles, for example, broke down the barrier between human and divine—but the honors given to Lysander set a precedent for worshiping rulers as divine, a trend that would pick up pace under Philip and Alexander in the coming century and would become more widespread in the three centuries before Christ.

In part, the Spartan failure to capitalize on their newfound prominence in the Aegean was due to the demands of foreign policy. Lysander's attention was focused more on events in Asia Minor, where a new Persian king, Artaxerxes II (*c.* 440–358 BC), ascended the throne in 404 BC and immediately faced a rebellion led by his brother, Cyrus the Younger (*c.* 424–401 BC). Lysander and the Spartans offered their support to Cyrus, and the pretender raised an army of Greek mercenaries, led by Klearchos and Xenophon. They were defeated in 401 at the Battle of Kunaxa, but the episode marked the beginning of a new period of Spartan aggression in the western satrapies of Asia Minor. The new Spartan king, Agesilaus II, pursued the same policies as Lysander, and in 396 a Spartan army marched into Persian territory. Artaxerxes' response was to dispatch an envoy, Timokrates of Rhodes, to stir up discontent in Greece against Sparta and to negotiate an alliance of Thebes, Athens, Argos, and Corinth to fight against the Spartans. The strategy was clear: if Sparta were threatened in the Peloponnese then the Spartans would be forced to withdraw from the western satrapies. For the next ten years the anti-Spartan alliance fought a series of skirmishes and battles that are collectively referred to as the Corinthian War (395–387 BC). The most notable events of the war were the death of Lysander at the indecisive Battle of Haliartos in 395, and a decisive defeat of a Spartan fleet in the Aegean, at the Battle of Knidos in 394.

Often seen as a coda to the Peloponnesian War, the Corinthian War is important for a number of reasons. In the first place, it marks a return of Persia to involvement in Greek affairs after three-quarters of a century of largely peaceful coexistence since the Battle of Eurymedon. The renewed involvement of the Persians is entirely understandable. By supporting pretenders, providing mercenaries, and even dispatching state-sanctioned expeditions, the Greeks were needlessly prodding the bear. It is difficult to find any justification, legal, ethical, or strategic, for the behavior of the Spartans. There had been no fresh moves by the Persians to invade or enslave Greek territories, and the Spartans were not looking to acquire an overseas empire. Booty was always welcome to the Spartans, but it was also a temptation that exposed internal conflicts. (During his Aegean campaigns, for example, Lysander amassed great wealth that he entrusted to Gylippos, who promptly stole part of it, leading to his condemnation and exile from Sparta.)

Ominously, the Great King and his satraps quickly realized that the Greeks could be bought or bought off, and over the next generation, Persian gold and Persian strategic interests would emerge as dominant factors in Greek international relations. In fact, the Corinthian War ended when the Great King decided that peace was a more effective means to achieving his goals than war. The terms of the peace negotiated by a Spartan ambassador, Antalkidas, in 386 BC reveal the new role of the Great King as power broker among the squabbling Greek states. For good reason the treaty is often referred to as the King's Peace:

King Artaxerxes thinks it just that the cities in Asia should belong to him, as well as Klazomenai and Cyprus among the islands, and that the other Greek cities should be left autonomous. Whichever party does not accept this peace, upon them I will make war, in company with those who do support it, by land and by sea with ships and money.

(Xenophon, *Hellenica* 5.1.31, trans. Brownson)

The Corinthian War and the Peace of Antalkidas (as the King's Peace is also known) forcefully underscore the limitations of the city-state system. The alliances that undergirded international relations among the Greek states were frequently short-lived and rarely effective, despite the solemnity with which they were ratified—less than a decade after urging the annihilation of Athens, for example, the Thebans and Corinthians formed an alliance with the Athenians

and opposed the Spartans. At most, alliances represented a cessation of hostilities. Were the Greek city-states doomed to a continuous cycle of warfare? Then and now observers have wondered: was the polis a dead end?

The question was made more pressing by the high-handed behavior of the Spartans in the years following the Peace of Antalkidas. They compelled the people of Mantineia to destroy their walls in 385 BC, and in the following year they disbanded the city entirely, forcing the inhabitants to disperse to small villages. This was not merely imposing a pattern of dispersed settlement that the Spartans themselves favored in Lakonia; Mantineia sits on the northern approaches to Lakonia, and Spartan intervention was designed to keep their potentially powerful northern neighbor weak. Then in 383 Phlius was compelled to take back exiles, a tactic often employed by hegemonial states to swing the balance of power internally within subordinate states in their favor.

Spartan aggression escalated during the 380s BC, as it became clear that, in the wake of the Peace of Antalkidas, they had returned to the favor of the Persian king. A pliant and unthreatening Sparta, from the point of view of Persia, excused Spartan abuses; the Spartans could assert their control within Greece, provided Persian interests were unaffected. The most outrageous example of Spartan adventurism came in 382, when a Spartan army under the authority of Phoibidas, while marching north, found the citadel of Thebes, the Kadmeia, undefended. Without even a pretext the Spartans simply occupied the Kadmeia. Spartan hegemony was no more subtle than that of Athens in the fifth century BC.

Athenian Diplomacy

The Athenian response to Sparta's aggressive policies is fascinating. From 384 BC to 379 BC, the Athenians negotiated a series of bilateral alliances with such states as Chios and Byzantion, large cities and islands that had served as key allies in the Delian League. An examination of the alliance with Chios reveals the care with which the Athenians went about rebuilding their network of alliances. After a preamble, poorly preserved, the text continues:

[...discussion which was held among the] Greeks, have been mindful to preserve, like the Athenians, the peace and the friendship and the oaths and the existing agreement, which the King swore and the Athenians and the Spartans and the other Greeks, and have come [announcing] good things for the People of Athens and the whole of Greece and the King, the People shall resolve: to praise the People of Chios and the ambassadors who have come; and the peace shall apply, and the oaths and the agreements which now exist; and to make the Chians allies on the basis of freedom and autonomy, not contravening anything that is written on the stelai about the peace, nor being persuaded if anybody else contravenes anything as far as possible. To put a stele on the acropolis in front of the statue; and on this to inscribe, that if anybody goes against the Athenians the Chians shall support with all their strength as far as possible, and if anybody goes against the Chians the Athenians shall support with all their strength as far as possible...

(*IG* II² 34, trans. Rhodes)

The terms of this alliance are striking. The Athenians scrupulously maintain that the treaty is in accordance with the broader terms of the King's Peace, and explicitly recognize that the alliance with Chios is to be on terms that guarantee the freedom and autonomy of the allied state. The Athenians were not only keeping an eye on the Spartans and the Persians, but were also looking back at the Delian League and the complaints of states, including Chios, who had revolted precisely because of hegemonial interference.

A collision between the reckless aggression of the Spartans and the cautious diplomacy of the Athenians—a direct inversion of their fifth-century practices—was bound to take place. In the spring of 378 BC, a young Spartan commander named Sphodrias led his men in a night march across Mount Kithairon and into Attica with the apparent intention of attacking the Piraeus at dawn. The raid was a fiasco. Dawn broke and the Spartans were exposed in the middle of the Thriasian plain, miles from their objective. They ignominiously retreated, and the Athenians swiftly denounced the incursion as an act of war. Whether Sphodrias's raid was a deliberate provocation or merely an opportunistic venture, modeled on the seizure of the Kadmeia, is unclear. At Sparta, Sphodrias was tried and acquitted, but the Athenians were now free to open their alliance to all. They issued a general invitation in 377 to all of the states of Greece to join a renascent alliance. The terms of the so-called Decree of Aristoteles can still be seen on a stele in Athens:

Aristoteles proposed: for the good fortune of the Athenians and the allies of the Athenians: so that the Spartans shall allow the Greeks to be free and autonomous and to live at peace, possessing securely all their own [territory], and so that [the peace and the friendship which the Greeks] and the King [swore] shall be in force [and endure] in accordance with [the agreements], the People shall resolve: if any of the Greeks or of the barbarians living in [Europe] or of the islanders who are not the King's, wishes to be an ally of the Athenians and the allies, it shall be permitted to him, being free and autonomous, living under the constitution which he wishes, neither receiving a garrison or a governor nor paying tribute, on the same terms as the Chians and Thebans and the other allies.

(*IG* II² 43, trans. Rhodes)

Debate still surrounds this second Athenian confederacy. Was it a kinder, gentler Delian League, or was it simply the fifth-century naval empire packaged to make it more palatable to the allies? There can be little doubt that the new emphasis on freedom and autonomy reveals shifts in the political vocabulary of the fourth century, but more than that, the fact that guarantees—promising no garrisons, no tribute, and no political interference—were written into this foundation charter (as it is often called), reveals that the Athenians were well aware that the second Athenian confederacy would be very different from its fifth-century predecessor. The allied states, for example, would meet in their own assembly, and thus had a collective voice to balance the decision-making power of the Athenians. It is true that the Athenian commanders operating in various theaters of war were able to levy "contributions" from allied states, but these never reached the levels of fifth-century tribute, and the new league was far less economically exploitative than the Delian League.

End of the Spartan Hegemony

The new Athenian maritime confederacy reflected the realities of the fourth century, in which the emergence of any one state as a hegemonial power led to the formation of a counter-balancing coalition. During the 380s BC, Sparta had enjoyed supremacy, but the 370s witnessed a decisive change of Sparta's fortunes as Athenian power once again proved a counterweight. The Athenian navy under Chabrias inflicted a major defeat on the Spartans at the Battle of Naxos in 376, and beginning in 375 the Athenian navy under Timotheus was able to operate freely in the waters off western Greece, enrolling many new allies in the Athenian confederacy. As it became more and more obvious that the mosaic of Greek city-states was locked into a seemingly endless cycle of war, the Greeks repeatedly tried to secure peace by formulating common peace treaties. These were treaties open to any independent state, and were designed to make peaceful coexistence possible between all the signatories. Such treaties were signed in 387/6 (the King's Peace), and again in 375, 371, 365 (possibly), 362/1, and 338/7. The grim succession of these treaties shows that a common peace (*koine eirene*, as the Greeks called such a treaty) was never a guarantee of lasting peace, yet the repeated efforts to find a way out of the cycle of interstate conflict also shows that the Greeks were trying to find a political solution to their quandary.

Negotiations were once again held in 371 BC between the major powers with a view to signing yet another common peace, when negotiations took an odd turn. On the eve of the signing of the treaty, the Thebans asserted that they were signing on behalf of all Boiotia, not just Thebes. Their insistence was based on the fact that Boiotia was a federal state, with a set of federal institutions—representative government, federal sanctuaries, federal coinage—and that Thebes represented all Boiotia in the negotiations. To some, however (and the Spartans in particular), one state signing on behalf of others amounted to a rejection of the autonomy of those states. The Spartans insisted on Thebes signing for themselves alone, a position which amounted to a rejection of their leadership of the federal state of the Boiotians. The talks collapsed. To enforce their authority and undermine the Thebans, the Spartans marched into Boiotia, where, in early July at the Battle of Leuktra, their army was roundly beaten by the Thebans, led by Epaminondas. The Spartan hegemony was over.

Regionalism and Panhellenism

With the defeat of Sparta and the death of one of its kings, Kleombrotos, Thebes emerged as the state best situated to assert hegemony within Greece. The ascendancy of Thebes, however, would be even shorter than Sparta's time as hegemon, although the Theban leaders were not lacking in ambition.

Between 371 BC and 362 BC, the Thebans projected their power well beyond central Greece. Led by two capable generals, Epaminondas and Pelopidas, the Thebans set about implementing a bold plan to break Sparta's regional power. Between 370 and 367, Boiotian armies invaded the Peloponnese three times, even going so far as to ravage large parts of Lakonia in 370. They took Sparta's port at Gythion, and liberated many of the neighboring communities of Sparta, the so-called *perioikoi*, thereby restricting Sparta's reserve of manpower. These accomplishments weakened Sparta both materially and symbolically, yet they were incidental compared to Epaminondas's

12.4 The walls of Messene, built in 369 BC. The circuit runs for over 9 kilometers (5½ mi.) and is punctuated with towers equipped with arrow slits and capable of holding artillery, such as catapults.

most significant accomplishments. He liberated the Messenian helots and oversaw the founding of a magnificent city, Messene, at the foot of Mount Ithome. At a stroke, Sparta's age-old hold on the southern Peloponnese was severed, and a powerful new Theban ally was installed on Sparta's western border. Messene's walls alone ran for over 9 kilometers (5½ mi.), meaning that in time of war thousands of inhabitants and their flocks could be safely protected from raiders (**12.4**). The impact on Sparta, which for centuries had relied on the produce of Messenia—"good to plow," as Tyrtaios called it—was devastating.

Epaminondas employed the same policy on Sparta's northern frontier in the central Peloponnese. Here in Arkadia the Theban commander managed to persuade Tegea and Mantineia, formerly the most powerful towns in the region, to cooperate in the founding of a new city, Megalopolis, which would serve as the center for a new Arkadian League. Both Tegea and Mantineia had suffered at various times from Sparta's aggression and were prepared to cooperate with Epaminondas. As with the Boiotian Federation, the Arkadian League would not replace the cities of the Arkadia, but represented another level of political affiliation designed to unify and

12.5 The Theater and Assembly Hall (Thersilion) at Megalopolis. The blocks of the Thersilion are column bases for a rectangular assembly area, 52.5 × 66.5 m (172 × 218 ft), in which ten thousand Arkadians met and deliberated.

strengthen the region. A political assembly called the Ten Thousand met at Megalopolis (**12.5**). The assembly was open to all Arkadians, and was probably identical in composition to the Arkadian army. As with Messene, by overseeing the formation of a powerful city on Sparta's borders, Epaminondas was engaged in a grand strategy of containment.

The founding of Megalopolis should be put into a broader context. It was not solely a city that Epaminondas was founding, but a federal state. Federations, usually known as koina (sing. koinon), were not a new development in the Greek world. There were both political and religious koina well attested as early as the Archaic period, but the fourth century BC saw a resurgence in federalism in Greece. Epaminondas favored the Boiotian model, in which a single city exercised leadership over a much larger region and satellite towns remained self-governing while participating in federal institutions. The Theban hegemony over Greek affairs was short-lived, but despite its short duration, the decade of Theban power reinvigorated federalism as a viable model for Greek political life. Small communities, such as the towns and tribes of northwestern Greece, favored it as a way of maintaining their identity while gaining strength in numbers. The koinon of Epeiros, for example, consisted of the Molossians, Thesprotians, and Chaones, and these in turn were made up of even smaller tribes. The Akarnanians lived in towns across western Greece and were united as a koinon, but remained quite separate and distinct from each other.

The tenacity of federalism should be kept in mind when judging the limitations of the polis. If the city-state represented the hold of separatism, sometimes called centrifugality, as each city jealously guarded its own territory, identity, and history, it is equally true that there was a centripetal tendency in Greek affairs, a process of fashioning common institutions and regional connections that resulted in ethnic identities as powerful as city affiliations. Increasingly from the fourth century BC onward, the people of the cities of Kalydon, Pleuron, and Oiniadai also referred to themselves as Aitolian. Moreover, this process of panregional unification would continue despite the political woes of the Greeks in the centuries to come. Even as the shadow of Rome was looming over Greece in the second century BC, Polybios could praise the "allied and amicable commonality" that had effectively united the Peloponnese under the control of the Achaian League. In time, the Peloponnese would use common weights and measures, enjoy common magistrates, councillors and juries. In fact the Achaian League's final manifestation would be as the Roman province of Achaia.

The Aitolian and Achaian Leagues are proof of the powerful hold of regionalism and federalism in Greek political life, but their ascent was by no means assured or predictable in the 360s BC. At that point Thebes enjoyed hegemony, so that yet again a coalition of the other major states—Sparta, Athens, and Corinth among them—formed to challenge the Thebans. The Athenian historian Xenophon was an eyewitness to these events and when the two sides drew up their armies outside Mantineia, in Arkadia, in 362 BC, it was as if all Greece was holding its breath awaiting the outcome. Xenophon captures the anticipation and uncertainty in his summation of the battle:

When these things had taken place, the opposite of what all men believed would happen was brought to pass. For since well-nigh all the people of Greece had come together and formed themselves in opposing lines, there was no one who did not suppose that if a battle were fought, those who proved victorious would be the rulers and those who were defeated would be their subjects; but...while each party claimed to be victorious, neither was found to be any better off, as regards either additional territory, or city, or sway, than before the battle took place; but there was even more confusion and disorder in Greece after the battle than before.

(Xenophon, *Hellenica* 7.1.26–27, trans. Brownson)

Forty years from the end of the Peloponnesian War and the Greeks had fought themselves to a standstill. No power—neither Athens, Sparta, nor Thebes—had proved itself capable of winning and holding supreme power. Indeed, subsequent events only underscored the weakness of Athens. The largest states of Athens' Confederacy went on to revolt in 357 BC and the Athenian campaign resulted in a succession of disasters. The fleet of Chabrias was defeated in 357. Timotheus was fined for failing to offer support to another general, Chares, who in turn received no financial support from Athens to prosecute the war. By 355, Athens had lost the majority of its most important allies and the city's power and finances were dramatically reduced. Regional federations were taking their place alongside the city-state as pieces in the great game of territorial politics, but unification on a broader scale was scarcely conceivable. The Olympic games was perhaps the nearest the Greeks came to a truly panhellenic institution, yet it also reinforced regional and city rivalries. It was apparent that the system of international politics as the Greeks knew it was not working. We can hear this in Xenophon's despondent summary of the Battle of Mantineia: the prevailing system of city-states and regional federations was the source of Greece's political woes. The fourth-century rhetor and public intellectual Isokrates realized that the system was

broken, yet his solution also reveals that the Greeks were prisoners of their own history:

As I kept going over these questions [namely, how could Athens avoid more pointless wars], I found that on no other condition could Athens remain at peace, unless the greatest states of Hellas should resolve to put an end to their mutual quarrels and carry the war beyond our borders into Asia.

(Isokrates, *Letter to Philip* 9, trans. Norlin)

And there we have the most imaginative solution to the paralysis condemning the Greeks to perennial interstate warfare: declare war on the Persians. What is perhaps most extraordinary in Isokrates' ruminations is that he sees this as a solution that will not only allow the Greeks to end their own strife, thereby unifying them, but will also supply the conditions by which Athens would remain at peace. Evidently peace really meant not fighting other Greeks. Fighting Persians was a horse of a different color altogether.

Philip of Macedon

It is significant that Isokrates' solution to the internecine warfare that bedeviled Greece was articulated in an open letter to Philip II of Macedon (382–336 BC) sent in 346 BC. If events in the 360s suggested that the prevailing system of city-states, federations, and alliances was ineffective, some were now wondering whether a single warleader might offer a solution to Greece's problems.

Philip, however, was an unlikely candidate. Born in 382 BC, Philip was one of the younger sons of Amyntas III. When his father died in 370, Philip was only twelve years old and the throne went to his older brother, Alexander III. During his teenage years Philip was a hostage first of the Illyrians and later of the Thebans, a fact that demonstrates the political weakness of Macedon even into the 360s, although his time in Thebes exposed him to the new tactical thinking of the Theban generals, lessons he was to build on. Upon the assassination of Alexander III, the throne went to another older brother, Perdikkas, who ruled until he died in battle in 360. Philip duly succeeded to the throne, an inexperienced twenty-two-year-old princeling in charge of a politically weak kingdom. The notion that he would transform both

Macedon and all of Greece would have seemed far-fetched at best.

At the time Philip succeeded to the throne in early 359, Macedon was not even regarded as fully Greek by those living in the south in such places as Athens. Thucydides spoke of the people of northern Greece as having old-fashioned ways, even wearing weapons, and often living in villages rather than cities. Although the Macedonians spoke Greek—funerary markers found in the Great Tumulus at Vergina leave no doubt about this—Athenians, Corinthians, and others who lived in the cities of southern and central Greece were not entirely convinced. As we saw in Chapter 4, when Alexander I, an early fifth-century Macedonian king, petitioned to compete in the Olympic games, which were open only to Greeks, the judges refused him entry until he presented a genealogy demonstrating that his ancestors came from Argos. The episode reveals a great deal: the Macedonians wanted to be considered Greek yet there were many who disputed this, so the neat solution was to concede the claim to the royal family alone: the king's claim to Greek identity was recognized, while the question of the ethnic identity of the ordinary shepherds and farmers of Macedon was put aside, although it is not clear whether they cared very much one way or the other about identity politics. In the second century AD, the Greek historian Arrian reported a speech by Alexander the Great (356–323 BC) that, even if fictional, reflects the deep changes that Philip engineered in Macedon:

For Philip found you vagabonds and destitute, most of you clad in hides, feeding a few sheep up the mountain sides, for the protection of which you had to fight with small success against Illyrians, Triballians, and the border Thracians. Instead of the hides he gave you cloaks to wear, and from the mountains he led you down into the plains, and made you capable of fighting the neighboring barbarians, so that you were no longer compelled to preserve yourselves by trusting rather to your inaccessible strongholds than to your own valor. He made you colonists of cities, which he adorned with useful laws and customs; and from being slaves and subjects, he made you rulers over those very barbarians by whom you yourselves, as well as your property, were previously liable to be carried off or ravaged.

(Arrian, *Campaigns of Alexander* 7.9, trans. Bohn)

In the fourth-century world of Philip and Alexander, the Greeks represented the high-status culture to which the Macedonians and other northern Greeks aspired. In the fifth century the Macedonians had patronized such poets as Pindar and Bacchylides, and in the fourth century they brought Greek playwrights, such as Euripides, to Macedon to serve as artists-in-residence. They brought Greek philosophers, such as Aristotle, to tutor the royal children, and they decorated their increasingly prosperous mansions and palaces with glorious mosaics made by Greek artists.

At the same time, however, it would be wrong to see Macedonian culture as no more than a fourth-century importation of southern arts; indeed, the earlier historical developments in this part of Greece are increasingly assuming a higher profile. Recent excavations, for example, by the Greek Archaeological Service at Aiani in Elymiotis, in the western part of Macedon, have shown that northern Greece shared in the cultural repertoire of the Greeks well before the fourth century: monumental architecture, the plastic arts (such as painting and sculpture; see **12.6**), and city planning. In a region once thought of as little more than a mountain canton, ruled by independent "feudal barons," archaeology has brought to light a thriving Greek city of the Archaic and Classical periods. Yet despite the thorough contacts between southern, central, and northern Greece, the Greeks of the south still preferred to see the north as a relic of Homer's world, citing how the great chieftains of Macedon still strengthened their dynasties by marrying each other's daughters. In their palaces, too, the Macedonian kings cultivated a drinking and feasting culture that resembled the world of the epic heroes but which frequently horrified guests from the south, who saw it as a sign of the semi-barbaric manners of their hosts. The fourth-century-BC historian Theopompos reflects the Athenian distaste for Philip's behavior in a famous description of a Macedonian feast:

But Philip, when the Athenian ambassadors had departed, sent for some of his companions, and he ordered them to call for the flute girls and Aristonikos the kithara player and Dorion the flutist and the others he was accustomed to drink with; for Philip brought around such people everywhere and had many implements at the ready for drinking parties and gatherings. For, being

12.6 Archaic kore head from Aiani, Macedonia, second half of sixth century BC. Terra-cotta

a lover of drink and intemperate in character, he also had a mass of buffoons around him, both musicians and comedians. Drinking through the entire night, he was very intoxicated and dismissed all the others. He continued his partying until it was daybreak, and then departed to the ambassadors of the Athenians.

(Athenaios, *Deipnosophists* 10.435B–C, trans. Morison)

A number of recent scholars studying this and many other reports of Philip's (and, later, Alexander's) heavy drinking have concluded that even though the sources that record this information are almost universally hostile to the Macedonians, nevertheless, carousing was a central feature of Macedonian court life. Some have suggested, plausibly, that the Macedonians were rejecting the quiet, quasi-philosophical symposia we associate with Plato's circle and were asserting a conscious link between Macedonian practice and the heroic world of Homer. In summary, Philip's reign would bring about a transformation and leave the Macedonians the most

powerful state in Greece, but it would not persuade an Athenian gentleman that the Macedonians were any less boorish.

Marriage and War

The key to Philip's success was a unique blend of canny diplomacy, tactical audacity, and an ability to exploit the weakness of his adversaries. Consider, for example, the early years of his reign. Two immediate problems loomed large: the first was the existence of a pretender to the throne, Argaios, who was supported by the Athenians, and the second was the need to secure the borders of his realm and protect it from raiding by tribes to the west and north. Argaios was killed in battle, but the solution to the border question was more innovative. Between 359 and 357 BC, Philip married Olympias (*c.* 375–316 BC), an Epirote princess and the daughter of Neoptolemos, king of the Molossians, thereby securing an alliance with the Molossians to the far west. Nearer (and on occasion a part of Macedon) was Elymiotis, where Philip married another princess, Phila. Further to the northwest were the Illlyrians, another tribal state with whom the Macedonians had perennial problems; Philip married Audata, daughter of Bardyllis, king of the Illyrians, ending fighting between the two sides. These marriages, however, were not sequential. In the manner of a true dynastic ruler, Philip kept many wives at a time, treating them for the most part as diplomatic pawns. The strategy was effective: over the course of three years he successfully fixed the western border of Macedonia and created stability within the kingdom.

The attempts to secure his control of a united Macedon also led Philip to look eastwards, which brought him into direct contact with the Athenians, whose interest in the region of Thrace were focused on the Athenian colony of Amphipolis. As we have seen in Chapter 8, the Athenian foothold in Thrace had been hard-won, and at least one colony at the mouth of the Strymon River, Ennea Hodoi, had been destroyed in the fifth century BC. In a deft move, Philip captured Amphipolis in 357 BC and offered to trade it back to the Athenians in exchange for the coastal city of Pydna, closer to the Macedonian heartland. Exactly how these negotiations were conducted is unclear—much later Demosthenes spoke of a secret pact between the two sides—but it is unlikely a formal treaty was ever signed. The result,

however, is not in doubt: Athens betrayed its ally, Pydna, by yielding it to Philip, yet Philip kept hold of Amphipolis. Philip had exposed the weakness of Athens: in contrast with their forefathers in the fifth century, the Athenians of the mid-fourth century had neither the means nor the inclination to put large expeditionary forces into the field. But if the Athenians were now more risk-averse, for Philip, the results were a first step toward territorial expansion. Pydna gave the Macedonians a port on the Thermaic Gulf, and holding Amphipolis gave Philip a base from which to move on Mount Pangaion in 356. Called to intervene in a local dispute, Philip took control of

the gold and silver mines of Mount Pangaion and renamed the place Philippi. The addition to the Macedonian treasury is said to have amounted to 1,000 talents per year.

Although Philip's diplomatic skills and marital prowess were important, battles are won by soldiers, and it was in the training of his army that Philip proved most innovative. Having observed the Theban generals Epaminondas, Pelopidas, and Pammenes while he was in Thebes as a teenage captive, Philip struck upon the most significant change in hoplite warfare in three hundred years. Doing away with the heavy shield of the hoplite as well as his 1.8-meter (6 ft) thrusting spear, Philip armed the men of the Macedonian phalanx with lighter bucklers and less body armor, but drilled them in fighting with pikes, known as ***sarissas***, whose length is estimated to have been 6 meters (20 ft). With the front three lines of the phalanx holding the sarissa in front with both arms, and the rear ranks holding theirs at various elevations, the phalanx presented an impenetrable front to the enemy (**12.7**). With skirmishers and cavalry to protect the flanks, a well-drilled Macedonian phalanx could destroy almost all lighter-armed formations, and it was not until the middle of the second century that the flexibility of the Roman legion proved itself to be a match for the Macedonians. Men had to train ceaselessly to acquire these skills, but the new wealth of Philippi made this possible. Courageous, well drilled, and regularly paid, Philip and Alexander's Macedonians may have been the world's most successful national army until the age of Napoleon.

An easy way to grasp Philip's success is to compare maps of Macedon in 359 BC with its territorial extent only eleven years later (**12.8** and **12.9**; see p. 314). A comparison of the two maps shows that Philip initially extended territorial control north over various Thracian and Illyrian tribes, including the Triballi,

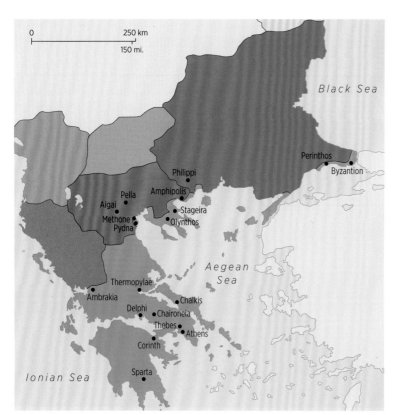

12.8 Map of Macedonia and its neighbors, 359 BC

Macedonia under control of Philip II (359 BC)

Independent Macedonian tribes

Greece and Greek-occupied Macedonian land

Illyria and Illyrian-occupied Macedonian land

Thrace and Thracian-occupied Macedonian land

Epirus, a Macedonian ally

Scythia

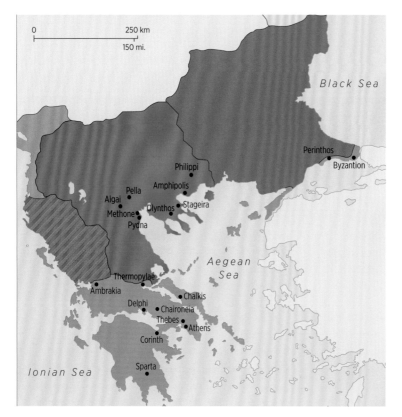

12.9 Map of Macedonia, 348 BC

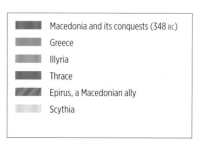

Macedonia and its conquests (348 BC)

Greece

Illyria

Thrace

Epirus, a Macedonian ally

Scythia

Agrianes, and Paionians, all tribes who dwelled in the areas of modern-day Serbia and western Bulgaria. Each tribe subsequently remained loyal to Philip; the Agrianes, in particular, contributed significant numbers of light-armed infantry for Philip and Alexander's armies. Illyria was subdued by war and marriage; Epirus was brought into alliance through marriage.

The other area in which Philip had managed to assert dominance was Thessaly, to the south of Macedon, a region rich in farmland and pasture. At the time Philip came to power it was divided into four regions dominated by large, aristocratic families, and it was one of these families—the Aleuadai of Larissa—who called on Philip to help them. The exact date is uncertain but seems to have coincided with the earliest period of Philip's rule, perhaps in 358 BC. Details of the subsequent military campaign are non-existent, but Philip left with two new wives, Philinna and Nikesipolis, who came from opposing sides of the conflict. As ever, Philip had proved himself an able negotiator.

The Third Sacred War

The final annexation of Thessaly, and the beginning of Philip's southern campaigns, (which would result in the total control of all Greece), occurred in 354 BC. It was in this year that Philip returned once again to Thessaly to help the Aleuadai, as Thessaly was still in a state of upheaval because of the rivalry between the ruling families of Larissa and Pherai. The Larissaians called on Philip while Pherai made an alliance with the generals in command of Phokis, further south.

In entering the conflict, however, Philip became embroiled not only in the war in Thessaly but also in the broader conflict known as the Third Sacred War (356–346 BC). This war was fought over the control of Delphi, which had been seized by the Phokians in 356 BC. The Amphiktyonic states, which had jointly controlled the sanctuary since the early sixth century BC, declared war on the Phokians. After plundering Delphi and melting down hundreds of dedications, the Phokian generals responded by raising a mercenary army with which they campaigned against the Boiotians to the east and Thessaly to the northwest. In 354, Philip was actually beaten in pitched battle by the Phokian general Onomarchos, but he withdrew, as he was fond of saying, like a battering ram, so that he could strike again all the harder. That same year he lost an eye at the siege of Methone, in southern Macedonia. Undeterred, Philip once again marched south in 353, and in the ensuing encounter, known as the Battle of the Crocus Field, Philip destroyed the Phokian army, including Onomarchos and six thousand men. Philip did not choose to press his advantage, although his election as ruler of Thessaly meant that he not only controlled territory south of Macedon as far as Thermopylae, but also that he now also had a vote on the Amphiktyonic Council. This would, in time, supply him with the pretext he needed to march south. He had punished Onomarchos and his men as temple-robbers, drowning the men he captured, and used his victory as propaganda, portraying himself as an instrument of Apollo's vengeance.

Instead of marching south, Philip continued to strengthen his position in the northern Aegean. For the next few years he extended his control of territory east of Macedonia through Thrace as far as the Hellespont. The Athenians viewed these events with increasing alarm, and the fourth-century orator Demosthenes took every opportunity possible to inveigh against Philip and his plans, being in no doubt that Philip's ultimate aim was to conquer all of Greece. The continuous expansion, however, seemed unstoppable. Philip sacked the city of Olynthos in 348 BC, a city that had recently formed an alliance with Athens because of the fear of Philip's expansion. His destruction of the city was so thorough that the ruins still visible today are those of the city abandoned after Philip enslaved its inhabitants. By some estimates the Athenians sent more than sixty ships to Olynthos, but they were too late to avert the Olynthian disaster, and by now Philip had learned that the merest suggestion of peace was enough to bring the Athenians to the negotiating table.

Now Philip once again turned his eyes toward central Greece. The Third Sacred War was still unfolding in its desultory way, now little more than annual skirmishes between the Phokians and the Thebans. Philip moved his army south in late 347 BC, and the Athenians began negotiations to secure a peace and prevent him marching any further. The record of these negotiations makes depressing reading. For months embassies travelled back and forth between Pella and Athens, and in the end the Athenians obtained a treaty, called the Peace of Philokrates, but it was not worth the stone it was carved on. Philip, on the other hand, had negotiated separately with the mercenary garrison that held Thermopylae. In exchange for safe passage to Crete, they abandoned their position and handed the most symbolic fort in Greece over to Philip. The final act was about to begin.

The Road to Chaironeia

With the Third Sacred War over, the Phokians defeated, and his domination of central Greece secure, Philip again demonstrated that he was playing a long game against the Greeks. At Athens passions were running high, as the Athenians began hurling recriminations at each other as to who bore responsibility for the debacle that had handed central Greece to Philip. Others held out hope that the peace might hold.

Rather than attack now, however, when the Athenians might turn their anger to resolve, Philip again shifted north and west. He campaigned for several years as far north as the Danube, and

founded cities in the region, anticipating a policy of urbanization that his son Alexander would employ across central Asia a decade later. In the west he consolidated his power by attacking the few cities, such as Kassope, that had held out against him. To the east he laid siege to the cities of Perinthos and Byzantion, thereby threatening to cut off Athens' grain supply. The city replied by rerouting a fleet under Chares to relieve the siege and dispatching a second fleet under Phokion to render assistance.

Philip now chose to drop all pretence. He declared war on Athens and seized a grain fleet waiting to enter the Bosporos and sail to Athens. He spent the campaigning season of 339 BC in the Danube region, where he was badly wounded in the leg, but in 338 he finally marched south. A Fourth Sacred War, instigated by the illegal cultivation of the Sacred Plain below Delphi by the men of Lokris, provided Philip with an excuse for bringing his army south. He was elected leader of the Amphiktyonic forces and ordered to lead an army against the Lokrians, but this was never more than a pretext. Coming south to Thermopylae, he continued into the Kephisos Valley and advanced unopposed all the way to Elateia. This city was located in eastern Phokis, well beyond Thermopylae, and the news that Philip had reached here meant two things: first, he had advanced further than Delphi and clearly had no intention of going in that direction, and second, that there was no natural choke-point between his army and either Thebes or Athens. To be stopped, Philip would have to be met on the open field of battle.

Demosthenes, who opposed Philip for most of his career, gave

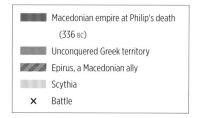

12.10 Map of Macedonian territory, 336 BC

a speech, *On the Crown*, delivered some years later, in which he paints a picture in words of the atmosphere in Athens when the news came that Philip had reached Elateia:

Evening had already fallen when a messenger arrived bringing to the presiding councillors the news that Elateia had been taken. They were sitting at supper, but they instantly rose from table, cleared the booths in the marketplace of their occupants, and unfolded the hurdles [wickerwork barriers], while others summoned the commanders and ordered the attendance of the trumpeter. The commotion spread through the whole city. At daybreak on the morrow the presidents summoned the Council to the Council House, and the citizens flocked to the place of assembly. Before the Council could introduce the business and prepare the agenda, the whole body of citizens had taken their places on the hill.

(Demosthenes, *On the Crown* 169,
trans. Vince, adapted).

As at the end of the Peloponnesian War, when facing annihilation, the Athenians responded soberly and magnificently. Faced with news that Philip was in the field, the Athenians met in democratic assembly. Demosthenes stepped forward and proposed that the Athenians immediately join forces with their old enemies, the Thebans, against the common threat of Philip. In August 338 BC, the two armies met at the western edge of the Boiotian plain, near the village of Chaironeia (**12.10**). That day one thousand Athenians would die, defeated by the right wing of the Macedonian phalanx, commanded by Philip himself. On the other wing the Thebans were routed by the Macedonian left, commanded by Philip's eighteen-year-old son, Alexander. Among the Thebans was an elite regiment of three hundred men, the Sacred Band. They died to a man. Their bones were buried beneath the Lion of Chaironeia (**12.11**).

As we shall see in the final chapter, Greek history after Philip's victory would play out on a vastly greater stage, and Alexander would take Greek culture across central Asia. This, however, would be a Macedonian version of Greek culture, and it is worth pausing to evaluate the accomplishments of the Greeks generally and the Athenians specifically in the one hundred and fifty years from Salamis to Chaironeia. History cannot be summed up in the tale of two battles, but they do provide markers that help us to define an

12.11 The Lion of Chaironeia. Originally made of five pieces of marble, the Lion commemorated the spot where the members of the Theban Sacred band were buried. Within the enclosure shown were found the skeletons of 254 men and their weapons. H: 3.8 m (12 ft 6 in.), sitting atop a pedestal 3 m (9ft 10 in.) high

age, and it is an epoch that, judged by the standards of contemporary societies in the fifth and fourth centuries BC, was extraordinary. A political culture based on the notion of participation by all adult male citizens took root, despite the hostility of conservative thinkers and aristocrats. That culture produced brilliant dramas: tragedies that resonate as powerfully today as ever they did to contemporary audiences, and comedies that show how an open society allows and encourages totally free speech, especially when it mocks power and the powerful. There is something very attractive about a society that spends more on public architecture than private mansions, that can advance science through observation, that values beauty as socially beneficial, and that believes, finally, that the unexamined life is not worth living. The free, independent, eloquent, petty, domineering, coercive, honest, and glorious society that lost to Philip deserves to be remembered. It was a golden moment in our human history.

12.12 The entrance to Tomb II, Vergina (Aigai), burial ground of Macedonian kings in the late fourth century BC.

Spotlight
Vergina: The Debate over Philip's Tomb

In the 1970s, the Greek archaeologist Manolis Andronikos excavated a great tumulus located in the Macedonian town of Vergina, the site of the ancient capital of Macedon, Aigai. Deep within the tumulus Andronikos excavated a series of tombs (**12.12**). Two were unplundered, and contained an astonishing range of precious vessels, weapons, armor, as well as furniture finished with gold leaf and ivory. Tomb II also contained gold boxes, called *larnakes*, in which had been placed the partially cremated bones of a man and woman of the very highest status (**12.13**). The bones had been collected from the funeral pyre, washed, wrapped in precious purple cloth and then placed in larnakes, one for the man and one for the woman, beneath exquisite golden wreaths (**12.14**).

The stunning quality of the goods in the tomb, and the approximate dates supplied by the burial goods, especially the pottery, led Andronikos to claim confidently that the male occupant of Tomb II was Philip II, King of Macedon and Alexander the Great's father. Philip was assassinated and given a royal burial in 336 BC. Greaves designed to protect a warrior's lower legs were found in the antechamber of the tomb and were of different lengths, a detail that seemed to fit with the report that Philip had been wounded in the leg three years before his death.

Forensic pathology was also used to build the case for the identification of the man in Tomb II as Philip. A reconstruction of the man's face matched a notch found in the upper right orbit (the man's eye-socket)

with reports in the ancient sources of Philip losing an eye in the siege of Amphipolis in 348 BC. Also drawing on contemporary depictions in ivory of Philip's face, the reconstruction seemed to offer a glimpse of the appearance of one of the most famous men in ancient Greece (**12.15**; see p. 320).

Despite this evidence, there have always been those unsure of the identification of the members of the Macedonian elite buried at Vergina. The use of a barrel vault in the tomb's construction fits more comfortably with a date after Alexander's conquest of the East, from where, it is usually argued, the technique of barrel-vaulting reached Greece. This would place Tomb II at least one decade after Philip's death. Similarly, the tomb was finished very hastily, as is shown by the fact that the plaster frieze painted over the tomb's entrance was still wet when the entire tomb was buried within the Great Tumulus. A significant number of scholars have adopted the view that it is more likely that Alexander the Great's half-brother, a puppet king who ruled as Philip III Arrhidaios (c. 356–317 BC), was buried in Tomb II with his wife, a Macedonian noblewoman named Eurydike (who incidentally was said by ancient writers to have been trained as a warrior). The greaves in the antechamber may have been those of the ill-fated young woman. Both Philip Arrhidaios and Eurydike were executed in late 317 BC by Olympias, mother of Alexander the Great, who continued to play an important role in Macedonian politics in the generation after Alexander's death. She championed the claim of her grandson, Alexander IV, although the young man would also be killed in the fighting between Alexander the Great's

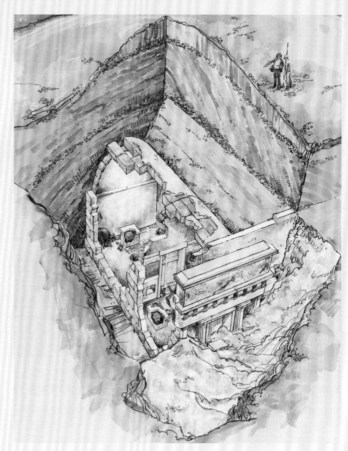

12.13 Cutaway reconstruction of Tomb II, Vergina, showing the location of *larnakes* in both front and back chambers

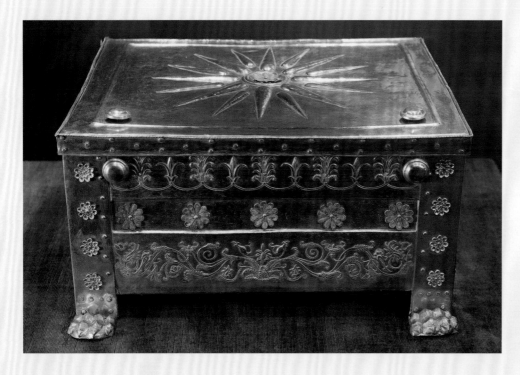

12.14 Golden larnax from Tomb II, usually identified with Philip II of Macedon, found and exhibited in Vergina, Greece

successors. In 309 BC, when the boy was about fourteen years of age, he was put to death by the Macedonian dynast Kassander. Along with Philip Arrhidaios and Eurydike, Alexander IV was given a royal burial, enjoying an honor in death that eluded him in life. Tomb III at Vergina is known as the Prince's Tomb, and was probably built to hold his last remains.

The puzzle of the tombs at Aigai received fresh attention in 2015, when a joint Spanish and Greek research team completed a study of the bones in Tomb I. These were uncremated bones, and the forensic scientists studying them concluded that the man buried in Tomb I was a tall (1.8 meters, or 5 ft 11 in.), middle-aged man around forty-five years of age. The bones of his left knee showed signs of severe trauma, which had healed three years before his death, leaving him a with a pronounced limp (**12.16**). Also in the tomb were the bones of a young woman around eighteen years of age, and the bones of a newborn

12.15 Head of Philip II of Macedon, carving from the Tomb of Vergina, Greece, fourth century BC. Ivory, H: 3.2 cm (1¼ in.)

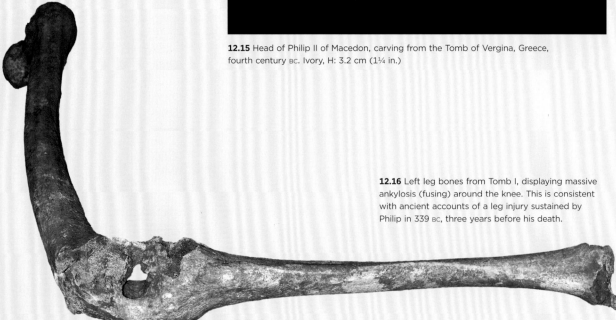

12.16 Left leg bones from Tomb I, displaying massive ankylosis (fusing) around the knee. This is consistent with ancient accounts of a leg injury sustained by Philip in 339 BC, three years before his death.

child. The chief researcher, Antonios Bartsiokas, has concluded, reasonably, that these are the bones of Philip II, the bride, Cleopatra, whom he married shortly before his death, and the child who might have become a threat to Alexander's succession.

The last piece of the puzzle concerns Alexander. If his father, his brother, and his son are all buried at Aigai, what became of Alexander's body? On this question our ancient sources are clear. After Alexander died in Babylon in 323 BC, his body was placed in an elaborate cortège and slowly taken back toward Macedon. When the funerary procession reached Syria, however, Ptolemy dispatched a flying column to intercept and kidnap the body. It was taken to Egypt, and there it was placed in a specially constructed funerary complex, referred to in later literature as the *Soma*, or "Body," in the center of Ptolemy's new Egyptian capital, Alexandria. In the manner of an embalmed pharaoh, Alexander's body became the focal point for a collection of sacred writings and other texts. In the case of the Egyptian pharaoh, Ramses III, his mortuary complex was later known as the Ramesseum; in Alexander's case, the complex is remembered as the Library of Alexandria. Never buried at Aigai, Alexander would not rest in the old Greece from which his family came, but in a capital of the new Hellenistic world he created. If, however, Tomb II does contain the burial of his half-brother, Philip Arrhidaios, then it is entirely possible that the famous iron cuirass found in the tomb was originally worn by Arrhidaios's more famous half-brother, Alexander the Great (**12.17**).

12.17 Armor found in Tomb II, Vergina. Traditionally the tomb's occupant is identified as Philip II. If, however, the tomb belongs to Philip III Arrhidaios, the armor may be that of his more illustrious half-brother, Alexander the Great.

356 BC
Birth of Alexander
the Great

336 BC
Alexander the Great
becomes King of Macedon

334 BC
Battle of the
Granikos River

333 BC
Battle of Issos

331 BC
Battle of Gaugamela

Chapter 13

Alexander the Great and the Hellenistic Age

Philip's defeat of the Greeks at Chaironeia is sometimes presented as the end of Greek freedom, but this is a skewed reading of Greek history. Philip died only two years later and the rise to power of his son Alexander saw a radical transformation of the Greek world, one that brought the Greeks back into conflict with their old enemy, Persia. The result was astonishing: within ten years, Greek Macedonian armies would conquer all of the Achaemenid realm. Even though Alexander died before he had the opportunity to rule a stable kingdom, his Successors, notably the Ptolemies and Seleukids, would carve out a series of world empires which would witness the fusing of Greek and non-Greek traditions across all of central Asia. Hardly remembered today, this Hellenistic world would represent a phase of Greek culture that was as rich and important as the Classical Age.

Alexander's Rise

In the aftermath of his victory over the Greeks at Chaironeia in 338 BC, Philip heeded the advice of Isokrates, who had suggested uniting the Greeks in a crusade against the Persians. He went to Corinth, where, instead of issuing orders as a conqueror, he convened a general meeting of representatives of the Greek states to plan the invasion. To Philip, it did not matter that the Persian invasion had occurred more than a century before he was born, or that in the last generation the Great King had brokered peace among the Greek states; a common enemy would unite the Greeks and allow Philip to repackage his hegemony as the captaincy of a grand Hellenic alliance, the League of Corinth.

At some point, probably in early 337 BC between the meeting of the League of Corinth and the opening of the Persian campaign, Philip returned to his capital, Pella, in Macedonia where he celebrated his most recent marriage to a girl named Cleopatra, daughter of a Macedonian nobleman named Attalos. At the wedding feast, Attalos raised his cup to toast the marriage, and prayed for a legitimate Macedonian heir. This was a direct insult to Olympias, an Epirote princess, and to her son, Alexander, who was not therefore fully Macedonian. The episode illustrates the tensions at court, which were perhaps to be expected in a dynastic setting where competing factions of royal women and their children vied for power. Alexander was clearly Philip's preferred son, having led the Macedonian left wing at Chaironeia a year earlier despite being only eighteen, but as a result of the insult, his mother Olympias withdrew from the Macedonian court and returned to her brother, Alexander of Epirus. If Attalos's remark had been designed to infuriate the queen, he had certainly succeeded. For a short period Philip and Alexander were also estranged, but Alexander was back in Pella by 336 BC and Philip was able to resume planning the invasion of Persia.

Philip's intentions were demonstrated by the fact that early in 336 BC he dispatched his subordinate, Parmenion, to secure a bridgehead at the Hellespont for the Graeco-Macedonian army he intended leading into Asia. It was also in that year that Philip gave his daughter, also named Cleopatra, to Alexander of Epirus in marriage, but the episode would end tragically. At a religious festival prior to the wedding ceremony, as his statue was carried into the theater behind statues of the twelve Olympians, Philip was cut down by an assassin. The increasing isolation of Olympias and the reports that Philip's young Macedonian bride either had or was about to bear him a child meant that a great deal of suspicion fell on Olympias and Alexander. Had they engineered the assassination? The killer was a royal guard named Pausanias, who claimed to have been raped by Attalos. Philip had deflected Pausanias's complaints, but it was rumored that Alexander had encouraged the guard's anger. Plutarch reports:

And so when Pausanias, who had been outrageously dealt with at the instance of Attalos and Cleopatra and could get no justice at Philip's hands, slew Philip, most of the blame devolved upon Olympias, on the ground that she had added her exhortations to the young man's anger and incited him to the deed; but a certain amount of accusation attached itself to Alexander also. For it is said that when Pausanias, after the outrage that he had suffered, met Alexander, and bewailed his fate, Alexander recited to him the iambic verse of the *Medea*: "The giver of the bride, the bridegroom, and the bride."

(Plutarch, *Alexander* 10.4, trans. Perrin)

Historians have debated whether to give any weight to these reports and questioned whether Alexander bears any responsibility for his father's death. No definitive conclusion is possible, but two aspects of the affair deserve comment. The first is that the longer Philip lived, the less secure became Alexander's position, especially if Philip fathered a son by a woman from the Macedonian elite. The second is that at the time of Philip's death Alexander was still extremely vulnerable, because of the various claims of other factions. In addition to the faction of Attalos and Cleopatra, there were also those who championed the claim of Amyntas IV, the child of Philip's older brother Perdikkas III. Philip had ruled as Amyntas's regent before declaring himself king more than twenty years earlier, but Amyntas was now near the age of thirty and could claim that the throne was rightfully his.

Alexander acted ruthlessly to assert his claim on the throne in the wake of Philip's death. The list of people executed in the early months of his reign includes Amyntas, Attalos, Cleopatra, Cleopatra's infant child, as well as two highborn Lynkestians named Heromenes and Arrabaios. Nor was his ruthlessness confined to dynastic rivals; when the Thebans responded to rumors that Alexander had died campaigning on Macedon's northern borders by going into revolt, Alexander marched south and sacked the city. Six thousand died and thirty thousand were sold into slavery, but in a gesture designed to show that he was no barbarian, the house of the poet Pindar (*c.* 520–*c.* 440 BC) was spared.

The Campaign in Asia

Alexander had secured his control of Macedonia by 334 BC and, as captain-general of the League of Corinth, had received a mandate to carry the war against the Persians into the enemy's territory. He crossed the Hellespont with an army numbering approximately 30,000 infantry and 5,000 horse and began the ten-year campaign of conquest that would define his legacy. There can be little doubt that Alexander was a brilliant tactician, but it is important to remember that Persia was a large, unwieldy territorial empire that was lightly ruled. The satrapal system was designed to guarantee the flow of tribute to the center and left defense in the hands of commanders who were trained to deal with uprisings and tax revolts, not foreign invasion. It was an easy target for a well-organized and determined attack from a Macedonian force that, despite being smaller, was superior in tactics and military technology. Two thousand years later Machiavelli understood such asymmetrical wars. His description of the strengths and weaknesses of the Ottoman empire applies equally to the Achaemenids:

Hence, he who attacks the Turk must bear in mind that he will find him united, and he will have to rely more on his own strength than on the revolt of others; but, if once the Turk has been conquered, and routed in the field in such a way that he cannot replace his armies, there is nothing to fear but the family of the prince, and, this being exterminated, there remains no one to fear, the others having no credit with the people; and as the conqueror did not rely on them before his victory, so he ought not to fear them after it.

(Machiavelli, *The Prince* 4, trans. Marriott)

In his first confrontation with the Persians, Alexander was still so far from the heartland of the empire that his opponents were the satraps of western Asia, not the Great King himself. At the Battle of the Granikos River in 334 BC in the Troad (northwestern modern-day Turkey), Alexander engaged the Persians with his cavalry while his infantrymen successfully forded the river. Once across, the Macedonian phalanx faced little resistance and, despite some fierce fighting between Alexander and the Persian commanders Spithridates and Rhoesaces, the Macedonians were overwhelmingly victorious. Alexander continued advancing through the region of modern-day Turkey, generally staying close to the coast. Many of the cities came over to him immediately: in quick succession he took Sardis, Ephesos, Miletos, and Halikarnassos. In Karia, the local queen, Ada, whose family had been satraps of the Persians but who also enjoyed a great deal of autonomy, took the unusual step of adopting Alexander as her son.

From the outset, Alexander strove to legitimize a campaign that was no more than military adventurism cloaked in the mantle of a vendetta. A propaganda war was being fought parallel to the military campaigns, with Alexander positioning himself as a liberator or a second Achilles, depending on the audience he was addressing. Keeping a copy of the *Iliad* by his pillow, for example, accorded with an image of the young king inspired by Homeric models, an image that made sense to Greeks and Macedonians. In such places as Egypt and Babylon, on the other hand, Alexander would present himself

as a legitimate successor of earlier dynasties, freeing subject people from the yoke of Persian rule. This need to make the campaign into something more than mere conquest expressed itself continuously in Alexander's behavior. For example, in 333 BC he marched his army through the Kilikian Gates in the southeastern corner of modern-day Turkey, and there engaged and defeated the Great King, Darius III (*c.* 380–330 BC), at the Battle of Issos. Having driven Darius from the field, capturing his wife, his daughters, and his personal baggage train, Alexander wrote to Darius and demanded that from now on the Persians address him as the Lord of Asia. Arrian records the letter Alexander sent to Darius:

Your ancestors invaded Macedonia and the rest of Greece and did us great harm, though we had done them no prior injury....As I have conquered in battle first your generals and satraps and now yourself and your own force, and am in possession of the country by the gift of heaven...you must regard me as Lord of Asia and come to me....And in future when you send to me, make your addresses to the king of Asia, and do not correspond as an equal, but tell me, as lord of your possessions, what you need.

(Arrian, *Anabasis* 2.14.8, trans. Brunt)

Evidently, punishing the Persians for the invasion of Greece, which had been Philip's justification for the war, was no longer enough. Alexander now aimed at possessing the suzerainty of Asia.

The speed of the Macedonian conquests almost defies comprehension, but even more stunning is how quickly Alexander responded to the new realities of power. In little more than one year of campaigning he had twice defeated the Persians in open battle and more than doubled the territory directly controlled by the Greeks. Still driven to go farther, he traveled down the coast of the eastern Mediterranean, taking the time to accept the surrender of Byblos and Sidon and to subjugate Tyre in 332 BC, which denied the Persians the seaports from which they could mount a rear attack upon the Aegean and Macedon itself. Not only did the campaign made good sense strategically, but also it allowed him to test a policy of tolerance that would prove useful in those areas where the Persians were seen as usurpers. The chief god of Tyre was Melqart, whom the Greeks identified with Herakles (see Chapter 10, p. 258). After capturing the city, Alexander spared those who had taken refuge in the god's temple and made sacrifices at the god's sanctuary as a devotee rather than as a conqueror. Gestures of this sort were facilitated by the fact that most of the religions of the Mediterranean were polytheistic and rarely defined by scriptures, meaning that a Greek and a Phoenician could find similarities between their gods without insisting that the other's gods were false. It also made it possible for Alexander, upon invading Egypt, to represent himself as pious, in contrast to such Persians as Cambyses, who was remembered for having dishonored the cult of Apis. The contrast went still further, as Alexander sought to reconfigure his leadership within the cultural context of each country. If the Achaemenids had trouble keeping control of Egypt which they had conquered,

Alexander would present his campaign not as the pacification of a conquered country, but as its restoration. He would honor the religious traditions of the Egyptians, so that while to the Greeks he remained Alexander, to the Egyptians he would be pharaoh.

The culmination of this policy of tolerance came with Alexander's visit to the oracle of Zeus Ammon at Siwah in the western Egyptian desert in early 332 BC. Zeus Ammon—a fusion of the Greek god Zeus and the Egyptian god Ammon—represented the spirit of syncretism that allowed Greek, Egyptian, and Libyan religion to blend. There is also evidence that this hybrid deity was known in the northern Aegean prior to Alexander's campaign, and a temple in his honor

13.1 Tetradrachm from Cyrene depicting Zeus Ammon, 480–435 BC. Silver, 17.16 grams

13.2 Tetradrachm of Lysimachos. Obverse: Alexander depicted with the horns of Ammon, 308–281 BC. Silver, 17.25 grams

was located at Aphytis in Chalkidike (in the northern Aegean) from the early fourth century BC. It is highly likely, therefore, that Alexander was familiar with Zeus Ammon even before he reached Egypt.

Accounts of what happened at Siwah vary, but Plutarch records that Alexander was greeted by the priest at the oracle as the "son of Zeus" ("*pai dios*"). Had the priest meant to say "My Child" ("*paidion*")? Or had Alexander arranged for an elaborate piece of political theater, which would allow him to start the rumor that Philip was his human father but that Zeus was his divine father? And did he believe the claim that he was divine? Those who regard Alexander as a megalomaniac point to the visit to Siwah as a significant stage in his disintegration, but flirting with divinity had been a part of the political posturing of the Greeks and Macedonians since the time of Lysander (see Chapter 12, p. 303). It was an age that believed in the superhuman powers of the divine man, the ***theios aner***. Alexander was neither the first not the last man of his age to blend a human and divine nature.

Alexander advertised his connection to Zeus Ammon by appropriating the god's most distinctive feature, ram's horns, for his own iconography. This can be seen by comparing the Cyrenean coin depicting the god (**13.1**) with the coin showing Alexander in profile (**13.2**). In both, the horn is prominently displayed. This fusion of elements is a fitting symbol for the merging of cultural identities that Alexander would attempt to accomplish.

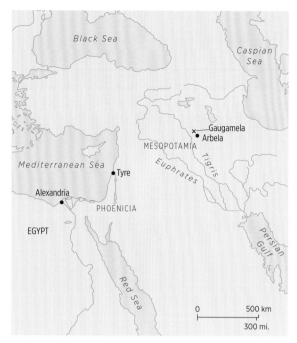

13.3 Map of Mesopotamia (Iraq), with location of Battle of Gaugamela, near Arbela (Irbil)

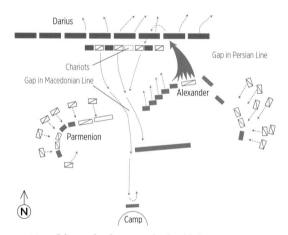

13.4 Map of the Battle of Gaugamela, the third major battle between Alexander the Great (blue) and the forces of the Persian king, Darius III (red). Solid blocks are infantry, white boxes with diagonal lines are cavalry.

13.5 (right) The Alexander Mosaic from the House of the Faun, Pompeii, *c.* 100 BC. The scene is usually identified as the moment Darius fled from the Battle of Gaugamela. The balance of power has shifted, and as the Persians are driven from the stage the Macedonians are poised to take control of the Achaemenid realm. The presence of the scene in a mosaic in Pompeii is evidence of the popularity of Alexander and his legendary status even in antiquity.

To Persia and Beyond

Having conquered Phoenicia and Egypt, Alexander resumed his advance eastwards, crossing through Mesopotamia until he faced the army of King Darius at the Battle of Gaugamela near Arbela (modern-day Irbil in Iraq) (**13.3**).

Reliable estimates put the Persian army at somewhere between 50,000 and 100,000 men, along with war elephants and scythed chariots (chariots with blades mounted on each side). The Macedonians fielded perhaps 30,000 heavy infantry, as well as light infantry, skirmishers, archers, and cavalry. In a typically daring move, Alexander advanced his line in **echelon** formation (staggered diagonally) to draw out the Persian line and create an opening in the center (**13.4**). Here, directly facing Darius, he drove a wedge of cavalry into the Persian line and caused them to break and flee. Only panicked calls for help from Parmenion on the Macedonian left prevented Alexander from pursuing Darius immediately.

Even so, the Macedonians had inflicted another shattering defeat upon the Achaemenid monarch. It would be the last encounter between Alexander and Darius. Arrian's account evokes the desperate atmosphere of the battle's aftermath:

After giving his horsemen rest until midnight, Alexander again advanced by a forced march towards Arbela, with the hope of seizing Darius there, together with his money and the rest of his royal property. He reached Arbela the next day, having pursued him altogether about seventy miles from the battlefield. But as Darius went on fleeing without taking any rest, he did not find him at Arbela. However the money and all the other property were captured, as was also the chariot of Darius a second time. His spear and bow were likewise taken, as had been the case after the battle of Issos.

(Arrian, *Anabasis* 3.15, trans. Chinnock)

In later times historians and artists would recognize that a seismic change had occurred when Darius fled from Gaugamela. Not only had the Great King been defeated for a second time, but this defeat represented what the Greeks regarded as the *kairos*, or critical moment, when the axis of the ancient world shifted (**13.5**). What had been a world in which the Achaemenids ruled a vast empire with the Greek states on its edge was now Alexander's world; Alexander had earned the epithet "great." The question to be answered was, how would he use that greatness?

Ruling the Achaemenid Empire

Alexander's generalship was based on audacity; how would he face the greater challenge of ruling? His treatment of Babylon, which he captured following Darius's defeat, illustrates his approach. He advanced upon the city in full battle order, using shock and awe tactics to intimidate the populace into submission,

yet once the gates of the city were opened to him he proved sensible to the feeling of his new subjects and ordered the restoration of temples, especially of the city's tutelary god, Bel. His appointment of Mazaios as governor was perhaps the most surprising step, since Mazaios was a Persian nobleman who had served as a satrap in western Asia, had been betrothed to Darius's sister, and had commanded the Persian left wing at Gaugamela. Alexander's decision to appoint him governor of Babylon therefore suggests that Alexander had already realized that governing the empire without the Achaemenid ruling class would be close to impossible, while favoring them offered the chance of continuity and stability. At the same time, it would be foolish to hand over military resources to the men he had only recently defeated, and so the command of troops stationed in Babylon was put into the hands of a Greek officer, Apollodoros of Amphipolis.

This separation of administrative and military spheres minimized the chance of any coordinated opposition arising. In similar fashion, the collection of tribute was assigned to yet another Greek, Asklepiodoros. Accordingly, local governance, military affairs, and financial administration were effectively separated into different compartments, allowing Persians and Greeks to share power. Another Persian nobleman, Mithrenes, who had surrendered to Alexander after the Battle of the Granikos River and subsequently fought on the Macedonian side, was rewarded with the governorship of Armenia. This represents a conspicuous feature of Alexander's system of governance: wherever possible he favored a continuation of the existing bureaucratic arrangements of the Achaemenid empire, installing loyal subordinates, whether Greek or Persian.

Maintaining the status quo, with the addition of Greeks and Macedonians in key roles, was pragmatic, but the scale of Alexander's conquests made dramatic, if not catastrophic, change unavoidable. It has been calculated, for example, that 200,000 talents entered the Greek world during his campaigns, the equivalent of billions of dollars in today's terms. The wealth encountered by the Macedonians was stupefying: recent estimates of the population of Mesopotamia around Alexander's time suggest the region had between 4.5 and 5 million inhabitants and produced 10,000 talents of agricultural revenue annually. Upon entering Babylon, the Macedonians came into possession of 5,000 talents' worth of

purple cloth and 40,000 talents of coined money. Considering that the tribute of the Delian League in 478 BC had been 480 talents, we can hardly avoid the conclusion that Alexander's campaigns generated a flow of wealth into the eastern Mediterranean of unparalleled proportions. With so much pure gold reaching the Mediterranean, the gold-to-silver standard dropped from 13:1 to 10:1. In the generations after Alexander, these economic repercussions, including inflation and fluctuating exchange rates, would continue to impact the royal economies of the Hellenistic world.

Such considerations were not Alexander's primary concern. After Gaugamela, Darius fled east, first into Persia and eventually into Baktria and Sogdiana in central Asia (**13.6**). Alexander continued a relentless pursuit, but before he could catch Darius, a Persian nobleman named Bessos killed the Great King and took his place. A Babylonian Chronicle recorded the bare details of these events in summer 330 BC:

[Month IV (July): Darius the king, from] his throne
    they removed him. Be[ssos]
[sat on the throne and Artaxerxes] as his name they named
    him, and Alexander and his troops
[pursued Bessos the rebel king. Alexander with] his few
    troops with the troops [of Bessos made battle.]
[Bessos] killed [Darius the king]. The Hanaean troops,
    his troops, which [...]
[... from Babylon (???) to (?)] Darius, the king, had gone,
    [were released.]

(*The Alexander Chronicle* (BCHP 1),
3–7, trans. Lendering)

Shortly afterwards Alexander caught up with Bessos, whom he mutilated and crucified. Having defeated the Achaemenids, taken control of their entire empire, and avenged the death of the last Great King, Darius, Alexander could fairly claim to be the legitimate and unchallenged ruler of the largest empire ever known.

The Eastern Provinces

The size and scale of Alexander's accomplishments only make the next phase of his conquests all the more difficult to explain. Rather than return either to a Persian capital—such as Susa, Persepolis, or Ekbatana—or to Macedon, Alexander chose to push further east, into the regions of modern-day

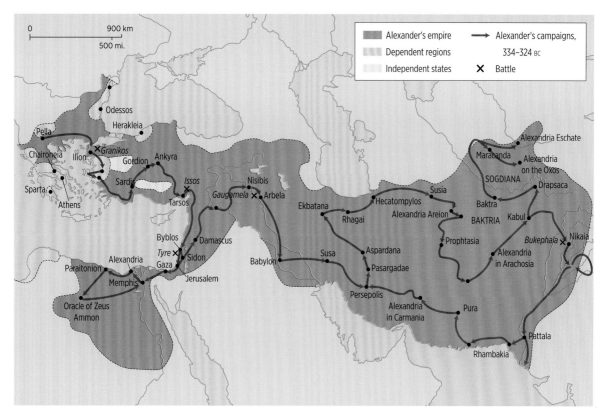

13.6 Map of the territory conquered by Alexander

Uzbekistan, Tajikistan, and Afghanistan, and up into the Hindu Kush. Ancient sources, many of which derive their information from men who marched with Alexander (such as Aristoboulos and Ptolemy, Alexander's bodyguard), fill their accounts of Alexander's campaigns in the Upper Satrapies with romantic tales of his marriage to Roxane, and his burning desire to outdo the hero Herakles by capturing the fort located on the rock of Aornos.

A more prosaic explanation for Alexander's continuing campaigns, however, is that Alexander was exploring the feasibility of marching further east. Precious trade goods, such as spices, emeralds, and silk, were brought across the Pamir Mountains along trade routes later known as the Silk Road, but to conquer the lands on the eastern, Chinese side of these mountains would have meant a massive investment of time and men. The passes into Xianjiang, such as the Irkeshtam Pass in Kyrgyzstan, traverse a beautiful but harsh landscape still referred to as the Roof of the World. Rather than risk such a dangerous venture, Alexander established a series of outposts on the western side of these mountains which he garrisoned with his veterans. These outposts of Hellenism were designed to protect and tax the trade coming overland from Xinjiang.

In time, many of these garrison towns (usually named "Alexandria") would grow into thriving settlements. In Afghanistan, for example, the city of Ai Khanum, whose ancient identity is still unknown, would boast city walls 3.2 kilometers (2 mi.) long, impressive towers, a large theater, a stoa, and a temple that blended Iranian and Greek design elements. The maxims of Delphi were carved over the entrance to the gymnasium, where the locals exercised under the watchful protection of Herakles (whose statue was found there) and read the works of Aristotle. Another fine example of Alexander's urbanization of central Asia is Khujand in Tajikistan, originally known as Alexandria Eschate ("the Farthest"). The city lies at the western end of the Fergana Valley and sits on a stretch of the Northern Silk Road running to Kokand and Kashgar, in western China.

The Greeks in these far reaches of Alexander's empire, sent there to secure the region and control

seen outside of Greece: the Graeco-Buddhist art of Gandhara. It was here that a Greek king, Menander (reigned *c.* 165–130 BC), would convert to Buddhism and win lasting glory not as a conqueror but as a sage known as Milinda. The coins of a second King Menander, who ruled perhaps a generation later, proudly identify him in Greek as King Menander the Just, while the reverse of these same coins say in Kharothshi: "Maharajasa Menadrasa Dharmikhasa, or Great King Menander, follower of the Dharma." The coin repeats the same message but to two different audiences, recalling the fluid interplay between identities that Alexander cultivated in his conquered territories. The coins of Menander also demonstrate a recognition of mutual intellectual interests: in the Hellenistic age Greek philosophers and Indian Buddhists were exploring similar philosophies of mind. Epicurus claimed that the just man was most free from disturbance, while the unjust was full of disturbance. This emphasis on avoiding disturbance, ***ataraxia***, also occurs in the popular Mahayana Buddhist text, *Heart of Perfect Mind Sutra*:

Bodhisattvas who practice
the Insight that Brings Us to the Other Shore
see no more obstacles in their mind,
and because there
are no more obstacles in their mind,
they can overcome all fear,
destroy all wrong perceptions
and realize Perfect Nirvana.   (trans. Thich Nhat Hanh)

13.7 Bodhisattva head. Pakistan, Kushan period (first–third century AD). Note that this sculpture dates to a time well after Greek domination of the region is over, but reflects the continuing influence of cultural contact with the Greek world. Schist, H: 32.5 cm (12¾ in.)

Statues of Lord Buddha from this region reveal the influence of the Greek canon, with the folds of drapery as carefully carved as we would find on a Greek statue. A Bodhisattva head from the Kushan period (**13.7**) is a fine example of the blending of Indian and Greek traditions that survived the end of the Greek kingdoms in Baktria and Sogdiana.

India and the Limit of Empire

By beginning the transformation of the intermittent trade across the Silk Road into a coherent trade network of cities linked by caravan routes, Alexander's policy of urbanization in Central Asia proved a more long-lasting legacy than his territorial conquests. Alexander, however, was always seeking the next battle. By 327 BC, he had turned south to the Indus

trade, were unwilling settlers, and after Alexander's death there were uprisings among the veterans who wished to come home. Other settlers came out from Greece, but the Greek political domination of the region was tenuous, especially after Seleukos I (*c.* 358–281 BC), the successor to Alexander who nominally controlled much of the territory east of Babylon, ceded the far eastern provinces to the Indian prince, Chandragupta Maurya. As political entities, these Graeco-Baktrian kingdoms would last no longer than about three hundred years, but the fusion of cultures in this region would produce perhaps the most beautiful expression of Greek culture ever

Valley where his relentless urge to fight other kings led him to conquer Taxiles and to face his last major foe, Porus, at the Jhelum River. The mythologizing of Alexander, begun by historians in his own entourage, fashioned these campaigns in northwestern India as confrontations between worthy and noble kings, but the reality is much less attractive. The region Alexander invaded was already the home of an ancient and venerable civilization, and one searches in vain for a point, much less a justification, for his expedition. His men evidently felt the same. Once Alexander had defeated Porus he immediately made plans for a descent into the Indus Valley. Appalled at the prospect of yet more fighting, and with no way of glutting Alexander's appetite for destruction,

his men rebelled and refused to continue. An apocryphal tale holds that Alexander wept for three days in his tent when he came to the end of his conquests, but far from weeping because he had no more worlds to conquer (as the legend has it), Alexander wept precisely because he knew that there were more worlds to conquer, from India to China. After Alexander's death, other Greeks would make the hard crossing into western China, but the Greek presence was only ever sporadic. Greek traders would still risk the journey along the Silk Road, however, along with Greek mercenaries from the kingdoms in Baktria, which perhaps explains why this beautiful textile found in Urumqi, in western China, probably represents a Greek warrior (**13.8**).

13.8 Detail of a wall hanging with warrior design, probably depicting a Greek warrior, *c.* second century BC–second century AD. Excavated from Sampul, Lop, Xinjiang Uygur Autonomous Region, China. Wool

Forced to turn back, Alexander engaged in a final campaign that was as costly as it was pointless. Marching his men through the Gedrosian desert in southern Iran, Alexander led his men on a series of sieges and attacks that risked his own and other men's lives for no strategic gain. His propaganda machine was able to mine the story of these battles for heroic vignettes—Alexander first across the wall, Alexander refusing to drink till every man had had his fill of water—but the reality was more prosaic. Alexander was a fighter and not suited to the business of governing; like his father, he was relentless in his need for a new enemy to beat. This was a pattern in the culture of the Macedonians and others from northern Greece. In the next generation, Pyrrhus of Epirus (319–272 BC) exhibited the same addiction to perpetual campaigning, leading his advisor, the philosopher Kineas, to ask Pyrrhus what he proposed to do if he conquered the Romans. Then conquer the Carthaginians, replied Pyrrhus. And then what, probed Kineas. Then my friend, we shall sit, relax, and enjoy our wine, replied Pyrrhus. And what, asked Kineas, is to prevent us from doing that right now? The point neatly made by the philosopher was that the kings of Macedon and Epirus lived for conquest. There was no deeper significance to their imperialism. It was war for the sake of war.

Death of Alexander and the Succession Crisis

Alexander had returned to Babylon by 324 BC. With ten years of fighting behind him, he would now be forced to wage peace, but no sooner had the realities of governing become clear than deep and possibly irreconcilable tensions within the army emerged. The Macedonian officer class treated each other as brothers—the elite cavalry regiment was known as "the Companions"—so that Alexander's pretensions to divinity were the subject of scorn. Here Alexander faced a dilemma: his Persian subjects were used to performing *proskynesis*, bowing before their superiors, but it was offensive to the Macedonians to bow before another man: the gesture appropriate to one audience was therefore an affront to the other.

There were other sources of conflict too. In February 324 BC, Alexander arranged for a mass wedding of Macedonian men and Persian women. Eighty of the Companions married the highest-ranking Persian women while Alexander legitimized and rewarded the marriages of 10,000 of his men, yet Alexander's plan to breed a master-race of Greeks and Iranians pleased no one: after Alexander's death virtually every one of the Companions repudiated his Persian bride. In fact, Alexander's attempts to introduce Persian customs only continued to infuriate his men, and in August 324 BC they mutinied. Alexander tried to stage-manage a reconciliation at Opis, close to modern-day Baghdad, where he announced that many of the veterans were being discharged with enough wealth to make them the envy of everyone in Macedon. Arrian recounts what happened next:

Alexander spoke these words with the clear intention of pleasing the Macedonians, but they felt Alexander now despised them and regarded them as completely unfit for service. It was not unreasonable for them to take exception to Alexander's words, and they had had many grievances throughout the expedition. There was the recurring annoyance of Alexander's Persian dress which pointed in the same direction, and the training of the barbarian "Successors" in the Macedonian style of warfare, and the introduction of foreign cavalry into the squadrons of the Companions. They could not keep quiet any longer, but all shouted to Alexander to discharge them from service and take his father on the expedition (by this insult they meant Ammon).

(Arrian, *Anabasis* 7.8, trans. Austin)

Alexander then berated the men and retired for two days to his tent, until finally his men implored his forgiveness. They were reconciled and Alexander organized a huge banquet to celebrate. The banquet was attended by nine thousand people from the various tribes and nations of the empire, and Alexander used the opportunity to pray for unity and harmony between the Macedonians and the Persians. Some have argued that Alexander was articulating an ideal of internationalism, but it is more likely that Alexander was attempting to set his empire on a more secure basis. His vision consisted of joint rule by the old and new masters of the empire.

Had Alexander lived, this fusion may have produced a truly fascinating world empire, but in June 323 BC Alexander died in Babylon. Whether the cause was malaria, typhoid, influenza, heavy drinking, or poison we cannot say; Alexander's death was as enigmatic as his life. He was a brilliant innovator in

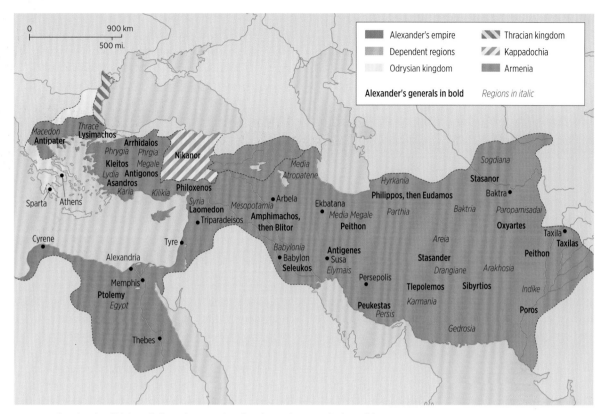

13.9 Map showing the division of Alexander's empire after the Settlement of Triparadeisos, 321 BC

military tactics, yet his reign was marked by purges and executions that suggest a level of deep insecurity and paranoia. At a drunken feast in Samarkhand, for example, a Companion named Kleitos rebuked the sycophants who were praising Alexander's exploits and pointed out that Philip's accomplishments had been as notable as Alexander's, a provocation that led Alexander to kill Kleitos with a javelin. The bond between Alexander and the ordinary soldiers of the Macedonian army was fierce, but potential rivals, such as Parmenion and his son, Philotas, were ruthlessly eliminated. Ultimately, attempts to psychoanalyse Alexander are futile, since we must rely on later and often unreliable sources and Alexander's own propaganda. Instead we are left with a breathtaking ten-year campaign that cost tens of thousands of lives but completely altered the shape of Greek history. For the next three hundred years, the entire eastern Mediterranean, Mesopotamia, modern-day Iran, and much of central Asia would be ruled by Graeco-Macedonian elites. This was the Hellenistic world, and it was a world entirely created by Alexander the Great.

The birth of the new world order was not easy. Alexander had died thousands of miles from Macedon and left a pregnant wife, Roxane; a mentally deficient half-brother, Arrhidaios; an army of 10,000 veterans under Krateros somewhere on the road back to Macedon; an army in Babylon of many more thousands of men blindly loyal to his family; and a cadre of ambitious officers eager to carve out their own portions from the carcass of Alexander's empire. Over the next few years meetings were held—first in Babylon and then in 321 BC in Triparadeisos—at which a series of arrangements were made that would shape the politics of the eastern Mediterranean (**13.9**).

Alexander was succeeded by Arrhidaios, who adopted the regnal name of Philip III. Roxane gave birth to a son, Alexander IV (323–310 BC), who was put in the charge of a guardian, Perdikkas. Antipater, one of Alexander's generals, was confirmed as regent in Macedon, and would eventually be succeeded by his son Kassander. The rest of the Triparadeisos agreement was a more straightforward distribution of territories, in which the old satrapies of the Achaemenid empire were assigned to various Greek and Macedonian commanders, some of whom were little more than rulers on paper, and most of whom disappear from history without leaving any dynastic legacy. The arrangements from Triparadeisos proved to be ephemeral because the reality was that most of the satrapal territories had to be reconquered if they were to be held by Alexander's Successors (the Diadochoi). This required a constant refiguring of alliances and plunged the eastern Mediterranean into a fresh round of wars. These wars of the Diadochoi would last for the next generation, during which time both Philip Arrhidaios and Alexander IV died: on December 25, 317 BC, Philip Arrhidaios was executed by Alexander's mother Olympias, and in 310 the twelve-year-old Alexander IV was murdered by Kassander. The bloodline of Philip and Alexander was gone, and the notion that the powerful Macedonian generals who ruled Alexander's empire were merely satraps for a supreme ruler was now revealed to all as an inconvenient fiction. Within the next five years most of the Diadochoi assumed the title of king.

The Ptolemies

Of the new Hellenistic kingdoms, that of the Ptolemies is the best known. A trusted Companion of Alexander, Ptolemy I Soter (or "Savior," *c*. 367–283/2 BC) as the founder of the dynasty was known), had been a bodyguard of the great man. In later sources Ptolemy is often depicted as almost another Alexander, but Ptolemy lived to write his memoirs and is one of the principal sources for later writers, so if he emerges as a hero of Alexander's campaigns we should hardly be surprised. What is certain is that Ptolemy deployed enormous skill in navigating the complexities of power and politics in the Hellenistic Age. Perhaps his smartest insight was that Egypt could be sealed off from much of the rest of Mediterranean world. To the west lay desert; to the east, desert and the Red Sea; to the south, cataracts (unnavigable stretches of shallow water); and to the north, the great Nile Delta. Movement throughout the kingdom essentially consisted of sailing up and down the Nile, which was easily controlled.

Ptolemy's reign over Egypt began aggressively. Knowing that a connection with Alexander conferred legitimacy, he raided Alexander's funeral cortège as it was slowly carrying the king's body from Babylon back to Macedonia. Alexander's corpse was kidnapped and brought back to Ptolemy's new capital, Alexandria, where Alexander's sarcophagus was installed in a monumental funerary complex. The body of Alexander, in the style of such pharaohs as Ramses, was surrounded by buildings housing holy writings and sacred texts. Under Ptolemy's successor, Ptolemy II (308–246 BC), this complex would be expanded, as texts from Athens and elsewhere were added, eventually forming the Library of Alexandria. The Library was one of the greatest institutions of the ancient world, an institution that owes its origins to a Greek inflection of an Egyptian practice.

The Library, in time, would emerge as the premier cultural institution of the Hellenistic Age. The head librarians included the poets Callimachus and Theocritus, who were responsible for some of the most influential poems of the period. Callimachus composed beautifully crafted hymns to the Olympian gods, taking an old genre and revitalizing it for the new age, in which the Greeks found themselves living around the Mediterranean and beyond in a diaspora vastly greater than before. For example, in his *Hymn to Apollo*, he uses the Doric associations of Apollo Karneios (a very early version of Apollo worshiped in Sparta and other Dorian regions) to link the Doric Greeks of old, venerable Sparta with the colonial Greeks of Thera and Cyrene, his own hometown in Libya. Using myth and geography, he gives a new definition to the geopolitics of the age.

Similar concerns occur in Theocritus's poetry. In Idyll 15, for example, Theocritus satirizes the accents of some Alexandrian matrons, whose broad Doric Greek was apparently quite distinctive:

SECOND STRANGER: For goodness sake, ladies, put
    a sock in it! What a cackle! Those broad alphas are
    too much!
PRAXINOA: Aargh! Where's this bloke from? What's it
    to you if that's how we talk? Order your slaves, not
    us! You're talking to a pair of Syracusans, thank you
    very much! We're Corinthians, as a matter of fact, by
    descent, just like Bellerophon. We talk Peloponnesian.
    Dorians, I assume, are allowed to speak Doric?
            (Theocritus, *Idyll* 15.87–94, trans. McInerney)

The poem is certainly funny, but also illustrative. The Hellenistic Age saw the emergence of a new form of Greek known as ***koine***, meaning "common," because it was spoken so widely around the eastern

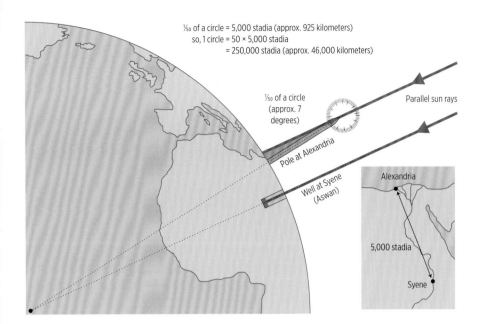

⅟₅₀ of a circle = 5,000 stadia (approx. 925 kilometers)
so, 1 circle = 50 × 5,000 stadia
= 250,000 stadia (approx. 46,000 kilometers)

⅟₅₀ of a circle
(approx. 7
degrees)

Parallel sun rays

Pole at Alexandria

Well at Syene
(Aswan)

Alexandria

5,000 stadia

Syene

13.10 Diagram illustrating Eratosthenes' calculation of the circumference of the Earth.

Mediterranean in all the communities of Greeks and those who aspired to be accepted by the Greeks. Greek then, as English now, served as a universal language, yet at the same time—just as in the context of recent globalization—older, distinctive, regional accents and dialects vigorously asserted themselves. Two episodes, however, demonstrate the importance of this new common language. The first is a petition written by a villager in Egypt to the regional governor complaining of his mistreatment at the hands of local thugs. The complaint, written in Greek by the village clerk, claims that the villager's complaints have fallen on deaf ears because he doesn't speak Greek; for his complaint to be heard, he had to have it translated into Greek. The second concerns a visit by the Greek philosopher Karneades (214–129 BC) to Rome in 155 BC, when he gave a series of public performances, delivering highly polished rhetorical speeches. On the first day he lectured on justice and the next day he spoke on the impossibility of justice. Outraged, the Romans expelled him. The story is sometimes taken to illustrate the gap between literal Romans, suspicious of rhetoric, and crafty Greeks, capable of arguing both sides of the same case, but the more significant point is that the Roman audience clearly understood the speeches delivered in Greek. If the Roman lower classes included many who had entered the Roman world as slaves from the Greek world, it also included many well-educated Romans who spoke and read Greek fluently.

Alexandria in particular became a generator of Greek culture, from the poetry of Apollonius—who composed a new epic for the age, the *Argonautica*, featuring an uncertain and anxious hero, Jason—to the scientific studies of Eratosthenes, who calculated the circumference of the Earth. Eratosthenes did this by measuring the angle of the shadow cast by a stick at Alexandria at precisely the same time as the sun shone directly down a well, casting no shadow, 5,000 stades (*c.* 575 mi) away at Aswan. Expressed as an arc of a circle, the distance allowed him to calculate the entire circle, or the Earth's circumference (**13.10**). Recent attempts to tease out Eratosthenes' reasoning and to render his measurements into modern equivalents suggest that his final calculation was within 10 percent of the correct figure, quite an accomplishment for a man whose most sophisticated instrument was a stick.

Greek Kings, Egyptian Kingdom

The Ptolemaic kingdom was, however, also Egyptian, and the living continuation of a cultural tradition much older than the Greeks. How did the Ptolemies reconcile the dual nature of their kingdom? The answer involved strict control of the population and the economy on the one hand and a powerful manipulation of Egyptian religion on the other. The economy inherited by the Ptolemies was a planned economy. Royal estates and temple properties alike were worked by peasants who owed a debt of corvée

13.11 Ptolemy as Egyptian pharaoh. Basalt, H: 64 cm (2 ft 1¼ in.)

labor to the crown, often in addition to a portion of their own produce. (Such arrangements, according to which peasants owed a fixed amount of unpaid labor to the crown, had long been a part of Egyptian society.) The regular inundation of the Nile and the close proximity of all productive land to the river made it possible to predict production, and the Ptolemies simply refined a system of close state control, setting production targets and sending officials to supervise every aspect of the rural economy, from planting to harvest. Instructions sent to a financial officer in the reign of Ptolemy II covered every imaginable topic: the registration of cattle (especially during the wet season); the transportation of goods to Alexandria;

inspections of canals, trees and calves; audits; and so forth. The degree of micromanagement is illustrated by this injunction concerning weaving: "Let all the looms which are idle be transported to the metropolis of the *nome* (administrative district), deposited in the store-house, and sealed up."

There were, however, some changes. New crops— such as grape and garlic—were introduced, and under the Ptolemies a great deal of land in the Fayyum, the depression west of the Nile, was reclaimed and distributed as estates to former military officers, policemen, and the army of bureaucrats who were part of the system. Demographic studies of the villages in the Fayyum, such as Berenike, reveal that outside Alexandria the Egyptians generally owned smaller plots of land and lived in smaller households. The Greeks, by contrast, lived on much larger estates, with households consisting of Greek families, their slaves and dependents. The picture we get from the thousands of papyrus documents preserved in Egypt's dry climate is of a system primarily devoted to maintaining production and royal revenue in which the Greeks exploited the land mercilessly. The system was rife with abuse, and this complaint of a group of stonemasons is typical:

To Kleon the architect, greetings from the dekatarchoi of the quarry-men from the landing place. We are being wronged by Apollonios the superintendent who has set us to work on the hard stone, not dividing it between us and the others, while he has assigned his own men the soft stone. As it is, we are being ruined by wearing out the edges of our tools. We beg you, so that we may obtain our rights, to measure out how much extra hard stone we have cut, so that it may be imposed in addition on the 140 quarry-men and we may not be oppressed. Farewell. [Address] To Kleon. [Docket] The dekatarchoi from the landing-place.

(SB XVIII 13881, trans. Bagnall and Derow)

Perhaps tellingly, petitions and tax dockets are the most common documents from Hellenistic Egypt, testifying to the tight control the Ptolemies exercised on every aspect of economic activity. The Ptolemaic economy was a continuation and extension of the centralized economy of the pharaohs, and it served the same purpose: maximizing the revenues to the crown. The corollary of this continuity was that the Ptolemies presented themselves to their Egyptian subjects as pharaohs, carving their names in cartouches (a loop that surrounds royal names in hieroglyphic writing) on the walls of pharaonic temples, and creating monumental sculptures that depicted them wearing the royal headdress of the pharaohs (**13.11**). Such imagery suggested that the Macedonians were simply the latest dynasty in a country that had been ruled by pharaonic dynasties for thousands of years. Following the same policy, the Ptolemies favored the traditional cults of the Egyptians: the Apis bull was still revered at Memphis, and festivals honoring the Egyptian gods were held according to the same religious calendar as in pharaonic times. The practical advantage of this was to win the support of the priestly caste whose authority was critical to the stability of Ptolemaic rule;

for an illiterate peasant who never left his village, the only difference between life under a pharaoh and life under Ptolemy would probably have been that the tax collector now had a Greek name. In Alexandria—polyglot, cosmopolitan, sophisticated, and convinced that it was the center of civilization—the Ptolemies went one step further and fashioned a new god for the age: Serapis. Blended from Apis and Osiris on the Egyptian side, the new god also resembled a version of Zeus and the popular fourth-century-BC god Asklepios (**13.12**). A mixture of old and new, of Egyptian and Greek, manufactured to appeal to Greeks and non-Greeks alike, he is the perfect face of Hellenism.

13.12 Bust of Serapis, the god favored by the Ptolemies. The god is frequently depicted, as here, wearing a *kalathos*, a symbol of fertility.

The Seleukids

The second of the major Hellenistic empires was the kingdom founded by Seleukos Nikator (c. 358–281 BC) ("the Victorious"). Originally a general in Alexander's army, he was awarded Babylon in the division of spoils at Triparadeisos but was driven out in the wars of the Diadochoi by Antigonus and was only able to take the city as a result of military aid from Ptolemy in 312 BC. Once established in Babylon, however, he began aggressively annexing territory all the way to Syria and east into the Upper Satrapies. By the time of his death in 281, his empire encompassed 3,000,000 square kilometers (1,200,000 sq. mi.) of territory (**13.13**), although his smartest decision may have been to cede the farthest eastern provinces to the Indian prince Chandragupta Maurya in exchange for five hundred war elephants. The Seleukids ruled an empire that bordered the Mediterranean, as did the Ptolemies, and just as Alexandria was located on the cusp of the Ptolemies' Nile-based kingdom, so too the Seleukids built new cities (such as Antioch and Seleukia) on the Orontes River, far from the old capitals of their realm in Babylonia and beyond but close to the Mediterranean coast. One historian has noted that the location of their cities suggests that these Hellenistic kings remained obsessed with the Mediterranean, as if they might have to quit their kingdoms and return to Macedon at any time.

The territory of the Seleukid realm shrank steadily over the next two centuries, usually seen as a mark of the kingdom's weakness. Ramsay and Erickson write, "Loss of territory and thus resources and manpower, diminished political clout in the face of Roman interference, and the Seleukid dynasty's apparent slide into dissolute luxury all make their impression upon the historian." The Seleukids, however, may also have understood Alexander's eastern policies better than modern-day historians. What need was there to undertake the expensive business of controlling vast amounts of relatively unproductive land, when you could concentrate on key nodes within a flourishing trade network? The key to real wealth in central Asia lay not in oil, wine, grain, or other agricultural staples, but in controlling and taxing the flow of luxury goods. This was why the Ptolemies developed a Red Sea port at Berenike and why the Seleukids concentrated on Palmyra and Dura Europus, the sites where the caravans emerged from the desert.

The Seleukids also understood, as did the Ptolemies, that the heartland of their empire, Babylonia, was an ancient region in which royal

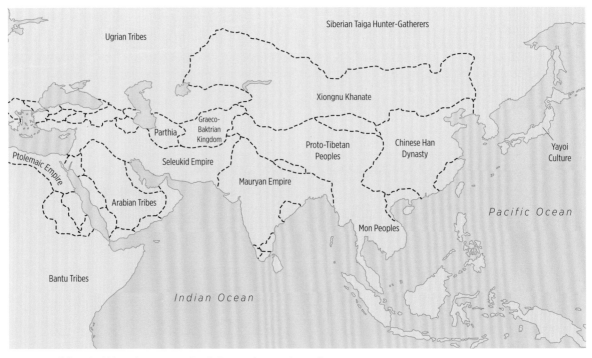

13.13 Map of the Seleukid empire *c.* 200 BC, in relation to other empires and states

power and divine authority had always gone hand in hand. Maintaining the goodwill of the priestly families was therefore crucial, and the restoration of temples was the most tangible expression of this policy of accommodation. Seleukos was succeeded by his son Antiochos I (*c.* 324–261 BC), who boasted of fashioning the first bricks for the restoration of Babylon's great ziggurat temples:

I am Antiochos, the great king, the legitimate king, the king of the world, the king of Babylon, the caretaker of the temples of Esagila and Ezida, the first born son of King Seleukos, the Macedonian, king of Babylon.

(ANET 3 317, trans. Pritchard)

The message was also conveyed by the chronicles kept by the Babylonian priests, who recorded the restoration project as follows:

...to the Bab[ylon]ians (of) [the assembly of Esa]gila he [gav]e and an offering on the ruin of Esagila they [arran]ged. On the ruin of Esagila he fell. Oxen and an offering in the Greek fashion he made. The son of the king, his troops, his wagons, and his elephants removed the debris of Esagila.

(Ruin of Esagila Chronicle, obverse ll. 3–8, trans. van der Spek and Finkel)

The Seleukid realm, however, was not only vastly bigger than Egypt, but also contained many different nationalities and languages. Administering the empire with a view to extracting wealth in tribute and taxes was therefore more complicated for the Seleukids than the Ptolemies, whose subject population of Egyptian peasants was broadly homogeneous. Some tributary regions, particularly in the north and south where the Seleukid empire bordered areas inhabited by nomads, remained virtually autonomous, provided they supplied troops, horses, and camels to the Seleukid army. In the Aegean and western Asia, however, where Seleukid kings (such as Antiochos III) persistently sought to establish control, dealing with a mosaic of Greek states presented a special challenge. Here the Seleukids adopted a very different posture, addressing the Greeks as benefactors. For example, when the Athymbrians sent an embassy to King Seleukos asking to have their tax-exempt status confirmed, the king wrote back:

[For our policy is always] through benefactions [to please] the citizens [of the Greek cities and by no means least] with reverence to join in increasing [the honors] of the gods, [so that we may be the object of good-will] transmissible for all time [to those who come after] us. We are convinced that even in previous times we have given [many great] proofs of [our] personal [reverence, and] now also, [wishing] to be consistent with [our actions from the beginning], [we grant] to all the temples which [have received the right of inviolability—].

(RC 9, trans. Bagnall and Derow)

Benefactions became the principal mode of competition among the Hellenistic kingdoms. The gifts they gave, from donations of grain during times of famine to subventions to pay for schools and such buildings as stoas (the broad porticoes favored by the Greeks as all-purpose civic buildings), allowed these powerful kings to position themselves as the philanthropic benefactors of the Greek states. In fact, older religious and cultural centers, such as Delphi, Delos, and Athens, were the main recipients of this generosity. The Hellenistic kings engaged in competitive gift-giving, representing a contest for legitimacy that paralleled the wars they fought over territory. Perhaps the most successful state in these propaganda wars was the kingdom of Pergamon, located in western Asia Minor.

Pergamon

The kingdom of Pergamon was founded by a eunuch named Philetairos (*c.* 343–263 BC). He had been placed in charge of a royal treasury located on the high akropolis of Pergamon by Lysimachos (*c.* 360–281 BC), a Successor of Alexander who had carved out a kingdom in Thrace and controlled the Hellespont. No doubt Lysimachos believed that a eunuch would be less likely to harbor dreams of establishing a dynasty, but he was proved wrong. When Lysimachos was killed at the Battle of Korupedion in 281 BC, Philetairos asserted his independence and founded a dynasty marked by an unusual degree of internal harmony. He was succeeded by his nephew Eumenes I, who in turn was succeeded by his cousin, Attalos I. Safe in their impregnable fortress, the Attalid kings transformed Pergamon from an insignificant fort into a cultural center that rivaled Alexandria.

One indication of their success was the buildings that they endowed in the major cities and sanctuaries of Greece. Notable among these was the Stoa of Attalos, a gift from Attalos II to the city of Athens in the middle of the second century BC (**13.14**). This stoa, which was rebuilt in the 1950s by a modern benefactor, John D. Rockefeller, delineates the eastern side of the Athenian Agora, and originally looked directly across toward the civic buildings on the western side of the Agora. If the old buildings represented democracy and Classical culture, the new one embodied royal patronage and Hellenistic culture.

The Attalids also employed architecture in Pergamon to proclaim their legitimacy as the protectors and continuators of Greek culture. For example, the temple of Athena on the Pergamon akropolis was entered through a Propylon that gave the same three-quarter profile of the temple as a visitor to the Athenian Akropolis might experience after passing through the Propylaia and seeing the Parthenon. On a lower terrace of the city, the Attalids also erected a monumental altar, known as the "Great Altar," with a frieze running around the top that told the story of Telephos, the mythical founder of Pergamon. This allowed the Attalids to connect with the great web of Greek myth in order to legitimize their rule. On the steps leading up to the altar, the sculptors carved statues in deep relief depicting the victory of the gods over the Titans, a traditional motif in Greek temple architecture that aligned the Greeks with the gods, symbolizing the dominance of order over all that was monstrous and chaotic. But instead of simply seeing the statues on top of a temple wall telling a story, the Pergamene reliefs are at eye level and are life-size, meaning that one engages with the

13.14 The Stoa of Attalos, Athens. Original built *c.* 150 BC, rebuilt *c.* 1950 AD

13.15 West frieze staircase, Great Altar of Pergamon, depicting the figures of Nereus, Doris, a Giant, and Okeanos spilling onto the steps, *c.* 160 BC. Marble

scenes almost as if one were not a spectator but a participant (**13.15**). The Great Altar perfectly captures the theatricality and monumentality that were characteristic of the Hellenistic Age.

The Attalids faced real threats from invading Gallic tribes in the middle of the third century BC, and the victory of Attalos I, who reigned from 241 to 197 BC, was commemorated by a monument adorned with sculptures of dying Gauls. Casting himself as a protector of Greek civilization, Attalos used the victory to justify adopting the title of king. His kingdom would remain a powerful independent state until 133 BC, when the last king of the dynasty, Attalos III, bequeathed Pergamon to the people of Rome.

The Coming of Rome

The most significant development in the political history of the Hellenistic world was the emergence of Rome as a Mediterranean power. At the time of the Macedonian overthrow of the Achaemenid empire, the Romans occupied a town on the banks of the Tiber in central Italy. According to their traditions, written down in annals kept by priests and family historians, they had expelled their Etruscan kings and founded a republic in 509 BC, exactly the same year in which the Athenians expelled their tyrants and founded their democracy. Sandwiched between the older, venerable Etruscan culture to the north, and the region of Magna Graecia to the south, where many of the cities were Greek-speaking, the Romans had been open to cultural influence from all sides for two hundred years. Their first military contact with the Greeks and Macedonians occurred in the early years of the third century BC, when Pyrrhus of Epirus, eager to emulate and perhaps outdo Alexander, chose to invade southern Italy and Sicily. He was invited by the people of Tarentum to join them in opposing Roman expansion into southern Italy, and in response to their invitation, landed in Tarentum in 280 BC

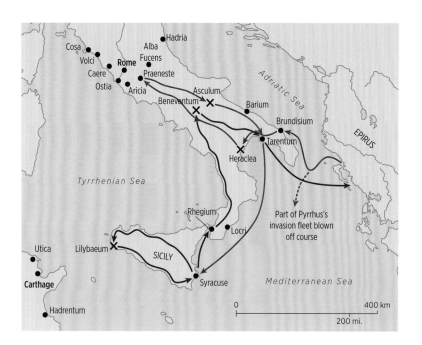

13.16 Map of Pyrrus's campaigns

Campaign of Pyrrhus from Epirus to Sicily

Campaign of Pyrrhus from Sicily to Epirus

with 20 war elephants, 3,000 cavalry, 2,000 archers, 500 slingers, and 20,000 soldiers. A map shows that this campaign was simply the next after his various campaigns in northern Greece (**13.16**), but what maps cannot show is the great disparity between the invading force and the Romans he encountered. At the Battle of Heraclea, in 280 BC, Rome lost 7,000 men, Pyrrhus 3,000. A year later, at Asculum, Rome lost 6,000 men and Pyrrhus 3,500. Each man lost weakened Pyrrhus to such a degree that in 278 Pyrrhus broke off the Italian campaign and crossed into Sicily to fight the Carthaginians.

The Roman perspective of these losses was different. According to Polybios, Roman manpower in the third century BC consisted each year of two consular armies of approximately 20,000 Roman infantry and 1,200 horse, two allied armies comprised of another 20,000 infantry and 2,000 horse as well as Sabine and Etruscan forces, on whom the Romans could call, of 50,000 infantry and 4,000 horse. Polybios relates that the Romans kept lists of those eligible for military service and that according to these rolls 250,000 soldiers from Rome and Campania could be mustered. If allies from further north rallied to the Romans, this meant the addition of another 40,000 soldiers. The Romans also kept in reserve 20,000 infantry and 1,500 horse plus 30,000 allied infantry and 2,000 horse. With other reserves and frontier forces added, the total number of men—

Roman or Italian—who were available could have amounted to more than 300,000 infantry and 10,000 horse. Of course, nowhere near this number was put in to the field for any one battle, but it explains why Pyrrhus could win battles but not the war: the Romans relentlessly sacrificed the lives of tens of thousands to defend their city. The Hellenistic east had had its first taste of the Roman war machine, and after the Battle of Beneventum in 275 BC, Pyrrhus would return to Greece with 8,000 infantry and 500 horse. His campaigns against Rome gave rise to the phrase "a Pyrrhic victory," meaning a victory won at a ruinous cost. Meanwhile, in 272, Rome sacked Tarentum, signaling the extension of a Roman sphere of influence into southern Italy, but also beginning the Hellenization of Rome as goods, art, and people from the Greek world were brought to Rome.

By the end of the second century BC, Rome's expanding power had brought it into conflict with the other great imperial presence in the western Mediterranean, Carthage. The two powers came into conflict in Sicily, the contact zone midway between them. Rome's victory in the First Punic War (264–246 BC) led to the incorporation of Sicily into Rome's territorial domain, its first overseas province. In the Second Punic War (218–202 BC), the Carthaginian general Hannibal (c. 247–c. 181 BC) inflicted crushing defeats on the Romans at Cannae, Trasimene, and Trebbia, yet once again the Romans managed to put massive armies into the field year after year. The defeat of Hannibal at the Battle of Zama in 202 BC freed the Romans to turn their attention to the eastern Mediterranean. In the east, meanwhile, the two principal opponents the Romans encountered were Philip V of Macedon (238–179 BC) and Antiochos III (c. 241–187 BC) of Syria. Historians still debate the underlying causes of Rome's expansion east, and causes of conflict with these Hellenistic princes. Interpretations depend on whether one approaches this from a Roman or a Greek point of view.

The Roman War Machine and Hellenistic Diplomacy

In the third and second centuries BC, Rome was being transformed into a war machine: policy was largely hammered out in the Senate, where former consuls, generals, and the heads of the great families chose to identify Rome's foes and to make the alliances that would benefit Rome's interests. These war policies and alliances were endorsed by the popular assemblies, not only because they were stacked in favor of the wealthy and influenced by Roman patronage, but also because war brought booty: the men who went off to war as poor farmers might hit the jackpot and return home with bags of silver and gold. The Roman nobility saw war as their personal testing ground and the means to winning *gloria* and office, meaning that war was always preferable to peace. Every year a fresh batch of praetors and consuls came into office, knowing that that year was their opportunity to win their place in Rome's catalogue of victorious generals. And behind all this lay all those territories subject to Rome, such as the colonies and the Italian allies, who provided manpower instead of paying monetary tribute. The Romans were able to call on large numbers of men who were increasingly loyal to their commanders because they brought them land and spoils from their successful campaigns. The Roman republican system, in other words, was well designed to fight wars.

On the Greek side, however, the Hellenistic world developed a diplomatic language and military practice over the third century BC that made international politics a matter of continuous negotiation, gift-giving, alliance, marriage, invasion, and retreat, but the Romans did not play by these rules. In short, Hellenistic kings and Roman generals approached the international politics of the eastern Mediterranean

with fundamentally different aims and objectives. When Antiochos III marched into Greece in 192 BC to liberate the Greeks, his campaign was an attempt to extend his territory. The Syrian War fought by the Romans against him, by contrast, was an opportunity for glory for the Roman commanders Manius Acilius Glabrio and Lucius Cornelius Scipio, and the chance to defeat a wealthy enemy. In the Peace of Apamea, signed in 188, after Antiochos's defeat a year earlier, Rome took 15,000 talents in reparations, but annexed no territory. The best illustration of these conflicting outlooks is the events of 196. The Romans, having defeated Hannibal, had sent armies to fight Philip V of Macedon (who had been an ally of Hannibal). The Romans were victorious, and in 196, at the Isthmian Festival that year the Roman commander Titus Quinctius Flamininus had the following proclamation read to the Greeks:

"The senate order and Titus Quintius the proconsul having overcome King Philip and the Macedonians, leave the following peoples free, without garrisons and subject to no tribute and governed by their countries' laws—the Corinthians, Phokians, Lokrians, Euboians, Phthiotic Achaians, Magnesians, Thessalians, and Perrhaibians." At once at the very commencement a tremendous shout arose, and some did not even hear the proclamation, while others wanted to hear it again. But the greater part of the crowd, unable to believe their ears and thinking that they were listening to the words as if in a dream owing to the event being so unexpected, demanded loudly, each prompted by a different impulse, that the herald and bugler should advance into the middle of the stadium and repeat the announcement, wishing, as I suppose, not only to hear the speaker, but to see him owing to the incredible character of his proclamation.

(Polybios, *Histories* 18.46, trans. Paton *et al.*)

There were no Roman troops in Greece by 194 BC; the promise of freedom was genuine. In the early second century BC, Rome was still resistant to the idea of direct rule of significant stretches of territory not originally considered to be Roman land. Yet the continued dynastic trouble in Macedon and further east inevitably drew Rome back again and again. Although Philip V had been defeated, the Romans soon faced fresh opposition in Macedon from his son Perseus, whom they duly defeated at the Battle of Pydna in 168. Macedon was subsequently partitioned into four states, but when this did not end the threat of rebellion, the Romans annexed the region in 146 and incorporated Macedon as a province of Rome under direct control of a Roman governor. In the same year, equally exasperated by the shifting alliances of Aitolians, Achaians, and Spartans in southern Greece, the Romans sacked Corinth, and eventually incorporated all of Greece south of Macedon into the new province of Achaia.

This gradual expansion of Roman influence further east witnessed a more profound transformation of Rome than of the Greeks. Conquest brought Greek philosophers and poets to Rome, as well as Greek artworks. Livius Andronicus, for example, translated the *Odyssey* from Greek into Latin, but contact with the Hellenistic east was also transforming the elite of Roman society as they spent more and more time negotiating (and fighting) with Hellenistic kings. A graphic illustration of the shifting roles Romans were required to adopt in relation to the Hellenistic kings is the episode in 168 BC when King Antiochos IV marched through Gaza to attack Egypt. When Antiochos arrived in Egypt, he found a Roman magistrate, Gaius Popillius Laenas, waiting for him with a message from the Senate of Rome, Ptolemy VIII's ally, ordering Antiochos to quit the country. When the king demurred, Laenas drew a line in the sand and demanded an answer before the king stepped out of the circle. Antiochos withdrew. Facing Rome, the most powerful Hellenistic prince had blinked. But if a single Roman magistrate, representing the Roman Republic, was expected to negotiate on equal terms with the kings of the eastern Mediterranean, what would happen once Romans began acting as the equals of these Hellenistic potentates?

Expansion of the Roman Empire

Pergamon had been incorporated as the Roman province of Asia by 133 BC, bequeathed by its last king, Attalos III. Bithynia soon followed in 74, also bequeathed to Rome by its last king, Nikomedes IV. Rome was drawn even more fully into eastern affairs in 88 when Mithridates VI of Pontos orchestrated the slaughter of eighty thousand Italian traders throughout Asia Minor. The event signaled a growing resentment of Rome's dominance, but also led to a fresh round of campaigning by Roman generals, notably Lucius Cornelius Sulla, who defeated Mithridates' army at Chaironeia and also sacked Athens mercilessly.

In all, the Greek east was becoming a persistent problem for Rome. On the one hand, the diplomatic complexity of the region and the increasing demands on the Romans to make alliances with a dizzying array of kings made it almost impossible to fashion a policy of coherent engagement, yet the opportunities for wealth and glory were an ever-present incentive for commanders to become involved in aggressive military campaigns. It was also true that these commanders were becoming increasingly influential in politics both home and abroad, a situation that created tension with the republican nature of Rome, as is illustrated by the career of Pompey. After three years of successful campaigning, Pompey presented the Roman Senate in 64 BC with 480,000,000 sesterces and a completely redrawn map of the east that would bring in 340,000,000 sesterces in annual revenue, almost doubling the taxes of the Roman state in one moment. Yet the Senate rejected this settlement, known as the eastern *acta*, precisely because it meant ratifying the accomplishments of one man and acknowledging his preeminent status.

The Hellenistic east provided Roman commanders with an opportunity to play out their competitions for status, honor, and recognition on a massive scale. Eventually, in the last generation of the Roman Republic, these competitions would pit Caesar against Pompey, then Antony against Octavian. The Senate proved incapable of mounting an effective resistance, and when it did try to thwart the ambitions of these commanders it only succeeded in driving them into an alliance with each other. The First Triumvirate, a cabal uniting Caesar, Pompey, and Crassus, was effectively created by senatorial intransigence. Equally powerless were the Hellenistic kings, whose dynastic rule was ineffective in challenging the encroachment of Roman ambitions. The last moment when the Hellenistic east might have become a unified Mediterranean state was with the alliance of Cleopatra VII and Marc Antony. Cleopatra, a Hellenistic queen from a Macedonian dynasty and the first of her family in three hundred years to learn Egyptian, seduced both Julius Caesar and subsequently Marc Antony, by whom she had three children (**13.17**). In their union, a Roman general began the final transformation into a Hellenistic prince. Antony's sons by Cleopatra, for example, were

13.18 Columns in the inner court of the Temple of Bel (Baal) in Palmyra, Syria. The columns and most of the temple were destroyed by ISIL in August, 2015.

named Alexander Helios and Ptolemy Philadelphus, while his daughter was named Cleopatra Selene and eventually was given in marriage to King Juba II of Mauretania, a dynastic marriage of exactly the sort favored by Hellenistic kings.

The climactic moment, and effectively the instant in which the Hellenistic world created by Alexander died, was at the Battle of Actium in 31 BC. Off the west coast of Greece, the fleets of Antony and Cleopatra were defeated by the Romans under Octavian. Within a short time the brilliant, extravagant Hellenistic couple was dead, having committed suicide, and the entire Mediterranean, both the Latin-speaking west and Greek-speaking east, was brought under the sway of a single Roman *imperium*, or empire, ruled by Octavian who shortly after adopted the imperial title of Augustus.

Hellenistic culture, of course, did not perish with the death of Cleopatra. The Greek east would

be incorporated into the provincial structure of the Roman empire, and Greek culture would continue to flourish in the Greek-speaking cities of the eastern Mediterranean. Libanios of Antioch, for example, was a brilliant scholar and rhetorician, a friend of the Emperor Julian, and an important figure in the preservation of the speeches of Demosthenes. He and other similar orators are often referred to as the Second Sophistic, a term coined by Philostratos in recognition of the brilliance of these intellectuals who often combined profound learning with an ability to speak persuasively in front of hundreds of people. They were the public intellectuals of their day and they testify to the vitality of urban, literary, and declamatory culture in the Greek east. Another figure who embodies the survival of Greek culture is Hypatia of Alexandria, the fourth-century-AD philosopher who lectured on Plato and Euclid, and kept alive the great Greek traditions of astronomy and mathematics. During her lifetime Christian fanatics destroyed much of the Library of Alexandria, and she would die in AD 415 at the hands of a mob outraged that a woman might walk openly among men practicing philosophy.

This Classical heritage is as fragile today as it was then. The destruction of libraries and the persecution of intellectuals both show how easily fanaticism can rob us of that heritage. This threat is constant and the damage often irreparable. In the second century AD, Palmyra, the caravan city on the edge of the Syrian desert, began to flourish as the result of the expansion of trade across the Silk Route. Arab, Mesopotamian, Greek, and Roman cultures blended in Palmyra, a fusion typical of the eastern Mediterranean world. A little under two thousand years later, in AD 2015, ISIL destroyed the Temple of Bel in Palmyra, reducing to a pile of rubble a building that once combined Greek and Roman architectural styles and housed a Semitic deity (**13.18**). In recent times the Mediterranean has seemed to exist as the fulcrum between Europe and Africa, and the most overt division has been between north and south, but this has not always been so. In antiquity the divide was more pronounced between east and west, yet there were once Greek-speakers from Marseilles to Alexandria. If the story of the Greeks in the Mediterranean tells us anything it is that political power is finally less lasting, and certainly less precious, than culture.

Spotlight
The Image of Alexander

Writing over four hundred years after Alexander's death, Plutarch offered this appraisal of the man whom the ancient Greeks and Romans regarded as the greatest general the world had seen:

> The outward appearance of Alexander is best represented by the statues of him which Lysippos made, and it was by this artist alone that Alexander himself thought it fit that he should be modelled. For those peculiarities which many of his successors and friends afterwards tried to imitate, namely, the poise of the neck, which was bent slightly to the left, and the melting glance of his eyes, this artist has accurately observed.
>
> (Plutarch, *Alexander* 4, trans. Perrin)

Plutarch recognized that Alexander controlled his image, choosing the Sikyonian sculptor Lysippos (*c.* 390–*c.* 300 BC) to produce official portraits, and that Alexander's physical style was copied by his successors: the leonine hair parted in the middle and combed up and back off his face (a style called the ***anastole***), the slight tilt of his head, and the far-away look he affected. In combination these suggested the ***pothos***, or yearning, that Alexander's biographers saw as the superhuman force driving him to ever greater acts of conquest (**13.19**).

Alexander may have been one of the earliest rulers to control his portraiture in such a way as to disseminate images of himself that projected not just an aura of power but of physical near-perfection: he seemed a young, beardless demi-god, capable of extraordinary deeds in the manner of Herakles, and of traveling to the far east, as did Dionysos. In fashioning

13.19 Bust of Alexander, from Pergamon, Turkey, second century BC. Note the lips slightly parted and the turn of the neck, physiognomic features designed to convey Alexander's yearning (pothos). Marble, H: 42 cm (1 ft 4½ in.)

13.20 Statue of Alexander, Lower Egypt, end of the fourth century BC. Bronze, H: 16.5 cm (6½ in.)

this image he was helped by artists in various media, such as Apelles the painter and Pyrgoteles the gem carver, but above all others, Lysippos.

This artist from Sikyon deliberately changed the proportions of head to body from the older canon of Polykleitos, who advocated 1:7, to a slender 1:8. Lysippos also adapted the *contrapposto* stance favored by Polykleitos, producing a posture at once more fluid and more dynamic. All these Lysippan features are displayed by a small bronze statue in the Louvre (**13.20**). (The statuette is probably a copy of a larger bronze portrait of Alexander holding a spear made by Lysippos *c.* 330 BC.)

So successful was this package of heroic ideas and associations that Alexander's Successors would legitimize their rule by evoking the same images. **13.21** shows a coin minted by Ptolemy, who carved an empire for himself out of Alexander's conquest of Egypt. This tetradrachm was minted *c.* 309 BC, by which time Alexander had been dead for more than a decade. The coin, however, depicts not Ptolemy but Alexander, wearing an elephant skin helmet in the manner of Herakles and his lionskin. The reverse of the coin names Alexander and shows Athena striding forward into battle. (This fusion of Alexander imagery and older Greek symbols is typical of the Hellenistic Age.) Ptolemy continued issuing coins as if serving as satrap for Alexander until *c.* 305 BC, after which, along with the other Successors, he adopted the title of king and issued coins in his own name.

13.21 Tetradrachm of Ptolemy, Alexandria, Egypt, *c.* 309 BC. Note the legend on the reverse: "[a coin] of Alexander." Silver, 15.65 grams

Of the many images of Alexander in different media, the one that most scholars believe actually captures the king's likeness is a herm statue found at Tivoli, east of Rome. Unearthed in AD 1779, the Azara Herm, as it is known, is a first- or second-century-AD Roman copy in marble of a bust that may have been cast in bronze by Lysippos himself (**13.22**). The Azara Herm shares some of the characteristic idealizing features of Alexander iconography but has a degree of individuation that brings us closer to the real Alexander.

13.22 The Azara Herm, a bust of Alexander the Great. Copy of the Imperial Roman era (first or second century AD) of a bronze sculpture made by Lysippos. Marble, H: 68 cm (2 ft 2¾ in.)

Because Hellenistic rulers relied so heavily on their connections to Alexander, his iconography permeated the artistic style of the entire age; the image of Alexander appears even outside the circle of the Successor dynasties. An example of his ubiquity is the so-called Alexander Sarcophagus, a burial container of carved marble from the late fourth century AD found in a necropolis outside Sidon in Lebanon in 1887 (**13.23**). Carved for a leading member of the local elite (possibly Abdalonymos, king of Tyre), the sarcophagus shows Alexander charging over his Persian adversaries at the Battle of Issos in 333 BC. The sarcophagus is notable for the traces of paint still visible on it.

Eventually, Alexander's image would become little more than decorative, especially for the Romans who conquered the Hellenistic eastern world he had created. This is illustrated by the fate of a monumental statue group made for Alexander by Lysippos in 334 BC to commemorate the recent victory of the Granikos River in the same year. The group was originally displayed in the sanctuary of Zeus in Dion, in southern Macedonia. After the Roman general Quintus Caecilius Metellus reduced Macedonia to the status of a Roman province in 146, the statues were brought to Rome to adorn the portico of Octavia. **13.24** shows a first-century-BC bronze miniature of Alexander the Great on horseback modeled after one of these statues. The conqueror of the world had become a charming centerpiece for a wealthy Roman's dinner table.

13.23 The Alexander Sarcophagus, Sidon, Lebanon, late fourth century AD. Marble, H: 1.95 m (6 ft 5 in.)

13.24 Statuette of Alexander on horseback, first century BC. Bronze and silver, H: 49 cm (1 ft 7¼ in.)

Glossary

Acrocorinth The akropolis of Corinth, which dominates the Isthmus of Corinth and thus helps to account for the perennial importance of the city in Greek history.

adelphoi nomoi Greek for "kindred law codes." This was how Plato described the Spartan and Cretan constitutional arrangements, which were acknowledged to be quite similar. The idea is further illustrated by the legend of Lykourgos's journey to Crete to study laws.

aegis The snake-fringed goatskin given to Athena by Zeus that features in the goddess's iconography, including the famous ivory-and-gold cult statue by Pheidias that resided in the Parthenon.

agoge The Spartan system of education, which focused upon physical and military training of male citizens from the age of seven until the age of twenty-nine. See also **homoioi**.

agora Literally, "the place of assembly," which came to connote the market-place of ancient Greek city-states, where one could expect to find structures associated with the administration of the city as well as shops and open areas for more casual public gatherings.

agoranomoi (sg. **agoranomos**) Officers of the Athenian democracy who made sure that legitimate weights and measures were used in marketplace transactions.

aidos Greek for "reserve," which was particularly cultivated by the Spartans, who generally discouraged open discussion.

aither/aether The Greek word for the upper air or atmosphere, where Aristophanes set his windbag-version of Sokrates in the comedy *Clouds*.

akropolis The term for the highest, most defensible part of a city, and applied specifically to the massive rock in central Athens on which stood the city's most important temples.

anarchia Literally, "period without an archon"; the Greek term for years in which the Athenians were unable to elect a chief magistrate due to *stasis* (civic strife). *Anarchia* was particularly an issue during the early years of the sixth century BC, before and after the legislative program of Solon.

anastole In sculpture, a hairstyle characterized by a middle part and combed up and back off the face;

associated in particular with portraits of Alexander the Great.

aparchai (sg. **aparche**) Literally, "first fruits," which the Athenians called the one-sixtieth of the tribute from Delian League members that they dedicated to Athena.

apeiron Literally, "boundless," which is what the philosopher Anaximander called the first principle of the universe. He considered that the universe itself was likewise boundless.

apostateres Literally, "Removers," a term used to describe a privilege of the Spartan kings and **Gerontes** ("Elders") in the rider to the Archaic Great Rhetra, which outlined the constitutional arrangement of the state. It seems that at some point after the drafting of the Great Rhetra, the right of veto was granted to the kings and elders, an indication of the reassertion of aristocratic authority after the conquest of Messenia.

apsidal A building the architectural form of which is characterized by a semi-circular end, such as is the case for the **heroon** of Lefkandi and some early Greek temples in the eighth century BC.

archagetes The epithet of Apollo that referred to his role as the sponsor of colonial foundations during the Greek Diaspora, c. 750–c. 500 BC. Typically, an individual or community would consult the oracle at Delphi prior to sending out an expedition. Additionally, the two kings of Sparta were known as the **Archagetai**.

Archaios Naos The Old Athena Temple on the Akropolis of Athens, constructed under the Peisistratids during the second half of the sixth century BC as the most important cult center of the city-state. It was destroyed by the Persians in 480 BC and succeeded by the Periklean Erechtheion in 421–407 BC.

Areopagus The "Hill of Ares" just below the Akropolis of Athens and to the northwest. It was here that the council made up of ex-archons met, and thus the hill gave its name to that council. The Areopagus was the main governing body of Athens until the reforms of Ephialtes (461 BC) stripped it of most of its functions.

arête The Greek word for "manly excellence," this was the quality most sought after and cultivated by Greek men and was part of a shared vocabulary of virtue.

aristeia From the Greek *aristos* ("best"), *aristeia* describes an account of the heroic accomplishments of an individual, such as Book 5 of Homer's *Iliad*, which recounts the *aristeia* of Diomedes.

aristoi Literally, "the best men," this term was used to describe the elite of an ancient Greek *polis*, especially during the Archaic period.

arrephoroi The two or four young girls who served Athena Polias on the Akropolis of Athens and helped with the weaving of Athena's **peplos**.

asebeia The Greek word meaning "impiety," which was a common charge against the sophists and philosophers—including ultimately Sokrates—during the fifth century BC at Athens.

Asklepieia (sg. **Asklepieion**) Sanctuaries of the god Asklepios that were centers of healing.

asty The Greek word for "city," meaning the urban center of a *polis* or city-state, as opposed to the surrounding agricultural and pasture lands.

ataraxia Literally, "lack of disturbance," the quality associated by the philosopher Epicurus with the just man.

Athenaioi Greek for "Athenians."

atimos Literally, "dishonored"; according to Solon's legislation, anyone convicted of attempting to establish a tyranny at Athens was to be declared *atimos*, which stripped him of all rights of protection.

atoma Literally, "uncuttable things"; the philosophers Demokritos and Leukippos hypothesized that the universe was made up of tiny particles imperceptible to the human eye, which were so small that they could not be cut.

aulos A kind of wind instrument; the most important musical instrument used by the ancient Greeks. Contests in virtuosity on the *aulos* were part of some agonistic festivals, including, for example, the **Panathenaia**.

basileus (pl. **basileis**) Greek for "king," which ultimately derives from a Mycenaean title referring to minor local officials. During the Early Iron Age it was applied to the ruling elite of burgeoning communities, and by the end of the Archaic period it was often applied to religious officials of

the **polis**, such as was the case for the Archon Basileus at Athens.

basilica (1) An important church; (2) A Roman building used for legal and commercial transactions.

Boulê The Greek word for the governing council of a city-state. At Athens, the *Boulê* consisted of 500 members selected by lot each year.

cabotage Seaborne trade characterized by the movement of ships and goods along the coast from one port to the next in succession.

caldera A cauldron-shaped depression formed in the wake of the eruption of a volcano, such as that on Thera c. 1628 BC.

cella The inner chamber of a Greek temple, where the cult statue was housed.

choregos A wealthy Athenian who produced a chorus for one of the dramatic festivals and paid for the entire production as a form of **liturgy** to the **polis**.

choris oikountes Literally, "those dwelling apart"; a class of privately owned slaves who lived apart from their masters and worked primarily in manufacturing.

city-state See **polis**.

contrapposto In sculpture, a standing statue characterized by having most of the weight placed on one foot, with the arms and shoulders opposed to the legs and hips.

corbeled vault A method of construction used in **tholos** tombs, characterized by a vault consisting of layers of stone superimposed one on top of the other, with each successive layer's stones extending out slightly further beyond the edge of the layer below. The entire structure is held together by the mound of earth placed above, which stabilizes the vault and counters the effects of gravity.

daimonion According to Sokrates, he possessed a "little spirit" (*daimonion*), which is generally taken to mean an inner voice with which he was constantly in dialogue.

damos See **demos**.

delphus Literally, "womb," which seems to be etymologically connected with the name of the sanctuary of Apollo at Delphi.

decarchies The oligarchies of ten men established by the Spartan Lysander in pro-Athenian democracies that opposed him. This represented a new kind of foreign policy that characterized Sparta after the defeat of Athens in the Peloponnesian War.

deme In Attica, *demes* were the local municipalities that formed the smallest subdivisions of the Athenian citizenry. At the time of the reorganization of Athens by Kleisthenes in 508 BC, they numbered 139.

demos A Greek word probably related to a root meaning "divide," originally associated with land-tenure in Mycenaean states (*damos*) and later broadening its scope to include the community at large and acquiring its more familiar meaning of "people." See also *kratos.*

demosioi Literally, "those belonging to the demos," the *demosioi* were the public slaves of Athens, owned by the state and charged with administrative duties. The *demosioi* were clerks, secretaries, and street-sweepers, and some even formed a rudimentary police force.

Demosion Sema The state cemetery of Athens located just outside the Dipylon Gate, where all citizens who died in war were buried. It was here that Perikles delivered his famous funeral oration.

diagnosis Along with **prognosis**, the observation of patients practiced by Hippokratic doctors before treatment.

diaulos In Greek athletics, the double **stadion** race, where the competitors sprinted two lengths of the stadium, down and back (approximately 400 meters or 1,300 ft). It was first instituted at Olympia in 724 BC.

diekplous A naval tactic whereby the attacking *trireme* changed the angle of attack and tried to shear off the oars of the enemy's vessel.

dikastikon A state fund of the Athenian democracy that paid for jury service.

dinos A term that describes a bowl used for mixing wine.

diolkos A limestone road built across the Isthmus of Corinth used in transshipping from the Gulf of Corinth and the western Mediterranean to the Saronic Gulf and the eastern Mediterranean. It connected the two ports of Corinth, Lechaion and Kenchreai.

Dionysia The civic festival held in honor of Dionysos at Athens in late March that featured contests in tragedy and comedy.

dithyrambs Hymns sung in honor of Dionysos whose origins are obscure but which were highly influential on the development of Attic tragedy.

doeroi/doerai In the Linear B texts, *do-e-ro* and *do-e-ra* (precursors to historical Greek **doulos** and **doule**, "slave") appear in a number of contexts, both sacred and profane. As in historical Greece, slaves seem to have been an integral part of Mycenaean economy and society.

dokimasia Under the Athenian democracy, *dokimasia* described the process whereby candidates for office were vetted; it originally belonged to the Areopagus, but after the reforms of Ephialtes in 461 BC it was transferred to the Boulê.

dolichos In Greek athletics, the long-distance race, which was first instituted in Olympia in 720 BC. It seems to have consisted of 20 or 24 lengths of the stadium, or around 7½–9 kilometers (4½–5½ mi.).

doulos (pl. **douloi**) Greek for "slave."

doxa The Greek word for "opinion, belief," which according to Aristotle was possessed by slaves, who did not exhibit *logos* ("reason").

drachma (pl. **drachmai**) Literally, "a handful," which originally referred to a handful of **obols** or metal spits that served as the earliest money of Greece. After coinage was adopted in the sixth century BC, the *drachma* was one of the standard units of the currency system. One *drachma* was a day's wage for a skilled workman in Classical Athens.

dromos The passageway leading to the entrance of a Mycenaean **tholos** tomb.

echelon A military formation that featured a staggered line; favored by Alexander the Great.

ekecheiria The sacred truce declared every four years during the month before the Olympic games, which guaranteed safe travel for all athletes and pilgrims.

Ekklesia The Greek word for the general assembly of a city-state, typically composed of all adult male citizens.

ekphora In an Athenian funeral, the *ekphora* (literally, "carrying out") was the second stage (after the **prothesis**), during which the body of the deceased was brought from the home to the gravesite.

ekphrasis In literature, *ekphrasis* is the detailed description of objects or works of art. In Homer, such scenes often preserve accurate accounts of

objects and weapons that were in use during the Late Bronze Age.

elasteros The Greek word for a "ghost" or "evil spirit" haunting a house.

elenchos The method of cross-examination favored by Sokrates, for which he became notorious.

engyê A word for a Greek marriage that means both "betrothal" and "contract." It was made between a man and the bride's father.

Enneakrounos The fountain house built by Peisistratos in the southeast corner of the Agora.

entablature The horizontal portion of a building resting on the columns and consisting of architrave, frieze, and cornice.

entasis In Greek architecture, the purposeful, cigar-shaped bulging of columns that corrects for the human eye's skewed perception of straight lines.

ephebes In an ancient Greek *polis*, the *ephebes* were the age-class comprised of those completing their first military service. In Athens, the ephebes served as border guards, whereas in Sparta they participated in the **krypteia**.

ephetai According to Drako's law on homicide, the fifty-one *ephetai* served as jurors and decided whether the accused acted intentionally or unintentionally.

ephors At Sparta, the five *ephors* ("overseers") were the leading magistrates elected yearly to manage the state's affairs. They are not present in the Archaic Great Rhetra and seem to have been instituted in the sixth century BC, after the conquest of Messenia.

erastes Literally, "the lover," the *erastes* was the adult (bearded), active partner in a homosexual relationship that had aristocratic, military, and initiatory overtones.

eristics The study of constructing effective arguments, taught by the sophists in Classical Athens.

eromenos Literally, "the beloved," the *eromenos* was the adolescent (unbearded), passive partner in a homosexual relationship that had aristocratic, military, and initiatory overtones.

ethnos (pl. **ethne**) An aggregate of communities that professed a common ethnic identity, such as the Aitolians or Arkadians, who all claimed descent from a common heroic ancestor.

eunomia Literally, "good order," the value that the Spartans believed characterized their society and which they attributed to the legendary lawgiver Lykourgos.

eupatridai Literally, "those descended from good fathers," as men from the wealthy and highborn families of Athens called themselves.

eusebeia Greek for "piety," which the Athenians considered to be their most essential quality and which was maintained through regular communal sacrifice to the gods.

euthyna In the Athenian democracy, the scrutiny of outgoing magistrates undertaken by the **Boulê**.

exegetai Officials who were responsible for the oral legal traditions of a community; they gradually lost significance as laws came to be written down. See also **Hieromnemones**.

genos (pl. **gene**) A clan made up of related households with common ancestral cults. Powerful *gene* had a considerable influence on the state in Archaic Athens.

Genesia A festival held in honor of the family dead; at Athens under Solon it became a public festival of the whole community.

gephyrismos Literally, "the Bridge"; part of the ritual of the Eleusinian Mysteries, during which the initiates were verbally abused at a river crossing.

Geronsia The Mycenaean word used to describe certain councils and associations.

Gerousia The senate of Sparta, comprised of twenty-eight elders and two kings, which proposed legislation to the assembly and eventually acquired the right to be **apostateres** (the right to veto).

gymnasiarch In the liturgies of democratic Athens, ten *gymnasiarchs* were chosen (one from each tribe) to finance festivals that featured torch-races, which included payment for all training and supplies.

Gymnetes Literally, "naked ones," which was the term for the agricultural slaves of Argos.

halter (pl. **halteres**) In the long-jump competition, *halteres* were weights held by the athlete in each hand to aid their attempt.

harmosts Governors installed by the Spartan Lysander in cities taken over from the Athenians after the Peloponnesian War. They typically commanded garrisons.

hegemon Literally, "leader," the word used to describe the chief **polis** (or individual) in an alliance of Greek states, a role that passed from Athens to Sparta to Thebes and finally to Philip II in the course of the Classical period.

Hekatompedon Literally, "a hundred-footer," the term used to describe an early temple on the Athenian Akropolis dating to the sixth century BC and associated with the Peisistratid tyrants. It may have been located on the site of the Parthenon.

hektemoroi Literally, "one-sixth men"; in Archaic Athens, the term used to describe men who had fallen into debt bondage and who were (most likely) required to pay one-sixth of their produce to the owners of the lands they worked.

helots A word connected to the Greek for "capture" and thus probably meaning something like "captives," this was the term used by the Spartans to describe the serf class drawn from, among others, their Messenian neighbors, who were reduced to this status during the Archaic period. The agricultural labor of the *helots* enabled the Spartans to develop their uniquely militaristic society.

Hellanodikai Literally, "Judges of the Greeks," who were in charge of organizing, administering, and judging the Olympic games every four years at Olympia. The *Hellanodikai* determined who was eligible to compete in the Games, the basic requirement for which was that the man in question was a Greek.

Hellenotamiai Literally, "Treasurers of the Greeks," which was the official title given to the men in charge of the treasury and finances of the Delian League, all of whom were Athenian.

heqetai In the Linear B archives, *heqetai* ("Companions") is the term used to describe men closely associated with the palatial administration; military and religious duties can be deduced from the tablets.

heroon A monument constructed in honor of a hero, as, for example, in the case of the Early Iron Age building at Lefkandi.

hetairai Literally, "female companions," the term used to describe high-class courtesans who were often found as entertainers (musicians, dancers, and conversationalists) at **symposia** in Athens.

hieromnemones Literally, "sacred-remembrancers," officials who were responsible for the oral legal traditions of a community, who gradually lost

significance as laws came to be written down. See also **exegetai.**

hierosyna The term used to describe the portion of a sacrifice reserved for the priest.

Hippeis Literally, "knights," the second class in the Solonian constitution of Athens, whose wealth had to be sufficient to maintain ownership of a horse. Under Solon's laws, only the *Hippeis* and **Pentekosiomedimnoi** could hold the archonship.

homoioi Literally, "equals"; the word used to describe full Spartan citizens or Spartiates, who had all completed their education in the **agoge**.

hoplites (pl. **hoplitai**; English "**hoplite**/**hoplites**") (1) Heavily armed infantrymen who drew their name from the large circular shield (*hoplon*) that they carried. Hoplites fought in close formation (the **phalanx**), which encouraged the development of an egalitarian ethos among those wealthy enough to afford their own equipment. (2) A race in the full armor of a hoplite.

horos (pl. **horoi**) Inscribed boundary stones that formed the borders of the Athenian Agora.

hubris Violent arrogance or pride, which according to Greek tradition will result in **nemesis** or divine retribution against the offender.

Hypomeiones At Sparta, an inferior class comprised of ex-Spartiates who for whatever reason (for example, failure to contribute to the **syssition**) had been demoted.

imperium The Latin word for empire.

kairos Literally, "critical moment"; used to describe the defeat of Darius III at Gaugamela by Alexander the Great in 331 BC, which was acknowledged to be a pivotal moment in history.

kalos Literally, "beautiful"; the term used by an **erastes** to describe his **eromenos**. The latter shed this characterization upon becoming a man.

katharsis According to Aristotle, a *katharsis* ("cleansing") was the aim of tragedy at Athens, by which he seems to have meant that negative emotions, such as pity and fear, would be purged through viewing the drama.

kinaidos The pejorative term used to describe the passive member of a homosexual relationship between two adult males (as opposed to the **erastes**/**eromenos** relationship, which was considered seemly).

kinesis Literally, "movement, commotion"; the term used by Thucydides to describe the

Peloponnesian War, which for him was the greatest *kinesis* that ever occurred.

kithara A guitar-like instrument, typically with seven strings and frequently translated as "lyre." Contests in virtuosity on the *kithara* were part of some agonistic festivals, including, for example, the **Panathenaia**.

klarotai The servile class in Crete, analogous to the **helots** in Spartan society and the **penestai** in Thessaly.

kleos The urge to win individual glory that characterizes the heroes of Homer's *Iliad* and *Odyssey*.

kleos aphthiton Literally, "undying fame"; the goal of any Homeric hero and the Greeks who emulated them: the glorious reputation that will live on after death.

kleroi (sg. **kleros**) Lots of land assigned to colonists.

klerosis ek prokritôn In the Athenian Democracy, from 487 BC archons were randomly selected from a list of candidates, a process described as *klerosis ek prokriton*.

knemides (sg. **knemis**) Bronze greaves, or shin guards, which protected the lower legs of a Greek **hoplite**.

koine Literally, "common"; the term for the dialect of Greek that emerged all across the Eastern Mediterranean beginning in the Hellenistic period.

Koine Eirene Literally, "common peace"; such general peace treaties that bound all Greek city-states were frequently struck in the fourth century BC but were never lasting or effective.

koinon (pl. **koina**) A political federation based on the communities of an **ethnos**, attested from the Archaic period and rising to prominence starting in the fourth century BC.

Koniopodes Literally, "dusty feet"; the term used to describe the agricultural slaves of Epidauros.

kore Literally, "daughter"; a statue of a young woman. Also a title given to the goddess Persephone, especially in connection with the cult at Eleusis that featured both her and her mother Demeter.

koreter The Mycenaean term describing governors of the various districts that made up the state centered upon Pylos.

krater A vessel used for mixing wine.

kratos The Greek word for "power" or "rule," which forms the second

element in *demokratia* (democracy or "rule of the people"). See also **demos**.

krypteia At Sparta, a subdivision of the **ephebes** who served as a kind of secret police charged with terrorizing the **helots**.

kykeon A drink administered to the initiates of the Eleusinian Mysteries that may have included the fungus ergot, a mild hallucinogen.

kylix (pl. **kylikes**) A high-stemmed, shallow goblet used in ancient Greek ritual drinking ceremonies beginning in Mycenaean times and continuing through into the historical period to include the **symposium**.

Kyria Ekklesia Each month, one of the meetings of the Assembly of Athens was labeled *kyria* or "authoritative," at which matters of great importance were debated.

larnakes (sg. **larnax**) Boxes used to house the remains of the deceased; at the Macedonian royal cemetery in Vergina, these were made of gold.

lawagetas Literally, "leader of the people"; this term is found in the Linear B documents and seems to refer to the official just below the **wanax**, whose duties may have included leading the army during times of war.

liturgy In democratic Athens, public services for which wealthy citizens were required to pay the costs. These included the upkeep of a **trireme**, the finance of a dramatic chorus, and service as **gymnasiarch**.

logistai In democratic Athens, the officers who served as public accountants and were required to publish a yearly audit.

logos A Greek word of many meanings, most basically "word" but extending to encompass "order," "meaning," and "rational thought"; Plato contrasted it with **doxa** ("opinion" or "belief").

magus (pl. **magi**) In Persian society, the **magi** were the priestly caste in charge of sacrifices and sacred lore.

Marathonomachoi Greek for "Men who fought at Marathon"; the heroized warriors whose deeds in battle against the Persians in 490 BC won them cult offerings in Athens.

medimnos A Greek unit of measurement which in Attica amounted to 52½ liters or 14 US gallons.

medize The Greek word used to describe those who had sided with the Persians during the wars of 490–479 BC.

megaron An architectural form consisting of a columned porch, vestibule, and large hall with a hearth in the center. The *megaron* has deep roots in the Aegean region, being found first in the Neolithic villages of Sesklo and Dimini and reappearing during the Late Bronze Age as the central feature of many of the Mycenaean palaces.

metoikion The tax paid by resident aliens (metics) of Athens, which amounted to 12 *drachmai* per year for a man and 6 for a woman.

metope A rectangular architectural element that fills the space between two triglyphs in a Doric frieze.

metropolis Literally, "mother city," the Greek word used to describe the city from which a colonial expedition had originated. For example, Corinth was the *metropolis* of Syracuse in Sicily.

misotyrannos Literally, "tyrant-hating," a characteristic ascribed to Sparta in the Archaic period and illustrated by the Spartan contribution to the expulsion of the Peisistratids from Athens.

misthos The term used to describe payment for jury service under the Athenian democracy.

mna (pl. **mnai**) A unit of currency; at Athens, it equaled 100 *drachmai*.

mystes Greek word for "initiate," used especially of the initiates of the Eleusinian Mysteries.

nemesis The divine retribution that awaited anyone who committed a sin of **hubris**.

niello A substance made of copper, silver, and lead sulphite used to produce the black highlights found on Mycenaean daggers. Especially notable examples were discovered in Grave Circle A at Mycenae.

Nostoi Epic poems whose theme was the returns of the Greek heroes from Troy, many of which included tragic elements.

nous Greek for "intellect, mind."

obai At Sparta, the villages that formed a subdivision of the state, alongside the **phylai** or tribes.

obol Derived from the Greek word for a spit ("*obelos*"), an *obol* was a coin worth one-sixth of a **drachma**.

oiketai The Greek term for household slaves, who wove cloth, cooked, and served as attendants of the master and mistress; their lot was typically better than that of agricultural slaves.

oikist The Greek term for the founder of a colony. The *oikist* typically consulted the oracle of Apollo before embarking on the expedition, and it was not uncommon for the colony to award him divine honors after his death.

oikos Literally, "household"; beginning in the Early Iron Age, the *oikos* was the standard patrilineal family unit consisting of a man, wife, children, house, and all dependents and chattels.

oinochoe A wine jug.

oliganthropia Literally, "shortage of human beings," which was the bane of Sparta beginning in the Classical period. Aristotle attributed this state of affairs to Spartan women.

omphalos Literally, "navel"; at Delphi, a stone was pointed out as the navel of the world, thus highlighting the belief that Delphi was the center of the world. The stone was believed to be the one swallowed by Kronos in lieu of Zeus.

orgeones Religious associations documented in Athens from the Archaic period onward; they saw to the rites of a god or hero.

Orpheotelestai Initiates in the mysteries associated with the hero Orpheus, who were buried with inscribed gold plates that served as passports to a blessed afterlife.

ostrakon A fragment of pottery upon which the name of a candidate for **ostracism** was inscribed (hence the name of the practice).

ostracism Instituted under the Athenian democracy, ostracism was a process whereby the Athenians could expel a leading figure for ten years. The man in question did not lose his property or citizenship.

paideia The Greek word for "education," which according to Isokrates defined what it meant to be culturally Greek in the fourth century BC.

Panathenaia The "All-Athens" festival, which was reorganized by Peisistratos in the sixth century BC to include contests in athletics, horsemanship, music, and poetry. The Greater Panathenaia was held every four years on Athena's birthday in July, and every year the Lesser Panathenaia was held on a smaller scale. Victors in the games received amphorae of olive oil as prizes.

pankration In Greek athletics, the "all-powerful" event combined boxing and wrestling; only eye gouging, groin grabs, and biting were outlawed. It was instituted at Olympia in 648 BC.

Paralos The state **trireme** of the Athenian democracy.

pelike A one-piece ceramic vessel used as a liquid container.

penestai The servile class in Thessaly, analogous to the **helots** in Spartan society and the **Klarotai** in Crete.

Pentekosiomedimnoi Literally, "500-measure men," the highest class under the Solonian constitution of Athens, whose origins may go back to the Early Iron Age. Under Solon's laws, only the *Pentekosiomedimnoi* and **Hippeis** could hold the archonship.

Pentekontaetia Literally, "fifty-year period," used to describe the period between the Persian invasion in 480 BC and the outbreak of the Peloponnesian War in 431 BC, during which Athens became a major imperial power with its domination of the Delian League.

peplos A garment for women in ancient Greece; every four years at the Panathenaia a new *peplos* was presented to the goddess Athena by the citizens of Athens as a birthday present.

periplous A naval tactic whereby a **trireme** circled round an enemy ship and rammed it in the rear.

perioikoi Literally, "dwellers round about"; in Spartan society, the *perioikoi* were inhabitants of the **poleis** of Messenia and Lakonia who were required to contribute troops for the army.

Perserschutt The German term for the archaeological deposit from the Akropolis that is associated with the Persian destruction of 480 BC.

phalanx Military formation consisting of ranks of closely packed, heavily armed infantrymen.

phoros Tribute paid by members of the Delian League to Athens.

phratry (pl. **phratries**) Literally, "brotherhood"; social groups in Athens that purportedly linked men of common descent, although the kinship may have been fictive. Acceptance by the *phratores* ("brothers") of a *phratry* was necessary for Athenian citizenship.

phyle (pl. **phylai**) Literally, "tribes"; one of the subdivisions of an ancient Greek **polis**, such as was the case in Sparta, where there were three, and Athens, where there were four in Archaic times but ten under the democracy. See also **obai**.

phylax play A kind of burlesque drama of Doric communities in Magna Graecia.

physis Greek for "nature."

pirradaziš The Persian term for the network of horse-changing posts along the Royal Road that ran from Sardis to Susa.

pinax (pl. **pinakes**) A painted tablet.

pithos A large ceramic jar used for storage in bulk and associated in particular with the magazines of Minoan and Mycenaean palaces.

plethra (sg. **plethron**) Units of measurement equivalent to either 100 feet in length or 900 m², used to describe plots of land assigned to colonists at, for example, Corcyra Melaina.

poletai In the Athenian democracy, officers responsible for public auctions of confiscated goods.

polis (pl. **poleis**) The Greek word usually translated as city-state and referring to an autonomous community of citizens, whose territory was comprised of an urban center and the surrounding agricultural and pasture lands, as well as any ports. Citizenship in a *polis* came to be acknowledged as a hallmark of Hellenic identity.

politeia Greek for the arrangement of laws and the extent of the franchise—more or less limited—equivalent to a state's constitution.

polos A headdress or crown worn by goddesses.

polyandry The practice whereby a woman has multiple husbands, which to a certain degree seems to have been practiced at Sparta, probably in order to avoid the division of family property.

porne (pl. **pornai**) Greek for "prostitute."

pothos Literally, "yearning, desire"; the superhuman force to which Alexander the Great's biographers attributed his drive to ever greater acts of conquest.

proedroi In the Athenian democracy, the executive board of nine men that rotated with every meeting of the **Boulê**.

prognosis Along with **diagnosis**, the assessment of patients undertaken by Hippokratic doctors before treatment.

proskynesis The custom of bowing before the Persian Great King, which caused a dilemma for Alexander the Great in the case of the Macedonians, who regarded the gesture as appropriate only for addressing a god.

prothesis In an Athenian funeral, the first stage, during which the body was laid out in the home while members of the household mourned. It was followed by the **ekphora**.

prytanis (pl. **prytaneis**) In the Athenian democracy, the fifty councillors from one of the ten tribes who served as presidents of the **Boulê** for one-tenth of the civic year. This duty rotated through the ten tribes over the course of the year.

rhapsodes Literally, "stitchers of songs," they were performers who specialized in the recitation of Homer. Contests in rhapsodic performance were instituted as part of the **Panathenaia** by Peisistratos and seem to have greatly influenced the form of the *Iliad* and *Odyssey* that we possess today.

rhyton (pl. **rhyta**) A ritual vessel with a spout used in libation ceremonies. During the Late Bronze Age, Minoans and Mycenaeans were noted for their use of *rhyta* in the form of bulls' and other animals' heads.

sarissa The long pike, estimated at 6 meters (20 ft) in length, which was used by soldiers of the Macedonian **phalanx** from the time of Philip II.

satrapy (pl. **satrapies**) A province of the Persian empire.

scholê Literally, "leisure," which is the origin of English "school"; the Greek word used to describe the leisurely pursuits available to the well-to-do of Classical Athens. These included philosophy and poetry.

Seisachtheia Literally, "Shaking off of Burdens," which Solon devised in 594 BC in order to relieve the crippling debts of the many Athenian citizens who had been relegated to the status of **hektemoroi**.

sitophylakes In the Athenian democracy, officials in charge of monitoring the grain supply to prevent price-fixing.

skyphos (pl. **skyphoi**) A drinking cup with two horizontally attached handles.

Soma Literally, "Body"; the funerary complex constructed in Alexandria to house the remains of Alexander the Great.

stadion The oldest event in Greek athletics: a straight sprint of a length of the stadium (192 meters, or 630 ft).

stamnos A broad-bellied ceramic vessel suitable for either storage or serving of liquids.

stasis The Greek word used to describe the civic strife that

characterized much of the public life of **poleis** during the Archaic period. See also **anarchia**.

stele (pl. **stelai**) A worked, standing stone slab (often engraved) used for marking graves and, in historical times, for publishing inscribed texts.

stichomythia In Greek drama, dialogue between two characters that features a line-for-line exchange and typically exhibits opposing viewpoints with an agonistic flair.

stoa A broad portico, the architectural form which was favored by the Greeks for all-purpose civic buildings.

stomion Literally, "mouth"; the entrance to the chamber of a Mycenaean **tholos** tomb, located at the end of the **dromos** or passageway.

symmories In fourth-century-BC Athens, twenty boards of sixty men each called *symmories* were instituted to share the burdens of financing a **trireme**, an important **liturgy**.

symposium (pl. **symposia**) An all-male drinking party with aristocratic overtones, typically devoted to carousing and drinking, with **hetairai** serving as entertainment (music, dancing, and conversation). Occasionally, the *symposium* served as a venue for the discussion of poetry and philosophy.

synoecism The process whereby multiple small communities—typically villages—coalesced into a single **polis** with an urban center and a single, unified political system.

syssition (pl. **syssitia**) In Sparta, the messes or eating clubs to which each Spartiate had to belong and contribute to from his estate worked by **helots**. The *syssition* included fifteen to twenty members, who were drawn from the various age groups and lived together.

telestai The Mycenaean term used to describe men who were significant landholders and may have performed religious duties.

Telesterion The Hall of Mysteries at Eleusis, which was periodically enlarged and thus mirrors the transformation of a private cult to one of the state.

tell An artificial mound built up by various layers of habitation on an archaeological site. Tells are particularly characteristic of the Neolithic period in Greece; the site of Troy, with its many layers of cities, is another good example. See also **tumulus**.

telos Literally, "the end"; according to Aristotle, the proper function or end of a relationship is mastery, such that

mastery defines all relationships and gives them a purpose.

temenos In Greek religion, the term for a sacred enclosure.

theios aner Literally, "divine man"; this idea emerged beginning in the time of the Spartan Lysander and contributed to the divinization of Alexander the Great.

theorikon A state fund of the Athenian democracy that subsidized theater tickets for those too poor to afford the price.

Thesmothetai Literally, "Law-setters"; in the Athenian democracy, these were the six officials in charge of seeing that the law was enforced.

Thetes The fourth and lowest class of the Solonian constitution of Athens, whose members were permitted to attend the Assembly.

thiasoi (sg. **thiasos**) Religious associations documented in Athens from the Archaic period onward; they saw to the rites of a god or hero.

tholos A circular structure, often a temple, or a beehive-shaped tomb covered by a corbeled arch.

thranites The top tier of rowers on a **trireme**.

to anthropinon Literally, "the human thing"; according to Thucydides, this is the governing principle of history, namely, that human nature does not change, and therefore future events will unfold similarly to events of the past.

to mythodes According to Thucydides, the "legendary" and "fabulous" element that characterized Herodotos's work and which Thucydides himself explicitly rejected.

trierarch A wealthy Athenian who maintained a **trireme** as a liturgy to the state. Occasionally, the *trierarch* also served as captain of the warship.

triglyph A tablet in a Doric frieze with three vertical grooves. Triglyphs alternate with **metopes**.

trireme A warship powered by rowers arranged in three tiers on each side of the ship and equipped with a bronze ram and sails for non-combat travel.

trittys (pl. **trittyes**) Literally, "third." After Kleisthenes' reorganization of Athens in 508 BC, the ten civic tribes were each composed of three *trittyes*, one from each region of Attica: the coast, the plain, and the city. This arrangement drastically reduced the power bases of the regional nobles and contributed to the strength of the Athenian democracy.

tumulus An artificial mound of earth, often associated with commemorative contexts in the archaeological record. See also **tell**.

Unterberg The lower citadel at Tiryns.

wanakteros An adjective found in the Linear B tablets denoting a commodity as associated with the **wanax**, roughly equivalent to English "royal."

wanax The term in the Linear B texts that refers to the ruler of the state. In later Greek (in the form *anax*) it is used especially of the Homeric heroes and deities.

Wappenmünzen Literally, "heraldic coins"; the term coined by German scholars to describe the earliest coinage of Athens in the sixth century BC, which featured heraldic blazons that probably represented the elite families of Athens.

xoanon An ancient cult statue made of wood, as was the case, for example, for the olive-wood statue of Athena kept in the **cella** of Athena Polias in the Erechtheion.

xenelasia Literally, "driving out foreigners"; a custom of the Spartans whereby they periodically expelled all foreigners from their territory in order to prevent the introduction of radical ideas and customs.

xenia Ritualized guest-friendship characterized by a particular reverence for hospitality. The relationship formed through bonds of *xenia* outlasted the individual and was inherited by his descendants. Violation of hospitality was counted among the gravest of sins, punishable by Zeus.

xiphos A short slashing sword used by **hoplites** at close quarters.

Zanes Literally, "Zeuses"; at Olympia, sixteen statues paid for with the fines exacted from cheaters in the Olympic Games.

Zeugitai Literally, "yokemen," who made up the third class of the Solonian constitution of Athens and were eligible to attend the Assembly.

Sources of Quotations

We have endeavored to credit rights owners where possible. The author and publisher apologize for any omissions or errors, which we will be happy to correct in future printings and editions of this book.

Chapter 1 Introduction: Why Study the Greeks?

p. 16 Homer, *The Iliad*, trans. Ian Johnston, http://records.viu.ca/~johnstoi/homer/iliad6.htm (Accessed April 20, 2017).

p. 17 Plato, *Symposium*, trans. Benjamin Jowett (Oxford: Clarendon Press, 1871).

p. 17 *Selected Poems of Rainer Maria Rilke*, trans. Stephen Mitchell (New York: Random House, 1982). Translation copyright © 1982 by Stephen Mitchell. Used by permission of Random House, an imprint and division of Penguin Random House LLC. All rights reserved.

p. 18 W. von Humboldt, *Geschichte des Verfalls und Unterganges der griechischen Freistaaten* (Leipzig: G. J. Göschen, 1896).

p. 19 Thucydides, *The Peloponnesian War*, trans. Benjamin Jowett (Oxford: Clarendon Press, 1881).

p. 20 Thucydides, *The Peloponnesian War*, trans. Benjamin Jowett (Oxford: Clarendon Press, 1881).

pp. 20–21 Ibid.

p. 23 Plato, *Republic*, 474c, trans. G. Vlastos, *Platonic Studies*, 2nd edn (Princeton, NJ: Princeton University Press, 1973).

p. 23 Aristotle, *Politics*, trans. Benjamin Jowett (Oxford: Clarendon Press, 1885).

pp. 23–24 Ibid.

p. 24 Osama bin Laden, "The sword fell," http://www.nytimes.com/2001/10/08/world/a-nation-challenged-bin-laden-s-statement-the-sword-fell.html (Accessed April 20, 2017).

p. 24 Osama bin Laden, "Let the world know," http://www.washingtonpost.com/wp-srv/nation/specials/attacked/transcripts/binladen_100801.htm (Accessed April 20, 2017).

p. 25 Herodotus, *The Histories*, trans. A. D. Godley (London: W. Heinemann, 1921).

p. 26 Victor Davis Hanson, "History and the Movie 300," http://carnageandculture.blogspot.com/2007/03/victor-davis-hanson-history-and-movie.html (Accessed April 20, 2017).

p. 28 Isokrates, *Panegyrikos* (Leipzig, Berlin: Teubner, 1903), trans. McInerney.

p. 28 Simonides of Keos, *The Spartan Epitaph*, (=Herodotos *The Histories* 7.228), trans. McInerney.

p. 28 Barack Obama, "Remarks by the President After Counter-ISIL Meeting, June 14,2016," https://obamawhitehouse.archives.gov/the-press-office/2016/06/14/remarks-president-after-counter-isil-meeting (Accessed April 20, 2017).

p. 29 Homer, *The Iliad*, trans. Lattimore (Chicago, IL: University of Chicago Press, 1951).

Chapter 2 Early Greece and the Minoans

p. 41 J. M. Galán, *Victory and Border: Terminology related to Egyptian Imperialism in the XVIIIth Dynasty* (Hildesheim: Hildesheimer Agyptologische Beitrage 40, 1995).

p. 46 K. T. Glowacki, "House, Household, and Community at LM IIIC Vronda," in *Building Communities: House, Settlement and Society in the Aegean and Beyond*, ed. R. Westgate, N. Fisher, and J. Whitley (London: British School at Athens, 2007), pp. 129–39.

p. 51 Richard A. Lovett, "'Atlantis' Eruption Twice as Big as Previously Believed, Study Suggests," National Geographic http://news.nationalgeographic.com/news/2006/08/060823-thera-volcano.html (Accessed July 11, 2017).

Chapter 3 Mycenae: Rich in Gold

p. 62 H. Schliemann, *Troy and its Remains* (London: John Murray, 1875).

p. 74 A.-F. Christidis (ed.), *A History of Ancient Greek: From the Beginnings to Late Antiquity* (Cambridge: Cambridge University Press, 2007).

p. 75 A. Vasilogamvrou, "The first Linear B documents from Ayios

Vasileios (Laconia)," in *Études Mycéniennes 2010*, actes du XIIIe colloque international sur les textes égéens. Sèvres, Paris, P. Carlier *et al.* (Rome: Fabrizio Serra editore, 2012), p. 43.

p. 78 R. Castleden, *Mycenaeans* (Abingdon: Routledge, 2005), p. 28.

p. 86 Homer, *The Iliad*, trans. Ian Johnston, http://records.viu.ca/~johnstoi/homer/iliad6.htm (Accessed April 20, 2017).

p. 89 A. H. Gardiner, *Egypt of the Pharaohs* (Oxford: Oxford University Press, 1961).

Chapter 4 The Iron Age

p. 99 Aleydis van De Moortel and Eleni Zahou, "2004 Excavations at Mitrou, East Lokris," in *Aegean Archaeology* 7, (2005): 39–48.

p. 100 Homer, *The Odyssey*, trans. I. Johnston, http://records.viu.ca/~johnstoi/homer/odyssey4.htm (Accessed April 20, 2017).

p. 102 F. Mora, "Nestor's cup," https://www.brown.edu/Departments/Joukowsky_Institute/courses/greekpast/4695.html (Accessed April 20, 2017).

p. 107 C. Fornara, *Archaic Times to the End of the Peloponnesian War* (Cambridge: Cambridge University Press, 1983).

p. 110 Herodotus, *The Histories*, trans. G. Rawlinson (London: J. Murray, 1897).

p. 111 Ibid.

p. 111 R. Meiggs and D. M. Lewis, *A Selection of Greek Historical Inscriptions to the End of the Fifth Century B.C.* (Oxford: Oxford University Press), trans. O. Murray in *Early Greece*, 2nd edn (Harvard: Harvard University Press, 1993), p. 109. Reprinted by permission of HarperCollins Publishers Ltd © 1978 Oswyn Murray.

p. 112 R. Meiggs and D. M. Lewis, *A Selection of Greek Historical Inscriptions to the End of the Fifth Century B.C.* (Oxford: Oxford University Press), p. 1969, trans. McInerney.

p. 113 *Supplementum Epigraphicum Graecum* IX 72, trans. J. McInerney in *The Cattle of the Sun: Cows and Herding in the World of the Greeks*

(Princeton: Princeton University Press, 2010).

p. 119 Pindar, *The Odes*, trans. C. M. Bowra (London: Penguin, 1969).

p. 120 Aeschines, *Speeches*, trans. C. D. Adams (Cambridge, MA: Harvard University Press, 1918).

p. 120 Pausanias, *Description of Greece*, trans. W. H. S Jones (Cambridge, MA: Harvard University Press, 1918).

Chapter 5 The Archaic Age: Sparta

p. 126 Strabo, *Geography*, trans. H. L. Jones (London: W. Heinemann, 1930).

p. 129 Homer, *The Odyssey*, trans. I. Johnston, http://records.viu.ca/~johnstoi/homer/odyssey8.htm (Accessed April 20, 2017).

p. 139 Plutarch, *Sayings of the Spartans* (=*Moralia*) 241c, 8, trans. S. Blundell, *Women in Ancient Greece* (Cambridge, MA: Harvard University Press, 1995).

p. 134–35 Plutarch, *Sayings of the Spartans* in *Moralia* vol. III, trans. F. C. Babbitt (Cambridge, MA: Harvard University Press, 1931).

p. 136 Plutarch, *Life of Lycurgus*, trans. P. Cartledge, *Sparta and Lakonia: A Regional History 1300–362*, 2nd edn (Abingdon: Routledge, 2002), p. 116.

p. 136 Thucydides, *The Peloponnesian War*, trans. Benjamin Jowett (Oxford: Clarendon Press, 1881).

p. 140 Alkman, *Greek Lyric, Vol. II: Anacreon, Anacreontea, Choral Lyric from Olympis to Alcman*, ed. and trans. D. A. Campbell, Loeb Classical Library Volume 143 (Cambridge, MA: Harvard University Press, 1989). Copyright ©1988 by the President and Fellows of Harvard College. Loeb Classical Library® is a registered trademark of the President and Fellows of Harvard College.

p. 140 Tyrtaios, *Elegy and Iambus*, trans. J. M. Edmonds (Cambridge, MA: Harvard University Press. London, 1931).

p. 141 Aristotle, *Politics*, trans. S. Pomeroy, *Spartan Women* (Oxford: Oxford University Press, 2002).

p. 142 Herodotus, *The Histories*, trans. A. D. Godley (London: W. Heinemann, 1921).

Chapter 6 The Archaic Age: Athens

p. 149 Herodotus, *The Histories*, trans. J. McInerney.

p. 152 Theogonis, *Elegies*, in *Greek Lyric: An Anthology in Translation*, trans. A. Miller (Indianpolis, IN: Hackett, 1996).

p. 153 Ibid.

p. 153 *IG* I³ 104, trans. S. Lambert and P. J. Rhodes, https://www.atticinscriptions.com/inscription/IGI3/104 (Accessed April 21, 2017).

p. 154 Solon, *Select Fragments*, trans. J. Porter, www.sayreschool.org/uploaded/faculty/bmorrish/Humanities...9/solontexts.doc (Accessed April 21, 2017).

p. 155 Ibid.

pp. 156–57 Josine Blok and A. P. M. H. Lardinois (eds.), *Solon of Athens: New Historical and Philological Approaches* (Amsterdam: Brill, 2006).

p. 157 Aristotle, *Ath. Pol.*, trans. J. F. McGlew, *Tyranny and Political Culture in Ancient Greece* (Ithaca, NY: Cornell University Press, 1993).

p. 159 Thucydides, *The Peloponnesian War*, trans. Camp.

p. 159 *IG* I³ 1092 bis, trans. R. E. Wycherly, *Literary and Epigraphical Testimonia, (Agora III)* (Princeton, NJ: ASCSA, 1957).

p. 164 Athenaios, C. Fornara, *Archaic Times to the End of the Peloponnesian War* (Cambridge: Cambridge University Press, 1983).

p. 164 J. Roisman and J. C. Yardley, *Ancient Greece from Homer to Alexander: The Evidence* (Oxford: Blackwell, 2011).

p. 164 Herodotos, *The Histories*, trans. McInerney.

p. 165–66 Josiah Ober, "Epistemic democracy in Classical Athens," ed. H. Landemore and J. Elster, *Collective Wisdom: Principles and Mechanisms* (Cambridge: Cambridge University Press, 2012), pp. 118–47.

p. 168 S. Cummings and J. Brocklesby, "Towards demokratia - myth and the management of organizational change in ancient Athens," *Journal of Organizational Change Management*, 10 (1997): 71–95.

Chapter 7 Persia

p. 172 Strabo, *Geography*, trans. H. L. Jones (London: W. Heinemann, 1930).

p. 175 *New American Standard Bible* (La Habra, CA: The Lockman Foundation, 1960).

p. 175 M. H. Crawford and D. Whitehead, *Archaic and Classical Greece: A Selection of Ancient Sources in Translation*, (Cambridge: Cambridge University Press, 1983).

p. 176 Herodotus, *The Histories*, trans. A. de Selincourt (Harmondsworth: Penguin, 1954).

p. 177 L. W. King and R. C. Thompson, *The Sculptures and Inscription of Darius the Great on the Rock of Behistûn in Persia* (London: British Museum, 1907).

p. 178 Herodotus, *The Histories*, trans. A. de Selincourt (Harmondsworth: Penguin, 1954).

p. 179 Ibid.

p. 183 Marathon Epigram, trans. Hartnett in S. B. Ferrario, *Historical Agency and the 'Great Man' in Classical Greece* (Cambridge: Cambridge University Press, 2014).

p. 188 Herodotus, *The Histories*, trans. R. Waterfield.

p. 190 Aeschylus, *Persians,* trans. H. W. Smyth (Cambridge, MA: Harvard University Press, 1926).

p. 191 Hippocrates, *Airs, Water and Places*, trans. F. Adams (London: Wyman and Sons, 1881).

p. 193 P. Bordes, *Jacques-Louis David: Empire to Exile* (New Haven: Yale University Press, 2005).

Chapter 8 Democracy and Empire

p. 200 Plutarch, *Cimon and Pericles*, trans. B. Perrin (New York: Scribner, 1910).

p. 202 *IG* I³ 52, trans. S. Lambert and P. J. Rhodes, https://www.atticinscriptions.com/inscription/IGI3/52 (Accessed April 22, 2017).

p. 203 Demosthenes, *On the Crown*, trans. J. McInerney.

p. 204 Aristophanes, *Wasps, The Complete Greek Drama, vol. 2,* trans. Eugene O'Neill, Jr. (New York: Random House, 1938).

p. 206 Demosthenes, *On the False Embassy*, trans. C. A. Vince and J. H. Vince (Cambridge, MA: Harvard University Press, 1926).

p. 207 *IG* I³ 1147, trans. S. Lambert and R. Osborne, https://www.atticinscriptions.com/inscription/IGI3/1147 (Accessed April 22, 2017).

p. 208 *IG* I³ 14, trans. S. Lambert and P. J. Rhodes, https://www.atticinscriptions.com/inscription/IGI3/14 (Accessed April 22, 2017).

p. 210 *IG* I³ 40, trans. S. Lambert and R. Osborne, https://www.atticinscriptions.com/inscription/IGI3/40 (Accessed April 22, 2017).

p. 211 Ibid.

p. 211 *IG* I³ 46, trans. S. Lambert and P. J. Rhodes, https://www.atticinscriptions.com/inscription/IGI3/46 (Accessed April 22, 2017).

pp. 212–13 Thucydides, *History of the Peloponnesian War*, trans. R. Crawley (London: J. M. Dent, 1910).

p. 213 Plato, *Gorgias*, trans. McInerney.

Chapter 9 Inclusion and Exclusion: Life in Periklean Athens

p. 223 Aeschylus, *The Suppliants*, trans. J. Lembke (Oxford: Oxford University Press, 1975).

p. 225–26 Demosthenes, *Against Midias*, trans. A. T. Murray (Cambridge, MA: Harvard University Press, 1939).

p. 227 Plutarch, *Pericles*, trans. T. Buckley, *Aspects of Greek History 750–323 BC: A Source-Based Approach*, 2nd edn (Abingdon: Routledge, 2010), p. 232.

p. 228 Plutarch, *Cimon and Pericles*, trans. B. Perrin (New York: Scribner, 1910).

p. 234 Plutarch, *Cimon and Pericles*, trans. B. Perrin (New York: Scribner, 1910).

p. 235 Hesiod, *Works and* Days, trans. H. G. Evelyn-White (Cambridge, MA: Harvard University Press, 1914).

p. 235 Semonides, *Women*, trans. Diane Arnson Svarlien, http://www.stoa.org/diotima/anthology/sem_7.shtml (Accessed April 22, 2017).

p. 235 Demosthenes, in *The Murder of Herodes and Other Trials*, trans. K. Freeman (New York: Hackett: 1994).

p. 235 Xenophon, *Economicus*, trans. J. McInerney.

p. 235 Thucydides, *History of the Peloponnesian War*, trans. R. Crawley (London: J. M. Dent, 1910).

p. 236 Lysias, *On the Murder of Eratosthenes*, trans. W. R. M. Lamb (Cambridge, MA: Harvard University Press, 1930).

p. 237 Aristophanes, *Wasps*, trans. McInerney.

p. 237 Demosthenes, *Against Neaira*, trans. K. Freeman, *The Murder of Herodes and Other Trials* (New York: Hackett: 1994).

p. 238 Herodotus, *The Histories*, trans. McInerney.

p. 238 G. Herdt, "Semen transactions in Sambia Culture," in *Ritualized Homosexuality in Melanesia,* ed. G. Herdt (Berkeley and Los Angeles: University of California Press, 1984), pp. 167–210.

p. 239 Strabo, *Geography*, trans. H. L. Jones (London: W. Heinemann, 1930).

p. 239 Aischines, *Against Ktesiphon*, trans. K. J. Dover, *Greek Homosexuality* (Cambridge, MA: Harvard University Press, 1989).

p. 241 Xenophon, *Ways and Means*, trans. E. C. Marchant (Cambridge, MA: Harvard University Press, 1925).

p. 241 Xenophon, *Memorabilia*, trans. E. C. Marchant (Cambridge, MA: Harvard University Press, 1925).

p. 241 Demosthenes, *Against Timocrates*, trans. A. T. Murray (Cambridge, MA: Harvard University Press, 1939).

p. 241 Aristotle, *Politics*, trans. Benjamin Jowett (Oxford: Clarendon Press, 1885).

p. 241 Schol. ad Aristot., *Aristotle in 23 Volumes*, vol. 22, trans. J. H. Freese. (London: William Heinemann Ltd., 1926).

p. 242 Lysias, *Against Pancleon*, trans. W. R. M. Lamb (Cambridge, MA: Harvard University Press, 1930).

Chapter 10 Religion and Philosophy: Belief and Knowledge in the Classical Age

p. 248 *IG* II² 1237, trans. S. Lambert and F. Schuddeboom, https://www.atticinscriptions.com/inscription/IGII2/1237 (Accessed April 22, 2017).

p. 249 *IG* II² 1514, trans. J. McInerney.

p. 250 Michael H. Jameson, David R. Jordan, and Roy D. Kotansky, *A Lex Sacra from Selinous* (Durham, NC: Duke University, 1993).

p. 248 *IG* II² 1262, trans. S. Lambert and F. Schuddeboom, https://www.atticinscriptions.com/inscription/IGII2/1362 (Accessed April 22, 2017).

p. 251 *SEG* 52.48A, trans. S. Lambert, https://www.atticinscriptions.com/inscription/Lambert2002/362-65 (Accessed April 22, 2017).

p. 252 *IG* II² 2499, trans. Kloppenborg, http://philipharland.com/greco-roman-associations/lease-of-the-temple-of-egretes-306305-bce/ (Accessed April 22, 2017).

p. 254 Homer, *The Odyssey*, trans. I. Johnston, http://records.viu.ca/~johnstoi/homer/odyssey8.htm (Accessed April 20, 2017).

p. 256 *The Homeric Hymns and Homerica*, trans. H. G. Evelyn-White (Cambridge, MA: Harvard University Press, 1914).

p. 257 W. K. C. Guthrie, *Orpheus and Greek Religion*, 2nd edn (London: Methuen, 1952).

p. 258 Theophrastus, *Characters*, trans. McInerney.

p. 259 M. Hamilton, *Incubation: Or, the Cure of Disease in Pagan Temples and Christian Churches* (London: St Andrews University Press, 1906).

p. 261 M. Lefkowitz and M. Fant (eds.), *Women's Life in Greece and Rome*, 3rd edn (Baltimore, MD: Johns Hopkins Press, 1992).

p. 261 *The First Philosophers: The Presocratics and Sophists*, trans. R. Waterfield (Oxford: Oxford University Press, 2000).

p. 262 *The Fragments of Parmenides, Revised and Expanded Edition*, trans. A. H. Coxon (Las Vegas, NV: Parmenides, 2009).

pp. 262–63 *Presocratics Reader: Selected Fragments and Testimonia*, ed. Patricia Curd; trans. Richard D. McKirahan, 2nd edn (Indianapolis, IN: Hackett Pub. Co., 2010).

p. 263 W. K. C. Guthrie, *The Sophists* (Cambridge: Cambridge University Press, 1971).

p. 263 R. Janko, "The Derveni Papyrus: An Interim Text," *Zeitschrift für Papyrologie und Epigraphik*, 141 (2002): 1–62.

p. 265 Aristophanes, *Clouds,* trans. P. Meineck (Indianapolis, IN: Hackett Pub. Co., 2000).

pp. 266–67 Thucydides, *The Peloponnesian War*, trans. Benjamin Jowett (Oxford: Clarendon Press, 1881).

p. 267 Ibid.

Chapter 11 The Peloponnesian War

p. 275 V. D. Hanson, "Democratic Warfare, Ancient and Modern," in *War and Democracy: A Comparative Study of the Korean War and the Peloponnesian War*, ed. D. R. McCann

and B. S. Strauss (Armonk, NY: M. E. Sharpe, 2001), pp. 3–33.

p. 275 E. D. Mansfield and J. Snyder, "Democratization and the Danger of War," in *International Security* 20 (1995): 5–38.

p. 275 D. Reiter and A. C. Stam, *Democracies at War* (Princeton, NJ: Princeton University Press, 2001).

p. 277 Plutarch, *Themistocles*, trans. McInerney.

p. 277 Xenophon, *Constitution of the Athenians*, trans. J. Moore in *Aristotle and Xenophon on Democracy and Oligarchy* (Berkeley and Los Angeles: University of California Press, 1975).

pp. 278–79 Thucydides, *The Peloponnesian War*, trans. McInerney.

pp. 280–281 Thucydides, *The Peloponnesian War*, trans. Benjamin Jowett (Oxford: Clarendon Press, 1881).

p. 282 Ibid.

p. 282 Thucydides, *History of the Peloponnesian War*, trans. R. Crawley (London: J. M. Dent, 1910).

p. 285 Ibid.

p. 285 (column 2) Thucydides, *History of the Peloponnesian War*, trans. P. Woodruff in *On Justice, Power, and Human Nature* (Indianapolis, IN: Hackett, 1993).

p. 286 Thucydides, *History of the Peloponnesian War*, trans. R. Crawley (London: J. M. Dent, 1910).

p. 288 Ibid.

p. 292 Xenophon, *Hellenica*, trans. C. L. Brownson (Cambridge, MA: Harvard University Press, 1918).

p. 294 B. Rankov, "Lessons of History: The good ship *Democracy*: The building of a trireme warship fleet had a deep effect on Athenian society," *The Independent* Sunday June 13, 1993, http://www.independent.co.uk/news/uk/lessons-of-history-the-good-ship-democracy-the-building-of-a-trireme-warship-fleet-had-a-deep-effect-1491503.html (Accessed April 24, 2017).

Chapter 12 Panhellenism and the Rise of Philip

p. 297 Xenophon, *Hellenica*, trans. C. L. Brownson (Cambridge, MA: Harvard University Press, 1918).

p. 298 Andrew Wolpert, *Remembering Defeat: Civil War and Civic Memory in*

Ancient Athens (Baltimore, MD: Johns Hopkins University Press, 2002).

p. 298 Lysias, *Against Eratosthenes*, trans. W. R. M. Lamb (Cambridge, MA: Harvard University Press, 1930).

p. 299 Aristophanes, *Clouds*, trans. McInerney.

p. 301 Xenophon, *Memorabilia*, trans. G. Boys-Stones and C. Rowe, *The Circle of Socrates: Readings in the First-generation Socratics* (Indianapolis, IN: Hackett Pub. Co., 2013).

p. 301 Xenophon, *Memorabilia*, trans. M. H. Crawford and D. Whitehead in *Archaic and Classical Greece: A Selection of Ancient Sources in Translation* (Cambridge: Cambridge University Press, 1983).

p. 301 Aeschines, *Speeches*, trans. M. H. Crawford and D. Whitehead, *Archaic and Classical Greece: A Selection of Ancient Sources in Translation* (Cambridge: Cambridge University Press, 1983).

p. 302 Plato, *Phaedo,* trans. H. Tredennick in *The Last Days of Socrates* (Harmondsworth: Penguin, 1954).

pp. 302–3 Plato, *The Apologia,* trans H. Tredennick in *The Last Days of Socrates* (Harmondsworth: Penguin, 1954).

p. 304 Xenophon, *Hellenica*, trans. C. L. Brownson (Cambridge, MA: Harvard University Press, 1918).

p. 304–5 *IG* II² 34, trans P. J. Rhodes, https://www.atticinscriptions.com/inscription/IGII2/34 (Accessed April 24, 2017).

p. 305 *IG* II² 43, trans P. J. Rhodes, https://www.atticinscriptions.com/inscription/IGII2/43 (Accessed April 24, 2017).

p. 309 Xenophon, *Hellenica*, trans. C. L. Brownson (Cambridge, MA: Harvard University Press, 1918).

p. 309 Isokrates, *To Philip*, trans. George Norlin, *Isocrates Vol. I, Loeb Classical Library Volume 209*, first published 1928 (Cambridge, MA: Harvard University Press, 1980). Loeb Classical Library® is a registered trademark of the President and Fellows of Harvard College.

p. 310 Arrian, *Anabasis*, trans. Bohn in *Readings in Ancient History*, ed. W. Stearns Davis (Boston, MA: Allyn and Bacon, 1912).

p. 310–11 Athenaios, *Deipnosophists* (= Theopompos BNJ 115 F 236), trans. W. Morison, http://proxy.library.upenn.edu:3217/entries/brill-s-new-

jacoby/theopompos-of-chios-115-a115?s.num=1&s.rows=20&s.f.s2_parent=s.f.book.brill-s-new-jacoby&s.q=theopompos (Accessed April 24, 2017).

p. 317 Demosthenes, *On the Crown*, trans. C. A. Vince and J. H. Vince (Cambridge, MA: Harvard University Press, 1926).

Chapter 13 Alexander the Great and the Hellenistic Age

p. 324 Plutarch, *Alexander*, trans. B. Perrin (Cambridge, MA: Harvard University Press, 1919).

p. 325 N. Machiavelli, *The Prince*, trans. W. K. Marriott (London: J. M. Dent, 1908).

p. 325 Arrian, *Anabasis of Alexander* in *Arrian Vol.* I, trans. P. A. Brunt, Loeb Classical Library Volume 236 (Cambridge, MA: Harvard University Press, 1976). Copyright © 1976 by the President and Fellows of Harvard College. Loeb Classical Library® is a registered trademark of the President and Fellows of Harvard College.

p. 329 Arrian, *Anabasis of Alexander*, trans. E. J. Chinnock (London: Hodder and Stoughton, 1884).

p. 330 *Alexander Chronicle* (BCHP 1), trans. J. Lendering, http://www.livius.org/sources/content/mesopotamian-chronicles-content/bchp-1-alexander-chronicle/? (Accessed April 24, 2017).

p. 332 "The Insight that Brings Us to the Other Shore" (Heart of Perfect Mind Sutra), trans. Thich Nhat Hanh https://plumvillage.org/news/thich-nhat-hanh-new-heart-sutra-translation/ (Accessed April 24, 2017).

p. 334 Arrian, *Anabasis of Alexander*, trans. M. M. Austin, *The Hellenistic World from Alexander to the Roman Conquest: A Selection of Ancient Sources in Translation* (Cambridge: Cambridge University Press, 1981).

p. 336 Theocritus, *Idyll* 15, trans. McInerney.

p. 339 SB XVIII 13881, trans. R. Bagnall and P. Derow in *Greek Historical Documents: The Hellenistic Period* (Chico, CA: Scholars Press for the Society of Biblical Literature, 1981).

p. 340 *Seleucid Dissolution: The Sinking of the Anchor*, ed. Kyle Erickson and Gillian Ramsey (Wiesbaden: Harrassowitz Verlag, 2011).

p. 341 J. B. Pritchard, *Ancient Near Eastern Texts Relating to the Old Testament* (Princeton, NJ: Princeton University Press, 1950).

p. 341 *Ruin of Esagila Chronicle* (BCHP 6; BM 32248 + 32456 + 32477 + 32543 + 76-11-17 unnumbered), trans. B. van der Spek and I. Finkel, http://www.livius.org/cg-cm/chronicles/bchp-ruin_esagila/ruin_esagila_01.html (Accessed April 25, 2017).

p. 341 *RC* 9, in *Greek Historical Documents: The Hellenistic Period*, trans. R. Bagnall and P. Derow (Chico, CA: Scholars Press, 1981).

p. 345 Polybius, *The Histories, Vol. V*, trans. W. R. Paton, F. W. Walbank and Ch. Habicht, Loeb Classical Library Volume 160 (Cambridge, MA: Harvard University Press, 2010–2012). Copyright © 2012 by the President and Fellows of Harvard College.

Loeb Classical Library® is a registered trademark of the President and Fellows of Harvard College.

p. 349 Plutarch, *Alexander*, trans. B. Perrin (Cambridge, MA: Harvard University Press, 1986).

Further Reading

Chapter 1 Introduction: Why Study the Greeks?

Cartledge, Paul, *The Greeks: A Portrait of Self and Others* (Oxford: Oxford University Press, 1993).

———, *Ancient Greece: A History in Eleven Cities* (Oxford: Oxford University Press, 2009).

de Ste. Croix, G. E. M., *The Class Struggle in the Ancient Greek World* (Ithaca, NY: Cornell University Press, 1981).

duBois, Page, *Out of Athens* (Cambridge, MA: Harvard University Press, 2010).

Hall, Edith, *Introducing the Ancient Greeks* (London: W. W. Norton, 2014).

Hall, Jonathan M., *Artifact and Artifice: Classical Archaeology and the Ancient Historian* (Chicago and London: Chicago University Press, 2014).

Hanson, Victor Davis, *The Other Greeks: The Family Farm and the Agrarian Roots of Western Civilization* (New York: The Free Press, 1995).

Horden, Peregrine and Nicholas Purcell, *The Corrupting Sea: A Study of Mediterranean History* (London: Blackwell, 2000).

Meier, Christian, *Athens: A Portrait of the City in its Golden Age* (New York: Metropolitan, 1998).

Snell, Bruno, *The Discovery of the Mind in Greek Philosophy and Literature* (New York: Harper, 1960).

Trittle, Lawrence A., *From Melos to My Lai: A Study in Violence, Culture and Social Survival* (London and New York: Routledge, 2002).

West, Martin L., *The East Face of Helicon: West Asiatic Elements in Greek Poetry and Myth* (Oxford: Clarendon 1997).

Chapter 2 Early Greece and the Minoans

Cadogan, Gerald, *Palaces of Minoan Crete* (London: Barrie and Jenkins, 1976).

Cappel, Sarah, Ute Günkel-Maschek, and Diamantis Panagiotopoulos (eds.), *Minoan Archaeology: Perspectives for the 21st Century* (Louvain-la-Neuve: Presses universitaires de Louvain, 2015).

Day, Leslie P., Margaret S. Mook, and James D. Muhly (eds.), *Crete beyond the Palaces: Proceedings of the Crete 2000 Conference* (Philadelphia, PA: INSTAP Academic Press, 2004).

Driessen, Jan, Ilsa Schoep, and Robert Laffineur (eds.), *Monuments of Minos: Rethinking the Minoan Palaces* (Austin: University of Texas, 2002).

Evans, Arthur, *The Palace of Minos: A Comparative Account of the Successive Stages of the Early Cretan Civilization as Illustrated by the Discoveries at Knossos* (London: Macmillan and Co., 1921).

Fitton, J. Lesley, *Minoans* (London: British Museum Press, 2002).

Hamilakis, Yannis (ed.), *Labyrinth Revisited: Rethinking "Minoan" Archaeology* (Oxford: Oxbow, 2002).

MacGillivray, Joseph Alexander, *Minotaur: Sir Arthur Evans and the Archaeology of the Minoan Myth* (New York: Hill and Wang, 2000).

Marinatos, Nanno, *Art and Religion in Thera: Reconstructing a Bronze Age Society* (Athens: D. & I. Mathioulakis, 1984).

Perlès, Catherine, *The Early Neolithic in Greece: The First Farming Communities in Europe* (Cambridge: Cambridge University Press, 2001).

Preziosi, Donald and Louise A. Hitchcock, *Aegean Art and Architecture* (Oxford: Oxford University Press, 1999).

Chapter 3 Mycenae: Rich in Gold

Allen, Susan Hueck, *Finding the Walls of Troy: Frank Calvert and Heinrich Schliemann at Hisarlık* (Berkeley and Los Angeles: University of California Press, 1999).

Bachhuber, Christoph and R. Gareth Roberts (eds.), *Forces of Transformation: The End of the Bronze Age in the Mediterranean* (Oxford: Oxbow, 2009).

Castleden, Rodney, *Mycenaeans* (London & New York: Routledge, 2005).

Chadwick, John, *The Decipherment of Linear B*, 2nd edn (London: Cambridge University Press, 1967).

———, *The Mycenaean World* (Cambridge: Cambridge University Press, 1976).

Dickinson, O. T. P. K, *The Aegean Bronze Age* (Cambridge: Cambridge University Press, 1994).

Galaty, Michael L. and William A. Parkinson (eds.), *Rethinking Mycenaean Palaces*, 2nd edn (Los Angeles: Cotsen Institute of Archaeology, University of California, 2007).

Latacz, Joachim, *Troy and Homer: Towards a Solution of an Old Mystery* (Oxford: Oxford University Press, 2004).

Schliemann, Heinrich, *Ilios: The City and Country of the Trojans* (New York: B. Blom, 1968).

Taylour, William, *The Mycenaeans* (New York: Praeger, 1964).

Voutsaki, Sophia and John Killen (eds.), *Economy and Politics in the Mycenaean Palace States: Proceedings of a Conference Held on 1–3 July 1999 in the Faculty of Classics, Cambridge* (Cambridge: Cambridge Philological Society, 2001).

Chapter 4 The Iron Age

Boardman, John, *The Greeks Overseas: Their Early Colonies and Trade*, 4th edn (London and New York: Thames & Hudson, 1999).

Clay, Jenny Strauss, Irad Malkin, and Yannis Z. Tzifopoulos (eds.), *Panhellenes at Methone: Graphê in Late Geometric and Protoarchaic Methone, Macedonia (ca 700 BCE)* (Berlin: Walter de Gruyter, 2017).

Deger-Jalkotzy, Sigrid and Irene S. Lemos (eds.), *Ancient Greece from the Mycenaean Palaces to the Age of Homer* (Edinburgh: Edinburgh University Press, 2006).

Descœudres, Jean Paul (ed.), *Greek Colonists and Native Populations: Proceedings of the First Australian Congress of Classical Archaeology Held in Honour of Emeritus Professor A. D. Trendall, Sydney, 9–14 July 1985* (New York: Oxford University Press, 1990).

Dickinson, O. T. P. K, *The Aegean from Bronze Age to Iron Age: Continuity and Change Between the Twelfth and Eighth Centuries BC* (London and New York: Routledge, 2006).

Dougherty, Carol, *The Raft of Odysseus: The Ethnographic Imagination of Homer's Odyssey* (Oxford: Oxford University Press, 2001).

Malkin, Irad, *Religion and Colonization in Ancient Greece* (Leiden: Brill, 1987).

———, *A Small Greek World: Networks in the Ancient Mediterranean* (Oxford: Oxford University Press, 2011).

Morris, I., *Archaeology as Cultural History: Words and Things in Iron Age Greece* (Malden, MA: Blackwell, 2000).

Raschke, Wendy (ed.), *The Archaeology of the Olympics: The Olympic and Other Festivals in Antiquity* (Madison: University of Wisconsin Press, 1988).

Sinn, U., *Olympia: Cult, Sport, and Ancient Festival* (Princeton, NJ: Markus Wiener, 2000).

Slater, William J. (ed.), *Dining in a Classical Context* (Ann Arbor: University of Michigan Press, 1991).

Tsetskhladze, Gocha R. (ed.), *Greek Colonisation: An Account of Greek Colonies and Other Settlements Overseas* I (Leiden: Brill, 2006).

Chapter 5 The Archaic Age: Sparta

Cartledge, Paul, *Sparta and Lakonia: A Regional History 1300–362 BC*, 2nd edn (London and New York: Routledge, 2002).

———, *The Spartans: An Epic History* (London: 4 Books, 2002).

Ducat, Jean, *Spartan Education: Youth and Society in the Classical Period* (Swansea: The Classical Press of Wales, 2006).

Ferrari, Gloria, *Alcman and the Cosmos of Sparta* (Chicago, IL: The University of Chicago Press, 2008).

Figueira, Thomas J. (ed.), *Spartan Society* (Swansea: The Classical Press of Wales, 2004).

Forrest, William George, *A History of Sparta 950–192 BC*, rev. edn (London: Bristol Classical Press, 1995).

Hodkinson, Stephen (ed.), *Sparta: Comparative Approaches* (Swansea: The Classical Press of Wales, 2009).

Hodkinson, Stephen and Anton Powell (eds.), *Sparta: New Perspectives* (Swansea: The Classical Press of Wales, 2009).

Luraghi, Nino, *The Ancient Messenians: Constructions of Ethnicity and Memory* (Cambridge: Cambridge University Press, 2008).

Luraghi, Nino and Susan E. Alcock (eds.), *Helots and their Masters in Laconia and Messenia: Histories, Ideologies, Structures* (Washington, D.C.: Center for Hellenic Studies, 2003).

Ogden, Daniel, *Aristomenes of Messene: Legends of Sparta's Nemesis* (Swansea: The Classical Press of Wales, 2004).

Powell, Anton (ed.), *Classical Sparta: Techniques Behind Her Success* (Norman: University of Oklahoma Press, 1989).

Chapter 6 The Archaic Age: Athens

Anderson, Greg, *The Athenian Experiment: Building an Imagined Political Community in Attica, 508–490 BC* (Ann Arbor: University of Michigan Press, 2003).

Anhalt, Emily Katz, *Solon the Singer: Politics and Poetics* (Lanham, MD: Rowman & Littlefield Publishers, 1993).

Blok, Josine H. and André P. M. H. Lardinois (eds.), *Solon of Athens: New Historical and Philological Approaches* (Leiden: Brill, 2006).

Fischer, Nick and Hans Van Wees (eds.), *Archaic Greece: New Approaches and New Evidence* (Swansea: The Classical Press of Wales, 1998).

Hignett, Charles, *A History of the Athenian Constitution to the End of the Fifth Century B.C.* (Oxford: Clarendon Press, 1952).

Kurke, Leslie, *Coins, Bodies, Games, and Gold: The Politics of Meaning in Archaic Greece* (Princeton, NJ: Princeton University Press, 1999).

Lavelle, Brian M., *Fame, Money, and Power: The Rise of Peisistratos and "Democratic" Tyranny at Athens* (Ann Arbor: University of Michigan Press, 2005).

Raaflaub, Kurt and Hans Van Wees (eds.), *A Companion to Archaic Greece* (Malden, MA: Wiley-Blackwell, 2009).

Sancisi-Weerdenburg, Heleen (ed.), *Peisistratos and the Tyranny: A Reappraisal of the Evidence* (Amsterdam: J. C. Gieben, 2000).

Shapiro, H. Alan, *Art and Cult Under the Tyrants in Athens* (Mainz am Rhein: P. von Zabern, 1989).

Snodgrass, Anthony, *Archaic Greece: The Age of Experiment* (Berkeley and Los Angeles: University of California Press, 1980).

Traill, John S., *The Political Organization of Attica: A Study of the Demes, Trittyes, and Phylai, and Ttheir Representation in the Athenian Council*, Hesperia Suppl. 14 (Princeton: American School of Classical Studies at Athens, 1975).

Chapter 7 Persia

Allen, Lindsay, *The Persian Empire* (Chicago, IL: University of Chicago Press, 2005).

Briant, Pierre, *From Cyrus to Alexander: A History of the Persian Empire* (Winona Lake, IN: Eisenbrauns, 2002).

Brosius, Maria, *The Persian Empire from Cyrus II to Artaxerxes I* (Kingston upon Thames: London Association of Classical Teachers, 2000).

Cawkwell, George, *The Greek Wars: The Failure of Persia* (Oxford: Oxford University Press, 2005).

Dandamaev, Muhammed A., *A Political History of the Achaemenid Empire*, trans. W. J. Vogelsang (Leiden: Brill, 1989).

Green, Peter, *The Greco-Persian Wars* (Berkeley and Los Angeles: University of California Press, 1996).

Harrison, Thomas, *Greeks and Barbarians* (London and New York: Routledge, 2002).

———, *Writing Ancient Persia* (London: Bristol Classical Press, 2011).

Hignett, Charles, *Xerxes' Invasion of Greece* (Oxford: The Clarendon Press, 1963).

Kuhrt, Amélie, *The Persian Empire [A Corpus of Sources from the Achaemenid Period]*, vol. 1 (London and New York: Routledge, 2009).

Skjærvø, Prods Oktor, *The Spirit of Zoroastrianism* (New Haven: Cornell University Press, 2011).

Waters, Matthew W., *Ancient Persia: A Concise History of the Achaemenid Empire, 550–330 BCE* (Cambridge: Cambridge University Press, 2014).

Chapter 8 Democracy and Empire

Boedeker, Deborah and Kurt A. Raaflaub (eds.), *Democracy, Empire, and the Arts in Fifth-Century Athens* (Cambridge, MA: Harvard University Press, 1998).

Constantakopoulou, Christy, *The Dance of the Islands: Insularity, Networks, the Athenian Empire, and the Aegean World* (Oxford: Oxford University Press, 2007).

Figueira, Thomas J., *The Power of Money: Coinage and Politics in the Athenian Empire* (Philadelphia: University of Pennsylvania Press, 1998).

Hansen, Mogens Herman, *The Athenian Democracy in the Age of Demosthenes: Structure, Principles, and Ideology*, 2nd edn (London: Bristol Classical Press, 1999).

Low, Polly (ed.), *The Athenian Empire* (Edinburgh: Edinburgh University Press, 2008).

Ma, John, Nicholas Papazarkadas, and Robert Parker (eds.), *Interpreting the Athenian Empire* (London: Duckworth, 2009).

Meiggs, Russell, *The Athenian Empire* (Oxford: The Clarendon Press, 1972).

Ober, Josiah, *Mass and Élite in Democratic Athens: Rhetoric, Ideology, and the Power of the People* (Princeton, NJ: Princeton University Press, 1989).

———, *The Athenian Revolution: Essays on Ancient Greek Democracy and Political Theory* (Princeton, NJ: Princeton University Press, 1996).

Raaflaub, Kurt A., *The Discovery of Freedom in Ancient Greece*, 1st edn, revised and updated (Chicago, IL: University of Chicago Press, 2004).

Raaflaub, Kurt A., Josiah Ober, and Robert W. Wallace (eds.), *Origins of Democracy in Ancient Greece* (Berkeley and Los Angeles: University of California Press, 2007).

Rhodes, Peter J., *The Athenian Boule* (Oxford: The Clarendon Press, 1972).

Roberts, Jennifer Tolbert, *Athens on Trial: The Antidemocratic Tradition in Western Thought* (Princeton: Princeton University Press, 1995).

Sinclair, Robert K, *Democracy and Participation in Athens* (Cambridge: Cambridge University, 1988).

Chapter 9 Inclusion and Exclusion: Life in Periklean Athens

Barringer, Judith M. and Jeffrey M. Hurwit (eds.), *Periklean Athens and its Legacy: Problems and Perspectives* (Austin: University of Texas Press, 2005).

Bresson, Alain, *The Making of the Ancient Greek Economy: Institutions, Markets and Growth in the City-States* (Princeton, NJ: Princeton University Press, 2016).

Blundell, Sue, *Women in Ancient Greece (*Cambridge, MA: Harvard University Press, 1995).

Cohen, David, *Law, Sexuality, and Society: The Enforcement of Morals in Classical Athens* (Cambridge: Cambridge University Press, 1991).

Csapo, E. and William J. Slater, *The Context of Ancient Drama* (Ann Arbor: University of Michigan Press, 1994).

Dover, Kenneth J., *Aristophanic Comedy* (Berkeley and Los Angeles: University of California Press, 1972).

Easterling, Patricia E. (ed.), *The Cambridge Companion to Greek Tragedy* (Cambridge: Cambridge University Press, 1997).

Finley, Moses I., *Economy and Society in Ancient Greece* (New York: Viking, 1981).

Fisher, Nicolas R. E., *Slavery in Classical Greece* (London: Bristol Classical Press, 1993).

Garlan, Yvon, *Slavery in Ancient Greece* (Ithaca, NJ: Cornell University Press, 1988).

Garland, Robert, *The Piraeus: From the Fifth to the First Century B.C.* (London: Duckworth, 1987).

Golden, Mark, *Children and Childhood in Classical Athens*, 2nd edn (Baltimore, MD: Johns Hopkins University Press, 2015).

Kennedy, Rebecca Futo, *Immigrant Women in Athens: Gender, Ethnicity, and Citizenship in the Classical City* (London and New York: Routledge, 2014).

Loraux, Nicole, *The Invention of Athens: The Funeral Oration in the Classical City*, 2nd edn (Cambridge, MA: MIT Press, 2006).

Osborne, Robin, *Athens and Athenian Democracy* (Cambridge: Cambridge University Press, 2011).

Samons, II, Loren J. (ed.), *The Cambridge Companion to the Age of Pericles* (Cambridge: Cambridge University Press, 2007).

Whitehead, David, *The Ideology of the Athenian Metic* (Cambridge: Cambridge Philological Society, 1977).

Chapter 10 Religion and Philosophy: Belief and Knowledge in the Classical Age

Bremmer, Jan N., *Initiation Into the Mysteries of the Ancient World* (Berlin: Walter de Gruyter, 2014).

Bruit Zaidman, Louise and Pauline Schmitt Pantel, *Religion in the Ancient Greek City* (Cambridge: Cambridge University Press, 1992).

Curd, Patricia and Daniel W. Graham, *The Oxford Handbook of Presocratic Philosophy* (Oxford: Oxford University Press, 2008).

Evans, Nancy, *Civic Rites: Democracy and Religion in Ancient Athens* (Berkeley and Los Angeles: University of California Press, 2010).

Kraut, Richard (ed.), *The Cambridge Companion to Plato* (Cambridge: Cambridge University Press, 1992).

McKirahan, Richard D. (ed.), *Philosophy Before Socrates: An Introduction with Texts and Commentary*, 2nd edn (Indianapolis, IN: Hackett Pub. Co., 2010).

Neils, Jenifer, *Worshipping Athena: Panathenaia and Parthenon* (Madison: University of Wisconsin Press, 1996).

Parker, Robert, *On Greek Religion* (Ithaca, NY: Cornell University Press, 2011).

Pedley, John, *Sanctuaries and the Sacred in the Ancient Greek World* (Cambridge: Cambridge University Press, 2005).

de Polignac, François, *Cults, Territory, and the Origins of the Greek City-State* (Chicago, IL: University of Chicago Press, 1995).

Schaeffer, Denise and Christopher Dustin (eds.), *Socratic Philosophy and Its Others* (Plymouth: Lexington Books, 2013).

Scott, Michael, *Delphi: A History of the Center of the Ancient World* (Princeton, NJ: Princeton University Press, 2014).

Sourvinou-Inwood, Christiane, *Athenian Myths and Festivals: Aglauros, Erechtheus, Plynteria, Panathenaia, Dionysia* (Oxford: Oxford University Press, 2011).

Chapter 11 The Peloponnesian War

Cawkwell, George L., *Thucydides and the Peloponnesian War* (London and New York: Routledge, 1997).

Connor, W. Robert, *Thucydides* (Princeton, NJ: Princeton University Press, 1984).

de Ste. Croix, G. E. M., *The Origins of the Peloponnesian War* (Ithaca, NY: Cornell University Press, 1972).

Hale, John R, *Lords of the Sea* (New York: Viking, 2009).

Hanson, Victor Davis, *A War Like No Other: How the Athenians and Spartans Fought the Peloponnesian War* (New York: Random House, 2005).

Kagan, Donald, *The Peloponnesian War* (New York: Viking, 2003).

Kallet, Lisa, *Money and the Corrosion of Power in Thucydides: The Sicilian Expedition and its Aftermath* (Berkeley and Los Angeles: University of California Press, 2002).

Mitchell-Boyask, Robin, *Plague and the Athenian Imagination: Drama, History, and the Cult of Asclepius* (Cambridge: Cambridge University Press, 2007).

Rengakos, Antonios and Antonis Tsakmakis (eds.), *Brill's Companion to Thucydides* (Leiden: Brill, 2006)

Shaw, J. T., *The Trireme Project: Operational Experience, 1987–90: Lessons Learnt* (Oxford: Oxbow, 1993).

Tritle, Lawrence A., *A New History of the Peloponnesian War* (Chichester: Wiley-Blackwell, 2010).

Viggiano, Gregory and Donald Kagan, *Men of Bronze: Hoplite Warfare in Ancient Greece* (Princeton, NJ: Princeton University Press, 2013).

Chapter 12 Panhellenism and the Rise of Philip

Archibald, Zofia, *Ancient Economies of the Northern Aegean: Fifth to First Centuries BC* (Oxford: Oxford University Press, 2013).

Buckler, John, *The Theban Hegemony* (Cambridge, MA: Harvard University Press, 1980).

———, *Philip II and the Sacred War*, Mnemosyne Suppl. 109 (Leiden: Brill, 1989).

Ellis, John R., *Philip II and Macedonian Imperialism* (London: Thames & Hudson, 1976).

Ferrario, Sarah Brown, *Historical Agency and the 'Great Man' in Classical Greece* (Cambridge: Cambridge University Press, 2014).

Hamilton, Charles D., *Agesilaus and the Failure of Spartan Hegemony* (Ithaca, NJ: Cornell University Press, 1991).

Hammond, N. G. L., *Philip of Macedon* (Baltimore, MD: Johns Hopkins University Press, 1994).

Lane Fox, Robin J., *Brill's Companion to Ancient Macedon: Studies in the Archaeology and History of Macedon, 650 BC–300 AD* (Leiden: Brill, 2011).

Mitchell, Lynette G., *Panhellenism and the Barbarian in Archaic and Classical Greece* (Swansea: University of Wales Press, 2007).

Roisman, Joseph and Ian Worthington (eds.), *A Companion to Ancient Macedonia* (Malden, MA: Wiley-Blackwell, 2010).

Ryder, Timothy T. B., *Koine Eirene: General Peace and Local Independence in Ancient Greece* (Oxford: Oxford University Press, 1965).

Sealey, Raphael, *Demosthenes and His Time: A Study in Defeat* (Oxford: Oxford University Press, 1993).

Worthington, Ian, *Philip II of Macedonia* (New Haven, CT: Yale University Press, 2008).

Chapter 13 Alexander the Great and the Hellenistic Age

Anson, Edward M., *Alexander the Great: Themes and Issues* (London: Bloomsbury Academic, 2013).

Boardman, John, *The Greeks in Asia* (London: Thames & Hudson, 2015).

Green, Peter, *Alexander to Actium: The Historical Evolution of the Hellenistic Age* (Berkeley and Los Angeles: University of California Press, 1990).

Gruen, Erich, *The Hellenistic World and the Coming of Rome* (Berkeley and Los Angeles: University of California Press, 1984).

Holt, Frank L., *Lost World of the Golden King: In Search of Ancient Afghanistan* (Berkeley and Los Angeles: University of California Press, 2012).

Kleiner, Diana E. E., *Cleopatra and Rome* (Cambridge, MA: Harvard University Press, 2005).

Lane Fox, Robin, *Alexander The Great* (New York: Dial Press, 1974).

Manning, Joseph G., *The Last Pharaohs: Egypt under the Ptolemies, 305–30 BC* (Princeton, NJ: Princeton University Press, 2010).

Pollitt, Jerome J., *Art in the Hellenistic Age* (Cambridge: Cambridge University Press, 1986).

Sherwin-White, Susan and Amélie Kuhrt, *From Samarkhand to Sardis: A New Approach to the Seleucid Empire* (London: Duckworth, 1993).

Thonemann, Peter, *The Hellenistic Age* (Oxford: Oxford University Press, 2016).

Waterfield, Robin, *Dividing the Spoils: The War for Alexander the Great's Empire* (Oxford: Oxford University Press, 2011).

Sources of Illustrations

Index